Human Rights and
United States Policy
toward Latin America

For Bill Keech,

with my best wishes

Lars Schoultz

March 1982

•

Human Rights and United States Policy toward Latin America

•

LARS SCHOULTZ

PRINCETON UNIVERSITY PRESS
PRINCETON, NEW JERSEY

To Jane, Karina, and Nils

CONTENTS

LIST OF TABLES

PREFACE

THIS is a book about human rights and United States policy toward Latin America. I have written it for two reasons. First, I hope it will contribute to an understanding of the process of U.S. foreign policy making. Despite the existence of a large body of literature that demonstrates how the decision-making process influences—some would say determines—what is decided, there are few empirical analyses of exactly how United States policy toward Latin America is created and implemented. Using the issue of human rights as a focus, this study attempts to narrow the gap between our knowledge of theory and practice by describing and analyzing the structure of foreign policy decision making, the rules and processes that officials have created to communicate and negotiate with one another, with the public, and with Latin American governments.

Second, this book examines the values that underlie the structure of United States policy toward Latin America. I began to write the proposal to conduct this study in late 1975, when it seemed that U.S. policy toward the Third World was oriented to support some of the most repressive governments imaginable. I began to write the concluding chapter on July 17, 1979, the day Anastasio Somoza fled Nicaragua at the urging of the Nicaraguan people and, in the end, the United States government. Sandwiched between those two dates were the human rights years in United States foreign policy, a period in which humanitarian values openly challenged the prevailing national security ideology. Rarely has so much data on the conflict of values in foreign policy been available for public examination, rarely has a challenge to the traditional value of anticommunism been so aggressive, and rarely has it been possible to identify with precision the manner in which values are defended, attacked, promoted, and compromised in the making of United States foreign policy.

The subject of United States policy toward human rights in Latin America is a difficult one to investigate dispassionately. Not only have human rights been frequently and intensively violated by a variety of Latin American governments during the past two decades but in several cases the United States government created, helped create, encouraged, or at least applauded the creation of the physical apparatus of repression and the ideological climate that encouraged its use. It would not be difficult for a study of United States policy toward human rights to become a diatribe. To avoid this I began to work with a number of rudimentary assumptions. I took it for granted that, other things being equal, citizens and their policy makers would prefer not to support repressive governments. But I also assumed that other things rarely if ever are equal in foreign policy making, and while with occasional but notable exceptions foreign policy officials are honorable people, these officials frequently find it impossible to pursue simultaneously humanitarian concerns and the host of other values they hold in common with the citizens and the interests they represent. I repeatedly note these competing values, but I leave to the reader the task of deciding whether his or her values are congruent with those of United States policy. I have attempted to present the data so that informed decisions can be made. While the reader will have no difficulty determining my views, the elaboration and defense of these views is not the purpose of this book. With the exception of the final pages of the conclusion, my purpose is to describe and analyze United States policy as it was and as it is, not as I would wish it to be.

This study is based upon interviews conducted during 1975, 1977 to 1978, 1979, and 1980 with officials of interest groups, the executive branch, and Congress. Although references are made to interviews as early as November 1975 and as late as April 1980, the bulk of the data was collected between December 1977 and December 1978. During that year I began by interviewing at least one representative of every interest group concerned with the issue of human rights and United States policy toward Latin America—sixty-three employees of business lobbies, Latin American governments, and a broad variety of nongovernmental organizations. I then turned to Congress and the executive branch, interviewing forty-seven executive branch officials at the assistant secretary level and lower who were charged with formulating and implementing United States policy toward human rights in Latin America and twenty-eight persons with similar responsibilities in Congress. Only four of the latter group were members of Congress. The others were evenly divided between legislative aides to individual members and staff personnel of foreign affairs and appropriations committees.

After it became clear that respondents were bored by the standardized questionnaire I had laboriously constructed, I began to tailor each interview to the interests and responsibilities of the respondent. I asked respondents what they did, how they did it, and why. I asked which tasks were emphasized and which were avoided; which bureaucratic actors were their friends and which their enemies; why some rules were obeyed and others ignored. Some of these interviews were short—the record was six minutes—but most lasted about an hour. A number of respondents were interviewed repeatedly, a few as many as a dozen times over the course of 1975 to 1980. Many have taken the time to read and criticize preliminary drafts of several chapters. Despite the fact that none of these officials was obligated to speak with me, none refused my request for an interview and only a very few evidenced any impatience with my intrusions. Although in many cases a promise of anonymity prevents the identification of individual respondents, this volume is basically their story.

The money to support my research was provided by a postdoctoral research award from the Joint Committee on Latin American Studies of the Social Science Research Council and the American Council of Learned Societies. To that benevolent committee and its two parent organizations, and to Louis Wolf Goodman, then of the SSRC, I am truly grateful. Other funds were generously supplied by the Public Concern Foundation, by Miami University's Faculty Research Committee and its Alumni Travel Fund, and by the University of Florida's Graduate School and its Center for Latin American Studies.

I am indebted to colleagues at three institutions for their support. The Dean of the College of Arts and Science at Miami University, C. K. Williamson, and the faculty of the Department of Political Science and its chairperson, Herbert Waltzer, encouraged my work at a time when other university officials would have preferred that I drop the subject of human rights. The faculty of the Department of Political Science at the University of Florida graciously permitted me to accept an unusual opportunity and begin a year's leave of absence less than four months after my initial appointment. And the Department of Political Science, the Institute of Latin American Studies, and the Institute for Research in Social Science at the University of North Carolina at Chapel Hill provided substantial assistance in manuscript preparation. Over the four years between the time I wrote my research proposal and the time I completed the conclusion, I received able editorial and typing assistance from Louisa Allen, Doris Atwater, Lydia González, C. L. Lassiter, Dotty Pearson, Debralee Poe, Hazel Pridgen, Betsy Roberts, Kathleen Stipek, Betsy Taylor, and Jean West.

My debt to a variety of Washingtonians is difficult to communicate. There are dozens of individuals who spent hours of their time answering my questions, introducing me to appropriate officials and sources of data, and then reading and criticizing the initial drafts of this volume. Within the U.S. government, Richard Feinberg, George Lister, and John Salzberg were extremely cooperative. At the Hispanic Division of the Library of Congress I was befriended and assisted by Georgette Dorn, John Hébert, Mary Ellis Kahler, Everett Larson, and Dolores Martin. Although one hesitates to publicize the location of a treasure, I must add my name to the list of the Hispanic Division's patrons who declare that there is no finer place on earth to study United States-Latin American relations. On the other side of Washington, I found Riorden Roett, who kindly opened the doors to the facilities of Johns Hopkins' School of Advanced International Studies. Among human rights interest group activists, Bruce Cameron, Joe Eldridge, Jo Marie Griesgraber, Tom Quigley, Brewster Rhodes, Ed Snyder, and Kay Stubbs were particularly helpful. Four Washington-based social scientists—John Bailey, Meg Crahan, Brian Smith, and Patricia Weiss-Fagen—read and criticized drafts of one or more chapters and assisted in clarifying a variety of research relationships as well.

In addition, Gayle Hudgens provided me with photocopies of the documents on U.S. covert actions in Brazil that she obtained through the Freedom of Information process; Tristram Coffin of the *Washington Spectator* identified initial persons to interview and reminded me repeatedly that the substance of policy rarely changes as rapidly or completely as the form in which it is presented to the public and to inquisitive researchers; and a number of social scientists outside Washington added their advice on how this work could be improved. I am especially grateful to my wife, Jane Volland, to two unusually helpful editors, Sandy Thatcher and Cathy Thatcher, to two uncommonly constructive critics, Yale Ferguson and Harrison Wagner, and in a variety of ways to Bill Ascher, Enrique Baloyra, Sam Fitch, Michael Fleet, Henry Landsberger, John Martz, Jim Prothro, Gene Wittkopf, and, as always, Federico Gil. In return for continual harassment from me, they have offered their persistent support, and for that I thank them all.

LIST OF ABBREVIATIONS

AACCLA	Association of American Chambers of Commerce in Latin America
ACC	American-Chilean Council
ADA	Americans for Democratic Action
AECB	Arms Export Control Board
AI	Amnesty International
AID	Agency for International Development
AID-LA	Bureau for Latin America, Agency for International Development
AIFLD	American Institute for Free Labor Development
ALESA	American League for Exports and Security Assistance
ALISA	American League for International Security Assistance
ARA	Bureau of Inter-American Affairs (formerly Bureau of American Republics Affairs)
CALC	Clergy and Laity Concerned
CCC	Commodity Credit Corporation
CCN	Consejo Chileno-Norteamericano
CIA	Central Intelligence Agency
COA	Council of the Americas
COHA	Council on Hemispheric Affairs
CRS	Congressional Research Service
DCC	Development Coordinating Committee
DEA	Drug Enforcement Administration
DIA	Defense Intelligence Agency
DISC	Domestic International Sales Corporation
DOD	Department of Defense
DSAA	Defense Security Assistance Agency
DSAC	Defense Security Assistance Council
EB	Bureau of Economic and Business Affairs
ECOSOC	United Nations Economic and Social Council
EDA	Excess Defense Articles
FARA	Foreign Agents Registration Act
FARS	Foreign Agents Registration Statement
FCNL	Friends' Committee on National Legislation
FICA	Federal Insurance Credit Association
FMS	Foreign Military Sales
FSO	Fund for Special Operations, Inter-American Development Bank

FY	Fiscal Year
GAO	Government Accounting Office
HA	Bureau of Human Rights and Humanitarian Affairs
HRWG	Human Rights Working Group
IBRD	International Bank for Reconstruction and Development (World Bank)
ICA	International Cooperation Administration
ICJ	International Commission of Jurists
IDA	International Development Association
IDB	Inter-American Development Bank
IDCA	International Development Cooperation Agency
IFC	International Finance Corporation
IMET	International Military Education and Training
IMF	International Monetary Fund
IO	Bureau of International Organization Affairs
IPA	International Police Academy
ITAR	International Traffic in Arms Regulations
ITS	International Trade Union Secretariat
JBUSMC	Joint Brazilian United States Military Commission
LASC	Latin American Strategy Committee
LOA	Letter of Offer and Acceptance
MAAG	Military Assistance Advisory Group
MAP	Military Assistance Program
MC	Office of Munitions Control
MDB	Multilateral Development Bank
MIPO	Multilateral Institutions Program Office
MNC	Multinational Corporation
MPC	Military Penal Code (Uruguay)
NAC	National Advisory Council on International Monetary and Financial Policies
NGO	Nongovernmental Organization
NSC	National Security Council
NSDM	National Security Decision Memorandum
OAS	Organization of American States
OMDB	Office of Multilateral Development Banks
OMB	Office of Management and Budget
OPIC	Overseas Private Investment Corporation
OPS	Office of Public Safety
PL	Public Law
PL480	Public Law 83-480 (Food for Peace)
PM	Bureau of Politico-Military Affairs
SAPRC	Security Assistance Program Review Committee
SAS	Office of Security Assistance and Sales

UNCTAD	United Nations Conference on Trade and Development
USCC	United States Catholic Conference
USDA	United States Department of Agriculture
WGMA	Working Group on Multilateral Affairs
WISC	Washington Interreligious Staff Council
WOLA	Washington Office on Latin America

Human Rights and
United States Policy
toward Latin America

INTRODUCTION

As WORLD WAR II drew to a close, the United States government appeared ready to make the protection of human rights an important component of its foreign policy. The nation was at the end of a war that had been fought in large measure to halt the violation of these rights, and it therefore seemed appropriate that international efforts to forestall further infractions should receive American support.[1] The appointment of Eleanor Roosevelt to the U.N. Commission on Human Rights underscored the nation's concern over the issue and guaranteed an energetic U.S. presence in that forum. Under the leadership of her delegation, Commission members labored more than two years to complete their initial task, the creation of the Universal Declaration of Human Rights. When the document was accepted by the General Assembly in the predawn hours of December 10, 1948, the presiding officer rose to congratulate U.S. officials for making the protection of human rights a cornerstone of American foreign policy. The assembled representatives of the world's governments responded with a standing ovation.

In the years between the beginning of the Cold War and the development of widespread opposition to the Vietnamese War, human rights all but disappeared as a component of United States foreign policy. On the domestic scene, the alleged incompatibility of human rights conventions with existing federal-state jurisdictional boundaries and the fears accompanying the relinquishing of the rights of domestic jurisdiction to international bodies influenced many groups (most notably the American Bar Association's Committee on Peace and Law through the United Nations) to oppose U.S. participation in human rights conventions. In international relations, the issue became increasingly politicized as ideological disagreements over the definition of human rights were reinforced by Cold War divisions. By the early

[1] "Human rights" is defined narrowly as the rights to life, liberty, and the integrity of the person in the sense that they cannot be denied without the impartial application of due process of law. The human rights violations upon which this study will focus are torture and other forms of cruel, inhuman, or degrading treatment, including prolonged detention without trial. This concentration upon certain human rights and the exclusion of others is not meant to imply that one group has a status superior to others; nor is it an arbitrary focus. Rather it reflects the fact that during the 1970s the U.S. government formulated its human rights policy primarily in terms of these antitorture rights. This volume is an analysis of the content of that policy, not a discussion of what one might wish the policy contained.

1950s, human rights had become no more than a propaganda weapon to be pulled out of a nation's arsenal whenever strategic considerations indicated it would be useful. The *coup de grâce* that formally eliminated human rights considerations from U.S. foreign policy came in 1953, when Senator John Bricker received the Eisenhower administration's commitment not to become a party to binding human rights agreements.

Throughout the 1950s and most of the 1960s, the nation's few human rights activists were dismissed as unrealistic (and often unreasonable) liberals, and their proposals were discarded as utopian. Then, for reasons that will be discussed at length in the following chapters, domestic political forces advocating a larger role for human rights slowly began to appear on the periphery of foreign policy decision making. By the late 1960s, human rights had clearly commenced its quiet resurgence as a component of American foreign policy, with primary emphasis upon U.S.-Third World relations. During the following decade, human rights considerations were added to the list of conditions under which the United States grants economic assistance, supplies military weapons, or supports loans by multilateral development banks. To accomplish these changes, human rights activists mobilized a substantial constituency through a number of extremely aggressive interest groups and created a State Department bureaucracy dedicated to increasing the impact of humanitarian considerations in United States foreign policy.

While the adversaries of human rights advocates were never rendered powerless, by the early 1970s they were on the defensive, engaged in holding actions rather than aggressively asserting policy preferences. In Congress, they were persons whose ideologies did not reflect the mainstream of U.S. public opinion, and their victories were won by parliamentary maneuvers rather than by the power of popularity. In the executive branch, they represented various parts of a disintegrating administration, the principals of which were unable to convince the public of their probity. By the mid-1970s, the remaining obstacles to the increased influence of human rights in American foreign policy were about to be removed.

Then Jimmy Carter became President in early 1977, and human rights promptly assumed an unparalleled prominence in foreign policy decision making: "Human rights," he announced on the thirtieth anniversary of the adoption of the Universal Declaration, "is the soul of our foreign policy." Human rights hardly replaced national security as the fundamental guiding principle of U.S. foreign policy, but where national security values were not threatened, human rights became a significant component of foreign policy decision making. American diplomats pursued the issue aggressively, using a variety of foreign policy instruments. Critics complained that each of these tools was employed inconsistently and that several of the nation's most powerful foreign policy instruments were not mustered into the effort to promote human rights. Everyone agreed, however, that human rights considerations had come to enjoy a substantial role in United States foreign policy in general and in U.S. policy toward Latin America in particular. One part of American foreign policy had changed. This book is an analysis of the nature of that change.

Analyses of how policy changes occur sometimes tend to underemphasize the reasons *why* change was necessary, for it is possible to examine organizational decision making with only cursory reference to the stimuli that created the need for decisions. One major argument of this book, however, is that the nature of an issue determines the values that impinge upon decision making and the process by which decisions are reached. Issues that arise out of crises involve values and decision-making procedures different from those that characterize routine issues, for example, just as national security issues involve procedures and participants different from humanitarian issues. Since the perception of an issue is crucially important in defining the bureaucratic environment in which United States policy is shaped, it is important to understand why human rights became the central issue of U.S.-Latin American relations in the 1970s. This requires a brief digression on what policy makers perceived as the objective reality of human rights in Latin America.

ORIGIN OF THE ISSUE

Statements by United States policy makers in the early and mid-1970s often explained lapses of respect for human rights as an indication of either a shortcoming of Hispanic political culture or, more frequently, an anomalous despotism. These were not novel interpretations: prior to the twilight of the tyrants in the 1950s, U.S. officials and academicians had been nearly unanimous in attributing human rights violations to the individual tyrannies of Batista, Pérez Jiménez, Perón, Rojas Pinilla, and Trujillo. Two decades later, there was a familiar ring to the arguments that human rights violations reflected lamentable individual excesses that responsible Latin American officials were powerless to halt. In mid-1974, for example, the Department of State informed Congress that "Chilean authorities have acknowledged instances of mistreatment of detainees; they have declared that such abuses are not sanctioned, and that persons responsible for them are

5

being tried and punished."[2] In late 1976, a State Department survey of human rights practices among foreign aid recipients reported that "Argentine leaders . . . are seeking to curb violations of human rights, but . . . they cannot yet control the situation."[3]

Significantly, the argument that human rights violations reflected individual excesses was offered only by the Nixon-Ford administration to counter proposals that the U.S. government halt aid or otherwise sanction the most repressive Latin American governments. But even if these officials disbelieved what they were saying—a debatable point—the fact that they would offer this argument to explain why the United States should not express its disapproval of rights violations indicates that their audience, primarily Congress, was thought to be susceptible to this time-honored interpretation.[4]

Generally, however, it was obvious by the mid-1970s that human rights violations in Latin America were the result of some dynamic other than the despotism of powerful individuals or the sadism of minor officials. At that time, such an interpretation may have described to a limited degree some of the hemisphere's more rudimentary political systems—Nicaragua until mid-1979, for example—but it failed to capture the essence of politics as they evolved during the 1960s and 1970s in many of the region's most important nations. And, very significantly, human rights conditions in these nations, particularly Brazil and later Chile, were the first to attract the attention of U.S. human rights activists. In retrospect, it was difficult to have missed the evidence that something more than a changing of the

[2] U.S. Congress, House, Committee on Foreign Affairs, Subcommittees on Inter-American Affairs and on International Organizations and Movements, *Human Rights in Chile*, 93d Cong., 2d Sess., June 12, 1974, p. 113. The statement was made by Harry W. Shlaudeman, who in 1976 became assistant secretary of state for inter-American affairs.

[3] U.S. Congress, House, Committee on International Relations, *Human Rights and U.S. Policy: Argentina, Haiti, Indonesia, Iran, Peru, and the Philippines; Reports Submitted to the Committee on International Relations, House of Representatives, by the Department of State*, 94th Cong., 2d Sess., December 31, 1976, p. 5.

[4] A former deputy assistant secretary of state for East Asian and Pacific affairs commented that the single purpose of human rights reports during 1975 to 1976 was to placate Congress. He noted: "After the reports were completed we had to talk with each embassy and explain that they [the reports] were just to satisfy liberals on the foreign aid committees." Interview with J. Owen Zurhellen, Jr., April 18, 1980, Asheville, North Carolina. The Carter administration also employed the argument that violations represented individual excesses but not in regard to any Latin American country. See, for example, the defense of institutionalized repression in Indonesia in U.S. Congress, *Country Reports on Human Rights Practices Report Submitted to the Committee on Foreign Relations, U.S. Senate, and the Committee on International Relations, U.S. House of Representatives, by the Department of State*, 95th Cong., 2d Sess., February 3, 1978, p. 225.

palace guard had occurred in the "developed" polities of Latin America—Argentina, Brazil, Chile, and Uruguay—where a vigorous pluralism was exchanged for the harshest of dictatorships. Previous crises among civilian political groups had encouraged military coups in these countries, so the exchange was not unique; the novel feature of post-Alliance politics in key Latin American nations was the type of government that emerged from these military takeovers. The transitory despotism of individual *caudillos* was replaced by a wholly distinct type of regime, aptly described as bureaucratic authoritarian.[5] United States policy toward human rights in Latin America was created in reference to this specific type of regime.

After the 1964 initiation of the bureaucratic-authoritarian model in Brazil, similar regimes were established in many of the major nations of Latin America, particularly in the southern cone of South America: Uruguay in 1972-1973, Chile in 1973, and Argentina in 1966 and again in 1976. These regimes were supported by the coercive powers of the military and the technocratic abilities of highly sophisticated civilian sectors, members of which characteristically prefer a minimum of interference by politicians and the public in the formulation and implementation of public policy. These bureaucratic-authoritarian regimes differed from previous forms of military authoritarianism in that their goal was not to halt fighting among rival groups of middle- and upper-class political elites or to seize power for the sake of personal gain but rather to destroy permanently a perceived threat to the existing structure of socioeconomic privilege by eliminating the political participation of the numerical majority, principally the working or (to use a broader, more accurate term) popular classes.[6] Bureaucratic-authoritarian regimes developed in response to increased popular political participation.

[5] Guillermo A. O'Donnell, *Modernization and Bureaucratic Authoritarianism: Studies in South American Politics* (Berkeley: Institute of International Studies, University of California, 1973), pp. 89-95.

[6] The term "popular classes" is meant as a rough translation of "*sectores populares.*" The term identifies the rural and urban working class, the lumpenproletariat, and much of the lower middle class in Latin America. For a discussion of the difficulties in identifying the supporters of popular governments in Latin America, see Lars Schoultz, "The Socioeconomic Determinants of Popular-Authoritarian Electoral Behavior: The Case of Peronism," *American Political Science Review* 71 (December 1977): 1423-1446.

The term "structure of privilege" is used throughout this volume to identify the groups or classes of citizens who benefit disproportionately from a society's existing distribution of power and wealth. It is intended to avoid the more value-laden terms generally associated with particular modes of economic production. As a socioeconomic category, the term was coined by Robert L. Heilbroner in *The Limits of American Capitalism* (New York: Harper and Row, 1965), pp. 70-75.

7

The history of Latin American politics during the past eighty years is characterized by the gradual emergence of new groups of political participants—the industrial bourgeoisie, the salaried middle class, the urban working class, and in some cases the peasantry—and their incorporation into governing coalitions previously composed only of traditional elites—agrarian interests, exporters, the Church hierarchy, and the military. Requirements for admission to the coalition were, first, a demonstration of political power and, second, a commitment not to threaten the existence of other coalition members. Except in instances of civil war or social revolution, groups were added but never subtracted from the governing coalition. Pluralism of this type prohibited substantial policy innovations because each coalition member enjoyed a veto over actions that it defined as threatening to its continued participation in politics. Twentieth-century Latin American politics therefore came to be characterized by the extraordinary variety of its participants—"a living museum" was Charles Anderson's felicitous phrase—and the immobility of its policy-making processes.[7] In Latin America and elsewhere, the rules governing politics functioned to discourage fundamental alterations in the existing structure of privilege.

While the policy-making process remained static, the distribution of political power in most Latin American societies was shifting in favor of groups whose power rested upon popularity. Until well into the twentieth century, coercion enjoyed an overwhelming advantage over popularity as a currency of Latin American political power. But then a series of fundamental socioeconomic changes—the growth of cities, the development of mass media, the birth of mass political parties, among others—encouraged higher levels of political awareness among groups whose previous passivity had dictated their exclusion from political activity. This political mobilization of new groups caused the balance between popularity and coercion to be struck anew. By the dint of their numbers and organization, the middle class and later the urban working class came to enjoy a substantially enlarged political influence during the twentieth century. As power was slowly redistributed in such a way that popularity challenged coercion as the dominant political currency, a new era of Latin American politics began.

Nothing could be more indicative of this changing power relationship than the ability of popular classes to place their representatives in the highest public offices. However different their ideologies and

[7] Charles W. Anderson, *Politics and Economic Change in Latin America* (New York: Van Nostrand Reinhold, 1967), p. 104.

policies may have been, the elections of Vargas and Quadros/Goulart in Brazil, Perón in Argentina, and Allende in Chile signaled the maturation of social groups whose claim to power rested predominantly upon popularity. Many of these leaders provided their followers with little more than symbolic rewards in exchange for their support, but even these offerings raised the political consciousness and expectations of traditionally passive social sectors. Other popular leaders did more to provide substantive benefits for their supporters. But each encouraged an intensification of the attitudinal shift that social scientists once called the revolution of rising expectations.

Since the growth rate of Latin American economies invariably lagged behind the surge in popular groups' expectations, the material desires that their representatives were pledged to fulfill had to be financed by the redistribution of existing wealth. Direct redistributions—for example, land reforms—could not occur because they violated the pluralist norm that prohibits the implementation of policies that destroy the power of existing political groups. Thus indirect redistributions— for example, extremely progressive social welfare legislation, price controls on basic commodities, and government-dictated wage adjustments—were attempted that tended to redistribute, albeit indirectly, the wealth of Latin American societies.

The problem, of course, was that these programs had to be financed. Redistributive legislation—tax increases—however indirect, threatened to alter the existing structure of privilege in Latin America. Trapped by the rules of Latin American pluralism, popular governments were left with no alternative other than to fund their supporters' expected rewards through expansionist monetary policies. The rewards were financed by printing money: money to meet increased government payrolls, money to pay for increased public welfare services, money to subsidize the production of commodities whose market prices were held below the costs of production. This activity invariably led to extraordinary inflationary pressures, which also threatened to alter the structure of privilege. It particularly damaged members of the middle class who were unable to hedge against rising costs, yet who were insufficiently poor to benefit from many of the inflation-financed government programs.

In addition to these ominous attempts to redistribute tangible assets, popular governments posed a more subtle threat to many members of the governing coalition. Popular governments tended to attack the symbols of privilege by which the upper and middle classes established their social identities. Labor relations boards were created to protect *peones* from the arbitrary power of landowners, mandatory service charges replaced voluntary tips, and legal rights were granted to domestic servants. Above all else, the deference of the working class toward the upper and middle classes was substantially eroded during the periods of popular governments. Perhaps more than any other change except unrestrained inflation, this symbolic diminution of social position convinced the groups that were to profit from the repression of human rights in the 1960s and 1970s that their social identities were endangered. To these privileged groups, social prestige (and the political power that in large measure determines its allocation) could not be divided indefinitely and still retain value: if everyone is permitted to stand on tiptoe, no one can see better.[8] Conditioned by generations of relative privilege, the traditional elites of Latin America and their emulative allies in other classes refused to acquiesce quietly to a redistribution of symbolic goods that had always been theirs alone. From the perspective of these groups, the fundamental rule of Latin American pluralism—do not threaten the existence of other coalition members—had been violated by governments whose political power rested upon popularity. To eliminate this threat, the power of popular governments had to be reduced.

But so long as popularity is used to select some members of the governing coalition and so long as the existence of coalition members cannot be threatened, the rules prohibit the devaluation of political power based upon popularity. Under these rules, if majority rule threatens to destroy minority privilege, the leaders of popular governments can be asked only to show restraint, to reduce voluntarily their redistributive activity. Where this proves unsuccessful, the political power of popularity can only be reduced by destroying democratic pluralism. Facing what they believed to be their own political extermination, coercion-based coalition members staged preemptive coups not against a specific government but against a type of regime: democracy. In Argentina, Brazil, Chile, and Uruguay, popularity was unable to match brute force.

The extreme animosity of these confrontations can be attributed in part to the apparent chaos created by policies of the popular governments. These policies were the results of a complex set of interrelated pressures: the desire for immediate improvements in the standard of living of the poor, the continuing demand that popular support be maintained to offset the power of rival political groups, the demonstrated unwillingness of international financial institutions to endorse or otherwise support any but the most orthodox monetary and fiscal programs, the continued control of domestic wealth by groups

[8] For the origin and generalized applicability of this metaphor, see Fred Hirsch, *The Social Limits to Growth* (Cambridge: Harvard University Press, 1974).

opposing popular governments, and the need to extract an economic surplus in order to invest for future growth. No Third World government operating in a pluralist political system has managed these pressures successfully for more than a short period of time. Forced to accede to the demands of every group able to exert substantial economic and political pressure, popular governments typically lose control over economic policy.

The great advantage of the bureaucratic-authoritarian regimes that replace popular governments is that they are able to eliminate some of the political pressures surrounding the formulation of economic policy. Because these regimes destroy the ability of popular groups to exert pressure on policy makers, they are able to implement economic policies that emphasize accumulation over distribution, growth over consumption, and (to a varying but generally lesser extent) a free market over government intervention in the production and distribution of goods. These are the traditional Western monetary and fiscal policies that command the respect of major public and private financial institutions, including the United States government. Once implemented, these orthodox policies cause prices of essential commodities to soar, government services to be curtailed, and unemployment to rise. The standard of living of social sectors that support popular governments is immediately and significantly depressed.

Just as privileged groups fight back when their political existence is threatened by a popular government, so the supporters of popular governments can be expected to resist first the destruction of their ability to participate in politics and then the economic shock treatment administered by bureaucratic-authoritarian governments. Given this potential opposition, government repression must focus upon the complex task of deterring political activity. Measures must be taken to forestall strikes, slowdowns, and demonstrations. Labor unions must be destroyed, political parties disbanded, media silenced, conversations monitored. It is at this point that the violations of human rights became notorious in many of the major nations of Latin America during the 1960s and 1970s. As an example, Table I.1 contains a selective list of major events related to human rights in Chile from September 1973 until early 1976. It is not a complete list, nor is it balanced, but it leaves no doubt about the fate of political pluralism in the nation that had been the pride of Latin American democracy. Table I.1 underscores the general fact that the subjection of any politically mobilized class entails an uncommon level of brutality because it involves not only the elimination of the class's current generation of political activists but also the destruction of those institutions (po-

11

INTRODUCTION

TABLE I.1
Selected List of Human Rights-Related Government Actions
Chile, 1973-1976

September 1973	Military deposes President Salvador Allende. Four-man military junta dissolves Congress, imposes martial law, a curfew, and strict press censorship. All Socialist and Communist party leaders are ordered to report to the Defense Ministry. All Marxist political parties declared illegal. All non-Marxist parties declared in recess. Eight hundred thousand-member Central Workers Confederation abolished. Scheduled wage increase cancelled. Work week increased from forty-four to forty-eight hours without extra pay. University autonomy suspended. All university rectors are replaced by government-appointed personnel. Schools of sociology, journalism, and education in all Chilean universities are closed. Technical schools are also closed on basis of allegations that they are "centers of leftism." Junta announces arrest of 7,000 persons, 300 deaths.
October	CIA Director William Colby testifies before Congress that 2,000 to 3,000 people have been killed in Chile, many by summary execution.
January 1974	Amnesty International charges that political arrests, torture, and executions without trial are continuing, many with the assistance of Brazilian police.
February	Junta chieftain Pinochet announces that a state of siege and curfew will remain in force, political activity will be banned for at least five years, and military control of the government will continue beyond that time.
April	Roman Catholic Church issues a formal declaration accusing the Chilean government of torture, characterizing Chileans as living in "a climate of insecurity and fear."
June	Junta breaks with Christian Democracy, imposing strict censorship on Radio Balmaceda, the party's major station.
August	President Pinochet announces that Marxist parties will be permanently outlawed. Three hundred persons from Santiago slums are arrested and sent to work in northern desert region.
September	Amnesty International issues eighty-page report, alleging that 5,000 to 30,000 persons have been killed, 6,000 to 10,000 remain prisoners. "The death toll is unprecedented in Latin American history." AI lists the most common forms of torture as "prolonged beatings with truncheons, fists, or bags of moist material, electricity to all parts of the body, burning with cigarettes or acid." Exiled General Carlos Prats and wife murdered in Buenos Aires.
December	Inter-American Commission on Human Rights issues a 175-page report charging Chilean government with "extremely serious violations" of ten fundamental human rights.
March 1975	State of siege extended. Government announces that the number of arrests since September 1973 has been 41,759 and that 5,154 still remain in custody. Government closes art exhibit by Luis Guillermo Nuñez at Santiago's French-Chile Institute. Government arrests Nuñez, whose work deals with alienation and loss of freedom.
August	Forty-four professors, students, and personnel at University of Chile arrested for "Marxist activities."
September	Episcopal Conference of Chile publishes report, "Gospel and Peace," condemning climate of fear and hatred.
October	Christian Democrat leader Bernardo Leighton and wife seriously wounded by gunfire in Rome.

INTRODUCTION

TABLE I.1 (cont.)

December	U.N. General Assembly adopts a resolution accusing Chile of "the institutionalized practice of torture." Government authorities at provincial level authorized to close temporarily any media that offend the government or "distort the truth."
February	U.N. Commission on Human Rights votes to accept the finding of a five-member
1976	panel that charges the Pinochet government with "barbaric sadism."
	Socialist leader Orlando Letelier murdered in Washington, D.C.

litical parties, labor unions, university faculties, peasant cooperatives) that could serve as centers of organized dissent.

In brief, the reason why large-scale human rights violations occurred in much of Latin America during the 1960s and 1970s was that the survival of bureaucratic-authoritarian governments depended upon the elimination of dissent by politically active citizens whose normal means of expression were destroyed and who probably would have refused to endure in silence a rapid, severe decline in their standard of living. As active dissenters were eliminated physically, potential dissenters were intimidated into silence.

During the 1960s and 1970s, leaders of repressive governments argued that their draconian measures, however lamentable, had no impact upon the typical citizen; rather their repression was directed at armed terrorists intent upon the violent overthrow of constitutional government. Thus it is extremely important to distinguish attempts by bureaucratic-authoritarian governments to cope with the problem of guerrilla warfare, on the one hand, from efforts to depoliticize large groups of citizens, on the other. While it is true that the new leaders inherited the problem of guerrilla insurgency from the popular governments they deposed, and that they took drastic, effective steps to eliminate the insurgency, it is also true that repressive governments went far beyond counterinsurgency. They eliminated at the same time the ability of popular classes to participate in liberal pluralist politics. A list of actions taken by Uruguayan authorities is particularly illustrative, because in Uruguay the Tupamaros were a credible threat to the government. As Table I.2 indicates, however, the authorities did much more than decimate the Tupamaros; they destroyed popular government.

During the 1960s and 1970s, the human rights violations by bureaucratic-authoritarian governments in Argentina, Brazil, Chile, and Uruguay were supplemented by more traditional forms of repression in other Latin American nations. The governments of Bolivia, El Salvador, Guatemala, Haiti, Nicaragua, and Paraguay were frequently

13

INTRODUCTION

TABLE I.2
SELECTED LIST OF HUMAN RIGHTS-RELATED GOVERNMENT ACTIONS
URUGUAY, 1972-1975

April *1972*	Congress declares a thirty-day "state of internal war," granting the President special powers to suspend individual liberties and to place the nation under martial law. Eight members of the Communist party are killed by police in a confrontation at party headquarters. At their funeral, Archbishop Partelli condemns the severity with which the war on the Tupamaros is being waged. President decrees strict censorship, banning "all forms of public criticism or censure of the decisions of the authorities in the fight against subversion."
June	Permanent Commission of Catholic Bishops writes President Bordaberry to protest both "inhuman treatment dealt some prisoners, whether linked to subversion or not," and "confessions extracted by means of terror." President responds that "conventional standards are not applicable. . . . Information is a decisive factor. . . . Information is obtained in some instances spontaneously . . . and in others after rigorous interrogations. I defend the rigor and severity of interrogations . . . which make possible bloodless victories."
July	State security law takes effect, cancelling state of internal war but subjecting accused subversives to military courts. Suspension of individual liberties continues.
October	Colorado party leader Jorge Batlle arrested for making remarks offensive to the morale of the armed forces.
January *1973*	Congress passes new education law, granting the President full control of all education. Appointments based upon merit are replaced by noncompetitive government appointments. The right of teachers and pupils to strike is revoked.
February	Following a severe crisis, President Bordaberry agrees to grant the military supervisory control of the government through a National Security Council.
April	Publication of three Montevideo dailies is suspended for violating military censorship by reporting on a proposed attempt to deprive Senator Enrique Erro of his parliamentary immunity.
June	President bypasses Congress and decrees an extension of the suspension of individual liberties. Congress refuses to impeach Senator Erro so that he can be tried by the military as a Tupamaro. Congress dissolved by the President. Military orders the arrest of Senator Erro. Schools are closed until late July, press censorship is tightened with a special prohibition on any report that "directly or indirectly attributes dictatorial goals to the executive power." All political meetings banned. Four hundred thousand-member National Workers Confederation is outlawed, its leaders arrested, its property confiscated. All strikes are outlawed, then controlled. Nineteen departmental (state) councils dissolved by the President. Troops occupy factories, banks, public offices, oil refineries, and schools.
July	New labor law is announced, with obligatory membership of all workers in a new labor confederation. Previous union leaders prohibited from holding office in the new confederation.
October	National University closed.
November	Leftist parties and organizations dissolved. Leftist media closed.
May *1974*	Newly functioning National University administration authorized to fire any university professor who lacks "a well-known affiliation for democracy."

14

TABLE I.2 (cont.)

June	Amnesty International and the International Commission of Jurists release a detailed report on torture in Uruguay.
January 1975	International Commission of Jurists charges Uruguayan government with increased torture. Amnesty International issues an additional protest.
April	Government dissolves federation of high-school teachers. Government arrests 1,800 workers at the Salto Grande hydroelectric project for attending a mass meeting. President Bordaberry announces on national TV that Uruguay will not participate in U.N. activities for International Women's Year because, among other reasons, such efforts "aggressively launch women into the arena of political battles that are occurring in the world today. . . . It is clear that at the root of all these attempts there is a materialist philosophy and underlying them is the Marxist conception of the state and society . . . to which we can in no way adhere."
July	Government announces that 20,000 books at the library of the Education and Culture Ministry's Council on Secondary Education have been destroyed in order to purge the schools of politically unacceptable texts. Included are books "whose content does not conform to the fundamental principles of patriotism" and "those books on mathematics and natural sciences, as well as language books, in which concepts prejudicial to the foundations of classical or Western thought may be introduced."

attacked by human rights activists in Washington and later by United States policy makers. But during most of these two decades, U.S. government officials tended to interpret repression as endemic in Latin America's most rudimentary political systems and to believe that elites were unable to respond positively to U.S. efforts on behalf of human rights. None of these nations was ignored, and after mid-1978 Nicaragua was a center of policy makers' attention, but in general the attitude in Washington was to overlook or at least not to sanction the repressive governments of the most traditional Latin American societies. As the following chapters will demonstrate, United States policy toward human rights in Latin America developed as a response to repression in the modern polities of Latin America.

Cuba was also attacked regularly for its human rights violations, yet the Castro government is included only infrequently in the following pages. This is not because the Cuban political environment was identified improperly as repressive of certain fundamental human rights, nor because revolutionary Cuba should be spared any criticism. Cuba is excluded because United States policy toward the Castro government was not based upon the regime's alleged repressiveness but rather upon its embrace of communism. Castro need not have shot a single *batistiano* nor jailed a single counterrevolutionary to provoke the extraordinarily hostile reaction of the United States. One former Senate staff member captured perfectly an attitude not restricted to members of Congress: "People in Congress don't think of Cuba . . . in terms

15

of Latin America now. They think of Cuba in terms of a whole lot of people down in Florida who will raise hell if you do anything about it; and they think of Cuba in terms of Africa; and they think of Cuba in terms of Russia. And it's only after you get all those things out of the way that you might find a handful of people who would think of Cuba as part of Latin America."[9] It is pointless to use the case of Cuba for insight into United States policy toward human rights; such an examination would yield instead an understanding of United States policy toward revolutionary socialist governments in Latin America.

ORGANIZATION AND SUBSTANCE

There are two major parts to this volume. The first is an analysis of the societal environment, or the constraints that political forces outside the United States government place upon the freedom of foreign policy decision makers. Within this part, the initial chapter is devoted to an analysis of *public opinion* toward United States-Latin American relations in general and toward U.S. policy regarding human rights violations in particular. Its basic message is that the public has few opinions about United States policy toward Latin America, a fact that will be familiar to many readers of this book. Many of the data in the chapter have never been presented with an analysis, however, and all of them contribute to subsequent discussions of the options available to policy makers. The chapter on public opinion is followed by a lengthy chapter on *interest groups*. It is divided into two sections, one describing the structure and goals of interest groups concerned with United States policy toward Latin America and the other analyzing their impact upon policy. That concludes the first part.

The second part is an analysis of the content and creation of U.S. policy toward human rights in Latin America. As the first part emphasizes the values that outside actors impose upon the policy-making process, the second concentrates upon the manner in which these values are accepted, rejected, or presaged by bureaucratic actors. Each of the six chapters emphasizes a different aspect of United States policy. Chapter 3, a discussion of *diplomacy* as a foreign policy instrument, distinguishes between the policies of the Nixon-Ford and the Carter administrations. Chapters 4 and 5 concentrate upon the use of *economic aid* as a tool to implement human rights policy. Both of

---

[9] Norman J. Ornstein, in "Congress and U.S. Foreign Policy toward Latin America," mimeographed transcript of a Conference on the United States, U.S. Foreign Policy, and Latin American and Caribbean Regimes, Washington, D.C., March 31, 1978, p. 11.

these chapters place major emphasis upon the role of Congress, a policy-making body whose power is typically underestimated in studies of U.S.-Latin American relations. Chapter 6 is an analysis of *military aid*, a major policy instrument and a source of continuing controversy. Unlike the other foreign policy instruments, many foreign policy analysts consider military assistance to be a principal cause of human rights violations. To understand the nature of this controversy, Chapter 6 includes an analysis of the changing values underlying military aid to Latin America. Chapter 7 examines attempts by the United States government to pursue the issue of human rights in the *multilateral development banks*, particularly the World Bank Group and the Inter-American Development Bank. There is also a discussion of human rights and the International Monetary Fund. Finally, Chapter 8 explores the extent to which four *linkages to the private sector* (the Export-Import Bank, the Overseas Private Investment Corporation, the Office of Munitions Control, and the American Institute for Free Labor Development) have been used to influence the level of repression of human rights.[10]

Within the six chapters of the second part is a discussion of every aspect of postwar United States policy toward human rights in Latin America. When combined with the analysis of societal values presented in part one, they form a comprehensive picture of United States policy toward the most prominent issue of inter-American relations in the 1970s.

[10] Missing from this volume is an analysis of the activities of the Central Intelligence Agency. It is absent because adequate reliable data on its activities are not available. It is unfortunate that a bureaucracy that has been a highly active foreign policy instrument must be mentioned only occasionally here, but the only alternative to exclusion is an analysis based primarily upon the examination of memoirs.

· 1 ·

LATIN AMERICA AND U.S.
PUBLIC OPINION

NEARLY three decades ago Gabriel Almond presented an impressive array of data to support his blunt declaration that the typical U.S. citizen is indifferent to foreign policy issues.[1] With the notable exception of American participation in the Vietnam War, little has been discovered in subsequent years to suggest that his assertion was incorrect.

In the specific foreign policy area of United States-Latin American relations, the data suggest that indifference is a more appropriate description of the pollsters than the polled. In its first thirty-six years (1935-1971), for example, the Gallup Poll did not ask a separate question about any Latin American nation, and during that same period the few existing inquiries by other polling organizations generally focused upon perceptions of major problems of U.S. foreign policy as opposed to Latin America per se—for example, Axis activity in Latin America, communist involvement in the Cuban revolution, and U.S. intervention in the Dominican Republic.[2] On the rare occasions when questions have been asked about Latin America, not only have they tended to be oriented toward a broader concern than attitudes toward a Latin American phenomenon, they have often been phrased improperly as well. One example of both of these aspects of polling is the October 1973 Roper Poll query: "What do you think— that his [Allende's] overthrow was good because he was a Marxist, or

[1] Gabriel A. Almond, *The American People and Foreign Policy*, rev. ed. (New York: Frederick A. Praeger, 1960), p. 53.

[2] The Gallup Poll has on occasion included a few Latin American countries on lists of nations that respondents were asked to scale from the "highest degree of liking" to the lowest. See, for example, George H. Gallup, *The Gallup Poll: Public Opinion 1935-1971* (New York: Random House, 1972), pp. 2104-2105, and *The Gallup Opinion Index*, November 1976, p. 4, and March 1980, p. 32. One rare survey of public opinion toward a Latin American government came in early 1975 in the form of a sixteen-nation survey of attitudes toward Chile. It was conducted by the Gallup Poll and financed by the Chilean government. The results indicated that by a margin of greater than 2 to 1 world public opinion viewed Chile as in worse condition under the Pinochet government than it had been under Allende. In a comparison survey, however, Gallup found that 64 percent of all Chileans thought they were "living better." *Miami Herald*, October 13, 1975. The Pinochet government subsequently became a regular purchaser of Gallup services.

bad because he was democratically elected?"[3] Given the low quality
and scarcity of data, it is not surprising that a recent volume that
surveys more than three decades of U.S. public opinion contains not
a single mention of Latin America, and no Latin American nation
figures among the fourteen countries discussed in the book's chapter
on foreign policy.[4]

The limited data that are available have little to demonstrate other
than that public opinion on issues of U.S.-Latin American relations
varies dramatically, sometimes over fairly brief periods. The April
1965 invasion of the Dominican Republic is an excellent example.
The event received premier coverage from the media, including multiple television appearances by President Johnson to explain why that
sovereign state required a unilateral incursion by 20,000 U.S. Marines.[5] In May, the Gallup Poll found that only 7 percent of the U.S.
public had no opinion of LBJ's actions. As used to be true of nearly
all major presidential initiatives in foreign affairs, an overwhelming
majority of respondents—76 percent—supported the invasion deci-

[3] The response: 19 percent good, 31 percent bad, 50 percent no opinion.
[4] Rita James Simon, *Public Opinion in America: 1936-1970* (Chicago: Markham,
1974).
[5] The President made three televised appearances to offer three separate explanations for the invasion. On April 28, 1965, he reported that the Dominican authorities "are no longer able to guarantee [U.S. citizens'] safety." He therefore "ordered
the Secretary of Defense to put the necessary American troops ashore in order to give
protection to hundreds of Americans who are still in the Dominican Republic and
to escort them safely back to this country." On April 30, Johnson broadened his
concern to include the welfare of non-U.S. citizens: "There is great danger to the
life of foreign nationals and of thousands of Dominican citizens, our fellow citizens
of this hemisphere." At this time he also noted that "there are signs that people
trained outside the Dominican Republic are seeking to gain control." On May 2, LBJ
was more specific:

> Communist leaders, many of them trained in Cuba, seeing a chance to increase
> disorder, to gain a foothold, joined the revolution. . . . A popular democratic
> revolution . . . was taken over and really seized and placed into the hands of
> a band of Communist conspirators. . . . The American nations cannot, must
> not, and will not permit the establishment of another Communist government
> in the Western Hemisphere. . . . Our goal, in keeping with the great principles
> of the inter-American system, is to prevent another Communist state in this
> hemisphere.

President Johnson then added a final explanatory sentence that characterized the
Vietnam-oriented mentality of U.S. foreign policy at the time: "I want you to know
and I want the world to know that as long as I am President of this country, we are
going to defend ourselves." *Public Papers of the Presidents of the United States: Lyndon
B. Johnson, 1965,* 2 vols. (Washington, D.C.: Government Printing Office, 1966),
1:461, 465, 471-474.

sion.[6] Six months later, one out of every five U.S. citizens had changed his or her mind about the wisdom of an invasion: 27 percent had no opinion on whether it was a good idea, 52 percent approved, and a nearly stable 21 percent continued to disapprove. In 1975, a decade after the fact, 9 percent thought the invasion was a "proud moment" in U.S. foreign policy, 20 percent thought it was a "dark moment," and 27 percent thought it was neither. A 43 percent plurality held no opinion on what the involvement signified.[7]

The case of United States policy toward the Cuban revolution is also revealing of the public's fluctuating attitudes toward inter-American relations. During the period 1959 to 1963, a substantial majority (about 65 percent) of the population repeatedly rejected the idea that the United States should invade Cuba, but the public's opinion of Fidel Castro dropped from 48 percent unfavorable to 81 percent unfavorable in fewer than ten action-packed months (June 1959 to May 1960). By June 1961, six of ten U.S. citizens thought we should boycott Cuban goods, and a year later 49 percent judged we should do something to rid the island of the Castro government: 10 percent favored the John Birch Society's solution of bombing the government into submission, 13 percent favored the Kennedy approach of an embargo ("starve them out" was the Gallup phrase), and 25 percent favored something short of war.[8] For more than a decade, a substantial majority of the public remained hostile to the Cuban government. In a 1971 Harris Survey, for example, 61 percent of the respondents opposed allowing Cuban cigars to be sold in the United States, while only 22 percent favored such a move.[9] But by the middle of the 1970s, the public had apparently changed its opinion of Cuba. In 1973, 51 percent of the respondents to one survey favored the resumption of diplomatic relations, while 33 percent were opposed.[10] Unfortunately,

[6] On the decline in the public's deference to presidential authority in foreign policy, see Daniel Yankelovich, "Farewell to 'President Knows Best'," *Foreign Affairs* 57 (1978): 670-671.

[7] *The Gallup Poll, 1935-1971*, p. 1942; Chicago Council on Foreign Relations, *American Public Opinion and U.S. Foreign Policy 1975*, ICPSR Codebook 5808 (Ann Arbor: Inter-University Consortium for Political and Social Research, 1977), p. 122.

[8] Only 22 percent thought the United States should do nothing. *The Gallup Poll, 1935-1971*, pp. 1624, 1681, 1721, 1787.

[9] *The Harris Survey Yearbook of Public Opinion 1971* (New York: Louis Harris and Associates, 1975), p. 95.

[10] The remaining 13 percent had no opinion. *Current Opinion* 3 (March 1975): 25. *The Harris Survey Yearbook of Public Opinion 1973* (New York: Louis Harris and Associates, 1976), p. 259. In 1975, a Roper Poll found only 45 percent favoring a resumption of relations with Cuba, while in the same year Harris reported the figure at 53 percent. In March 1977, Gallup reported that 53 percent of its respondents wished to resume relations, while only 32 percent were opposed to the idea. *The*

none of these soundings of public opinion probed the reasons for these attitudes; thus they told policy makers very little about citizens' views of the Cuban revolution other than that they fluctuate.

In addition to the observation that public opinion on issues of U.S.-Latin American relations fluctuates quite dramatically, a number of studies have supported the common proposition that the public is largely uninformed about foreign affairs.[11] To a somewhat lesser extent, this evaluation characterizes opinions on domestic issues as well. In the mid-1970s, Philip Converse portrayed the public's attitudes as "wretchedly informed and feebly structured. . . . popular levels of information about public affairs are, from the point of view of the informed observer, astonishingly low."[12] When this low level of knowledge is combined with the observation that opinions about foreign affairs tend to fluctuate more in reference to the passing of time than to observable changes in international relations, it is justifiable to question whether survey results measure public opinion or, indeed, whether public opinion can be said to exist on most questions of United States policy toward Latin America. This questioning has led authorities such as Daniel Yankelovich to conclude that most public opinion polls measure "what the public believes prior to having considered a foreign policy issue in depth."[13] The issue of human rights provides significant support for this interpretation.

HUMAN RIGHTS

There are relatively few data on United States citizens' attitudes toward the international protection of human rights, and estimates of public

Gallup Opinion Index, July 1977, p. 28; *American Public Opinion and U.S. Foreign Policy 1975*, p. 140. The desire to resume diplomatic relations did not mean that the public changed its generally low regard for Cuba, however. In a mid-1976 Gallup Poll, only 15 percent of the respondents held favorable views of Cuba, the lowest rating for any of twenty-five nations, including the People's Republic of China and the Soviet Union. See *The Gallup Opinion Index*, November 1976, p. 13.

[11] See the list of sources provided in Robert Weissberg, *Public Opinion and Popular Government* (Englewood Cliffs, N.J.: Prentice-Hall, 1976), p. 136n; *Roper Reports 75-7*, p. A.

[12] Philip E. Converse, "Public Opinion and Voting Behavior," in *Handbook of Political Science*, ed. Fred I. Greenstein and Nelson W. Polsby (Reading, Mass.: Addison-Wesley, 1975), 4: 78-79.

[13] Yankelovich, "Farewell to 'President Knows Best'," p. 690. For a more systematic treatment of this issue, see George F. Bishop et al., "Pseudo-Opinions on Public Affairs," *Public Opinion Quarterly* 44 (Summer 1980): 198-209, where it is argued that "for a significant segment of the population (a third?) we may be measuring not much more than their general positive or negative affect toward the government, rather than specific beliefs about the policy alternatives contained in our questions" (p. 208).

opinion are therefore highly speculative. Many foreign policy makers believe that citizens are concerned about human rights in an abstract sense but that their level of interest in the issue of U.S. policy toward human rights violations is extremely low. There are some data to support this perception. First, at a fairly abstract level, the public favors government efforts to promote human rights. For example, 85 percent of the respondents to a 1974 Harris Survey said it was important that the United States be a leader in moral values, and 70 percent said the United States should help to bring a democratic form of government to other nations.[14] While this appears to be an impressive commitment to encourage one type of human rights, it is quite possible that these responses indicate less a desire to promote human rights than a perception of the United States as the guardian of values associated with these rights. This is a most important distinction.

The perception of the United States as a self-appointed protector of noble values stems from a peculiar sense of historical innocence, a belief that the United States is not like other nations but rather exceeds them in the nobility of its purpose and the purity of its past. To John F. Kennedy, this special blessing implied an obligation: "We are still the keystone in the arch of freedom," he told his final audience in November 1963. Later that same day he was scheduled to tell a Dallas audience that "we, in this country . . . are—by destiny rather than choice—the watchmen on the walls of world freedom."[15] In 1965, his successor reminded a White House audience that "history and our own achievements have . . . thrust upon us the principal responsibility for the protection of freedom on earth."[16] Although President Carter altered the established terminology from "freedom" to "human rights," in his inaugural address he associated his administration with the vision of his predecessors: "Ours was the first society openly to define itself in terms of both spirituality and human liberty. It is that unique self-definition which has given us an exceptional appeal—but it also imposes on us a special obligation, to take on those moral duties which, when assumed, seem invariably to be in our own best interest."

This elite perception of the United States as *the* nation possessed of a historic role to enhance human rights is echoed in public opinion. More than six of every ten respondents to the 1974 Harris Survey

[14] *American Public Opinion and U.S. Foreign Policy 1975*, pp. 103, 110. See also *Public Opinion* 2 (March/May 1979), pp. 24, 28.

[15] *Public Papers of the Presidents of the United States: John F. Kennedy, 1963* (Washington, D.C.: Government Printing Office, 1964), pp. 890, 894.

[16] *Public Papers of the Presidents of the United States, Lyndon B. Johnson, 1965*, I:181.

agreed that the world was dependent on the United States to set moral examples; conversely, an equal proportion said that the United States was "not at all" dependent upon other nations for moral examples. Similarly, 82 percent of the respondents expressed a belief that the world was dependent upon the United States to supply the learning necessary "to improve the quality of life," while 59 percent asserted that the United States had nothing whatever to learn from the rest of the world about improving the quality of life for its citizens.[17] To many Americans, the protection of human rights is a special moral obligation, accepted in much the same way that Kipling's Britain accepted its burden to civilize the nonwhite people that history had not favored.

And, as with Victorian England, much of the U.S. public does not perceive its role as essentially protective, as a guardian of human rights and a stationary beacon to guide others; rather, citizens believe their government should take positive, aggressive measures to promote human rights. For example, 67 percent of the Harris Survey respondents favored putting pressure on governments that violate human rights, and 62 percent said the United States should not support authoritarian governments that have overthrown democratic regimes. More than seven of every ten citizens agreed that "it is morally wrong to back military dictatorships that strip people of their basic rights, even if that dictatorship will allow us to set up military bases in that country."[18] This question merits particular attention because it forces respondents to consider a potential cost for speaking out against the violation of human rights. Bases or no bases, the public prefers that its government move positively to dissociate itself from and deny support to repressive military dictatorships.

As the following chapters demonstrate, the question has never been phrased in the context of human rights versus military bases in Latin America but rather in terms of human rights versus communism. The loss of a military base is a relatively small price to pay to promote human rights. When the costs are raised to include the loss of a country to communism, however, the public becomes less enthusiastic about the international protection of human rights. More than 80 percent of the 1974 Harris Survey respondents agreed that the containment of communism should be an important component of foreign policy, and 70 percent said that a communist Latin American country would be a threat to the United States. As a result, slightly more than half of the respondents were willing to support repressive governments

[17] *American Public Opinion and U.S. Foreign Policy 1975*, pp. 96, 98.
[18] Ibid., pp. 120, 123-124.

24

if a communist takeover were the alternative.[19] When the values of human rights and anticommunism conflict, the latter emerges dominant in United States opinion.

Other data suggest that the threat of communism remains a lodestar of public opinion on foreign policy issues. Using survey data from the Potomac Associates, Watts and Free found that the fear of this threat reached an all-time high of 86 percent in 1964. It then fell to 69 percent in 1974 but subsequently rose to 74 percent in 1976.[20] Given this high level of concern, it is not surprising that U.S. citizens are reluctant to climb out on a limb for human rights in Latin America, at least when the perceived risk is an increased threat of communism. And given this fear, it is certainly no accident that, as the next chapter demonstrates, lobbyists employed by repressive Latin American governments consistently argue that human rights violations are an unfortunate but inevitable response to communist subversion.

In addition to their willingness to aid repressive regimes in order to frustrate communism, a plurality of citizens prefers that the United States not address the human rights issue in such a way that other important foreign policy considerations are jeopardized. In late 1974, for example, 40 percent of the respondents to the Harris Survey said that the Soviet Union's treatment of Jews is none of our business. Two years later, when asked how they felt about the Carter administration's early criticisms of repression in the Soviet Union, 38 percent of the respondents to a *New York Times*/CBS News Poll disapproved, 26 percent approved, and 36 percent were not sure how they felt. These and similar survey results prompted Yankelovich to conclude

[19] Opposed were 32 percent. Charles William Maynes et al., *U.S. Foreign Policy: Principles for Defining the National Interest* (New York: Public Agenda Foundation, 1976), p. 76. By 1978, the proportion in favor of aid to repressive but anticommunist dictators had risen to 57 percent. *Public Opinion* 2 (March/May 1979), p. 26. Once again, however, the manner in which a question is worded may determine much of the public's reaction. In the *U.S. Foreign Policy* survey, 57 percent of the respondents believed that it was proper for the United States to support socialist (as opposed to communist) governments that respect the basic political rights of their people (p. 120).

[20] William Watts and Lloyd A. Free, "Nationalism, Not Isolationism," *Foreign Policy*, no. 24 (Fall 1976), pp. 11, 23. Parenthetically, the public is evenly divided on the question of whether to "take all necessary steps, including the use of armed force, to prevent the spread of communism to any other parts of the free world." In 1976, 44 percent of the public favored this idea, while 43 percent rejected it. Eight years earlier, 57 percent favored taking "all necessary steps" to stop communism, while 29 percent were opposed. In a 1977 address, President Carter suggested that the fear of communism had diminished among the public, but he offered no data to support his assertion. *Weekly Compilation of Presidential Documents* 13 (May 30, 1977): 774.

that, in relations with the Soviet Union, "there is little support for a sacrifice of vital American interests in defense of human rights."[21]

Not only does support for humanitarian initiatives decline when human rights is placed in conflict with either communism or détente, it also drops somewhat less precipitously when the pursuit of human rights might hamper the functioning of capitalism. As of 1974, a plurality of citizens (44 percent) thought that it is justified for the United States to back governments that believe in free enterprise but not in democracy.[22] In the most glaring human rights issue of the 1970s, apartheid in South Africa, the public was willing to use moderate pressure (halt arms sales, restrain new business investment, make private corporations pressure the South African government) to end apartheid but reluctant to pay a high economic price for such activity: 47 percent of the public were opposed to pushing for black rule in South Africa if it meant a reduction in the supply of vital minerals, compared to 37 percent who approved, and 51 percent of the public opposed forcing U.S.-based corporations to close their operations in South Africa, compared to 21 percent who approved.[23] As the discussion of human rights and the Export-Import Bank in Chapter 8 demonstrates, the high value citizens place upon domestic prosperity affects efforts to increase the influence of human rights in United States foreign policy.

Finally, the large proportion of respondents who are undecided on these human rights-related questions indicates that, as with most foreign policy issues, the issue of human rights is not of central concern to the public. Some policy makers and interest-group activists often overlook this fact when they address the issue. In particular, they argue that a policy of promoting human rights, even one that fails in its primary objective, should nonetheless be pursued since it ennobles the public spirit. Government support of human rights is said to have "an immense emotional appeal because it reflects the hopes and aspirations of mankind"; policy makers are urged to "take into account the debilitating effects of the internal dissonance which a policy patently devoid of moral content is bound to generate in the United States."[24] Statements such as these ignore the public's low level of

---

[21] American Public Opinion and U.S. Foreign Policy 1975, p. 119; New York Times, April 29, 1977, p. 16; Yankelovich, "Farewell to 'President Knows Best'," p. 680.

[22] American Public Opinion and U.S. Foreign Policy 1975, p. 120.

[23] Yankelovich, "Farewell to 'President Knows Best,' " pp. 685-686.

[24] The first remark is by Thomas Buergenthal, "International Human Rights: U.S. Policy and Priorities," Virginia Journal of International Law 14 (Summer 1974): 617. The second is by Tom J. Farer, "United States Foreign Policy and the Protection of Human Rights: Observations and Proposals," Virginia Journal of International Law 14 (Summer 1974): 627. See also U.S. Congress, House, Committee on Foreign Affairs,

interest in the issue of human rights, its high fear of communism, and the normal economic anxieties that characterize participants in market economies. Given the extent to which human rights violations in Latin America have been justified as a response to communism, and given the extent to which proposals to encourage a stronger U.S. human rights policy have been viewed as harmful to the domestic economy, the dissonance to which human rights activists refer will probably be restricted to a relatively small portion of the public.

In summary, it appears that strong public pressure did not develop during the 1970s to increase the importance of human rights considerations in United States policy toward Latin America. "Public concern for the human rights problem has probably never been very widespread or intense," lamented Richard Bilder in 1974. "Most Americans are not aware of these problems. Of those that do know, most probably do not really care. The probability that these attitudes will change seems low."[25] After those words were written, United States human rights policy underwent a profound change, coming to influence nearly all aspects of U.S.-Latin American relations, yet there is no evidence that the public became more concerned about the issue. The protection of human rights, like other aspects of United States policy toward Latin America, remained a matter of minor public interest.

Foreign Aid

Although there are few survey data on either U.S.-Latin American relations or U.S. human rights policy, there is a considerable body of relevant survey research on foreign aid, a principal instrument used by the U.S. government to implement its human rights policy. Two types of questions about the foreign aid program have been asked repeatedly, one of which probes the public's approval of the concept of foreign assistance. Over the years a slim majority of the public at large and a significantly larger majority of the voters have supported the basic concept of foreign aid. The first effort to assess citizens' opinions in this area was posed by George Gallup in 1941 when he asked: "Do you think the United States should send money to Central and South American countries to help them build up their industries, railroads, and defenses?" While the meaning of responses to this question are clouded by the reference to national defense in a prewar

Subcommittee on International Organizations and Movements, *International Protection of Human Rights*, 93rd Cong., 1st Sess., 1973, p. 192.

[25] Richard B. Bilder, "Human Rights and U.S. Foreign Policy: Short-Term Prospects," *Virginia Journal of International Law* 14 (Summer 1974): 604.

atmosphere, 58 percent of the public responded in favor of aid to Latin America, while 22 percent opposed the idea. From March 1949 to March 1955, the following question was asked seven times: "In general, do you think it is a good policy for the United States to try to help backward countries in the world raise their standard of living or shouldn't this be any concern of our government?" The average level of support for aid was 72 percent. During the twelve-year period from 1956 to 1968, the public was asked eight times whether it favored or opposed the U.S. aid program. The average level of approval was 56 percent; about one-third of the respondents consistently opposed foreign assistance.[26]

On the other hand, the public is highly critical of the administration of American aid programs. In late 1974, for example, 70 percent of the respondents to one survey said that economic aid never reaches the people who need it, while only 9 percent believed that most aid "ends up helping people." Fully 65 percent said that it is distributed to the wrong nations, and 51 percent said that the United States was pouring its money into a bottomless hole. Specifically, 66 percent thought aid makes the rulers of foreign countries rich. This perception of an inefficient, corrupt aid administration may account for some citizens' dislike of the aid program. In one survey, only a slim majority (53 percent) favored aid in the abstract sense, but 79 percent said they would favor aid if the money "ended up helping the people" living in Third World countries.[27]

When surveys probe citizens' approval or disapproval of particular types of aid, there is no general pattern. The public is highly sympathetic to the need for humanitarian relief and aid to address the most basic human needs. This is true when survey questions refer to aid to specific nations (such as the noncommunist countries in Asia, and famine relief in either India or Communist China) or to specific programs (including those which encourage birth control). In general, about nine out of ten citizens favor providing emergency food and medical supplies to other nations in case of natural disasters such as floods or earthquakes. Although the respondents to a July 1977 *New*

---

[26] Alfred O. Hero, Jr., "Foreign Aid and the American Public," *Public Policy* 14 (1965): 113; *American Public Opinion and U.S. Foreign Policy 1975*, p. 88; *The Gallup Poll, 1935-1971*, pp. 265, 1546-1547, 1802-1803, 1932, 1995; Michael Kent O'Leary, *The Politics of American Foreign Aid* (New York: Atherton Press, 1967), p. 138; Weissberg, *Public Opinion and Popular Government*, p. 156. The last question has not been asked in recent years.

[27] *American Public Opinion and U.S. Foreign Policy 1975*, pp. 90-91; *Roper Reports* 75-10, p. C.

York Times/CBS News Poll overwhelmingly opposed the idea of giving "financial assistance" to Vietnam, 69 percent of the same respondents favored giving Vietnam food and medicine.[28]

When considering less altruistic programs, public support for the foreign assistance program is low. This is particularly true of military aid. Near the end of American military activity in Vietnam, a Harris Survey revealed that a substantial majority (64 percent) of the public wanted to eliminate grant military aid and 52 percent opposed military sales programs. Only 35 percent favored continuing military aid. The reasons for this hostility were diverse and multiple: 77 percent said military aid involves the United States too deeply in other people's affairs, 75 percent said it makes other nations too dependent on us, 67 percent said it aggravates relations with other countries, and over 50 percent said it is detrimental to our own economy and, in any event, fails to contribute to our national security. In other words, with the exception of serving as a "good substitute for the use of American troops" (a proposition agreed to by 45 percent of the respondents), military aid was thought to confer few benefits on the United States. A plurality of citizens (48 percent) felt military assistance does not even help prevent the spread of communism.[29]

The public was extremely ambivalent about the impact of military aid upon recipients. About six out of ten citizens said it helps dictators use military power against their own people, and the same proportion believed that military aid leads to military dictatorships. Yet the public was about evenly divided on the proposition that military aid strengthens our political friends abroad, and a substantial majority (68 percent) believed that military aid helps the national security of recipient countries. A plurality (48 percent) thought that military aid helps people in other countries to live better.[30]

The second question asked repeatedly concerns the size of the U.S. aid budget. At an abstract level, public opinion has generally favored foreign aid, but as Robert Dahl noted three decades ago, more could be learned about citizen support for the program if pollsters were to ask instead: "Would you like to pay higher taxes?" On the concrete question of monetary outlays, the public's response is clear: too much

[28] *The Gallup Poll, 1935-1971*, pp. 978-979, 1330, 1711, 1772, 2185; *American Public Opinion and U.S. Foreign Policy 1975*, p. 91; *New York Times*, July 29, 1977, p. 22.
[29] *American Public Opinion and U.S. Foreign Policy 1975*, pp. 91-94; *Roper Reports* 75-8, p. 25, and 76-10, p. 8. For similar data for 1978, see *Public Opinion* 2 (March/May 1979), p. 28.
[30] *American Public Opinion and U.S. Foreign Policy 1975*, pp. 91-93.

money is being spent on foreign aid.[31] One well-phrased question that links aid to its costs was posed by the Gallup Poll in 1965: "President Johnson has proposed that Congress set aside about $3.4 billion for aid to countries in other parts of the world, or about 3 percent of the total annual budget. Would you like to see this amount increased or decreased?" Almost 50 percent of the respondents favored a decrease, 23 percent opted for a stable level of spending, and only 6 percent favored an increase in the foreign aid budget.[32] In Table 1.1, responses to items of a similar nature indicate that only briefly in the mid-1950s did the "about right" category challenge the majority position of "too much."

During the 1970s, the public agreed overwhelmingly that the foreign aid program was overfunded. In an October 1978 *Time*/Yankelovich survey, 75 percent of the population asserted that the United States was spending too much on foreign aid, while a mere 4 percent thought the current appropriation was too little. Only a miniscule proportion of the population has ever believed that the United States has provided too little foreign assistance.[33] Of the 72 percent of the respondents to one Gallup Poll who favored an overall decrease in public spending, the largest single group (30 percent) thought that cuts should be made specifically in the aid budget.[34] On three different occasions during the period 1969 to 1975, citizens were asked what they would like to eliminate or reduce in federal government spending. On two of these occasions, foreign aid was first; on the other occasion, it was second to Vietnam war spending. On the other hand, if more money were to be available for expenditures by the federal government, the *last*

---

[31] Robert A. Dahl, *Congress and Foreign Policy* (New York: Harcourt, Brace, 1950), p. 269; David A. Baldwin, *Economic Development and American Foreign Policy, 1943-1962* (Chicago: University of Chicago Press, 1966), p. 263. Ironically, 1977 was the first year in the history of AID's programs in Latin America in which repayments on previous loans exceeded new loan authorizations. During fiscal year 1977 (FY1977) the U.S. Treasury received $176.5 million in repayments from Latin America, while new loans totaled $106.6 million. U.S. Congress, House, Committee on International Relations, *Foreign Assistance Legislation for Fiscal Year 1979*, 95th Cong., 2d Sess., March 1978, pt. 7, p. 42.

[32] There were only minor changes in responses to this same question when it was asked two years later in May 1967. *The Gallup Opinion Index*, June 1967, p. 11.

[33] *Time*, October 23, 1978, p. 29; Weissberg, *Public Opinion and Popular Government*, p. 157; *Roper Reports* 74-1 p. c; *American Public Opinion and U.S. Foreign Policy 1975*, p. 71.

[34] The grouping of government operations—a combination of government salaries and government personnel—outweighed foreign aid as the most attractive target. O'Leary, *The Politics of American Foreign Aid*, p. 23; *The Gallup Poll, 1935-1971*, p. 1589.

TABLE 1.1

ARE WE SPENDING TOO MUCH, TOO LITTLE, OR ABOUT THE RIGHT AMOUNT ON FOREIGN AID?

	1952	1953	1954	1957	1965	1967	1971	1973	1974	1975	1976	1977	1978
Too much	60%	20%	25%	37%	49%	51%	71%	76%	73%	75%	67%	66%	67%
About right amount	28	57	56	48	33	30	13	14	15	14	20	24	24
Too little	2	9	8	2	6	8	4	2	4	3	3	3	4
Don't know/no opinion	10	15	11	13	12	11	14	8	7	8	9	7	6

SOURCES: *Roper Reports*, nos. 74-1, 75-10, 76-1, 77-1; Robert Weissberg, *Public Opinion and Popular Government* (Prentice-Hall, 1976), p. 157; *Public Opinion* 2 (March/May 1979), p. 28.

NOTE: Totals other than 100 percent are due to rounding.

place citizens would spend it would be on foreign aid. In a 1975 Gallup Poll, citizens were ten times more likely to add money to welfare programs (which were themselves relatively unpopular) than to increase foreign aid appropriations.[35]

When citizens are asked more complex questions about the aid program than whether they favor it or whether they want to spend less on it, the level of informed opinion declines precipitously and the proportion of respondents who refuse to express any opinion rises. In a question asked in 1958 (and not posed since), only six percent of the population could give a rough idea of how much foreign aid the President had requested. The public has little or no understanding of the legal objectives of aid, the various emphases of the programs, or the countries receiving large aid distributions. In short, opinions on foreign aid do not appear to be tightly integrated components of the typical citizen's worldview. Quite the contrary, these opinions tend to be highly unstable and profoundly responsive to citizens' opinions on other issues of greater salience, particularly taxes.[36]

Perhaps because of this low salience, responses to questions about foreign aid are characterized by an acquiescence bias, a tendency to select affirmative responses to all questions on a single subject. This was first noticed by Rita Simon, whose interest was aroused when she observed that respondents to one poll favored both an aid appropriation equal to that of the previous year *and* a cut in foreign aid spending. In the 1974 Harris Survey, many of the respondents who damned the administration of aid programs because funds were siphoned off by corrupt leaders (70 percent) also praised aid because it aids the economy of other nations (77 percent) and specifically helps the people in other countries to live better (70 percent). More than 20 percent of the respondents believed both that aid never reaches the people who need it *and* that aid helps people in other countries to live better. This illogical response pattern is commonly found when respondents are disinterested in a questionnaire item. Not surprisingly,

[35] *The Harris Survey Yearbook of Public Opinion 1970* (New York: Louis Harris and Associates, 1971), p. 498; *The Harris Survey Yearbook of Public Opinion 1971*, p. 59; *Roper Reports 75-10*, p. C; George H. Gallup, *The Gallup Poll: Public Opinion 1972-1976*, 2 vols. (Wilmington, Del.: Scholarly Resources, 1978), 1:656. For a general analysis, see Burns W. Roper, "The Limits of Public Support," *Annals* of the American Academy of Political and Social Science, vol. 442 (March 1979), pp. 40-45.

[36] *The Gallup Poll, 1935-1971*, p. 1546. Limited data from other Western industrialized nations suggest that the majority of their citizens are equally uninformed about their own aid programs. Hero, "Foreign Aid and the American Public," p. 113; Paul G. Clark, *American Aid for Development* (New York: Praeger, 1972), p. 61; David B. Truman, "The Domestic Politics of Foreign Aid," *Proceedings* of the Academy of Political Science, vol. 27 (January 1962), p. 70.

then, in one 1971 poll, foreign aid ranked last on a list of citizens' problems, slightly behind their second least pressing concern, the control of pornography.[37]

No one viewing data such as these can disagree that citizens have a low intensity of opinion about foreign aid. It was V. O. Key who first traced the policy implications of such findings, concluding that "the foundation in public opinion for an aggressive American policy of leadership in the economic development of the free world appears . . . to be thin."[38]

To state that the general public has a negligible commitment to the foreign assistance program is not to assert that citizens have few preferences about the norms governing the distribution of aid. Citizens favor technical assistance over either capital or military aid, they favor economic aid over military assistance, and they prefer to assist Latin America over either Asia or Africa. In addition, many citizens have a fairly clear idea of the type of country to which aid should be directed: they would aid nations that are supportive of United States foreign policy. In 1966, the Gallup Poll asked: "Suppose another country— which is receiving foreign aid from the United States—fails to support the United States in a major foreign policy decision such as Vietnam?" Almost 45 percent of the respondents would have cut aid completely and another 30 percent would have reduced aid, while only 16 percent would have continued an existing aid program. A decade later, the Harris Survey reported that 61 percent of the respondents to one poll agreed that "we should give foreign aid only to our friends, and not to countries which criticize the United States."[39]

These data suggest that the public supports the use of nondevelopmental foreign policy criteria to assist in aid decision making. But, as with other aspects of opinion on foreign aid, there is an inconsistency in opinions related to these strings. The public rejects the general concept of giving aid for "political purposes," yet there is widespread approval of some specific political uses of aid—reductions for failure

[37] Simon, *Public Opinion in America*, pp. 167-168. Acquiescence bias has been found to have a profound effect and to have very little impact. For the former position, see M. Jackman, "Education and Prejudice or Education and Response Sets?" *American Sociological Review* 38 (1973): 327-339; for the latter, see James D. Wright, "Does Acquiescence Bias the 'Index of Political Efficacy'?" *Public Opinion Quarterly* 39 (Summer 1975): 219-226. The 1971 poll data are reported in *The Harris Survey Yearbook of Public Opinion 1971*, p. 55.

[38] V. O. Key, Jr. *Public Opinion and American Democracy* (New York: Alfred A. Knopf, 1961), pp. 214-215.

[39] Hero, "Foreign Aid and the American Public," pp. 81, 84, 88, 93; *The Gallup Poll, 1935-1941*, p. 1995; *American Public Opinion and U.S. Foreign Policy 1975*, p. 118.

to support United States foreign policy or reductions to discourage military coups, for example.[40]

When probed in any detail, this subject of strings—the use of economic aid for purposes other than socioeconomic development—inevitably introduces the more general topic of intervention in the internal affairs of recipient governments. "Intervention" is a tainted word that elicits predictable responses from the public. In one of the early questions regarding foreign assistance, the Gallup Poll asked: "If we lend England and other nations food or money, do you think we should insist on having something to say about the way they run their affairs?" A plurality of 48 percent opposed intervention.[41] Nearly three decades later, a 1974 Harris Survey reported that 60 percent of its respondents thought it was "wrong for the United States to intervene in the internal affairs of Chile and to try to destabilize the government," while only 18 percent favored the intervention. In addition, the public agreed by an overwhelming margin (83 percent to 7 percent) on the very abstract principle that "every country should have the right to determine its own government by itself without outside interference from other countries."[42]

These responses are balanced, however, by the results from another poll from the late 1970s, in which the respondents agreed by a plurality of 59 percent to 21 percent that the CIA should be allowed to continue working "inside other countries to try to strengthen those elements that serve the interests of the United States and to weaken those forces that work against the interests of the United States."[43] In the same survey, respondents were about evenly divided on whether to maintain/expand or to reduce "secret political operations of the CIA." As for the case of Chile, in late 1974, a 40 percent plurality thought CIA involvement there was a "dark moment" in United States foreign policy, but 35 percent were unsure how to assess that particular intervention.[44] Combining these data with those in the preceding par-

[40] Joan M. Nelson, *Aid, Influence, and Foreign Policy* (New York: Macmillan, 1968), p. 28.

[41] Forty-one percent believed that the United States should intervene. *The Gallup Poll, 1935-1941*, p. 687.

[42] *Current Opinion* 3 (January 1975): 1.

[43] Twenty percent of the respondents were opposed to these CIA activities. *Public Opinion* 2 (March/May 1979), p. 25. For 1974 data on the same question, see *Current Opinion* 3 (January 1975), p. 1. Moreover, in April 1975, the respondents to a Harris Survey narrowly approved (34 percent to 32 percent) of the way Secretary of State Kissinger was "handling relations with Chile." *Current Opinion* 3 (May 1975): 41. See also *American Public Opinion and U.S. Foreign Policy 1975*, p. 141.

[44] *American Public Opinion and U.S. Foreign Policy 1975*, pp. 73, 121.

agraph leads to the conclusion that the public perceives various reasons for intervention, some acceptable, others unacceptable.

Joan Nelson once suggested that the public views an intervention as acceptable if the goal is the establishment of order and constitutional government or the defeat of communism and unacceptable if it is designed to influence the outcome of normal political processes.[45] This interpretation assumes an interest that apparently does not exist in the minds of most survey respondents; the data are unclear and contradictory because the public has no strong feelings about the subject. When a question is phrased in inflammatory terms—as in the question on the CIA in Chile in the preceding paragraph—or when established principles such as self-determination are mentioned, the public gives a response that is consonant with the best tradition of liberal pluralism. But when (as in the preceding paragraph) the questions are phrased in a frame of *Realpolitik*, the public responds with a *Realpolitik* answer. No survey has ever been able to demonstrate that the public cares enough about the question of intervention to form a consistent opinion regarding its advisability, unless (as in Vietnam) the intervention involves significant personal costs to large numbers of citizens.

In fact, no survey has been able to demonstrate that the public has a consistent, coherent opinion regarding any aspect of inter-American relations. There are several reasons why citizens might lack a coherent set of opinions about Latin America. First, with the few exceptions noted in the following chapter, there are no politically mobilized ethnic or expatriate groups in the United States concerned primarily with U.S.-Latin American relations. The lack of a politically active community working to focus attention upon these relations should not be overemphasized as a cause of the low level of public concern, but it probably is a contributing factor.[46] While Americans with Hispanic surnames form the second largest minority group in the United States—5.3 percent of the population—and could be quite visible in attempts to influence United States foreign policy, the representatives of the organized Hispanic communities feel compelled to direct their political energy toward ameliorating the relative deprivation of their constituents. Issues such as bilingual education that affect the ability of Hispanic-Americans to cope with U.S. society are at present more important to them than the problems of Latin America or of U.S.-

[45] Nelson, *Aid, Influence, and Foreign Policy*, p. 111.

[46] Compare President Carter's 1978 speech proclaiming National Hispanic Heritage Week, in which he remarked that "Americans have come to recognize the important role of the Hispanic community . . . in our efforts to achieve understanding, mutual respect and common purpose with the Spanish-speaking nations of this hemisphere." *Congressional Record*, September 16, 1977, p. E5623.

Latin American relations. When an official of the League of United Latin American Citizens testified before Congress in April 1978, for example, he spoke not about economic aid to Latin America—the subject of the hearing—but about AID's shortcomings in implementing an affirmative action program for citizens with Hispanic surnames.[47] In another example, a State Department human rights conference in February 1978 attracted the representatives of virtually every ethnic group in the United States, including many Hispanic-Americans, yet only a few Hispanic-Americans attended the conference session on Latin America, and those few persistently diverted the discussion to the question of their constituents' domestic human rights.

Of course it is also important to remember that Latin America is not an ethnic group or a nation but a geographic region and that the national divisions of the region serve to fragment efforts by Hispanic-Americans to generate public interest in Latin America. As a result, attempts to raise the public's awareness of U.S.-Latin American relations are almost invariably oriented toward national rather than regional loyalties. Thus when New York's Dominican expatriates staged demonstrations over electoral fraud in the Dominican Republic in May 1978, they were not joined by the Mexican, Haitian, or Puerto Rican communities. There is no more reason for Mexican-Americans and Cuban-Americans to jointly address the issue of military aid to Uruguay, for example, than for Polish-Americans and Irish-Americans to join with Greeks to influence American policy toward Cyprus.

The crisis orientation of United States foreign policy is a further explanation for public indifference toward Latin America, a region on the periphery of nearly all major foreign policy crises. While the 1965 Dominican intervention and the 1973 Chilean coup may be exceptions to this general rule, the Cuban missile crisis is the only clear post-World War II instance in which Latin America was centrally involved in a major crisis of world politics. Significantly, the crisis involved Cuba only because that was where the missiles were physically placed, not because Cuba had a major role to play in its resolution. Latin America is an isolated part of the world, yet close enough so that the United States can exercise the privilege of the powerful to protect weaker neighbors from potential crises. Europe, the Middle East, Africa, Southeast Asia, and East Asia are all "exposed" in a way Latin America will never be, and thus the vulnerability of Latin America to crisis-causing (and public opinion-producing) forces is relatively low.

[47] U.S. Congress, House, Committee on Appropriations, Subcommittee on Foreign Operations and Related Agencies, *Foreign Assistance and Related Agencies Appropriations for 1979*, 95th Cong., 2d Sess., 1978, pt. 3, pp. 243-248.

The crisis orientation of U.S. foreign policy and the absence of politically powerful ethnic or expatriate groups probably contribute to the low level of public interest in Latin America, but social scientists typically overlook these factors and concentrate upon a third explanation for the lack of coherent public opinion on foreign policy issues: incompetence as a consequence of complexity. Gabriel Almond has argued that "there are inherent limitations in modern society on the capacity of the public to understand the issues and grasp the significance of the most important problems of public policy. This is particularly the case with foreign policy, where the issues are especially complex and remote."[48] Following Almond, more recent textbooks continue to explain indifference or ignorance as a function of complexity, concluding that a complex world requires "so much expertise that it would be utopian to expect extensive citizen competency."[49] Interpretations that stress such structural obstacles as the need for secrecy or the rapidity with which crises develop encourage the belief that, given the complexity (secrecy, urgency) of foreign policy issues, citizens are hopelessly incompetent. Even if they tried to improve, they would not do much better.

This explanation for the low level of public interest in U.S.-Latin American relations often defines indifference as unfortunate (a debatable point), while simultaneously placing the blame for this alleged failure where it might not belong. It seems more reasonable to deposit the responsibility at the feet of the nation's leaders, to require that they detail exactly why its citizens *should* care whether the United States has a policy toward every imaginable issue in every country on earth. This is not to deny that there are issues of importance about which the public has an identifiable stake and might therefore want to have an opinion. There is probably good reason to be dismayed when, for example, in a 1977 poll, respondents who were asked to rank a list of items of "serious threat to future generations" placed the "increasingly widening gap between the underdeveloped and the developed nations" next to last, just one percentage point ahead of "the prospects for increasing numbers of devastating earthquakes."[50] But in general, it is difficult to argue with the nine of every ten citizens who feel that America's real concerns should be at home, not abroad, and it is understandable why only about 5 percent of the public regularly cites foreign policy issues among their dominant concerns, com-

---

[48] Almond, *The American People and Foreign Policy*, p. 5.
[49] Weissberg, *Public Opinion and Popular Government*, p. 139.
[50] *Roper Reports*, 77-2, p. C.

pared to 80 percent who mention domestic or personal economic issues.[51]

Thus while foreign policy officials create and implement a variety of policies toward Latin America, the polls tell us that the typical United States citizen is busy deciding whether to purchase frozen french fried potatoes or to make them fresh at home. It seems perfectly rational for members of the public to give more attention to the quality of the food on their plates than, for example, to the nature of the Uruguayan government, since U.S. officials have never made (and probably cannot make) a compelling case that the vital interests of the United States are involved in that nation. Until such an explanation is forthcoming, it seems arrogant to assume that the public's priorities are misplaced. Since it is extremely rare for the public to be confronted with an issue of inter-American relations that impinges upon their daily lives, there is little reason to expect the structure of poll responses to be internally consistent or for opinions to display ordered priorities. There is little reason to expect anything except indifference. Citizens probably have few opinions about U.S.-Latin American relations because there is no rational reason why they should take the time to create them.

THE IMPACT OF PUBLIC OPINION ON POLICY

Public opinion may be said to have an impact on policy only if it serves to alter the preferred behavior of foreign policy officials.[52] Using this definition, it is difficult to identify an instance where public opinion has clearly influenced the making of United States policy toward Latin America. Perhaps the nearest that surveys of public opinion have come in recent years to exerting an impact upon the Latin American policy of the United States was the 1978 battle over Senate ratification of the Panama Canal treaties. As with most data on issues of inter-American relations, the opinion data relating to the treaties could be variously interpreted, enabling each side to claim

[51] *American Public Opinion and U.S. Foreign Policy 1975*, p. 118; Maynes et al., *U.S. Foreign Policy: Principles for Defining the National Interest*, p. 81. Moreover, the public's mood appears to be shifting toward increased concern for domestic rather than international issues. In 1964, 55 percent of the respondents to a Potomac Associates poll agreed that "we shouldn't think so much in international terms but concentrate more on our own national problems and building up our strength and prosperity here at home." By 1972, the proportion in agreement had risen to 73 percent, where it remained in 1976. Watts and Free, "Nationalism, Not Isolationism," p. 17.

[52] Bernard C. Cohen, *The Public's Impact on Foreign Policy* (Boston: Little, Brown, 1973), p. 28.

that its position accurately reflected public opinion.[53] The low impact of opinions upon policy is encouraged by the limited quantity of data and their inconclusive nature, but there are also features of the policy-making process that influence the impact of the few unambiguous opinions that do exist.

The Executive Branch

Administration policy makers continue to lay great emphasis upon "the need for public support," a phrase that Cohen found so common in the early 1970s "that it begins to look like one of the pillars on which the whole structure of decision making rests."[54] Virtually every executive branch official whom I interviewed asserted that public opinion played an important role in decision making on United States policy toward Latin America. Further discussion tended to reveal that what many officials mean when they assert that public opinion influences foreign-policy making is that the public acts indirectly to set the broad limits within which officials must operate. Public opinion therefore is seen as a *constraint* upon policy makers rather than an interference in daily decision making on specific issues. The systematic analysis of this proposition may not be possible.[55] For limits to be set and identified, the public must know the range of policy options being considered, the issue each option is expected to resolve, and the consequences of each option's implementation. Some options—destroying Havana with nuclear weapons, for example—are clear, and the public probably does set limits on their use. But other options that are documented components of United States policy toward Latin America—military invasions, assassination plots, economic destabilization—are only presented to the public after the fact. In these cases, the attentive public can grumble and threaten to grumble even louder if policy makers reimplement the offending policy, but that is to set a limit after it has been exceeded.

Given foreign policy officials' professed interest in public opinion polls, it is surprising that the bureaucracy charged with formulating and implementing foreign policy has an extremely rudimentary mech-

[53] For the antitreaty poll results, see *Congressional Record*, February 27, 1978, p. S2385; March 7, 1978, pp. S3109-S3111; and March 10, 1978, pp. S3397-S3401, S3427-S3430. For the protreaty results, see *Congressional Record*, March 10, 1978, pp. S3402-S3405. An insightful analysis of the role of public opinion in the Senate debate is Maurice L. Farber, "Canal Issue Shows the Risks of Opinion Polling," *Los Angeles Times*, March 7, 1978, pt. 2, p. 5.

[54] Cohen, *The Public's Impact on Foreign Policy*, p. 139.

[55] Bernard C. Cohen and Scott A. Harris, "Foreign Policy," in *Handbook of Political Science*, ed. Fred I. Greenstein and Nelson W. Polsby (Reading, Mass.: Addison-Wesley, 1975), 6:413; Cohen, *The Public's Impact on Foreign Policy*, pp. 18, 139.

anism for collecting, analyzing, and disseminating public opinion. It was not always this way. From the beginning of the Cold War until 1957, the Department of State regularly commissioned surveys on issues of specific concern to policy makers. Over time, Congress became increasingly uncomfortable with this activity, primarily because the only results the members ever saw were those that supported the administration. Their criticism became so severe that the polls were discontinued.

The analysis of independently gathered poll data continued under the Public Opinion Studies Division (formerly Public Studies Division) of the Bureau of Public Affairs, but its significance decreased dramatically over the two decades following World War II. From 1946 to 1952, the division was staffed by nineteen to twenty-five employees, from 1953 to 1961 by ten to twelve employees, and from 1961 to 1965 by only six. In 1965, it suffered the supreme bureaucratic ignominy of being downgraded from a division to a single position, that of the Public Opinion Advisor in the Office of Plans and Management of the Bureau of Public Affairs.[56] Since 1975, the informal status of the position seems to have increased somewhat. In the late 1970s, the occupant was a Foreign Service Reserve (FSR) officer with a Ph.D. in sociology; his assistant was also a FSR with a Ph.D. in political science. While both were recognized by other foreign policy officials as competent analysts of public opinion, there was little familiarity with their work. Their influence as analysts of public opinion probably suffers from the fact that they are part of the Bureau of Public Affairs, whose primary mission is to tell the public what to think, not to learn what the public thinks.

In the 1970s, no regular attempt was being made to survey public opinion on issues of United States policy toward Latin America. By 1972, the systematic treatment of public opinion had been reduced to counting the mail, separating it into issue-areas, and then dividing each pile into "favorable" and "unfavorable" stacks.[57] In 1978, the

[56] Cohen, *The Public's Impact on Foreign Policy*, pp. 45-46, 67.

[57] There are occasional ad hoc efforts to sample public opinion on issues of foreign policy. One of the most fascinating examples occurred in early 1976, when Secretary of State Kissinger asked four of his aides (one deputy undersecretary and three assistant secretaries) to conduct a series of "town meetings." At each of the five major cities they visited, the four officials conducted a day-long discussion with attentive constituents: local businesspersons, labor leaders, academicians, and ethnic group representatives, all of whom were selected by local world affairs councils and universities. In addition, parts of the proceedings were televised, with viewers calling in questions to be answered on the air. Finally, the public opinion advisor conducted telephone surveys of three hundred citizens in each city. The four State Department officials reported to the Secretary of State that "many citizens are distressed at what they

ratification of the Panama Canal treaties was the only subject on which the Bureau of Inter-American Affairs (ARA)[58] was receiving this type of information from the Bureau of Public Affairs, and in an interview one official remarked that the only reason for reading the correspondence was to determine which form letter should be sent in response.

Within ARA there appears to be a general disregard for the entire concept of polling, a feeling that the issues facing policy makers are too complex to be answered with a simple "approve" or "disapprove." When asked whether public opinion offers general guidelines by specifying desirable *values* with which to weigh policy on these more complex or specialized issues, most respondents replied either that value-identification was the role of elected officials or that the State Department was already fully aware of the public's values. How, then, can officials become aware of opinions regarding values without asking about them? The responses varied—"We all read widely" was offered more than once—but they invariably indicated a belief that in their daily activities the State Department's Latin Americanists absorb public opinion without having to make any special effort. Cohen's research suggests that this phenomenon is not restricted to ARA. "Intuition," he found, "is the prevailing mode of opinion evaluation in the State Department."[59]

Having said this, it is important to add the major caveat that the level of attention to public opinion varied significantly among the State Department bureaus charged with formulating and implementing United States policy toward human rights in Latin America during the late 1970s. This is probably not an indication that some bureaus were staffed with individuals committed to the norm of responsiveness while others lacked such people, but rather that public opinion sometimes reinforced the existing views of one bureau at the expense of others. When that occurred, the bureau so blessed enlisted the public as its ally in the fight to have its position become public policy. One organization that regularly used its perceptions of public opinion to buttress its own positions was the Bureau of Human Rights and Humanitarian Affairs (HA), despite the fact that, as we have seen, in the 1970s citizens had very limited and ambivalent opinions about the role of the United States in the international protection of human

---

perceive as a failure to uphold American ideals as an integral part of this country's foreign policy." Memorandum to Secretary of State Kissinger from Atherton, Reinhardt, Matlock, and Placke, June 24, 1976.

[58] The use of ARA as the official cable abbreviation and the informal shortened title of the Bureau of Inter-American Affairs is a holdover from the period prior to October 1949, when its title was the Bureau of American Republics Affairs.

[59] Cohen, *The Public's Impact on Foreign Policy*, p. 64 (and on the risks of intuition, see p. 72).

rights. What HA tended to offer as public opinion were statements that reflect consensually held attitudes—for example, that the public wants its government to protest human rights violations. Other components of the policy-making apparatus also muster public opinion into the bureaucratic fray whenever certain claims—that the public opposes aid to nations that expropriate property without compensation or that the public wants the government to fight communism in Latin America—seem appropriate.

To summarize the discussion so far, two obstacles—the low level of public interest in U.S.-Latin American relations and the lack of a means for collecting and disseminating the few opinions that do exist—hamper the ability of public opinion to influence the Latin American policy of the United States. Despite the obvious fact that these are significant deterrents to increased public impact on foreign policy, they are not the only reasons why the public enjoys a limited influence on policy. One further problem remains: the value that the foreign policy bureaucracy places on isolation from public pressure. My perception is that citizens could be perfectly informed about relations with Latin America, opinion surveys on human rights could be conducted hourly, and still the public would have difficulty influencing United States policy toward human rights violations in Latin America because policy makers are unwilling to act on what they hear.

No one can prove that foreign policy officials would ignore informed public opinion if it existed, but a striking number of observers have come to this conclusion after working with the officials who manage U.S. relations with Latin America.[60] To these officials, foreign policy formulation is often viewed as an art form—an "arcane craft" in one official's terms—that only professionals are able to practice. This attitude, the artist syndrome, produces people who value insulation. Thus if the public were interested and informed, it would still face formidable communications problems. As Cohen has demonstrated, "The interested, active, and involved public . . . is seen as embodying a variety of negative characteristics: it is held to be suspicious, hostile, and critical, above all else; but it is also resentful, prejudiced, unrepresentative, dogmatic—a monster. The public debate on issues is seen mostly as uninformed but also as irrelevant, narrow, inaccurate, unrealistic, and unreasoned."[61] The only possible role for this type of citizen is that of playing a supporting role, of agreeing with the de-

[60] U.S. Department of State, *Diplomacy for the 70's: A Program of Management Reform for the Department of State*, Publication 8551 (Washington, D.C.: Government Printing Office, 1970); Yankelovich, "Farewell to 'President Knows Best'," p. 688; Cohen, *The Public's Impact on Foreign Policy*, pp. 57-58.

[61] Cohen, *The Public's Impact on Foreign Policy*, pp. 57-58.

cisions of those who know best. It is unimportant if little support can be found for a given policy, for apathy is the equivalent of acquiescence. But if there is active opposition to a policy, then policy changes are not considered. Instead officials view their task as either attempting to convince the public that its opinions are wrong or, more commonly, simply persevering in a hostile environment. This attitude is extraordinarily prominent in the Bureau of Inter-American Affairs. The reasons offered for disregarding hostile public opinion invariably have some reference to specialized knowledge ("They haven't seen the cables"), to complexity ("Other issues are involved here than just human rights"), or to sensitivity ("These are delicate negotiations"). Policy makers concerned with Latin America want to be left alone to work out unselfish professional responses to specialized, complex, sensitive issues within the framework of their own value structure.

Congress

While the influence of public opinion on the foreign policy decisions of Congress is quite different from its impact on the executive branch, an analysis of these differences must begin by noting that the quality and quantity of formal public opinion are identical for both branches of the government.[62] Like the executive branch, Congress possesses few data to gauge general public opinion on foreign policy issues. And also like the executive branch, Congress has never developed a mechanism by which to collect, analyze, and disseminate among its members those data that do exist.[63] It is at this point that the similarities end, however, because Congress receives a special type of public opinion: messages from home. To many members, the receipt of communications from constituents is the rough equivalent of concerned public opinion, an "issue public" in Converse's terminology.[64] This is particularly true of letters on subjects not covered by public opinion polls,

[62] This discussion is concerned with the impact of public opinion on the legislative role of Congress as it relates to foreign policy issues, not with the role of Congress as a conduit of public opinion to the executive branch.

[63] But members are often close students of polling. According to Erikson and Luttbet, during one sixteen-year period (1954-1970), the proportion of members of the House of Representatives who used public opinion surveys increased from 11 to 74 percent. Robert S. Erikson and Norman R. Luttbeg, *American Public Opinion: Its Origins, Content, and Impact* (New York: Wiley, 1973), p. 268. For a contrary opinion on congressional interest in polls, see "Congress and U.S. Foreign Policy towards Latin America," mimeographed transcript of a Conference on the United States, U.S. Foreign Policy, and Latin American and Caribbean Regimes, Washington, D.C., March 31, 1978. It must be emphasized that there are few polls on Latin America available to assist members in reaching decisions.

[64] Philip E. Converse, "The Nature of Belief Systems of Mass Publics," in *Ideology and Discontent*, ed. David E. Apter (New York: Free Press, 1964), p. 245.

which include most foreign policy legislation. It is all but axiomatic of letters concerning United States policy toward Latin America.

A number of members are regularly contacted by their constituents about various aspects of United States-Latin American relations. The representative from Florida's fourteenth congressional district is continually in contact with his Miami constituents regarding U.S.-Cuban relations, and the subject of U.S.-Mexican relations sporadically generates a considerable amount of pressure upon representatives from districts situated along the border or from districts with large chicano populations such as California's twenty-fifth congressional district. Members from districts containing disproportionate numbers of liberal activist citizens (major universities, New York's Upper East Side, the San Francisco Bay Area) at times receive substantial correspondence from constituents on humanitarian subjects. In addition, occasional crises or controversies involving Latin America are capable of generating relatively large amounts of mail, as the flood of correspondence on the 1978 Panama Canal debate demonstrated to many senators.

Overall, however, most congressional offices receive very few communications on any aspect of United States policy toward Latin America. Unlike mail sent to the executive branch, the few messages that are sent receive some attention. In virtually every member's office, each letter is read by at least one person, who then drafts a reply. Many members read a substantial portion of their mail, others read less of it. Of those members who fall into the latter group, nearly all receive some form of summary from their aides that outlines the issues being addressed and the position of the writers.[65] At the very least, Congress hears what it defines as public opinion.

Members of Congress may occasionally be willing to adjust their votes on an issue (particularly an obscure issue) to please their communicating constituents. In theory, a single letter has the potential to determine a member's position; a series of letters from concerned constituents is almost certain to be considered before a vote is cast, particularly if the letters do not appear to be part of an orchestrated campaign. Typically, however, the impact of correspondence from constituents depends almost entirely upon the nature and extent of

[65] There are exceptions to this rule. One of the most notable occurred during the course of the debate over ratification of the Panama Canal treaties, when an aide to treaties opponent Senator James Allen responded to critical correspondence with: "Your letter has been received and placed in Senator Allen's crackpot file. There are quite a few letters from Massachusetts in this file. Evidently, your state is a melting pot for neurotics, cranks and other individuals with subnormal mentalities." Allen subsequently apologized to the several persons who received these letters, noting that he had not seen them and, if he had, "they would not have been answered as they were."

counteracting pressures. In the specific area of United States policy toward human rights violations in Latin America, there have always been several factors competing with constituent pressure for a member's vote. The most important of these is interest-group pressure. Another is pressure from the executive branch. The Nixon, Ford, and Carter administrations all lobbied vigorously against nearly every piece of human rights legislation during the 1970s. At times, this proved to be a decisive factor, for a large number of members of Congress, especially in the House of Representatives, are willing to defer to the leadership of the President in foreign affairs. Thomas 'Doc' Morgan, who chaired the House Committee on Foreign Affairs from 1959 to 1977, consistently held that the views of his committee were subordinate to those of the executive branch: "The President is solely responsible for foreign policy, and it needs to be on a bipartisan basis."[66] A key participant in the U.S.-Nicaragua debate of the late 1970s, Representative Charles Wilson of Texas, provided perhaps the best recent expression of this deferential attitude: "I have grown up with the idea all of my life, and I still believe, that disagreements among American policy-makers, in so far as possible should stop at the water's edge. . . . The Executive has the responsibility for the conducting of foreign policy in this country, and I say that he should indeed have the final say-so if he has got the responsibility. He needs the authority."[67]

It is also important to note that a number of legislators have their own beliefs on issues of personal salience, and they will be unmoved by almost any amount of constituent pressure. In regard to human rights legislation aimed at Latin America during the 1970s, the opposition of Charles Wilson and Robert Lagomarsino and the support of Donald Fraser, Tom Harkin, and Edward Kennedy were so firm that no amount of public opinion could have changed their votes.

Regardless of these considerations, we must return to the crucial datum that, as measured by the quantity of constituent correspondence, United States policy toward Latin America is an issue of exceedingly low salience to most citizens. One obvious implication of

[66] "Senate, House Committees Differ on Foreign Affairs," *Congressional Quarterly Weekly Report* 28 (November 20, 1970): 2825; Dahl, *Congress and Foreign Policy*, p. 147.

[67] *Congressional Record*, September 16, 1977, p. H9559. Miller and Stokes found that this disposition to follow an administration's advice nearly neutralized the correlation between members' roll-call behavior and their perceptions of constituent preferences. Warren E. Miller and Donald E. Stokes, "Constituency Influence in Congress," *American Political Science Review* 57 (March 1963): 51. Representative Wilson's deference did not extend to the Carter administration's policy toward Nicaragua.

this fact is that a member of Congress typically remains unaware of constituent attitudes if indeed such attitudes exist. This is congruent with Miller's and Stokes' finding that the correlation between constituency attitudes and representatives' perceptions of constituency attitudes on the subject of foreign involvement is extremely low— only +.19 compared to a correlation of +.63 on the subject of domestic civil rights.[68] Another implication is that most members of Congress can cast ballots on issues of U.S.-Latin American relations without fear of retaliation by the electorate. Perhaps this has been best demonstrated by Congress-constituent interaction on foreign aid. One comparison of votes by 116 representatives in the Eighty-fifth Congress and the opinions of their constituents reveals "almost no correlation between constituent attitudes and either the roll-call votes or the attitudes of Congressmen pertinent to foreign aid." The data further demonstrate that members consistently exaggerate the extent to which their own positions and those of their constituents are congruent and that success of members at the polls depends little, if at all, on their foreign aid votes. As a result, many legislators vote as they please on foreign aid issues, even when they feel that most of their constituents disagree with them.[69]

There is no certainty that the impact of public opinion on the subject of the protection of human rights in Latin America is equivalent to that on foreign aid, but both are issues upon which the members of Congress receive few communications from their constituents. Perhaps public opinion sways an occasional vote on an issue involving United States policy toward human rights in Latin America. When faced with competing forces, however, the low intensity of public opinion probably means that such occasions are few.

The data on human rights and other issues of inter-American relations suggest that public opinion occupies an extremely limited amount of space in the societal environment surrounding the formal and informal processes by which United States policy toward Latin America is created. The insignificance of public opinion can be attributed to several interacting invariables, including the low salience of Latin America among the public, an elitist value system among State Department officials, and the host of competing pressures upon policy makers. It is probably a mistake to believe that any single variable bears primary responsibility for the minor influence of public opinion. Some variables are more prominent than others, some are logically

[68] Miller and Stokes, "Constituency Influence in Congress," p. 52.
[69] Hero, "Foreign Aid and the American Public," pp. 109, 112-114.

prior to others, but all contribute to the unimportance of public opinion. The nation's political structure is mined with obstacles to an effective role for public opinion in the area of United States policy toward Latin America. Imbedded as they are in the ground that supports the current decision-making apparatus, these obstacles will probably continue indefinitely to limit the public's impact upon the nation's policy toward Latin America.

· 2 ·

INTEREST GROUPS

UNTIL quite recently, relatively few interest groups specialized in foreign policy in general or United States policy toward Latin America in particular. One former executive branch official recalled, for example, that in the early 1960s the lobbies dedicated to influencing foreign policy were limited to domestic business leaders seeking protective tariffs, national minorities pursuing extremely narrow interests, and occasional church-related groups championing humanitarian concerns.[1] Latin Americanists know that a list this brief is incomplete, of course, for the literature on inter-American relations is packed with references to the efforts by individual multinational corporations to influence United States policy on a variety of incidents or issues. But in the past, these efforts were sporadic. Prior to 1960, an ongoing, institutionalized attempt by the business community or by any other group to affect United States policy toward Latin America was so unusual as to be a rarity.

Over the course of the 1960s and 1970s, the number and variety of corporations and voluntary membership associations attempting to influence foreign policy grew dramatically; nowhere was this growth greater than in the area of United States policy toward Latin America. By 1980, a foreign policy official with so much as a minor concern for Latin America was likely to be under at least periodic siege by a fairly large assortment of lobbyists representing one of three types of groups: Latin American governments, U.S.-based business organizations, and nongovernmental human rights organizations. The purpose of this chapter is to describe these groups' activities and then to analyze their impact upon policy.

LATIN AMERICAN GOVERNMENTS

While direct attempts by Latin American governments to influence United States policy have generally been minimal, embassy lobbying is not an unknown phenomenon. There is a near-perfect consensus

[1] Roger Hilsman, *The Politics of Policy Making in Defense and Foreign Affairs* (New York: Harper and Row, 1971), pp. 69-70. For a comprehensive summary of the early analyses of foreign policy interest groups, see Lester W. Milbrath's "Interest Groups and Foreign Policy," in *Domestic Sources of Foreign Policy*, ed. James N. Rosenau (New York: Free Press, 1967), esp. p. 247.

among officials at the State Department that the most effective Latin American embassies are those of Brazil and Venezuela. Diplomats of these two nations are said to be sensitive to trends in United States politics, to understand how these trends affect their interests, and to know how to negotiate solutions to differences and to avoid confrontations. When Venezuela faced a quota reduction following the failure to meet its 1973 sugar allotment, for example, its ambassador invited the entire House Committee on Agriculture to Caracas for an on-site inspection. Venezuela kept its quota.[2] When the Brazilian shoe industry faced the imposition of a surcharge on exports to the United States, the Brazilian government sent its diplomats to negotiate with Treasury officials, whereas representatives of other Latin American governments limited their contacts to the State Department. In the end, reports Albert Fishlow, "instead of a duty that might have been as large as 24 percent, close Brazilian cooperation with the Treasury resulted in a levy of 4.8 percent applicable to the vast majority of firms."[3]

But clearly these nations' representatives are not omnipotent. In 1974, Venezuela could not avoid being included in Congress's punitive denial of GSP tariff advantages to OPEC members, nor could Brazil convince the Carter administration to cease its early opposition to Brazil's purchase of a nuclear capability from West Germany. It may be that Brazilian and Venezuelan diplomats appear effective in influencing United States policy primarily because they are compared to other Latin American embassies. No doubt part of their effectiveness stems from the importance of these two nations to U.S. strategic and economic interests, not from the skills of their diplomatic representatives.

Diplomats from other Latin American nations make occasional efforts to influence United States policy. They urge congressional staff members to invite their partisans to testify at committee hearings, they host visits by members of Congress, and they engage in straightforward efforts to influence the decisions of State Department officials. In the past two decades, however, these efforts by Latin American governments to lobby in Washington have been few. During the 1950s and 1960s, when the allocation of the U.S. sugar quota spelled the difference between prosperity and depression for several Caribbean

[2] Robert A. Pastor, "U.S. Sugar Politics and Latin America: Asymmetries in Input and Impact," in the *Report* of the Commission on the Organization of the Government for the Conduct of Foreign Policy (Washington, D.C.: Government Printing Office, 1975), vol. 3, app. I, p. 228.
[3] Albert Fishlow, "Flying Down to Rio: Perspectives on U.S.-Brazil Relations," *Foreign Affairs* 57 (Winter 1978-1979): 397-398.

dictatorships, the sugar lobby was extraordinarily active in its lobbying efforts.[4] In the 1970s, five Latin American governments (Argentina, Chile, Nicaragua, Guatemala, and Haiti) maintained fairly regular access to policy makers through professional lobbyists, but only the first three of these engaged in an intense campaign to influence American foreign policy. Only the Nicaraguan lobby could compare with the highly professional, free-spending sugar lobby of the earlier era.

Argentina

In the 1970s, the Argentine lobby consisted of a publicity effort by the highly regarded public relations firm of Marstellar, Inc., formerly Burson-Marstellar. Following the March 1976 coup against the Perón government, the Argentine junta's human rights violations came under intense scrutiny in the U.S. media. Noting this unfavorable coverage, Argentina entered into a one-year contract with Marstellar in June 1976 in an attempt to forestall the development of a reputation for brutality. For $1,100,000 plus advertising expenses, Marstellar undertook an eight-nation campaign that focused upon the United States, where $590,000 of the original $1.1 million was spent. Marstellar's task was "to assist in promoting confidence in and good will toward the country and its government. The promotion of such confidence and good will . . . would presumably be reflected in the attitudes of the U.S. government toward Argentina." After the initial year, the Argentine Ministry of Economy renegotiated the contract with terms that varied from year to year; in 1978, Marstellar was paid $848,000 in fees, expenses, and project charges. Marstellar found this relationship sufficiently attractive to warrant opening an office in Buenos Aires.[5]

---

[4] The 1963 Senate hearings into influence peddling by Rafael Trujillo revealed an intricate, sophisticated lobbying apparatus. U.S. Congress, Senate, Committee on Foreign Relations, *Activities of Nondiplomatic Representatives of Foreign Principals in the United States*, 88th Cong., 1st Sess., Feb.-May 1963, pts. 3-5.

[5] Department of Justice Foreign Agent Registration Statement (FARS), June 1976. The Foreign Agents Registration Act of 1938 (FARA) requires agents of certain foreign organizations to register and report on their activities to the Department of Justice. In addition to an initial Foreign Agent Registration Statement, agents are required to file semiannual supplemental statements of activities. For a description and analysis of these reporting procedures, see U.S. Congress, Senate, Committee on Foreign Relations, *The Foreign Agents Registration Act, A Study Prepared by the American Law Division, Congressional Research Service, Library of Congress*, 95th Cong., 1st Sess., August 1977; and U.S. General Accounting Office, *Effectiveness of the Foreign Agents Registration Act of 1938, As Amended and Its Administration by the Department of Justice*, Report B-177551 (Washington, D.C.: General Accounting Office, March 13, 1974); Burson-Marstellar FARS, June 1976; Burson-Marstellar FARA supplemental statements October 23, 1977 and April 23, 1978.

Very little of Marstellar's public relations activity was oriented directly toward influencing policy makers. In late 1976, representatives of the firm met with Robert Zimmerman, the Director of East Coast Affairs in the State Department's Bureau of Inter-American Affairs, but the meeting was more a courtesy call than an effort to influence policy. Marstellar also monitored congressional hearings on repression in Argentina but took no active part in the proceedings.

From the beginning, a major focus of Marstellar's work was to encourage multinational corporate investment in Argentina. While nearly all Latin American governments engage in this promotional activity, under Marstellar's guidance Argentina became unusually aggressive during the immediate postcoup period. In cooperation with the Council of the Americas, a business-sponsored interest group whose activities are discussed later in this chapter, the firm arranged radio and television interviews in five cities for an expert on investment opportunities in Argentina, provided media support for three Council of the Americas workshops on investment in Argentina, and created a "trade and investment communications program" for the Argentine ambassador and his staff.

Marstellar has always been recognized as an expert in press relations, and it is in this area that the firm directed most of its attention.[6] The goals of these efforts were to influence members of the "interpretive" press and to gain media exposure for its clients. In carrying out its mission, the firm demonstrated considerable expertise and an enviable set of contacts. Marstellar arranged for an appearance by General Videla on ABC's "Good Morning America" in September 1977, when the junta chieftain was in the United States to witness the signing of the Panama Canal treaties, organized UPI and Reuters interviews for Raúl Lanusse, vice president of the Banco de la Nación Argentina, arranged an NBC radio interview for the president of Vinos Argentinos, sponsored a visit to Argentina by ABC-TV's "American Sportsman," and arranged for interviews by the *Christian Science Monitor*, the *Journal of Commerce*, and UPI with Minister of Planning General Ramón Díaz Bessone.

Marstellar was also responsible for a small advertising campaign, one part of which was an impressive full-page advertisement in the *New York Times* and the *Washington Post* on April 6, 1977. Signed by sixteen Argentine business groups but paid for by the Argentine government, the ad marked the first anniversary of the Videla coup.[7]

[6] An absolutely fascinating Marstellar report detailing the strategy to be followed in improving Argentina's image was obtained by Amnesty International and reprinted in the *Congressional Record*, October 14, 1978, pp. S12435-S12447.

[7] Burson-Marstellar FARA supplemental statement, April 23, 1977, attachment III.

51

Under the headline "A Year of Peace," the text depicted the government as grounded upon popular support and oriented both toward freeing Argentines "from the consequences of years of social, political and economic strife" and "insuring the validity of human rights to the population." Although most of the copy was devoted to the simple message that the trains were now running on time in Argentina, the Marstellar product appeared highly sophisticated when compared to similar ads by other Latin American governments.

The firm was equally adept in its efforts to attract the attention of journalists. Upon learning that *Time* magazine was sending an editor to Buenos Aires in early 1977, Marstellar employees sought him out, briefed him on Argentina, and offered their assistance in arranging interviews. Throughout the late 1970s, the firm arranged for groups of journalists from Canada, Great Britain, and the United States to travel to Buenos Aires for interviews with Argentine leaders. Although some journalists paid their own way, Marstellar made roundtrip tickets and housing at the posh Plaza Hotel available to reporters whose editors had no prohibition against accepting financial aid from interested parties. Each of the groups was provided with extraordinary access to public officials; in late 1976, for example, one group of North American reporters held a ninety-minute interview with General Videla.[8]

Chile

In distinct contrast to the limited indirect efforts by the Videla government to influence United States policy toward Argentina, in late 1973 the Chilean junta initiated a broad variety of public relations and lobbying activities in the United States. In the area of media relations, Chile entered into agreements with three firms between 1973 and 1975. The first of these was Worden and Company, a Washington, D.C. company whose clients included the Nicaraguan government of Anastasio Somoza. For two and a half years beginning in 1973, Jane Worden and her associates collected $1,200 per month plus expenses for assisting the Chilean ambassador to counter unfa-

---

[8] In general, reports by the subsidized journalists were much more favorable toward the Videla government than those of nonsubsidized journalists. In a series of articles for the *Christian Science Monitor*, for example, subsidized reporter James Nelson Goodsell seemed almost eager to explain the government's position. "From blue-collar workers to the affluent upper classes," he reported, "the people of Argentina increasingly are looking to the military government for solutions to longstanding economic and social problems—and finding them." *Christian Science Monitor*, October 13, 1978, pp. 12-13. For a contrary opinion at about the same time by nonsubsidized writers, see Karen DeYoung and Charles A. Krause, "Our Mixed Signals on Human Rights in Argentina," *Washington Post*, October 29, 1978, pp. C1-C2.

vorable attitudes toward the Chilean junta. Activities included editing and producing a newsletter, *Chile Today*, counseling responses to various antijunta articles in the press, drafting advertisements, reprinting and disseminating statements favorable to the junta (the embassy's favorite was one written by MIT economist Paul Rosenstein-Rodan), and arranging interviews for the ambassador and other spokespersons.[9]

The second public relations effort began in July 1974, when a contract was signed with Dialog, a subsidiary of the U.S. advertising giant J. Walter Thompson, for assistance in the development of an effective communications program. This contract was a direct result of the poor quality of earlier attempts by the junta to make its case with paid advertisements such as the crude Worden-produced ad on "The Real Story of the Persecution of Doctors in Chile."[10] For an annual retainer of $96,000 plus expenses that were expected to total between $700,000 and $900,000 per year, Dialog agreed to "bring to the attention of government leaders, intellectuals and other decision-makers in the United States and certain other countries accurate information and pertinent material about the objectives, actions and achievements of the Government of Chile, its institutions and its people."[11]

Then in late September 1974, before the program had begun, Dialog reconsidered its agreement, ostensibly because "certain J. Walter Thompson offices were threatened with internal disruption and violence from the outside including, in at least one case, the threat of bombing."[12] Another reason for asking Chile to relieve the company of its contractual obligations may have been the damage such a notorious client could have had upon the firm's image. The decision to drop the Chilean account was made soon after news of the firm's contract was published in an article by Lewis Diuguid in the *Washington Post*.[13]

J. Walter Thompson was sorely missed, for the series of embassy-sponsored ads in major American newspapers in late 1974 were notable only for their sledgehammer subtlety. In response to an unfavorable report by a Geneva-based human rights group, the embassy announced in half-page ads: "We rejoice over the present communique of the

[9] Worden and Company FARS, February 1, 1974, and FARA supplemental statements, August 1, 1974 and August 1, 1975.

[10] *New York Times*, February 24, 1974, sec. 4, p. 5.

[11] Dialog FARS, October 2, 1974.

[12] Ibid.

[13] *Washington Post*, September 13, 1974, p. A12. For an example of how the reputation of a public relations firm can suffer from association with an unsavory client, see John E. Cooney, "Public-Relations Firms Draw Fire for Aiding Repressive Countries," *Wall Street Journal*, January 31, 1979, pp. 1, 30.

International Commission of Jurists since it demonstrates the latter's relationship with the Soviet Union and its allies in the pursuance of identical objectives. . . . We are, indeed, appreciative of this new falsehood, this grotesque lie."[14] Two days later, an unusually tasteless half-page ad attacked a *Washington Post* story describing the execution by dismemberment of folk singer Víctor Jara at Estadio Chile in September 1973:

> Victor Jara was never famous or popular in Chile, except during the official activities of the Communist Party. But even his own party treated him as a second-rate musician, mainly because of some peculiar aspects of Jara's private behavior, which were not compatible with Chile's traditional moral code of behavior, a code respected even by militants of the nation's Communist Party. Jara's limited popularity decreased after 1970 when he was arrested by the police when he was found in the company of homosexuals. [15]

Another ad, sponsored by a group called "Acción de Mujeres de Chile" with an embassy address, attempted to discredit the Unidad Popular government through personal attacks upon its leader: "Never could anyone explain why Salvador Allende did not trust the poor soul that appeared as his wife. . . . He gave a fleet of more than 50 automobiles to his secretary-confidant-companion, not to his wife. . . . The truth is that Salvador Allende never treated Hortensia Bussi the way a normal man treats his wife."[16] In distinct contrast to Marstellar's efforts on behalf of Argentina, scurrilous attacks upon individuals associated with the Allende government became the hallmark of the Chilean junta's public relations campaign.

Finally, in October 1975, the embassy of Chile contracted with a retired Kennecott Copper public relations specialist, Lester Ziffren, to "assist in strengthening understanding and economic relations between the United States and Chile." For $2,500 per month plus expenses, Ziffren agreed to perform a variety of fairly mundane tasks. Most of his time was spent translating into English the public statements of Chilean officials and advising Chilean diplomats on antijunta activities in the United States.[17]

In addition to its various public relations campaigns, the Pinochet government also made direct attempts to influence United States pol-

[14] *Washington Post*, November 8, 1974, p. A16.
[15] *Washington Post*, November 10, 1974, p. A11.
[16] *Washington Post*, December 10, 1974, p. A20.
[17] Lester Ziffren FARS, October 1, 1975, and FARA supplemental statements, May 25, 1976, November 25, 1976, May 25, 1977, and November 25, 1977.

icy toward Chile. The first effort in this area began in January 1974, when the Chilean ambassador hired as a lobbyist a retired vice president of Anaconda Copper, Henry Gardiner, who, like Ziffren, had specialized in public relations during his corporate career. During the year and a half that he was employed by the embassy, Gardiner received $16,800 "to counteract critical comments and publicity of the Chilean government." Gardiner spent a considerable amount of time contacting members of Congress, their staffs, and executive branch officials.[18]

By far the most exotic component of the Chile lobby was Dumitru G. Danielopol, a Romanian painter and free-lance journalist hired in January 1975 by the Chilean military attaché, General Enrique Morel, to "inform members of Congress, the United States Government, the New York and Washington news media of the activities, aspirations, and accomplishments of the Government of Chile." During the thirteen months he was employed (first at $10,000 plus expenses for six months, later at $750 per month), Danielopol met with Morel two or three times a week, furnishing him with reports on a variety of topics. His work with U.S. government officials was limited to contacting a few members of Congress and a single member of the White House staff. Most of Danielopol's time was consumed in urging a truly extraordinary variety of conservative political groups to support the Chilean junta. Also notable was the enthusiasm with which Danielopol set about his work. Lamenting that "there are today some elements who are no longer interested in a strong America with a sacred responsibility to guard the hemisphere," he attempted to demonstrate the validity of his hypothesis that U.S. national security required support for the Chilean government: "One has only to look at the country's coastline which stretches along a large part of the West Coast of South America. This coast cannot be dominated by a hostile power. Important sea lanes would be in jeopardy."[19]

In 1975, Chile launched a major effort to counter antijunta attitudes among U.S. policy makers. In March, the New York public relations firm of Marvin Liebman was hired by Nena Ossa of the Consejo Chileno-Norteamericano (CCN) to create an organization of U.S. citizens to improve United States-Chilean relations. Allegedly funded by voluntary contributions by private Chilean businesspersons, the Santiago-based CCN agreed to pay Liebman $3,000 per month plus expenses until the organization he was to organize became self-suffi-

[18] Henry E. Gardiner FARS, January 17, 1974, and FARA supplemental statements, July 21, 1974, January 21, 1975, and March 1, 1975.

[19] Dumitru G. Danielopol FARS, January 10, 1975, and FARA supplemental statements, July 21, 1975 and January 21, 1976.

cient. Thus was born the American-Chilean Council (ACC).[20] In December 1978, the Justice Department filed a civil fraud suit against Liebman and the ACC, charging them with violations of the Foreign Agents Registration Act of 1938. According to the Justice Department complaint, the sole purpose of the ACC "is to disguise the business relationship that exists between the Chilean government of Gen. Augusto Pinochet and its American public relations representatives." In letters seized by the Justice Department, Liebman referred to the ACC as a "front group" and to the group's members as "letterhead names."[21]

Until it ran afoul of the law, the Council engaged in a variety of activities. Its initial interest was in linking the antijunta lobby in the United States to the Soviet Union through a series of fairly turgid pamphlets whose titles included "Key Targets of Soviet Diplomacy: Chile and Peru," "The Soviet Offensive Against Chile," "Soviet Penetration of Latin America," and the best of them all: "Communists Sponsoring Anti-Chile Lobby." Soon after its founding, the ACC broadened its scope and hired L. Francis Bouchey, a public relations consultant with links to the ultraconservative Council for Inter-American Security, to be its Washington representative.[22] Bouchey's task was to contact members of Congress, congressional staffs, and opinion leaders, concentrating upon securing "passage of legislation affecting Chile which the American-Chilean Council judges desirable." Bouchey terminated his relationship with the ACC at the end of September 1976, but not before he had performed activities that would implicate him along with Liebman in a Justice Department complaint alleging fraudulent fund raising.

By late 1976, the Council's annual budget was approaching $117,000, of which $100,000 was supplied by the CCN. At no time during the 1970s were voluntary contributions by U.S. citizens substantial, despite Council chairperson John Davis Lodge's pleas for funds to "counteract the leftist propaganda campaign against Chile." For example, of the $181,700 received by the ACC during the twelve-

[20] American-Chilean Council FARS, March 31(?), 1975.

[21] *Washington Post*, December 19, 1978, p. A18.

[22] At one point in the 1970s, Bouchey's public relations firm and the Council for Inter-American Security shared the same building in Washington. The Council is an amorphous organization that counts among its founding members Roger Fontaine, a principal spokesperson for the far-right position in U.S.-Latin American relations. For an illuminating statement by one of the Council's associates, a retired army general and former chairperson of the Inter-American Defense Board, see U.S. Congress, House, Committee on International Relations, Subcommittee on Inter-American Affairs, *Arms Trade in the Western Hemisphere*, 95th Cong., 2d Sess., June-August 1978, pp. 65-105.

month period ending September 30, 1978, more than 81 percent came directly from the CCN.[23] In addition to covering administrative fees, the costs of producing pamphlets (such as "Chile's Economy Gaining Momentum," reprinted from *International Finance*, a publication of the Chase Manhattan Bank), and Bouchey's retainer, the money was disbursed to U.S. journalists for airline tickets to Chile and to Nena Ossa for a variety of travel and other expenses.

The final component of the undistinguished Chile lobby was the Washington law firm of Anderson, Pendleton, McMahon, Peet and Donovan. For an initial retainer of $1,250 per month beginning in mid-1976, the firm provided the Chilean embassy with legal counsel and professional lobbying. In the former category, the firm represented the Chilean government before the Department of Justice in regard to the investigation into the assassination of Orlando Letelier, performed research of the law of libel and the subject of letters rogatory for the ambassador, studied the legal implications of the Harkin human rights amendment, and examined the subject of arms export licenses.[24]

The firm's unsuccessful lobbying efforts focused upon blocking congressional initiatives to reduce or eliminate aid to the Chilean government. Its tactic was to encourage conservative members of Congress (the modal ADA rating of the members approached was an extremely conservative "5")[25] who might be wavering in their support for aid to Chile. These efforts were mostly inconclusive, as, for example:

> On May 27 [1976] Kenneth Robinson and Edmund Pendleton met with Edward Kenny in the offices of the Senate Armed Services Committee. We asked his advise [sic] as to what Chile should do to improve it's [sic] position. Kenny indicated that Senator Thurmond strongly opposes communist governments and therefore supports Chile, even though he was not sure whether the Chilean Government was repressive or not. Kenny suggested

[23] American-Chilean Council FARA supplemental statements, March 31, 1978 and September 30, 1978. Lodge served as chairperson pro tem while Leibman searched for a replacement for the first ACC chairperson, the late Spruille Braden.

[24] Anderson, Pendleton and McMahon FARS, June 9, 1976, and FARA supplemental statements, May 9, 1977 and November 9, 1977.

[25] At the end of each session of Congress since 1947, the Americans for Democratic Action (ADA) has given each member of Congress a score computed on the basis of his or her vote on twenty key issues selected by ADA personnel. The range of scores is 0 to 100, with high scores indicating a liberal voting record. A member's ADA score is widely accepted as a reasonably accurate (but not infallible) indicator of his or her ideological position.

the need for a better briefing of the Congressmen with the facts on Chile.[26]

Once all United States aid was halted, these lobbying efforts also ended. During the Nixon-Ford administration, Anderson, Pendleton, McMahon, Peet and Donovan also maintained close contact with the Department of Treasury. Since at that time Treasury's position on United States-Chilean relations was nearly identical to that of the government of Chile, no effort was made to influence its policy.

Nicaragua

Until 1978, United States government ties to the Somoza family in Nicaragua were characterized by an uncommon cordiality. The Somozas' ability to maintain this relationship was in no small measure the result of their close relations with United States policy makers, including in the 1970s a number of members of Congress led by Representatives John Murphy of New York and Charles Wilson of Texas.[27] Unlike the Argentine and Chilean lobbies, the Nicaraguan lobby enjoyed direct access to the floors of Congress.

For as long as anyone can remember, the Somoza government maintained a public relations/lobbying effort in the United States. In 1963, for example, the lobby was so visible that the Senate Foreign Relations Committee investigated alleged influence peddling by President Luis Somoza.[28] After the devastating 1972 earthquake, the major component of the Nicaraguan lobby became the Comité Nacional de Emergencia, formed to obtain funds to rebuild Managua. The lobby did its work quietly and efficiently, there was no organized opposition, and the Somoza family regularly received the aid that, critics would later allege, was instrumental in freeing the foreign exchange necessary

[26] Anderson, Pendleton and McMahon FARA amendment to registration statement, May 1977; FARA supplemental statement, November 9, 1977.

[27] Murphy and Anastasio Somoza Debayle were classmates in military preparatory school. Both received B.S. degrees from the U.S. Military Academy at West Point, but they attended at different times. In 1977, the Department of Justice conducted an inquiry into alleged improprieties by Murphy in the course of arranging financing for an oil refinery to be built in Nicaragua by a Somoza-controlled corporation. During the 1970s, Murphy was also one of the staunchest supporters of the Park dictatorship in South Korea. On one occasion, he publicly endorsed the jailing of Korean presidential candidate Kim Dae Jung because the latter was "seriously hampering the Park government's ability to function." *New York Times*, October 26, 1977, p. 25; *Congressional Quarterly*, June 5, 1976, p. 1456. One of the members of Congress implicated in the Justice Department's Abscam bribery case, Murphy was defeated in his 1980 bid for reelection.

[28] See *Activities of Nondiplomatic Representatives of Foreign Principals in the United States*, pt. 11., *supra* n. 4.

to buy arms (much of it on credit from the U.S. government) needed to repress domestic political opposition. By 1975, however, as perceptive an observer of American politics as Anastasio Somoza could foresee that future support would not come at its traditional low cost. When Congress began to take substantial measures to curtail aid to repressive governments, President Somoza moved to reinforce his lobby.

In May 1975, the government of Nicaragua entered into an agreement with Sullivan, Sarria and Associates, a Ft. Lauderdale public relations firm. With a first-year budget of $336,000, Sullivan agreed to launch a publicity program to improve the image of the Somoza government in the United States. Through newsletters, press releases, radio and television reports on Managua reconstruction, a sixteen-page "Businessman's Dialogue With the New Nicaragua" in *Business Week*, AP and UPI press interviews with Somoza, press coverage of visits by Somoza to Louisiana, South Carolina, and his alma mater at West Point, and an address to the Chicago World Trade Conference, in one year the public relations firm placed an enormous amount of news about Nicaragua before the American public. So taxed was the firm that it had to subcontract part of its effort to Warren Weil Public Relations in New York and Worden and Company in Washington, D.C.[29]

In 1976, part of Sullivan, Sarria was spun off as an independent firm under the name of the Nicaragua Government Information Service. Ian MacKenzie, a former executive vice president of Sullivan, Sarria and later president of another Somoza-related New York public relations firm, MacKenzie-McCheyne, became the chief public relations representative of the Nicaraguan government. From June 1976 to June 1977, the Nicaragua Government Information Service received $205,000 from Somoza to pursue tasks it had assumed from Sullivan, Sarria. In addition to adding at least five new members to the staff, MacKenzie contracted with two influential Georgia lawyers, Bobby Lee Cook and Irwin Stolz, to conduct an independent human rights investigation in Nicaragua. Although he could not even spell "Nicaragua," Cook discovered that aid had been denied the Somoza government "by virtue of unfair and distorted allegations." Working at the rate of $1,000 per day each plus expenses, Stolz and Cook

[29] Some of this publicity was counterproductive as, for example, when it was revealed that Somoza's Chicago limousine bill reached $3,036 at a time when he was seeking aid for earthquake recovery. Sullivan, Sarria and Associates FARS, June 1975; Worden and Company FARS, May 1976; Warren Wiel Public Relations FARS, undated.

prepared a twenty-eight-page report for MacKenzie that was never distributed publicly.[30]

In total, the Nicaraguan government spent $571,000 to improve its public image in the United States during the two-year period from mid-1975 to mid-1977. This level of spending continued through mid-1979, when Somoza was overthrown.

As in the case of the Chilean government, Nicaragua's public relations efforts were supplemented by an active lobbying campaign. Unlike the Chilean authorities, however, the Somoza government chose as its lobbyists two Washington-wise attorneys, William Cramer and Fred Korth. In April 1975, the Nicaraguan development board, the Instituto de Fomento Nacional, contracted with the law firm of Cramer, Haber and Becker (later Cramer, Visser, Lipsen and Smith) for advice on United States policies affecting the economic development of Nicaragua. For $2,000 per month the firm agreed to hold discussions "with the proper agencies and government officials in the United States" but not to engage in "political activities."[31]

In mid-1976, liberals in Congress achieved major victories in their drive to reduce aid to repressive Latin American governments, with a reduction in economic aid to Chile and a prohibition on military aid to both Chile and Uruguay. Exulting over the Uruguayan vote, Edward Koch boasted that if Latin America's human rights violators "don't get the message, then next year on to Nicaragua."[32] The Somoza government got the message, but it hardly reacted the way Koch would have approved; instead it began to augment its Washington lobby. In late spring 1977, the Nicaraguan-American Trade Council (formerly the American-Nicaraguan Council and, before that, the Citizens for the Truth About Nicaragua) registered as a lobbying organization with Congress. The two principals of the Council were Charles Lipsen, a law partner of William Cramer, and Raymond Molina, a Cuban exile and participant in the Bay of Pigs invasion.[33]

[30] MacKenzie-McCheyne, Inc. FARS, October 1, 1976, Bobby Lee Cook FARS, August 1977, and FARA supplemental statement, February 24, 1978. After a misunderstanding regarding fees, Cook refused compensation. Although concrete evidence is lacking, Cook may have been employed by President Somoza as a favor to U.S. Representative Larry MacDonald of Georgia, whom Cook had defended in a federal probe of MacDonald's alleged hoarding of arms. Cook was hired by Somoza shortly after MacDonald visited Nicaragua in 1977. Stolz received highly unfavorable publicity for his efforts. See Jack Anderson, "Five Rose-Colored Days in Nicaragua," *Washington Post*, January 25, 1979, p. DC9.

[31] Cramer, Haber and Becker FARS, April 1975.

[32] House Report 94-1228, p. 49.

[33] For an understanding of Mr. Molina's political views and his financial relations with the Nicaraguan government, see his statement in U.S. Congress, House, Com-

The efforts by the Council were at first unsuccessful, for in mid-1977 the House Committee on Appropriations reported a foreign assistance bill that deleted military aid to Nicaragua. Liberal committee members had been able to convince a bare majority of their colleagues that the Nicaraguan government was too repressive to receive military aid. Facing a rising tide of congressional interest in human rights and clear evidence that Koch and his allies were capable of fulfilling their threat of a year earlier, the government of Nicaragua (as opposed to the Instituto de Fomento Nacional) responded by retaining Cramer, Haber and Becker. Somoza paid the firm $50,000 for seven months (June to December 1977) to "attempt to convince the U.S. government, including the U.S. Congress, that the elimination of economic and/or military assistance to Nicaragua was not in the mutual and best interest of the U.S. and Nicaragua."[34] By early 1978, attorney Cramer was being paid at the rate of $150,000 per year by the Nicaraguan government.

Cramer, an eight-term former member of Congress from Florida and an influential Washington attorney who counted among his clients the Republican National Committee, started to contact his friends on Capitol Hill. He approached more than forty members of Congress, concentrating upon individuals who would be willing to work to convince wavering colleagues to vote on behalf of Nicaragua. In addition, the firm sent a telegram to every member of the House shortly before the floor debate on the aid appropriations bill. It declared in part that

> Nicaragua, one of our staunchest friends, as proved by its votes in the U.N. and by being the country for the training and staging of the Bay of Pigs invasion, should not be named by Congress as the only Latin American country which desires to continue such aid to be cut off. To the world, it appears that the United States, while making overtures to Communist Cuba, is penalizing its staunchest friend, a country that Castro wants to turn Marxist. Alleged violations of human rights being circulated are second-hand, hearsay and unproven. Such violations are largely attributable to the Marxist-terrorists in Nicaragua.[35]

The efforts of Cramer and his associates were supplemented in May 1977 when another Washington attorney, Fred Korth, read in the newspaper of the proposal to halt aid to Nicaragua. He immediately

---

mittee on Appropriations, Subcommittee on Foreign Operations and Related Agencies, *Foreign Assistance and Related Agencies Appropriations for 1978*, 95th Cong., 1st Sess., 1977, pt. 3, pp. 18-24.

[34] Cramer, Haber and Becker FARS, June 1977.

[35] Ibid.

began an independent lobbying effort on behalf of the Somoza government. A former Secretary of the Navy, Korth was another of the large number of lawyers in Washington in the 1970s who moved in and out of public service, in the process establishing personal contacts that were later valuable in pursuing the interests of clients. In 1977, the clients of the legal firm of Korth and Korth included investors with financial interests in Nicaragua. Korth, however, chose to ignore his pecuniary interests in the preservation of the status quo in Nicaragua. Instead, he emphasized that the best interests of the United States required support for the Somoza government. Writing in the third person, he explained:

> Upon learning of the proposal to eliminate foreign military and other aid to the Republic he has become convinced from his own investigation that such action would be detrimental to the relationship between the United States and Nicaragua. Fred Korth firmly believes that the Republic of Nicaragua and President Somoza are among the best friends that the United States has in all of Latin America. It is with this thought that Fred Korth asked the permission of President Somoza to make representation to the members of Congress. There was no discussion of any fee nor is there any anticipation of any compensation of any character or reimbursement of expenses for this service.[36]

In the late 1970s, Korth was one of the handful of people who denied that the Somoza regime was repressing its citizens' rights. Three months before the 1978 civil war erupted, Korth reported that "everything was quite peaceful" as he drove about Managua.[37]

Korth's work on behalf of the Somoza government was crucial. It was he who convinced fellow Texan Charles Wilson to champion the Somoza government in the House. In 1977, Wilson was upset with what he called the "flaming radical left" in the State Department's Bureau of Human Rights and Humanitarian Affairs. After Korth showed Wilson copies of the opposition newspaper, *La Prensa*, which demonstrated to the latter's satisfaction the falsity of State Department allegations concerning human rights violations, Wilson agreed to help restore the aid that had been cut by the subcommittee.[38] During the ensuing months, Korth became the principal contact between Wilson and Somoza. Following the vote in June 1977, Korth escorted Wilson and Representative George M. O'Brien to lunch and dinner with

[36] Korth and Korth FARS, May 11, 1977; Korth and Korth FARA supplemental statement, November 11, 1977.
[37] Ibid.
[38] Telephone interview with Fred Korth, Washington, D.C., November 27, 1978.

President Somoza. A year later, in May 1978, he again acted as an intermediary during Wilson's effort to end the Carter administration's embargo on aid to Nicaragua.[39] In addition, Korth took advantage of a friendship with Senate staffer William H. Jorden to obtain an interview with the chairperson of the Appropriations Subcommittee on Foreign Operations, Senator Daniel Inouye, to urge him to support military aid to Nicaragua. Although Inouye fought resolutely against a cut in military aid to Somoza during Senate consideration of the 1977 aid appropriations bill, he insisted that the meeting with Korth did not determine his position.[40]

By the time the question of military aid to Nicaragua came to a vote before the full House, the Nicaraguan lobby had finished its work. Coincidentally, at the same time, the Washington human rights lobby was exhausted following a successful campaign to reduce military aid to Argentina. With the help of votes from Murphy's Merchant Marine and Fisheries Subcommittee, Wilson's fellow Texans (including such prominent liberals as Barbara Jordan), all but one of Cramer's former colleagues from Florida, and a confusing letter of support from a Carter administration official, an amendment was passed to restore the $3.1 million in military aid to Nicaragua that the Appropriations Committee had eliminated.[41] The key votes were cast by conservatives who normally vote for all aid reductions. Of the forty-one members who voted to cut aid to Argentina on June 22 and to restore aid to Nicaragua on June 23, twenty-six had conservative ADA ratings of less than twenty.

Under normal circumstances, the long-term effectiveness of the Nicaraguan lobby could have been expected to persist. It enjoyed all the crucial components of an effective lobby, plus until 1978 its client was free from the reputation of extreme brutality that the Argentine and Chilean governments had earned. But the late 1970s was not a period of normalcy in foreign assistance policy making. Faced with substantial congressional hostility toward Nicaragua, a growing anti-Somoza attitude within the Department of State, and a need to practice its own human rights preaching, the Carter administration dropped to $150,000 its fiscal year (FY) 1979 military aid request for Nicaragua. After consultations with a few members of Congress,

[39] Korth and Korth FARA supplemental statement, Nov. 11, 1977.

[40] "I took no action with reference to United States assistance to Nicaragua that I would not have taken had I not seen Mr. Korth." Letter from Senator Daniel K. Inouye, May 23, 1978.

[41] Ex-Representative Jordan asserted that her vote to arm Somoza reflected a desire to pursue "the best interests of U.S. defense" and that no lobby influenced her position. Letter from Barbara Jordan, February 26, 1979.

the Nicaraguan lobby decided not to fight for an increase to normal levels. Its strategy became that of increased public relations efforts (including the employment of another public relations expert, Norman Wolfson, to produce the *Nicaragua Update* and other press materials) and a low profile on Capitol Hill until the human rights issue passed from the scene. When the end came in mid-1979, the lobby was still at work attempting to convince the Carter administration that Somoza was the only alternative to communism in Nicaragua.

Other Latin American Lobbies

Aside from the ubiquitous trade-promotion lobbies, in the 1970s the only other Latin American lobbies were those of Haiti and Guatemala. In mid-1977, the Haitian government of Jean-Claude Duvalier retained the law firm of Peabody, Rivlin, Lambert and Meyers for $2,000 per month to influence U.S. policy makers. Officials of the Department of State, AID, the Overseas Private Investment Corporation, the House Committee on International Relations, and the Senate Committee on Foreign Relations were the particular foci of the firm's activities. The topics discussed with these officials included trade, foreign aid, immigration, and human rights.[42] Although the Haitian government was recognized by policy makers as among the most repressive in Latin America, it was also identified as governing the most poverty-stricken people in the hemisphere. These two facts combined to produce a general belief among members of both the State Department and Congress that Haiti was existing at the very margins of civilization and therefore that efforts to promote respect for human rights would be fruitless. There is no evidence that Peabody, Rivlin, Lambert and Meyers contributed to the prevalence of this attitude. Whatever the cause of Haiti's immunity, the firm that represented it faced none of the challenges that confronted the representatives of the governments of Argentina, Chile, and Nicaragua.[43]

By June 1977, the government of Guatemala had become concerned about the combined efforts by Congress and the new Carter administration to incorporate human rights considerations into United States foreign policy. Outraged by a State Department report on human rights practices, Guatemala rejected U.S. military aid in 1977. At the same time, the growing interest in human rights in Washington and Guatemala's generally poor record in this area led the Guatemalan ambassador in Washington to hire an attorney, Sheldon Z. Kaplan,

[42] Peabody, Rivlin, Lambert and Meyers FARS, August 1, 1977, and FARA supplemental statement, September 29, 1977.

[43] The Haitian government of Jean-Claude Duvalier also hired the U.S. public relations firm of Edelman International to reform its image in the United States.

to represent his government's interests.[44] For $25,000 per year, Kaplan reported to the embassy on U.S. foreign policy initiatives, particularly in the area of foreign aid. He also lobbied on behalf of Guatemala, but, as in the case of Haiti, his efforts were probably unnecessary. During the 1970s, there was very little active opposition to the Guatemalan government by human rights groups or within the United States government.

U.S. BUSINESS ORGANIZATIONS

The Carter administration's human rights policy was implemented in part by the withdrawal of goods and services from repressive Latin American governments; consequently U.S.-based multinational corporations were frequently affected by human rights decisions. Facing a loss of markets, corporate lobbyists and corporate executives often worked to decrease the influence of human rights considerations in foreign policy decisions. In 1977, for example, executives of Massachusetts-based Kollmorgan Corporation contacted House Speaker Thomas O'Neill and Representative Silvio Conte to complain that the State Department had refused to grant an export license for their pending sale of submarine periscopes to the repressive Argentine government of General Videla. O'Neill and Conte informed Secretary of State Vance in late October that their corporate constituent was being harmed by the Carter administration's human rights policy; the license was granted on November 3. In 1978, with the assistance of sympathetic members of Congress, officials of Allis-Chalmers Corporation lobbied against an executive branch decision to block a $270 million Export-Import Bank loan to Argentina for the purchase of Allis-Chalmers turbines. In this case, too, the corporate lobby was successful.[45]

Examples such as these are not plentiful, however, and thus it is impossible to generalize about the effectiveness of corporate lobbying against human rights decisions. Under the Carter administration, the success of the business lobby appeared to vary directly with the size of the proposed transaction and the inoffensiveness of the proposed sale item. Given the chronic U.S. balance of payments deficit, most efforts by human rights activists to block large sales of nonmilitary items were regularly overcome by concerted business lobbying. On relatively small sales and sales of items related to human rights vio-

[44] Sheldon Z. Kaplan FARS, June 24, 1977.
[45] See the discussion in U.S. Congress, Senate, Committee on Foreign Relations, Subcommittee on Western Hemisphere Affairs, *Latin America*, 95th Cong., 2d Sess., October 1978, pp. 54-55, 217-218.

lations, the probability of successful business lobbying decreased greatly. As in the case of Kollmorgan Corporation, the outcome of conflicts over these less-important efforts often appeared to be determined more by the position of a corporation's allies in Washington than by the substance of the proposed transaction.

Aside from their efforts to influence decisions on individual export sales, few corporations lobbied directly on the general issue of human rights and United States policy toward Latin America. Instead, they used their associations to perform this task for them. The two most significant of these associations—the Council of the Americas and the Association of American Chambers of Commerce in Latin America—merit individual consideration.

The Council of the Americas

The Council of the Americas (COA) is a nonprofit business association supported by over two hundred-member corporations with investments in Latin America. It is the nation's most influential nongovernmental organization with a specific interest in Latin America. Its corporate members represent 90 percent of U.S. equity in Latin America and include virtually every major multinational corporation based in the United States.[46] David Rockefeller has always been the single dominant figure associated with the Council, although he relinquished many of his responsibilities in the late 1970s. One of the Rockefeller's former employees at Chase Manhattan Bank, Henry R. Geyelin, is COA president.

Although the Council represents the entire ideological range of the American business community, it is dominated by what might be termed "enlightened liberalism." In the late 1970s, leading members of the board of trustees included Robert O. Anderson, the chairman of Atlantic Richfield, and Donald M. Kendall, the chairman of Pepsico, as well as such respected, easily recognized corporate leaders as C. Douglas Dillon (Dillon, Reed and Company), General James M. Gavin (formerly chairman of Arthur P. Little), and Ernest C. Arbuckle (Wells Fargo Bank). Each of the sixty-five members of the Council's board was a president, chairman, or senior vice president of a major multinational corporation. At the administrative level, about a dozen persons formed the largest full-time staff of any interest group concerned with U.S.-Latin American relations. The Council has always been fortunate to attract a number of able, knowledgeable professionals. Money is one of the reasons it has been able to do so—at the end

---

[46] In addition, the Council has about twenty-five diverse organizational members, including the Center for Inter-American Relations, the National Association of Manufacturers, and the Inter-American Bar Association.

of the 1970s the Council's annual revenues were close to $1 million, four or five times larger than those of any other Latin America-related lobbying organization.

The Council's major strength lies in its ability to link executives of member corporations and foreign policy makers at the highest levels of government. COA pioneered this type of direct lobbying, which has now become an important feature of the U.S. business lobby.

> Ten years ago business lobbying . . . was fairly inept. It was done solely by corporations and a couple of trade associations that were highly ideological, extremely conservative, unwilling to compromise, and not knowledgeable about the Congressional process. They were basically ineffective when they did lobby. . . . We've seen enormous changes in business lobbying in the last few years. There is more sophistication, and a much more broadly based effort. We have new groups such as the Business Roundtable, which is composed of the chief executive officers of the largest corporations in the country. They do their own lobbying, and that's much more effective. The average lobbyist—business or labor—who comes to a Senate office will talk to the staff person; the Senators just don't have time for them. If the chief executive officer of U.S. Steel comes to Washington, he walks right into the Senator's office and can make his views known. . . . Business may have been beleaguered a few years ago, but they're doing just fine now.[47]

In the area of United States-Latin American relations, the opinion of a COA-affiliated executive is often the only nongovernmental view a major policy maker will hear. The Council of the Americas is the only component of the Latin America-related lobby with direct access to virtually every executive branch policy maker, including the President. On May 7, 1973, for example, the COA chairperson and executive vice president briefed Secretary of State William Rogers and assistant secretary of state for inter-American affairs Jack Kubisch prior to the Secretary's official tour of Latin America. No other group interested in U.S. policy toward Latin America ever briefs the Secretary of State; in fact, no other such group even talks with the Secretary of State. On June 7, 1973, Council trustees met with Pres-

---

[47] Norman Ornstein in "Congress and U.S. Foreign Policy towards Latin America," mimeographed transcript of a Conference on the United States, U.S. Foreign Policy, and Latin American and Caribbean Regimes, Washington, D.C., March 31, 1978, pp. 25-26. For a further elaboration of Ornstein's views, see Norman J. Ornstein and Shirley Elder, *Interest Groups, Lobbying and Policymaking* (Washington, D.C.: Congressional Quarterly, 1978).

ident Nixon to gain his endorsement of a business advisory committee on United States policy toward Latin America. At that meeting were the presidents or board chairpersons of Dupont, Manufacturers Hanover Trust, Chase Manhattan Bank, Wells Fargo Bank, Standard Oil of California, Kennecott Copper, Owens-Illinois, United Brands, and Alcoa. Not only did Mr. Nixon agree with the idea but he permitted the Council to name the committee and ordered that his administrators listen to its advice. On July 19, 1973, following up on its meeting with the President, COA trustees met with William Jorden, who as Henry Kissinger's Latin Americanist on the National Security Council staff at the time was helping to supervise the destabilization of the Allende government in Chile, "to discuss mechanisms whereby the Council might improve its informal advisory role to the United States Government on Latin American policy." Included in this meeting were representatives of both ITT and Kennecott Copper, two companies whose investments in Chile had recently been nationalized.[48]

Nineteen seventy-six was another typical year for the Council. Reviewing its activities, COA president Geyelin reported that "the trustees, advisory boards, and staff met regularly over the year with senior officials of the United States Government Departments of State and Commerce, the White House staff, and with leaders of the U.S. Congress." The Council's 1976 *Annual Report* presents an impressive eleven-page list of these meetings. On June 16, for example, Augustine R. Marusi, Council (and Borden Corporation) chairperson and three Council trustees met with Treasury Secretary William Simon to discuss the Secretary's trip to Latin America. They then rushed to the Department of State to meet with William D. Rogers, undersecretary of state for economic affairs, and Harry W. Shlaudeman, assistant secretary of state for inter-American affairs, "to review proposals from the OAS meeting in Santiago." The Council did not voice its support for the human rights initiatives taken at the OAS meeting but rather stressed its members' belief that economic issues should not be "politicized" by human rights considerations. The COA representatives indicated their support for the approach employed by Treasury Secretary Simon, who during his trip to Chile raised the issue of human rights but also praised the Pinochet government for "clearly establishing the bases for economic development."[49] What is more important than the substance of these COA-administration conversations, however, is the fact that they actually occurred. They demonstrate that the Coun-

[48] Council of the Americas, *1973 Annual Report.*
[49] Council of the Americas, *1976 Annual Report.*

68

cil holds a completely unrivaled ability to present its opinions to government decision makers.

Added to the political power of its member corporations is a second reason for the strength of the Council: the expertise it brings to the policy-making process. This expertise is evident in its basic knowledge of the issues of United States-Latin American relations and in its sophisticated lobbying techniques. The best indicator of the Council's expertise on important issues is the series of papers prepared by the four advisory groups established with President Nixon's approval. These groups focused upon science and technology, investment dispute mechanisms, raw materials and energy, and extraterritorial application of United States laws. Members of each group were selected by COA personnel on the basis of their familiarity with the issue. The Council's 1975 position paper on hemispheric trade, for example, is a distillation of the views of 180 corporate members obtained in consultative workshops held in eight major U.S. cities in 1974 and 1975. It provided policy makers with a clear statement of the issues and a concise set of suggestions for implementing a freer system of interchange.[50] After preparing position papers, Council members met for prolonged discussions with their counterparts in the executive branch in groups of about twenty. With these and similar efforts, the goal is to encourage government officials to take the Council's views into account when formulating policy. In many cases that require highly specialized knowledge, these are the only nongovernmental views available to decision makers.

In terms of lobbying expertise, the Council has mastered the art of befriending key government personnel. COA regularly honors a high-ranking administration official at its annual meeting. In the 1970s, these included Charles Meyer, assistant secretary of state for inter-American affairs, Kenneth Rush, deputy secretary of state, Daniel P. Moynihan, ambassador to the United Nations, and Anthony P. Solomon, under secretary of the treasury for monetary affairs. William D. Rogers was feted twice, in 1974 as assistant secretary of state and in 1976 as undersecretary of state for economic affairs. On the latter occasion, he was introduced to two hundred Council members by David Rockefeller and presented a plaque thanking him for his contribution to U.S.-Latin American understanding.

The Council also seeks to befriend officials at the lower levels of government, inviting newly appointed ambassadors to visit COA headquarters for briefings by staff members, visiting staff members of

[50] U.S. Congress, Senate, Committee on Foreign Relations, Subcommittee on Western Hemisphere Affairs, *U.S. Relations with Latin America*, 94th Cong., 1st Sess., February 1975, pp. 215-223.

congressional committees to offer help in arranging visits to Latin America and interviews with corporate executives, and seeking out little-known officials overlooked by other interest groups. In the 1970s, Representative Gillis W. Long, chairperson of the Subcommittee on Inter-American Economic Relations of Congress's Joint Economic Committee rarely saw any lobbyists regarding Latin America, but in 1976 the entire executive committee of the Council sat down with him for an exchange of views on hemispheric relations and for a discussion of his committee's upcoming hearings on Latin America. There is no other lobbying group in Washington that communicates so frequently with so many government officials as the Council of the Americas.

The third reason for the strength of the Council is its extremely careful choice of issues. COA weighs with some precision the relative costs and benefits of every position it takes. As expected, the Council stands squarely for lower tariffs on goods produced in Latin America, for increased authority for OPIC, for increased concessional aid to Latin America, and against restrictions on foreign investment by either the United States or Latin American nations. Somewhat unexpectedly, it urged that greater flexibility be added to both the Hickenlooper and González amendments.[51] The Council was one of the leading proponents of a renegotiated Panama Canal treaty. Once the new treaties had been signed by President Carter, the Council worked more actively than any other interest group to assure their ratification by the Senate. The COA staff not only did its best to de-fuse potential opposition to the treaties by some Council members, it brought its most influential corporate members to Washington to lobby on behalf of the treaties. Perhaps the Council's major triumph, however, has not been in achieving specific policy ends but in encouraging within the government an ideological bias in favor of a government policy supporting private investment in Latin America.[52] It is probably correct that this predisposition has always existed among many policy

[51] Marie Thourson Jones, "The Council of the Americas and the Formation of American Foreign Policy," in the *Report* of the Commission on the Organization of the Government for the Conduct of Foreign Policy (Washington, D.C.: Government Printing Office, 1975), vol. 3, app. I, pp. 248-249. See also the Council's unpublished survey of members, 1970. Robert H. Swansbrough, *The Embattled Colossus: Economic Nationalism and United States Investors in Latin America* (Gainesville: University of Florida Press, 1976), pp. 195, 211; C. Fred Bergsten, Thomas Horst, and Theodore H. Moran, *American Multinationals and American Interests* (Washington, D.C.: Brookings Institution, 1978), p. 391.

[52] See Jones, "The Council of the Americas and the Formation of American Foreign Policy," p. 249.

70

makers; what is less clear is whether it would be as strong as it is without the persistent reinforcement of the Council.

In the 1970s, the Council refused to take a public position on the issue of human rights.[53] Earlier, in 1968, COA lobbied actively against a United States protest to Brazil over the promulgation of the extremely repressive Fifth Institutional Act.[54] Beginning about 1976, however, the staff decided that the Council's corporate members would object to lobbying against efforts to protect human rights. On the other hand, staff members never entertained the notion of lobbying on behalf of these efforts, for, as one COA briefing paper noted, the Carter human rights policy "had a detrimental effect on some U.S. business interests abroad."[55] Thus the Council found itself in the anomalous position of taking no open stand on a major issue of U.S. Latin American relations.

The Council nevertheless was deeply involved in attempting to influence United States policy toward repressive Latin American governments in the 1970s. Having decided against an anti-human rights stance, COA ignored the issue while pursuing an alternative approach: the legitimation of repressive governments. This was accomplished by providing representatives of governments such as those of Argentina, Brazil, and Chile with access to leading U.S. corporate executives and the U.S. media. On April 5, 1976, for example, Chilean Finance Minister Jorge Cauas, accompanied by the Chilean Minister of Planning and the President of the Central Bank, addressed over one hundred COA members in New York. On February 14, 1978, the Council arranged for Cauas, then ambassador to the United States, to participate on a panel during a COA conference for corporation executives on Latin America's business outlook. The panel, entitled "What Latin American Governments Want from Foreign Investors," was composed primarily of ambassadors from Latin America's most repressive regimes.[56] At the conclusion of the conference, Ambassador Cauas hosted a reception for participants.

The Council made similar efforts on behalf of the Argentine military government of General Jorge Videla. Less than two months after the March 1976 coup initiated one of the bloodiest periods of repression

[53] See, for example, the very ambivalent position taken by the Council's executive director in *Latin America*, p. 52, *supra* n. 45.

[54] See Jones, "The Council of the Americas and the Formation of American Foreign Policy," p. 249.

[55] Samuel L. Hayden, "Human Rights Briefing Paper," mimeographed (Washington, D.C.: Council of the Americas, 1978).

[56] In addition to Cauas, other panelists included the ambassadors of Uruguay, El Salvador, and Brazil.

71

in Latin American history, the Council arranged for the president of the U.S. Chamber of Commerce in Argentina and five prominent Argentine businessmen to brief representatives of thirty COA-member corporations on recent developments in Argentina. Shortly thereafter, on June 22, 1976, the Council sponsored the first major address on economic policy in the United States by the Argentine Minister of Economy, José Martínez de Hoz. It was attended by more than three hundred business leaders.

In addition, the Council of the Americas urged U.S. policy makers to sympathize with the leaders of Latin America's repressive governments, generally by emphasizing the dire economic conditions these governments inherited from their predecessors. In May 1977, for example, the Council's senior Latin American advisor, Esteban A. Ferrer, spoke out against officials' apparent unwillingness to recognize that "these countries are giving their most gallant effort to overcome 150 years of mismanagement."[57] The implication of statements such as these was that human rights violations, if not excusable, were at least understandable given the draconian economic measures required for responsible fiscal management.

The Association of American Chambers of Commerce in Latin America

Since its founding in 1967, the Association of American Chambers of Commerce in Latin America (AACCLA) has grown to become an organization of sixteen U.S. Chambers of Commerce in Latin America. Each AACCLA member functions like its United States counterpart as a private, nonprofit, voluntary association supported principally by local membership dues. AACCLA speaks not for Latin American business interests but for United States businesses with financial interests in Latin America. The Association therefore is properly considered a subsidiary of the United States Chamber of Commerce rather than an independent association. Since 1969, the U.S. Chamber of Commerce has provided AACCLA with its support staff and with offices in Washington.

AACCLA's principal objective is to encourage trade and investment between Latin America and the United States. Most of its activities focus upon creating a favorable climate for this intercourse by influencing United States foreign policy in areas affecting multinational corporations. In the 1970s, its specific interests included increases in the authorization and appropriation for OPIC and the Export-Import Bank, changes in the 1974 Trade Act to extend trade preferences to

[57] *Journal of Commerce*, May 27, 1977, p. 9.

Ecuador and Venezuela, revision of various laws to provide medicare benefits, social security, and an increase in tax exclusions for citizens residing abroad, and a number of rather minor alterations in customs laws and tariff schedules. To achieve these ends, the Association employed an executive secretary who functioned both as a facilitator for members wishing to present their views to U.S. officials and as a lobbyist for the Association.

When political repression became the central issue of United States policy toward Latin America in the late 1970s, AACCLA adopted a business-as-usual approach to human rights protection. Typical of this approach was its policy on multilateral development bank loans adopted at the Association's 1977 meeting in Costa Rica. After deciding that they could not avoid taking a position on what many members considered a partisan political issue, the Association declared that "AACCLA shares U.S. governmental interest in fostering respect for human rights. However, in pursuit of this objective AACCLA does not support any action that affects normal lending practices and policies of international financial institutions. AACCLA strongly believes that the activities of these institutions should be carried out solely on the basis of sound economic considerations."[58]

The implementation of this and other policies on related human rights issues led AACCLA to work actively against the incorporation of human rights considerations into United States foreign policy. In 1977, for example, the Association lobbied both the executive branch and Congress against proposed aid reductions for Argentina, El Salvador, and Uruguay. Although some of this activity responded to pressures from the Association's members, in general AACCLA preferred to solicit the aid of its members rather than to respond to their demands. Its favored strategy was to bring members to Washington for private talks with executive branch officials. On the occasions when it attempted to influence Congress, AACCLA used fairly rudimentary techniques, such as sending form letters to entire committees. In 1977, it mailed each member of the House Banking Committee a general plea that they not "impose punitive human rights constraints on the [Export-Import] Bank's ability to fulfill its basic functions" by adding a human rights amendment to pending Eximbank legislation (H.R. 6415).

In addition to AACCLA and the Council of the Americas, during the 1970s a variety of industry associations occasionally attempted

---

[58] For a detailed statement of AACCLA's human rights policy, see *Latin America*, pp. 53-59, *supra* n. 45.

to influence United States policy toward human rights in Latin America. One of the largest of these was the American League for Exports and Security Assistance (ALESA), an aerospace industry lobby that concentrated upon obtaining government support for the exports of about forty major aerospace firms and a few aerospace-related labor unions. Under the leadership of Joseph E. Karth, a nine-term member of Congress, ALESA particularly encouraged government credit subsidies for the export of military hardware, an emphasis that regularly conflicted with the Carter administration's human rights policy. Since cuts in military aid and rejections of arms export license requests were used frequently to implement U.S. human rights policy, Karth and ALESA worked to halt the policy.[59] ALESA and the other industry associations were relatively minor actors on the human rights issue, however, especially when compared to the Council of the Americas.

HUMAN RIGHTS ORGANIZATIONS

Until the early 1970s, the attempts by business lobbyists and Latin American governments to influence United States policy toward Latin America went uncontested. With the exception of an occasional confrontation between rival business interests or the U.S. labor movement over issues such as tariffs, runaway shops, and commodity price supports, the field was clear of significant competition.

This was particularly true of the human rights issue. Surveying three decades of human rights activity, Louis Henkin commented sadly in 1974 that "increasingly, the constituency in the United States supporting the international human rights effort has seriously weakened."[60] At the time, most efforts to promote a stronger role for human rights in United States foreign policy were produced not by interest groups but by a handful of members of Congress, particularly Donald Fraser and Edward Kennedy, and they were effectively neutralized by the Nixon-Kissinger foreign policy bureaucracy. A number of nongovernmental organizations (NGOs) were actively working to decrease support for repressive dictatorships in the Third World, but Vietnam remained the central issue and none of the NGOs had placed major

[59] See U.S. Congress, House, Committee on Foreign Affairs, Subcommittee on International Organizations, *Human Rights and U.S. Foreign Policy*, 96th Cong., 1st Sess., 1979, pp. 441-454; *Arms Trade in the Western Hemisphere*, pp. 43-64, 261-277, *supra* n. 22. Before 1979, ALESA was called the American League for International Security Assistance (ALISA).

[60] Louis Henkin, "The United States and the Crisis in Human Rights," *Virginia Journal of International Law* 14 (Summer 1974): 665.

emphasis upon the still-obscure question of human rights in Latin America. The full dimensions of the Nixon administration's involvement in the events leading to the 1973 coup in Chile were as yet largely unpublicized, with the consequence that concern over the abuses of the Pinochet junta was more unfocused outrage than an organized attempt to alter United States policy. Henkin was correct.

By 1977, the combined interest groups concerned with the repression of human rights in Latin America had become one of the largest, most active, and most visible foreign policy lobbying forces in Washington. The reasons for this growth are probably many. Among those that seem particularly important are the end of American participation in the Vietnam war and not only the liberation of interest-group resources that had focused exclusively on that issue but the perception by many political activists that human rights was a logical extension of the civil rights movement. Whatever may have caused the explosion of lobbying interest in human rights, it is certain that by 1976 a new ingredient had been added to the traditional recipe by which United States policy toward Latin America is concocted.

At the end of the 1970s, there were about seventy to eighty voluntary groups in the United States with a major interest in human rights violations in the Third World. Approximately fifteen concentrated upon Latin America. Many of these human rights NGOs were founded in the 1970s, and it is therefore difficult to write about them with confidence, particularly in those cases where a group remains the organizational vehicle of one or two dominant individuals. At the beginning of the 1980s, an atmosphere of impatience and impermanence surrounded many of the Washington human rights interest groups. Therefore what follows here is simply a description of interest group activity on behalf of human rights during the 1970s and an outline of the most dynamic members of the Washington-based Latin American lobby at the beginning of the 1980s. The former topic may be addressed with some confidence; the latter should be recognized as tentative.

The Human Rights Working Group

As the Washington human rights lobby expanded rapidly during the mid-1970s, coordination of human and financial resources became a major problem. This difficulty was resolved in part by Jacqui Chagnon of Clergy and Laity Concerned (CALC). Using the skills of group coordination acquired over the course of more than a decade of civil rights and antiwar activity, she assumed a leadership role in forming a discussion group that in January 1976 became the Human Rights Working Group (HRWG) of the Coalition for a New Foreign and

Military Policy. Chagnon was soon joined by Bruce Cameron of the Americans for Democratic Action as the Working Group's cochairperson. They, along with Coalition codirector Brewster Rhoads, an antiwar activist who previously directed the Coalition to Stop Funding the War, formed the original leadership of the Human Rights Working Group.[61]

During the important human rights years of the middle and late 1970s, the HRWG united a broad range of religious, peace, human rights, research, professional, and social action organizations. At one point, the Working Group had seventy organizational participants, about a third of which were actively involved in all HRWG activities. About half of the participants were unable to join the parent Coalition for a New Foreign and Military Policy, whose antiwar origins and liberal-left orientation were suspect by some organizations' constituents. But by 1977, human rights had entered the mainstream of American politics; as a result, virtually every Washington-based NGO concerned with promoting humane values in United States foreign policy had become a member of the Group.

The HRWG met monthly throughout the middle and late 1970s to receive reports from its steering committee and its subcommittees and to make decisions on future actions. Working Group decisions were passed to the Action Committee of the parent Coalition, which determined how to utilize its national network and office personnel. Once it decided to focus on a particular aspect of an issue—almost invariably upon securing passage (or defeat) of a piece of legislation— the Coalition contacted its network of members, provided them with educational material on an issue, and urged them to contact their members of Congress.

Although much of the Coalition staff's energy was directed toward encouraging grassroots activity by its membership, the HRWG itself performed an entirely different task: coordination of the human rights community in Washington. The HRWG provided a forum for groups with differing ideological and tactical perspectives to air their disagreements and to determine the most efficient use of their resources. The existence of a forum where differences could be debated, some priorities selected, and activities coordinated was a successful innovation of the traditionally divided political left in the United States,

[61] Like the HRWG, the parent Coalition was established in early 1976 through a merger of the Coalition to Stop Funding the War and the Coalition on National Priorities and Military Policy. At the end of the 1970s, half a dozen staff members and several interns were operating the Coalition on an annual budget in excess of $100,000.

and it probably contributed to the successful lobbying of human rights interest groups.

Washington Office on Latin America

Of the many Human Rights Working Group members with a specific interest in human rights in Latin America, two—the Washington Office on Latin America (WOLA) and the Council on Hemispheric Affairs (COHA)—merit special attention. WOLA's development was a natural outcome of the work of the Latin American Strategy Committee (LASC), an ad hoc group of church-related activists who met in the late 1960s to explore the relationship between United States foreign policy and political repression in Latin America. LASC's founders include some of the most prominent Latin America-oriented human rights activists in the United States—Thomas Quigley, Morton Rosenthal, Brady Tyson, Philip Wheaton, and William Wipfler. Much of their prominence can be traced to LASC's attacks upon the Brazilian military dictatorship, upon the alleged subversion of the free labor movement in the Dominican Republic by the American Institute for Free Labor Development, and upon the police training programs of AID's Office of Public Safety. Although LASC became inactive in the mid-1970s, for a few years after its founding it was the only Washington-based organization concerned exclusively with human rights in Latin America.

The idea of founding a new Washington center for information and political action on United States policy toward Latin America developed slowly out of conversations among Joseph Eldridge, a young Methodist minister who had been removed from his duties in Chile following the 1973 coup, William Brown, a retired New York businessman concerned with human rights violations in Central America, and LASC representatives. WOLA opened its offices in the Methodist Building on Capitol Hill in early 1974, with Brown working for free, Eldridge supported by the Methodist church, and with church groups contributing a few hundred dollars for office supplies and postage. By 1978, WOLA had ended its always-informal ties to LASC, and William Brown had returned to New York. But the Office had increased its staff to seven moderately liberal Latin Americanists plus a few interns and occasional volunteers with special interests in particular issues. At the end of the 1970s, WOLA was supported primarily by about twenty-five religious groups, among which the Maryknoll Fathers and Brothers stand out as particularly enthusiastic benefactors.

WOLA engages in several types of activities. First, it acts as an informal link between Latin American citizens and the Washington foreign policy bureaucracy. Typical of this linkage was a mid-1978

77

visit to the United States by the Paraguayan opposition leader Domingo Laino. WOLA arranged for him to meet with a broad variety of government officials in both Congress and the executive branch to describe human rights conditions in Paraguay.[62] Second, WOLA monitors United States policy toward Latin America, giving testimony before congressional committees and publishing analyses of government activities affecting Latin America along with summaries and commentaries on events in Latin America. In addition to its extremely informative bimonthly *Latin America Update*—by far the most reliable source of information on humanitarian issues in Latin America—WOLA publishes occasional reports on particular issues, such as a special 1977 analysis of the Panama Canal treaties. The staff also provides the media with more general services regarding Latin America: current information, background studies, and analyses of news events. Third, it collaborates with other nongovernmental organizations with interests in human rights but limited expertise in Latin America. WOLA shares its resources, collaborates on joint research and education projects, and contributes heavily to the efforts of the Human Rights Working Group. Of the thirteen 1978 State Department human rights reports for which the HRWG issued counter-reports, for example, four were produced by WOLA.

WOLA is Washington's most respected Latin America-oriented human rights interest group. Within the State Department's Bureau of Human Rights and Humanitarian Affairs, WOLA is known for having factual information and, unlike many human rights NGOs, for understanding the positions of its allies within the executive branch. Congressional aides tend to view WOLA as a knowledgeable, dedicated lobby, always prodding but rarely offensive. Despite its slight leftward tilt, WOLA has become the organization that government officials can contact for a correct answer or an informed opinion on a question regarding United States policy toward Latin America. Of the NGOs concerned specifically with hemispheric relations, in the late 1970s only the Council of the Americas and WOLA could claim that distinction. Unlike the Council of the Americas, which obtained its position of eminence largely by standing in the shadow of its powerful corporate constituents, WOLA gained its influence among

[62] Immediately upon his return to Paraguay, Laino was kidnapped on the streets of Asunción. Working through Congress, WOLA launched a major effort to secure his release. "There have been calls from all over the Hill," reported one harassed State Department official. "There is a tremendous amount of pressure and outrage." *Washington Post*, July 8, 1978, p. A9.

policy makers by providing the most reliable data available in the United States on repression of human rights in Latin America.[63]

The Council on Hemispheric Affairs

The second major interest group with a specific interest in human rights and Latin America is the Council on Hemispheric Affairs (COHA), another relatively new organization founded in New York in 1975. Like WOLA, COHA represents the liberal-left persuasion in foreign policy analysis. Unlike WOLA, during the 1970s COHA invested little of its resources in lobbying Congress or mobilizing and assisting other members of the Washington human rights community. While COHA did not ignore Capitol Hill, it preferred to use the mass media to exert pressure on executive branch personnel. From its inception, COHA was recognized for its ability to see that its views reach the readers of major newspapers in both the United States and Latin America. COHA's director, Laurence R. Birns, once remarked that "reality exists in the media. To talk about human rights without a background radiation is a hopeless task."[64] COHA's central strategy was to use the Carter administration's verbal commitment to human rights to pressure individual members of the foreign policy bureaucracy to become more active in promoting these rights. The implicit threat was that if a targeted official failed to respond as requested, she or he would be featured in newspaper articles as an unresponsive bureaucrat.

In addition to human rights issues, COHA concentrated upon improving the quality of diplomatic personnel assigned to manage United States relations with Latin America, particularly by attempting to influence presidential appointments. In 1977, it gained brief attention for its opposition to Terence Todman's nomination as assistant secretary of state for inter-American affairs. Todman had been selected over COHA's candidate for the position, United Auto Workers' official Esteban Torres.[65] In addition to challenging Todman's nomination, COHA actively opposed Senate confirmation of his predecessor, Harry W. Shlaudeman, because of his alleged complicity in the

[63] See, for example, the evaluation of a former staff member of the Senate Foreign Relations Committee in "Congress and U.S. Foreign Policy towards Latin America," p. 20, supra n. 47.

[64] Interview with Laurence Birns, January 27, 1978. Birns is particularly noted for his insightful discussions of the September 1973 coup in Chile. See his "The Death of Chile," New York Review of Books, November 1, 1973, pp. 32-34; and "Chile in The Wall Street Journal," The Nation 217 (December 3, 1973): 581-587.

[65] Although only COHA openly opposed his confirmation by the Senate, virtually all human rights activists were soon in agreement with COHA's evaluation that Todman was a poor choice to head ARA.

destabilization of the Allende government in Chile.[66] COHA also commented on many Carter ambassadorial appointments, sometimes negatively but more frequently with praise.

In the 1970s, COHA consisted of Birns, an occasional associate, and a few student interns, none of whom were committed to either cooperative action with other NGOs or to grassroots organizing of its own constituency.[67] They preferred instead to work directly with Washington political elites and especially with the mass media. By the time of my interviews in 1978, most foreign policy officials had learned that COHA lacked an active constituency, and many were annoyed by its strident approach to lobbying. In late 1977, the staff of the House Foreign Affairs Subcommittee on Inter-American Affairs declared Birns *persona non grata* in the subcommittee's offices, and at least one member of COHA's prestigious board of directors resigned in protest over the breadth of COHA's attacks. When it was founded in 1975, COHA was known only by its board, which included Kalman Silvert, Donald Fraser, James Abourezk, and Leonard Woodcock. Their prestige made COHA a force that could not be ignored. Within a few years, COHA had become identified primarily as the organizational vehicle of its articulate but abrasive director. As a result, the organization appeared to have a limited influence upon policy makers.

Friends' Committee on National Legislation

In addition to the Washington Office on Latin America and the Council on Hemispheric Affairs, which concentrate exclusively upon inter-American relations, during the 1970s, two broader-based interest groups stood at the forefront of efforts to increase the influence of human rights considerations in United States policy toward Latin America. The first of these was the Friends' Committee on National Legislation (FCNL), a lobby supported by about forty Quaker meetings and related Friends' organizations throughout the United States. Since its founding in 1943, FCNL has been among the most prominent

[66] U.S. Congress, Senate, Committee on Foreign Relations, *Shlaudeman Nomination*, 94th Cong., 2d Sess., May 25 and June 10-11, 1976, pp. 10-15.

[67] COHA attempted to attract the attention of the U.S. Hispanic community. In the 1970s, several chicano leaders were associated with the organization, including the president of the National Congress of Hispanic-American Citizens, who saw in COHA an institution that Hispanic Americans could use to demonstrate that they are no longer "content to be a passive and ignored factor when it comes to formulating and executing policy for the Latin American region." With the presidents of three major unions sitting on its board of trustees, COHA was also the only interest group of its type with ties to the U.S. labor movement. Council on Hemispheric Affairs, "For the Freedom of Thought and Person" (New York: Council on Hemispheric Affairs, 1977[?]), p. 2.

Washington interest groups promoting increased attention to such issues as domestic civil rights and humane foreign policy. In the latter category, FCNL has been active in promoting a reduction in military spending through congressional defeat of major funding for new weapons systems, the withdrawal of troops from foreign countries such as South Korea where U.S. security is not directly threatened, disarmament, and, especially, opposition to U.S. participation in the Vietnamese war. Representative Robert Kastenmeier once labeled FCNL as "the conscience of the anti-war movement in the country," a significant accolade given the large number of organizations that opposed that military adventure.[68] While a number of interest groups in Washington share similar political commitments, for many years FCNL has ranked with the Americans for Democratic Action as the most effective lobby of its type on Capitol Hill.

FCNL representatives labored in two ways to increase the importance of human rights in United States policy toward Latin America. First, they were actively involved in attempting to influence legislation on human rights issues. In fact, the Committee was probably the first major interest group to devote attention to the issue, and it has contributed its resources to virtually every major human rights battle since 1975. The original Harkin human rights amendment governing economic aid (PL94-161, Sec. 310) was written in FCNL offices, and it was FCNL's executive secretary, Edward Snyder, who found a sponsor (Harkin) for it in the House of Representatives. FCNL also helped write the 1976 and 1977 amendments that strengthened the human rights provisions of the military assistance program.[69] Second, FCNL assisted in organizing and coordinating the efforts of like-minded interest groups. As cochairperson of the Coalition for a New Foreign and Military Policy, Snyder filled the crucial role of a mediator, soothing ruffled feathers, arranging compromises, and finding common ground upon which groups with divergent ideologies and operational styles could stand together. One human rights lobbyist referred to Snyder as "the glue that holds together the whole [liberal] foreign policy community," an evaluation echoed by many members of the Washington human rights lobby.

[68] James L. Adams, *The Growing Church Lobby in Washington* (Grand Rapids, Mich.: Eerdmans, 1970), esp. pp. 209-285. James A. Nash, "Church Lobbying in the Federal Government: A Comparative Study of Four Church Agencies in Washington," Ph.D. dissertation, Boston University, 1967; E. Raymond Wilson, *Uphill for Peace* (Richmond, Ind.: Friends United Press, 1975).

[69] The specific legislation was Sec. 502B of the Foreign Assistance Act of 1961, amended in 1976 by Sec. 301 of PL94-329 and Sec. 112 of the Agricultural Trade Development and Assistance Act of 1954, added in 1977 by Sec. 203 of PL95-88.

Without intending to overemphasize the role of specific individuals, it is difficult to ignore the evidence that the expertise of Edward Snyder was a principal resource of the human rights lobby in the 1970s. An attorney who practiced law only briefly following graduation from Yale, Snyder joined FCNL in 1955 and assumed the position of executive secretary in 1962. By the time the human rights issue arose, he had been cultivating friendships on Capitol Hill for two decades, learning which battles could be won, which would be lost, and which should be fought anyway. When a major interest in human rights developed in Congress in the early 1970s, Snyder had more friends on Capitol Hill than all the other human rights lobbyists combined, and he knew which of them to approach with help, encouragement, and prodding. Later in the 1970s, Snyder turned his primary attention to a reduction in U.S. military spending, and other relatively young antiwar and civil rights activists became the key lobbyists for human rights issues. For a few crucial years, however, his was the major voice of the Washington human rights lobby.

Americans for Democratic Action

The second general interest group with a specific commitment to increasing the human rights component of United States foreign policy during the 1970s was the Americans for Democratic Action (ADA), one of the oldest and best-known lobbies in Washington. Founded in 1947 to encourage liberal domestic and foreign policies, ADA has always maintained a special interest in promoting humanitarian values in United States foreign policy. In the 1960s, it was among the first political groups of national prominence to take a firm stand against participation in the Vietnam war, and for the ensuing decade was a major participant—more often an organizer—of nearly every antiwar activity. In domestic politics, ADA participated actively in the civil rights movement; indeed, its representatives were responsible for placing the first civil rights plank in the Democratic party platform in 1948. Thus when United States support for repressive Latin American regimes became a major foreign policy issue in the mid-1970s, it was probably inevitable that ADA would become involved.

Encouraging this participation was Bruce Cameron, one of ADA's registered lobbyists and a person of unusually acute political instincts. Until 1975, Cameron had been a leader of the Ann Arbor chapter of the Indochina Peace Campaign. With the war concluded, he decided that ADA's traditional interest in a humane foreign policy could be refocused upon United States aid to repressive governments, especially if it were to focus initially upon relations with the extraordinarily brutal Chilean junta. Meanwhile, in early 1976 the newly formed Human Rights Working Group lacked a specific focus for its considerable potential energy. It therefore needed no persuasion by Cameron to pursue a reduction in aid to Chile as its first major attempt to influence human rights policy. With data supplied by the Center for International Policy, Cameron was able to provide Representative Donald Fraser, the most influential liberal on the House Committee on International Relations and the president of ADA, with evidence of the disproportionate flow of aid to the Pinochet government. Fraser used these data to convince a group of liberal members of the committee, informally known as the Whalen Caucus, to reduce the Ford administration's aid program. The Caucus approved an amendment to the 1976 military assistance authorization bill that set a $25 million ceiling on economic aid to Chile.[70] When the full committee met to mark up the bill, the restriction was adopted without opposition, and soon thereafter the ADA-sponsored amendment became law (PL94-329, Sec. 406). Encouraged by this success, Cameron led the ADA into every subsequent human rights battle. In addition to his work as the cochairperson of the HRWG, Cameron became the primary lobbyist for all legislative activity on behalf of human rights.

Amnesty International

Amnesty International (AI) opened its Washington office in mid-1976, primarily to be near sources of information. As a matter of policy, AI did not lobby directly on behalf of human rights during the 1970s. As a matter of fact, however, from the beginning AI representatives have been active participants in the Washington human rights movement. AI's Washington staff members act as conduits, transferring data to London and New York headquarters, analyzing the local climate for implementing AI recommendations, exchanging information and supporting other NGOs, and assisting individuals to contact government officials on behalf of friends or relatives who are missing or imprisoned.

However important these activities may be, they are all peripheral to AI's principal focus upon research and publicity. AI first reported on a specific human rights abuse in Latin America in 1966, when it reported on prison conditions in Paraguay. Six years passed before AI again focused its attention on Latin America, publishing in September 1972 its *Report on Allegations of Torture in Brazil*, which caused the government of Brazil to prohibit any mention of AI in the nation's press. Later that year, Amnesty launched its Campaign for the Ab-

---

[70] In 1976, there was no economic assistance bill to which the restriction could have been attached. Since no similar rise had occurred in military aid to Chile, the Caucus decided to concentrate upon the enormous jump in economic assistance.

olition of Torture, in which several Latin American nations were to figure prominently. The December 1973 *Amnesty International Report on Torture* accused several Latin American regimes of systematically torturing their citizens in order to suppress dissent. In 1974, three major reports—two on torture in Chile, one on torture in Uruguay—provided heretofore unavailable evidence of the systematic abuses of these two governments. In February 1976, AI launched its first world-wide campaign against torture in a single country, Uruguay, by pub-lishing the names of tortured and torturers alike and by circulating an international petition calling for an independent investigation. Later that year, in November, an Amnesty mission visited Argentina to investigate abuses of human rights by the Videla government. The mission's remarkable report on Argentina, published in March 1977, stands to date as the masterpiece of its genre, possibly the most com-prehensive public evidence ever assembled by a NGO on human rights violations by any Latin American government. Included in ninety-two pages is an eighteen-page list of "disappeared" persons, their date of abduction, and other pertinent details.

It is difficult to overestimate the influence of the AI reports on U.S. human rights policy during the 1970s. With a Nobel Peace Prize added to its credits and a reputation for impartial documentation of human rights abuses around the globe, AI helped to create a receptive attitude among members of Congress to general human rights legislation and to country-specific reductions in foreign assistance. In particular, AI publicity contributed significantly to a change in the nature of the debate over United States policy toward Argentina, Chile, and es-pecially Uruguay. Prior to the AI report on obscure Uruguay, the debate in the United States focused upon whether Uruguay deserved to be singled out as a gross violator; after the report, it centered on what the response should be to the accepted fact that the Uruguayan government was among the most repressive on earth. No one can estimate exactly how significant this contribution was, of course. Per-haps Representative Koch would have been able to eliminate aid to Uruguay even if AI had not launched its worldwide campaign against that nation's torturers shortly before he made his successful attempt; perhaps not. What is certain is that Koch had taken no interest in Uruguay until AI asked that he submit its report on torture in Uruguay for publication in the *Congressional Record*. Perhaps WOLA would have been able to convince key members of the Senate Appropriations Subcommittee on Foreign Operations to halt aid to Uruguay without the data provided by AI; perhaps not. What is certain is that in this case and others Amnesty International was able to provide policy makers and other interest groups with reliable research backed by an unsurpassed reputation for integrity.[71] In the 1970s, the debate over U.S. policy toward repressive governments was sometimes won or lost on the empirical question of the severity of human rights violations. This was the question AI could answer with authority.

The International Commission of Jurists

As with Amnesty International, the provision of information on human rights abuses was the International Commission of Jurists' (ICJ) principal contribution to United States foreign policy in the 1970s. The Commission devoted a considerable amount of attention to Argentina, Chile, and Uruguay. Two ICJ reports on Chile were among the first to document precisely the brutality of the Pinochet government. One was published in September 1974, providing not only such specific examples of illegal decisions by military tribunals as executions under decrees applied retroactively but also details of torture methods. The second report, issued in October 1974, so infuriated the Chilean ambassador to the United States that he paid for the opportunity to brand the ICJ investigators as liars in half-page ads in the *Washington Post* (November 8) and the *New York Times* (November 17).

In February 1967, a scandal erupted when it was revealed that a number of private voluntary organizations had been funded indirectly by the Central Intelligence Agency. At the time, the press focused upon CIA infiltration of the National Student Association, but the ICJ was also accused of being a front for the CIA. Since that time, the work of the ICJ has been hampered by allegations of linkages to various governments and especially to the CIA. In 1967, ICJ secretary-general, Nobel laureate Sean McBride, issued a carefully worded statement to the effect that the ICJ had received money from an obscure organization known as the American Fund for Free Jurists, but that the money was provided without strings. There was no public accounting of the Fund's finances. Further charges of CIA involvement were leveled at the ICJ in mid-1975, when ex-CIA agent Philip Agee published his diary and placed the Commission on a long list of organizations allegedly directed by the CIA. In a press release, the ICJ secretary-general once more asserted that the Commission "is not controlled, financed or influenced by the CIA in any way, and has no connection whatsoever with the CIA." But no response was made

---

[71] Conservative writers occasionally complain that AI prefers to attack conservative dictatorships. See Stephen Miller, "Politics and Amnesty International," *Commentary* 65 (March 1978): 57-60; Raymond D. Gastil, *Freedom in the World: Political Rights and Civil Liberties 1978* (New York: Freedom House, 1978), pp. 28-30. For AI's response, see Andrew Blane, "The Individual in the Cell: A Rebuttal to 'Politics and Amnesty International'," *Matchbox*, Winter 1979, pp. 5-6, 19-20.

to Agee's specific claims of ICJ-CIA collaboration in Latin America, particularly in Ecuador where in 1961 the CIA allegedly arranged the schedule for a visit by the ICJ secretary-general when he was laying the groundwork for an Ecuadorian affiliate. Nor was there a rebuttal to the assertion that the affiliate's directorate was composed of CIA agents.[72] Agee's association with the CIA ended in 1969, and there have been no subsequent claims that the ICJ continues to receive Agency funds.

When it was founded in 1952, the ICJ would have been a prime target for CIA funding, since its original goal was to inquire into abuses of justice in Eastern Europe. During the 1970s, eighteen governments underwrote more than half of the ICJ budget by funding the Commission's national sections, which forwarded the money to the international secretariat in Geneva. The United States contribution, made openly under the Mutual Educational and Cultural Exchange (Fulbright-Hays) Act, amounted to less than $50,000 per year.

Church Groups

Any discussion of interest groups concerned with human rights in Latin America would be incomplete if it failed to mention the central role of an enormous variety of churches and church-related organizations. Of the thirty-six formal members of the Coalition for a New Foreign and Military Policy in 1978, for example, nearly half were church-related, and a majority of the remainder were at least partially funded by churches. Church activity on behalf of human rights was coordinated through other coalitions as well. Under the leadership of William Wipfler, the National Council of Churches took an early and aggressive interest in the issue of human rights in Latin America. In addition, both the Foreign Policy and Military Spending Task Force of the 120-member Washington Interreligious Staff Council (WISC) and the Interreligious Task Force on U.S. Food Policy gave considerable attention to the question of political repression in Latin America.[73] Individual denominations also participated in human rights lobbying efforts. The Church of the Brethren, the Jesuit Conference, the Mennonite Central Committee, the United Methodist Church, and the United Presbyterian Church all devoted significant attention to human rights problems in United States policy toward Latin America.

During the crucial period of human rights activism between 1975

[72] Philip Agee, *Inside the Company: CIA Diary* (Middlesex, Eng.: Penguin Books, 1975), p. 169.

[73] See, for example, the latter organization's position in *Congressional Record*, April 1, 1977, p. S5356, with an elaboration in *Foreign Assistance and Related Agencies Appropriations for 1978*, pt. 3, pp. 267-303, *supra* n. 33.

and 1978, one church-related interest group, Clergy and Laity Concerned (CALC), became an extremely important component of the Washington human rights lobby. It was founded in 1966 by a highly visible group of civil rights leaders, including Martin Luther King, Jr., to seek an end to the American intervention in Vietnam and to assist draft resisters. Following the termination of the war, CALC expanded its interests to include all aspects of foreign and domestic policy that might be supportive of political repression in the Third World. For example, CALC, along with the American Friends' Service Committee and the Federation of American Scientists, led the successful battle against funding for the B-1 bomber. Under the leadership of Jacqui Chagnon, CALC's Washington office was instrumental in coordinating the capital's growing human rights lobby and in focusing the lobby's attention upon the most serious human rights problems in the noncommunist world. As noted earlier, it was Chagnon who formed the HRWG, which she directed as cochairperson until her departure in early 1978. After that, CALC continued to participate actively in human rights lobbying efforts, particularly those involving pre-1979 Iran, the Philippines, South Africa, and South Korea, but it ceased to direct the human rights movement.

The Office of International Justice and Peace of the United States Catholic Conference (USCC) was a second important church-related component of the Washington human rights lobby during the 1970s. The work of the USCC advisor for Latin America, Thomas Quigley, was particularly important in translating Catholic social doctrine into action supporting a stronger human rights component in United States foreign policy. For nearly two decades, Quigley has steered the USCC into virtually every major battle of U.S.-Latin American relations, from early opposition to the Brazilian military government, to the formation of LASC, WOLA, and COHA, to the demise of AID's Office of Public Safety, to the human rights legislation governing aid to repressive governments.

Finally, during the 1970s several groups concerned with human rights in a particular country actively attempted to influence various aspects of foreign assistance programs. These organizations focusing upon individual Latin American nations tended to have short institutional lives; they often represented the work of a handful of highly motivated individuals who, short of funds but long on indignation, worked furiously throughout one or more sessions of Congress and then either joined broader-based human rights interest groups or simply decided to try no further. Prominent exceptions to this generalization were the various Chilean groups, particularly the Chile Committee for Human Rights led by Isabel Letelier. These committees invested

87

an enormous amount of energy in achieving a dissociation of the U.S. government from the Chilean military regime. Simply by remaining active, Letelier served as a constant reminder that the Chilean government challenged the integrity of the American legal order by assassinating both her husband and Ronnie Karpen Moffitt at Washington's Sheridan Square in September 1976.

These, then, were the most active Latin America-related human rights interest groups in Washington during the 1970s.[74] No mention has been made of the several functional organizations (the Inter-American Press Association, the Federation of American Scientists, PEN International) whose efforts to promote respect for human rights in Latin America were limited in scope to protecting institutions or individuals directly related to the organizations. Nor has there been a discussion of the many research-oriented centers (particularly the Center for International Policy and the Institute for Policy Studies) that not only provided the data for other interest groups but often engaged in more direct forms of lobbying. The *Human Rights Internet Reporter*, an extraordinarily valuable communications medium founded by political scientists Laurie Wiseberg and Harry Scoble, has also received scant mention. All of the major nongovernmental actors concerned with the issue of United States policy toward human rights in Latin America during the 1970s have been described, however, and it is now time to turn to an analysis of their attitudes, their strategies, and their impact upon policy.

ATTITUDES

One characteristic of nearly all representatives of interest groups concerned with United States policy toward human rights in the 1970s was a commitment to liberal pluralism. Within this broad ideological

[74] In the 1970s, other interest groups concerned with political repression in a single Latin American nation included the Argentine Commission for Human Rights (Washington) and the Argentine Information and Service Center (New York and Berkeley), the American Friends of Brazil (Berkeley) and the Liberation Brazil Committee (London), the National Chile Center (New York) and the Chile Legislative Center (Washington), the Friends of Haiti (New York), Paraguay Watch (Washington), and a large number of representatives of Latin American political parties living in exile in the United States. There were also a variety of country-specific human rights groups focusing on non-Latin American nations. Finally, a number of groups of anti-Castro Cuban exiles actively attempted to influence United States foreign policy, but only one of these (Of Human Rights) worked in Washington on the human rights issue. The *Human Rights Internet Reporter* is an invaluable source of information on the activities of virtually every interest group concerned with human rights.

category there were individuals representing most points on the traditional left-right political continuum. Most representatives of Latin
American governments classified themselves as Ronald Reagan or
Richard Nixon Republicans, particularly on foreign policy issues.
None considered the 1977/1978 Panama Canal treaty revision a
change for the better, all thought highly of Henry Kissinger's foreign
policy realism, and most believed that their adversaries (the human
rights activists) were out to destroy America's ability to lead what they
invariably called the Free World. It is more difficult to characterize
the ideological commitments of the representatives of business interests, although they were predominantly bunched near the center of
the United States political spectrum. Among the variety of human
rights activists, most identified themselves as radical reformists, but
few demonstrated any values not common to mainstream liberals. It
is true that many proposed radical solutions for the problems of Latin
America, but their approach to political issues in the United States
was decidedly reformist. A large number of these activists viewed the
problems of the Third World as caused, in part, by the United States—
by its economic demands for raw materials, markets, and cheap labor,
and by its political need to maintain hemispheric hegemony for the
sake of national security—but in virtually no case was there a belief
that radical transformation of the Third World required a prior transformation of the United States. What the United States must do,
they suggested, is reform its foreign policy. Most of these activists
described themselves as liberal Democrats and were therefore radical
in the sense that Senator Edward Kennedy would be radical. They
were not the radical Marxists their adversaries believed them to be.

On the core values of liberalism—what Louis Hartz has identified
as the liberal tradition in the United States—the differences among
interest group representatives were minor. Because of this value consensus, nearly all interest group lobbyists agreed on the rules of the
political game. There was a near-perfect consensus across the entire
range of interest groups that the existing rules were appropriate or, at
worst, in need of minor reform. Then and now these rules emphasize
the importance of unfettered pluralism, with every viewpoint entitled
to representation, and an overwhelming emphasis upon individualism
and therefore competition. No one believed that this basic pluralist
framework within which the United States reaches its political decisions should be altered in any significant way. Instead, the task of
each interest group is to improve its individual position of influence
within the inviolate framework. Politics was viewed as the last great
example of a free market, where the enterprising (and, if possible,
well-financed) interest group could sell its better foreign policy mouse-

89

trap to people in need of such a commodity. Viewed from this perspective, politics, like the market Adam Smith described, was seen as a neutral vehicle that every interest exploited to the extent that its leaders were capable of satisfying a need. As a consequence, the political debate was over who should operate the vehicle and in which direction it should be driven, never over whether it was sufficiently sound to be on the road.

A second notable characteristic of interest group lobbying on the issue of human rights in Latin America was the highly variable level of personal commitment. The leaders of human rights groups were enormously involved. It was striking to note the extent to which the U.S. citizens involved in the human rights issue were former civil rights activists, antiwar organizers, ex-Peace Corps volunteers, and liberal religious leaders. The Latin Americans within the human rights lobby were invariably former targets of repression themselves. They were people who bore physical and emotional bruises, who will always remember the day they, their spouses, or children were tortured or murdered in Santiago, Montevideo, Buenos Aires, or Washington. These were people who at times wept when they talked of their experiences. Their commitment appeared total.

Some of the representatives of Latin American governments displayed a level of dedication equal to that of the human rights activists. It would be churlish to suggest that this represented no more than a desire to remain employed, although in some cases such a suggestion would be fairly accurate. For $1.1 million per year, for example, the Argentine government purchased a considerable amount of intellectual talent but little commitment from Marstellar, Inc. But the truly dedicated members of these interest groups were primarily volunteers who viewed themselves as defending the Free World from communism. For example, Raymond Molina of the Nicaraguan lobby was a Cuban exile who trained in Nicaragua prior to participation in the Bay of Pigs invasion. Marvin Liebman of the Chile lobby devoted most of his professional life to anticommunist crusades, including work as the secretary of the Committee of One Million Against the Admission of Communist China to the United Nations.[75] Several members of the Nicaraguan lobby, in particular, were absolutely convinced that Western Civilization depended upon continued support for the Somoza government, if for no other reason than such support served as an indication of America's determination to deter communism. These

[75] See *Activities of Nondiplomatic Representatives of Foreign Principals in the United States*, pt. 7, p. 700, *supra* n. 4.

lobbyists labored with exemplary vigor to convince others that their analysis was correct.

The lowest level of personal involvement in the question of United States policy toward human rights in Latin America was displayed by the leaders of business interest groups; they had almost no commitment whatsoever to the issue. The principal reason for this disinterest seemed to be a desire not to be identified as an opponent of an issue with such a strong emotional appeal as human rights. Human rights legislation, for example, was perceived by nearly all corporate lobbyists as contrary to the interests they were employed to protect, and quite understandably their inclination was to work against its passage. But one lobbyist for an energy conglomerate characterized the general attitude of business groups when he explained why he declined to fight against the 1978 human rights amendment to the OPIC authorization, despite the fact that it would almost certainly expose his firm to an otherwise insurable risk in a major Chilean investment: "Politically, we're not going to win because of the issue. It would kill our effectiveness on the Hill if [our firm] became known as an 'anti-human rights lobby.' Even if we won on OPIC, and we could, in the long run it would hurt us." For this reason, business lobbyists generally decided to ignore the issue. Their commitment was to being inconspicuous.

This observation introduces a third notable feature of the interest groups concerned with United States policy toward Latin America: the variable nature of their appeals. No one acted publicly in opposition to a policy of promoting human rights, for by late 1976 the mobilization of opinion in Washington was so in favor of increasing the influence of human rights that it would have been futile to make a contradictory appeal. Yet it was evident that some employees of Latin American governments opposed granting human rights to their employers' political opponents. These representatives believed that political repression was legitimate when it served to deny opposition leaders—invariably referred to as "Marxists" or "communists"—access to constitutionally prescribed channels of political participation. This, of course, was a significant departure from a basically liberal perspective on political activity.

The dilemma of wanting to advocate the curtailment of human rights but knowing that such a position would be indefensible was resolved by the single tactic that has ingratiated innumerable repressive governments with United States policy makers since World War II: red-baiting. If it is true that one cannot openly espouse political repression, it is equally correct that, historically, the best way to attract sympathetic attention from the United States government is to become the target of a credible communist conspiracy. A few years ago, many analysts believed that the Red Scare technique had lost its effectiveness.[76] But events outside Latin America, particularly U.S. involvement in Zaire in 1978, indicated that even an administration oriented toward human rights would support an uncommonly repressive government if it could be demonstrated that a change in government might involve a victory for communism.

Other values in addition to anticommunism were used to direct the attention of policy makers away from human rights. One of these was an appeal that officials not "politicize" an economic issue such as development assistance or OPIC insurance. This argument appeared to have a limited impact, however, for by the late 1970s most policy makers appeared to understand that the global distribution of resources is, inevitably, a political question. Another appeal emphasized many citizens' stereotyped understanding of Latin American society, explaining political repression as a product of an inherently inferior political culture. As one business lobbyist noted, "I know there are human rights problems. I think there are very few people who will assert that there aren't problems. It's a question, though, of trying to understand the circumstances that surround a country's trials and tribulations. Democracy as we know it is just not in the vocabulary of Latin Americans. You can't have true safeguarding of civil liberties unless you've got a democracy. It just doesn't exist in Latin America, and it never existed." Statements such as this had as their goal the elimination of human rights as a concern of United States policy. If Latin America is preordained to suffer repressive governments, why then should the United States adopt a policy of encouraging the impossible?

The representatives of human rights groups naturally adopted a distinct appeal in their effort to influence policy; they stressed the humanitarian aspect of the issue. In the past, efforts of lobbies emphasizing altruistic values have been deprecated because their strategies rely heavily upon vague appeals for justice.[77] In general, foreign policy

[76] On May 22, 1977, President Carter noted that his administration would not permit the fear of communism to dictate U.S. foreign policy: "We are now free of that inordinate fear of communism which once led us to embrace any dictator who joined us in our fear. . . . For too many years we've been willing to adopt the flawed and erroneous principles and tactics of our adversaries, sometimes abandoning our own values for theirs." *Weekly Compilation of Presidential Documents* 13 (May 30, 1977): 744.

[77] Abraham F. Lowenthal and Gregory F. Treverton, "The Making of U.S. Policies toward Latin America," mimeographed (Washington, D.C.: Woodrow Wilson Center of the Smithsonian Institution, January 10, 1978), p. 18; Harry Weiner, "U.S.-Brazil Relations: Non-Governmental Organizations and the Fifth Institutional Act," in the *Report* of the Commission on the Organization of the Government for the Conduct

officials clearly are less receptive to pleas based upon humanitarian values than to those such as anticommunism that relate directly to national security concerns. But over the course of the 1970s, groups making appeals for humanitarian causes noticed a greater willingness among foreign policy officials to listen and even to solicit their proposals. They discovered that many of these officials were speaking favorably of the need for greater justice in United States policy toward Latin America. After describing his 1977 effort to enlist the support of a State Department desk officer in seeking the release of a political prisoner, one human rights lobbyist summed up the new outlook of foreign service personnel: "This would never have happened five years ago. The same people we deal with now would not have helped us then. They know . . . that we are able to vault above them anytime we want, able to make it unpleasant for them not to cooperate. Thus, on the basis of duress, they have opened up to us. Now we have very nice professional relationships with these people."

This evaluation is not intended to contradict the earlier experience of a representative of the National Council cf Churches, who in 1969 found that his efforts to increase the importance of human rights in American foreign policy fell on deaf ears: "The desk officers thought of me as a pain in the butt that they had to tolerate in the interests of maintaining good public relations."[78] While United States policy changed during the 1970s, it remained very difficult for foreign policy officials to respond to requests for a general emphasis on humanitarian issues. Given a vague plea for a more humane foreign policy, the response in the late 1970s would have been much the same as it was a decade earlier. But the pleas of human rights activists also changed. They became less general; they demanded specific actions—the release of a specific prisoner, the elimination of a specific aid program, the opposition to a specific multilateral development bank loan proposal. Once human rights activists learned that appeals for justice became significant only when attached to concrete proposals, they changed the nature of their appeals.

STRATEGIES

The dominant feature of most interest groups' strategies to influence United States policy toward Latin America has been their reliance upon Congress, an observation that substantiates V. O. Key's earlier

of Foreign Policy, vol. 3, app. i (Washington, D.C.: Government Printing Office, June 1975), p. 250.

[78] Weiner, "U.S.-Brazil Relations," p. 254.

assertion.[79] Adler and Bobrow once calculated that interest groups concerned with foreign policy devote more time to Congress than to the executive branch by a ratio of about four to one.[80] This is an accurate assessment of the emphasis of Latin American governments and of human rights interest groups throughout the 1970s. On the question of foreign aid allocations, for example, one human rights lobbyist asserted that "the real question comes with Congress—who's going to do the best job lobbying with Congress to get the aid bill through or to get it cut—that's where the fight comes." Few human rights lobbyists attempted to influence the budget process in the executive branch.

The four-to-one ratio clearly overestimates the amount of time that business lobbyists devoted to Congress during the 1970s. After years of carefully cultivating close contacts with the White House staff and State Department officials, the Council of the Americas worked effectively through the executive branch, exerting little energy in lobbying Congress. When asked why no member of Congress had been invited to speak at the Council's annual banquet, one COA representative responded that they preferred to concentrate upon key decision makers. With the exception of the representatives of the Council of the Americas and a few individual corporations, however, in the 1970s most lobbyists concerned with United States policy toward Latin America concentrated upon Congress.

There is a logic to this strategy, of course: groups concentrate upon Congress because its members are relatively open to influence. Foreign policy discussions within the executive branch tend to focus upon how best to create policy from guidelines that flow downward from higher administration officials rather than on how to accommodate domestic interest groups. As one desk officer told Cohen: "Our business is to figure out what the best policy is for the United States; it is *not* to let every group which has its own political interest in that policy have it."[81] As this view suggests, State Department officials

[79] V. O. Key, Jr., *Politics, Parties, and Pressure Groups*, 4th ed. (New York: Thomas Y. Crowell, 1958), p. 147. Other scholars have also noted that interest groups have an aversion to lobbying the executive branch: Bernard C. Cohen, *The Influence of Non-Governmental Groups on Foreign Policy-Making* (Boston: World Peace Foundation, 1959), p. 13; Stephen Krasner, "Business-Government Relations: The Case of the International Coffee Agreement," *International Organization* 27 (Autumn 1973): 511-512; Pastor, "U.S. Sugar Politics and Latin America: Asymmetries in Input and Impact," p. 230; Weiner, "U.S.-Brazil Relations," p. 254.

[80] Kenneth P. Adler and Davis Bobrow, "Interest and Influence in Foreign Affairs," *Public Opinion Quarterly* 20 (Spring 1956): 96.

[81] Bernard C. Cohen, *The Public's Impact on Foreign Policy* (Boston: Little, Brown, 1973), pp. 63, 157.

tend to view with jaundiced eyes any perspective outside the main-stream of current in-house policy. All Washington policy makers will receive the views of virtually anyone, for no one wants to risk need-lessly alienating citizens and their elected representatives in Congress. But from behind their huge desks these apparently attentive individuals in the State Department tend to see outsiders as acting in pursuit of narrow, self-serving interests and as uninformed about the complexity of any given issue.[82]

On the other side of Washington, however, members of Congress were faced with voting openly and continually on an ever-widening number of issues affecting U.S.-Latin American relations during the 1970s. Yet very few of the 535 members were regularly prepared to make informed choices. Not only were individual members personally unfamiliar with the issues but the congressional leadership typically refused to become involved on either side of minor questions such as aid to Nicaragua or human rights amendments to Eximbank legisla-tion. Only once in the 1970s—during ratification of the 1978 Panama Canal treaties—did the leadership actually lead on an issue related to inter-American affairs. Therefore on most issues affecting Latin America there was a large pool of uncommitted votes held by members who simply did not have the time or the inclination to care much about how they were cast. On an issue of relatively low salience to them and their leaders, and absolute indifference to most of their constituents, members could afford to permit lobbyists to influence their votes, especially if, as in the case of Nicaragua, the lobbying effort was mediated by other members of Congress.

And, of course, lobbyists are experts on obscure policy questions. They can help members of Congress. They are, as a young John Kennedy once noted, "necessarily masters of their subject and, in fact, they frequently . . . provide useful statistics and information not otherwise available."[83] Despite the increase in congressional staffs, members continue to rely upon lobbyists for briefs, memorandums, and legislative analyses. Once they have drafted proposed legislation, lobbyists then find witnesses to testify and even provide committee members with questions for hostile witnesses. Because nearly every conceivable Latin America-related interest group can find some mem-ber of Congress to accept these services, most lobbying on Latin American issues takes place on Capitol Hill.

In the late 1970s, therefore, a situation developed that was some-what akin to several adversaries reluctantly grasping the tail of a

---

[82] Weiner, "U.S.-Brazil Relations," pp. 155, 250.

[83] Congressional Quarterly, *The Washington Lobby*, 2d ed. (Washington, D.C.: Congressional Quarterly, 1974), p. 6.

generally docile but erratic tiger. Of the groups concerned with United States policy toward Latin America, the first to cling to Congress were those involved in the human rights movement—CALC, FCNL, and later WOLA and ADA—groups that found the Nixon-Ford executive branch impenetrable. Left unchallenged, these human rights activists threatened to accentuate the beast's autonomous tendency to veer in directions not favored by repressive Latin American governments. Thus the representatives of these governments and (to a much lesser extent) the business lobby also grabbed hold. Just to protect an employer's interests, lobbyists for Latin American governments were forced to concentrate their activities on Capitol Hill. This required enormous energy, for during the years 1975 to 1979 human rights activists were intent upon attaching general or country-specific amendments to a broad variety of legislation, all of which could damage the interests of repressive Latin American governments. When rivals court Congress on an issue of United States-Latin American relations, only the uninformed remain inactive.

But by 1978, there was considerable evidence that Congress had done about as much as it could or would to promote a larger role for human rights in United States policy toward Latin America, and, in addition, that the executive branch was somewhat more accessible to human rights activists than it had been for at least a decade. The point had been reached where the human rights lobby was not only obtaining a fairly low return on its investment in Congress but also failing to exploit the emerging opportunities in the Carter administration. "Sure, it's nice to be respectable on the Hill," lamented one key lobbyist, "but now we get calls for information from legislative aides which we can't turn down, even if it means changing the whole office's plans for the day. They want reliable information, always immediately, and always hand-carried." As the decade ended, the human rights lobby continued to spend four out of every five lobbying hours concentrating upon (and doing the staff work for) Congress.

One of the reasons why the human rights lobby was reluctant to disengage was that it could not afford to leave Capitol Hill to the representatives of repressive Latin American governments. Conversely, these representatives had no alternative but to concentrate upon Congress. Until 1977, there was little need for the lobbyists of Latin American governments to attempt to influence the executive branch, for, as the following chapters will demonstrate, the Nixon-Ford administration maintained extremely cordial relations with the hemisphere's most repressive regimes. With the inauguration of the Carter administration's human rights policy, however, lobbyists for repressive governments soon found that their executive branch allies were being replaced by less friendly faces whose aggressive support for human rights was often quite threatening. And, after the first year of the new administration, the allies who remained at work in the executive branch became less prominent in their support for repressive regimes. The representatives of Latin American governments were forced to do what human rights activists had done during the Nixon-Ford years—turn to friendly faces in Congress for support.

IMPACT

If by "impact" is meant action that serves to alter the preferred behavior of foreign policy officials, then it must be admitted that it is impossible to measure with confidence the impact of interest groups upon foreign policy decisions.[84] Using the data at hand, it is possible to analyze the policy-making process in those cases where a particular decision resembled the preferred outcome of an interest group that actively lobbied on the issue. In most cases, the reader must then decide whether a similar decision would have emerged had the interest group not been involved.

Business Interest Groups

Obvious problems of data collection have always hampered research into the manner in which private economic interest groups attempt to influence foreign policy. On occasions when the activities of business lobbies have become public, they have suggested that these groups enjoy an unrivaled impact upon policy decisions affecting relations with Latin American governments. Unfortunately, it is difficult to determine whether these revelations are sensational because they permit an infrequent glimpse of the normal operations of economic interest groups or because they are infrequent, period. The case of ITT's attempt to encourage the Nixon administration's opposition to the Allende government is an excellent example, rarely equalled in the annals of interest-group influence over United States policy toward Latin America.[85] Most analysts now recognize that ITT's efforts served not to create but to reinforce the already strong anti-Allende dispo-

---

[84] Robert H. Trice, *Interest Groups and the Foreign Policy Process: U.S. Policy in the Middle East*, Sage Professional Papers on International Studies 02-047 (Beverly Hills, Calif.: Sage Publications, 1976), p. 72; Cohen, *The Public's Impact on Foreign Policy*, p. 28. A good general introduction to research on the subject of interest group impact on foreign policy is Barry B. Hughes, *The Domestic Context of American Foreign Policy* (San Francisco: W. H. Freeman, 1978), ch. 6.

[85] U.S. Congress, Senate, Committee on Foreign Relations, Subcommittee on Multinational Corporations, *The International Telephone and Telegraph Company and Chile, 1970-71*, 93d Cong., 1st Sess., June 21, 1973.

sition of the Nixon administration, but it is nonetheless impressive to note the extent to which ITT could command the attention of nearly any government official, including the President. While it may be tempting to assume that the fireworks accompanying the ITT-Chile scandal and similarly spectacular displays of corporate lobbying describe the typical *modus operandi* of business organizations seeking to influence the Latin American policy of the United States, there are few data upon which to base such an assumption. My belief is that the example is atypical.

It was previously noted that individual corporations rarely sought to influence decision making on issues concerning the repression of human rights during the 1970s. Thus it is inappropriate to study corporate lobbying on the issue of United States policy toward human rights violations in order to assess the impact of business upon decision makers. A more revealing approach is to examine attempts to influence policy on an issue of greater salience to corporations: uncompensated expropriations. In terms of legislation, the outstanding examples of this type of lobbying are two amendments to the Foreign Assistance Act of 1961, both of which were sponsored by the late Senator Bourke B. Hickenlooper.

The first was added to the Foreign Assistance Act in 1962. It required the President to suspend assistance to any country that expropriated property owned by any United States citizen or corporation unless the offending government took appropriate steps within six months to provide "equitable and speedy compensation for such property in convertible foreign exchange."[86] The amendment was sponsored by Senator Hickenlooper, but it was written by Monroe Leigh, an attorney whose Washington legal firm of Steptoe and Johnson had at the time a commission to protect United Fruit's Honduran property from a threatened nationalization.[87] Leigh is an example of the sizable corps of Washington attorneys who move in and out of government service. Between his association with two prestigious law firms (Covington and Burling, 1947-1951, and Steptoe and Johnson, 1959-1974 and 1977 to present), Leigh was a member of the U.S. mission to NATO (1951-1953), a Defense Department attorney (1953-1959),

[86] PL87-565, Sec. 301 (d) (3).

[87] Leigh modeled the Hickenlooper amendment after the Johnston-Bridges amendment to the Mutual Security Act of 1959. For an excellent discussion of the latter amendment, see Charles H. Lipson, "Corporate Preferences and Public Policies: Foreign Aid Sanctions and Investment Protection," *World Politics* 28 (April 1976): 400. According to Leigh, his task was made easier by the fact that many members of Congress were surprised that the Johnston-Bridges language was not included in the Kennedy administration's aid proposal, which became the Foreign Assistance Act of 1961. Interview with Monroe Leigh, Washington, D.C., June 6, 1978.

and the legal advisor of the Department of State (1975-1977). Monroe Leigh knows at least one of the principals involved in any major foreign policy decision. Since he regularly sails the ship of state himself, he is on familiar terms with most of the crew and virtually all of the important passengers.

The second Hickenlooper amendment, often and more correctly called the Sabbatino amendment, was added to the Foreign Assistance Act in 1964. Its purpose was to negate a ruling by the Supreme Court that upheld the act of state doctrine—that U.S. courts could not adjudicate disputes arising out of an act of a foreign state, specifically the Cuban government's nationalization of property owned by U.S. corporations. According to the second Hickenlooper amendment [PL88-633, Sec. 301(d)(4)], no court could invoke the act of state doctrine to avoid making a determination on the merits of a case arising out of the confiscation of property. The initial motivation for this amendment was the desire of a corporation (Texaco) to obtain compensation for expropriated property in Cuba, but other corporations were also involved. It was written by a group of corporate executives and their attorneys, specifically Monroe Leigh and Timothy Atkeson of Steptoe and Johnson, Cecil Olmstead of Texaco, Malcolm Wilkey of Kennecott Copper, and John Laylin of Covington and Burling. Leigh convinced the other participants that a separate bill would face more opposition than an amendment to the foreign aid authorization. The amendment was drafted and refined in the offices of Steptoe and Johnson and then presented to Senators Fulbright and Hickenlooper, senior members of the Committee on Foreign Relations, both of whom accepted it as written. Although Senator Hickenlooper has received primary credit for the amendment, neither he nor his staff wrote a word of it and, in fact, it was Senator Fulbright who ordered the committee staff to add it to the bill that eventually became the Foreign Assistance Act of 1964.[88]

Examples such as these suggest that effective lobbying depends in large measure upon personal contacts and that effective lobbyists are individuals who, like Monroe Leigh, have been in Washington for some time and who know which government officials to approach with their problems.[89] But more is required for effective lobbying than

[88] Interviews with Pat Holt, former chief of staff of the Senate Committee on Foreign Relations, Bethesda, Md., May 1, 1978, and with Monroe Leigh, Washington, D.C., June 6, 1978.

[89] Parenthetically, nearly all of these lobbyists are middle-aged, male, white, and clean-shaven. Fulfilling most of these requirements in the 1970s were several competent agents of Latin American governments and one major human rights activist (Edward Snyder), but by far the largest number worked for business interest groups.

a simple knowledge of the workings of official Washington and a set of well-placed contacts. The role of a lobbyist is best viewed as that of mobilizing decision makers to support actively a position that they already hold in common with the interest group. The task is not so much that of convincing decision makers of the wisdom of a given position—although much of that clearly occurs—as it is of alerting them to the existence of a mutually perceived problem and then encouraging them to act. In the nature of this task lies the strength of business interests in influencing United States policy toward Latin America.

Briefly stated, the principal reason why close working relationships are common between business lobbyists and foreign policy officials is that within the government it is relatively easy to find people who hold values similar to those of the business community. No small proportion of these officials are actually business executives themselves, on leaves of absence or between jobs with law firms or major corporations. This is certainly not to deny that foreign policy officials pursue additional values that are often of relative unimportance and sometimes harmful to economic interest groups, but that is not the point to be made in this context. Rather the crucial observation is that the values of corporate enterprise dominate American society, including that part of it which makes foreign policy.[90] Therefore business lobbyists are guaranteed at least a hearing for their opinions. Or as one Council of the Americas lobbyist responded to the question of why he had relatively easy access to members of Congress, "the Hill is much more receptive—let's face it—to the Establishment, because they are part of the Establishment themselves."

Given this reality, it is not surprising that one study of three cases of U.S. economic policy toward Latin America concluded that business groups were "able to shape policy in conformity with their interests." And as Stephen Krasner's study of the U.S. coffee industry clearly demonstrates, "with an unambiguous economic interest at stake . . . corporate action was decisive and effective" in using business-minded members of Congress to overcome the occasional resistance of the executive branch.[91] Given the dominant value system of contemporary society, it is to be expected that the positions of business lobbyists and foreign policy makers will often be congruent on issues directly affecting United States business interests in Latin America.

[90] Cohen, The Influence of Non-Governmental Groups on Foreign Policy-Making, p. 14.

[91] R. Harrison Wagner, United States Policy toward Latin America: A Study in Domestic and International Politics (Stanford: Stanford University Press, 1970), p. 123; Krasner, "Business-Government Relations," p. 515.

Unlike expropriations or tariffs, humanitarian issues such as human rights are not clearly and directly related to business concerns, and the impact of business lobbyists is consequently more difficult to discern. This uncertainty is best demonstrated by the ambivalent interpretation of the impact of the Council of the Americas upon United States policy toward human rights in Latin America. No one is able to gauge the value of having the Council sponsor economic presentations to the American corporate community by representatives of the hemisphere's most egregious violators of human rights. The 1977 COA *Annual Report* contains photos captioned "President Pinochet Ugarte of Chile chats with COA members at reception," "Argentine Ambassador Jorge Aja Espil, Treasury Secretary W. Michael Blumenthal and Argentine President Rafael Videla at Council luncheon," "Argentine President Videla in conversation with Rafael Miguel of Dow Chemical," and "Pepsico Chief Executive Officer Don Kendall and Ambassador Sevilla Sacassa [sic] of Nicaragua." It is simply not possible to determine how much desperately needed foreign exchange flowed into Argentina and thereby supported the Videla government following the Council's presentation of economy minister Martínez de Hoz to the New York financial fraternity. The efforts of the Council of the Americas to legitimize the repression of human rights by associating its enormous prestige and the prestige of its member corporations with the most abusive governments in the hemisphere are unmeasurable in their impact. But it is difficult to think of them as insignificant. All that can be said with certainty, however, is that by encouraging a business-as-usual approach to relations with repressive regimes, the Council did nothing to encourage the government to incorporate human rights considerations in its policy toward Latin America.

Viewed from another perspective, however, the Council indirectly and passively encouraged the incorporation of human rights considerations in United States foreign policy by not opposing the numerous human rights initiatives in the 1970s. COA could not have lobbied successfully against the general human rights sections added by Congress to foreign assistance legislation, nor could it have dissuaded the Carter administration from making human rights a hallmark of its foreign policy. But the Council could have tempered many specific human rights initiatives had it decided to mobilize an opposition movement using the political power of its constituent members. It probably could have dissuaded President Carter from authorizing the important symbolic aid reductions to Argentina and Uruguay in February 1977, and it probably could have reversed the administration's decisions not to support a number of multilateral development bank

101

loans to Argentina in 1977 to 1978. These were hotly contested policy decisions, and the Council's influence could have contributed to a different outcome. In the Congress, the active opposition of the Council probably would have led to the defeat of several country-specific aid reductions in 1975 to 1978. The silence of the Council of the Americas on the human rights issues of the 1970s was viewed by many policy makers as an indication that the business community was not opposed to the increased influence of human rights in United States policy toward Latin America. In a government that sometimes appears to operate in response to the law of anticipated reactions, the importance of this silence should not be overlooked.

Latin American Governments

No generalizations are possible regarding the impact of the representatives of repressive Latin American governments; each nation's lobby must be considered separately. The Argentine lobby was almost entirely a public relations campaign, and it therefore had no observable impact upon policy. The Chilean lobby was an inept effort. Despite the fact that the various groups that comprised it were spending an estimated $250,000 yearly to influence U.S. policy, in 1978 very few officials even knew that such a lobby existed. On the infrequent occasions when a policy maker could identify one of the lobby's components, that component was either the embassy newspaper advertisements, which were universally considered vulgar, or the American-Chilean Council. The Council was known only by its newsletter, which was thought to be a fund-raising vehicle to attract money from conservative citizens, not an effort to influence policy.

The impact of the Chilean government's Washington attorneys and its individual lobbyists—Gardiner, Danielopol, Ziffren—was undoubtedly minimal. Perhaps their primary service was to comfort the beleaguered Chilean authorities stationed in Washington. When a series of anti-Chile amendments was being added to U.S. foreign aid legislation, Danielopol wrote his employer: "I believe I have made considerable progress in the past six months in clearing the way for a counter-attack on the information front. Chile's enemies and critics continue to be vocal, but there is a growing appreciation in Washington and throughout the United States of the dangers and absurdities of leftist rule. . . . The struggle will not be easy, but it will be worthwhile. It is a pleasure to work with you, General, and I look forward to a long association."[92] Given the strength of the political forces allied against them, there probably was little that these indi-

---

[92] Letter from Dumitru G. Danielopol to General Enrique Morel, August 11, 1975.

viduals could accomplish. Miracles could not be expected of a handful of employees charged with overcoming the reputation of the Pinochet government.

Although miracles are not the stock-in-trade of Washington lobbyists, sophisticated tactics, plentiful supplies of money, and access to strategically placed friends can occasionally create them, as was demonstrated by the Nicaraguan lobby in the late 1970s. The crucial difference between the Nicaraguan and Chilean lobbies appears to have been the access the former enjoyed to key members of Congress. In particular, the case for Nicaragua was strengthened immeasurably once lobbyist Fred Korth convinced Charles Wilson to become Somoza's champion in the House. Although not a powerful member of that body, Wilson held a seat on the key appropriations subcommittee on foreign operations. In 1978, he used that position to hold the omnibus FY1979 foreign aid appropriations bill hostage until the Carter administration freed previously authorized funds for Nicaragua. There was never any evidence that Wilson could have made good on his threat to defeat the entire aid appropriation—it is one thing to have the power to restore a military aid request for a single country for a single year; it is quite another to convince Congress to scrap the entire foreign assistance program. Nevertheless, Wilson was able to obtain concessions from the Carter administration, perhaps because few of his colleagues in Congress cared enough about aid to Nicaragua to call his bluff once the administration had capitulated.

The Nicaraguan case suggests that a repressive Latin American government can temporarily avoid punitive measures from the United States by employing lobbyists who are able to enlist the support of strategically placed legislators. Should the situation arise where the opposition also enlists the support of strategically placed members, then the issue can become a significant battle. There exists no better example of this than the 1977 struggle over the Nicaraguan military aid appropriation, the details of which were just presented. In the end, Representative Koch and his anti-Somoza forces were out-voted in the House by Representatives Wilson and Murphy and their pro-Somoza allies. But Koch forced Wilson, Murphy, and ex-Representative Cramer to use all of their persuasive skills in order to win the vote.

This feat could not be repeated indefinitely. Thus in early 1978, the Nicaraguan lobby did not fight to restore the military aid authorization that the Carter administration reduced from its typical $3 to $4 million to $150,000. Instead, through Representative Wilson it attempted to force the release of embargoed pipeline aid, negotiating directly with the executive branch and ignoring Congress altogether.

Despite the resistance of several senior officials, the Carter administration yielded to this pressure. But even then the success of the Nicaraguan lobby was transient. By mid-1978, no amount of lobbying could mask the obvious fact that human rights conditions in Nicaragua were continuing to degenerate. After the September civil war, Nicaragua's plight became highly salient in the executive branch, and relations between the United States and the Somoza government deteriorated to their lowest point in history. After September, Somoza's few remaining supporters in the administration were convinced that dissociation from the regime was mandatory if the United States wished to establish friendly relations with any subsequent Nicaraguan government.[93] When 1979 began, Peace Corps volunteers were leaving, the embassy staff was being reduced by half, and economic aid was slowing to the barest trickle. The Nicaraguan lobby seemed absolutely powerless to halt these attacks by the executive branch. It won the battle in Congress but lost the war with the Carter administration.[94]

Human Rights Interest Groups

In an early study of the influence of interest groups upon foreign policy, Bernard Cohen identified as powerless "large national organizations commonly placed in the categories of civic, professional, women's, ideological, and even religious groups."[95] Another student of foreign policy making divided foreign policy interest groups into two categories, economic and noneconomic, and concluded that the impact of the latter was slight.[96]

One of the reasons offered to explain the relative lack of success of humanitarian interest groups is their leaders' rudimentary under-

[93] See, for example, the statement by President Nixon's ambassador to Nicaragua, James Theberge, in *Latin America*, p. 44, *supra* n. 45.

[94] This is not to suggest that the Carter administration adopted a clear policy of hostility toward Somoza; in fact, the policy was quite ambivalent. But in late 1978, the administration decided that Somoza had to leave office. Thereafter, the ambivalence in U.S. policy stemmed from the administration's inability to decide (1) how hard to push Somoza, and (2) which anti-Somoza forces to support. These two questions, in turn, were related to perceptions of U.S. security interests, not to a desire to prolong the Somoza government.

[95] Cohen, *The Influence of Non-Governmental Groups on Foreign Policy-Making*, p. 16. Cohen subsequently became less certain about the impact of interest groups on foreign policy. See Bernard C. Cohen and Scott A. Harris, "Foreign Policy," in *Handbook of Political Science*, ed. Fred I. Greenstein and Nelson W. Polsby (Reading, Mass.: Addison-Wesley, 1975), 6: 413. On this issue, cf. Trice, *Interest Groups and the Foreign Policy Process*, p. 72.

[96] Lester W. Milbrath, "Interest Groups and Foreign Policy," in *Domestic Sources of Foreign Policy*, ed. James N. Rosenau (New York: Free Press, 1967), pp. 247-248.

standing of the political process. For example, Lowenthal and Treverton noted as late as 1978 that "non-governmental groups in the United States which do not have specific economic interests at stake show little sense of where decision-making power lies within the U.S. government."[97] Although this may be an accurate characterization of some noneconomic lobbies, it does not describe human rights interest groups in the late 1970s. Like the representatives of business groups and some of the representatives of repressive Latin American governments, by 1978 the human rights lobby had an extremely sophisticated understanding of the decision-making process. Nearly all of the principal human rights lobbyists could describe precisely where important relevant decisions were made in both Congress and the executive branch, who made them, why they did so, over whose opposition, and with whose support. They knew who gets angry at meetings, who is asked not to smoke, and who likes to sit next to whom. One can learn more about the making of United States policy toward Latin America in a day with the staff of the Washington Office on Latin America than in a week with the employees of any other organization in Washington, including the State Department. If in previous years human rights lobbyists were ignorant of the functioning of the foreign policy process, this is no longer the case.

In addition, these lobbyists may not ever have been as naive as has been purported. The accumulated evidence suggests that human rights lobbyists were close to correct in viewing the Nixon-Ford administration as an inflexible bureaucracy dedicated to preserving the status quo in Latin America, regardless of the level of repression that might require. Certainly it is true that the executive branch has always controlled United States policy toward Latin America, but with whom were human rights lobbyists to speak before 1977? Charles Meyer? Harry Shlaudeman? Lincoln Gordon? The Johnson and Nixon-Ford administrations employed a small quota of liberals but, as the following chapters will demonstrate, they were not allowed to speak out on human rights until late 1975—November 1975 was the date of William D. Rogers ice-breaking speech on human rights—and it is quite doubtful whether they ever had a significant impact upon policy decisions. Given this reality, it seems entirely rational that the human rights lobby went to Congress to obtain the legislation necessary to make the executive branch pay attention to its positions.

Every piece of human rights legislation that passed the Ninety-fourth and Ninety-fifth Congresses (1975-1978) did so with the active

[97] Lowenthal and Treverton, "The Making of U.S. Policies toward Latin America," p. 18; Weiner, "U.S.-Brazil Relations," pp. 250-255.

support of human rights interest groups. When they were disinterested in a particular battle or distracted by other concerns, human rights proposals were defeated. There is no way to determine whether this concomitant variation between lobbying effort and legislative success is spurious, but there are several individual cases to substantiate the suggestion that some of the success can be explained by interest group activity. Of all the human rights legislation passed by Congress during the 1970s, the halt in military training for Argentina provides the clearest example of the impact of human rights interest groups. In 1977, military aid to Argentina was a major focus of the Human Rights Working Group, and member organizations worked with extraordinary persistence to influence wavering members of Congress. The Argentine Commission on Human Rights, led by Olga Talamante, Gino Lofredo, and Bob Barber, the Americans for Democratic Action, the Mennonite Central Committee, and the Washington Office on Latin America were particularly active. Amnesty International provided an enormous amount of documentary evidence to substantiate allegations of gross violations of human rights.

Of particular value were the personal visits to members of Congress by citizens who had been subjected to the junta's brutality. On the floor of the House, members who were usually quiet spoke emotionally of these interviews, all of which were arranged by human rights interest groups. They had a telling effect. Representative William Lehman told his colleagues of the treatment received by the daughter of two Mennonite missionaries:

> In September, 1976, she was kidnapped by several men in plain clothes [and] placed in a concentration camp. During the ten days she spent in this camp, she was repeatedly beaten, given electric shocks, and raped. . . . How many more stories like this one are waiting to be told? How many more victims are dead or still languishing in prisons? . . . Let us not condone these travesties of human rights by continuing to provide military training assistance to Argentina.[98]

Representative Don Bonker addressed his colleagues with a similar personal story:

> Yesterday, for the first time, I had the opportunity to see the personal dimension of what goes on and the extent of the brutality in Argentina when a young girl came to my office, a dark Christian girl, who had always lived in Argentina. She was taken out of her house into captivity in a remote part of the city. She was

[98] *Congressional Record*, June 27, 1977, p. H6345.

subjected to brutal repeated torture and without cause. Mr. Chairman, once we grasp the personal significance of what is going on in Argentina, I do not think there is any way we can rationalize our continued support for military training there. In fact, the girl told me that she had heard about the military training which they got, most of it from the United States.[99]

Other members rose to relate similar individual stories, stories that began, as Norman Mineta's did, with the preface, "please let me share with you my own personal involvement in a nightmare experienced by a constituent of mine . . . at the hands of Argentine Government,"[100] Members who ordinarily exhibited little interest in foreign affairs worked with some enthusiasm against aid to Argentina. One legislative aide recalled the meeting at which the daughter of the Mennonite missionaries described her rape by Argentine military officers to an extremely powerful member of Congress: "When the girl had finished her story neither he [the member] or I knew what to say to her. He looked over at me and his eyes were ablaze, simply livid. I knew right then that there was no way those goose-stepping perverts were getting a cent out of us that year."

In addition to the Argentine case and a variety of related examples involving specific countries, there are other indicators of the influence of the human rights lobby. If business-group lobbying effectiveness is indicated by the Hickenlooper amendments, for example, then the Harkin amendment (and, indeed, much of the subsequent human rights legislation of the 1970s) is an equal demonstration of the prowess of human rights interest groups. Most amendments followed the same legislative route from lobbyist's pen to the statute books. Since 1975, the human rights lobby has been the primary source of legislative initiatives regarding United States policy toward human rights in the multilateral development banks, the International Monetary Fund, OPIC, and the Export-Import Bank. In addition, the human rights lobby filled an information vacuum, providing sympathetic policy makers with virtually all of the data that were instrumental in linking U.S. foreign policy to the repression of human rights by Latin American governments. It is unknown how much of these and similar efforts ultimately contributed to the decisions by Congress, but the evidence suggests that there is no longer any justification for dismissing as ineffective the efforts of all lobbies concerned with humanitarian issues. The conventional wisdom is obsolete.

Nothing in the preceding paragraphs is meant to suggest that the

[99] Ibid.
[100] *Congressional Record*, May 22, 1977, p. H4790.

human rights lobby has enjoyed the same level of influence as the business lobby, however, for it is clearly much weaker. On several occasions it was defeated badly—on aid to Nicaragua in 1977, on human rights amendments covering the Export-Import Bank and United States participation in the International Monetary Fund in 1978. On a variety of occasions, it saw initial legislative victories turn into defeats when the administration or rival interest groups were able to influence higher-level officials, particularly key members of congressional conference committees. What the human rights lobby exploited with its substantial energy was a respectable, significant issue that arose at an opportune moment. But mainstream foreign policy officials were able to provide only a vague commitment to human rights. Whenever competing values—anticommunism, the balance of payments, corporate profits, national security—entered the dispute over United States policy toward human rights violators, the influence of human rights lobbyists decreased rapidly. In those cases where competitive values were not particularly evident, however, the human rights lobby appeared to have a significant influence on policy. These cases were sufficiently numerous to suggest that without the active involvement of human rights interest groups the following chapters on United States human rights policy would have been written much differently.

· 3 ·

DIPLOMACY AND HUMAN RIGHTS

MOST of the witnesses who appeared at the initial human rights hearings by Representative Donald Fraser's Foreign Affairs Subcommittee on International Organizations and Movements in 1973 noted that the policy of the Nixon administration was to denigrate humanitarian values in foreign policy making. Fresh from a tour as her nation's representative to the U.N. Commission on Human Rights, Rita Hauser told of how "we speak out against violations of countries we are not particularly close to . . . and we are largely silent . . . when human rights violations occur on the part of our allies." Richard Falk lamented that human rights maintained such a low priority that they were all but excluded from foreign policy decision making, an evaluation echoed by a second specialist in international law, Tom Farer, who characterized human rights as "the stepchildren of United States foreign policy." "The best guarantor of an aborted career in the defense and foreign policy establishments," he observed, "is a marked concern for the humanitarian consequences of national behavior."[1]

It should be noted at the outset that while some administrations clearly place greater emphasis than others upon the promotion of human rights, in no case has a commitment to increase the importance of human rights considerations in foreign policy been to deny the legitimacy of other competing values. Thus the importance of human rights is always a function of the other potential interests and values that impinge upon any given policy decision. In all administrations, the question policy makers address is not whether to incorporate human rights into the decision-making process but rather how much influence human rights should have in relation to a host of other potentially conflicting variables. The question is not human rights versus no human rights; instead it is human rights versus national security versus friendly relations with existing regimes versus economic benefits to the domestic economy versus humanitarian aid to impov-

[1] U.S. Congress, House, Committee on Foreign Affairs, Subcommittee on International Organizations and Movements, *International Protection of Human Rights*, 93d Cong., 1st Sess., 1973, pp. 233, 250, 113, respectively. This chapter is a revised version of "United States Diplomacy and Human Rights in Latin America," in *Latin America, the United States, and the Inter-American System*, edited by John D. Martz and Lars Schoultz (Boulder: Westview Press, 1979), pp. 173-206. Reprinted by permission.

erished people. At some extreme, there probably would be a near-perfect consensus in any administration that United States policy ought to emphasize human rights values above all others, but in most cases differing circumstances and disparate assessments of the importance of human rights encourage differing human rights policies.

The issue of United States policy toward human rights violations in Latin America was never discussed directly by President Nixon. This in itself is significant, for a presidential address serves as one of the principal mechanisms by which a President informs the executive branch of the concerns he wishes to emphasize. When President Nixon did approach the subject of human rights indirectly, he emphasized his greater interest in other potentially competing values, particularly the stability of existing relationships: "The United States has a strong interest in maintaining cooperation with our neighbors regardless of their domestic viewpoint. . . . We hope that governments will evolve toward constitutional procedures but it is not our mission to try to provide except by example, the answers to such questions to other sovereign nations. We deal with governments as they are."[2] Except for this comment and a similar one near the end of his presidency,[3] Mr. Nixon was silent on the issue of human rights in Latin America.

The principal Nixon administration spokesperson on human rights was Henry Kissinger. Until 1975, he commented upon the issue only in response to direct questioning. At his 1973 confirmation hearing, Kissinger was asked about the administration's intentions in light of the increasing levels of repression among America's allies. He responded: "In our bilateral dealings we will follow a pragmatic policy of degree. If the infringement on human rights is not so offensive that we cannot live with it, we will seek to work out what we can with the country involved in order to increase our influence. If the infringement is so offensive that we cannot live with it, we will avoid dealing with the offending country."[4] At the time Kissinger was making this argument, human rights violations in many countries with which the United States was closely allied (Chile, Indonesia, Iran, the Phil-

[2] U.S. Congress, Senate, Committee on Foreign Relations, Subcommittee on Western Hemisphere Affairs, *United States Policies and Programs in Brazil*, 92d Cong., 1st Sess., May 4, 5, and 11, 1971, p. 290.

[3] U.S. President (Nixon), *U.S. Foreign Policy for the 1970's: Shaping a Durable Peace; A Report to the Congress, May 3, 1973* (Washington, D.C.: Government Printing Office, 1973), p. 118.

[4] See *International Protection of Human Rights*, p. 507, *supra* n. 1. This position is not significantly different from that advanced by the administration of Lyndon Johnson. See James D. Cochrane, "U.S. Policy toward Recognition of Governments and Promotion of Democracy in Latin America since 1963," *Journal of Latin American Studies* 4 (November 1972): 278.

ippines, South Korea, Uruguay) were reaching new levels of intensity. When he and President Nixon failed to make an issue of these violations, the foreign policy bureaucracy concluded correctly that the administration wished to emphasize values other than human rights in its relations with repressive governments. In July 1974, the particular issue of diplomatic intervention on behalf of human rights appeared to be settled for the duration of the Nixon-Ford administration. In that month, the American ambassador to Chile, David Popper, broached the subject of torture and other abuses during the course of a meeting with the Chilean minister of defense. In the margin of the cable describing the discussion, Kissinger scrawled an instruction to his aide: "Tell Popper to cut out the political science lectures."[5]

Then in mid-1975, the Ford administration began to propose a change in the importance of human rights in United States foreign policy. Once again, Secretary of State Kissinger was the principal administration spokesperson. During his final year and a half in office, he asserted repeatedly that there were limits to the extent to which governments engaged in the systematic repression of their citizens' human rights could be "congenial partners" with the United States.[6] The impetus for this changed rhetoric is uncertain, although many factors probably contributed; certainly congressional pressure would be among the most prominent of these. Many observers agreed with David Weissbrodt, the legal scholar who chronicled the Kissinger human rights policy most carefully, that the Secretary's "rhetoric may not have been translated into his policies."[7] Nonetheless, the fact is that the human rights policy enunciated by the "late" Kissinger differed substantially from that of the "early" Kissinger.

The most vivid example of this difference came in his June 1976 speech entitled "Human Rights and the Western Hemisphere" to the sixth general assembly of the Organization of American States (OAS) in Santiago, Chile. He began: "One of the most compelling issues of our time, and one which calls for the concerted action of all responsible peoples and nations, is the necessity to protect and extend the fundamental rights of humanity."[8] Kissinger's speech concentrated exclusively upon human rights. There exists no parallel to this address in the first seven years of the Nixon-Ford administration. The message

[5] *New York Times*, September 27, 1974, p. 18.

[6] David Weissbrodt, "Human Rights Legislation and U.S. Foreign Policy," *Georgia Journal of International and Comparative Law*, supplement to vol. 7 (Summer 1977), pp. 237-238.

[7] Ibid., p. 237n.

[8] *Department of State Bulletin* 75 (July 5, 1976): 1.

to American diplomats was that the value of human rights in United States policy toward Latin America had increased considerably.

It is of absolutely crucial importance to note, however, that throughout the period from 1969 to 1977 Kissinger consistently voiced his belief that human rights concerns must remain secondary to the maintenance of peace and world order. The best example of his understanding of this subordinate relationship appeared in a 1976 speech in which he acknowledged that "it is our obligation as the world's leading democracy to dedicate ourselves to assuring freedom for the human spirit. But responsibility compels also a recognition of our limits. Our alliances . . . serve the cause of peace by strengthening regional and world security. If well conceived, they are not favors to others but a recognition of common interests. They should be withdrawn when those interests change; they should not, as a general rule, be used as levers to extort a standard of conduct or to punish acts with which we do not agree."[9] Overall, the message from the Secretary of State to his diplomats was that human rights, while deserving of greater attention, should not distract foreign policy officials from the pursuit of their more traditional national security interests.

Once out of office, Kissinger placed this position in sharper focus in commenting upon the obvious difference between his human rights policy and that of the Carter administration. Speaking as a private citizen in 1977, he warned the new policy makers to "maintain the moral distinction between aggressive totalitarianism and other governments which, with all their imperfections, are trying to resist foreign pressures or subversion and which thereby help preserve the balance of power in behalf of all free peoples."[10] This statement appears to confirm Rita Hauser's evaluation that during the Nixon administration the United States had friends—"free peoples" in Kissinger's lexicon—whose human rights practices were irrelevant to United States policy because these allies were engaged in a struggle to maintain a higher value, the balance of power. The human rights behavior of "aggressive totalitarianisms," conversely, was morally distinct: their abuses could not be counterbalanced by the value of maintaining freedom. It is upon this logic that American policy toward the inter-

[9] *Department of State Bulletin* 75 (November 15, 1976): 603. For an earlier statement about the potential costs of supporting human rights in the Soviet Union, see *Department of State Bulletin* 69 (October 29, 1973): 529.

[10] *Washington Post*, September 25, 1977, p. C3. The following year Kissinger was the guest of Argentina's General Videla for the World Cup soccer matches, at the end of which he held a news conference and criticized the Carter administration for not understanding that human rights are a necessary casualty in the battle against terrorism. *Washington Post*, June 26, 1978, p. A18.

national protection of human rights was based during the Nixon and Ford administrations.

If one were to search for the single most prominent difference between the foreign policy of the Carter administration and that of its immediate predecessors, surely the distinction would be the policy on human rights protection. Candidate Carter's first major speech emphasizing human rights and foreign policy came on September 8, 1976, during an appearance before the national convention of B'nai B'rith: "We cannot look away when a government tortures people, or jails them for their beliefs or denies minorities fair treatment or the right to emigrate. . . . We should begin by having it understood that if any nation . . . deprives its own people of basic human rights, that fact will help shape our own people's attitude towards that nation's government."[11] During the second preelection debate in October 1976, Carter accused the Ford administration of ignoring "in our foreign policy the character of the American people" and of acting "contrary to our longstanding beliefs and principles." Responding to President Ford's statement that the United States "does not condone . . . repressive measures" in South Korea, Carter noted "that Mr. Ford didn't comment on the prisons in Chile," where "his administration overthrew an elected government and helped to establish a military dictatorship."

Thereafter, statements about human rights became a prominent feature of the Carter campaign. By the time of his inauguration, no one was startled to hear him assert that "our commitment to human rights must be absolute." Perhaps the most-quoted passage from his inaugural address concerned human rights: "Because we are free, we can never be indifferent to the fate of freedom elsewhere. Our moral sense dictates a clearcut preference for those societies which share with us an abiding respect for individual human rights."[12] Even if President Carter had done nothing else on the issue, he would have been noted for bringing human rights to the center of diplomatic exchange. After January 1977, United States diplomats knew that the

[11] In earlier speeches—to the Chicago Council on Foreign Relations on March 15, 1976, and particularly to the Foreign Policy Association of New York City on June 23, 1976—Mr. Carter emphasized the need to "restore the moral authority of this country in its conduct of foreign policy" by discarding "policies that strengthen dictators or create refugees, policies that prolong suffering or postpone racial justice." During the course of the New York speech, he advocated that the United States "take the lead in establishing and promoting basic global standards of human rights." The B'nai B'rith speech in September, then, was notable for its emphasis on human rights considerations, not for its uniqueness. Only after this speech did the media firmly identify the issue of human rights as a major feature of the Carter campaign.

[12] *Department of State Bulletin* 66 (February 14, 1977): 121-122.

value of human rights had risen dramatically in American foreign policy.

Once human rights came out of the closet, the perennial question arose over their relative value. The Latin Americanist on U.N. ambassador Andrew Young's staff observed that "those of us who had been outside came in with lots of ideas about what was wrong and about what ought to be, but not many ideas of how to go about it."[13] Gingerly, they groped their way. At his February 8, 1977, news conference, the President noted that he was "reserving the right to speak out forcefully whenever human rights are threatened," but then he finished this sentence by adding "—not every instance, but when I think it's advisable." In stark contrast to his inaugural address, this suggested that President Carter had a relative rather than an absolute commitment to increasing the value of human rights in United States foreign policy.

The question then became the same one that had faced all previous administrations: How much of a commitment? The first attempt at an answer was made by Secretary of State Cyrus Vance when he appeared before the Senate Appropriations Subcommittee on Foreign Operations on February 24, 1977. He announced that the administration planned to reduce aid to Argentina, Ethiopia, and Uruguay because of their gross violations of human rights. Absent from the Secretary's statement was any suggestion that human rights had the absolute value that the President had mentioned in his inaugural address. Instead Vance noted that while human rights considerations would receive greater attention, as with previous administrations they would be incorporated in United States policy on a country-by-country basis: "In each case we must balance a political concern for human rights against economic or security goals."[14] At his initial appearance before the U.N. General Assembly in March 1977, President Carter again emphasized the relative value of human rights in United States foreign policy by asserting that human rights would not interfere with progress in certain other areas, especially arms control.

The important point, though, is that the President actually addressed the issue of human rights and pledged the support of his administration for improved human rights practices. These presidential affirmations continued over the course of the late 1970s. One of the

---

[13] Tom Quigley et al., *U.S. Policy on Human Rights in Latin America (Southern Cone): A Congressional Conference on Capitol Hill* (New York: Fund for New Priorities in America, 1978), p. 41.

[14] U.S. Congress, Senate, Committee on Appropriations, Subcommittee on Foreign Assistance and Related Programs, *Foreign Assistance and Related Programs Appropriations Fiscal Year 1978*, 95th Cong., 1st Sess., 1977, pp. 161, 196.

strongest occurred in December 1978, when the President took advantage of the thirtieth anniversary of the Universal Declaration of Human Rights to emphasize his commitment: "As long as I am President, the government of the United States will continue throughout the world to enhance human rights. . . . No force on earth can separate us from that commitment. . . . Our human rights policy is not a decoration. It is not something we have adopted to polish up our image abroad, or to put a fresh coat of moral paint on the discredited policies of the past. . . . Human rights is the soul of our foreign policy."[15] From the beginning then, it was obvious that the President and his major advisors held a near-perfect consensus that human rights should be given a greater relative value than they had during the Nixon-Ford years. The answer to the question, "How much emphasis?" was "Quite a bit more."

Once this had been determined, a number of ancillary issues had to be clarified before U.S. diplomats could implement the administration's policy. One such issue—the selection of the type of human rights to be given major emphasis—was settled by Secretary of State Vance at his Law Day speech at the University of Georgia in April 1977. The Carter administration, he declared, would concentrate first upon the right to be free from governmental violation of the integrity of the person; second, upon the right to the fulfillment of basic human needs; and third, upon the right to enjoy civil and political liberties. Noting that problems might arise over which of these rights should be given primary emphasis, he indicated that the first set of rights was mentioned first because it was to be treated by American diplomats first: "We may justifiably seek a rapid end to such gross violations as those cited in our law: torture, or cruel, inhuman or degrading treatment or punishment, or prolonged detention without charges. . . . The promotion of other human rights is a broader challenge. The results may be slower in coming."[16] After this address, no one misunderstood where diplomats should concentrate their efforts on behalf of the international protection of human rights.

A second issue—the relationship between terrorism and governmental human rights violations—had particular significance for Latin America. It too was clarified by Secretary Vance, this time at the seventh general assembly of the Organization of American States in June 1977. In that forum, Vance presented a vigorous rebuttal to the contention that human rights abuses were an unfortunate but necessary

[15] *Department of State Bulletin* 79 (January 1979): 1-2.
[16] Cyrus Vance, "Human Rights and Foreign Policy," *Georgia Journal of International and Comparative Law*, supplement to vol. 7 (Summer 1977), pp. 223-224, 228. *Department of State Bulletin* 79 (January 1979): 1.

by-product of the war against terrorism. In direct contrast to the position of his predecessor, the Secretary of State rejected the legitimacy of combating terrorism with counterterrorism: "If terrorism and violence in the name of dissent cannot be condoned, neither can violence that is officially sanctioned. Such action perverts the legal system that, alone, assures the survival of our traditions. The surest way to defeat terrorism is to promote justice in our societies—legal, social and economic justice. Justice that is summary undermines the future it seeks to promote. It produces only more violence, more victims, and more terrorism."[17] At the same meeting, the United States cosponsored a resolution that reflected the Carter administration's refusal to recognize terrorism as an excuse for repression.

Finally, the manner in which the Carter administration handled four specific events in 1977 and early 1978 served to clarify the limits of the new emphasis upon human rights in United States policy toward Latin America. First, any fears that the President would project a fundamentalist view of human rights protection were put to rest on March 9, 1977. A day earlier Brady Tyson, a Methodist minister, history professor, and aide-de-camp to U.N. ambassador Andrew Young appeared at a Geneva meeting of the U.N. Commission on Human Rights and expressed "our profoundest regrets" at the role of public and private United States groups in the overthrow of the Allende government in Chile. He further expressed sorrow that such regrets could not "contribute significantly to the reduction of suffering and terror that the people of Chile have experienced." Tyson was immediately called home for instruction in diplomatic procedures.[18] At his news conference the following day, President Carter repudiated both Tyson and his own charge in the October 1976 preelection debate that the United States "overthrew an elected government and helped to establish a military dictatorship" in Chile. Between October and March he discovered the lack of "any evidence that the U.S. was involved in the overthrow of the Allende government in Chile." He said little about the human rights violations of the Pinochet government. To American diplomats, the content of this message was that the United States would not attempt to atone—or even apologize—

[17] *Department of State Bulletin* 77 (July 18, 1978): 70; *New York Times*, September 17, 1977, p. 6.

[18] The instruction consisted of a four-hour discussion with assistant secretary of state for international organization affairs, Charles W. Maynes, during which Tyson steadfastly resisted Maynes's demand that he resign. Maynes, incidentally, was the author of a 1976 study urging "U.S. support for defending human rights more vigorously." Charles William Maynes et al., *U.S. Foreign Policy: Principles for Defining the National Interest* (New York: Public Agenda Foundation, September 1976), p. 15.

for human rights abuses to which Americans may have contributed. To avoid such responsibility, it was permissible to ignore earlier statements.

The second event was the September 1977 ceremonial signing of the new Panama Canal treaties, attended by nearly all of the hemisphere's chiefs of state. President Carter spoke individually with each of the leaders, including Chile's Pinochet and Argentina's Videla, thereby signaling his belief that the need for hemispheric solidarity on other important issues—in this case, the canal treaties—was of sufficient importance to override the damage done to human rights by such meetings.

The third event was an extraordinarily ill-timed letter sent by President Carter to Nicaraguan President Somoza in July 1978, less than two months before the beginning of the full-scale civil war that eventually toppled Somoza's government. The purpose of the letter was to praise Somoza's improvements in the area of human rights. It was drafted by a National Security Council staff member whose inexperience in Latin American affairs was only exceeded by his self-confidence, and cabled to Managua over the strong opposition of the Department of State. But the United States ambassador was ordered to deliver the letter, and every United States diplomat learned it was the Carter policy not to pressure client governments whose leaders were willing to make a verbal commitment to improving human rights practices.

The fourth and surely the most widely received human rights message to U.S. diplomats came in the form of a demonstration of what happens to half-hearted participants. The individual in question was the assistant secretary of state for inter-American affairs, Terence A. Todman, a career diplomat. Under his direction, ARA initially opposed the use of public diplomacy to pursue aggressively the protection of human rights in Latin America. In fact, Mr. Todman's public statements constituted something of a reverse human rights policy. This was demonstrated clearly on two occasions.

First, upon completion of a trip to Chile in October 1977, he remarked that the Department of State was encouraged "by recent evidence that the trend away from democracy may be ending," citing as an example of this trend the Chilean government's "public commitment to a timetable" for elections. No such timetable existed. Within a week, the State Department took the unusual step of presenting a detailed rebuttal to Todman's statement. It noted that the assistant secretary "has tried to emphasize the readiness of our Government to recognize progress" and "to avoid the development of a sterile adversary relationship." Nonetheless, the Department argued

117

that "at no time did he allege that the human rights situation in the Southern Cone countries was satisfactory," and even if he did give that impression, "the Department continues to be disappointed with the lack of political freedom in Chile."[19] Todman's second major break with the Carter administration came in February 1978, during the course of a speech at the Center for Inter-American Relations in New York. There he presented a list of ten "tactical mistakes" that the United States must avoid "if we are truly to help and not hinder the cause of promoting human rights and alleviating suffering."[20] Among these were the practices of "condemning an entire government for every negative act by one of its officials" and of "holding entire countries up to public ridicule and embarrassment." Shortly thereafter, Mr. Todman was asked to leave his post and accept the ambassadorship to Spain.

The general message that emerged from these actions was that human rights would have a significant place in nearly all foreign policy decisions but that the amount of significance would depend upon the nature of other variables involved and, therefore, the countries involved. As it happened, many of the truly egregious human rights violators were outside the U.S. sphere of influence—the United States had no diplomatic relations with Cambodia or Uganda, for example. Other major violators were of such importance to American strategic and economic interests that administration officials concluded that human rights values could not be pursued vigorously. In this category were the repressive governments of Indonesia, Iran, the Philippines, and South Korea. This left the nations of Latin America, linked to the United States by two centuries of intimate intercourse and, with the possible exceptions of Brazil and Mexico, lacking any of the strategic significance that exempted other nations from diplomatic pressure on behalf of human rights.

Once the Carter administration recognized that a universal, absolute standard of human rights would conflict with other foreign policy values to an intolerable extent—once the administration adopted a case-by-case approach to human rights abuses—attention shifted to the nations of Latin America. By the end of 1977, it was clear that the United States' efforts to protect human rights were to be concen-

[19] U.S. Congress, House, Committee on International Relations, Subcommittee on International Organizations, *Human Rights and United States Foreign Policy: A Review of the Administration's Record*, 95th Cong., 1st Sess., October 25, 1977, pp. 30-31.

[20] Terence A. Todman, "The Carter Administration's Latin American Policy: Purposes and Prospects," speech at the Center for Inter-American Relations, New York, February 14, 1978.

trated upon Latin America's repressive governments. With the policy direction set, U.S. diplomats began to implement their superiors' directions.

POLICY IMPLEMENTATION

A common feature of the literature on foreign policy implementation is an assertion that diplomats tend to avoid doing as they are told. Instead of implementing the policies of a given administration, diplomatic personnel are said to be engaged in "cookie pushing" or in operating their "foreign affairs fudge factory." Relating to the diplomatic corps is likened to "pushing on a marshmallow" or shaking a "bowl of jelly."[21] Having become accustomed to accusations that American diplomacy is being handled by people who are most frequently likened to various kinds of junk food, students of foreign policy tend to sympathize with senior foreign policy officials such as Arthur Schlesinger, Jr., who lamented that he and his President were kept from accomplishing their admirable goals in Latin America because the State Department hired persons "for whom the risks always outweighed the opportunities."[22] After investment banker Earl E. T. Smith completed his tour as President Eisenhower's ambassador to Cuba, he wrote: "I have reached the conclusion that the structure of organization in the State Department is faulty by law. No President, no Secretary of State, no matter how sincere and purposeful, can protect the United States from the damage of this day-to-day operation by the lower officials. These men . . . protect each other as though they belonged to a fraternity."[23]

The following discussion of the implementation of the human rights component of American foreign policy is intended to suggest that these characterizations of the foreign policy bureaucracy are incorrect. These stereotypes have encouraged the belief that foreign policy failures result from the operation of a malfunctioning system when, as we shall see in the case of human rights, the system is capable of functioning quite well. United States diplomats are able implementors of whatever policy high-ranking officials decide to pursue. Their premier characteristic appears to be their responsiveness, their willingness

---

[21] See, for example, Richard J. Barnet, *Roots of War* (New York: Atheneum, 1972), p. 116; Earl E. T. Smith, *The Fourth Floor: An Account of the Castro Communist Revolution* (New York: Random House, 1962), p. 227; Quigley et al., *U.S. Policy on Human Rights in Latin America (Southern Cone)*, p. 74.

[22] Arthur M. Schlesinger, Jr., *A Thousand Days: John F. Kennedy in the White House* (Boston: Houghton Mifflin, 1965), p. 414.

[23] Smith, *The Fourth Floor*, p. 23.

to adapt to changing policy orientations; malfunctions occur when policy is obscure or contradictory—when there is incomplete or incompetent direction by senior foreign policy officials. Thus it is wrong to assert that obstructionist diplomats are to blame for the Kennedy administration's policy failures in Latin America. That responsibility rests with Schlesinger and his fellow New Frontiersmen, the leaders who could never quite surrender to their liberal instincts. Of the Dominican crisis in 1961, the President told Schlesinger: "There are three possibilities in descending order of preference: a decent democratic regime, a continuation of the Trujillo regime or a Castro regime. We ought to aim at the first, but we really can't renounce the second until we are sure we can avoid the third."[24] Ambassador Smith's own record indicates that United States policy toward the rebellion against the Batista government was unusually ambiguous. Perhaps Schlesinger and Smith would have reached a different conclusion about the efficiency of the diplomatic corps had their policies been less ambivalent. Operating under the very different but similarly clear policies of the Nixon and Carter administrations, United States diplomats ably implemented their instructions in the area of human rights in Latin America. As Charles Frankel once noted, the gap between policy statements and policy implementation is smallest when there is a clear understanding throughout the diplomatic corps of the spirit of an administration's policy.[25]

Bilateral Diplomacy

Within the Department of State, the two bureaus charged with using diplomacy to implement United States policy on human rights in Latin America are the Bureau of Inter-American Affairs and the Bureau of Human Rights and Humanitarian Affairs.

ARA's primary task is the maintenance of smooth relations with the various governments of Latin America. It is responsible for the day-to-day diplomatic interaction with Latin America, the staffing of embassies and consulates, and the general observation of activities in the region that might affect United States interests. Because of the nature of the Bureau's duties, ARA officials have always been reluctant to raise publicly the issue of human rights abuses. Thus the following statement by a Nixon administration assistant secretary of state for inter-American affairs, Jack Kubisch, verbalizes a widely held attitude: "It is one thing for our newspapers or for private citizens to make charges or make complaints or appeal to the Chileans. It is something

[24] Schlesinger, A Thousand Days, p. 769.
[25] Charles Frankel, High on Foggy Bottom: An Outsider's Inside View of the Government (New York: Harper and Row, 1968), pp. 187-188.

else for U.S. government officials or the Executive branch to lean hard publicly on a regime since to do so might make them feel that they are required to dig in their heels and resist us publicly, or not have anything to do with us, or discuss the matter with us."[26] It is doubtful that this attitude is simply a manifestation of an ideological affinity between ARA and the hemisphere's right-wing repressive governments. Although it could reflect a willingness to accept repression as an alternative to disorder and revolution, it is at least as plausible to suggest that the attitude stems from the simple perception that, as Kubisch stated, if the United States publicly presses a Latin American government too hard on a sensitive issue such as human rights, the government might indeed decide "not to have anything to do with us." Should that occur, ARA will have failed in its primary mission of maintaining smooth relations.

Because the officials of ARA have as their principal task the preservation of effective working relationships with all recognized Latin American governments, regardless of their level of repressiveness, the Bureau has always preferred a special type of diplomatic interaction called quiet diplomacy. Quiet diplomacy is to ARA what Foreign Military Sales credits are to the Defense Security Assistance Agency or volunteer placement is to the Peace Corps—the standard means of conducting relations with Latin American governments. But there are various types of quiet diplomacy. During the Nixon-Ford years, diplomatic interaction over human rights issues was of a perfunctory nature. Secretary Kissinger's assistant secretary of state for inter-American affairs, William D. Rogers, liked to compare his marital experience and the Nixon-Ford administration's activities on behalf of human rights. He contended that he was much more willing to accept his wife's criticisms of his social misbehavior if she waited until they were alone in bed rather than chastising him publicly. Following this approach, Rogers argued that he could be more successful by tactfully suggesting rather than by openly demanding that a repressive regime relent.[27]

Readers of some maturity will recognize that private criticism by most spouses displays a wide range of intensity. The quiet diplomacy ARA had in mind during the Nixon administration was not modeled after George and Martha's connubial interaction in *Who's Afraid of Virginia Woolf?* Take, for example, the half-hearted response from William Roundtree, the American ambassador to Brazil, when Senator

[26] U.S. Congress, Senate, Committee on the Judiciary, Subcommittee to Investigate Problems Connected with Refugees and Escapees, *Refugee and Humanitarian Problems in Chile*, 93d Cong., 1st Sess., September 28, 1973, p. 41.

[27] Interview with William D. Rogers, November 6, 1975, Washington, D.C.

Frank Church inquired whether ARA had expressed concern over the evidence that the Brazilian dictatorship was systematically exterminating all dissent: "To the government, yes. I might say that the Department of State here in Washington has mentioned its concern to the representatives of Brazil, and the various members of the mission . . . have indicated concern regarding these stories."[28] To the Nixon-Ford administration, quiet diplomacy on behalf of human rights involved only the most circumspect protestations.

This style of quiet diplomacy contrasts vividly with that which occurred under the Carter administration. In 1978, for example, the deputy assistant secretary of state for inter-American affairs, Richard Arellano, was asked the same question as Ambassador Roundtree regarding the repressive activities of El Salvador's White Warriors Union. He responded by describing a far more aggressive form of quiet diplomacy: "Repeatedly, upon instructions from Washington, the Embassy has made formal démarches, sent protest notes and otherwise actively sought to impress upon Salvadorean authorities and others the abiding concern of the American people and Government with the human rights ramifications of developments in El Salvador."[29] It is worth noting that few of the national security concerns which might have prompted a relatively mild approach to the Brazilian government's human rights violations applied at the time to tiny El Salvador. But even in those instances where national security was a minor consideration—Uruguay in the mid-1970s for example—the Nixon-Ford administration's form of quiet diplomacy was notably lacking in aggressiveness.

Despite these differences in tone and contentiousness, it should be emphasized that under any administration ARA strives to conduct diplomatic relations in such a way that relations are not strained. While under the Carter administration the Bureau occasionally accepted the risk of straining relations, even then its opposition was apparent. In fact, throughout the late 1970s, the Bureau maintained its reputation for renitency on the human rights issue. Much of this reputation was undeserved, for the Carter ARA regularly used quiet diplomacy in defense of human rights. But because it was quiet, ARA's diplomacy often went unnoticed, and thus the Bureau's reputation came from its open efforts to protect existing aid programs from attacks by Congress and the Bureau of Human Rights and Humanitarian Affairs. Given its responsibility to maintain contact, access, and in-

[28] *United States Policies and Programs in Brazil*, pp. 281-282, *supra* n. 2.

[29] U.S. Congress, House, Committee on International Relations, Subcommittee on International Organizations, *Religious Persecution in El Salvador*, 95th Cong., 1st Sess., July 21 and 29, 1977, p. 34.

fluence with all Latin American governments, it is difficult to imagine how the Bureau could have behaved otherwise. Its often-criticized "curator mentality"—the desire to protect existing relationships—will probably never disappear from ARA or, indeed, from any of State's regional bureaus.[30]

The Bureau of Human Rights and Humanitarian Affairs, the second executive branch bureaucracy responsible for implementing United States policy toward human rights in Latin America, is a relatively new organization. The idea of creating a human rights bureau grew out of a 1968 recommendation from the Commission on the Observance of Human Rights Year that the President appoint an assistant for human rights. The following year, Senator Edward Kennedy's Judiciary Subcommittee on Refugees advocated the creation of a Bureau of Humanitarian and Social Services. Soon thereafter, the President's Task Force on International Development urged the establishment of such a bureau, and in 1971 the Nixon administration included in its foreign assistance message a recommendation that Congress authorize its creation. The administration was not upset when Congress ignored the request.[31]

The subject next received attention in 1973, when Representative Donald Fraser introduced a resolution (H.R. 10455) to establish a Bureau of Humanitarian Affairs in the Department of State. While the House failed to give his proposal serious consideration, in the same year Senator Kennedy convinced the Senate to add to its version (S. 1443) of the Foreign Assistance Act of 1973 an expression of the sense of Congress that the State Department should create a Bureau of Humanitarian and Social Services. The House bill contained no such provision, and the conference committee rejected Kennedy's

[30] I. M. Destler, *Presidents, Bureaucrats, and Foreign Policy: The Politics of Organizational Reform* (Princeton: Princeton University Press, 1974), p. 248. That such a mentality is not peculiar to ARA is demonstrated, for example, in the testimony of the personnel of the Bureau of East Asian and Pacific Affairs on the issue of repression in Indonesia. See U.S. Congress, House, Committee on International Relations, Subcommittee on International Organizations, *Human Rights in Indonesia and the Philippines*, 94th Cong., 1st and 2d Sessions, 1975-1976, pp. 105-107; U.S. Congress, House, Committee on International Relations, Subcommittee on International Organizations, *Human Rights in Indonesia: A Review of the Situation with Respect to the Long-Term Political Detainees*, 95th Cong., 1st Sess., 1977, p. 23.

[31] Throughout the period 1969 to 1975, the Nixon-Ford State Department opposed the formal creation of a bureau for humanitarian affairs, voicing its doubts that "inserting an additional bureau into the picture would increase the effectiveness of the Department's work in this sphere." See *International Protection of Human Rights*, pp. 321, 506, *supra* n. 1. State could not oppose the administration's 1971 recommendation that a bureau be created, of course, but it made no effort to promote the idea.

123

initiative.[32] The Senate tried again in 1976, and this time the House accepted its suggestion. Thus the International Security Assistance and Arms Export Control Act [PL94-329, Sec. 301(b)] authorized the position of the Coordinator for Human Rights and Humanitarian Affairs, providing it with responsibility for advising the Secretary of State on "matters pertaining to human rights and humanitarian affairs . . . in the conduct of foreign policy." Congress indicated the importance it wished to attach to this position by stipulating that the coordinator was to be appointed by the President with the advice and consent of the Senate.

Prior to the creation of the Office of the Coordinator, responsibility for the diplomatic aspect of human rights protection rested with the State Department's Bureau of International Organization Affairs (IO) and, to a lesser extent, with the Office of the Legal Advisor. This reflected State's conception of its human rights duties as primarily technical: the preparation of instructions for United States representatives to international human rights commissions and the creation of policy toward international human rights agreements. At the time of the initial Fraser Subcommittee hearings in 1973, IO had assigned one foreign service officer to work full time on human rights, assisted part time by a junior officer. In the Office of the Legal Advisor, there was one assistant legal advisor for human rights.[33]

Soon after the hearings were completed, a human rights officer was designated in every regional bureau. It is not known whether the purpose of this move was to please congressional critics or to promote a larger role for human rights in United States foreign policy. But it is instructive to note that each of these new human rights officers was initially expected to continue with his or her previous tasks (most were labor specialists) and to perform human rights functions as well.[34]

[32] House Report 93-664, p. 54.

[33] See *International Protection of Human Rights*, pp. 506-507, *supra* n. 1; John Salzberg and Donald D. Young, "The Parliamentary Role in Implementing International Human Rights: A U.S. Example," *Texas International Law Journal* 12 (Spring-Summer 1977): 274.

[34] As a further indication of the limited importance given to regional human rights activity, the 1975 State Department telephone directory did not list the human rights officers. Beginning in 1977, ARA's human rights officer was listed immediately after the assistant secretary of state, with the title of special assistant and human rights officer. Similar examples are plentiful. The term "human rights" does not appear in a September 1976 publication that describes in some detail the duties and organization of the Department of State, but by 1978 the State Department was publishing separate booklets on the subject of human rights and foreign policy. U.S. Department of State, Bureau of Public Affairs, Office of Media Service, *Foreign Policy and the Department of State*, Publication 8869 (Washington, D.C.: Department of State, September 1976); U.S. Department of State, Bureau of Public Affairs, Office of Public Communication,

In addition to the creation of these regional human rights officers, IO's human rights officer was upgraded to deputy director of the U.N. Political Affairs Office, and another officer was assigned to work as his assistant. Finally, in April 1975, the State Department anticipated Congress's directive and appointed a coordinator for humanitarian affairs in the office of the deputy secretary of state.[35] The 1976 congressional action mentioned above changed the title of the coordinator, made the position subject to Senate confirmation, and guaranteed that it could not be abolished without congressional approval.

Despite these structural changes, human rights officials had little impact on policy determination during the Nixon-Ford administration. The initial coordinator, James M. Wilson, Jr., was noted for his low visibility during his brief tenure. Most of his first year in office was devoted to the problem of Vietnamese refugees; thereafter he spent much of his time attempting to convince Congress not to pass human rights legislation. In his only public statement on human rights and diplomacy, he offered an opinion of diplomatic interaction which differed not at all from that of his colleagues in ARA: "In every instance . . . human rights problems are likely to be a unique result of a special set of circumstances. There will be few general prescriptions that will apply equally well to all countries. A case-by-case approach . . . is essential. . . . bilateral diplomacy remains the basic weapon for promotion of human rights. . . . This requires deft diplomacy of the highest order. We have to retain contact and influence and yet try to persuade governments who feel fiercely besieged [by terrorists]."[36] Responding to congressional demands for an activist human rights policy that would include the use of a variety of foreign policy tools, Wilson urged instead that the United States concentrate upon "quiet and friendly persuasion" to combat human rights abuses.[37]

At the initiative of the House of Representatives, in mid-1977

Human Rights and U.S. Foreign Policy, Publication 8959 (Washington, D.C.: Department of State, December 1978).

[35] State informed Representative Fraser of its intentions in August 1974. The first coordinator actually started work in June 1975.

[36] U.S. Congress, Senate, Committee on Foreign Relations, *Foreign Assistance Authorization: Arms Sales Issues*, 94th Cong., 1st Sess., June, November, and December, 1975, pp. 465-466.

[37] Interview with James M. Wilson, December 15, 1978, Washington, D.C.; *Foreign Assistance Authorization: Arms Sales Issues*, p. 467, *supra* n. 36. Wilson was never confirmed by the Senate, and his only scheduled appearance before Congress was cancelled due to lack of time and perhaps interest on the part of the senators involved. As a reward for a job that they considered poorly done, Carter administration officials exiled Wilson, an FSO-1, to the Education and Relocation staff. Wilson is remembered by several ARA officials as the person who helped to block the issuance of a visa to Peruvian political activist Hugo Blanco.

Congress included in its Foreign Relations Authorization Act (PL95-105) an amendment upgrading the position of the coordinator to that of an assistant secretary of state, a move that was strongly endorsed by the Carter administration. HA quickly became the center of human rights activities in American foreign policy and an unusually aggressive State Department bureaucracy. Most of HA's considerable bureaucratic strength stemmed, of course, from President Carter's emphasis upon the international protection of human rights, an emphasis that was most evident in United States policy toward Latin America. Because of this commitment, HA's staff grew by both quantitative and qualitative measures. The two-person staff under the Ford administration was almost immediately augmented by five new human rights officers, and further additions were made as needs became identified. By the end of 1978, HA had at least one expert covering each aspect of United States policy toward Latin America.

In qualitative terms, two Carter appointees were particularly significant. As the first assistant secretary of state for human rights and humanitarian affairs, Patricia Derian set the tone of HA's activities. A civil rights activist, a founder of the Mississippi Civil Liberties Union, and an organizer of the biracial Loyalist Mississippi Democratic Party that successfully challenged the all-white Mississippi delegation for seating at the 1968 Democratic party convention, Ms. Derian is a person of unusually strong will. If President Carter wanted an assistant secretary who could present forcefully the case for human rights and who was not intimidated by established bureaucratic procedures, there could have been few better choices than Derian.[38] Until early 1980, her principal associate was Mark Schneider, the deputy assistant secretary for human rights. Through Schneider, HA enjoyed extremely close relations with several members of Congress who had been working for years to enlarge the human rights component of U.S. foreign policy. A former Peace Corps volunteer with service in El Salvador, Schneider had served as an aide to Senator Edward Kennedy, where he performed most of the staff work that resulted in a number of Senate-sponsored hearings, resolutions, and laws on repression in post-Allende Chile.

Under Derian, HA concentrated upon building its staff and its

---

[38] Derian was criticized by human rights activists for conceding on some issues. In 1978, for example, she defended the Carter administration's aid request for the very repressive Marcos government in the Philippines because, as she told Congress, "the Philippine bases are of vital importance to the security of the United States." U.S. Congress, House, Committee on Appropriations, Subcommittee on Foreign Operations and Related Agencies, *Foreign Assistance and Related Agencies Appropriations for 1979*, 95th Cong., 2d Sess., 1978, pt. 2, p. 444.

expertise in specific policy areas such as foreign aid. But interspersed with these activities was an ongoing attempt at direct bilateral diplomacy on behalf of human rights, including a number of meetings with the leaders of Latin America's most repressive governments. Unlike officials at ARA, whose démarches and private conversations expressed profound concern over human rights violations but never went so far as to offend foreign leaders, HA was willing to push the issue beyond the bounds of normal diplomatic intercourse. Derian characterized her diplomatic conversations with leaders of repressive governments as "a very serious kind of thing. It's not just talk. It is always extremely tense."[39] She was one of the few United States diplomats to elaborate publicly upon her discussions:

> What happens is that we begin a meeting, and this is at the official level, with long statements about the concern and affection and importance of human rights to the country involved. All countries say that they are great defenders of and believers in human rights. Then we have a kind of pause in the discussion and they explain whatever the crisis is in the country that causes them to violate human rights. No country really admits it is a human rights violator. All countries, or representatives of countries, profess to care as much as we do. They often hold up their own constitutions and pronounce them better than ours. Then they explain their crisis, which threatens their society, and next say that as soon as they get on the other side of this crisis they will begin to observe human rights again, but during this interval it is necessary for them to take extraordinary measures.
>
> Then I talk respectfully about what they mean by extraordinary measures. There is ordinarily a great breakthrough because I use the word "torture" in places where this is applicable, and it is applicable in far too many places. I talk about the specific kinds that they do, the names of places where people are detained, the names of people who are missing, the names of people who are no longer in detention but are not [at liberty], who have suffered various kinds of abuses and mistreatment.
>
> Then we come to a kind of reality facing. Mostly an explanation that they are not responsible, that we have to understand things are so terrible and intense in the place that people at a lower level are moved by their own overriding emotions to take these actions on their own. Then I talk about responsibility. If you hold high office you must take the full responsibility and the

[39] "Foreign Policy and Human Rights," speech to the National Foreign Policy Conference on Human Rights, Washington, D.C., February 27, 1978.

blame. Then we generally start all over again and go through the whole thing again. That is generally the end of the first encounter.[40]

To Latin American leaders accustomed to exchanges with United States diplomats who emphasize the maintenance of smooth relations, Ms. Derian's brand of quiet diplomacy must have come as a surprise.

Multilateral Diplomacy

In addition to their bilateral activities, United States diplomats worked through the United Nations and the Organization of American States to implement U.S. policy toward human rights in Latin America during the 1970s. For most of the Cold War period, however, multilateral diplomacy has not been a favored tool of American policy makers. In 1974, Louis Henkin lamented that "the United States has remained largely outside the international human rights program. It has been for this country a peripheral aspect of its United Nations activities, themselves increasingly peripheral, and conducted by officials peripheral to the seats of power and the major concerns of United States foreign policy."[41] This is not to suggest that the United States has always ignored the United Nations in addressing its human rights concerns; indeed, the United States dominated the early human rights activities of the U.N., providing the major impetus for the human rights provisions of the Charter and much of the initiative for the Universal Declaration of Human Rights and the Genocide Convention. In addition, the United States was instrumental in urging the creation of the U.N. Commission on Human Rights, and it enjoys an excellent but largely unrecognized record of sponsoring improvements in the Commission's procedures. Given the Cold War attitudes of American policy makers and the decline of United States hegemony in the United Nations, it was probably inevitable that U.S. participation in multilateral human rights activities peaked early. Still, the decline in United States interest in multilateral diplomacy to protect human rights was impressive in its dimensions.[42] The nadir was reached during the Nixon administration.

The general policy of the Nixon-Ford administration toward human rights issues in the United Nations was to protect American allies

[40] Quigley et al., *U.S. Policy on Human Rights in Latin America (Southern Cone)* pp. 53-54.

[41] Louis Henkin, "The United States and the Crisis in Human Rights," *Virginia Journal of International Law* 14 (Summer 1974): 666.

[42] The best analysis by far of United States policy toward human rights issues in intergovernmental organizations through 1970 is Vernon Van Dyke, *Human Rights, the United States, and World Community* (New York: Oxford University Press, 1970).

from criticism.[43] Since the only major Latin American human rights issue to arise in the U.N. during the 1970s was that of Chile, it is upon this single case that the entire record of the Nixon-Ford administration stands. There is some question as to the content of that position. In his March 1976 testimony before Congress, Secretary of State Kissinger asserted that at his direction the United States "voted in the United Nations with the majority on the issue of human rights in Chile."[44] Contrary to the impression Kissinger may have left with Congress, what he must have meant by this statement is not that the United States consistently voted with the majority or that it regularly voted with the majority but that it *once* voted with the majority. The record is fairly unambiguous, and it indicates that the Nixon-Ford administration obstructed the efforts of the United Nations to assess the situation in Chile and to promote increased respect for human rights. This position appears congruent with other aspects of that administration's policy toward post-Allende Chile.

To begin, in early 1974 the Social Committee of the U.N. Economic and Social Council (ECOSOC) adopted its first resolution on Chile, a mild statement calling upon the government of Chile to "restore and safeguard basic human rights." The measure passed by a vote of 41 to 0, with two abstentions: Chile and the United States. The resolution was then passed to the parent ECOSOC, where it was adopted by consensus. According to one active observer, California Supreme Court Justice Frank Newman, in the ECOSOC deliberations, the contribution of the United States to the resolution "was to make it as weak as conceivable."[45]

[43] Thus, for example, in 1972, the United States, with the United Kingdom, South Africa, and Portugal, opposed seven of the eight General Assembly resolutions on southern Africa and colonialism, and it abstained on the eighth. *International Protection of Human Rights*, p. 168, *supra* n. 1. The Nixon protectionist policy continued into the Ford administration, as demonstrated by the December 1976 vote against a resolution to investigate the annexation of East Timor by Indonesia. See U.S. Congress, House, Committee on International Relations, Subcommittees on International Organizations and on Asian and Pacific Affairs, *Human Rights in East Timor and the Question of the Use of U.S. Equipment by the Indonesian Armed Forces*, 95th Cong., 1st Sess., March 23, 1977, p. 17.

[44] U.S. Congress, House, Committee on International Relations, *Report of Secretary of State Kissinger on His Trip to Latin America*, 94th Cong., 2d Sess., March 4, 1976, p. 20.

[45] U.S. Congress, House, Committee on Foreign Affairs, Subcommittee on International Organizations and Movements, *Review of the U.N. Commission on Human Rights*, 93d Cong., 2d Sess., 1974, pp. 42, 92; U.S. Congress, House, Committee on Foreign Affairs, Subcommittees on Inter-American Affairs and on International Organizations and Movements, *Human Rights in Chile*, 93d Cong., 2d Sess., December 1973 and May-June 1974, p. 130; Salzberg and Young, "The Parliamentary Role in Implementing International Human Rights," pp. 258-259.

In October 1974, the General Assembly's Social, Cultural and Humanitarian Committee voted 83 to 9 to urge the Chilean government to restore human rights and to free political prisoners. The United States abstained. The following month, the General Assembly passed two resolutions on human rights in Chile. One called upon the government of Chile "to release all persons who have been detained without charge or imprisoned solely for political reasons." The resolution passed by a vote of 90 to 8. The United States abstained, calling the resolution "unbalanced." The second resolution requested freedom for Clodomiro Almeyda, Chile's foreign minister under Allende and the president of UNCTAD III. Again the United States abstained.

Finally, on November 11, 1975, the United States voted with the majority on an issue of human rights in Chile, when the General Assembly's Social, Cultural and Humanitarian Committee recommended by a vote of 88 to 11 that the General Assembly express its "profound distress at the constant, flagrant violations of human rights, including the institutionalized practice of torture" in Chile.[46] This vote occurred as part of a broader effort by the Ford administration to distance itself from the Pinochet government. The Chilean junta was a particularly vulnerable target for a variety of reasons: its unusual brutality, its 1975 decision to support (and later abstain on) the U.N. resolution equating Zionism with racism, its refusal to permit a U.N. human rights investigating team to enter Chile, and its repression of all domestic political opposition. Of additional consequence was the negative connotations of an association with the Chilean junta during the upcoming United States presidential contest and, perhaps, a belief that the United States should speak out on the issue of human rights abuses.

Thus in his June 8, 1976, speech to the foreign ministers of the OAS, Secretary of State Kissinger addressed the subject of human rights with unusual frankness. Although he noted the conclusion of the Inter-American Commission on Human Rights that "the infringement of certain fundamental rights in Chile has undergone a quantitative reduction" and that "Chile has filed a comprehensive and responsive answer [to the Commission's charges of institutionalized torture] that sets forth a number of hopeful prospects," he expressed the dismay of the U.S. government that violations continued to occur: "In the United States, concern is widespread in the executive branch,

[46] Salzberg and Young, "The Parliamentary Role in Implementing International Human Rights," pp. 260-261; U.S. Congress, Senate, Committee on the Judiciary, Subcommittee to Investigate Problems Connected with Refugees and Escapees, *Refugee and Humanitarian Problems in Chile, Part III*, 94th Cong., 1st Sess., October 2, 1975, pp. 106-108; *New York Times*, November 7, 1974, p. 6.

in the press, and in the Congress, which has taken the extraordinary step of enacting specific statutory limits on United States military and economic aid to Chile. The condition of human rights . . . has impaired our relationship with Chile and will continue to do so. We wish this relationship to be close, and all friends of Chile hope that obstacles raised by conditions alleged in the report will soon be removed."[47]

Except for the periodic vilification of Cuba, this was at the time the strongest formal statement any OAS member had made against the internal human rights violations by another member government. Aside from this activity in support of human rights in Chile, however, the Nixon-Ford administration demonstrated little interest in using multilateral diplomacy to promote the observance of human rights in Latin America or elsewhere.

In their use of multilateral diplomacy as a foreign policy tool to promote human rights, there is little to differentiate the Nixon-Ford and the Carter administrations. In the United Nations, the major difference was in the level of rhetoric. On March 17, 1977, President Carter chose the U.N. General Assembly for the site of his first major foreign policy speech as President. Although he spoke on several topics, his remarks were noted for their emphasis on human rights. To demonstrate his administration's commitment to human rights, the President signed and promised to seek Senate ratification of the two U.N. human rights covenants, and he continued his predecessors' attempts to obtain ratification of both the Genocide Convention and the Treaty for the Elimination of All Forms of Racial Discrimination. In addition, he pledged to support efforts by the United Nations to improve its human rights machinery. Specifically, he proposed moving the U.N.'s human rights division back to New York headquarters from Geneva, and he promised to support efforts to establish the post of U.N. high commissioner for human rights.

Beyond these initial activities, the Carter administration did not emphasize the use of the United Nations to promote respect for human rights in Latin America. This reflects in part a desire to address the issue of Latin American human rights violations in the OAS, where U.S. diplomatic power is far greater than in the United Nations. But even on non-Latin American human rights issues, the Carter administration appeared to view the United Nations as a relatively unimportant arena. For example, the administration continued the practice of appointing part-time representatives to the U.N. Commission on Human Rights. These individuals were often selected because they

[47] *Department of State Bulletin* 75 (July 5, 1976): 4.

were underemployed party loyalists, particularly recently defeated members of Congress, rather than experts in the field of human rights or persons with a significant influence upon United States foreign policy. In the area of human rights, the Carter administration initiated little of significance in the United Nations.[48]

Less than a month after his initial speech to the U.N. General Assembly, President Carter gave his first address to the Permanent Council of the Organization of American States. Unlike some of his predecessors who have taken advantage of their initial appearance at the OAS to announce a new Latin American policy, President Carter's speech was basically a catalogue of problems affecting inter-American relations, nearly all of which were economic in nature. Special emphasis was placed upon human rights, however. He told the delegates that "our values and yours require us to combat abuses of individual freedom, including those caused by political, social, and economic injustice. Our own concerns for these values will naturally influence our relations with the countries of this hemisphere and throughout the world. You will find this country eager to stand beside those nations which respect human rights and promote democratic values."[49] In addition to this relatively mild statement, the President signed the American Convention on Human Rights on June 1, 1977.

The Carter administration's use of the OAS to encourage respect for human rights can best be pictured as an extension of the policy begun in 1976 by the Ford administration. Its major effort occurred in mid-June 1977, at the organization's seventh general assembly on the Caribbean island of Grenada. The human rights issue totally dominated the meeting. Secretary of State Vance went far beyond the Kissinger statement at Santiago in 1976, presenting a strong rebuttal to the popular contention that human rights abuses were a necessary part of the war against terrorism. In addition, the United States cosponsored (and helped obtain the necessary votes for) a resolution that stated in part that "there are no circumstances which justify

[48] This is not to suggest that no progress was made in the U.N. during the Carter administration. For a review of the administration's record, see U.S. Congress, House, Committee on Foreign Affairs, Subcommittee on International Organizations, *Review of the 35th Session of the United Nations Commission on Human Rights*, 96th Cong., 1st Sess., April 9, 1979. Overall, however, little dramatic progress was made. This led most human rights activists to agree with one analysis of the Carter administration's record in international organizations: "One can only regret that more leadership has not been shown to date and only hope that more will be forthcoming in the future." Frederic S. Pearson, J. Martin Reynolds, and Keith E. Meyer, "The Carter Foreign Policy and the Use of International Organization: The Limits of Policy Innovation," *World Affairs* 142 (Fall 1979): 94.

[49] *Department of State Bulletin* 76 (May 9, 1977): 454.

torture, summary executions or prolonged detention without trial contrary to law."[50] The Secretary of State then proceeded to link the provision of United States foreign assistance to the recipient's level of respect for human rights, noting that aid would be useless in an environment of extreme repression. Finally, Vance met privately with the foreign ministers of nearly all OAS member states, urging the representatives of repressive regimes to take seriously his public comments. Each of these statements was a significant extension of the human rights policy of the preceding administration.

But beyond this initial effort in 1977, multilateral diplomacy through the OAS did not become a prominent tool to implement United States policy toward human rights. OAS members soon became aware that the Inter-American Commission on Human Rights was fully supported by the United States and that the reports of the Commission could no longer be ignored as they had been for years. The necessary resolutions and declarations were made; there was little more that the OAS could do to promote human rights. There was never a question about the possibility of the OAS punishing an individual member, for most Latin American governments have always considered the level of respect for human rights an internal political matter. In addition, many nations were understandably suspicious of the role of the United States in the human rights effort. One need not know much about U.S.-Latin American relations to recognize why Latin Americans might be wary of the motivations behind yet another United States crusade in Latin America. So while Latin America's repressive regimes could not prevent the United States and several hemispheric allies from making human rights the major issue in the OAS, they could make concrete action extremely difficult to accomplish.

Recognizing this reality, the Carter administration decided to invest its diplomatic resources in bilateral efforts to promote human rights in Latin America. And, as the preceding pages have attempted to demonstrate, bilateral diplomatic activity on the issue of human rights in Latin America changed substantially in both substance and implementation. Nevertheless, it is possible to contend that the change was merely cosmetic, that words are cheap, and that the fundamental values orienting United States policy, particularly the maintenance of hegemony, remained unaffected. What changed during the 1970s, some critics might suggest, was the need for the United States to support repressive regimes in the major countries of Latin America.

[50] The resolution passed by a vote of 14 to 0, with 8 abstentions (Argentina, Brazil, Colombia, Chile, El Salvador, Guatemala, Paraguay, and Uruguay) and 3 absences (Bolivia, Honduras, Nicaragua).

Were President Carter to have perceived a threat such as that which Lyndon Johnson discerned in Brazil or Richard Nixon sensed in Chile, perhaps values other than human rights would have characterized his administration's diplomatic activity in Latin America.

There is little in the preceding discussion to confirm or reject this hypothesis. By its nature, diplomacy is primarily a verbal interaction, mere words. The efficacy of the tool depends entirely upon the perceptions of repressive Latin American governments of the cost involved in ignoring the words. The words then have only a latent content. Diplomacy is the means whereby a threat is communicated, not the threat itself. The threats can be many: to reduce military and economic aid, to oppose loans in multilateral development banks, to interfere with private economic transactions, to initiate covert actions. Thus the test of whether any diplomatic initiative is genuine or cosmetic can only be determined by measuring the extent to which these threats are carried out when diplomacy is ignored. Until the data on the linkage between words and deeds are presented in the following chapters, it would be inappropriate to praise as humane or to denigrate as meaningless the Carter administration's diplomacy on behalf of human rights.

· 4 ·

ECONOMIC AID: PARTICIPANTS
AND PROCESSES

ALTHOUGH there are a variety of forms of concessional aid, in recent decades, most United States bilateral economic assistance has flowed to Latin America through the Agency for International Development (AID) and the Food for Peace program (PL480, a shortened title of the program's initial authorizing legislation, Public Law 83-480 of 1954).[1] Of the $346 million in economic aid that the United States provided Latin America in FY1977, for example, $187 million (54 percent) was from AID and $113 million (33 percent) was from the Food for Peace program. Over the first seventeen years of the Foreign Assistance Act period, 1961 to 1977, AID accounted for $6.75 billion (68 percent) and Food for Peace for $2.05 billion (21 percent) of the $9.9 billion in bilateral economic aid to Latin America.

United States economic aid to Latin America has fluctuated dramatically since World War II. During the era of postwar relief and the Marshall Plan (1946-1952), bilateral economic assistance to Latin America averaged $28 million per year. It consisted primarily of technical experts working in the areas of food production, health and sanitation, and education.[2] During the Mutual Security Act period

[1] Bilateral economic assistance is defined as official bilateral grants and loans on concessional terms for development purposes as designated by the Development Assistance Committee of the Organization for Economic Cooperation and Development. By this definition, the Peace Corps, refugee assistance, Inter-American Foundation projects, and the International Narcotics Control program are formally considered part of total U.S. bilateral economic assistance. Excluded from the category of bilateral economic aid are Export-Import Bank loans and guarantees, short-term credits under the Commodity Credit Corporation Charter Act, Overseas Private Investment Corporation direct loans, and private trade agreements under Title I of PL480.

[2] On the subject of economic aid to Latin America in the pre-1961 period, see William A. Brown and Redvers Opie, *American Foreign Assistance* (Washington, D.C.: Brookings Institution, 1953); Merle Curti and Kendall Birr, *Prelude to Point Four: American Technical Missions Overseas, 1838-1938* (Madison: University of Wisconsin Press, 1954); James G. Maddox, *Technical Assistance by Religious Agencies in Latin America* (Chicago: University of Chicago Press, 1956); Arthur T. Mosher, *Technical Cooperation in Latin American Argriculture* (Chicago: University of Chicago Press, 1957); and especially Philip M. Glick, *The Administration of Technical Assistance: Growth in the Americas* (Chicago: University of Chicago Press, 1957). Also of value is U.S. Congress, House, Select Committee on Foreign Aid, *Final Report on Foreign Aid*, 80th Cong., 2d Sess., 1948.

(1953-1961), economic aid to Latin America increased fivefold to an annual average of $149 million. Between passage of the Foreign Assistance Act of 1961 and 1978, bilateral economic assistance to Latin America averaged $619 million per year. The heyday of the aid program to Latin America occurred in the 1960s, during an era in which entire nations were targeted to be "showcases" for U.S.-directed economic development. As Congress discovered, creating such exhibits was not an inexpensive activity, particularly when a foreign war and a domestic war on poverty broke out and began to compete for scarce financial resources. Bilateral economic aid to Latin America peaked at $888 million in 1966 and since then has declined considerably. AID's $190 million obligation to Latin America in FY1977 was the lowest in the history of the Agency. Since then, AID expenditures in Latin America have increased somewhat: $233 million in FY1978 and $245 million in FY1979. For FY1980, the Carter administration requested $230 million; for FY1981, it requested $275 million. Throughout the 1960s and 1970s, Food for Peace shipments remained substantial, with fluctuations primarily reflecting the level of U.S. grain surpluses.[3]

PURPOSES OF ECONOMIC AID

The Development Assistance section of the Foreign Assistance Act of 1961 declared the purpose of the U.S. economic aid to be to assist "people of less developed friendly countries of the world to develop their resources and improve their living standards, to realize their aspiration for justice, education, dignity, and respect as individual human beings, and to establish responsible governments."[4] Congress made cosmetic changes in this statement during its major revisions of the Act in 1967 and 1973 (deleting, for example, the word "friendly"), but at the beginning of the 1980s the formal purpose of the program remained essentially unchanged.[5]

The goals of the second major component of economic aid, Food for Peace, are substantially different: to dispose of U.S. farm surpluses, including tobacco, and in the process to promote United States foreign

[3] These amounts are in current dollars. If they were adjusted to reflect their real purchasing value, the growth in aid since World War II would appear smaller and the decline since 1966 would appear much more substantial.

[4] PL87-195, Sec. 102.

[5] The current (1980) wording of this portion of the statement of policy asserts that economic aid is meant to "assist the people of less developed countries in their efforts to acquire the knowledge and resources essential for development and to build the economic, political, and social institutions which will meet their aspirations for a better life, with freedom, and in peace."

policy.[6] Over time, the self-serving language in a law funded by the annual foreign assistance appropriation act became something of an embarrassment to its author, Senator Hubert Humphrey, and in 1966, he obtained Congress's approval to broaden the goals to include combatting hunger and malnutrition.[7] Despite this and a few other minor changes, the basic purpose of PL480 remains what it was in 1954.

These formal statements of purpose are supplemented by a large number of legally binding congressional guidelines, including such goals as promoting "the involvement of the people in the development process" and encouraging other countries "to increase their contributions to development programs."[8] These are very general purposes, of course, and their direct pursuit occupies little of aid officials' time. But other congressional policy directives are so specific that they cannot be ignored. These directives vary widely, from attempts to implement Congress's notions of appropriate development policies ("assistance shall be utilized to encourage regional cooperation") to efforts to strengthen the U.S. economy ("assistance shall, whenever practicable, be constituted of United States commodities and services furnished in a manner consistent with other efforts of the United States to improve its balance of payments position"). These formal statements of policy do not exhaust the efforts by Congress to specify the purposes of the U.S. economic aid program, for a new foreign assistance authorization act is produced annually or biannually, and each provides aid officials with new orders or advice on the goals they should be pursuing.[9] Some of these amendments require the executive branch to take or to avoid taking a specified step, while others are strongly worded suggestions—"consideration shall be given to excluding aid to any country which . . ." or "it is the sense of the Congress that the President shall. . . ."

Given the cardinal rule that AID officials must always appear to heed the advice of the body that authorizes its existence, a congressional suggestion is really an order to do something or, critics argue,

[6] PL83-480, Sec. 2.

[7] PL89-808, Sec. 2(A).

[8] PL87-195, Sec. 102.

[9] From 1962 to 1969 the economic aid portion of the Foreign Assistance Act of 1961 was revised annually, after which time Congress initiated sporadic attempts to make authorizations on a biennial basis. There are no foreign assistance authorization acts for 1970, 1972, or 1976. In recent years, the law has been given new names: in 1975, 1977, and 1978, it was called the International Development and Food Assistance Act; in 1979, it was named the International Development Cooperation Act. All foreign assistance authorization acts essentially amend the original Foreign Assistance Act of 1961. Foreign aid appropriations continue to be made on an annual basis.

to seem to be doing something. Foreign aid is probably the most investigated activity of the federal government; consequently, as one former AID administrator noted, the Agency is "largely oriented toward defending itself against critics."[10] In particular, aid officials must endure an annual series of inquisitions by congressional committees, at the conclusion of which Congress alters the purpose of economic aid. In the FY1962 foreign aid appropriations bill, for example, Congress expressed its wish that "in the administration of these funds great attention and consideration should be given to those nations which share the view of the United States on the world crisis."[11] AID officials can be fairly certain that in hearings the following year the member interested in this amendment (in this case, Representative Otto Passman) will inquire about its implementation. If the member is someone who dislikes the aid program with a fervor most people reserve for mass murderers (as Otto Passman did), and if that member is chairperson of the House Appropriations Subcommittee on Foreign Operations (as Otto Passman was), then AID had better have a good answer. So AID has to assign people to follow "the world crisis" and to be prepared to explain what types of "attention and consideration" have been given to nations that share with the United States a common view of it. For those officials, the purpose of AID has been changed.

Some of these mandated changes are short-lived and therefore of limited influence upon aid programs, but others tend to persist indefinitely. Beginning in 1964 and continuing through the 1970s, for example, the foreign assistance appropriations bill annually required that no refugee assistance be provided to assist migration to any Western Hemisphere nation by "any person not having a security clearance based on reasonable standards to insure against Communist infiltration in the Western Hemisphere."[12] Not only did this provision severely hamper efforts to provide refugee assistance for Latin American dissidents, but, as in the case of "the world crisis," this provision ne-

---

[10] John Hannah in U.S. Congress, House, Committee on Appropriations, *Foreign Assistance and Related Agencies Appropriations for 1971*, 91st Cong., 2d Sess., March 18, 1970, pt. 2, p. 167. As part of their survival strategy, AID officials have developed a keen ability to stroke the egos of the appropriate members of Congress. Not atypical is AID administrator Herman Kleine's paean to Representative Dante Fascell in 1971: "I have in mind your own statement, Mr. Chairman, in Costa Rica before the Partners of the Alliance in which you pointed out considerably more eloquently—than I could possibly hope to—that Latin America is in the throes of a modernizing process." U.S. Congress, House, Committee on Foreign Affairs, Subcommittee on Inter-American Affairs, *New Directions for the 1970's—Part 2: Development Assistance Options for Latin America*, 92d Cong., 1st Sess., 1971, p. 93.

[11] PL87-329, Sec. 112.

[12] PL88-634 through PL95-481.

cessitated a diversion of resources, this time on a continuing basis, from the myriad other objectives that aid officials might have pursued.

In brief, a simple reading of the legislation governing U.S. aid programs reveals that economic aid is intended to be a multipurpose implement of foreign policy.[13] Certainly one purpose has been to increase the material well-being of poor people in the Third World, but there are other goals as well. A list of the most transparent non-developmental, "political" purposes would include aid to help allies in Latin America win elections (Chile in 1964), consolidate their government following the seizure of power (Brazil after 1964), and survive crises that threaten their continued exercise of power (the Dominican Republic after 1965, Bolivia after 1971). Aid has been used to purchase votes in intergovernmental bodies, particularly the OAS, to secure military base rights, and to obtain the help of foreign troops. Although in these cases aid is properly considered an inducement, under different circumstances economic assistance can serve as a stick as well as a carrot. According to Joan Nelson, at the extreme this has included the use of aid "to alter the composition of a government outside the context of elections."[14] Little has changed since Senator Frank Church noted more than a decade ago that "every kind of conduct by a foreign government that we view as mischievous ends up in some kind of penalty provision that is attached to the aid program."[15]

The evidence to support the claim that economic aid serves as a flexible instrument of foreign policy is now so massive that further

[13] Support for this assertion includes Edward S. Mason, *Foreign Aid and Foreign Policy* (New York: Harper and Row, 1964), p. 3; Joan M. Nelson, *Aid, Influence, and Foreign Policy* (New York: Macmillan, 1968), p. 23; William Reynolds Sanford, "The Decision-Making Process in the Alliance for Progress," Ph.D. dissertation, University of Southern California, 1972, p. 305; Abraham F. Lowenthal, "Foreign Aid as a Political Instrument: The Case of the Dominican Republic," *Public Policy* 14 (1965): 141-160.

[14] Nelson, *Aid, Influence, and Foreign Policy*, p. 93. See also President's Committee to Study the United States Military Assistance Program, *Composite Report* (Washington, D.C.: Government Printing Office, August 17, 1959), pp. 170-171.

[15] U.S. Congress, Senate, Committee on Foreign Relations, Subcommittee on Western Hemisphere Affairs, *Rockefeller Report on Latin America*, 91st Cong., 1st Sess., November 20, 1969, p. 31. It should be noted that the United States has no monopoly on the use of aid as a foreign policy tool. The highly respected Swedish aid program is equally predicated upon the notion that aid recipients must behave in the way the Swedish government deems appropriate. One critical commentator has asserted that the most distinctive feature of the Swedish aid program is "its moralistic and even sanctimonious tone." Goran Ohlin, "Swedish Aid Performance and Development Policy," in *European Development Policies*, ed. Bruce Dinwiddy (New York: Praeger, 1973), p. 56.

discussion simply serves to divert attention from the more important questions of whether this is desirable and, if it is, which foreign policy goals should enjoy primacy in determining the nature of the United States aid program.[16] One important response to this question came in the 1963 report of the Presidential Committee to Strengthen the Security of the Free World, which was chaired by General Lucius D. Clay. The Clay Committee focused upon the contribution of economic assistance to increased national security:

> There should be no doubt . . . of the great value of properly conceived and administered foreign aid programs to the national interest of the United States and of the contribution of the foreign assistance dollar in such programs to the service of our nation's security. We live in a world in which poverty, sickness, instability and turmoil are rife and where a relentless Communist imperialism manipulates this misery to subvert men and nations from freedom's cause. A foreign aid program is one instrument among many with which we and other developed countries adequately can afford and vigorously must use in the defense and advancement of free world interests.[17]

This view continues to be held by many influential members of Congress. For example, one of the reasons why the long-time (1959-1977) chairperson of the House Committee on Foreign Affairs, Thomas "Doc" Morgan, refused to separate the economic and military aid bill into two separate bills was that to him they both had the same purpose: "to prevent war and maintain our security."[18]

Given the existence of this perspective, it is not surprising that the aid program developed as a response to crises that were thought to threaten national security. Point Four was a direct response to the

[16] For some of the best evidence, see Charles H. Lipson, "Corporate Preferences and Public Policies: Foreign Aid Sanctions and Investment Protection," *World Politics* 28 (April 1976): 397; Steve Weissman, *The Trojan Horse: A Radical Look at Foreign Aid* (San Francisco: Ramparts Press, 1974), p. 11; Michael J. Francis, "La ayuda económica de Estados Unidos a América Latina como instrumento de control político," *Foro Internacional* 12 (April-June 1972): 433-452. Social science has made some progress in understanding the linkage between politics and economic aid since Hans Morgenthau noted in 1962 that "the very assumption that foreign aid is an instrument of foreign policy is a subject of controversy." Hans J. Morgenthau, "A Political Theory of Foreign Aid," *American Political Science Review* 56 (June 1962): 301.

[17] U.S. Committee to Strengthen the Security of the Free World (Clay Committee), *The Scope and Distribution of United States Military and Economic Assistance Programs* (Washington, D.C.: Department of State, March 20, 1963), p. 4.

[18] "Senate, House Committees Differ on Foreign Affairs," *Congressional Quarterly Weekly Report* 28 (November 20, 1970): 2828.

Greek and Turkish crises of 1947, the Alliance for Progress resulted at least in part from the crisis provoked by the Cuban revolution, and during the Cold War era the country-specific economic aid programs to Bolivia, Brazil, Colombia, the Dominican Republic, Indonesia, the Philippines, South Korea, South Vietnam, Taiwan, and Zaire were all responses to perceived challenges to national security. And these are only the cases about which the evidence is absolutely unequivocal. One searches in vain through the history of United States economic aid, from Lend-Lease through the Marshall Plan and the Mutual Security Act to the present day for an example of a major aid program being initiated without the accompanying rationale of enhancing national security. Beyond this core obligation to assist in protecting national security, economic aid programs have been used to carry out a variety of less-central tasks: the protection of investors, the promotion of trade, and, of course, the development of less-wealthy economies. In the 1970s, a further task, the promotion of human rights, was added to the list of aid's purposes. Before turning to that specific issue, however, we need to focus upon the governmental actors involved in aid decision making.

AID DECISION MAKERS

Executive Branch

An impressive number of actors are involved in the day-to-day operation of the various economic aid programs, from AID personnel overseas who help to formulate host-government requests, to the President who issues policy guidelines or, very infrequently, resolves disputes upon which his subordinates are deadlocked. Despite the existence of a highly pluralistic and often-fragmented bureaucratic process, however, the number of officials who control aid decision making in the executive branch are few.

In a formal sense, the Agency for International Development participates in nearly all economic aid decisions. Even when decisions are made at the highest levels of government, AID is at least consulted on policy changes.[19] This formal participation tends to mask the fact that the Agency's control over economic aid to Latin America, while never strong, decreased dramatically during the 1970s. Part of this decrease can be attributed to the perception by administration and congressional authorities that AID was incapable of managing economic development, a perception that encouraged the search for such alternative mechanisms as the multilateral development banks, the

[19] Policy changes linked to covert action are exceptions to this rule.

Inter-American Foundation, and private voluntary organizations to provide aid to Latin America. In addition, AID's influence over economic aid to Latin America declined as a result of the Agency's decision to "graduate" relatively wealthy countries. By 1980, AID had ended or was ending its programs in Argentina, Brazil, Chile, Colombia, Mexico, Uruguay, and Venezuela, and its programs in Ecuador and even Paraguay were very small. Multilateral development banks and the private sector had assumed the principal responsibility for the external financing of all the relatively wealthy Latin American countries. As a consequence, the number of AID employees worldwide plummeted from 27,000 in FY1968 to 8,733 in FY1979, with much of this reduction occurring in staffs assigned to Latin America. The AID mission in Brazil, once among the largest in the world, dropped from about 400 employees in late 1966 to about 200 in 1972; then it declined further to 62 in early 1977.[20] At the beginning of the 1980s, only a handful of AID employees remained in Brazil.

The Bureau of Inter-American Affairs is another aid-related bureaucracy that experienced a decline in prestige and power in the 1970s, but throughout the decade it maintained a major influence over economic aid to Latin America. ARA's influence has always been difficult to isolate and examine, however, because it is exerted through such informal channels as budget meetings and discussions between State Department country directors and AID officials. It is probably correct to assert that ARA has always held a veto over any executive branch economic aid proposal that originates, as virtually all proposals do, at the assistant secretary level and below. The Bureau's opinion is often solicted but not always heeded on proposals originating above this level or in the Congress. ARA does not have the power to force its own aid proposals upon either the Department of State or the executive branch; its power is essentially negative in that it can block most aid proposals. Whenever it wishes to initiate a program, the Bureau is subject to a number of checks from competing bureaucracies.

For a variety of somewhat peculiar reasons, in the late 1970s the Bureau of Human Rights and Humanitarian Affairs became AID and ARA's most obvious executive branch rival in decision making on economic aid to Latin America. Most of HA's considerable bureaucratic strength reflected President Carter's emphasis upon the international protection of human rights. At the same time, AID and ARA chose to pursue a policy of not permitting human rights violations to interfere with "normal" relations, including the provision of economic

[20] John W. Tuthill, "Operation Topsy," *Foreign Policy*, no. 8 (Fall 1972), pp. 62-85.

aid. Thus both AID and ARA were out of step with the Carter administration's policy at exactly the time that HA was cutting its bureaucratic teeth, and it cut them by gnawing on economic aid programs to Latin America. Specifically, in 1977 HA demanded and obtained the right to review all aid proposals. Once included in the decision-making process, HA could issue a reservation by refusing to "sign off" on any proposal. Because of its status as a bureau—the organizational equivalent of ARA—HA could thereby force any decision up to a higher level, which in the case of economic aid was the Interagency Committee on Human Rights and Foreign Assistance, chaired by deputy secretary of state Warren Christopher. This ability to affect policy by refusing to agree to proposals was exploited with such vigor that by 1978 HA had become a major influence upon the size and nature of United States assistance programs to Latin America.

Although issues of economic aid to Latin America have an extremely low priority in United States foreign policy, on occasion the President becomes involved directly in aid decision making. The President sets the general tone of an administration's economic assistance programs. President Kennedy's support for the Alliance for Progress and President Carter's promotion of human rights are examples of presidential initiatives that profoundly influenced the amount and direction of aid. There are also instances when the President makes decisions on very specific issues of aid to Latin America, but when this occurs the issues generally reflect a national security concern rather than an interest in foreign aid. For example, in 1962 President Kennedy's desire to forestall "an actual or potential threat of internal subversion or insurgency" led him to order AID to "initiate the necessary studies and interdepartmental coordination looking toward early establishment of an international police academy under Government management."[21] Following the 1970 Chilean elections, President Nixon met with National Security Advisor Kissinger, Attorney General Mitchell, and CIA Director Helms on September 15, 1970 to determine his administration's policy toward Chile. According to the now-famous notes Mr. Helms took during the meeting, one decision was to "make the economy scream," a decision implemented in part by an aid embargo.[22]

In addition to AID, ARA, HA, and the President, a variety of other executive branch bureaucracies influences decisions on bilateral

[21] National Security Action Memorandum #177, August 7, 1962.

[22] A photocopy of Helms's handwritten notes is included in U.S. Congress, Senate, Select Committee to Study Governmental Operations with Respect to Intelligence Activities, *Intelligence Activities*, vol. 7, 94th Cong., 2d Sess., December 4 and 5, 1975, p. 96.

economic aid. The National Security Council staff, the Department of Agriculture, the Office of Management and Budget (OMB), and several additional bureaus within the State Department, particularly the Bureau of Economic and Business Affairs, all have opportunities to influence economic aid policies. The Department of Agriculture chairs the interdepartmental committee on Food for Peace, for example, and so monopolizes the available information on agricultural supplies that it holds a de facto veto over the size of the PL480 program. OMB stands in the middle of the path between all aid agencies and the congressional appropriations committees. Given the general tendency for Presidents to support OMB's decisions to reduce slightly the size of the aid budget—typical was the FY1979 reduction from AID's request for $1.78 billion to $1.65 billion—and the near-certainty that Congress will further reduce rather than increase aid requests, a decision by OMB in effect limits the size of the aid budget. Overall, however, the influence of these bureaucratic actors is significantly less than those who have been given the primary responsibility for creating and implementing the executive branch's policies on economic aid to Latin America. While their influence cannot be ignored, neither should it be overemphasized. The power to make governmental decisions on economic aid is not as widely dispersed as a list of the participating executive bureaucracies would suggest.

As part of his administration's reorganization plan, in 1979 President Carter created a new bureaucracy—the International Development Cooperation Agency (IDCA)—to coordinate most economic aid programs. In the remaining years of the Carter administration, IDCA served as a supervisory agency for AID, the Overseas Private Investment Corporation, U.S. participation in United Nations aid programs, and in certain aspects of six multilateral development banks. Overall, however, this change was simply procedural: IDCA replaced the State Department as the bureaucracy that channeled AID's budget requests.

Congress

As in most matters of federal policy, in economic aid there are two authorities, the executive branch and the Congress. As a result, the United States often has two economic aid policies, one reflecting the wishes of Congress and the other responding to the goals of the administration; most often, policy is a single compromise between what the President desires and what Congress will permit. History indicates that the President can circumvent the restrictions and guidelines imposed by Congress, especially in cases of perceived crises, but in the day-to-day operation of the various assistance programs, Congress exerts a signficant influence upon the direction and scope of the nation's aid. Nowhere has this influence been used more successfully than in promoting the issue of human rights.

Although the volume and scope of legislation on foreign aid is prodigious, only a few congressional actors are involved in economic aid decision making. There is no sizable bloc of members supporting aid, and the opponents of foreign assistance programs are primarily conscientious objectors to all nondefense federal spending who periodically focus their attention on economic aid legislation. Indicative of this general indifference is the fact that between 1961 and 1976, when Congress revised its budget procedures, not once could the body muster the energy to complete work on the aid appropriations bill before the beginning of the fiscal year for which it was to apply. In 1972 and again in 1975, there were no foreign aid appropriations bills until March, three months before the end of the fiscal year, in 1976, the appropriations bill became law on the last day of the fiscal year, and FY1980 ended before Congress could pass the appropriations bill.[23]

Despite this low level of concern, foreign aid legislation has become Congress's principal instrument for making foreign policy toward the Third World. By 1979, the original Foreign Assistance Act of 1961 had become an extraordinarily complex 160-page document, with each page containing at least half a dozen instructions to the executive branch. Some of this legislation concerns specific recipient nations or even specific projects within a specific country, but in general Congress concentrates upon broad questions of policy and especially upon the level of aid appropriations.[24] The issue of appropriations is often unclear, however, since questions of foreign policy easily become confused with those that relate to frugality. It is not unusual for Congress to slash the administration's foreign aid request by anywhere from 10 percent to 40 percent, and it is certain that these cuts would be even deeper were it not true that aid to Israel forms a large portion of the aid budget and were there not a continual series of national

[23] This tardiness typically reflects the inability of the managers to gather the votes necessary for passage of the bills. In addition, decisions on aid appropriations often must be deferred until disputes over authorizing legislation are resolved.

[24] In the early years of the aid program, Congress often expressed its disapproval of specific projects and countries in nonspecific terms. For example, Nelson notes that the FY1963 appropriations bill contained a general prohibition against any project costing more than $100 million, although the prohibition was designed to express disapproval of the state ownership of the proposed Bokaro steel mill in India. Nelson, Aid, Influence, and Foreign Policy, pp. 56-57. By the mid-1970s, this reluctance to be straightforward was overcome, and thereafter Congress often prohibited or reduced aid to specific countries.

145

security crises (Vietnam, Cambodia, Laos, Brazil, the Dominican Republic) to provide the rationale to combat further aid reductions. In the thirty-one years between World War II and 1979, Congress reduced the executive branch aid request by an average of 17.6 percent. In only one of those years did Congress fail to exercise its prerogative to cut the President's request.[25]

Traditionally, there are only one or two individual experts on Latin America in Congress. In the 1950s and 1960s, the principal Latin Americanists were Senators Bourke Hickenlooper and Wayne Morse. In the 1970s, Representative Dante Fascell was the only one of 535 members who could claim to be reasonably conversant on most of the major issues of U.S.-Latin American relations. From 1969 to 1974, Fascell was chairperson of the House Foreign Affairs Subcommittee on Inter-American Affairs. But when the committee abolished regional subcommittees as part of its reorganization in 1975, he became chairperson first of the now-defunct Subcommittee on Political and Military Affairs and then, when Wayne Hays was forced to resign from Congress in September 1976, of the Subcommittee on Foreign Operations, the most powerful subcommittee on the committee. Fascell declined to return to his former subcommittee when regional subcommittees were reestablished in 1977. Regardless of who was chairing the Subcommittee on Inter-American Affairs, however, during the 1970s Dante Fascell remained the key person in the House on issues affecting Latin America. Fascell held a reputation among his colleagues of being a skillful negotiator and an able legislative manager. He was, as one commentary suggested, "a man worth watching for those who enjoy seeing a legislative job well done."[26]

Ideologically, in the 1970s, Fascell was a liberal Democrat whose overall ADA rating fluctuated around 75 to 85, although on foreign policy issues he was fairly erratic. He opposed most human rights legislation. In 1975, he voted against passage of the Harkin amendment to forbid economic aid to countries with governments that consistently violate their citizens' human rights. In 1976, he voted for an amendment to prohibit military sales to Chile. In 1977, he opposed all three major human rights initiatives, voting against an amendment to require U.S. representatives to multilateral development banks to oppose loans to repressive governments, against an amendment to prohibit funds to Argentina for military training, and for an amend-

[25] U.S. Department of State, Agency for International Development, *Congressional Presentation Fiscal Year 1980* (Washington, D.C.: Agency for International Development, 1979), main vol., p. 198.

[26] Michael Barone, Grant Ujifusa, and Douglas Matthews, *The Almanac of American Politics 1978* (New York: E. P. Dutton, 1977), p. 185.

TABLE 4.1
APPROPRIATION HISTORY FOR ECONOMIC ASSISTANCE, FY1948-FY1979
(millions of dollars)

Fiscal Year	Appropriation Request	Appropriated by Congress	Percentage of Request Appropriated
1948-49	$7,370.0	$6,446.3	87.5%
1950	4,280.2	3,728.4	87.1
1951	2,950.0	2,262.5	76.7
1952	2,197.0	1,540.4	70.1
1953	2,499.0	1,782.1	71.3
1954	1,543.2	1,301.5	84.4
1955	1,788.5	1,528.8	85.5
1956	1,812.8	1,681.1	92.7
1957	1,860.0	1,749.1	94.0
1958	1,964.4	1,428.9	72.8
1959	2,142.1	1,933.1	90.2
1960	2,330.0	1,925.8	82.7
1961	2,875.0	2,631.4	91.5
1962	2,883.5	2,314.6	80.3
1963	3,281.3	2,573.9	78.5
1964	3,124.6	2,000.0	64.0
1965	2,461.7	2,195.0	89.2
1966	2,704.5	2,463.0	91.1
1967	2,469.0	2,145.5	86.8
1968	2,630.4	1,895.6	72.1
1969	2,498.5	1,380.6	55.3
1970	2,210.0	1,424.9	64.5
1971	2,008.0	1,733.9	86.4
1972	2,355.2	1,718.2	73.0
1973	2,256.6	1,644.2	73.7
1974	1,884.2	1,632.6	86.7
1975	2,948.7	2,049.8	69.5
1976	3,216.5	3,168.9	98.5
1977	3,328.1	3,156.6	94.9
1978	3,531.6	3,750.0	106.2
1979	3,863.0	3,718.2	96.2

SOURCE: Agency for International Development.
NOTE: Amounts include all economic assistance under the Foreign Assistance Act of 1961 and predecessor legislation, excluding funds for International Narcotics Control, Investment Guaranty Program, and Overseas Private Investment Corporation.

ment to restore military aid funds to Nicaragua that had been deleted in committee.[27] And although in the past he urged the government

[27] The 1975 vote was on H.R. 9005, September 10; the 1976 vote was on H.R. 13680, March 3; and the 1977 votes were on H.R. 5262, June 17, and on H.R. 7797, June 22 (Argentina) and 23 (Nicaragua). Despite his 1976 vote against aid to Chile, Fascell was reluctant to criticize either the Nixon administration's support of the

147

not to retaliate for expropriations of U.S. property by Latin American governments, he also provided persons who would do so with ammunition by offering his opinion that the motivation for nationalizations is nothing more than "political satisfaction."[28] In an earlier era, Fascell joined the anti-Castro hysteria that swept Congress. In 1961, it was his proposal that authorized the President to establish a total embargo on Cuban-U.S. trade. "The amendment," he announced to his colleagues who approved it without debate, "is very simple, very clear, and very necessary."[29]

The Foreign Affairs Committees. Most of the responsibility for Congress's contribution to United States policy toward Latin America rests with its foreign affairs committees: the House Committee on Foreign Affairs and the Senate Committee on Foreign Relations.[30] The two committees on appropriations also have a major foreign policy role, since they determine how much of the money authorized by the foreign affairs committees will actually be made available to the executive branch. Beyond these generalities, the question of committee jurisdiction is a constant feature of congressional foreign policy making. In the House, seventeen of the twenty-two committees deal with aspects of foreign policy, and all but three of the Senate's nineteen committees have some jurisdiction over foreign affairs. There is no single rule governing the procedures by which proposed bills are referred to one committee or another. Jurisdictional disputes are resolved by joint, consecutive, or simultaneous referrals.[31]

Pinochet regime or its destabilization of the Allende government. When Harry Shlaudeman, the deputy chief of the U.S. mission in Chile from 1969 to 1973, was called before the Committee on Foreign Affairs in June 1974, his responses to questions were (as subsequent investigations were to demonstrate) something less than candid. Fascell made a special effort to commend Shlaudeman. U.S. Congress, House, Committee on Foreign Affairs, Subcommittees on Inter-American Affairs and on International Organizations and Movements, *Human Rights in Chile*, 93rd Cong., 2d Sess., December 1973, May and June 1974, pp. 129, 137.

[28] See *New Directions for the 1970's*, p. 267, *supra* n. 10.

[29] *Congressional Record*, August 18, 1961, p. 16292.

[30] During the Ninety-fourth and Ninety-fifth Congresses (1975-1979), the Committee on Foreign Affairs was called the Committee on International Relations.

[31] For example, in the Senate, all "area" resolutions such as the Cuban resolution of 1962 and the Tonkin Gulf resolution of 1964 are referred jointly to the Committee on Foreign Relations and the Committee on Armed Services. The 1975 foreign aid authorization bill was referred consecutively to the Committee on Agriculture after being reported by Foreign Relations. Beginning in 1975, the Senate adopted the technique of simultaneous referral to expedite congressional action. In cases of simultaneous referral, a bill is not placed on the calendar for consideration by the full Senate until it has been reported by all committees. U.S. Congress, House, Committee on International Relations, Special Subcommittee on Investigations, *Congress and*

As a result of overlapping jurisdictions, some of the most important issues of United States policy toward Latin America are argued outside the foreign affairs committees. One study of the Ninety-third Congress (1973-1974) estimated that nearly 40 percent of the committee hearings on Latin America were held by nonforeign affairs committees.[32] In 1954, for example, the Export-Import Bank Act was revised to permit long-term loans for capital goods, a revision that has had an enormous impact upon trade between the United States and Latin America. The bill came out of the Senate Banking and Currency Committee, whose chairperson, Homer Capehart, had earlier conducted a study tour of Latin America to assess the potential impact of the proposed legislation.[33] In the House, the Banking Subcommittee on International Development Institutions and Finance is responsible for authorizing legislation related to United States participation in the Inter-American Development Bank and other multilateral development banks (MDBs). But the Committee on Foreign Affairs has oversight responsibility for the MDBs, i.e., it can hold hearings but has no jurisdiction over proposed changes in authorizing legislation. Another Banking subcommittee, this one on International Trade, Investment and Monetary Policy, enjoys jurisdiction over two institutions of major importance to U.S.-Latin American relations: the Export-Import Bank and the International Monetary Fund (IMF). In many cases, these jurisdictions reflect a logical division of labor based upon the nature of the subject, but in other cases jurisdictions are determined by extraneous factors that stop just short of caprice. The essential point, however, is that Congress makes an input into U.S. policy toward Latin America from many directions.

Within the two foreign affairs committees, there are a number of subcommittees that exercise authority over various aspects of U.S.-Latin American relations. During most of the 1970s, the House Committee on Foreign Affairs had eight subcommittees, four based on geography and four on functional aspects of foreign policy. Each of the latter had some authority over various aspects of United States

---

Foreign Policy, 94th Cong., 2d Sess., January 2, 1977, p. 20. For a comprehensive study of Senate committee jurisdictions, see U.S. Congress, Senate, The Senate Committee System: First Staff Report to the Temporary Select Committee to Study the Senate Committee System, 94th Cong., 2d Sess., July 1976.

[32] Robert A. Pastor, "Congress' Impact on Latin America: Is There a Madness in the Method?" in the Report of the Commission on the Organization of the Government for the Conduct of Foreign Policy, vol. 3, app. 1 (Washington, D.C.: Government Printing Office, June 1975), p. 261.

[33] R. Harrison Wagner, United States Policy toward Latin America: A Study in Domestic and International Politics (Stanford: Stanford University Press, 1970), pp. 101, 11-16, respectively.

policy toward Latin America. Thus efforts by the Subcommittee on Inter-American Affairs were supplemented by the oversight activities of the Subcommittees on International Economic Policy and Trade (Export-Import Bank, OPIC, MDBs, commodity agreements) and International Security and Scientific Affairs (military aid, foreign intelligence, arms control).[34] In many cases, the competition between regional and functional subcommittees was resolved by the technique of joint hearings. Studies of the OAS, for example, were typically a combined effort by the Subcommittees on Inter-American Affairs and International Organizations. On the other hand, during the Ninety-fifth Congress (1977-1978), the conservative Subcommittee on Inter-American Affairs regularly declined the invitation of the liberal Subcommittee on International Organizations to cosponsor hearings on human rights violations in specific Latin American countries. During previous years it had occasionally accepted such invitations.

The House Subcommittee on Inter-American Affairs is perhaps best known for its obscurity. With the exception of the period when Fascell was chairperson, during the 1960s and 1970s the subcommittee was almost completely peripheral to policy making on Latin America. Few people even noticed when it was disbanded during the Ninety-fourth Congress, and upon its revival in 1977 the subcommittee promptly reassumed the position it had cemented during the mid-1960s under Armistead J. Selden as the least prestigious foreign affairs subcommittee. Between 1977 and 1981, the subcommittee chairperson was Gus Yatron. He obtained his subcommittee post strictly on the basis of seniority, having had no prior interest in Latin America and having never been a member of the subcommittee. Ideologically, Yatron was typical of previous chairpersons: overall he was fairly conservative, with an ADA rating that fluctuated around 30 to 45; on issues of foreign policy, he was extremely conservative. If his 1977 ADA were computed only on the basis of foreign policy votes (and adjusted to retain the scale of 0 to 100), it would have been 14.

Frequent membership changes make it difficult to generalize over time about any House subcommittee, but the Ninety-fifth Congress

[34] A Subcommittee on International Development existed from 1977 to 1979, during which time its chairperson, Michael Harrington, was so far to the left of mainstream opinion in the House that his subcommittee posed no significant threat to the power of any other subcommittee. When Harrington resigned from Congress, committee chairperson Clement Zablocki abolished the subcommittee. In the 1970s, the Subcommittee on International Organizations, commonly referred to as the Fraser Subcommittee, enjoyed enormous influence as the center of the movement to incorporate human rights considerations into United States foreign policy. When Donald Fraser gave up his House seat in 1979 during the course of an unsuccessful bid for the Senate, he was replaced as subcommittee chairperson by Don Bonker.

was fairly typical for the Subcommittee on Inter-American Affairs, except that during this session the Subcommittee was composed of seven members, several fewer than in the past. Like its chairperson, it too tilted strongly toward the right. In support of Yatron's conservatism was Andy Ireland, Eligio (Kika) de la Garza, and Robert Lagomarsino, with 1977 ADAs of 15, 5, and 0, respectively. Benjamin Gilman normally professed moderate views (1977 ADA of 50), but his principal interest in the subcommittee—narcotics control—led him into an alliance with conservatives who promote a power politics approach toward all issues of U.S.-Latin American relations. Of the two remaining members, one (Fascell) was liberal and highly involved and the other (Cardiss Collins) was equally liberal but disinterested. She rarely attended meetings of the subcommittee for, as one of her aides put it, "a black woman representing Chicago's West Side has better things to do with her time." Although some members of the subcommittee had been to Latin America, only Fascell and de la Garza spoke Spanish. Of the seven, probably only Fascell could have completed a list of the countries of Latin America without the help of an atlas. In 1979, the subcommittee was expanded to nine members. A conservative Democrat (de la Garza) was replaced by an equally conservative Republican (Tennyson Guyer) but two new members (Benjamin Rosenthal and Gerry Studds) had very liberal 1978 ADAs of 90 and 95, respectively. Nonetheless, the conservatives (Yatron, Ireland, Gilman, Guyer, Lagomarsino) continued to outnumber the liberals. None of the new members was familiar with United States policy toward Latin America.

Throughout the 1960s and 1970s, the subcommittee concentrated upon aspects of inter-American relations that were believed to have a negative impact upon the United States. Its hearings were dominated by discussions of narcotics control, undocumented immigrants, and aid-financed competition for U.S. industries. Yatron was also particularly upset over Cuban activities in Africa and post-Somoza Nicaragua, just as before him Fascell worried about Cubans in Latin America.[35] In addition, the subcommittee stood solidly against efforts

[35] U.S. Congress, House, Committee on International Relations, *Foreign Assistance Legislation for Fiscal Year 1979*, 95th Cong., 2d Sess., March 1978, pt. 7, pp. 74-76, 92-99; U.S. Congress, House, Committee on Foreign Affairs, Subcommittee on Inter-American Affairs, *Assessment of Conditions in Central America*, 96th Cong., 2d Sess., April and May, 1980; U.S. Congress, House, Committee on Foreign Affairs, Subcommittee on Inter-American Affairs, *Impact of Cuban-Soviet Ties in the Western Hemisphere, Spring 1980*, 96th Cong., 2d Sess., March-May 1980. Fascell, too, was concerned about Cubans in Africa. See U.S. Congress, House, Committee on International Relations, *Foreign Assistance Legislation for Fiscal Year 1979*, 95th Cong., 2d Sess., February and March 1978, pt. 1, p. 61.

by the Carter administration and other members of Congress to promote respect for human rights by means other than quiet diplomacy. Although not all members of the subcommittee voted against the human rights legislation of the 1970s, none of the legislation originated in the subcommittee and, in addition, some subcommittee members were among the strongest opponents of human rights initiatives. In the June 1977 effort to cut military aid to Somoza's Nicaragua, for example, only Collins cast an anti-Somoza vote.

Chairperson Yatron was particularly opposed to human rights as a focus for United States policy toward Latin America. Yatron criticized Secretary of State Kissinger for his June 1976 statements against repression in Chile. He felt it odd that the Secretary would criticize a government "with which our relations have been at least cordial if not friendly" and warned that further comments by the administration would violate U.S. commitments to nonintervention in Latin America.[36] Yatron and Lagomarsino were the most enthusiastic supporters of assistant secretary of state Terence Todman. When Todman read his list of "don'ts" to chastise human rights proponents during the course of a speech at the Center for Inter-American Relations on February 14, 1978, Yatron called him before the subcommittee "to commend you for your statement that you made in New York." Lagomarsino added that "your conclusion, the list of things we should and should not do, makes a lot of sense,"[37] Shortly thereafter, Todman was fired for his opposition to an aggressive policy to protect human rights.

The subcommittee under Representative Yatron in the late 1970s was not substantially different from what it was in earlier years, for it has always tended to concentrate not upon the problems of Latin America but upon the issues related to Latin America that might threaten the United States. This perspective has had an important impact upon economic aid to the region. Note, for example, the values expressed during the course of a 1971 hearing on "Development Assistance Options for Latin America," when Representative Fascell inquired of the State Department whether there was any truth to the "rumors that a Cuban who at one time served under Castro is being considered for a position in the OAS. . . . There has been a good deal of sentiment in the Congress that as long as the U.S. is the chief contributor in financing the OAS, the man directly responsible for auditing and accounting should be a U.S. citizen. Do you believe that

[36] U.S. Congress, House, Committee on International Relations, *Report of Secretary of State Kissinger on His Visits to Latin America, Western Europe, and Africa*, 94th Cong., 2d Sess., June 17, 1976, p. 30.

[37] See *Foreign Assistance Legislation for Fiscal Year 1979*, pt. 7, p. 11, *supra* n. 35.

placing a Cuban citizen in such a job would detract from the concept of maintaining effective control by the U.S.?"[38]

The subcommittee also has a tendency to be petty, although that trait declined somewhat after H. R. Gross retired in 1974. Consider, for example, the following exchange during a hearing whose purpose, according to Fascell, was "to discuss multilateral assistance to Latin America":

> Mr. Gross. Am I correctly informed that the Germans loaned us $5 billion recently?
>
> Mr. Petty. [Assistant Secretary of the Treasury]. The Germans bought some special Treasury bonds. They have agreed to buy $5 billion. I am not sure they actually bought them yet.
>
> Mr. Gross. What interest rate? I will tell you. Six percent.
>
> Mr. Petty. It was calculated at the rate of 90-day bills at the time, or 180-day bills. It is about 6 percent. In other words, if the Treasury—
>
> Mr. Gross. Can I, an American, buy a Treasury bill today and get 6 percent?
>
> Mr. Petty. Yes, sir.
>
> Mr. Gross. Like hell I can.
>
> Mr. Petty. A Treasury bill, or a Treasury bond?
>
> Mr. Gross. A Treasury bill.
>
> Mr. Petty. They are probably just below 6 percent now. Our Treasury bonds are above 6 percent, and our Treasury notes are about 6 percent.
>
> Mr. Gross. I will bet you I can't get over 5¼ percent.
>
> Mr. Petty. I hope not. I would like to get the rate down.
>
> Mr. Gross. You are willing to pay the Germans, but you don't want to pay me or any other American.
>
> Mr. Petty. If we compare maturities of the German borrowing which is a 5-year note, with what it costs—
>
> Mr. Gross. I will be surprised if you got the Germans to take on a 5-year note.
>
> Mr. Petty. They just did.
>
> Mr. Gross. I don't think they did.[39]

That this type of discussion regularly occurred in the 1960s and 1970s during hearings on United States aid to Latin America is indicative of the subcommittee's hebetudinous character.

[38] The State Department replied that the individual in question had fled Cuba in early 1960, after breaking with the Castro government in 1959. See *New Directions for the 1970's*, p. 176, *supra* n. 10.

[39] Ibid., pp. 131, 95, respectively.

During most of the 1970s, the Senate Committee on Foreign Relations was divided into four functional subcommittees (Arms Control, Oceans, and International Environment; Foreign Assistance; Foreign Economic Policy; and International Operations) and five geographic subcommittees.[40] As in prior decades, these subcommittees were extremely weak. Proposed legislation, resolutions, treaties, and nominations have traditionally been considered by the full committee on the theory that most issues of foreign policy should not be divided by geographic or substantive content. In addition, the committee's long-time (1959-1975) chairperson, J. William Fulbright, viewed with considerable favor the notion of concentrating power in the chairperson. In the 1970s, exceptions to this rule were Frank Church's Subcommittee on Multinational Corporations (now International Economic Policy) and Hubert Humphrey's Subcommittee on Foreign Assistance. The latter subcommittee was created in 1975 at a time when it appeared that Senate support for foreign aid legislation had all but disappeared. Humphrey was asked to conduct studies and hearings that would lead to a reorganized aid program, and he agreed to accept the task only if given his own subcommittee staff and jurisdiction over foreign aid and MDB legislation. As a result, the Subcommittee on Foreign Assistance gained control over a number of issues affecting Latin America: AID programs, the Peace Corps, the Overseas Private Investment Corporation, and the MDBs. The Subcommittee on International Economic Policy obtained responsibility for the IMF and multinational corporations, leaving the Subcommittee on Western Hemisphere Affairs with the task of overseeing general relations with the American nations, including Canada, on such issues as boundary disputes, treaties, and the OAS. Its most important activity during the 1970s was assisting to secure Senate ratification of the Panama Canal treaties in 1978.

Under the leadership of John Sparkman during the human rights years of 1975 to 1979, the Senate Committee on Foreign Relations declined dramatically in both its activities and influence. In 1978, the *Almanac of American Politics* noted acerbically that "Sparkman is one who has seldom questioned what the Executive Branch was up to. Indeed, Sparkman seems to float almost obliviously through some meetings; and his main function now may be to prevent Frank Church . . . from taking control of the Committee's staff."[41] During his last

---

[40] From 1950 to 1975, the committee maintained consultative subcommittees—one for each assistant secretary of state. As the number of assistant secretaries expanded and the various tasks of foreign relations were dispersed among other executive departments, the arrangement had to be abandoned.

[41] Barone et al., *Almanac of American Politics 1978*, p. 2.

year in Congress, Sparkman took virtually no part in the Panama Canal debate, leaving most of the job of managing the treaties to Church, who assumed the committee chair in 1979. Church's record of activism on foreign policy issues—particularly his opposition to the Vietnam war and his prolonged investigations of both multinational corporations and the CIA—lent credence to his promise to restore the committee's traditional position of prominence, but the promise went unfulfilled.

The Subcommittee on Western Hemisphere Affairs (until 1969, American Republics Affairs) has generally enjoyed a number of advantages denied its counterpart in the House. In the 1970s, perhaps the most important of these was that it operated in a relatively sympathetic environment. While there was no senator whose expertise on Latin America rivaled that of Dante Fascell, there was a larger proportion of members with an interest in Latin America than existed in the House. Senators Chiles, Church, Javits, and Kennedy all had more than a passing knowledge of the region, and on certain issues—Kennedy on refugees and U.S.-Chilean relations, Church on multinational corporations and U.S.-Brazilian relations—they were acknowledged experts. In addition, many key senators had long been advocates of a more progressive, experimental policy toward Latin America. In 1960, Senator Mike Mansfield gave a major speech on Latin America in which he observed that "for anyone who knows the countries to the south and looks to the present and the future rather than to the past, I believe it is apparent that change is as desirable as it is inevitable. I do not think acquiescence in unnecessary misery and vicious repression and exploitation find any echo in the finest traditions of this Nation."[42] Senator Church, too, was a long-time proponent of a policy that addressed the central issues of Latin American politics. In 1960, for example, he told his colleagues that "you have got to have land reform. That means taking land away from a relatively small group of very wealthy people and distributing it to a great many peasants. That is an awfully hard thing to do when the government and the society in that country are controlled by those who own the land."[43] These are far different matters than those that relate to the rate of interest on Treasury bills sold to Germans or the reliability of an individual Cuban. At times during the 1970s, the Subcommittee on Western Hemisphere Affairs was petty and vindictive, but not with the same frequency and whimsicality that were hallmarks of the House Subcommittee on Inter-American Affairs.

[42] *Congressional Record,* August 8, 1960, p. 15947.
[43] U.S. Congress, Senate, Committee on Foreign Relations, *American Republics Cooperation Act and Other Subjects,* 86th Cong., 2d Sess., August 15, 1960, p. 78.

A previous advantage of the Senate subcommittee—its relative stability—was lost by the 1970s. Senators still do not come and go as rapidly as members of the House, however, and as a consequence the subcommittee has had a fairly stable membership, even though there were eight different chairpersons between 1953 and 1980. Bourke Hickenlooper led the subcommittee for two years when the Republicans were the majority party in the Senate (1953-1955), and he remained on the subcommittee until 1968. Parenthetically, it is perhaps unfortunate that his record is indelibly linked to an amendment that smacks of the Big Stick mentality, for his views on this subject were certainly no different than those held by the vast majority of his colleagues, and on some other subjects he antedated what many persons would consider progressive changes in Senate attitudes. He was a supporter of the Bolivian revolution of 1952—returning home from a trip to La Paz, he commented that if life were as hard and politics as corrupt in his home state there would have been a revolution in Des Moines long ago—and, unlike most senators, he was not enthusiastic about the covert activity in Guatemala that culminated in the overthrow of President Arbenz in 1954. He traveled widely in Latin America and studied it conscientiously.

Senator Hickenlooper was succeeded as subcommittee chairperson by Theodore Francis Green, whose age and other duties soon forced him to yield his position to the very liberal Wayne Morse. Morse, who led the subcommittee until he was defeated for reelection in 1968, was one of the very few members of Congress who attempted to keep the Alliance for Progress from becoming an anticommunist bludgeon. He too knew Latin America well, the last subcommittee chairperson of whom that statement can be made. Frank Church filled Morse's position, but then in 1972 he resigned to head the Subcommittee on Multinational Corporations. During his tenure as subcommittee chairperson, Church was not particularly interested in the job, and he made only limited attempts to learn about its subject. Church became involved in the issue of repression in Brazil, however, initiating the long series of congressional studies of the relationship between United States aid and the repression of human rights by the Brazilian government.

Church's replacement as subcommittee chairperson was Gale McGee, who served until he was defeated for reelection in 1976. Probably the most notable feature of the subcommittee during McGee's tenure was its inactivity.[44] McGee is remembered by many State De-

[44] The only major hearings by the subcommittee during this period were U.S. Congress, Senate, Committee on Foreign Relations, Subcommittee on Western Hem-

partment and congressional staff personnel as the person who worked to quiet the concern of a few Senate liberals (Abourezk, Kennedy, Cranston) over U.S.-Chilean relations in the 1970s. Senate hearings on United States policy toward postcoup Chile were held by Kennedy's Judiciary Subcommittee on Refugees because McGee refused to address the issue. In addition, Senator Church's Subcommittee on Multinational Corporations held the 1973 hearings on the ITT-Chile scandal, once again because McGee was uninterested in the subject.

The selection of Paul Sarbanes as subcommittee chairperson during the Ninety-fifth Congress (1977-1979) was indicative of the priority the Senate gives to Latin America. When Sarbanes entered the Senate in 1977, he joined nine other Democrats on the full Committee on Foreign Relations. There were nine subcommittees, none of which chairperson Sparkman wanted to lead, so Sarbanes immediately became a subcommittee chairperson, a position some members of the House wait a decade or more to obtain. And since none of the other nine Democrats wanted to chair the Subcommittee on Western Hemisphere Affairs, the member with the least seniority on the committee had to accept the task. While subcommittee chairperson, Sarbanes joined Frank Church in assuming the formidable task of ushering the Panama Canal treaties through the Senate. In the process, he demonstrated the extraordinary capacity for work that earlier had earned him a Rhodes scholarship. He never missed a hearing by the full committee, and during the months the treaties were before the Senate he was almost always present, answering questions, responding to criticisms, and demonstrating that he was a quick learner. Once the treaties were approved, the subcommittee became quiescent. Like Yatron, prior to 1977 Sarbanes had no experience whatever with U.S.-Latin American relations (during his six years in the House he won special praise for his work on committee reform and for his participation in the Nixon impeachment hearings) and, also like Yatron, he is a Greek-American who would have preferred any of the other eight subcommittees, a fact demonstrated by his move in 1979 to the Subcommittee on International Economic Policy. Sarbanes' replacement in the Ninety-sixth Congress, Senator Edward Zorinsky, was again the Democratic member of the Foreign Relations Committee with the least seniority.[45]

---

isphere Affairs, *U.S. Relations with Latin America*, 94th Cong.,1st Sess., February 1975.

[45] Although the subcommittee shares a low prestige rating with its counterpart in the House, in one respect during the 1970s it differed significantly: ideologically the Senate subcommittee has stood to the left of the House Subcommittee on Inter-American Affairs. In 1976, the mean ADA of its five members was 61, in 1977, it was 71, in 1978, 65—generally about twice the ADA of the House subcommittee.

Congress recognized long ago that the probability of unwise legislation would be greatest on issues of low salience to members and their constituents. "Above all," wrote Robert Dahl in 1950, "the Congressman lacks expert advice on policy. . . . It is probably fair to say that the future of Congress as a policy-making institution rests on its willingness and capacity for attaining and using the knowledge of experts."[46] Following Dahl's advice, the foreign affairs committees have sought to compensate for their lack of interest by hiring staff members to follow the issues and develop the expertise necessary to assist members to formulate coherent policy. Although this has proven to be a felicitous solution in some areas, in the area of United States policy toward Latin America it was a thorough failure during the 1970s, for the two foreign affairs committees persistently chose to employ persons who were either unfamiliar with or disinterested in Latin America.

The staff of the House Subcommittee on Inter-American Affairs has never been distinguished by its knowledge of Latin America or of U.S.-Latin American relations. When he assumed the subcommittee chair, Representative Yatron appointed as its staff director a person who had never been to Latin America, who neither spoke nor read Spanish or Portuguese, and who, in an interview nearly a year after assuming his post, displayed virtually no knowledge of the executive branch actors other than ARA that were responsible for creating and implementing United States policy toward Latin America. An example of how this basic lack of knowledge translates into poor staff work is the staff-submitted amendment to the FY1979 foreign assistance authorization bill that would have provided aid for military training of civilians:

> Mr. Lagomarsino. I have one question about the language you suggest we include regarding extension of the IMET [International Military Education and Training] program to civilian sectors. Could somebody inform me what we are possibly talking about there? How do we extend IMET to civilians?
> Mr. de la Garza. Where did it come from?
> Mr. Yatron. I believe the staff recommended it. . . . We have Mr. Herbert Gelber from the Foreign Service with us. Perhaps you would like to comment on this Mr. Gelber?

In February 1976, five of the Senate subcommittee's eight members voted to prohibit military sales to Chile, compared to only one anti-Pinochet vote on a similar amendment in the House in March 1976. The Senate subcommittee's ADA rating would have been 69 in 1976 had not Howard Baker joined the subcommittee and lowered its average with his ADA of 5. The next lowest ADA rating was 45, and four of the eight members were above 75.

[46] Robert A. Dahl, *Congress and Foreign Policy* (New York: Harcourt, Brace, 1950), pp. 138, 242.

Mr. Gelber. We have clearly no intention to use any such authority. . . . There is no proposal on our side to do this.[47]

In another example, when Representative Ireland voiced concern over the kidnapping in Venezuela of William Niehous, an Owens-Illinois Corp. employee, the staff identified the unfortunate person as "the Owens, Ill., executive." At the time the man had been held captive for twenty-five months and had received considerable attention from the press, including an active campaign by Jack Anderson.[48]

Morton Halperin observed two decades ago that "the Senate Foreign Relations Committee is determined to play a major role in policy making, yet lacks the requisite expertness."[49] Despite an enormous growth in the size of its professional staff—by the late 1970s, it numbered over sixty—Halperin's observation remained as true on the subject of United States policy toward Latin America in the 1970s as it was in the 1960s.[50] For a lengthy period, Pat Holt was the committee staff Latin Americanist, but he abandoned the job when he became committee chief of staff, and subsequently retired in 1977. For the remainder of the decade, the executive assistant to the chief of staff served as a nominal Latin Americanist. He was not known for the enthusiasm with which he approached the subject of U.S. policy toward Latin America, however, and he was particularly apathetic on the issue of human rights. Although there were a number of people on the staff who specialized in subjects related to Latin America, it is fair to say that until 1980 the committee had no Latin Americanist in the sense of someone who followed events in the region, who identified emerging issues and problems, and who advised the subcommittee leaders on how to best invest their limited time.[51] In an effort to fill this intellectual gap, in 1980, the Committee hired

[47] See *Foreign Assistance Legislation for Fiscal Year 1979*, pt. 7, pp. 104-105, *supra* n. 35.

[48] Ibid., p. 16. Niehous escaped in late June 1979, after three and a half years in captivity.

[49] Morton H. Halperin, "Is the Senate's Foreign Relations Research Worthwhile?" *American Behavioral Scientist* 4 (September 1960): 21.

[50] Neither Halperin nor I mean to imply that Congress would be wise to abdicate its policy-making role in favor of a group of technocrats. To the contrary, Congress's professional staff might better be conceived as a link between experts from the administration and from outside the government, on the one hand, and the members of Congress, on the other. Rather than answer the questions, the staff should be prepared to ask the questions that need to be answered.

[51] Each member of the subcommittee employs one or more aides who focus on foreign affairs, but only the chairpersons' aide is expected to devote much time to Latin America. Given the tendency for senators to leave the subcommittee whenever their seniority permits, there is little incentive for even the chairperson's staff to exert the energy necessary to become thoroughly familiar with U.S. policy toward Latin America.

Barry Sklar as its staff Latin Americanist. A specialist with long experience with the Congressional Research Service, Sklar is among the
most competent Latin Americanists in Washington.

On the other hand, the number of staff members with an interest
in human rights grew substantially in the 1970s. Generally speaking,
they appeared to be both emotionally and intellectually committed
to their subject. In several cases these staff members were also quite
knowledgeable, and they were often supervised by members of Congress who were interested in the issue of human rights. The result was
several extremely effective legislative teams. One such team was that
of Senator Kennedy and Mark Schneider. Until Schneider left to join
the Carter administration in 1977, he was largely responsible for the
thousand and one details that underpinned Senator Kennedy's campaign against U.S. support for the Pinochet government. Between
1973 and 1979, the team of Representative Fraser and John Salzberg
was at the center of human rights activity in the House, and they were
briefly complemented by Representative Edward Koch and Charles
Flynn. Salzberg engineered the lengthy series of hearings by the House
Foreign Affairs Subcommittee on International Organizations that are
generally credited with raising the issue of human rights and U.S.
foreign policy during the 1970s. A soft-spoken Quaker with a Ph.D.
in political science, Salzberg maintained contact with virtually everyone who had an interest in the human rights component of United
States foreign policy. It was he whom interest group representatives
approached first when they needed help from Congress on a human
rights issue.

Some commentators have suggested that legislative aides such as
Schneider, Salzberg, and Flynn were the principal impetus behind the
human rights movement in Congress and that they were "more radical
and more committed to human rights issues than the legislators themselves."[52] This is simply incorrect. Not only do these statements un-
derestimate the commitment of members such as Fraser, Kennedy,
Solarz, McGovern, and Koch, they also ignore the fact that few if
any legislators are so malleable as to be pushed into such controversial,
extremely time-consuming positions simply because they are lobbied
by their aides. If anything, just the opposite was true in the 1970s.
Members concerned with human rights selected aggressive aides who

[52] "For the Record: The Human Rights Lobby in the USA," *Latin America* 10
(October 15, 1976): 315. See also Philip L. Ray, Jr. and J. Sherrod Taylor, "The
Role of Nongovernmental Organizations in Implementing Human Rights in Latin
America," *Georgia Journal of International and Comparative Law*, supplement to vol.
7 (Summer 1977), p. 497.

were equally concerned with the issue, and then closely supervised their staff work.

In addition to seeking help from committee and personal staffs, members of Congress can seek assistance from the Government Accounting Office (GAO) and the Congressional Research Service (CRS) of the Library of Congress. The GAO has been particularly valuable in its oversight studies of the Agency for International Development. One such study of AID's compliance with the ban on police training, for example, provided Congress with detailed information on AID's observance of the formal wording rather than the spirit of Congress's directive.[53] The Foreign Affairs and National Defense Division of CRS performs a broad variety of research tasks, advising individual members and their aides and on occasion providing staff members to accompany congressional tours of Latin America.

In the past, congressional committees contracted with outside experts, generally university professors, to perform research or provide advice on specific topics related to U.S.-Latin American relations. The growth of professional committee staffs made the expense of these research contracts more difficult to justify and, in addition, the studies themselves were often too theoretical to be of direct value to policy makers.[54] In the 1970s, the use of outside experts on Latin America was generally restricted to their participation in hearings, although this may have reflected the low salience of Latin America in United States foreign policy rather than a decline in the perceived utility of independent advisors. When the Panama Canal treaties became a major issue in 1977 to 1978, several senators consulted outside experts on the treaties. Former assistant secretary of state William D. Rogers had a particularly important role in advising minority leader Howard Baker to support ratification of the treaties.

The Appropriations Committees. The major remaining congressional actors influencing U.S. economic aid to Latin America are the foreign operations subcommittees of the two appropriations committees. Foreign aid appropriations are always made on an annual basis, with all military and economic aid requests considered in a single bill.

[53] U.S. General Accounting Office, *Stopping U.S. Assistance to Foreign Police and Prisons* (Washington, D.C.: General Accounting Office, February 19, 1976), Report number ID-76-5.

[54] Exceptions were the series of reports commissioned in 1967 and 1968 by Senator Morse's Foreign Relations Subcommittee on American Republics Affairs. See, for example, the committee print of Robert Dockery's excellent study of U.S. influence upon organized labor in Latin America. U.S. Congress, Senate, Committee on Foreign Relations, Subcommittee on American Republics Affairs, *Survey of the Alliance for Progress: Labor Policies and Programs*, 90th Cong., 2d Sess., July 15, 1968.

In fulfilling its function in the House, the Committee on Appropriations clearly overshadows the Committee on Foreign Affairs in its influence upon both the nature and size of the U.S. aid program.[55] Perhaps one reason for this relative strength is the subcommittee structure. Unlike foreign affairs subcommittees, the House Appropriations Subcommittee on Foreign Operations (like other House appropriations subcommittees) is extremely powerful; the full committee is generally little more than a rubber stamp for its subcommittees' decisions.[56] Rather than following the authorization procedure of dividing authority for the foreign aid program first among a variety of subcommittees and then between the subcommittees and the full committee, the appropriations process places responsibility for the entire foreign aid program upon a single subcommittee or, more accurately, upon a single subcommittee chairperson.

The House Subcommittee on Foreign Operations was once the personal fiefdom of Otto Passman, who held that his major duty in life was to reduce the administration's foreign aid requests. Explaining why he felt obliged to recommend a 21 percent cut in the Kennedy administration's FY1962 aid request, Passman noted that "my primary function . . . is to cut and prune this ever-growing foreign aid plant of ours."[57] Passman's power to conduct budgetary surgery rested in part upon a friendship with committee chairperson Clarence Cannon, who permitted Passman to pack his subcommittee with antiaid representatives. When Cannon died in 1964, George Mahon became chairperson, and Mahon's former colleague on the Texas delegation, Lyndon Johnson, convinced him to revamp Passman's subcommittee. Two proaid northern Democrats and the unenthusiastic but moderate Clarence Long replaced two antiaid southern Democrats, thereby ending the subcommittee's fundamental hostility to foreign aid.[58] Passman

[55] This has been the case since at least the 1960s. See Heyward Moore, Jr., "Congressional Committees and the Formulation of Foreign Aid Policy," Ph.D. dissertation, University of North Carolina, 1965, p. 62.

[56] Holbert Carroll, *The House of Representatives and Foreign Affairs* (Pittsburgh: University of Pittsburgh Press, 1966), p. 153; Richard F. Fenno, Jr., "The House Appropriations Committee as a Political System: The Problem of Integration," *American Political Science Review* 56 (June 1962): 316; H. Field Haviland, Jr., "Foreign Aid and the Policy Process: 1957," *American Political Science Review* 52 (September 1958): 710.

[57] *Congressional Record*, September 5, 1961, p. 18134.

[58] William L. Morrow, "Legislative Control of Administrative Discretion: The Case of Congress and Foreign Aid," *Journal of Politics* 30 (November 1968): 989; Elizabeth Brenner Drew, "Mr. Passman Meets His Match," *The Reporter* 31 (November 19, 1964): 40-43; Barbara Hinckley, *Stability and Change in Congress* (New York: Harper and Row, 1971), pp. 161-162.

continued as chairperson, however, and his hostility remained strong and dominant despite the changes in the subcommittee's composition.

In 1976, an aging Passman was defeated in his primary bid for reelection. Representative Long became subcommittee chairperson and, ipso facto, probably the most powerful member of the House on foreign aid issues. A mildly liberal Democrat who taught economics at Johns Hopkins before being elected to the House in 1962, Long was not fundamentally opposed to the aid program in the 1970s; neither was he an enthusiastic supporter of it.[59] In the final years of the 1970s, his attitude toward aid and his behavior toward aid officials came to resemble that of his predecessor, suggesting that the bureaucratic role rather than the individual incumbent determines the behavior of chairpersons. In particular, Long projected the same outspoken arrogance that once characterized his predecessor. He made fun of witnesses at hearings who did not share his vocabulary skills, he joined conservative subcommittee members in attacks upon Carter administration representatives, he lectured and bullied distinguished witnesses when he disliked their attitude toward what were often incredibly inane questions, and he was inclined to concentrate upon trivia.[60]

One AID official speculated that Long became engrossed in trivia in the 1970s because of his grass-roots approach to fact finding. Rather than talk with aid officials overseas when on study missions, Long preferred (using his own analogy) to act like the Caliph of Bagdad in the *Arabian Nights*, who disguised himself as an ordinary citizen and went out to talk to the people. Masquerading as a Third World peasant, Representative Long collected information and then returned to Washington with a considerable store of unrelated facts, which he proceeded to discuss with any aid official who had the misfortune to be called before his subcommittee.[61]

If Long's goal was to infuriate aid officials in the executive branch, my interviews suggest that he was enormously successful by the late 1970s. Among many AID officials he became known as "The Cur-

---

[59] See, for example, his statement in U.S. Congress, House, Committee on Appropriations, Subcommittee on Foreign Operations and Related Agencies, *Foreign Assistance and Related Agencies Appropriations for 1979*, 95th Cong., 2d Sess., 1978, pt. 1, p. 917. Although Long was generally considered a liberal, his voting record was fairly erratic. In the 1970s, his ADA rating fluctuated between the mildly conservative (1978 = 40) and the mildly liberal (1977 = 65).

[60] Ibid., pt. 1, pp. 635, 657, 663, 674; pt. 2, pp. 445, 446; pt. 3, p. 243.

[61] Apparently Long's cover was less than secure, for on one occasion in the Andes the local residents were waiting for his arrival to inspect an AID-financed road project: "They shot off a lot of fireworks in my honor and I was very pleased. I was very much moved by it. Apparently they remembered me and named the highway after me." Ibid., pt. 1, pp. 674-675, 823.

mudgeon," and the mention of his name in the presence of one Treasury official triggered a cascade of four-letter words offensive even to the hardened sensibilities of a social scientist. Perhaps part of this animosity reflected Long's detailed supervision of aid administrators. Like Passman, Long and his staff reevaluate on an annual basis virtually every aspect of the foreign aid program. The subcommittee hearings, which ran to 3,500 printed pages in six volumes in 1979, regularly force the administration to defend publicly its entire economic and military assistance package.[62] Were it not for the subcommittee, many of the most controversial components of the aid program would remain unpublicized and uncriticized.

On the issue of human rights, Long was among the first legislators to adopt the position of using aid not to deter or to halt repression but rather to dissociate the United States from the most grievous violators.[63] He therefore supported most proposals to cut aid to repressive regimes. In particular, he emerged as an outspoken critic of the State Department's position that aid to needy people should be continued regardless of the nature of their government: "Every conceivable abomination has been perpetrated in the name of the poor and the needy. . . . Must we continue to pay tribute and ransom for these people no matter how few they are? . . . The world is full of poor people, isn't it? . . . We have plenty of people we can help without having to pay tribute to a bunch of ruthless dictators."[64] Long did not lead his subcommittee on human rights issues during the 1970s, however; rather he followed the preferences of other strong subcommittee members. During the brief period (1975-1977) when Edward Koch was Long's colleague, the subcommittee rivaled the Fraser subcommittee as the center of prohuman rights activity in the House. When Koch left the House to become mayor of New York, human rights remained a major subcommittee focus, but the antihuman rights (and strong pro-Somoza) influence of subcommittee member Charles Wilson grew dramatically. While Long concentrated upon his favorite aid project—light capital technology—Wilson assumed the leadership role on the subcommittee in the area of human rights. Long abdicated his role so far as to permit Wilson to embarrass the Carter adminis-

[62] The page total is somewhat misleading, for the subcommittee regularly pads its work. In the 1978 hearings, for example, one set of letters is printed no fewer than three times, consuming 64 pages out of 125. Ibid., pt. 1, pp. 439-451, 490-513, 535-564. Compare also pp. 30-41 and 1101-1112.

[63] "I don't think you are going to change those tyrannical regimes." U.S. Congress, House, Committee on Appropriations, Subcommittee on Foreign Operations and Related Agencies, *Foreign Assistance and Related Agencies Appropriations for 1978*, 95th Cong., 1st Sess., 1977, pt. 2, p. 375.

[64] Ibid., pp. 374-375.

tration by holding hearings on human rights in Panama at the same time the Senate was considering ratification of the Panama Canal treaties.[65]

The Senate Appropriations Subcommittee on Foreign Operations is far tamer than its counterpart in the House.[66] As in the House, chairpersons of appropriations subcommittees enjoy substantial autonomy in decision making; only rarely are they checked by the subcommittee members, the full committee, or the Senate. Under Senator Daniel Inouye in the 1970s, the Subcommittee on Foreign Operations continued to perform the role it established two decades ago—that of an appeals board for executive branch officials who wished to overturn the decisions of the House. The Senate subcommittee could not be classified as an enthusiastic supporter of foreign aid programs, but it generally voted to reinstate much of the money cut by the House from the administration's requests. During the six-year period from 1958 to 1963, for example, the House Committee on Appropriations made an average annual cut of 22 percent in the administration's overall aid request. The Senate Committee on Appropriations restored about half of this amount. On economic aid, the House cuts were even deeper—an average cut in the Development Loan Fund of 36 percent—but the Senate restored all but 16 percent.[67]

The 1970s saw a repetition of this pattern. In FY1977, the Ford administration asked for $5.8 billion, the House passed a bill providing for $4.8 billion, Inouye's subcommittee reported a bill for $5.3 billion, and House-Senate conferees agreed upon $5.1 billion. For FY1978, the Carter administration asked for $7.6 billion, the House appropriated $6.7 billion, the Senate provided $6.85 billion, and the House-Senate conference committee agreed upon something in between—in

[65] Another Democratic subcommittee member protested the timing of the hearing, asserting that its only purpose was to demonstrate that human rights violations were occurring in other Central American nations in addition to Nicaragua. Wilson supported the treaties but later announced he would lead the House fight to block implementing legislation unless the Carter administration ceased its hostility toward the Somoza government. *Foreign Assistance and Related Agencies Appropriations for 1979*, pt. 1, pp. 161, 961, 979, *supra* n. 59; *Washington Post*, December 7, 1978, p. A26.

[66] The subcommittee has had difficulty deciding on a name. Until 1975 it was the Subcommittee on Foreign Operations; in 1976 and 1977 it was the Subcommittee on Foreign Assistance and Related Programs; in 1978 it was the Subcommittee on Foreign Operations once more; in 1979 and 1980 it was the Subcommittee on Foreign Assistance and Related Programs. With the exception of bibliographical citations, this volume accepts common usage and refers to the subcommittee as the Subcommittee on Foreign Operations.

[67] Moore, "Congressional Committees and the Formulation of Foreign Aid Policy," pp. 125, 144.

this case $6.77 billion. This congressional minuet of slash-restore-compromise became something of a ritual, with the House permitted the luxury of venting its full fury in the knowledge that the Senate would balance its excesses. Some executive branch officials became active participants in this procedure, of course, requesting more money than their agencies needed in recognition that a substantial budget cut was so certain that an honest request would place the programs they wished to pursue in danger. Other aid officials, especially those from the Treasury Department in search of money for MDBs, could not employ this procedure, since their needs were set publicly.

In the 1970s, the Senate subcommittee viewed the subject of human rights with ambivalence. On the one hand, its members did "not believe that our interest is served by the support of dictatorial regimes in the name of stability," since "such short-sighted policies only forestall instability and assure that, when events do occur, they will happen with explosive impact." On the other hand, the subcommittee was reluctant to terminate aid to even extremely repressive governments. It argued with some passion that "to sever all ties would be to cut ourselves off from the peoples of these countries and to leave them under the dark night of oppression. We can stand afar and curse the darkness, or we can try to bring them light."[68] Given this ambivalence, the issue of human rights was ignored whenever possible.[69]

When it could not be ignored, the subcommittee took the path of least resistance. In 1976, it agreed to accept a House-sponsored cutoff of aid to Uruguay but only because some House members and interest groups were more active in support of the reduction than the Ford administration was in opposing it. In 1977, it refused to consider an aid reduction for Nicaragua after the Somoza lobby had demonstrated in the House that it was more powerful than the collectivity of human rights activists. With an apparent commitment to offend as few people as possible, Senator Inouye's subcommittee generally limited its human rights action to the voicing of platitudes. After weighing the variety of alternatives in 1977, for example, Senator Inouye decided that the appropriate course would be to issue a statement that would "encourage the Administration to hold steady in its determination . . . to reform the policies which have, on occasion, awarded liberal grants and loans

[68] Senate Report 95-352, pp. 20-21.

[69] The voluminous (1518 pages) hearings of the subcommittee on FY1976 aid appropriations contain no mention of human rights by either subcommittee members or administration witnesses. Only the public witnesses on abuses in South Korea and the Philippines broached the subject. U.S. Congress, Senate, Committee on Appropriations, Subcommittee on Foreign Operations, *Foreign Assistance and Related Programs Appropriations Fiscal Year 1976*, 94th Cong., 1st Sess., 1975.

to repressive regimes which violate human rights."[70] Even here the subcommittee did not commit itself to an autonomous policy; its words were copied from the President's foreign assistance message to Congress.

In summary, during the 1970s there was little evidence to suggest that the four congressional committees that bore major responsibility for the foreign aid program to Latin America were prepared to assist the executive branch or other interested members of Congress in creating a stable, coherent policy toward Latin America. Congressional authority over aid decisions was fragmented, and the fragments were uncoordinated except in the most rudimentary fashion. The vast majority of members of Congress remained disinterested in both foreign aid and Latin America, and it was only with charity that the level of staff expertise on Latin America could be characterized as modest. Because decisions were made affecting a subject about which few cared and even fewer were informed, almost inevitably the results were unpredictable. This is old news, of course. In 1950, Dahl began his study of Congress and foreign policy with the observation that "the national legislature . . . is remarkably ill-suited to exercise a wise control over the nation's foreign policy."[71] In 1965, Heyward Moore added to Dahl's indictment of Congress but was relieved to note that its level of wisdom was irrelevant because it had no impact upon policy. He found that the foreign aid committees "performed a negligible role in initiating policy and did not materially alter the content of foreign aid policy through modification or veto."[72] During the 1970s, these characterizations continued to be valid in most instances. On the issue of human rights and economic aid to Latin America, however, both Dahl and Moore were proven incorrect. The following chapter analyzes how human rights became an exception to the rule of congressional impotence in foreign affairs.

[70] Senate Report 95-352, p. 21.

[71] Dahl, *Congress and Foreign Policy*, p. 3. See also Sanford, "The Decision-Making Process in the Alliance for Progress," pp. 300-301.

[72] Moore, "Congressional Committees and the Formulation of Foreign Aid Policy," p. 248.

· 5 ·

ECONOMIC AID AND
HUMAN RIGHTS

DURING the course of the 1960s and 1970s, the relationship between United States economic aid and human rights violations by recipient governments underwent a remarkable transformation. While the aid program was regularly criticized as supportive of repressive Latin American governments throughout most of this period, by the late 1970s economic aid had become a principal foreign policy tool with which the United States was attacking the hemisphere's most repressive regimes. The purpose of this chapter is to analyze the process by which this change occurred. To do so, it is useful first to concentrate upon the allegations that aid assisted in the creation and support of governments that repressed their citizens' human rights and then to discuss the role of aid in United States human rights policy.

CREATING REPRESSIVE GOVERNMENTS

When a political crisis develops in Latin America, the strong tendency of the United States government is to support Latin American political groups that share with the United States a perception of the crisis as a threat to hemispheric stability and, ipso facto, to United States security. Generally this has meant support for the existing structure of socioeconomic privilege rather than for those groups that challenge it. Not every Latin American nation has developed the raw political divisions that result in extreme levels of repression of human rights, but where such divisions create a crisis, the United States typically stands with those groups that suppress attacks upon the status quo—in the 1970s, aid was forthcoming for the Uruguayan police and not the Tupamaros, for the Nicaraguan National Guard and not the Sandinistas, for the Argentine military and not the Montoneros.

At times, however, a crisis generated by a Latin American government is perceived as a threat to the United States. When this occurs, the relationship between aid and repression becomes more complex, for it is difficult to continue aid and at the same time to use aid to attack a threatening government. On rare occasions it may be possible, as, for example, in 1963 and 1964 when the United States withdrew aid from the Brazilian federal government of João Goulart and redirected it to states with friendly governors—the "islands of sanity" policy.[1] But this response was highly atypical; economic aid is a government-to-government arrangement.[2] Given the centralized nature of most Latin American regimes, it is generally impossible to find an alternative to the national government as a recipient of economic aid. If foreign policy officials wish to support with economic aid those groups that would repress a perceived threat to the United States, they must first help to place the repressors in power.

Economic aid can be used to create a repressive government only in a negative sense: by withdrawing aid from a relatively nonrepressive government in order to undermine its control of political power. This is done infrequently, since only rarely does a threat to the United States assume control of a Latin American government. Two uncontestable examples of the use of aid to undermine relatively nonrepressive but threatening governments are Brazil under Goulart and Chile under Allende. There are other cases (Peru in the 1960s and Bolivia in 1970 and 1971, for example) about which suspicion is justified but evidence is less substantial. But in the cases of Brazil and Chile there is no question that economic aid was halted or curtailed drastically because policy makers perceived the governments as threats to U.S. security. In both cases a coup ensued, and an unusually repressive government proceeded to destroy the supporters of the overthrown regime.

The defense of this interpretation of the relationship between aid and the repression of human rights rests upon an understanding of two related issues. The first concerns causality. The response to the question of whether a halt in aid causes the overthrow of regimes such as those of Allende and Goulart is, I believe, no. United States economic aid programs are not capable of this high level of influence in major Latin American nations. Certainly a dramatic decline in aid hurts, for if it does nothing else it signals a government's domestic opposition that the United States has embarked upon a policy of hostility. But aid reductions also have a more measurable impact: the loss of funding for a wide variety of government activities such as agricultural extension services and urban health care. These and similar nonprofit pro-

---

[1] U.S. Congress, Senate, Committee on Foreign Relations, Subcommittee on Western Hemisphere Affairs, *United States Policies and Programs in Brazil*, 92d Cong., 1st Sess., May 4, 5, and 11, 1971, pp. 278-279; Albert Fishlow, "Flying Down to Rio: Perspectives on U.S.-Brazil Relations," *Foreign Affairs* 57 (Winter 1978-1979): 392.

[2] There are exceptions to this rule, such as Title II PL480 distribution through private voluntary organizations. Nevertheless, in all cases, the recipient governments must agree to permit any aid activity.

grams are the means by which many popularly elected Latin American regimes maintain the support they require in order to govern. These services generally survive the withdrawal of aid, but the lost funding is typically replaced by expansionist monetary policies. This in turn accelerates inflation and reduces domestic and international financial support for welfare-oriented governments such as those of Goulart and Allende. A major decline in aid is much more than a minor annoyance to many Latin American governments, especially those that devote substantial resources to improving the living conditions of their poorest citizens. Nevertheless, it is probably accurate to assert that most Latin American regimes could survive U.S. hostility if the only action against them were a substantial diminution of economic assistance.[3] Used alone, the withdrawal of economic aid is a relatively weak instrument to fight governments perceived as threatening. Used in conjunction with the entire United States arsenal, however, economic aid can make a contribution to achieving the ends of U.S. policy.

The second issue is a slight variation on the theme of causality: it is sometimes argued that when the United States withdraws economic aid to undermine a government's financial health it does not necessarily create a repressive government in its place.[4] This was the position offered in November 1975 by the Latin Americanist on the State Department's policy planning staff. When pressed by a group of academicians on the issue of U.S. hostility toward the Allende government, he shouted: "Look, we didn't mean for the junta to run wild." Probably not. Policy makers most likely would have preferred a quiet coup, a few planeloads of exiles, a brief military caretaker to supervise the transfer of power to a new government led by a Frei or an Alessandri. But this was not the choice, anymore than a similar choice was available in Brazil in 1964. The choice was someone like Allende or someone like Pinochet, for threats cannot be repressed without a fight in highly mobilized Latin American political environments. To dismiss the development of repressive regimes as merely an unfortunate by-product of a policy designed to undermine a perceived threat to the United States is to ignore clear evidence that the only political forces capable of destroying popularly elected threats such as Goulart

[3] This is not necessarily true of such Latin American nations as Bolivia and the Dominican Republic, where governments have come to depend upon United States aid to fulfill the basic needs of large segments of their populations.

[4] In addition, the United States cannot be said to have caused or encouraged repression if it helps to undermine a threatening regime that is also repressive. In this circumstance, the United States is encouraging the repression of different groups for different reasons by a different regime—certainly no small distinction—but it is not creating repression.

or Allende are those that tend to "run wild." To undermine the threat is to assist in creating the repression.

Rather than continue to pursue this argument abstractly, the premier cases of Brazil and Chile can be used to illustrate the relationships between aid reductions and the creation of repressive governments. Whatever their shortcomings may have been, the governments of João Goulart and Salvador Allende were not based upon the systematic extermination of their opposition; the regimes that replaced them were. Thus in April 1964, Brazil experienced a change in government from one that was relatively nonrepressive to one that ruled when necessary through terror and intimidation. In September 1973, Chile underwent a similar governmental shift. Prior to these two events, the United States had halted what had been substantial economic aid programs. The information in Table 5.1 provides fairly clear evidence of these aid reductions in the case of Chile. In interpreting Table 5.1, note that Salvador Allende's Popular Unity government ruled Chile for half of FY1971, all of FY1972 and FY1973, and two months of FY1974.[5] The data for Brazil are more difficult to interpret because of the relatively brief period (less than six months) during which aid was halted. As the following discussion indicates, however, incontrovertible evidence exists to demonstrate that aid was withdrawn in an effort to undermine the Goulart government.

Aid officials have never denied that aid was halted to both governments.[6] Thus the question has never been whether aid was reduced, but why. In the case of Brazil, the official who supervised the reduction, AID's William A. Ellis, explained that Brazil failed to live up to an economic agreement: "Unfortunately, Goulart, for political reasons, failed to support the stabilization program upon which U.S. program loans and IMF standby support were predicated. . . . the Government of Brazil: agreed to a 70 percent wage increase for government employees; was unable to contain other government expenditures; would not reduce the treasury cash deficit; and could not make significant

---

[5] The relatively small increase in FY1974 can be attributed to the lengthy bureaucratic process that delays the reinitiation of most aid programs. The initial aid to the Pinochet government was in the form of Commodity Credit Corporation and Export-Import Bank credits, which involve very simple government loan procedures. Eximbank loans to Chile increased from $3.1 million in FY1973 to $57.0 million in FY1974. U.S. Congress, Senate, Select Committee to Study Governmental Operations with Respect to Intelligence Activities, *Covert Action in Chile 1963-1973*, 94th Cong., 1st Sess., 1975, p. 34.

[6] See *United States Policies and Programs in Brazil*, pp. 163, 186, *supra* n. 1; U.S. Congress, Senate, Committee on the Judiciary, Subcommittee to Investigate Problems Connected with Refugees and Escapees, *Refugee and Humanitarian Problems in Chile*, 93d Cong., 1st Sess., September 28, 1973, p. 38.

TABLE 5.1

U.S. ECONOMIC AID TO CHILE, FY1962-FY1978

(millions of dollars)

Year	AID	Food for Peace	Total
1962	$142.7	6.6	$149.3
1963	41.3	22.0	63.3
1964	78.9	26.9	105.8
1965	99.6	14.2	113.8
1966	93.2	14.4	107.6
1967	15.5	7.9	23.4
1968	57.9	23.0	80.9
1969	35.4	15.0	50.4
1970	18.0	7.2	25.2
1971	1.5	6.3	7.8
1972	1.0	5.9	6.9
1973	.8	2.5	3.3
1974	5.3	3.2	8.5
1975	31.3	62.4	93.7
1976	20.6	56.8	77.4
1977	.6	31.5	32.1
1978	.2	5.6	5.8

SOURCE: Agency for International Development.

strides to implement the program upon which further release of U.S. program loan funds was predicated."[7] In the case of Chile, assistant secretary of state Jack Kubisch also cited economic considerations to explain the reduction in aid: "After the [Allende] government was in office and defaulted on its repayments, for purely economic and commercial reasons alone, it is understandable why additional credits were not made available."[8] The Department of Agriculture had a different but equally nonpolitical reason for reducing Food for Peace shipments to Chile: "We have expenditure limitations on Public Law 480," a Department spokesperson asserted in 1971, "so we must carefully review all programs."[9]

[7] See United States Policies and Programs in Brazil, pp. 186, 163, supra n. 1.

[8] See Refugee and Humanitarian Problems in Chile, p. 38, supra n. 6. AID officials argued further that existing legislation—the Hickenlooper and González amendments—forced them to halt assistance. U.S. Congress, House, Committee on International Relations, Subcommittee on International Organizations, Chile: The Status of Human Rights and Its Relationship to U.S. Economic Assistance Programs, 94th Cong., 2d Sess., April-May 1976, p. 25.

[9] U.S. Congress, House, Committee on Foreign Affairs, Subcommittee on Inter-American Affairs, New Directions for the 1970's—Part 2: Development Assistance Options for Latin America, 92d Cong., 1st Sess., 1971, p. 227.

After some time, it became evident that these economic explanations were at best incomplete. It was widely believed from the beginning that the Johnson administration encouraged the Brazilian coup because of the Goulart regime's slide to the left; therefore few people were surprised when an enterprising young history student forced the declassification of President Johnson's national security files on Brazil and found documents to prove what most people had long suspected: the United States was concerned about something quite different from Goulart's fiscal irresponsibility. A covert military operation, code-named "Brother Sam," was prepared to assist the Brazilian military to oust a government headed not toward economic problems but toward communist domination.[10] But AID's Ellis knew all along that the problem with Brazil was only superficially economic, for he noted that the crucial factor was that Brazil had become "ripe for political developments which might be antithetical to our interests."[11] To combat these developments, aid was stopped.

In the case of Chile, several congressional investigations amassed overwhelming evidence that the United States government was implacably hostile to the socialist government in Chile and that the hostility was not passive. Once investigators found President Nixon's direct order to destroy the Chilean economy, it took little effort to discover that one way this was implemented was through a cut in economic aid. Standing by its earlier argument that the assistance was terminated for purely economic reasons, AID claimed ignorance of any noneconomic motivation.[12] Although Department of Agriculture officials were never reexamined, the data belie the earlier claim of PL480 officials—that reductions in aid to Chile stemmed from the pressure of expenditure limitations. Despite the reduced levels of U.S. food stocks in 1973 and 1974, the years 1970 through 1973 were near-

[10] Gayle Hudgens Watson, "Our Monster in Brazil: It All Began with Brother Sam," *Nation* 224 (January 15, 1977): 51-54. I am indebted to Ms. Hudgens for providing me with photocopies of the documents she obtained through the Freedom of Information process. For a contrasting perspective on Brother Sam, see Vernon A. Walters, *Silent Missions* (Garden City, N.Y.: Doubleday, 1978), pp. 384-387. For the most complete documentation of U.S. policy toward Goulart's Brazil, see Phyllis R. Parker, *Brazil and the Quiet Intervention, 1964* (Austin: University of Texas Press, 1979).

[11] See *United States Policies and Programs in Brazil*, p. 165, *supra* n. 1. The American ambassador to Brazil, Lincoln Gordon, also noted in 1966 that to him "it had become clear for many months before his [Goulart's] deposition that his purpose was to put an end to constitutional government in Brazil in the interest of establishing some sort of political dictatorship." Gordon added his belief that the 1964 coup was designed "to preserve and not destroy Brazil's democracy." U.S. Congress, Senate, Committee on Foreign Relations, *Nomination of Lincoln Gordon to be Assistant Secretary of State for Inter-American Affairs*, 89th Cong., 2d Sess., February 7, 1966, pp. 7-8.

[12] See *Chile: The Status of Human Rights*, p. 30, *supra* n. 8.

normal for PL480 shipments to Latin America. There was only a severe limitation for Chile.[13]

While most of the relevant documents remain classified, some aspects of the decisional process are now part of the public record. They indicate that there is no clearly established process by which policy makers decide to cut aid to threatening governments. One reason for this is that such decisions are infrequent; rarely has a single administration had more than one such opportunity arise in Latin America. Thus there is no need to institutionalize a procedure. In addition, it was only in the 1960s that the economic aid program assumed substantial proportions. The tool is relatively new. Finally, the process of halting aid to undermine a threat has not been formalized because reductions are but one part of an integrated effort that includes various forms of intervention, some of which violate international law. Consequently, policy deliberations remain secret and the number of participants kept to a minimum.

In the case of Chile between 1970 and 1973, the policy decisions were made by President Nixon and National Security Advisor Kissinger. The bureaucratic entity that created and supervised the overall campaign against Allende's government was the National Security Council, which at the time enjoyed broad powers of policy formulation as well as responsibility for the coordination and monitoring of overseas operations. The reduction in economic aid became official policy in mid-September 1970, as a part of a broader program of economic hostility. This initial decision was formalized in early November 1970 by National Security Decision Memorandum (NSDM) number 93, which was signed by the President. Only the very highest government officials participated in formulating this policy. The task of implementing the halt in economic aid fell to the Latin Americanist on the National Security Council staff. It was coordinated with other forms of hostility through interagency task forces, all under the close supervision of Kissinger and Treasury Secretary John Connally.[14]

While the ambassadors to Chile (first Edward Korry and later Nathaniel Davis) were at least informed and enthusiastic implementors of Washington's policy, they had a negligible role in policy formulation. On June 18, 1970, months prior to the Popular Unity electoral victory, Korry submitted a two-phase proposal to both the State Department and the CIA to increase funding for anti-Allende candidates

---

[13] U.S. Agency for International Development, *U.S. Overseas Loans and Grants and Assistance from International Organizations: Obligations and Loan Authorizations, July 1, 1945-September 30, 1976* (Washington, D.C.: Agency for International Development, 1977), pp. 33-61, esp. pp. 33, 41.

[14] See *Covert Action in Chile*, pp. 25, 27, 33, 35, *supra* n. 5.

and to provide $500,000 to bribe members of the Chilean parliament in the event that its vote became crucial. On the specific topic of an aid reduction, Korry later informed the defense minister of the outgoing Frei government that "not a nut or bolt would be allowed to reach Chile under Allende."[15] Both Korry and Davis participated in embassy meetings on the implementation of NSDM-93.

The principal executive branch organizations in charge of aid to Latin America participated only marginally in the policy-making process. Although it is difficult to believe they could have remained ignorant of at least the basic contours of policy, both AID and ARA claim to have known nothing about the entire Chilean operation. To this day, their spokespersons stand by earlier statements that aid reductions were a natural consequence of Allende's economic policies. They deny knowledge of NSDM-93.[16]

The data are less clear on the origin of United States hostility toward the Goulart government, but, as in the case of Chile, a reduction in economic aid was but one part of a complex series of efforts that culminated in the 1964 coup. It is probable that the general policy was set by President Johnson and his closest advisors, especially fellow-Texan Thomas Mann, the administration's chief Latin Americanist. It appears that lower levels of the executive branch were excluded from decision making. AID and ARA officials maintain that aid was reduced because of the Goulart regime's failure to fulfill its obligations under the Bell-Dantas stabilization agreement. Unlike the Chilean case, however, the U.S. ambassador to Brazil, Lincoln Gordon, played an important policy-making role.

Given its lack of interest in inter-American relations, it is hardly surprising that Congress had no role in the decision-making process. Few legislators rose to support the Allende government, and none assisted that of Goulart. Several members encouraged the executive branch to cut aid in both cases. In early 1962, for example, a Brazilian state government expropriated an ITT-owned utility in Porto Alegre. Less than a week later, one member took to the floor of the House with a speech entitled "Private Enterprise Versus Socialism in South America," which complained that "our Government has thus far taken

[15] Ibid., pp. 20-21, 33. For Ambassador Davis's understanding of events, see Nathaniel Davis, "U.S. Covert Actions in Chile, 1971-1973," *Foreign Service Journal* 55 (November and December 1978).

[16] See *Chile: The Status of Human Rights*, p. 30, *supra* n. 8. One respected foreign policy analyst believes that the State Department was fully aware of U.S. policy. See Tad Szulc, *The Illusion of Peace: Foreign Policy in the Nixon Years* (New York: Viking Press, 1978), p. 646.

no step . . . to rescind or defer foreign aid to Brazil in order to bring about a reversal of this act of outright confiscation." He continued:

> In my judgment, gentlemen, the State Department protest is an inadequate response to this flagrant takeover of American properties. . . . At the very moment these outrageous events were taking place in Brazil our Government and the Government of Brazil were engaged in negotiations looking toward our granting to Brazil $1 billion in current foreign aid. . . . Is it truly in the interests of the United States to provide foreign aid through the governmental officials of Latin American countries who follow communist theories and who refuse—as did Brazil at Punte [sic] del Este—to even denounce communism in our hemisphere?[17]

Legislators did more than make speeches: in 1962, they added the Hickenlooper amendment to the Foreign Assistance Act to deter expropriation by requiring the President to halt aid to countries that nationalized U.S. property without adequate compensation. Although the amendment was not the direct result of the ITT-Brazil dispute, it reinforced the tone of the Johnson administration's policy toward Brazil.[18]

Similarly, the congressional hearings on Chile during the Allende years contain statements urging the President to protect American interests (and national security) through the economic aid program. One Representative, for example, criticized U.S. support for multilateral loans to Chile's Catholic and Austral universities—the only such loans approved during Allende's presidency—because they would help Chileans "to learn more about communism."[19] Finally some members with oversight responsibility for intelligence activities were aware that the Nixon administration was working to oust Allende and that one aspect of that effort was an elimination of economic aid, but the briefings they received were vague and the members charged with oversight apparently expressed little desire to know what specific steps were being implemented. Ambassador Korry was of the opinion that Congress approved of the administration's policy. When asked by the Senate Select Committee on Intelligence to testify regarding covert action in Chile, Korry reminded the committee chairperson, Senator Frank Church, that he (Church) had deliberately avoided becoming involved in U.S.-Chilean relations when he was chairing the Foreign Relations Subcommittee on Western Hemisphere Affairs during the Allende years: "Your wash must be pinned on the same sunlit line

---

[17] *Congressional Record*, February 22, 1962, pp. 2615-2616.
[18] Fishlow, "Flying Down to Rio," p. 392.
[19] See *New Directions for the 1970's*, pp. 16-17, 46, *supra* n. 9.

with mine. . . . Is it unfair to compare your looking-the-other-way in 1969-70 to a sentry asleep on duty on the eve of battle? Is it not right to inquire how such a negligent guard turns up as presiding judge in the resultant court-martial?"[20] Congress may not have been involved in making decisions to reduce aid to Brazil and Chile, but it fortified the policies of the executive branch.

Supporting Repressive Governments

The process by which the United States employs economic aid to support repressive governments is significantly different from the process that leads to the creation of political repression. One obvious reason for this difference is that the latter involves active hostility toward an existing government, while the former demands only active friendliness. Assistance to friendly governments does not have the de facto illegitimacy of hostile intervention. If a repressive government requests aid and the United States is disposed to provide it, the policy debate centers upon the wisdom or (less frequently) the morality of the move, not its legality. Conversely, the use of aid to destabilize a regime is always publicly condemned, for it is interference in the internal political affairs of another state and therefore prohibited by the charter of the OAS. For this reason, President Nixon was forced to hide the truth about his administration's policy toward Allende's Chile. Six months after he signed NSDM-93, Nixon wrote to Congress that "we will not be the one to upset traditional relations. . . . we are prepared to have the kind of relationship with the Chilean government that it is prepared to have with us."[21] But no one needed to lie about providing aid to the Pinochet government because every sovereign state retains the right to determine openly which governments should receive its foreign assistance. What was needed in the case of aid to the Pinochet government was a justification.

Out of this distinction comes the second reason why the use of aid to support repression differs from that which leads to the creation of repression: supportive aid is easier to justify during the policy-making process. This is because Latin American governments identified as gross violators of human rights also tend to adopt economic policies favored by aid officials. Specifically, as one ARA official told Congress during the course of a favorable report on the Pinochet government:

[20] Roger Morris, *Uncertain Greatness: Henry Kissinger and American Foreign Policy* (New York: Harper and Row, 1977), p. 243.
[21] *Public Papers of the Presidents of the United States: Richard M. Nixon, 1971* (Washington, D.C.: Government Printing Office, 1972), pp. 246-247.

"The Chileans pay their bills."[22] Not only do repressive regimes tend to pay their foreign debts, they also tend to welcome foreign capital. In addition, they keep government services at "realistic" levels, which is believed to check inflation. Unrestrained inflation, in turn, is viewed by aid officials as the principal hinderance to orderly economic growth.

By the mid-1970s, welfare-related phrases such as "aid for the poorest of the poor" peppered the public statements of aid spokespersons, but Congress was more effective in legislating new directions for AID than in encouraging new attitudes among aid officials. Most of the officials I interviewed in 1978 continued to view gross economic growth as an overwhelmingly important measure of "development" and a relatively unfettered market economy as the most appropriate means for fostering this growth. Such a perspective encourages the tendency to excuse repression when it is accompanied by economic growth. The post-1971 Bolivian government of Hugo Banzer was by most accounts among the most repressive in the history of a country that is noted for its repressive governments, for example, but rather than emphasize this repression, AID applauded the economic growth that occurred after all political opposition had been exterminated: "Recent growth has been helped immeasurably by the relative political calm which the country has experienced since 1971. President Hugo Banzer, who took control through a military coup in that year has been in power longer than any previous Bolivian leader and Bolivia is currently as well-off economically as it has ever been."[23] Perhaps the best public example of this attitude was Assistant Secretary of State Charles Meyer's assertion that torture and other abuses by the Brazilian government should be viewed in a relative perspective, that is, relative to the nation's high rate of economic growth.[24]

The United States has used its economic aid programs in two distinct ways to support political repression in Latin America: direct support

[22] See *Chile: The Status of Human Rights*, p. 36, *supra* n. 8.

[23] U.S. Congress, House, Committee on Appropriations, Subcommittee on Foreign Operations and Related Agencies, *Foreign Assistance and Related Agencies Appropriations for 1979*, 95th Cong., 2d Sess., 1978, pt. 1, p. 904.

[24] For Meyer's statement, see *New Directions for the 1970's*, p. 265, *supra* n. 9. For an example of how this ideology functions to direct aid to governments with market-oriented development policies, see pp. 112-113. Given this ideology, it is not difficult for many of these governments to elicit additional sympathy by pointing to the financial crises they inherited when they seized power. Given the U.S. economic offensive against the Allende government, there was no small irony in assistant secretary of state William D. Rogers' use of this argument as a rationale for aid to the Pinochet government. U.S. Congress, Senate, Committee on the Judiciary, Subcommittee to Investigate Problems Connected with Refugees and Escapees, *Refugee and Humanitarian Problems in Chile, Part III*, 94th Cong., 1st Sess., October 2, 1975, pp. 48-49.

to equip a repressive regime and indirect support to help maintain a repressive government in power.

Direct Support of Repression

The major direct program to support repression through economic aid, AID's Office of Public Safety (OPS), was halted in 1975, but for two decades it and its predecessors provided arms and training to any Latin American police force that shared the U.S. fear of insurgency. Although a rudimentary public safety program began in 1954 with the provision of technical assistance, like other forms of economic aid, it only became a major aid activitity during the 1960s. OPS was established in late 1962 in response to a direct order from President Kennedy: "The U.S. should give considerably greater emphasis to police assistance programs in appropriate less developed countries where there is an actual or potential threat of internal subversion or insurgency; to this end . . . AID should envisage very substantial increases in the global level of the FY1963 program, with further increases in subsequent years where there is a demonstrated need. The DOD [Department of Defense] should also give, where appropriate, increased emphasis to the police aspect of existing MAP programs."[25]

From a small team of technical advisory personnel, OPS grew rapidly to an intricate bureaucracy supplying arms and training to the police forces of fifty-two nations throughout the world. By 1963, OPS had established its International Police Academy (IPA) in an unused Georgetown trolley-car barn, its advisors were stationed or scheduled to be stationed in nearly every Latin American country save Cuba, and its budget was one of the fastest growing in Washington. By 1966, 10 percent of all AID technicians in Latin America were public safety officers, a figure four times higher than the number of AID officials working in the area of health and sanitation. In that year, internal security programs consumed 38 percent of all AID commitments.[26]

The OPS program in Brazil was particularly active. U.S. police training began in Brazil in 1959 but accelerated dramatically after the 1964 coup. In 1965, for example, the United States established from

[25] National Security Action Memorandum #177, August 2, 1962.

[26] U.S. Agency for International Development, *FY1966 Annual Report to the Congress* (Washington, D.C.: Agency for International Development, 1967), p. 38. See also Richard P. Claude, "Human Rights in the Philippines and United States Responsibility," Working Paper No. HRFP-5 of the Center for Philosophy and Public Policy, University of Maryland, College Park, Md., February 3, 1978; and U.S. General Accounting Office, *Stopping U.S. Assistance to Foreign Police and Prisons*, Report ID-76-5 (Washington, D.C.: General Accounting Office, February 19, 1976); Joan M. Nelson, *Aid, Influence, and Foreign Policy* (New York: Macmillan, 1968), pp. 37-38.

scratch the Brazilian federal police organization and in one year provided it with such an enormous amount of equipment that its coercive
abilities immediately made it a mainstay of the Castelo Branco government. At its peak, OPS stationed 23 advisors in Brazil, most of
whom were involved in in-country training to supplement the hundreds of higher-ranking Brazilian officers (641 between 1963 and 1971)
who studied at the IPA in Washington.[27]

Criticism of this close relationship between U.S. police training
and the repressiveness of the Brazilian government was viewed by AID
as a public relations problem, as AID's answer to a question from
Senator Church clearly demonstrates:

> Q. Do you know the source of the equipment the police used
> when they occupied the University of Brasilia in 1968 that had
> "USA" stenciled on it?
> A. Subject equipment were olive-drab canvas pouches for car-
> rying gas masks. . . . the masks were loaned to the military police
> by the Brazilian army. Following the incident, U.S. Aid Public
> Safety advisors discussed the subject with Secretary of Public
> Safety for the Federal District and he made the decision to have
> all the U.S. markings on these pouches painted over with black
> paint. He later issued orders to the military police commander
> to make certain that all equipment on loan from the Brazilian
> Army be checked and U.S. markings be painted over.[28]

By 1970, congressional inquiries and a number of nongovernmental
analyses had raised serious objections to the continuation of OPS. A
1971 Senate Foreign Relations staff report concluded that the major
result of the OPS program in Guatemala and the Dominican Republic
was to identify the United States with political violence. In 1970, the
kidnapping and assassination of OPS advisor Dan Mitrione by the
Tupamaros in Uruguay triggered new concern about the program. At
the same time, allegations that the IPA taught torture as part of its
curriculum became so numerous that Congress asked the GAO to
perform an independent review. While the GAO found no evidence
of instruction in torture beyond showing the movie "Battle of Algiers,"
by 1973 so much other evidence had been collected on OPS support
for repressive Third World regimes that congressional critics were
encouraged to attempt to legislate the institution out of existence.[29]

[27] See United States Policies and Programs in Brazil, pp. 3-51, supra n. 1.
[28] Ibid., pp. 240-241.
[29] Claude, "Human Rights in the Philippines," pp. 17-18; "Building a Better
Thumbscrew," New Scientist 59 (July 19, 1973): 139-141; Thomas Lobe, "Adventures
in Social Control in the Third World," in United States National Security Policy and

In particular, the demise of OPS was accelerated by its relationship with the South Vietnamese police. In 1964, there were 10,000 national police in South Vietnam; by 1973, the number had risen to 120,000. Virtually all of this growth in personnel and a parallel growth in hardware and facilities had been financed by AID. The straw that eventually broke OPS's back was the discovery in 1970 of the AID-financed tiger cages on Con Son Island. In subsequent hearings, witness after witness came to Congress with statements deploring OPS linkages to the Vietnamese police. Typical was the commentary of John Champlin, an Air Force doctor:

> The paralysis in these prisoners was primarily due to severe nutritional deficiency coupled with prolonged immobilization. Each man had spent months or years without interruption in leg shackles while subsisting on a diet of three handfuls of milled white rice and three swallows of water per day. This combination of prolonged immobilization and starvation has to my knowledge never occurred before on such a scale. A computer review of 1200 medical journals and a personal search through medical literature on the health of POW's produced *no* descriptions similar to the above. Their paralysis together with the causitive conditions are unique in the history of modern warfare, and the U.S. bears a heavy burden of complicity.[30]

Statements such as this were supplemented by internal U.S. government memoranda that indicated that AID officials had full knowledge of the conditions OPS was financing. One such memo was written in 1964 by Frank Walton, AID's public safety director in South Vietnam: "In Con Son II, some of the hardcore communists keep preaching the 'party' line, so these 'Reds' are sent to the tiger cages in Con Son I where they are isolated from all others for months at a time. This confinement . . . may include immobilization—the prisoner is bolted to the floor."[31]

It is possible that OPS could have been saved if the State Depart-

---

Aid to the Thailand Police, University of Denver Graduate School of International Studies, Monograph Series in World Affairs, vol. 14, bk. 2 (Denver, 1977), pp. 3-11; Penny Lernoux, "Church Cowed by Uruguayan Military," mimeographed report (New York: The Alicia Patterson Foundation, 1975), p. 8; *Stopping U.S. Assistance to Foreign Police and Prisons*, p. 16, *supra* n. 26.

[30] U.S. Congress, House, Committee on Foreign Affairs, Subcommittee on Asian and Pacific Affairs, *The Treatment of Political Prisoners in South Vietnam by the Government of the Republic of South Vietnam*, 93d Cong., 1st Sess., September 13, 1973, p. 20.

[31] Ibid., p. 21. The tiger cages were not built by OPS but by the French during their occupation of Indochina. OPS advisors supervised their use, however.

ment had ended its support for the most flagrant violators of human rights and pushed for continued aid to more reputable governments. Instead, State denied that a problem existed. In 1973, after several members of Congress had seen the tiger cages with their own eyes and after *Life* magazine had published photographs of their maimed inhabitants alongside the AID personnel who were in charge of prison oversight, assistant secretary of state Marshall Wright told Congress: "The goal of the U.S. assistance and advisory programs to the South Vietnamese Directorate of Corrections has been to help South Viet-Nam develop a more humane prison system, and we believe this goal has been substantially achieved. . . . We cannot accept the recent allegations by some that our programs in this area are supporting a prison system based on torture and the suppression of legitimate dissent."[32]

AID then asked Congress for money to establish in South Vietnam "a central records system containing 12 million biodate documents and 115 million dossiers," a program that would place two-thirds of the South Vietnamese population under the surveillance of police computers.[33] The insensitivity of this request was too much for the dwindling number of members who supported President Nixon's Vietnamization program to overcome. In September 1973, Senator James Abourezk announced he would offer an amendment to the foreign assistance authorization to end aid to police forces in foreign countries. Passage of the amendment became the focus of every antiwar group in the country, although it is questionable whether their lobbying efforts were necessary. The amendment became law in December.[34] The following year, the Foreign Assistance Act of 1961 was further amended to prohibit training of foreign police in the United States.[35] On March 1, 1975, the International Police Academy was converted into a training center for the Customs Service, and on July 1, 1975, AID's Office of Public Safety was outlawed.

The only type of police aid that Congress did not prohibit was that used for curbing the international flow of narcotics, and part of OPS survived on the basis of its antidrug expertise. Abuses of this limited charter soon developed. In 1975, for example, the Senate Committee on Appropriations noted with alarm the dramatic growth in police equipment exports for narcotics control and suggested that much of it "is possibly being used for purposes unrelated to the control of drug

[32] Ibid., p. 60.
[33] Ibid., p. 16.
[34] PL93-189, Sec. 2 (3).
[35] PL93-559, Sec. 30.

traffic."[36] In 1976, a GAO investigation concluded that "commodities furnished to police units under the public safety program are now being provided to the same units under the narcotics program."[37] The study indicated that Third World drug control police units were receiving basic police equipment—radios, vehicles, revolvers, handcuffs, cameras, binoculars, office equipment—and that these units were sharing facilities with other police and military organizations, thereby rendering impossible any attempt to identify precisely the amount of narcotics control aid used to support the repression of human rights.[38]

Indirect Support of Repression

AID and Food for Peace are the major programs of economic aid that support repressive governments in Latin America. This, of course, is a highly controversial assertion, for very little agreement exists on the political implications of some types of economic assistance. For example, there are two polar views of the $212 million in economic aid that the United States sent the Somoza government betweeen 1962 and 1977: either the United States government provided each Nicaraguan citizen with about one hundred dollars to improve living standards in this poverty-stricken country or it helped to make the government of Anastasio Somoza one of the most repressive in the hemisphere. Reality probably rests somewhere on a continuum between these two extremes, depending upon the specific economic aid program being considered. OPS to Nicaragua was clearly pinned against the repression-supporting edge, but what about Food for Peace? Except to people who hold the doctrinaire position that all aid to a repressive government is supportive of repression, the answer is unclear. It is unclear whether hunger encourages or discourages urban squatters to resist repression of their attempts to seize land. It is unclear

[36] Senate Report 94-39, p. 88.

[37] See *Stopping U.S. Assistance to Foreign Police and Prisons*, p. 22, *supra* n. 26.

[38] The primary responsibility for assisting Latin American police in the control of narcotics traffic rests not with the State Department or AID but with the Justice Department's Drug Enforcement Administration (DEA), an organization whose analysis is beyond the scope of the present study. It should be noted, however, that by 1978, the DEA had developed an unsavory reputation in Latin America by paying Bolivian, Brazilian, and Uruguayan police and paramilitary personnel to kidnap and torture the persons it believed to be drug dealers, and some reports had begun to identify the Justice Department as a violator of human rights in Latin America. Some of these allegations have been proven and admitted, but there is no evidence on the extent to which such allegations characterize DEA behavior. See in particular the fascinating note by James B. Smith, Jr., in the *Texas International Law Journal* 11 (Winter 1976): 137-146; David Weissbrodt, "Human Rights Legislation and U.S. Foreign Policy," *Georgia Journal of International and Comparative Law*, supplement to vol. 7 (Summer 1977), p. 254.

whether an infusion of PL480 food will inevitably cause a decline in local market prices and, even if it does, it is unclear whether the consumers' pleasure outweighs the producers' anger. It is even unclear whether a PL480-induced price decline makes peasants rebellious or so concerned with starvation that they spend more time laboring in the fields and less time working to overthrow a tyrannical government. The political implications of aid designed to meet basic needs remain speculative.

There are occasions, however, when *changes* in economic aid disbursements are such that the only possible conclusion is that the United States government has made a formal policy decision to support a Latin American government that is engaged in the gross repression of its citizens' human rights. For example, the first significant United States financial aid to Guatemala began shortly after the CIA-assisted overthrow of the Arbenz regime in 1954. Between 1954 and 1955, U.S. aid skyrocketed from $463,000 to $10,708,000, a one-year increase that made Guatemala second only to famine-plagued Bolivia in the receipt of United States aid.[39] In the context of the times, it is difficult to conceive of a reason for this aid increase other than support for the repressive Castillo Armas government.[40] The pattern of AID expenditures in Brazil during the 1960s is so discontinuous that a similar conclusion seems warranted. From a total of $15 million in FY1964 (which ended three months after the anti-Goulart coup), AID expenditures jumped to $122 million in FY1965 and did not dip below that level until 1970, when Brazil's graduation from the economic aid program began. No other Latin American country has ever experienced sustained gross or per capita aid increases approaching these changes in the Brazilian program.

When confronted with examples of anomalous changes in aid disbursements coincident with the inception of repression, aid officials typically deny the existence of any unusual activity. The following dialogue between Representative Donald Fraser and AID's Herman Kleine in 1976 is characteristic of many I had with lower-ranking AID officials:

> *Mr. Fraser.* Why should the United States have been so interested in helping out the economic problem in Chile? What

[39] U.S. Department of Commerce, Office of Business Economics, *Foreign Grants and Credits by the United States Government: December 1955 Quarter* (Washington, D.C.: Department of Commerce, April 1956), p. 523.

[40] R. Harrison Wagner, *United States Policy toward Latin America: A Study in Domestic and International Politics* (Stanford: Stanford University Press, 1970), p. 211.

interest was there on the part of the United States to step in with all these programs?

Mr. Kleine. The similar interest that it has collaborating with governments within this region. The fact of a change in government, I do not think should lead to a decision that we should not cooperate. The government was eligible, it was interested.

Mr. Fraser. We were not helping the prior government. Then there was a coup. A new government came in; it was having economic distress. What interests of the United States were to be served by stepping in at that point and bringing to bear all of the different programs that we were able to help them out?

Mr. Kleine. There is a humanitarian interest in helping in a situation such as that. There are the usual interests in desiring to maintain good and close relationships with governments in this hemisphere.[41]

The case of Chile merits special attention, for the initial human rights battles in the mid-1970s focused upon the Nixon-Ford administration's support of the Pinochet government. The strongest evidence that the United States used economic aid to support repression in post-Allende Chile is to be found in the Food for Peace program. During 1973 and 1974, United States food reserves were at unusually low levels, and worldwide PL480 authorizations during FY1974 were at their lowest level in a decade. But less than a month after the 1973 coup—early in FY1974—the Department of Agriculture approved Chile's request for a $24 million non-PL480 Commodity Credit Corporation loan for the purchase of wheat.[42] This was eight times the total commodity credit offered to Chile during the three Allende years, and it set a pattern that was to continue when more PL480 supplies were available during the remaining years of the Nixon-Ford administration. In FY1975, Chile received 48 percent of all Food for Peace aid to Latin America, 40 percent in FY1976, and 28 percent in FY1977.[43] By way of comparison, in the typical year of FY1968, Chile received 12 percent of PL480 aid to Latin America; under Allende in FY1972, six percent of Latin America's total Food for Peace aid went to Chile. With about three percent of Latin America's population and, according to one study,[44] no more than its proportional share of

---

[41] See Chile: The Status of Human Rights, pp. 31-32, supra n. 8.

[42] See Refugee and Humanitarian Problems in Chile, p. 54, supra n. 6.

[43] The Ford administration proposed to ship to Chile an even larger share of PL480 food. In the FY1976 budget request, Chile was to receive 53 percent of all PL480 food to Latin America—85 percent of all Title I and 10 percent of all Title II. See Refugee and Humanitarian Problems in Chile, Part III, p. 113, supra n. 24.

[44] Ibid., pp. 11ff.

hungry people, Chile received an absolutely extraordinary amount of food aid during the initial years of the Pinochet regime. In the three-decade history of the PL480 program, the only similar instances of radically skewed distributions to relatively small populations occurred in Indochina during the Vietnamese war and South Korea during the 1970s.

Aid officials were forced to justify this distribution before subcommittees chaired by two influential members of Congress, Representative Donald Fraser and Senator Edward Kennedy, both of whom could be characterized as enraged over the Nixon-Kissinger policy toward Chile. Five years after the 1973 coup, Senator Kennedy's face still reddened visibly and his voice rose several octaves at the mention of Chile. Former Representative Fraser was always less excitable, but he too remained open in his loathing of pre-1977 American policy toward Pinochet's Chile. Because of this intense animosity, the administration sent its best people to Capitol Hill to explain the Chilean government's food requirements. In 1975, assistant secretary of state William D. Rogers, a Democrat who willy nilly became the spokesperson for Secretary of State Kissinger's Latin American policy, appeared before Kennedy's judiciary subcommittee on refugees and attributed the rise in PL480 shipments to crop failures.[45] Within a year, the Ford administration shifted the blame from production shortfalls to the demands of the Pinochet stabilization program: "The cornerstone of the Government of Chile's economic recovery program is the controlling of inflation, which at the end of fiscal year 1973 was the highest in the world at 500 percent per annum. PL480 Title I proceeds freed scarce foreign exchange which was needed to finance essential imports and thereby curb inflation,"[46] Specifically, the Chileans financed their arms imports. By 1977, Chile had become one of the best customers of U.S. arms manufacturers—fifth in the world behind Iran, Israel, Saudi Arabia and Jordan.[47] Noting that arms purchases probably were not essential imports and certainly did not help curb inflation, Representative Fraser concluded that "one of the major benefits to Chile of Public Law 480 Title I loans is to indirectly assist Chile in purchasing arms from the United States."[48]

[45] Ibid., pp. 48-54. On Rogers' more moderate early positions, see his *The Twilight Struggle: The Alliance for Progress and the Politics of Development in Latin America* (New York: Random House, 1967), esp. pp. 287-288.

[46] U.S. Congress, Senate, Committee on Agriculture, Nutrition, and Forestry, Subcommittee on Foreign Agricultural Policy, *Future of Food Aid*, 95th Cong., 1st Sess., April 4 and 5, 1977, p. 46.

[47] *New York Times*, October 16, 1977, sec. IV, p. 3.

[48] See *Chile: The Status of Human Rights*, p. 2, *supra* n. 8.

The process by which the United States government decides to support repressive governments differs substantially from the process by which decisions are made to support the creation of repressive regimes. During the 1960s and 1970s, decisions to channel increased amounts of aid to repressive governments appeared to emerge from the various aid bureaus with a minimum of direction. These decisions responded to a set of extremely obvious cues from high-level officials. At a news conference three days after the 1964 Brazilian coup, for example, President Johnson could hardly restrain his delight over the fall of Goulart, telling reporters that "this has been a good week for this hemisphere." "While the problems are immense there," he continued, "we are prepared to join with our friends in the world in trying to help Brazil face up to them and meet them. . . . We have seen the transition in Brazil."[49] Johnson's statements were reinforced by additional words of approval from the most powerful Latin Americanist in the State Department since Nelson Rockefeller, assistant secretary of state Thomas Mann. Meanwhile, Ambassador Gordon and the Brazilian minister of finance quickly revived the massive program loans that were then the fashion at AID. The first of these was signed in June 1964 for $50 million, followed by another in December for $150 million.[50]

This was all that lower-level officials needed to know about policy. With only minimal direction they apparently moved to reinitiate the aid programs that had been halted during the last months of the Goulart government and to begin new ones. The AID staff in Brazil was increased at the ambassador's request and, as a natural consequence of people doing their jobs, the mission started a flow of funding requests northward to Washington headquarters. The requests flowed through the executive branch budget bureaucracy and then on to Capitol Hill as part of the administration's foreign aid request. With the notable exception of Senator Wayne Morse, during the 1960s Congress ignored the question of supporting repression in Brazil with economic aid.

Decision making in the case of Chile in 1973 was not dissimilar from that of Brazil a decade earlier. Two days after the coup, a State Department spokesperson said "we will have to work with the generals and it makes no sense to issue some moral statement about democ-

[49] *Public Papers of the Presidents of the United States: Lyndon B. Johnson, 1963-64* (Washington, D.C.: Government Printing Office, 1965), pp. 437-438.

[50] Another $150 million was made available in February 1966, $100 million in March 1967, and finally $75 million in May 1968. See *United States Policies and Programs in Brazil*, p. 185, *supra* n. 1.

187

racy."[51] A week later, assistant secretary of state Kubisch told a House Foreign Affairs subcommittee that "if the Chileans want our help and we can give help, it would be my hope and expectation that we would do everything we could to provide it."[52] Kubisch also told Senator Kennedy's subcommittee on refugees that "it is quite apparent that Chile is going to need considerable aid and if it adopts a sensible government I would expect that aid to be given."[53] Less than two months after the coup, the Chilean minister of finance arrived in Washington, where he found government officials ready to entertain his economic aid proposals.

The activity that ensued in both the Brazilian and Chilean cases was not the product of a tightly controlled decision-making cabal in the White House, the State Department, or the National Security Council staff. Unlike the secret high-level plotting that must characterize policy making on efforts to undermine nonrepressive governments, the decisions to support repressive governments with economic aid can be and were made openly but without much discussion. There were no memoranda filtering up or filtering down the aid bureaucracy, no convening of committees, yet everyone involved apparently knew what policy would be. In interview after interview, State Department respondents said there simply was no question how the United States would respond to requests for economic aid to Chile or Brazil following the coups against Allende and Goulart.

Although there are no data to support any specific explanation of how this knowledge is acquired, it is probable that lower-level aid officials knew what policy would be because they are extremely good at perceiving even subtle changes in statements by the President or other senior decision makers. Like most employees, lower-level foreign policy officials adapt their behavior to accommodate their superiors' preferences. Adaptability is encouraged by the fact that aid officials who refuse to be accommodating are "selected out" of their jobs, so that officials who remain tend to profess values that are not particularly different from those of their superiors. These officials jointly perceive threats and they jointly perceive the elimination of threats. Lower-level officials need direction in dealing with threats that are in control of a foreign state, since the destabilization of governments is at least improper, probably illegal, and certainly too sensitive for minor officials to handle. But prior to 1977, it was not necessary to tell aid officials what United States policy should be toward a strongly anticommunist but repressive Latin American government.

[51] *New York Times*, September 14, 1973, p. 8.
[52] *Journal of Commerce*, September 21, 1973, p. 1.
[53] *Miami Herald*, September 30, 1978, p. 1.

Because Congress must authorize aid programs and appropriate funds with which they can be pursued, in theory it could have become involved in the policy-making process at a fairly early stage. But in the case of Brazil, Congress became concerned about the relationship between aid and repression very slowly. This was probably inevitable given members' low level of interest in U.S.-Latin American relations, but it is significant that there was no policy of systematically excluding Congress from decision making; Congress excluded itself. Conversely, a number of members acted almost immediately to express their concern over human rights violations by the Pinochet government, indicating that by the mid-1970s Congress had overcome any reluctance to force its way into the decision-making process. It is to an analysis of the resurgence of congressional activism that we now turn.

Pre-1977 Human Rights Activity

While economic aid programs have always served as a means to encourage certain types of behavior by Third World recipients, the Charter of Punta del Este was unique in that it publicly formalized the reciprocal obligations linking donors and Latin American recipients. Specifically, the Alliance for Progress made aid contingent upon recipients instituting certain specific policies, which were called reforms. President Kennedy told the representatives of Latin American governments that "if the countries of Latin America are ready to do their part, and I am sure they are, then I believe the United States, for its part, should help provide resources of a scope and magnitude sufficient to make this bold development plan a success."[54]

In the initial years of the Alliance, certain Latin American governments were called upon to do "their part" by reducing their human rights violations. United States aid was used inconsistently to achieve this end, however, with primary attention focused upon the least powerful nations in the region. Thus in 1963, the United States decided against a major aid program in poverty-stricken Haiti as a protest against the repressiveness of the Duvalier regime, while in Brazil a year later an increase in repression appeared to coincide with an increase in aid. Stung by charges that the Johnson administration's policy penalized only the weak, in 1964, assistant secretary of state Thomas Mann replied that "we cannot put ourselves in the doctrinaire straitjacket of automatic application of sanctions to every unconstitutional regime which arises in this hemisphere." Foreshadowing the

[54] *Public Papers of the Presidents of the United States: John F. Kennedy, 1961* (Washington, D.C.: Government Printing Office, 1962), p. 172.

189

Nixon administration's argument a decade later, Mann rejected the use of aid reductions to attack repressive governments as illegal intervention in the "internal political developments in other countries."[55]

During the 1960s, the only well-researched example of an aid reduction in response to increased repression in a major Latin American nation occurred in late 1968 and early 1969, when $188 million in economic aid to Brazil was placed "under review" (as was a vague military aid request for destroyer escorts) following promulgation of the Fifth Institutional Act. Weiner tells us that during the four-month suspension, the Agency for International Development and other State Department entities engaged in a vigorous internal debate over the proper response to evidence that all dissent in Brazil had become illegal. State's Office of Regional Economic Policy championed the view that the United States should only consider the Brazilian government's compliance with loan and grant agreements in formulating aid policy. Conversely, AID's Office of Development Programs argued that Alliance objectives could not be met in an environment of extreme repression. This disagreement was left unresolved and the aid requests left unprocessed by the lame-duck Johnson administration. By March 1969, the new Nixon officials had familiarized themselves with the issue, and they decided to resume the aid programs.[56]

From the beginning, then, the policy of the Nixon administration was to minimize what came to be called "human rights considerations" in economic aid decision making. Early in his administration, President Nixon declared his intention to overlook political repression in Latin America: "The United States has a strong interest in maintaining cooperation with our neighbors regardless of their domestic viewpoint. . . . We hope that governments will evolve toward constitutional procedures but it is not our mission to try to provide except by example,

[55] *Department of State Bulletin*, June 29, 1964, p. 999. An expanded treatment of this issue is provided by James D. Cochrane, "U.S. Policy toward Recognition of Governments and Promotion of Democracy in Latin America Since 1963," *Journal of Latin American Studies* 4 (November 1972); 278. For a comparison of the Nixon and Johnson policies, see U.S. Congress, Senate, Committee on Foreign Relations, Subcommittee on Western Hemisphere Affairs, *Rockefeller Report on Latin America*, 91st Cong., 1st Sess., November 20, 1969, p. 13.

[56] Harry Weiner, "U.S.-Brazil Relations: Non-Governmental Organizations and the Fifth Institutional Act," in the *Report* of the Commission on the Organization of the Government for the Conduct of Foreign Policy, vol. 3, app. 1 (Washington, D.C.: Government Printing Office, June 1975), pp. 252-253; *United States Policies and Programs in Brazil*, p. 189, *supra* n.1; U.S. Congress, House, Committee on Foreign Affairs, Subcommittee on Inter-American Affairs, *New Directions for the 1970's: Toward a Strategy of Inter-American Development*, 91st Cong., 1st Sess., March-May 1969, p. 571.

the answers to such questions to other sovereign nations. We deal with governments as they are."[57] President Nixon's stated policy quickly filtered through the aid bureaucracy. Citing the illegality of intervention, officials rejected the suggestion that the United States employ aid to influence the level of political repression. In mid-1973, for example, assistant secretary of state Kubisch noted that the administration's goal was to "avoid anything which smacks of a tutorial or patronizing approach toward Latin America."[58]

After American complicity in the destruction of the Allende government became a matter of public record, increased congressional interest in the human rights violations of aid recipients forced higher-level officials to enter the controversy. Secretary of State Kissinger developed two arguments against linking aid distributions to the recipients' levels of respect for human rights. He warned repeatedly against "temptations to crusade," for, like Kubisch, Kissinger did not wish to insult the maturing nations of Latin America.[59] When the audience was appropriate, he also advanced the Cold War belief that a halt in aid to repressive governments could damage national security, since "such withdrawal, or even the threat of withdrawal, depreciates the strength of the mutual defense relationship which we share with our allies and offers encouragement to potential enemies."[60] Halfway through its final year in office, the Ford administration moderated somewhat its view that human rights violations were the internal affair of each sovereign state. But it used quiet diplomacy and not aid as the foreign policy instrument to advance its position. There never was a time when the Nixon-Ford administration accepted economic aid reductions as a tool to discourage human rights violations.

While there is no evidence that the views of AID officials differed significantly from those of higher-level decision makers, during the mid-1970s the Agency experienced a slow awakening of interest in the issue of human rights. In responding to the initial spate of congressional concern over assistance to repressive regimes, AID insisted that reductions in foreign aid were inappropriate responses to human rights

[57] See *United States Policies and Programs in Brazil*, p. 290, *supra* n. 1. President Nixon reaffirmed this policy near the end of his administration. U.S. President (Nixon), *U.S. Foreign Policy for the 1970's: Shaping a Durable Peace; A Report to the Congress, May 3, 1973* (Washington, D.C.: Government Printing Office, 1973), p. 118.

[58] *Miami Herald*, July 20, 1973, p. 1.

[59] U.S. Congress, House, Committee on International Relations, *Report of Secretary of State Kissinger on His Trip to Latin America*, 94th Cong., 2d Sess., March 4, 1976, p. 8.

[60] U.S. Department of State, *The Secretary of State*, March 26, 1976, p. 4.

violations.[61] Unlike their superiors in the State Department and the National Security Council, however, AID personnel were not unconcerned about the rising level of political repression in the hemisphere. These officials were merely continuing the firmly established practice of following orders. The social and political variables considered in aid decision making have always been selected by officials outside AID, in the executive branch and in Congress. Thus the Agency was (and remains) unprepared to incorporate any independent sociopolitical analysis, including the analysis of human rights behavior, into its internal decision-making processes. But AID officials listen attentively to the opinions of members of Congress, and by 1975 the Agency recognized that it could no longer ignore demands that human rights be considered in aid decisions. In an August 1975 letter to all assistant administrators and heads of departments, AID administrator Daniel Parker urged his personnel to "address the problem of human rights with imagination and compassion. . . . I urge you and your staffs to begin developing human rights programs immediately."[62]

Nonetheless, AID was trapped between congressional demands that greater attention be given to human rights and senior executive branch officials' insistence that the subject be ignored. AID resolved this dilemma by centering its human rights efforts on convincing Congress that it was doing all it could to promote human rights rather than on encouraging aid recipients to alter their repressive policies. One memo that is suggestive of this effort was written in early 1976 by the AID policy planning chief: "The country teams indicate the human rights environment in each nation is unique and must be considered in [sic] its own terms. The U.S. should watch out for local sensitivities if we hope to maintain a constructive relationship with the country. . . . Governments receiving U.S. aid that wished to uphold human rights have probably been helped to do this. But if the desire is not present to start with, it is unlikely that economic assistance will do much for human rights in the short or medium term."[63] Only after the Ford administration had been voted out of office did AID officials finally incorporate human rights considerations in their decision making.

Internal AID memoranda indicate that Congress was the reason why the Agency and other executive departments began to give increased attention to the level of political repression in recipient na-

---

[61] U.S. Congress, House, Committee on Foreign Affairs, Subcommittee on International Organizations and Movements, *International Protection of Human Rights*, 93d Cong., 1st Sess., 1973, p. 819.

[62] See *Chile: The Status of Human Rights*, pp. 164-165, *supra* n. 8.

[63] Ibid., p. 116.

tions.[64] This congressional concern has taken two forms: general human rights sections added as amendments to foreign assistance legislation and country-specific aid prohibitions. While both forms of legislation became prominent in the 1970s, each was used in the 1960s as well. Section 501 of the Foreign Assistance Act of 1964 (PL88-633) stands as the first human rights clause in foreign aid legislation. It was a mild sense-of-Congress statement that the United States "deeply believes in the freedom of religion for all people and is opposed to infringements of this freedom anywhere in the world."[65] Two years later, the Foreign Assistance Act of 1966 (PL89-583) directed aid officials to take into account "the degree to which the recipient country is making progress toward respect for the rule of law, freedom of expression and of the press, and recognition of the importance of individual freedom, initiative, and private enterprise." All but the last three words of this provision resulted from an initiative by Senators Robert Kennedy and Ernest Gruening.[66]

During the 1960s, the only major country-specific actions by Congress on behalf of human rights in Latin America were expressions of concern by individual members about human rights violations in Brazil. In October 1965, Senator Wayne Morse called for a cut in economic and military aid as a protest against the government's Second Institutional Act.[67] Thereafter Senator Frank Church took an active interest in the relationship between Brazilian repression and the United States aid programs, and in the House, the Fraser Subcommittee gave major attention to Brazil during its initial human rights hearings in 1973. In neither body did the hearings serve as the basis for subsequent legislation.[68] In general, prior to 1973, neither

[64] See, for example, the documents published in ibid., pp. 167-169.

[65] This provision had an anticommunist focus. As passed by the Senate (S.1188), the amendment condemned the persecution of Jews in the Soviet Union; in conference, the House insisted on the more diplomatic generalized language.

[66] Added during floor debate, the Kennedy-Gruening amendment was the first of what became a battery of human rights amendments to the Foreign Assistance Act that bypassed the Senate Committee on Foreign Relations. The amendment applied only to aid for Latin America. *Congressional Record*, July 26, 1966, pp. 17057-17064. The Foreign Assistance Act of 1966 also contained a remarkable prohibition on aid to countries officially participating in international conferences planning subversion. Its purpose was to punish participants in the 1966 Tricontinental Conference in Havana.

[67] See *International Protection of Human Rights*, p. 646, *supra* n. 61.

[68] U.S. Congress, Senate, Committee on Foreign Relations, Subcommittee on American Republics Affairs, *Survey of the Alliance for Progress: Labor Policies and Programs*, 90th Cong., 2d Sess., February-March 1968, pp. 73-74; Robert A. Pastor, "Congress' Impact on Latin America; Is There a Madness in the Method?" in the *Report* of the Commission on the Organization of the Government for the Conduct

the House nor the Senate was particularly concerned with human rights violations in Latin America. Indicative of this neglect were the "New Directions" hearings by the House Foreign Affairs Subcommittee on Inter-American Affairs. Out of a total of 1,132 pages of hearings, the question of human rights surfaced infrequently and, when it did, it was almost immediately passed over in favor of other topics.[69]

It is difficult to pinpoint with precision the sequence of events in 1973 that served to make human rights the major focus of Congress's annual review of economic assistance legislation. As Patricia Fagen has suggested, the September coup in Chile and the widespread allegations of U.S. complicity served to increase congressional concern, and the end of the lengthy debate over aid to South Vietnamese prisons also contributed to the general focus upon political repression and aid.[70] It is probably not incorrect to suggest that the human rights movement was in large measure a continuation and a generalization of the antiwar movement. Nearly all of the principal congressional human rights activists were involved in antiwar activities in the years before 1973. In 1970, for example, Representative Tom Harkin, at the time a congressional aide, arranged (with Don Luce of Clergy and Laity Concerned) for the first inspection by U.S. legislators of the notorious Vietnamese penal colony on Con Son Island. His *Life* magazine photos of prisoners staring up through the bars of their tiger cages were among the most vivid reminders of American aid projects in that unhappy land.[71] Other congressional human rights leaders— Abourezk, Badillo, Drinan, Fraser, Kennedy, Koch, McGovern—were also outspoken opponents of United States involvement in Vietnam.

By general consensus, major credit for raising the level of congressional concern for human rights is given to the set of hearings held in 1973 by the House Foreign Affairs Subcommittee on International Organizations and Movements. Representative Donald Fraser's subcommittee held fifteen hearings with forty-five witnesses between

of Foreign Policy, vol. 3, app. 1 (Washington D.C.: Government Printing Office, June 1975), p. 264; *United States Policies and Programs in Brazil, supra* n. 1; *International Protection of Human Rights*, pp. 188-217, 643-680, *supra* n. 61. In addition, the issue of repression in Brazil was raised in 1966 during the confirmation hearing for assistant secretary-designate and former ambassador to Brazil, Lincoln Gordon. At that hearing, Senators Morse and Edward Kennedy praised Gordon's actions in Brazil. See *Nomination of Lincoln Gordon*, pp. 3, 9, *supra* n. 11.

[69] See *New Directions for the 1970's*, pp. 162-164, 265, *supra* n. 9; *New Directions for the 1970's: Toward a Strategy of Inter-American Development*, p. 571, *supra* n. 56.

[70] Patricia Weiss Fagen, "U.S. Foreign Policy and Human Rights: The Role of Congress," in *National Control over Foreign Policy Making*, ed. Antonio Cassese (Leyden: Sijthoff and Noorhoff, 1979).

[71] *Life* 69 (July 17, 1970): 2A, 26-31.

August and December. The subcommittee's interest continued into the Ninety-fourth Congress (1975-1976), when no fewer than forty hearings were held on various aspects of human rights and United States policy toward eighteen different countries. Although the subcommittee exercised no jurisdiction over United States policy toward Latin America, it reviewed the status of human rights in Argentina, Brazil, Chile (three hearings), Cuba, El Salvador, Haiti, Nicaragua, Paraguay, and Uruguay.

These hearings served three purposes. First, they permitted Representative Fraser to claim expertise in a specific policy area in much the same way that Representative Dante Fascell claimed nearly exclusive knowledge of Latin America. As a result, for several years Fraser determined the fate of most if not all human rights questions in the House. His support was almost invaluable, his opposition difficult to overcome. Second, the hearings lent credibility to the subcommittee's proposed legislation regarding human rights and foreign aid policy during the crucial aid authorization markup sessions by the Committee on Foreign Affairs. And finally, the subcommittee hearings were a means by which the government could investigate human rights violations at a time when the executive branch would have preferred to ignore the subject. When combined with the implicit threat of aid reductions, this publicity may have helped to moderate some repressive measures and to forestall others.

The initial legislation of the 1970s linking human rights and foreign aid was a relatively innocuous section in the Foreign Assistance Act of 1973 (PL93-189, Sec. 32). PL93-189 was one of the two major revisions that have been made in the Foreign Assistance Act of 1961, and as a result it contained many new sections, including the much-discussed New Directions policy statement. Section 32, a Senate initiative, went almost unnoticed. It was in the form of a simple declaration: "It is the sense of Congress that the President should deny any economic or military assistance to the government of any foreign country which practices the internment or imprisonment of that country's citizens for political purposes." Although there were a number of other human rights clauses related to military aid and to specific countries in PL93-189 and in the Foreign Assistance Act of 1974 (PL93-559), Section 32 was the only general legislation by the Ninety-third Congress (1973-1974) that tied economic aid to the recipients' respect for their citizens' human rights.

The Harkin amendment (Sec. 116 of the Foreign Assistance Act of 1961) is today the cornerstone of human rights legislation related to U.S. bilateral economic assistance. Created by the liberal Ninety-fourth Congress as part (Sec. 310) of the International Development and Food Assistance Act of 1975 (PL94-161), the amendment is the prime product of the liberal-isolationist coalition that determined the fate of most human rights legislation during the 1970s. In 1975, the Committee on International Relations reported the foreign assistance authorization bill to the House without a human rights clause. Edward Snyder of the Friends Committee on National Legislation and Joseph Eldridge of the Washington Office on Latin America then drafted an amendment that provided for a halt in economic aid to countries engaged in gross violations of internationally recognized human rights unless the aid would directly benefit needy people. Then they set out in search of a sponsor. They found Representative Tom Harkin, a freshman critic of aid to repressive regimes, who forcefully presented the case for the human rights amendment on the floor.

The Harkin amendment appeared to be doomed, however, as two powerful leaders of the Committee on International Relations—first Dante Fascell and then Clement Zablocki—rose to express their opposition. At that crucial moment, immediately after the House liberal foreign affairs establishment had expressed its disapproval, Representative Wayne Hays stood up and announced his support for the Harkin initiative. Hays, the powerful chairperson of the International Relations Subcommittee on International Operations, was noted for both his scathing criticism of the State Department and his venomous hatred of foreign aid recipients. (In the 1975 foreign aid debate he characterized the government of Sri Lanka as led by "that miserable Bandaranaike woman, who is only exceeded in her miserableness by the head of the Government of India, to whom we are also giving a handout.") He told his friends on the floor:

> This must be . . . the one-thousandth time I have heard somebody get up, as the gentleman from Florida [Fascell] did, and say, 'Oh, this is a good amendment. It's a great idea. It ought to be done, but it's too hard for the bureaucrats to do.'
>
> Now, that it a lot of baloney. The only reason we got this bill down here really mainly, the reason they are pushing it downtown is so that the bureaucracy can stay in business. God knows they do little enough now and to give them one little additional thing to do is not going to hurt them any. It may even get them to working for a change.
>
> I will guarantee that anyone can go down and walk through that foreign aid agency and find 20 percent of them asleep, 20 percent reading newspapers, 20 percent out for coffee, 20 percent in the various men's or lady's rooms, and another 20 percent are

taking a vacation; so you have darn near nobody there at any given time. . . .

So what is wrong with this amendment? It is well-intentioned. It may do some good. The bureaucracy may enforce it a little bit. We ought to put their feet to the fire and give them a chance to try it.[72]

Hays' remarks were followed by those of John Ashbrook, a leader of the House conservative block, who noted: "It is far beyond the time when we ought to cut off these giveaways generally, but until this House is more enlightened in our own self-interest, we should at least cut off aid to repressive regimes."[73] With this strange collection of bedpersons, the House passed the Harkin amendment by the substantial margin of 238 to 164.[74]

Harkin and other human rights activists had caught the congressional foreign affairs leaders and administration officials unprepared, but in the Senate the leadership was fully ready to do battle. Attempts to insert a Harkin-type human rights amendment into the Senate foreign aid authorization bill failed both in Senator's Humphrey's Foreign Relations Subcommittee on Foreign Assistance and in the full Foreign Relations Committee markup. Again FCNL's Snyder and others drafted a slightly modified Harkin-type amendment that Senator McGovern proposed in a dissenting additional view in the committee report to the full Senate. The formal amendment was offered on the floor by Senator Abourezk. During the debate, Senator McGovern spoke for the liberal wing of the Democratic party:

> I think nothing has damaged the support of the American people for aid programs more than our identification . . . with corrupt and brutal regimes overseas. Perhaps a body of experts can find reasons why it is acceptable for us to be sending money into a country whose prisons are jammed with political dissenters, or whose leaders amuse themselves by tearing people's fingernails out. But I do not think the American people will or should accept

[72] *Congressional Record*, September 19, 1975, p. H8609. The Representative sitting next to Hays at that moment recalled that Hays' decision to speak was apparently made quite quickly. As Harkin spoke, Hays put down some papers he was reading, nodded vigorously, and said to anyone listening: "That boy's got a good idea." Interview with Representative Ned Pattison, Washington, D.C., December 2, 1978.

[73] *Congressional Record*, September 19, 1975, p. H8609.

[74] I have been unable to discover evidence that Section 116 resulted from Congress's dismay over the Department of State's failure to implement Section 32. It is probable that the liberal Ninety-fourth Congress would have passed the Harkin amendment even if the Ford administration had vigorously implemented Section 32. Compare Weissbrodt, "Human Rights Legislation and U.S. Foreign Policy," p. 241.

it. We must notify such governments in unmistakeable terms that our aid is on the line, not only because it is morally right, but because it is true. Unless we begin standing for at least these fundamental human rights, I think the entire program could wither, and these hopeful new aid directions could die, for want of public support.[75]

Without the support of liberal senators, the bill's floor managers faced the prospect of the entire aid bill being defeated. Senators Humphrey and Case therefore reluctantly accepted the amendment, and it passed by voice vote. The Harkin amendment goes well beyond the weak "sense of Congress" declaration of Section 32 to a mandatory prohibition of aid to repressive governments, unless the President determines that such aid will directly benefit needy people. It is upon this amendment that all efforts to limit economic aid to Latin America's most repressive regimes have been based since 1975.

During the period leading up to 1977, the question of country-specific aid denials centered upon the human rights abuses of the Chilean government.[76] In 1973, Congress added Section 35 to the foreign assistance authorization bill, urging the President to (1) request the government of Chile to respect human rights, (2) support U.N. efforts to protect Chilean refugees and political prisoners, (3) support emergency relief needs in Chile, and (4) request the Inter-American Commission on Human Rights to undertake an immediate inquiry into the events following the September 1973 coup. Section 35 was primarily the work of Senator Edward Kennedy. As approved by the Senate, his amendment included a statement of the sense of Congress that military and economic aid should also be reduced. The House had no similar provision in its bill. Because he was not a member of the Committee on Foreign Relations, Kennedy was not among the conferees who met to reconcile the two versions. Senator Humphrey refused to fight for the Kennedy language when House conferees, especially Foreign Affairs chairperson "Doc" Morgan and Clement Zablocki, expressed their disapproval. The aid cutoff was rewritten as a request that the President ask the government of Chile to protect human rights.[77] Timing was one reason for the weak language: the legislation was completed two months after the coup, before

[75] *Congressional Record*, November 4, 1975, p. S19197.

[76] Country-specific denials for other reasons are common additions to aid legislation. In chronological order beginning with 1961, Cuba, Indonesia, the United Arab Republic, the Palestine Liberation Organization, Greece, Pakistan, India, Ecuador, Laos, North Vietnam, South Vietnam, and Turkey experienced aid reductions or cutoffs prior to action against Chile in 1974.

[77] House Report 93-664, pp. 53-54.

the full human rights implications of the Pinochet government's policies had been documented.

By the following year, there was no longer any doubt about the regime's brutality, and although the executive branch lobbied vigorously it was unable to prevent Congress from authorizing what was to be the smallest amount of economic aid to Chile in the 1974 to 1977 period.[78] The Nixon administration had requested $84.9 million for Chile in FY1975, of which $63.6 million was to be economic aid and the remainder military assistance. The Senate Foreign Relations Committee trimmed the total figure to $65 million and then, upon recommittal, to $55 million, none of which could be military aid. The House then passed a prohibition on military aid but made no restriction on economic assistance. The House-Senate conference committee struck a strange compromise. It restricted economic aid to $25 million but supplemented this reduction by deleting the words "or any other" in a key phrase in the Senate bill that limited "the total amount of assistance that may be made available for Chile under this or any other law." This left unaffected a variety of aid programs, including Food for Peace. Nixon administration officials lobbied for this modification on the grounds that certain semiconcessional aid programs that also benefited U.S. producers and investors (Overseas Private Investment Corporation insurance, Commodity Credit Corporation loans) should not be affected. This argument was sufficient to convince Representatives Morgan and Zablocki and Senator Sparkman. The liberal conferees (Senators Church and Humphrey, Representative Fascell) offered little opposition to the deletion.

When the heavily Democratic Ninety-fourth Congress convened in 1975, it appeared inclined to restrict further aid to Chile, which by then had come to be seen as a major disaster of the Nixon-Kissinger foreign policy. But when the International Development and Food Assistance Act of 1975 (PL94-161) became law, the economic aid ceiling had not been lowered but raised from $25 million to $90 million. For the second year in a row Edward Kennedy took to the Senate floor to challenge the weak bill reported by the Foreign Relations Committee. After asserting that the $25 million limitation enacted the previous year had been interpreted by the Kissinger State Department to permit total FY1975 economic aid disbursements to Chile of $112 million, he was successful in setting ceilings on economic aid to Chile of $90 million (FY1976) and $50 million (FY1977), along with a tighter definition of economic aid to include housing guarantees and PL480 Title I sales. There were additional clauses designed to

[78] PL93-559, Sec. 25.

close loopholes in earlier legislation. The House bill contained no limitation on aid to Chile, but House conferees agreed to the Senate's $90 million limitation for FY1976.[79] The Senate agreed to defer action on FY1977 assistance.

The implementation of the 1974 and 1975 limitations on aid to Chile will probably stand for some time as the classic example of executive branch contempt for congressional directives on foreign aid. The Ford administration clearly wished to continue its aid programs to Chile without any ceiling. The task of determining how to circumvent the limiting legislation fell to AID's general counsel. He disposed of the $25 million ceiling for FY1975 by interpreting narrowly the phrase in the Senate-House conference report on PL93-559 which stated that the purpose of Section 25 was to "limit the funds that could be used for assistance to Chile." Specifically, AID determined that $30 million in housing guarantees were excluded from the $25 million ceiling because a housing guarantee does not require the expenditure of funds. The $30 million was a U.S. government protection for private investors against losses. Nonetheless, encouraged by the government guarantee, United States investors sent $30 million into the Chilean economy.[80]

To circumvent the $90 million ceiling for FY1976, AID's general counsel produced twelve pages of prolix legalese in which a distinction was made among the terms "signed," "authorized," and "delivered."[81] This was done despite evidence from the conference committee report that Congress meant something quite simple: no more than $90 million in aid should reach Chilean shores in FY1976.[82] The effect of AID's legal opinion was to permit the verb in Section 320 ("made available") to be defined in such a way that AID could ignore the law. For example, in 1976, AID told Congress that it "formally authorized" the previously mentioned $30 million housing guarantee on June 30, 1975, the day before Section 320 took effect, even though the contracts for the loan were not signed until January 26, 1976. Thus in 1975, AID asserted that the $30 million was not aid as defined by PL93-559. Then a year later AID agreed that the $30 million was aid as defined by PL94-161 but that it was not part of the $90 million ceiling for FY1976 because "made available" in this case meant "authorized" in FY1975 rather than "signed" in FY1976.[83] AID officially claims to have made available $78.3 million in economic aid to Chile during FY1976. In reality,

[79] PL94-161, Sec. 320.
[80] See Chile: The Status of Human Rights, p. 16, supra n. 8.
[81] Ibid., pp. 79-91.
[82] House Report 94-691, p. 40.
[83] Ibid., pp. 94-95.

no one outside the executive branch—especially no one in Congress—
has any idea how much economic aid actually reached Chile during
that year.

By 1976, some form of showdown between Congress and the Ford-
Kissinger State Department was inevitable. Although there was no
economic aid authorization bill in 1976, Congress adopted the unusual
approach of amending the military assistance legislation to limit economic aid to Chile. In the House, the process of reducing aid was
greatly facilitated by a series of hearings by the Fraser Subcommittee
which, in the words of the House report, "substantiates the record of
gross violations of human rights occurring in Chile."[84] In the Committee on International Relations, Representative Fraser's amendment
to limit FY1977 economic aid to $25 million passed unanimously, and
the full House made no attempt to delete or to weaken its provisions.
Perhaps the most significant aspect of the House bill was the sense of
distrust of the executive branch that rested between the lines of the
extraordinary explanatory language of its report:

> Sec. 407 [of the 1976 bill] also amends section 320 [of 1975's
> PL94-161] to make clear that the limitations apply to all forms
> of assistance of any kind, direct or indirect, including, without
> limitation, grants, loans, housing and other guaranties, insurance
> by the Overseas Private Investment Corporation (OPIC) or other
> agencies and programs under title I of Public Law 480 (food for
> peace), with the sole exception of humanitarian aid provided
> through private voluntary agencies under title II of Public Law
> 480. The limitation applies to assistance furnished by all de-
> partments, agencies, or instrumentalities of the United States,
> including, without limitation, the Export-Import Bank, OPIC,
> and the Commodity Credit Corporation.[85]

In the Senate, Hubert Humphrey's Foreign Relations Subcommittee
on Foreign Assistance included no limit on economic aid to Chile.
But once again Senator Humphrey took note of the dissatisfaction of
liberal senators and introduced an amendment on the Senate floor to
limit economic aid to Chile to $30 million. The Humphrey amend-
ment provided Chile with an additional $38 million when the Pres-
ident could certify to Congress that the government of Chile no longer
engaged in human rights violations, was willing to permit investigations of human rights practices, and had informed prisoners' families

---

[84] House Report 94-1144, p. 47.
[85] Ibid., pp. 46-47

ECONOMIC AID AND HUMAN RIGHTS

of the conditions and the charges against their relatives. The Senate definition of economic aid was similar to that of the House.

The House-Senate conferees agreed to split the difference, limiting FY1977 economic aid to Chile to $27.5 million. The potential addition of $38 million was reduced to a potential $27.5 million. The major change by the conference committee resulted from heavy administration lobbying of International Relations chairperson Morgan. The president of the Export-Import Bank and other high-level officials from OPIC and the Department of Agriculture requested an exemption from the ceiling. As one of his last major acts in Congress before retiring, Morgan obliged. He insisted that "economic aid" be redefined, with the result that the conference report included not the above quotation from the House report but rather: "The ceiling . . . is not intended to apply to usual commercial-type, non-concessional Overseas Private Investment Corporation insurance, Export-Import Bank loans, guaranties and insurance, and credits through CCC." This was a most significant change.

The issue of economic aid to Chile illustrates some of the most crucial aspects of decision making on United States policy toward human rights in Latin America. Of primary importance, of course, was the active role of Congress; nowhere else in the area of United States human rights policy has it been more aggressive. But regional foreign affairs subcommittees in both the House and Senate were inactive—indeed in 1975 and 1976 the House Subcommittee on Inter-American Affairs did not exist—and the task of supporting and opposing the aid cuts fell to members with no formal responsibility for policy toward the area. Instead, members with functional responsibilities (Fraser and human rights, Kennedy and refugees) were the primary proponents of aid limitations, which the Democratic foreign affairs leadership (Morgan and Zablocki in the House, Humphrey in the Senate) and the Republican administration contested. In this process, many more key decisions occurred on the floor and in conference than in committee markup, where major aid battles are typically won or lost. As is the case with much legislation, conference committees served as the administration's court of last resort, and in virtually every instance the overall impact of compromises by conferees was to lessen restrictions on economic aid to repressive governments. Finally, the case of economic aid to Chile demonstrates that an administration with a will can find a way to circumvent congressional limitations in foreign assistance legislation. By the time Congress became aware of and closed the loopholes, the Pinochet regime had exterminated its opposition and no longer required the support of the United States economic aid program.

202

The Carter Administration and Congress

However much the pre-Carter State Department and AID officials may have talked about human rights in public forums and however much they may have passed memos on human rights among one another, human rights considerations did not influence decisions on economic aid to Latin America until the change in administrations in 1977. The tone of the Carter policy on economic assistance was set in late February 1977, when Secretary of State Vance told a Senate subcommittee that the administration would reduce its aid request for Uruguay, specifically mentioning human rights as the cause of the reduction.[86] A few days later, the State Department announced that the cut would be from the Ford administration's $220,000 in FY1977 to $25,000 in FY1978.

While virtually all Carter administration officials publicly accepted the importance of human rights considerations in economic aid policy making, few were willing to permit *their* programs to be cut. Thus undersecretary of state Richard Cooper expressed concern over the level of human rights violations by repressive governments but simultaneously remarked that there was no reason to cease providing violating regimes with economic assistance.[87] Other officials adopted the approach of the Ford-Kissinger era, asserting that the level of repression in any given country was not so bad as experts claimed and that, even if they were correct, encouraging signs pointed to future improvements.[88] Terence Todman, for example, affirmed that he was "100 percent behind the doctrine" of linking economic aid to human rights behavior in Latin America but then spent the better part of his brief career as assistant secretary of state trying to block aid reductions to the hemisphere's most repressive regimes. For help in his efforts he relied upon every conceivable rationale, from the "needy-people" argument ("All you're doing is adding to their misery") to the assertion that U.S. hostility toward repressive governments may contribute to a deterioration in human rights behavior.[89] Undersecretary of state

[86] U.S. Congress, Senate, Committee on Appropriations, *Foreign Assistance and Related Programs Appropriations Fiscal Year 1978*, 95th Cong., 1st Sess., 1977, p. 196. Military aid for Argentina and Ethiopia was reduced at the same time. Congress had already prohibited military aid to Uruguay for FY1977.

[87] Lewis M. Simons, "U.S. to Skirt Rights Issue in Aid to Friends," *Washington Post*, September 11, 1977, p. A23.

[88] See, for example, the testimony by deputy assistant secretary of state Robert B. Oakley in U.S. Congress, House, Committee on International Relations, *Foreign Assistance Legislation for Fiscal Year 1979*, 95th Cong., 2d Sess., February 15, 1978, pt. 4, pp. 58-60.

[89] U.S. Congress, House, Committee on International Relations, *Foreign Assistance Legislation for Fiscal Year 1978*, 95th Cong., 1st Sess., March-April 1977, pt. 7, p. 73; *Washington Post*, December 17, 1977, p. A17.

Cooper also subscribed to this latter theory, arguing that the Harkin amendment "in the long run may have the effect of worsening human rights."[90]

Following the lead of the President, AID actively supported the policy of linking economic assistance to human rights performance. In 1977, the new AID administrator, former Ohio governor John Gilligan, indicated that he had no idea how to implement this policy, but he was clearly eager to make an effort.[91] For the guidance of officials submitting proposals for FY1979 funding, AID informed overseas personnel that "economic assistance is to be used to foster basic human rights. High priority is given to activities within the scope of A.I.D.'s new initiatives in human rights. If there is any question about a government's human rights conduct, all activities proposed . . . must be shown to benefit needy people."[92] Such an order would never have been sent to the field during the previous administration.

At the same time that AID indicated its willingness to accept the legitimacy of human rights criteria in aid decision making, it had no desire to halt its existing programs. Agency officials were particularly quick to question the effectiveness of aid reductions. AID deputy administrator Abelardo Valdez expressed his agency's doubts "about the effectiveness of cutting off economic aid as a means to force better human rights performance. In the first place our programs are generally not large enough to constitute effective leverage, at least in Latin America. In the second place the impact is probably felt more by the people the programs are aimed toward rather than by their own governments. I do believe there are cases in which a regime's record is so reprehensible that we should dissociate ourselves from it. I would simply argue that economic assistance directed at the poor should be one of the last cords to be cut, not one of the first."[93]

As expected, the newly created Bureau of Human Rights and Humanitarian Affairs enthusiastically supported the administration's policy of linking economic aid and human rights considerations. Like

[90] U.S. Congress, House, Committee on Banking, Finance, and Urban Affairs, Subcommittee on International Development Institutions and Finance, *International Development Institutions—1977*, 95th Cong., 1st Sess., 1977, p. 68.

[91] U.S. Congress, House, Committee on Appropriations, Subcommittee on Foreign Operations and Related Agencies, *Foreign Assistance and Related Agencies Appropriations for 1978*, 95th Cong., 1st Sess., 1977, pt. 2, pp. 154-159.

[92] U.S. Congress, House, Committee on International Relations, Subcommittee on International Organizations, *Human Rights and United States Foreign Policy: A Review of the Administration's Record*, 95th Cong., 1st Sess., October 25, 1977, p. 36.

[93] Tom Quigley et al., *U.S. Policy on Human Rights in Latin America (Southern Cone): A Congressional Conference on Capitol Hill* (New York: Fund for New Priorities in America, 1978), pp. 17-18.

AID's Gilligan, the new HA officials were fairly uncertain about how to pursue their assigned task of monitoring the human rights component of U.S. foreign policy, but their attention quickly focused upon economic aid programs. At first HA viewed the threat of aid reductions as a tool to force decreases in recipients' levels of political repression. Assistant secretary of state Patricia Derian told Congress that "what we have tried to do is measure . . . : Will this do any good? Will it make a difference if we deprive people of aid money, on the basis of human rights?"[94] By 1978, this goal had proven to be unrealistic—aid or no aid, most of Latin America's most repressive governments refused to alter their policies—and the argument advanced by AID's Valdez thus appeared increasingly reasonable. At that point, HA began to speak of aid reductions as a tool not to reduce repression but to dissociate the United States from repressive regimes. By 1978, in fact, the word "dissociate" had become the most frequently used verb in the lexicon of human rights officials. "What we must do," asserted Derian, "is see to it that we don't contribute to the violations."[95]

This slight change in emphasis from deterrence to dissociation was highly significant, for it permitted HA to disregard the potential impact of aid reductions upon the level of political repression. To arguments by AID officials that a particular program was too small to provide effective leverage, HA replied that, given the intransigence of a repressive government, U.S. policy should be designed to reduce ties to the regime, not to improve its human rights practices. With the support of higher-level officials, particularly deputy secretary of state Warren Christopher, HA used this argument to assume a major role in bilateral aid decision making.

As a result of these changes in policy, personnel, and bureaucratic structure, the distribution pattern of economic aid to Latin America changed dramatically. The FY1979 budget request, the first for which the Carter administration could be held fully responsible, continued major aid reductions to repressive regimes along with substantial increases for relatively nonrepressive governments. Economic aid to Chile and Nicaragua in particular dropped precipitously during the early years of the Carter administration. In addition, aid programs in Latin American nations with relatively repressive governments (Bolivia, Guatemala, Haiti) were redesigned to reach only the neediest

[94] U.S. Congress, Senate, Committee on Foreign Relations, Subcommittee on International Operations, *Foreign Relations Authorization Act*, 95th Cong., 1st Sess., April 1977, p. 225.
[95] Speech to the American Bar Association's National Institute on International Human Rights Law, Washington, D.C., April 26, 1978.

social sectors. The FY1979 aid budget request also contained major aid increases for the relatively nonrepressive governments of Costa Rica, Guyana, and Jamaica. Many of these changes resulted from congressional actions, but it is important to recall that similar congressional initiatives had little noticeable impact upon the preceding administration.

With the addition of the Harkin amendment to the Foreign Assistance Act in 1975, Congress had concluded its major battle to force the incorporation of human rights considerations into economic aid decision making. Thereafter Congress was content to refine and extend the existing human rights language in bilateral economic aid legislation. The International Development and Food Assistance Act of 1977 (PL95-88) contained two refinements. One revised the Harkin amendment to require (1) the AID administrator to consult with HA before determining whether a country is eligible to receive assistance, and (2) the Secretary of State to report annually to the Congress on the status of basic human rights in countries that receive economic aid. This extended the reporting requirements established in 1976 for countries receiving military aid. The second refinement was an extension of the Harkin amendment to include Food for Peace. The 1975 amendment applied only to economic aid under Part I of the Foreign Assistance Act of 1961. PL95-88 amended the Agricultural Trade Development and Assistance Act of 1954 (PL83-480) by adding a new Section 112 to prohibit Title I sales of agricultural commodities to repressive governments unless the food would directly benefit needy people.

Perhaps the most interesting aspect of these two revisions is the ease with which they were adopted. The revision of the Harkin amendment was accomplished without any controversy whatever. It was added to the economic aid bill by the Senate Committee on Foreign Relations, passed by the Senate, and accepted in conference by the House without a single substantive revision. There was no opposition from the executive branch. The extension of the Harkin amendment to include Food for Peace was equally effortless. The proponents of the PL480 amendment, including FCNL's Edward Snyder, who helped Representative Stephen Solarz's aides to draft the language, feared opposition from the Department of Agriculture, which regularly protests any threat to foreign marketing opportunities. Their fears were unfounded. In early 1977, human rights was the policy with which a new administration wished to reassert United States leadership in international relations, and Congress and the various executive departments were eager to display their support. The 1977 PL480 amendment is the only human rights legislation that any administration has

206

endorsed prior to passage.[96] The amendment was proposed by Representative Solarz before both the House Committee on International Relations and the Senate Agriculture Subcommittee on Foreign Agricultural Policy, passed by the full House, and accepted in conference by the Senate.

In the course of extending human rights language to PL480, Congress made a major contribution to the body of human rights law by redefining the concept of aid to needy people. The original Harkin language permitted economic aid to continue if the President determined that the aid would benefit needy people, and even the reductions in economic aid to Chile in 1975 and 1976 provided exceptions for food aid through private voluntary agencies. Underlying these "needy-people" clauses was a desire to avoid punishing the oppressed in order to teach the oppressors a lesson. As Representative Solarz noted, "we ought to be helping the poor people all over the world. The fact that they have a repressive regime should not mean they are denied the opportunity to eat."[97]

The problem was that some administration officials interpreted the needy-people clause as a loophole permitting various types of assistance to regimes that otherwise would be ineligible on the basis of their human rights records. These arguments in favor of overlooking human rights abuses were often offered by champions of the trickle-down approach to economic aid. In urging a restoration of aid to Chile, for example, Representative Charles Wilson of Texas, perhaps the major congressional opponent of human rights legislation, argued: "I don't think we serve the cause of human rights by making the Chilean peasants drink dirty water. . . . The rich can only drink so much water. So surely some of this clean water is getting to the poor."[98] Another opponent of human rights-related aid reductions, assistant secretary of state Todman, advanced the economic-development-ends-torture argument, suggesting that human rights violations are caused by the lack of fulfillment of basic needs. Thus the provision of aid can eliminate "the kind of conditions that are the world's most widespread source of deprivation of basic human rights."[99]

[96] In a letter to the chairperson of the Agriculture Subcommittee on Foreign Agricultural Policy, the State Department approved the amendment, but it wanted Congress to know that the "procedure [reporting] provisions are unnecessary and may add to administrative burdens." The Carter administration supported other human rights legislation but only as a compromise to defeat more stringent proposals. See *Future of Food Aid*, p. 84, *supra* n. 46.

[97] Ibid., p. 73.

[98] *Foreign Assistance and Related Agencies Appropriations for 1978*, pt. 2, p. 159, *supra* n. 91.

[99] Terence A. Todman, "Statement before the Subcommittee on Inter-American Affairs, House International Relations Committee," mimeographed, March 1, 1978.

In any event, the original clause in the Harkin amendment was vague. Its legislative history was unclear, and while some key members of Congress called it a major loophole, others insisted that it was a stringent stipulation.[100] The Ford administration preferred the former interpretation, defining the term in such a way that assistance could be provided to any regime. Adopting Representative Wilson's argument, in early 1976 AID's legal counsel wrote an opinion that

> the decision on whether assistance will directly benefit needy people . . . should be based upon the 'principal purpose' of the assistance. If the principal purpose is to benefit the needy people . . . then . . . the intent of Congress has been carried out, notwithstanding that the intended class of beneficiaries may not be the initial recipient of resources provided to the project.[101]

Using this definition, AID effectively ignored the Harkin amendment.

In 1977, the issue of what constitutes aid to needy people was joined over the question of extending the Harkin amendment to the Food for Peace authorization. This was a particularly appropriate place to decide the issue. Food aid is clearly beneficial to needy people, yet the process of providing this aid under Title I is such that recipient governments can make at least a temporary profit by the transaction. The Department of Agriculture (USDA) provides a purchasing government with low-interest, long-term credit through the Commodity Credit Corporation (CCC). The recipient government then purchases the food in the United States and disposes of it on its domestic markets, typically through sales to wholesalers at the prevailing market price, and pockets the proceeds until the CCC loan must be repaid.[102] The government also profits whenever the proceeds of a sale exceed the cost of the food. Although data on this spread are unavailable, there is nothing to keep recipient governments from selling at a profit the food they have purchased from the United States.

Representatives Solarz, Fraser, and others focused their criticism upon the time lag provided by CCC repayment schedules. This lag,

[100] See *Chile: The Status of Human Rights*, p. 21, *supra* n. 8. For an example of congressional confusion on this issue, see *International Development Institutions—1977*, p. 105, *supra* n. 90.

[101] See *Chile: The Status of Human Rights*, p. 114, *supra* n. 8. For an example of this logic's impact on aid programs, see U.S. General Accounting Office, *Impact of U.S. Development and Food Aid in Selected Developing Countries*, Report ID-76-53 (Washington, D.C.: General Accounting Office, April 22, 1976).

[102] In FY1977, for example, PL480 sales of $15 million of wheat to Chile were financed for twenty years at an annual interest rate of 3 percent, with a two-year grace period before the first payment. U.S. National Advisory Council on International Monetary and Financial Policies, *Annual Report, 1977*, p. 353.

they asserted, permits some regimes to use the proceeds of PL480 sales to finance the costs of political repression.[103] For this reason, the needy-people clause in the 1977 PL480 authorization was crafted to ensure that such aid to a repressive regime reached the poor. First the word "directly" was placed before the phrase "benefit needy people," and then the entire phrase was defined in some detail: "An agreement [for PL480 food] will not directly benefit the needy people . . . unless either the commodities themselves or the proceeds from their sale will be used for specific projects or programs which the President determines would directly benefit the needy people of that country."[104] The House report was even more explicit, defining the term "specific projects or programs" as those in the area of agricultural development, rural development, nutrition, health services, population planning, food distribution, education, housing, public works, conservation and storage, and credit and marketing facilities.[105]

When the law entered into force on October 1, 1977, an interagency group headed by deputy secretary of state Christopher began a lengthy review of food aid policy. For two months, the flow of PL480 food was nearly halted. At the end of the review, eleven of the twenty-eight countries scheduled to receive PL480 aid in FY1978 were judged to be nonrepressive of human rights. PL480 aid to the remaining seventeen countries required "human rights clearance," which essentially meant a new CCC contract clause specifying in some detail how the commodities would be used to help the needy. Of the four FY1978 recipients in Latin America (Haiti, Honduras, Jamaica, and Peru), Haiti and Honduras were placed in the category requiring special clearance.

By 1978, Congress and the executive branch had accomplished about as much as could be expected in linking human rights considerations to bilateral economic assistance to Latin America. They had reached agreement on the principle that bilateral economic aid was to be halted or reduced to Latin American countries that engaged in a consistent pattern of gross violations of fundamental human rights, unless such aid directly benefited needy people. Moreover, the two branches had agreed upon tentative definitions of the various terms of this agreement. These understandings served to accelerate the decline in the level of economic aid to Latin America that had begun

[103] See *Future of Food Aid*, p. 72, *supra* n. 46; *Chile: The Status of Human Rights*, pp. 21-22, *supra* n. 8.
[104] PL95-88, Sec. 112(a).
[105] House Report 95-240, p. 49.

in 1966. With the exception of relatively small programs to the economically least-developed Latin American nations and a few projects in such showcase countries as Costa Rica and Jamaica, by the end of the 1970s, bilateral economic aid had become a minor instrument of United States policy toward Latin America.

· 6 ·

MILITARY ASSISTANCE

In 1958, EIGHT members of the Senate Foreign Relations Committee wrote President Eisenhower to request that he reduce the proportion of military aid in the United States foreign assistance program. The President responded by creating the Draper Committee to study the matter. A year later, the committee reported that world conditions called for an increase rather than a decrease in military aid to the Third World. The committee argued that the relative size of the military aid component of foreign aid programs was an unimportant issue, since in its view economic and military aid were complementary: "Without internal security, and the general feeling of confidence engendered by adequate military forces, there is little hope for any economic progress. Nor does the maintenance of military strength in a less developed country, particularly when we cushion its impact with Defense Support, necessarily inhibit economic growth."[1] Moreover, the report continued, economic and military assistance are not only complementary but interchangeable: "It should be noted that both military and economic assistance increase the total resources available to the recipient country. . . . a recipient country may shift internal resources from economic to military uses or vice versa in accordance with the local government's appraisal of their relative importance, which may not always be the same as our own."[2]

For at least two decades, the arguments set forth in the Draper Report oriented the policy debates over United States military aid to Latin America. Groups supporting substantial programs of military assistance used the report's conclusions as a primary justification for their position; those challenging the growth or questioning the importance of military aid were forced to refute the report's assertion

[1] President's Committee to Study the United States Military Assistance Program, *Composite Report* (Washington, D.C.: Government Printing Office, August 17, 1959), pp. 150-151. This conclusion might have been expected given the committee's composition: of nine members, three were retired generals, one a retired admiral, and one a former assistant secretary of defense. Defense Support is an early term for Security Supporting Assistance, which since 1978 has been part of the Economic Support Fund. Security Supporting Assistance is economic aid designed to promote U.S. security and other interests in militarily unstable or politically sensitive areas of the world, principally the Middle East.

[2] Ibid., p. 151.

211

that military and economic aid were complementary or interchangeable.

This debate grew increasingly acrimonious during the 1970s, as the level of repression of human rights in Latin America appeared in many cases to coincide with military coups against civilian governments. Under normal circumstances, the armed forces and the police hold a monopoly or near-monopoly on the organized power to coerce, and in Latin America the police are typically subservient to, if not a part of, the military establishment. Thus the growing concern over widespread governmental violations of basic human rights seemed inevitably to involve an examination of the political role of the region's military forces. One product of such an examination was the observation that, with the sole exception of Cuba, all of Latin America's military establishments had received assistance from the United States. Moreover, some of the most repressive governments received by far the largest amount of aid. With these basic observations as evidence, it was argued that military assistance programs were contributing to the increased level of repression in Latin America. The purpose of this chapter is to assess the content and impact of this argument. The approach is to examine first the purposes of military aid, then the procedures by which military aid policy is made and implemented, and finally the relationship between military aid and the repression of human rights.

It was only after its victory in the Spanish-American War that the United States began to compete with European powers for the market in educating and equipping Latin American military forces. Although the competition was formally inaugurated when officers were assigned to train Cuban soldiers following that nation's independence in 1902, the United States military aid program remained small during the initial years of the twentieth century. The next assistance after the Cuban training mission was an agreement with Brazil permitting two navy officers to serve as instructors at the new Naval War College in Rio de Janeiro. Then in 1920, Congress granted the executive branch broad authority "to detail officers of the United States naval service to assist the Governments of the Republics of South America in naval matters," and the President immediately sent the first official U.S. military advisory group to Latin America: a four-person mission to Lima to assist in the reorganization of the Peruvian navy. Shortly thereafter, in 1922, nine naval officers became advisors to the Brazilian navy.

In 1926, Congress expanded the President's powers to provide military aid by authorizing the use of land as well as sea forces in advisory and training capacities. Despite this authorization, the interest of the

United States in the Latin America military remained small until the 1930s. As late as 1938, Washington had stationed only six military attachés in the twenty countries of Latin America. But in that year, the State Department decided to pursue aggressively the displacement of European, particularly German, military advisors, and from 1938 until the early 1970s United States military aid programs to Latin America grew dramatically. By 1942, military missions had been established in all of South America except Paraguay and Uruguay, and by the end of World War II there were military missions in all Central American and Caribbean countries except El Salvador and Nicaragua.[3] When Paraguay (1943), El Salvador (1947), Uruguay (1951), and Nicaragua (1952) requested military assistance, the formal ties between the United States and Latin American militaries were complete. In the process, most European missions were displaced.[4]

In many cases, very close ties developed between the United States and Latin American military establishments. The case of Argentina, the Latin American nation that has traditionally been most independent from United States military influence, is illustrative. In that nation, a continuous United States advisory presence began in 1934, when the navy assisted in the establishment of the Argentine Naval War College. Between 1950 and 1978, Argentina received more than a quarter of a billion dollars in military aid, and more than four thousand Argentine officers and enlisted men were trained by United States military personnel.[5] Table 6.1 describes the magnitude of military assistance to Latin America during the period 1961 to 1978; Table 6.2 provides information on the specific aid recipients.

Although the term military assistance is subject to a variety of definitions, four distinct types of aid are of primary importance.[6]

(1) The *Military Assistance Program* (MAP) accounted for most military aid to Latin America from the passage of the Mutual Security

[3] Nicaragua, of course, was subject to a nearly continuous U.S. military occupation from 1912 to early 1933, and other Caribbean nations were also exposed to the U.S. military acting as occupation forces.

[4] Unfortunately, the two best historical analyses of military aid to Latin America are unpublished: Raymond Estep, "United States Military Aid to Latin America," mimeographed (Maxwell Air Force Base, Ala.: Aerospace Studies Institute, Air University, September, 1966); Frank R. Pancake, "Military Assistance as an Element of U.S. Foreign Policy in Latin America, 1950-1968," Ph.D. dissertation, University of Virginia, 1969.

[5] U.S. Department of Defense, Defense Security Assistance Agency, *Fiscal Year Series, December 1978* (Washington, D.C.: Defense Security Assistance Agency, 1978), pp. 200-201. This bound computer printout is an invaluable source of historical data on the magnitude of the military aid program.

[6] The U.S. government now uses the euphemism "security assistance" instead of "military assistance."

TABLE 6.1
MILITARY ASSISTANCE TO LATIN AMERICA, FY1950-FY1978
(thousands of dollars)

Fiscal Year	Total	FMS	MAP	EDA	IMET
1950	$ 1,154	$ 1,154	—	—	—
1951	9,597	9,597	—	—	—
1952	94,032	10,071	46,500	37,461	—
1953	75,031	17,575	34,926	22,456	74
1954	37,052	11,769	16,669	7,513	1,101
1955	37,435	11,930	13,922	9,408	2,175
1956	53,478	19,990	22,799	7,965	2,724
1957	64,441	22,112	30,179	8,525	3,625
1958	64,586	22,147	22,098	17,092	3,249
1959	46,002	8,208	28,997	2,957	5,840
1960	87,645	30,165	38,656	14,063	4,761
1961	68,713	7,341	49,862	3,673	7,837
1962	91,863	18,047	47,723	10,976	15,117
1963	61,498	11,849	32,918	8,245	8,486
1964	81,411	16,547	45,535	7,685	11,644
1965	116,326	42,784	54,027	9,515	10,000
1966	109,972	24,511	64,219	10,537	10,705
1967	109,376	52,041	42,268	4,144	10,923
1968	53,849	26,193	16,273	2,501	8,882
1969	45,522	23,367	12,146	2,079	7,930
1970	47,428	25,027	9,259	5,530	7,612
1971	71,845	49,409	5,813	8,685	7,938
1972	130,023	106,443	5,885	9,510	8,185
1973	130,851	110,265	5,463	7,110	8,013
1974	259,999	214,138	6,417	31,360	8,084
1975	201,504	184,229	6,744	1,941	8,590
1976	109,802	91,351	5,800	2,358	10,293
1977	95,048	84,888	3,143	27	6,990
1978	88,147	80,943	205	—	6,999
Total	2,443,630	1,334,091	668,446	253,316	187,777

SOURCE: U.S. Department of Defense, Defense Security Assistance Agency, *Fiscal Year Series, December 1978* (Washington, D.C.: Defense Security Assistance Agency, 1978), pp. 197-265. Bound computer printout.

NOTE: Figures include Cuba. Data are for the year in which commitments were made, with delivery normally occurring one or more years later.

Act in 1951 until the late 1960s. In the typical year of 1964, for example, 56 percent of the $81 million in military aid to Latin America was provided by MAP. Then in 1969, the Nixon Doctrine formally announced a new emphasis on allies' self-reliance, a policy that greatly accelerated the existing trend from grant aid to credit and cash sales. When the Air Force revised its MAP handbook in 1970, for example,

TABLE 6.2

MILITARY ASSISTANCE TO LATIN AMERICA BY COUNTRY, FY1950-FY1978

(thousands of dollars)

Country	Total	FMS	MAP	EDA	IMET	Students Trained
Argentina	$251,628	$200,347	$ 34,020	$ 4,375	$12,886	4,017
Bolivia	59,023	1,983	33,125	10,075	13,840	4,650
Brazil	597,871	291,160	207,163	83,092	16,456	8,659
Chile	313,455	192,081	80,468	24,010	16,896	6,883
Colombia	150,933	34,985	83,163	17,902	14,883	7,500
Costa Rica	3,122	1,176	930	115	901	696
Dominican Republic	37,929	2,176	21,701	3,902	10,150	4,108
Ecuador	128,519	73,986	31,992	10,354	12,187	5,504
El Salvador	16,815	3,520	5,014	2,454	5,827	1,971
Guatemala	61,786	31,264	16,332	6,732	7,458	3,334
Haiti	5,075	1,243	2,427	195	1,210	622
Honduras	25,902	10,070	5,634	1,996	8,202	3,219
Mexico	24,027	21,469	7	50	2,501	906
Nicaragua	30,172	5,627	7,758	5,233	11,554	5,670
Panama	15,866	5,198	4,604	1,674	4,390	4,706
Paraguay	28,091	727	9,458	11,188	6,718	2,017
Peru	297,058	182,743	74,956	20,277	19,082	7,904
Uruguay	87,942	19,872	41,008	20,433	6,629	2,806
Venezuela	257,405	243,063	33	324	13,985	5,540

SOURCE: U.S. Department of Defense, Defense Security Assistance Agency, *Fiscal Year Series, December 1978* (Washington, D.C.: Defense Security Assistance Agency, 1978), pp. 197-265. Bound computer printout.

it added the instruction that henceforth "Foreign Military Sales must be substituted for grant aid under the Military Assistance Plan whenever a country can afford to pay . . . for the equipment it needs."[7]

The shift from grant to credit aid was encouraged by Congress, which had always been reluctant to pay for Latin America's military expenditures. In the Foreign Assistance Act of 1962 [PL87-565, Sec. 201(a)], it ordered the President to end MAP aid "to any country having sufficient wealth to enable it . . . to maintain and equip its own military forces." The Foreign Assistance Act of 1974 [PL93-559, Sec. 17(a)] expressed the sense of Congress that MAP "should be reduced and terminated as rapidly as feasible," and in 1976 Congress

[7] U.S. Air Force, Directorate of Military Assistance and Sales, *Information and Guidance on Military Assistance Grant Aid and Foreign Military Sales*, 12th ed. (Washington, D.C.: U.S. Air Force, 1970), p. 16; U.S. Congress, Senate, Committee on Appropriations, *Department of Defense Appropriations, Fiscal Year 1976*, 94th Cong., 1st Sess., April 8, 1975, pp. 169-260.

finally decided upon a four-year plan to phase out MAP grants. In making this decision, Congress found no opposition from the executive branch. Indeed, MAP aid to Latin America had declined from a high of $64 million in FY1966 to less than $1 million in FY1978. In terms of military aid to Latin America, by 1980 MAP was a defunct program.[8]

At the same time that MAP aid was being terminated, however, other forms of concessional assistance were being developed to enable poor countries to continue their purchases of military equipment. In 1980, the undersecretary of state for security assistance, Matthew Nimetz, noted that "although the trend away from grants will not change radically, we will in the coming years need to consider methods of introducing some element of concessionality into our military assistance programs." Noting that "some of our most important recipients are among the poorest in annual per capita income," including Bolivia and Colombia in Latin America, Nimetz then listed several financing techniques currently in use that have the effect of continuing MAP.[9]

(2) In Congress's 1976 revision of the security assistance program, the *International Military Education and Training* (IMET) program was separated from MAP assistance and retained as a grant aid program. Since then, IMET has provided the Pentagon with the authority to train Latin American military personnel in the United States, Panama, and elsewhere in Latin America.

(3) By the early 1970s, the *Foreign Military Sales* (FMS) program had become the largest of the four components of military aid to Latin America, accounting for 92 percent of total military aid of $88 million in FY1978. FMS is actually two programs, credit and cash.[10] The former is the larger, providing loans from the Department of Defense

[8] Section 105 of the International Security Assistance and Arms Export Control Act of 1976 (PL94-329) terminated as of FY1978 the authority for grant military assistance other than training, with the exception that Congress may authorize such aid to specified countries in specific amounts. The following year, the International Security Assistance Act of 1977 (PL95-92) authorized $228 million in grant aid to eight nations, none of which was in Latin America. The Carter administration's FY1979 military aid request contained MAP grants for four nations: Jordan, the Philippines, Portugal, and Spain.

[9] Speech to the Aerospace Industries Association's International Council, San Diego, California, April 9, 1980.

[10] Whether for credit or cash, by law [PL90-329, Sec. 43(b)] all FMS transactions are designed to be self-supporting. Credit terms are set at a rate slightly higher than the prevailing market rate for U.S. government securities, which is invariably much lower than any commercial loan rate. In addition, the costs to a recipient government include a 3 percent charge for administration, but in the late 1970s, the Pentagon was unable to provide data to indicate the total costs—including, for example, personnel retirement benefits—of the FMS program.

(DOD) to Latin American governments to purchase United States military equipment and services, including technicians and training. These loans can be either direct (DOD-funded) or indirect (DOD-guaranteed). In the case of guarantees, since 1973 funds have been loaned to foreign governments by the government-owned Federal Financing Bank, which requires a 10 percent guarantee from the Department of Defense. This leverage permits the DOD to finance arms sales far in excess of congressional appropriations. The second FMS program, cash sales, is in reality a commercial sales program that passes through the DOD procurement process. FMS processing is mandatory for the sale of classified or government-manufactured military equipment or for commercial sales valued at over $100 million. FMS is also preferred by purchasers who believe there is more security in dealing with the United States government rather than with commercial suppliers.

(4) *Excess Defense Articles* (EDA) is a small (about $100 million annual volume worldwide) program for the disposal of obsolescent or unneeded military equipment. EDA has never been a large component of military aid to Latin America—in FY1978, there were no new EDA commitments to the region for the first time since 1951—and, as might be expected, the recipient nations have often been the poorest in the region.

THE PURPOSE OF MILITARY ASSISTANCE

The purpose of military aid has always been to assist friendly governments to defend themselves against threats to the national security of the United States. In the early 1960s, this purpose was supplemented by other goals—making military personnel subservient to civilian authorities, encouraging them to carry out civic action programs, introducing them to a superior form of social organization ("a beneficial exposure to American institutions," reported the Senate Committee on Foreign Relations in 1960)—but these were soon dropped in favor of the unchanging goal of aid to oppose threats to United States national security.[11]

During the post-World War II era, this threat has been perceived in three distinct forms. In the period between World War II and the late 1950s, the perceived menace was extrahemispheric communist aggression. A 1953 policy statement by the Department of State noted

[11] U.S. Congress, Senate, Committee on Foreign Relations, *Mutual Security Act of 1960*, 86th Cong., 2d Sess., 1960, p. 6. For an excellent general survey of aid rationales, consult Michael J. Francis's "Military Aid to Latin America in the U.S. Congress," *Journal of Inter-American Studies* 6 (July 1964): 389-404.

217

that the United States was giving military aid to Latin American countries because of three fundamental facts:

1. This hemisphere is threatened by Communist aggression from within and without;

2. The security of strategic areas in the hemisphere and of inter-American lines of communication is vital to the security of every American Republic; and

3. The protection of these strategic areas and communications is a common responsibility. [12]

Although the aggression was expected to be internal as well as external, the congressional hearings on military aid clearly indicate that invasion was the major fear. As late as 1959, one Defense Department official told Congress that "the most positive threat to hemispheric security is submarine action in the Caribbean Sea and along the coast of Latin America. We can expect raider attacks against strategic bases, sea communications and coastal installations, and the mining of ports and approaches." [13]

Nonetheless, some members of Congress noted that military aid might be used by unscrupulous dictators to repress dissent and maintain themselves in power rather than for defense against an invader. These fears were based upon a slow but perceptible shift in the attitudes of aid officials, a change that was completed prior to Castro's overthrow of the Batista government. As the threat of an invasion by extrahemispheric forces grew dimmer during the course of the 1950s, a second type of threat—domestic insurgency—gradually developed in the minds of aid officials. In 1958, President Eisenhower's Secretary of Defense, Neil McElroy, signaled an official shift in rationale when he told the Senate that military aid to Latin America "is primarily for the purpose of the maintenance of internal security and also a very modest preparation for defense against any incursion from offshore." [14] When this modification was opposed by the Senate, particularly by Senators Church and Morse, aid officials told Congress that "the maintenance of internal security in the Latin American Republics does not come within the purview of the military assistance program in Latin America." [15]

[12] U.S. Department of State, Office of Public Affairs, *Military Assistance to Latin America* (Washington, D.C.: Department of State, January 1953), p. 1.

[13] U.S. Congress, House, Committee on Appropriations, *Mutual Security Appropriations for 1960*, 86th Cong., 1st Sess., 1959, p. 736.

[14] U.S. Congress, Senate, Committee on Foreign Relations, *Mutual Security Act of 1958*, 85th Cong., 2d Sess., 1958, p. 24.

[15] U.S. Congress, House, Committee on Foreign Affairs, *Mutual Security Act of 1959*, 86th Cong., 2d Sess., 1958, p. 24.

The Cuban revolution then interceded to destroy all arguments against counterinsurgency as a legitimate purpose of military aid. The concept of hemispheric defense was abandoned in favor of internal security, which quickly became the single goal of military aid to Latin America. By 1962, for example, the Department of Defense announced that "in recognition of the fact that the principal threat faced in Latin America is Communist subversion and indirect attack, the primary emphasis of the military assistance program was changed from hemispheric defense to internal security in FY1962. . . . The danger of internal subversion has not diminished; . . . rather, it has increased significantly. This threat is not peculiar to one or two or even a few of the Latin American countries. It exists in every country."[16]

To improve the capabilities of Latin American military forces to control insurgents, the United States shifted support away from conventional defensive weapons. By 1967, Secretary of Defense McNamara could tell Congress that the Pentagon was providing "no tanks, artillery, fighter aircraft, or combat ships. The emphasis is on vehicles and helicopters for internal mobility [and] communications equipment for better coordination of in-country security efforts."[17] For a brief period, there was a division of labor in the aid effort: AID's OPS concentrated upon increasing the ability of Latin American police forces to cope with urban unrest, while military aid programs were aimed primarily at combatting a Vietnam-type rural insurgency. Over the course of the 1960s, however, the focus of military aid was broadened beyond rural counterinsurgency to a more generalized internal security capability, with the accent on communications, intelligence, and similar noncombat activities.

The use of military aid to combat domestic insurgency did not enjoy the near-universal acceptance that hemispheric defense had claimed in the early years of the Cold War. To some members of Congress, the concept of aid for the purpose of maintaining internal security smacked of intervention, of choosing sides in internal disagreements. But this view was held by a fairly small minority. When Congress wrote a new Foreign Military Sales Act (PL90-629) in 1968, the purposes of military credits were listed as (1) internal security, (2) legitimate self-defense, (3) participation in collective defense efforts, and (4) civic action. Critical members of Congress remained vocal, however, forcing administration officials to justify assistance to repressive regimes. At first, these officials relied upon the reformist image

[16] U.S. Congress, Senate, Committee on Foreign Relations, *Foreign Assistance Act of 1962*, 87th Cong., 2d Sess., 1962, p. 420.

[17] U.S. Congress, House, Committee on Foreign Affairs, *Foreign Assistance Act of 1967*, 90th Cong., 1st Sess., 1967, p. 118.

of the Alliance for Progress, borrowing the Draper Report's conceptualization of military aid as an instrument to guarantee the effectiveness of economic aid: "As the Alliance achieves success, we can be assured that the extremists will use every means available to them—including subversion, terrorism, and civil war—to defeat it. Therefore, if the Alliance for Progress is to have its chance, the governments must have the effective force required to cope with subversion, prevent terrorism, and deal with outbreaks of violence before they reach unmanageable proportions."[18]

Then, when the Alliance was abandoned, the executive branch was left with its single straightforward reason for military aid: the traditional containment of communism.[19] But for a time in the 1970s, this hoary rationale retained little of its former attractiveness. In 1977, the assistant secretary of state for inter-American affairs had to admit that he could think of "no strategic concerns that are vital to the safety and well-being of the United States" in Latin America.[20] Earlier, in 1971, Henry Kissinger had ranked the nations of the noncommunist world on the basis of their need for military aid to contain communist advances, and all of Latin America was given the lowest priority.[21] The 1960s and 1970s saw the defeat of nearly all potential threats to United States security through internal communist subversion of Latin American governments, and the probability of an external attack upon Latin America came to be considered negligible by everyone. For the moment, there were very few communists left to contain.

With neither external nor internal threats in evidence, the United States adopted its third postwar reason for military aid to Latin America: to maintain, in the words of the army chief of staff, "reasonable relationships with people upon whom we are in some degree dependent."[22] The use of military aid to maintain access and influence with the Latin American armed forces existed prior to the 1970s. Secretary of Defense McNamara can be credited with bringing this

[18] See *Foreign Assistance Act of 1962*, p. 420, *supra* n. 16.

[19] See, for example, *The Rockefeller Report on the Americas* (Chicago: Quadrangle Books, 1969), p. 6.

[20] U.S. Congress, House, Committee on International Relations, *Foreign Assistance Legislation for Fiscal Year 1978*, 95th Cong., 1st Sess., 1977, pt. 7, p. 66.

[21] John P. Leacacos, "Kissinger's Apparat," *Foreign Policy*, no. 5 (Winter 1971-1972): 17.

[22] U.S. Congress, Senate, Committee on Appropriations, *Department of Defense Appropriations, Fiscal Year 1976*, 94th Cong., 1st Sess., 1975, pt. 2, p. 118. See also U.S. Congress, Senate, Committee on Foreign Relations, Subcommittee on Western Hemisphere Affairs, *Rockefeller Report on Latin America*, 91st Cong., 1st Sess., November 20, 1969, pp. 9, 12; U.S. Congress, House, Committee on Appropriations, Subcommittee on Foreign Operations and Related Agencies, *Foreign Assistance and Related Agencies Appropriations for 1976*, 94th Cong., 1st Sess., 1975, pt. 4, pp. 5-6.

rationale to the center of the security assistance program. In 1965, he told Congress that the United States provided military aid to Latin America because military officers were "the coming leaders of their nations. It is beyond price to the United States to make friends with such men."[23] Cuts in military aid have been opposed because they "would greatly reduce United States influence on significant elements of host governments," funding for military advisors has been supported because they "extend U.S. influence," and specific country programs to Argentina, Ecuador, El Salvador, and Venezuela have all been supported by the goal of securing access and influence with the Latin American military.[24] A proposed cut in aid to Argentina for human rights violations was opposed by the Ford administration, for example, because military aid enabled the United States "to influence the course of events by maintaining this contact with Argentina rather than by not doing it."[25] In the 1970s, the primary response to proposals that the United States reduce its military aid programs was that to do so would reduce the nation's influence in the Third World.

Thus as the other rationales disappeared, only the goal of maintaining access and influence with Latin America's military establishments remained to justify the military aid program to Latin America. The remainder of this chapter is an analysis of how the political ramifications of this influence became a major focus of the human rights activity of the 1970s. Before continuing this discussion, however, it is necessary to describe the participants and their roles in military aid decision making.

Decision Making

The formal process of military aid decision making is a model of bureaucratic precision, operating continuously to export armaments and military training to the noncommunist world. In theory, the process begins when a foreign government, having decided to procure some items for its armed forces from or through the United States government, sends a request to the Department of State.[26] Operating

[23] U.S. Congress, House, Committee on Foreign Affairs, *Foreign Assistance Act of 1965*, 89th Cong., 1st Sess., 1965, p. 782.

[24] Michael J. Francis, *Military Assistance and Influence: Some Observations* (Carlisle Barracks, Pa.: Strategic Studies Institute, U.S. Army War College, 1977), p. 4.

[25] See *Foreign Assistance and Related Agencies Appropriations for 1976*, pt. 4, p. 272, *supra*, n. 22.

[26] Prior to October 1977, a request could also be sent through military channels to the Department of Defense. After that date, all requests for items of significant combat equipment have been transmitted by the ambassador to the Department of State rather than by military assistance personnel to the Defense Security Assistance Agency (DSAA).

within the budgetary and other restrictions determined by Congress during the authorization and appropriation processes, the State Department determines, in consultation with the Defense Department and other interested agencies, whether the proposed acquisition is in the general interest of the United States. If so, State permits one of the three military branches to prepare a letter of offer and acceptance (LOA or, more commonly, DD Form 1513). If the proposed sale or grant exceeds a certain value, at this point Congress is informed of the proposed transfer and given thirty days to veto it through a concurrent resolution. Should Congress not object or should the transaction be below the limits of congressional veto authority, the LOA is sent to the foreign government. Upon acceptance of the offer, the appropriate military service then provides the aid by either supplying goods from its own stocks or, much more frequently, by contracting with a U.S. corporation to manufacture the goods.

Behind this straightforward procedure is an intricate web of formal and informal bureaucratic relationships. More than a year after assuming her position as assistant secretary of state for human rights and humanitarian affairs, Patricia Derian sounded a theme about military assistance that was absent from discussions of her bureau's impact upon bilateral or multilateral economic aid: "It is incredibly complex. There are so many arms, so many pieces. It has taken us an incredibly long time just to get a handle on the steps that are involved."[27] Actually, the military aid decision-making bureaucracy is not particularly complex, but, as with economic aid, there are many points of access to the process.

Executive Branch

The principal executive branch participants in military aid decision making are the Departments of State and Defense. Overall authority for military assistance rests with the undersecretary of state for security assistance, science, and technology. Although the undersecretary enjoys far less prestige and power than the other two undersecretaries (political affairs and economic affairs), that such authority should rest with a high State Department official is indicative of State's interest in military aid.[28] Although the undersecretary has an extremely small staff, she or he is aided by the Bureau of Politico-Military Affairs (PM), where the day-to-day responsibility for supervising all arms transfers is located. PM's director is generally among the most powerful officials in the State Department at the assistant secretary level.

[27] Speech to the American Bar Association's National Institute on International Human Rights Law, Washington, D.C., April 26, 1978.

[28] The position was created in 1972 as the undersecretary for coordinating security assistance programs.

The Bureau of Politico-Military Affairs is itself divided into seven offices, one of which, the Office of Security Assistance and Sales (SAS), is the central military aid bureaucracy within the State Department. In one sense, SAS serves essentially as a conduit; it has the responsibility for consulting with all the interested executive branch agencies and bureaus before transmitting to the DOD a decision on any military aid proposal. In addition, SAS staff members scrutinize each aid request, concentrating upon such politico-military variables as the existence of a military threat, the regional arms balance, and the anticipated benefits to the United States.

As with economic aid decision making, any government agency or bureau can become involved in the decision-making process simply by informing SAS that military aid is related to its area of responsibility. Once notified, SAS is obligated to obtain approval of the bureau before a decision can be reached. For this reason, PM maintains a full staff of regional and functional liaison officers, and each regional and functional bureau in the State Department has a military assistance liaison officer. ARA's military aid activities are supervised by its Office of Regional Political Programs. Interestingly, both the ARA official in charge of relations with PM and the PM official in charge of relations with ARA are often active-duty military officers on assignment to the Department of State. During the Carter administration, the Bureau of Human Rights and Humanitarian Affairs also participated actively in military aid decision making, especially when a transfer involved one of the "problem governments" that HA had identified as unusually repressive. HA also maintains permanent representation on the interagency Arms Export Control Board, which will be discussed shortly.

The Department of Defense is the second executive branch organization with a major responsibility for military assistance programs, and the size of its commitment is impressive. Whereas in 1975 the Department of State had assigned about 50 people to spend the greater amount of their time on military aid programs, the Department of Defense had given the same task to no fewer than 2,100 employees. This difference reflects DOD's responsibility for administering the various programs. Whereas State holds the ultimate responsibility for authorizing arms transfers, the Pentagon and the individual services actually provide the aid, contracting with both foreign governments and domestic producers, supervising the delivery and use of equipment, and controlling the various aid programs so that congressional directives are not violated.

The Defense Security Assistance Agency (DSAA) coordinates the various programs of the three military branches. It in turn is supervised by the Defense Security Assistance Council (DSAC), of which the director of DSAA is the secretary. The DSAC meets about once a month to advise the Secretary of Defense on security assistance matters and to coordinate overall DOD policy on arms transfers. Generally, DSAA operates with a minimum of supervision.

Perhaps the best way to understand how these bureaucracies interact is to follow an aid request through the channels, in this case an FSM request: in the late 1970s, such requests were being processed at the rate of about eight thousand per year. Once a week, every week of the year, DSAA sends SAS a computer printout of all the FMS requests it has received from overseas during the preceding week. SAS adds to the DSAA list any requests received by the State Department and then distributes copies to every interested agency. Within the State Department, this normally includes AID, the office of the Secretary of State, the undersecretary for political affairs, and the legal advisor, plus all of the regional and functional bureaus. Copies are also sent out to the NSC staff, the Departments of Treasury and Commerce, the CIA, and OMB. Any one of these agencies or bureaus is permitted five days to notify SAS of a reservation regarding any proposed sale on the printout. Typically there is no objection, and SAS notifies DSAA to proceed with the sale. DSAA, in turn, authorizes the appropriate military service to prepare a formal letter of offer.

If any agency indicates its opposition to the sale, this process stops. A challenging agency is required to provide a statement of the nature of its opposition within five days after issuing a reservation; generally it accompanies the reservation. It may be a detailed document demonstrating, for example, that the proposed recipient is a gross violator of human rights, or it may be a simple declaration that the proposed sale is not congruent with some aspect of the administration's policy on arms transfers. During the late 1970s, the Bureau of Human Rights and Humanitarian Affairs often placed proposed transfers "under review," a delaying tactic that avoided the need to issue a formal objection. In most cases, the deputy director of PM first tries to resolve the dispute. If unsuccessful, PM sends the matter up the hierarchy to the undersecretary of state for security assistance, along with an action memorandum (itself fully cleared with all relevant agencies) giving the position of PM and other bureaus on the proposed sale. The undersecretary makes a decision by accepting or modifying the action memorandum. These decisions are formally announced in a memorandum signed by the Secretary of State or the deputy secretary.

In the meantime, if the contested sale is significant in its sensitivity or size, all of the informal channels are clogged with communicating officials in search of allies and a common strategy. In the 1970s, ARA, PM, and Defense were frequently at odds with the Bureau of Human

Rights and Humanitarian Affairs. When it felt strongly opposed to a transfer, HA made up for its youth and lack of allies by going over everyone's head to the deputy secretary of state, Warren Christoper, who was known for his general sympathy for human rights concerns. Nearly every bureau or agency also seeks out friends on Capitol Hill to ask for help. At the same time, the private contractor who stands to gain by the sale has its members of Congress at work and often talks with members of the White House staff as well. Eventually a decision of some sort is made, even if it is a decision not to make a decision. Then the dust settles, the next DSAA printout arrives at SAS, and the entire process begins anew. Each case is treated as unique, so applicable precedents are few in number. As a result, it is only by accident that any two consecutive decisions reflect the same values and policies.

One long-standing question regarding this process concerns the relative influence of State and Defense in military assistance policy making. During the 1950s, there was no question about which bureaucracy was king of the military aid mountain: the Department of Defense determined the military aid budget, with only minor assistance from the Department of State. In 1952, assistant secretary of state Edward G. Miller, Jr., told Congress that the administration's $62.4 million military aid request for Latin America was "the amount the Joint Chiefs of Staff have decided upon," and in 1957 assistant secretary of state Henry Holland noted that the proposed military aid budget for Latin America was determined by the Pentagon, although it was "in the judgment of the Department of State—we are not military men, of course—a reasonable sum."[29] By the late 1960s, however, the Department of Defense was unwilling to accept primary responsibility for aid decision making. Secretary of Defense Robert McNamara noted in 1967 that "every military sale made is either consonant with overall policy established by the Department of State or specifically subjected to a careful . . . review within the U.S. government before a negotiation is instituted."[30] By 1975, the DOD was refusing to take *any* responsibility whatever for military aid de-

---

[29] Francis, "Military Aid to Latin America," p. 395. On the deference of the State Department to the Defense Department on military aid matters, see Miles D. Wolpin, *Military Aid and Counterrevolution in the Third World* (Lexington, Mass.: D.C. Heath, 1972), p. 200. On the general reluctance of State to assert its authority in nontraditional areas of foreign affairs, see I. M. Destler, *Presidents, Bureaucrats, and Foreign Policy: The Politics of Organizational Reform* (Princeton: Princeton University Press, 1974), p. 160.

[30] U.S. Congress, House, Committee on Foreign Affairs, *Foreign Assistance Act of 1967*, 90th Cong., 1st Sess., 1967, p. 312.

cisions. Department officials regularly asserted that they worked only under the direction of the State Department.[31]

It is clearly a mistake to take such disclaimers of responsibility at face value. By the 1970s, Defense may not have determined the military aid budget, but for several reasons it had hardly become the passive conduit that administration officials would have had Congress believe. First, overseas military assistance advisory groups (MAAGs) are the source of many aid requests. General Howard Fish, the colorful former director of DSAA, agreed that MAAGs "may be called upon to express an opinion" on military procurement by host countries but insisted that "it is basic Department of Defense policy that foreign military sales will not be promoted by MAAG/MILGP personnel."[32] On the other hand, in 1978 the DSAA manual for officials involved in MAP and FMS activity stated that "the essential role of the MAAG is to assist the foreign government in making its decisions."[33] In addition, a 1975 GAO report on the activities of fourteen such groups concluded that "MAAG efforts are devoted heavily to foreign military sales and dialog. . . . Foreign Military Sales efforts include assistance in interpreting sales procedures, developing requests, and coordinating letters of offer; coordinating purchased training programs; consulting with U.S. contractors on market potential and sales presentation; providing technical data to the host military; and serving as a troubleshooter during the contract period."[34] Because aid requests from overseas form the decision-making agenda, the Department of Defense has a major impact upon United States military assistance policy.

Second, the Department of Defense exercises significant influence upon both general military assistance policy and the fate of specific agenda items through its membership on the Arms Export Control Board. Created in January 1978, the AECB is simply a renamed (and slightly enlarged) Security Assistance Program Review Committee (SAPRC), which was itself created in 1971 to oversee military aid

[31] U.S. Congress, House, Committee on International Relations, *Foreign Assistance Legislation for Fiscal Year 1979*, 95th Cong., 2d Sess., February-March 1978, pt. 1, pp. 485-486; U.S. Congress, House, Committee on Foreign Affairs, Subcommittee on Inter-American Affairs, *Cuba and the Caribbean*, 91st Cong., 2d Sess., July-August 1970, p. 92; *Department of Defense Appropriations, Fiscal Year 1976*, p. 192, *supra* n. 7.

[32] See *Department of Defense Appropriations, Fiscal Year 1976*, p. 241, *supra* n. 7.

[33] U.S. Department of Defense, Defense Security Assistance Agency, *Military Assistance and Sales Manual*, publication 5105.38-M (Washington, D.C.: Department of Defense, August 1, 1978), pt. 1, p. D-1.

[34] U.S. General Accounting Office, *Assessment of Overseas Advisory Efforts of the U.S. Security Assistance Program*, Report ID-76-1 (Washington, D.C.: General Accounting Office, October 31, 1975), p. 10.

policy. The AECB is chaired by the undersecretary of state for security assistance, with participation by interested bureaus in the Department of State and Defense. Additional members are drawn from the Joint Chiefs of Staff, OMB, the Arms Control and Disarmament Agency, the NSC staff, the CIA, AID, and the Departments of Treasury and Commerce. The decisions of the AECB are advisory, with final authority vested in the undersecretary of state. Although the AECB has a number of functions in the area of arms transfer policy, its principal activity is the crucial negotiation of the military aid budget. The AECB's predecessor, SAPRC, tended to meet frequently over the course of several weeks about four months before the military aid request was presented to Congress and then to suspend operations until the next budget cycle required its active participation.[35]

The third reason for the significant influence of the Department of Defense in military aid decision making is the strength of a number of less formal linkages that facilitate the expression of military views in the State Department. Most participants at a given level in the executive branch seem to know one another well. The directors of DSAA and PM are in daily contact, for example, as are their immediate subordinates. In addition, the Department of Defense has infiltrated the Department of State's military aid decision-making process by taking maximum advantage of the State/Defense exchange program, which sends foreign service officers to work for extended periods in the Department of Defense and military officers to Foggy Bottom. Although not a large program (in 1978, there were eight State Department officials at Defense and sixteen military officers at State), the military officers are placed in positions where their expertise indicates they can best contribute to furthering the foreign policy interests of the United States. Not surprisingly, therefore, these officers simply assume many of State's military aid responsibilities. Of the sixteen officers participating in the program in late 1978, one was assigned to the policy planning staff and ten were assigned to PM. The remaining five were assigned to regional bureaus, where their duties focused upon military aid. In ARA in the late 1970s, for example, a military officer had exercised a major decision-making role on every piece of military equipment going to Latin America through commercial or government channels for as long as anyone could remember. One single army colonel filled this post for five years during the 1970s, an unusually long tenure that served to make him ARA's acknowledged expert on military aid and foreign policy.

[35] See *Department of Defense Appropriations, Fiscal Year 1976*, pp. 173, 219, *supra* n. 7.

227

Because of these close relationships, on issues of military assistance it is probably incorrect to view State and Defense as separate bureaucracies. Although State is now publicly in command of military aid decision making, Defense is assured of significant if not overwhelming influence on any issue that it selects as important.

Congress

The congressional committees that authorize and appropriate funds for military assistance are the same as those responsible for economic aid. The House Committee on Foreign Affairs and the Senate Committee on Foreign Relations authorize the expenditure of funds, and the two committees on appropriations provide that portion of the authorization that they determine to be necessary. In addition, within these four committees, the same set of subcommittees reviews executive branch requests for both military and economic aid.[36]

The two basic laws authorizing military assistance are the Foreign Assistance Act of 1961 and the Arms Export Control Act of 1968. Until 1968, all military aid was authorized by the former act, but then Congress placed military sales under a new Foreign Military Sales Act (PL90-629), which in 1976 was renamed the Arms Export Control Act. This act authorizes FMS credit and cash sales, while the Foreign Assistance Act authorizes MAP and IMET programs. Disposal of EDA is authorized by both laws. In addition to their general function of determining what proportion of an authorization to fund, the appropriations committees also exercise control over military aid by earmarking specific funds and prohibiting the expenditure of others.

In the past, however, the executive branch enjoyed considerable flexibility in the distribution of aid funds because the annual appropriations bill did not specify dollar amounts of aid for specific nations. The military assistance presentation document submitted to Congress at the beginning of each budget cycle provided the administration's proposed dollar distribution by country, but the President was not bound to distribute the funds exactly as stipulated. By the end of the

[36] An exception to this rule is the House Foreign Affairs Subcommittee on International Security and Scientific Affairs, which holds general hearings on military aid. Its sister Subcommittee on Inter-American Affairs holds similar hearings on military aid to Latin America, however. Digressions from established procedures are particularly likely to occur when committee chairpersons develop interests in subjects normally covered by subcommittees. In 1975, for example, the chairperson of the Senate Committee on Appropriations decided to hold hearings on FMS in conjunction with DOD appropriations. But these departures are fairly rare. In the example at hand, Senator McClellan focused upon the impact of FMS on U.S. defense readiness, and the Appropriations Subcommittee on Foreign Operations went ahead with its more comprehensive hearings on the general subject of U.S. military aid.

1970s, there were limits on this flexibility. Between 1971 and 1979, Section 653 of the Foreign Assistance Act of 1961 required the administration to notify Congress prior to providing a recipient nation aid in excess of 10 percent of the amount previously programmed. The foreign assistance appropriations act for FY1979 (PL95-481) prohibited aid disbursements for any country in amounts not justified or in excess of amounts previously justified to the Congress unless both committees on appropriations are notified fifteen days in advance.

Beyond the authorization and appropriations processes, the major power of the Congress to control military aid decisions lies in the veto it holds over FMS sales of any major defense equipment valued at more than $7 million or any defense articles or services valued at more than $25 million.[37] The executive branch is required to advise Congress of any such sale prior to the issuance of a letter of offer; Congress then has thirty days to reject the proposed sale through a concurrent resolution. In practice, Congress rarely considers exercising its authority to block a proposed sale. The 1978 battle over the sale of jet aircraft to several Middle Eastern countries was an exception, yet it demonstrated that Congress in general and the House in particular are extremely unwilling to embarrass the President by a public rejection. Once formal notification of a proposed sale reaches Congress, most members feel that it is too late to do anything but agree.

A number of additional legislative restrictions constrain the executive branch's freedom in military aid decision making. These number about twenty-five, ranging from the denial of aid to governments that violate their citizens' human rights to the requirement that FMS credits be repaid within twelve years.[38] Because many (but not all) of these restrictions are rigidly enforced, the ability of Congress to authorize and appropriate funds should not be viewed exclusively as a passive function of accepting or rejecting administration initiatives. In general, however, congressional-executive interaction on military programs is not particularly conflictive; it is clearly more cordial than that on economic assistance.[39] The State Department would prefer Con-

---

[37] The term "major defense equipment" is defined as "any item of significant combat equipment on the U.S. Munitions List having a nonrecurring research and development cost of more than $50,000,000 or a total production cost of more than $200,000,000." PL94-329, Section 215.

[38] A list of these restrictions as of 1975 can be found in *Department of Defense Appropriations, Fiscal Year 1976*, pp. 242-243, *supra* n. 7.

[39] High levels of agreement do not always exist, of course. In the 1960s, the executive branch was thought by some members of Congress to be distorting the cost of the Vietnam War by hiding expenditures in the aid program. *Foreign Assistance Act of 1967*, p. 14, *supra* n. 30. In the period 1961 to 1975, Congress appropriated an average of 78 percent of the administration's economic aid request, in contrast

gress not enact restrictions on the export of sophisticated weapons systems, on regional ceilings, or on funds for certain nations, for examples, but, when compared to economic aid, Congress has enacted relatively few stringent restrictions on the use of military assistance.

THE VALUE OF MILITARY ASSISTANCE

As concern grew during the 1960s and 1970s over the relationship between military aid and the repression of human rights by recipient Latin American governments, the debate centered around two separate questions: the impact of aid upon the political behavior of Latin American militaries and the political value to the United States of the influence its aid is meant to purchase. Each question merits detailed consideration.

The Impact of Military Aid Upon Politics

As the size of MAP and FMS programs in Latin America declined during the 1970s, the basic means of developing and maintaining access to Latin American military establishments became the International Military Education and Training program. Between the inception of its grant military training program in 1950 and 1978, the United States instructed more than 81,000 Latin American military personnel at a cost of about $190 million.[40] At its peak in FY1962, the United States paid for the training of nearly 9,000 Latin American military officers and enlisted personnel. Between 1964 and 1976, the number of students fluctuated between 3,000 and 4,000 per year. This number declined to 2,610 in FY1977 and then to a two-decade low of 1,858 in FY1978. Nevertheless, at the beginning of the 1980s there were hundreds of military personnel on active duty in virtually every Latin American country except Cuba who had participated in these training programs, and in all of the larger nations and several smaller ones (Guatemala, Honduras) they numbered in the thousands.

Many Latin American officers and some enlisted personnel have been trained in the continental United States, and an even larger number have received in-country training from the Department of Defense or private U.S. contractors under MAP or the FMS program,

---

to 84 percent of the MAP request during the same years. In two years (1965 and 1966), more military aid funds were appropriated than the administration had requested, and in 1959, Congress authorized a blank check for the first and only time, giving the executive branch "such funds as may be necessary" in FY1961 and FY1962.

[40] The figure of $190 million represents costs paid by the United States. Many Latin American governments pay for all or part of their students' tuition. *Fiscal Year Series, December 1978*, p. 198, *supra* n. 5.

but the major site of IMET programs for Latin America has been Panama. In what was until 1979 the Panama Canal Zone, there are four military schools devoted exclusively to training Latin American military personnel: the Army School of the Americas, the Inter-American Air Force Academy, the Navy Small Craft Instruction and Technical Team, and the Inter-American Telecommunications Network School.[41] The last two of these schools are of relatively minor significance; the other two have always been the major components of IMET to Latin America. The School of the Americas opened in Fort Gulick in 1949, six years after the Inter-American Air Force Academy, the oldest of the schools in Panama, was founded at Albrook Air Force Base.[42]

For FY1979 the Carter administration proposed to pay for the training of 576 students from eleven Latin American countries in Panama at a total cost to the United States of $8.25 million (or $14,328 per student). It is difficult to compare this budget request with those of prior years, since in 1978 the DOD changed accounting procedures by adding a separate line item for the fixed costs of operating the schools. These costs were previously distributed among the various participating countries.[43] The total FY1979 request for IMET in Latin

[41] Under the 1978 Panama Canal treaties, the Small Craft Instruction School, the Telecommunications Network School, and the Inter-American Air Force Academy can continue to operate until the year 2000. The School of the Americas can continue to operate for five years after ratification, i.e., until 1982, during which time its future must be negotiated with Panama. If no agreement can be reached, the Pentagon will be obliged to close the school. In 1978, the undersecretary of state for security assistance informed Congress that in this event "the U.S. Government would continue to be able to provide the same type of training now conducted at the School of the Americas at other U.S. military facilities in Panama" until the final transition in 2000. It is unlikely that a dispute will arise over this interpretation, for in the late 1970s, the Department of Defense ceased objecting to moving all U.S. training facilities in Panama to the United States. U.S. Congress, House, Committee on International Relations, *Foreign Assistance Legislation for Fiscal Year 1979*, 95th Cong., 2d Sess., March 1978, pt. 7, pp. 19-20; U.S. Congress, House, Committee on Appropriations, Subcommittee on Foreign Operations and Related Agencies, *Foreign Assistance and Related Agencies Appropriations for 1979*, 95th Cong., 2d Sess., 1978, pt. 2, p. 122; *Foreign Assistance Legislation for Fiscal Year 1978*, pt. 7, p. 76, *supra* n. 20.

[42] The Inter-American Air Force Academy did not begin to train large numbers of Latin American military personnel until the early 1960s.

[43] This change reflected the tenor of the times, for it resulted from congressional prohibitions on training students from countries ruled by repressive governments. While enrollments dropped, the schools continued to incur certain fixed costs that the Department of Defense did not want to pass along in the form of tuition hikes. For FY1981 the administration requested that $4.6 million (51 percent) of the $9.1 million IMET budget for Latin America be allocated to pay the fixed costs of U.S. military schools in Panama.

America exceeded that of FY1978 by $1.4 million and that of FY1977 by $1.0 million. The number of students trained in Panama declined significantly, however, from 2,229 in FY1977, to 1,116 in FY1978, to 576 in FY1979.

The central controversy surrounding the U.S. military schools in Panama has concerned the impact of training upon the political behavior of Latin American military personnel and, therefore, upon the nature of course material. In the early 1960s, the schools led the transition from training for protection against external armed attack to instruction in counterinsurgency. New courses were offered in riot control, intelligence, psychological warfare, counterguerrilla operations, and public information.[44] This emphasis on populace control continued into the 1970s. In 1971, for example, a Senate committee investigating alleged abuses of human rights by the Brazilian military found that the United States provided training on "censorship, briefings on the CIA, clandestine operations, communism and democracy, cordon and search operations, counterguerrilla operations, defoliation, electronic intelligence, the use of informants, insurgency intelligence, counterintelligence, subversion, countersubversion, espionage, counterespionage, interrogation of prisoners and suspects, handling mass rallies and meetings, intelligence photography, polygraphs, populace and resources control, psychological operations, raids and searches, riots, special warfare, surveillance, terror, and undercover operations."[45]

There can be no questioning of the fact that the IMET program teaches Latin American military personnel how to control their nations' citizens, but the Department of Defense has denied with uncommon vehemence the charges that it instructs Latin Americans on the repression of dissent. DSAA's General Fish complained in 1977 that critics were "uninformed" and "misguided": "We . . . examine the curricula carefully to ensure that it meets the very highest standards of American democratic principles. We are not teaching ideology. We are teaching technical skills. But, to the extent that there is any input at all from a philosophical standpoint, it is very carefully examined to make sure that proper democratic principles are supported."[46] The courses cited by General Fish as typical were all quite technical: rotor/

---

[44] See Francis, "Military Aid to Latin America," p. 403.

[45] U.S. Congress, Senate, Committee on Foreign Relations, Subcommittee on Western Hemisphere Affairs, *United States Policies and Programs in Brazil*, 92d Cong., 1st Sess., May 1971, p. 89.

[46] *Foreign Assistance Legislation for Fiscal Year 1978*, pt. 7, p. 69, *supra* n. 20.

propellor repairman, tank driver training, etc.[47] Despite Fish's statement, his successor, General Ernest Graves, found it necessary to purge twenty-one questionable courses from the various schools' curricula in late 1977. He then told Congress that "the remaining courses provided by Canal Zone Military Schools consist of professional/management training for foreign students having leadership potential and technical training in aircraft maintenance and avionics/support by the U.S. Air Force Inter-American Air Force Academy."[48] Throughout the 1960s and 1970s, the Department of Defense rejected categorically any suggestions that IMET programs included inappropriate subjects.

At the same time it was issuing these denials, the DOD continually modified the curricula at the schools to eliminate the most suggestively titled courses. By FY1978, the full list of courses for Latin American military personnel, an imposing forty-nine-page document in the form of a computer printout, was dominated by essentially technical subjects: underwater demolition training for Peru, advanced aerospace medical training for El Salvador, and parachute rigging for Haiti.[49] But there were several courses that could easily be classified as instruction in populace control, including counterinsurgency, urban warfare, commando operations (for Somoza's National Guard), and military intelligence.[50] This last subject was the most popular on the course list; most Latin American countries sent at least one officer to the United States or Panama for some type of training in intelligence operations.

Of greater interest than the titles of the courses is their content, specifically their ideological content. Few recent data are available in this area, but in 1969 Miles Wolpin discovered that the syllabus for a course innocuously titled "Automotive Maintenance Officer" included instruction in "fallacies of the communist theory, communist front organizations in Latin America, and communism vs. democracy."[51] In the late 1970s, DOD officials asserted that all traces of

[47] Ibid., p. 70; U.S. Congress, House, Committee on International Relations, *International Security Assistance and Arms Export Control Act of 1976*, 94th Cong., 2d Sess., March-April 1976, p. 146.

[48] *Foreign Assistance Legislation for Fiscal Year 1979*, pt. 2, p. 214, *supra* n. 41.

[49] While the impression gained from reading the list is that the United States is training for twenty-first-century technocratic warfare, it must be remembered that the purpose of such training is not to educate but to gain influence with Latin American military establishments.

[50] In some cases, FY1978 course names were changed from FY1977 in order to minimize the emphasis on the control of dissent. "Military Intelligence Interrogator" was dropped, for example, but the subject of "interrogation techniques" was incorporated in the five-month course for military intelligence officers.

[51] Wolpin, *Military Aid and Counterrevolution*, p. 78.

233

ideological instruction had been purged from IMET and that only technical and managerial courses comprised the various schools' curricula. This may have been true. Outside the Department of Defense, however, there was no one in Washington who knew what specifically was being taught; all that was known was the titles of the courses and the content of a few of them. Congressional oversight of IMET course content was extremely superficial.

Neither the critics nor the supporters of the IMET programs have found it necessary to be informed about the specific content of IMET courses to reach a conclusion about their political impact upon Latin American societies and upon U.S.-Latin American relations. Those who approve of IMET rest their case on three assumptions regarding the results of the training. The first assumption is that the schools make students more capable soldiers. Statements to this effect are generally accompanied by an altruistic goal beyond the increased ability to coerce, as when the Department of Defense suggested in 1975 that IMET training had "assisted Latin American countries to establish a degree of security which is conducive to orderly social development and nation building."[52]

The second argument is that IMET training creates new values among the students, indoctrinating them, as Secretary of Defense Robert McNamara said in 1962, "with democratic philosophies, democratic ways of thinking, which they, in turn, take back to their nations."[53] By the 1970s, the DOD recognized that a single training course probably could not effect major changes in individuals' value systems, but it nevertheless endorsed this extraordinarily ethnocentric assumption. As the commander of the U.S. Southern Command explained in 1974, "we endeavor . . . to ensure that the schools create an appreciation and understanding of our values. We do not look for this process to effect any sudden reversal of the deep-rooted cultural and social traditions of Latin American societies, but we think the schools have contributed something worthwhile to the quality of life in this hemisphere."[54]

The third assumption of IMET supporters is that training provides the United States with political influence over the trainees, i.e., that it adds to the ability of the United States to influence the internal

---

[52] U.S. Department of Defense, "Response to Senator Mike Mansfield: Information for Consideration by the Commission on the Organization of the Government for the Conduct of Foreign Policy," in the *Report* of the Commission on the Organization of the Government for the Conduct of Foreign Policy (Washington, D.C.: Government Printing Office, June 1975), vol. 5, app. N, p. 256.

[53] See *Foreign Assistance Act of 1962*, p. 76, *supra* n. 16.

[54] See *Cuba and the Caribbean*, p. 61, *supra* n. 31.

affairs of Latin American societies. This assumption enjoyed an over-whelming popularity among Pentagon officials throughout the 1960s and 1970s. It was stated in its most blatant form by the deputy assistant secretary of defense in 1964: "When the chips get down and you see who is supporting a U.S. position, whether it be in the U.N. or in some dispute that is going on in the country, or whether it be a problem of a new government and its attitude toward the United States; we can see—I think I can report confidently—that those who have been trained here have a greater friendliness for us."[55] By the 1970s, U.S. officials were couching this argument in more circumspect language. The DOD spoke of training that fosters "pro-U.S. attitudes through exposure to our customs and culture."[56] But while the descriptive phrases may have changed, the training in 1978 was expected to produce roughly the same results as in 1964: "We think that the general program is a good program because it gives people who are going to be eventually in leadership positions a chance to receive broad training in the American schools. This in the long run will be a positive thing from our standpoint by developing these kinds of contacts with people who are obviously going to be leaders in their country."[57] This evaluation by Secretary of State Vance was shared by congressional proponents of United States military training programs.[58]

No empirical evidence exists to support any of these three assump-tions. Indeed, it is conceivable that IMET training may produce as much opposition as support for the United States and its policies toward Latin America.[59] But what is of importance here is the *per-ception* by most policy makers that the benefits of the IMET program are the professionalization of the Latin American military, the incul-cation of democratic values, and above all else the creation of influence over Latin American political behavior.

Critics of IMET hold exactly the opposite beliefs. First, they agree that military training increases the abilities of students to perform

[55] U.S. Congress, House, Committee on Foreign Affairs, Subcommittee on Inter-national Organizations and Movements, *Winning the Cold War: The U.S. Ideological Offensive—U.S. Government Agencies and Programs*, 88th Cong., 2d Sess., January 1964, p. 1031.
[56] See "Response to Senator Mike Mansfield," p. 255, *supra* n. 52.
[57] *Foreign Assistance Legislation for Fiscal Year 1979*, pt. 1, p. 65, *supra* n. 41.
[58] *Foreign Assistance Legislation for Fiscal Year 1979*, pt. 7, p. viii, *supra* n. 41.
[59] Luigi Einaudi, "U.S. Relations with the Peruvian Military," in *U.S. Foreign Policy and Peru*, ed. Daniel A. Sharp (Austin: University of Texas Press, 1972), p. 46; U.S. Congress, House, Committee on Foreign Affairs, Subcommittee on National Security Policy and Scientific Developments, *Military Assistance Training*, 91st Cong., 2d Sess., October-December, 1970, p. 129.

technical tasks, but while IMET supporters refer to the increased capacity to coerce as professionalization, a positive value, critics contend that this technical proficiency has regularly been used to repress human rights in Latin America. IMET critics argue that to teach counterinsurgency techniques to, say, the members of Alfredo Stroessner's palace guard is not conducive to "orderly social development and nation building" but rather to the repression of political dissent in Paraguay.[60] These critics note that IMET graduates frequently become directors of repressive intelligence bureaucracies or assume related tasks involving the repression of human rights. In its 1976 report on human rights in the Philippines, for example, Amnesty International identified half of the torturers as former IMET students.[61] But these findings have been few. No one can state with certainty whether a direct relationship, causal or coincidental, exists between IMET training and subsequent acts of torture committed by the trainees.

Recognizing the argument that IMET instruction can be used to increase a government's proficiency at repressing its citizens' rights, the State Department simply responded that it had prohibited military training for police functions.[62] This response missed the critics' point entirely because it was based upon the erroneous notion that Latin American governments separate police and military functions. The military either is the police, directs the police, or works alongside the police in nearly every Latin American country. In the 1960s and 1970s, the military held primary responsibility for intelligence and internal security. It operated the detention camps and the interrogation centers. It often repressed dissent. In adopting a policy of training only those military officers who have nonpolice functions, the State Department advertised either an extraordinary ignorance of Latin America or, more likely, a contempt for the intelligence of the congressional and nongovernmental groups whose concern the policy was intended to assuage.

On the question of technical competence, then, the unresolved issue remains whether it is more important (1) to continue training Latin American military personnel in order to secure influence, with the clear knowledge that some trainees, at some time in their careers,

---

[60] See, for example, John Duncan Powell, "Military Assistance and Militarism in Latin America," *Western Political Quarterly* 18 (June 1965): 382-392; Aristide R. Zolberg, "The Military Decade in Africa," *World Politics* 25 (January 1973): 320-331.

[61] Richard P. Claude, "Human Rights in the Philippines and United States Responsibility," Working Paper No. HRFP-5 of the Center for Philosophy and Public Policy, University of Maryland, College Park, Md., February 3, 1978, p. 24.

[62] U.S. Congress, House, Committee on International Relations, Subcommittee on International Organizations, *Human Rights and United States Foreign Policy: A Review of the Administration's Record*, 95th Cong., 1st Sess., October 25, 1977, p. 43.

might be called upon to use their newly acquired skills to repress human rights, or (2) to cease training these personnel, sacrificing potential influence, so that they will be less efficient in their repression or, at the very least, less identified with the United States.

While critics of IMET programs agree with the assumption that training fosters new values among students, they disagree over what these values might be. To Robert McNamara's suggestion that students acquire democratic values, they argue that a U.S. military base is low on the list of sites at which such values might best be transmitted. They claim that the United States military is best equipped to promote Cold War national security values, blending socialism and communism into a single ideological threat whose mere existence justifies whatever repression is necessary to ensure its extirpation.

As with the proponents of IMET activity, critics of IMET programs prefer to rest their case upon the third assumption, that the provision of training purchases political influence with the trainees. By its very nature, IMET programs provide United States government officials with access to the most competent Latin American military personnel, and there is evidence that IMET graduates tend to become national leaders. One report on the careers of foreign graduates of the Army Command and General Staff College found that one-third eventually became generals, that 20 had become heads of state, that 153 had reached the rank of minister, ambassador, or legislator, and that 152 had become chiefs of staff.[63] In 1974, the DOD revealed that 170 graduates of military schools in Panama "are heads of government, cabinet ministers, commanding generals, chiefs of staff and directors of intelligence."[64] Nearly everyone agrees that IMET programs provide some access to the best potential talent in the Latin American military. The question that critics raised in the 1960s and 1970s was the ends to which this access was directed, and it is to that question that we now turn.

The Political Value of Influence

The provision of military assistance quite obviously involves human interaction between U.S. officials and recipient military personnel. Much of this intercourse begins during the training of Latin American military personnel in the United States and Panama, but the primary focus of ongoing contacts is in Latin American countries, where over the years military assistance advisory groups have established perma-

[63] Similar conclusions were drawn from a study of career patterns of graduates of the Air Force Command and Staff College. See *Foreign Assistance Legislation for Fiscal Year 1979*, pt. 7, p. ix, *supra* n. 41.

[64] See "Response to Senator Mike Mansfield," p. 255, *supra* n. 52.

nent institutional ties to Latin America's military forces.[65] Interaction between MAAGs and host country military personnel occur on an extremely broad variety of topics. A 1975 GAO report on the activities of military aid personnel in three Latin American countries (Chile, Colombia, and Venezuela) estimated that MAAG officers devote 31 percent of their time to administration, 25 percent to advisory effort (basically military-managerial advice), 12 percent to assisting FMS, 3 percent to end-use monitoring (inspecting U.S.-provided equipment to determine its condition and use), and 29 percent to dialog. "Dialog," the study reported, "consists of influence, representation, and information exchange. Influence is generally described as a means to develop rapport so that the host military will more readily accept suggested improvement and the American way."[66]

It is difficult to estimate the influence that accrues to the United States as a result of dialogs between United States military personnel and their hosts in Latin America. Clearly the potential for developing influence exists, for MAAG officers work extremely closely with their counterparts. Most have their offices in the host country's defense ministry building. Until 1978, the admiral in charge of the United States navy mission in Brazil was a rear admiral in the Brazilian navy, and ten other U.S. naval officers were concurrently officers in the Brazilian navy. Until 1958, in fact, all MAAG personnel were paid directly by the foreign government to which they were assigned.[67]

The specific form of MAAG-host interaction has developed slowly over the course of the six decades since Congress authorized military advisory activity in Latin America, with each bilateral arrangement

[65] In 1978, there were MAAGs in all Latin American countries except Cuba, Mexico, Costa Rica, Uruguay, and Paraguay. In the last three countries, MAAGs had been replaced by a single military assistance advisor to the ambassadors. MAAGs, military groups (milgroups), military missions, joint military advisory groups, mutual defense assistance groups, and defense attaché augmentation for security assistance are all terms for groups of people serving roughly the same purpose—the implementation of U.S. military assistance programs. Some members of Congress are confused by the variety of titles given to a single task, and they along with suspicious social scientists believe that the DOD may be attempting to circumvent congressional restrictions on MAAG activity. *Foreign Assistance Legislation for Fiscal Year 1979*, pt. 2, p. 117, *supra* n. 41. The military attachés assigned to all U.S. embassies normally do not perform MAAG functions. Their tasks are to observe and record local activity for the DOD and the ambassador. See *Foreign Assistance Legislation for Fiscal Year 1978*, pt. 7, p. 76, *supra* n. 20.

[66] See *Assessment of Overseas Advisory Efforts of the U.S. Security Assistance Program*, pp. 9-11, *supra* n. 34.

[67] Since passage of the Mansfield amendment to PL85-477, foreign governments have paid the U.S. Treasury for MAAG services and the advisors have received their pay through normal U.S. military channels.

differing in varying ways from all the others. The optimum relationship was established with Brazil. Until it was unilaterally dismantled by Brazil in 1977 and 1978, the most highly institutionalized MAAG activity was the Joint Brazilian United States Military Commission (JBUSMC), which provided the United States government with access to all decision-making levels of the Brazilian military establishment.[68] In 1971, the chief of the U.S. delegation to the JBUSMC, Major General George S. Beatty, described its functioning:

> The commission does not conduct frequent formal or plenary meetings; however, cooperation and coordination between the senior U.S. and Brazilian members and their respective staffs is carried out on a daily basis. The organization constitutes a ready, available, and receptive forum at all levels of the Brazilian Armed Forces for dialog concerning matters of joint interest and has, over the years, contributed to the understanding and the friendship toward the United States on the part of Brazilian officers ranging today from young staff officers to senior army commanders and cabinet ministers. . . . Briefly stated, the mission of the U.S. delegation to JBUSMC is to assist, as part of the U.S. country team in Brazil, in achieving U.S. policy objectives. . . . the chairman and head quarters staff of the U.S. delegation, JBUSMC, are co-located with the Brazilian delegation in a Brazilian Government building in Rio de Janeiro. The Army, Navy and Air Force sections of JBUSMC are physically located in their respective Brazilian ministry buildings. This provides daily contact with Brazilian counterparts at all levels from action officer to Cabinet minister. The atmosphere has been and is today one of friendly cooperation and mutual respect in dealing with whatever matters may arise.[69]

One product of MAAG activity in Vietnam was a reassessment by Congress of the entire concept of stationing military personnel abroad in advisory roles. The Foreign Assistance Act of 1971 (PL92-226, Sec. 512) expressed the sense of Congress that "the need for large United States military assistance advisory groups and military aid missions in foreign countries has diminished substantially during the last few years" and therefore ordered a 15 percent reduction in the total number of MAAG personnel. But this mandatory reduction applied only to 1971

[68] The JBUSMC was not a MAAG, but U.S. military officers assigned to the commission performed MAAG functions. Established during World War II, the JBUSMC was recognized in 1955 as the principal agency for military collaboration between the two countries in a formal exchange of notes. 6 UST 4103.

[69] See United States Policies and Programs in Brazil, pp. 52-53, supra n. 45.

239

and 1972, and in 1973 the Senate, at the Nixon administration's urging, voted to repeal the entire section, including the sense-of-Congress statement. The House agreed somewhat reluctantly. Large MAAGs continued to operate as late as 1975 in seventeen Latin American countries.

But then, in 1976, Congress reorganized the U.S. military aid program, and in the process critics of military assistance programs were able to establish the principle that Congress would annually set specific limits upon the size and distribution of MAAG personnel.[70] To date, Congress has not fully exercised this authority. In 1976, the total number of MAAGs for FY1977 was limited to 34, each of which could be composed of no more than three members. In 1977, Congress was less inclined to wrap these loose bonds around hands of a new Democratic administration, and it therefore decided not to specify the countries that would be authorized to have MAAGs during the upcoming fiscal year. Instead, the FY1977 limit on the number of MAAGs (34) was exchanged for a limit on the total number of MAAG personnel (865) for FY1978, and the administration was freed to establish MAAGs of any size in any country receiving MAP plus seven other countries (including Brazil and Panama). In addition, Congress authorized the administration to assign up to six members of the armed forces to any other country receiving military aid.[71] For FY1979, Congress reduced the authorized number of MAAG personnel from 865 to 790.[72]

Partially as a consequence of this legislation, the executive branch reduced MAAG activity dramatically in the late 1970s. The number of MAAGs worldwide with more than six military personnel dropped from 33 in FY1977, to 15 in FY1978, and to 14 in FY1979. In Latin America, only the group in Panama retained more than six officers. In twenty-nine other countries MAAGs were reduced to a maximum of six members, and in another twenty-six countries MAAG functions were assigned to the defense attachés. In the special case of Brazil, the changes were particularly dramatic: U.S. military personnel dropped from 81 in 1969, to 56 in 1971, to 46 in 1975, to 32 in 1978, and to 6 in 1979.[73] Worldwide, the number of MAAG personnel

---

[70] PL94-329, Sec. 104. Congressional control over the naming of specific countries to receive MAAGs was deferred until FY1978.

[71] PL95-92, Sec. 7.

[72] PL95-384, Sec. 9.

[73] Most of the early declines reflected the need for fewer personnel as grant aid programs were terminated. See *United States Policies and Programs in Brazil*, p. 276, *supra* n. 45; *Department of Defense Appropriations, Fiscal Year 1976*, p. 334, *supra* n. 7.

declined irregularly from 7,200 in 1960, to 1,269 in FY1977, and then to 775 in FY1979.

By the end of the 1970s, concern developed in the Department of Defense and Congress that these reductions had caused too great a decline in United States influence with Latin American militaries. Supporters of the cuts responded that MAAGs had been notoriously overstaffed, with most MAAG personnel performing the mundane tasks of monitoring end-use and writing reports of activities while the important work of maintaining influence was conducted by a few in-country officers supported by the DSAA in Washington. Critics of MAAG activity therefore expressed disappointment that Congress reduced only the number of MAAG personnel and not the number of MAAG functions.[74] Given these functions and the professional interaction they imply, the close working relationships between United States and Latin American military personnel probably did not disappear because the military clerks were sent home. U.S. military officers continued to act as Latin America's link to the most complete and sophisticated arsenal on earth, working alongside their hosts and establishing the contacts that provide the United States with access to perhaps the most significant political force in the majority of Latin American countries.

This access can be used to attempt to influence two types of decisions by Latin American military personnel: technical and political. In the area of technical decisions on training, staffing, procurement, and management techniques, MAAG personnel are sometimes thought to act as passive conduits, sending requests from Latin American militaries up the line to Washington and acting to ensure that the paperwork on aid programs is processed expeditiously. The contrary was true during the 1960s and 1970s: MAAG personnel were directly involved in determining the training and materiel to be requested from the United States. In 1964, a deputy secretary of defense noted that "the program of military assistance training is worked out very much the same way the military materiel program is worked out, and that is we attempt through our military assistance advisory groups . . . to work out with them the types of military goals that they have in mind, what military organization is needed to face the threat concerned, what the composition of this military threat should be. And from this begins to fall out the training requirements. . . . Actually, our experience is that they pretty faithfully follow our recommendations as to what they should do."[75] By the late 1970s, Latin American

[74] Congress prohibited one MAAG function: the promotion of the purchase by any foreign country of U.S.-made military equipment. PL95-384, Sec. 9 (h).
[75] See *Winning the Cold War*, pp. 1028-1029, *supra* n. 55.

militaries possessed a higher level of technical expertise than they did in 1964, but in 1977 DSAA's General Fish observed that decision making by host-country militaries was still heavily influenced by MAAG personnel. The content of IMET programs, he said, was determined by "what are called training conferences. . . . I would say fundamentally it is their initiative as to what will be taught. I am saying that wrong. It is not coming out the way I really want to say it. We work together. We wouldn't teach something because they requested it, if we thought it was inappropriate."[76] The notion that the Latin American militaries use MAAG personnel as no more than checkout clerks at an arms supermarket is probably inconsistent with reality.

Influence over technical decisions is of secondary importance to the political influence that develops out of MAAG activity. Quite obviously, this influence can be used to implement a broad variety of political goals, but in the 1960s and 1970s, MAAGs became a controversial component of the overall military aid program because they were linked to one specific political activity: the physical repression of Latin Americans holding political beliefs that conflicted with those of the United States government. It is upon this particular use of influence over Latin American military establishments that the next few pages concentrate. While the available evidence warrants this concentration, it should be emphasized that the influence gained through military aid need not be used for this particular purpose. That political influence provided by military aid has been used to encourage the repression of human rights is both true and unfortunate; it is not inevitable.

Less than two months prior to the 1970 Popular Unity electoral victory in Chile, the United States army general in command of all MAAGs in Latin America was asked what he would do "if the election were held and the Communists actually took over power?" He replied: "I just hope it doesn't happen. As you know, our record of recovery of countries that have gone down the drain is practically nil. We haven't gotten any of them back once they have gone. That is what we have got to stop."[77] How is the electoral process to be stopped and the army's mission accomplished? General Mather's answer captures perfectly the value of MAAGs to U.S. foreign policy decision makers: "The military in Latin America play a very definite role in the political process. . . . Given that, then I have an excellent channel to that very important element in the political process. . . . this can be of

[76] Foreign Assistance Legislation for Fiscal Year 1978, pt. 7, p. 71, supra n. 20.
[77] See Cuba and the Caribbean, p. 99, supra n. 31.

significant assistance in the conduct of our relations in support of our national purpose. . . . The MilGroup contacts have, on occasion and for short periods, been the best channel open."[78] It must be, then, that occasionally the United States uses the influence purchased by its military aid programs to encourage Latin American military officers to overthrow a democratic government. There is no other way for an election to be nullified by the military. If a coup is in fact subsequently attempted against a constitutional regime, it is proper to assert that the military assistance programs have at the very least contributed to or enhanced the probability of a coup.[79] Whether such coups would have occurred without the urging of the United States is a question about which one can only surmise.

Considerable speculation in this area has centered upon the coups in the Dominican Republic (1963), Bolivia (1964), and Brazil (1964),[80] but the instance about which the record seems uncommonly clear is the attempt to stage a preemptive coup in Chile in September and October 1970, immediately after the popular election but prior to the congressional election and subsequent inauguration of Salvador Allende. In the course of its investigation of the CIA, the Senate Select Committee on Intelligence Activities produced irrefutable evidence that "the United States Government supported and sought to instigate a military coup to block Allende."[81] From this evidence the committee produced an unusually detailed chronology of events:

> On September 15, 1970, President Richard Nixon informed CIA Director Richard Helms that an Allende regime in Chile would not be acceptable to the United States. The CIA was instructed by President Nixon to play a direct role in organizing a military coup d'etat in Chile to prevent Allende's accession to the Presidency. . . . Between October 5 and October 10, 1970, the CIA made 21 contacts with key military and Carabinero (police) officials in Chile. Those Chileans who were inclined to stage a coup were given assurances of strong support at the highest levels of the U.S. Government, both before and after a coup. One of

[78] Ibid., p. 92.

[79] Cf. Ernest W. Lefever, "The Military Assistance Training Program," *Annals of the American Association of Political and Social Science*, Vol. 424 (March 1976), pp. 85-95.

[80] See, for example, George Thayer, *The War Business: The International Trade in Armaments* (New York: Simon and Schuster, 1969), pp. 199-200; *Military Assistance Training*, p. 128, *supra* n. 59; Wolpin, *Military Aid and Counterrevolution*, p. 135.

[81] U.S. Congress, Senate, Select Committee to Study Governmental Operations with Respect to Intelligence Activities, *Supplementary Detailed Staff Reports on Foreign and Military Intelligence, Book IV*, 94th Cong., 2d Sess., April 23, 1976, p. 121.

the major obstacles faced by all the military conspirators in Chile was the strong opposition to a coup by the Commander-in-Chief of the Army, General Rene Schneider, who insisted the constitutional process be followed. As a result of his strong constitutional stand, the removal of General Schneider became a necessary ingredient in the coup plans of all the Chilean conspirators. . . . An unsuccessful abduction attempt was made on October 19, 1970, by a group of Chilean military officers whom the CIA was actively supporting. A second kidnap attempt was made the following day, again unsuccessfully. In the early morning hours of October 22, 1970, machine guns and ammunition were passed by the CIA to the group that had failed on October 19. That same day General Schneider was mortally wounded in an attempted kidnap on his way to work. The attempted kidnap and the shooting were apparently conducted by conspirators other than those to whom the CIA had provided weapons earlier in the day.[82]

This example may appear irrelevant to the issue being discussed, as some group other than that supported by the CIA was also attempting an anti-Allende coup; that is, encouragement from the United States was unnecessary.[83] The facts indicate otherwise, for the United States supported, financed, and perhaps incited *both* known groups of conspirators, one led by retired General Roberto Viaux and the other by General Camilo Valenzuela, commander of the important Santiago garrison. On October 13, 1970, CIA headquarters cabled its Santiago station to pass Viaux $20,000 in cash and a promise of $250,000 in life insurance in exchange for which Viaux was to kidnap Schneider.[84] Three days later, the CIA switched its allegiance to the Valenzuela group, apparently because Viaux commanded no troops. CIA headquarters ordered its Santiago station "to get a message to Viaux warning him against precipitate action." It is this sentence that Secretary of State Kissinger uses as proof that he was interested in "turning off the coup plans."[85] Yet the very same cable (Cable 802, Headquarters to Station, October 16, 1970) contained the *additional*

[82] U.S. Congress, Senate, Select Committee to Study Governmental Operations with Respect to Intelligence Activities, *Alleged Assassination Plots Involving Foreign Leaders: An Interim Report*, 94th Cong., 1st Sess., November 20, 1975, pp. 225-226.

[83] This was the position of Vice President Walter Mondale, who condemned U.S. policy toward Chile but argued that "the guy was killed by others." Remarks to a Seminar of Editors from the American Press Institute, Washington, D.C., February 23, 1979.

[84] See *Alleged Assassination Plots Involving Foreign Leaders*, p. 241, *supra* n. 82.

[85] Ibid., pp. 243, 251.

instructions: "It is the firm and continuing policy that Allende be overthrown by a coup. It would be much preferable to have this transpire prior to 24 October but efforts in this regard will continue vigorously beyond this date. . . . There is great and continuing interest in the activities of Valenzuela et al. and we wish them optimum good fortune."

On October 22, Viaux's group killed Schneider. Viaux was convicted of being the "intellectual author" of the murder and received a twenty-year prison sentence. Valenzuela was convicted of knowledge of a conspiracy to prevent Allende's assumption of office and sentenced to three years in exile.

What is of importance here is the manner in which the United States military was employed by the Nixon administration to foment the coup attempt. The CIA implemented the operation directed by Kissinger's now-famous Forty Committee, but the Agency lacked access to the Chileans who could ensure its implementation:

> The CIA Station in Santiago had inadequate contacts within the Chilean military to carry out its task. However, a U.S. military attaché in Santiago knew the Chilean military very well due to his broad personal contacts among the Chilean officers. Following a proposal by the Chief of Station, the CIA decided to enlist the attaché in collecting intelligence concerning the possibility of a coup and to use him as a channel to let the interested Chilean military know of U.S. support for a coup. [CIA Deputy Director of Plans Thomas] Karamessines described this procedure for the [Senate Intelligence] Committee:
>
>> We also needed contact with a wider segment of the military, the senior military which we had not maintained and did not have, but which we felt confident that our military representative in Chile had. . . . And we got the approval of the DIA [Defense Intelligence Agency] to enlist the cooperation of the attaché in our effort.
>
> General Cushman [deputy director of the CIA] requested the assistance of the attaché, and General Philpott [deputy director of the DIA] signed a letter that authorized transmission of the message directing him [the attaché]:
>
>> to work closely with the CIA chief, or in his absence, his deputy, in contacting and advising the principal military figures who might play a decisive role in any move which might, eventually, deny the presidency to Allende. Do not, repeat, not, advise the Ambassador or the Defense Attaché of this

245

message, or give them any indication of its portent. In the course of your routine activities, act in accordance with the Ambassador's instructions. Simultaneously, I wish—and now authorize you—to act in a concerted fashion with the CIA chief. This message is for your eyes only, and should not be discussed with any person other than those CIA officers who will be knowledgeable. CIA will identify them.[86]

Upon receipt of this cable, the attaché began to exploit his influence within the Chilean military. On October 5, he "informed both an Army General . . . and an Air Force General of the pro-coup U.S. policy." On October 7, the attaché "approached members of the War Academy in Santiago who in turn asked him to provide light weapons." In fact, the attaché was the conduit to both groups of conspirators, serving initially as a contact to Viaux and later fulfilling the unpleasant task of informing General Valenzuela that his $50,000 fee from the CIA would not be forthcoming until the kidnapping had been completed.[87]

This lengthy example illustrates the extraordinary value of the military aid program to foreign policy decision makers. Only U.S. military personnel had access to the single Latin American political force capable of attempting a coup. In the case in question, the access was provided by a U.S. military attaché under the direction of the DIA rather than by a MAAG official, but the access was undoubtedly facilitated by the military aid program, including IMET and MAAG activity.

In the case of Chile, aid-generated influence was used purposefully to support and perhaps to create the Chilean military's opposition to a democratic transition between civilian governments. But, again, U.S. influence with the Latin American military need not be used for this purpose. In 1978, it was employed quite differently, when the people of the Dominican Republic selected opposition candidate Antonio Guzmán as their president. This prompted the Balaguer government and its military supporters to threaten to overturn the electoral results. The Carter administration sent the chief of the U.S. Southern Command, Major General Dennis McAuliffe, to inform the Dominican general staff that a coup would do irreparable damage to United States-Dominican relations. The preference of the Dominican electorate was honored. Thus military aid is a neutral instrument of foreign policy *in the sense* that it provides access and influence with the Latin American military establishments. Then foreign policy makers must determine which values to pursue with their influence. And,

[86] Ibid., pp. 235-236.
[87] Ibid., pp. 240, 244.

as the following discussion of the use of military aid to promote human rights indicates, the specific values to be pursued are not predetermined. But *in the sense* that military aid inevitably increases the ability of military forces to coerce, such assistance can never be considered a neutral instrument of foreign policy. Lamentably, it is not possible for even the best-intentioned U.S. administrations to pursue the goal of access and influence without simultaneously increasing the coercive power of the military.

HUMAN RIGHTS AND MILITARY ASSISTANCE

The Issue

To provide military aid to a government that bases its existence upon the repression of its citizens' human rights is to support the repression of human rights, since any government sustained primarily by threats of physical force is obviously strengthened by the acquisition of greater amounts of force or, in the case of military training, by the acquisition of the skills necesary to employ coercion. In the 1960s and 1970s, the executive branch officials charged with explaining the existence of this support typically argued that, while they lamented the violations of human rights by recipient governments, other foreign policy considerations required that the repressiveness of certain governments be overlooked. Within this general argument were three specific defenses of continuing to support repression with military aid.

The first of these was succinctly summarized in 1975 by army chief of staff Fred W. Weyand, when a member of Congress asked him why the United States should continue offering FMS credits to gross violators of human rights: "If we don't sell it to them," he responded, "they buy it from someone else."[88] This is a time-honored argument that has served as the prime response to critics of U.S. military assistance by all recent administrations.[89] This is also a controversial question upon which there are no reliable data. As a result, opinions

[88] See *Department of Defense Appropriations, Fiscal Year 1976*, pt. 2, p. 118, *supra* n. 22.

[89] On the Nixon administration's use of this argument, see *Rockefeller Report on Latin America*, p. 35, *supra* n. 22; U.S. Congress, House, Committee on Foreign Affairs, Subcommittee on Inter-American Affairs, *Aircraft Sales in Latin America*, 91st Cong., 2d Sess., April 1970, p. 3. In 1980, the Carter administration's assistant secretary of state for inter-American affairs, William G. Bowdler, told Congress that "we can offer them the opportunity to purchase equipment in the United States and to send officers to us for training in its reasonable and humane use; or we can opt out. If we do opt out, we should be under no illusion that other countries, particularly those hostile to us, will follow our lead." Statement before the Senate Committee on Foreign Relations, April 16, 1980. On the use of this argument by the Eisenhower administration, see Francis, "Military Aid to Latin America," p. 398.

differ. At one 1977 congressional hearing, the assistant secretary of state for inter-American affairs stated his conviction that buyers had gone elsewhere, while the next witness, DSAA's General Fish, gave the following opinion: "It is really a judgment call, and reasonable people can disagree, and the Secretary may disagree. I administer the program. I watch it closely. I believe that many countries in Latin America that come to us for arms—and we turn down—are reluctant to go into the embrace of the [Soviet] bear. They do not want the kinds of equipment and the supply relationship that they can get with some of their other suppliers. So the result is that they cut their buy back considerably."[90] In addition, the deputy assistant secretary of state for inter-American affairs told Congress in 1978 that General Weyand's fears had not been confirmed. "The number of times we failed to supply arms and someone else came in to supply them," he said, "is fairly limited."[91]

Interestingly, in the 1970s this issue split the conservatives in Congress. One member concerned about the loss of markets and influence was E. W. Bill Young, a leader of House members opposed to closer ties with leftist regimes such as those of Angola, Cuba, and Mozambique. In 1977, he expressed his fear that the Carter administration's human rights campaign had so angered the Brazilian military that Brazil would turn to the Soviet Union for military aid.[92] The equally conservative William Goodling attempted to assuage Young's fears: "I vote against all of them [military aid bills] and I know they always say, 'Oh, but the other side will supply.' Let the other side supply. The best way to eliminate that kind of philosophy [communism] and that kind of government that they are trying to bring upon the world . . . is let them collapse economically and they sure will if they have to try to pick up our burden. . . . then we won't have to have meetings like this because we won't have any involvement."[93]

The second defense of aid to repressive regimes is that because the full range of consequences of military aid remains unclear, it may be possible that such aid actually promotes human rights. In 1975, for example, the Department of State suggested that "suppression of hu-

[90] Foreign Assistance Legislation for Fiscal Year 1978, pt. 7, pp. 80, 67, respectively, supra n. 20.

[91] See Aircraft Sales in Latin America, p. 3, supra n. 89.

[92] U.S. Congress, House, Committee on Appropriations, Subcommittee on Foreign Operations and Related Agencies, Foreign Assistance and Related Agencies Appropriations for 1978, 95th Cong., 1st Sess., 1977, pt. 1, p. 778.

[93] U.S. Congress, House, Committee on International Relations, Subcommittees on International Organizations and on Asian and Pacific Affairs, Human Rights in East Timor and the Question of the Use of U.S. Equipment by the Indonesian Armed Forces, 95th Cong., 1st Sess., March 23, 1977, p. 22.

man rights . . . is in many cases symptomatic of a basic insecurity on the part of a government in a particular country. It is possible, there-fore, that U.S. security assistance, by contributing to the economic stability of such a country or by enhancing its sense of security from outside attack, may serve to improve local attitudes toward the pro-tection of human rights."[94] The notion that military aid increases a nation's sense of security was the Nixon-Ford administration's primary argument against reducing military aid to the Pinochet government of Chile. The Peruvian government's purchase of twenty-two T-55 tanks from the Soviet Union provided the referent for such an ar-gument. One hundred years after the War of the Pacific, the State Department insisted that aid to Chile must continue because Peru had revanchist notions.[95]

The third and most widely voiced argument in favor of ignoring human rights considerations is that since the purpose of aid is to provide access to governments with which the United States must interact on a broad variety of issues, a halt in military aid would have the effect of damaging the entire relationship between the United States and the recipient government. This, too, is a time-honored argument. It was first employed in conjunction with the national-security argument of defense preparedness. In the 1950s, the Depart-ment of Defense argued that access to raw materials and base rights bears "no relation to the type of government which rules the nation capable of contributing to these requirements."[96] In the late 1970s, this statement could not have been made about Latin America by a policy maker who wished to remain employed by the Carter admin-istration, but administration officials continued to argue that access to military bases and raw materials was an appropriate justification for military aid to repressive regimes elsewhere in the world, especially in the Middle East and East Asia. This suggests that the argument was not being permanently discarded from United States policy toward Latin America but merely mothballed, to be returned to active duty when a threat to the strategic posture of the United States develops in the hemisphere.

Defense preparedness is not the only reason used to support the

[94] U.S. Congress, House, Committee on International Relations, Subcommittee on International Organizations, *Human Rights in Indonesia and the Philippines*, 94th Cong., 1st and 2d Sessions, December 18, 1975 and May 3, 1976, p. 110.

[95] See *International Security Assistance and Arms Export Control Act of 1976*, pp. 174-175, *supra* n. 47; U.S. Congress, Senate, Committee on Foreign Relations, *Foreign Assistance Authorization: Arms Sales Issues*, 94th Cong., 1st Sess., 1975, pp. 466-467. At least one member of Congress repeated the argument. *Congressional Record*, Feb-ruary 18, 1976, p. S1888.

[96] *Congressional Record*, August 1, 1957, p. 13408.

assertion that military aid continue to repressive Latin American governments in order to retain access. Following his 1958 tour of the hemisphere, Milton Eisenhower reported to his brother that if the United States were to withdraw aid from Latin America's dictators it would "paralyze the conduct of all foreign relations."[97] ARA officials in particular have always been wary of dissociating the United States from repressive governments by reducing military aid. In 1959, the assistant secretary of state for inter-American affairs told Congress that aid should continue despite human rights violations because "the maintaining of relations, including military relationships with a country, does not imply approval of the type of government which it happens to have."[98] In the 1970s, the clearest statement of this position came from assistant secretary of state Todman:

> The United States for many years has maintained close working ties with the Latin military. . . . This long association has developed an arms relationship with the Latin American countries that has helped us maintain access to their military establishments, a matter of importance since 15 Latin and Caribbean nations today are governed by or under the aegis of the armed forces. Security assistance to these governments thus is a political tool that provides us an opportunity to exert some influence on their attitudes and actions. It is, in short, a means of protecting or advancing our interests, which are many and varied. . . . We hope . . . that the executive branch will be allowed leeway to work with the military in Latin America, using the traditional tools of a relatively modest security assistance program to take advantage of whatever opportunities we might have to advance the cause of human rights and our other, real interests in the hemisphere.[99]

This is the argument ARA used throughout the 1970s to oppose reductions in military assistance for human rights considerations.

The Congressional Initiative

Prior to 1977, a handful of members of Congress repeatedly urged that reductions in military aid be employed to express disapproval of human rights conditions in Latin America. In 1957, Representative Charles Porter demanded that the Eisenhower administration "stop all eco-

---

[97] G. Pope Atkins, *Latin America in the International Political System* (New York: Free Press, 1977), p. 109.

[98] See Francis, "Military Aid to Latin America," p. 401.

[99] *Foreign Assistance Legislation for Fiscal Year 1978*, pt. 7, p. 68, *supra* n. 20.

nomic and military aid to the despotisms in Latin America."[100] Also in 1957, a House Foreign Affairs Committee report on Latin America noted that U.S.-supplied arms were supporting a variety of unpopular regimes and urged that aid to these governments be reassessed.[101] In 1962, Senator Ernest Gruening charged that military aid to Latin America was undermining the democratic goals of the Alliance for Progress; in 1965, Senator Wayne Morse asked for a cutoff in military and economic aid to Brazil as a protest against the Second Institutional Act; and in 1969, Senator Frank Church voiced his concern over increases in military aid to human rights violators in Latin America.[102]

These early pleas on behalf of human rights went largely unheard by Congress and several administrations whose perceptions of Latin America were dominated by the national security concern of containing communism. Prior to 1973, the issue of human rights violations in Latin America was discussed infrequently in Congress, and when the subject did arise it was not generally linked to military aid programs. In the 1,132 pages that comprise the New Directions hearings by the House Foreign Affairs Subcommittee on Inter-American Affairs during 1969 to 1971, for example, no one mentioned the idea of using military aid to attack repressive Latin American governments.[103] Indeed, as late as 1975 the Senate Committee on Appropriations held lengthy hearings on the FMS program without considering the relationship between military aid and human rights.[104]

There was one specific human rights clause added to military assistance legislation in the 1960s, a policy statement in the Foreign Military Sales Act of 1968 (PL90-629) that stated: "It is . . . the sense of Congress that sales and guaranties . . . shall not be approved where they would have the effect of arming military dictators who are denying social progress to their own people." Three years later, the phrase

---

[100] A freshman member without any prior interest in Latin America, Porter apparently became concerned about U.S. policy toward Latin America when one of his constituents was murdered, allegedly by the Trujillo government in the Dominican Republic. *Congressional Record*, August 1, 1957, pp. 13405, 13409.

[101] Francis, "Military Aid to Latin America," pp. 400-401.

[102] U.S. Congress, House, Committee on Foreign Affairs, Subcommittee on International Organizations and Movements, *International Protection of Human Rights*, 93rd Cong., 1st Sess., 1973, p. 646; *Congressional Record*, August 2, 1962, pp. 14409-14440; *Rockefeller Report on Latin America*, supra n. 22, pp. 9-20.

[103] U.S. Congress, House, Committee on Foreign Affairs, Subcommittee on Inter-American Affairs, *New Directions for the 1970's: Toward a Strategy of Inter-American Development*, 91st Cong., 1st Sess., March-May 1969, p. 571; U.S. Congress, House, Committee on Foreign Affairs, Subcommittee on Inter-American Affairs, *New Directions for the 1970's—Part 2: Development Assistance Options for Latin America*, 92d Cong., 1st Sess., 1971.

[104] See *Department of Defense Appropriations, Fiscal Year 1976*, supra n. 7.

"denying social progress" was replaced by "denying the growth of fundamental rights or social progress."[105] Although Congress soon learned that the Nixon administration chose to emphasize the non-binding nature of such legislation, it was not until 1973 that disaffection with the Nixon-Kissinger military aid policy became sufficiently strong to enable the passage of new human rights legislation.[106]

Although 1973 can be considered the year that the human rights issue became the central focus of the foreign assistance program, of the four human rights amendments added to the Foreign Assistance Act of 1973 (PL93-189), only Section 32—a request that the President deny aid to governments holding political prisoners—was directly related to military aid. In 1973, there also were several unproductive attempts to link military aid to respect for human rights. Senator Abourezk made an unsuccessful proposal to ban (rather than express the sense of the Congress that the President ban) aid to any country with political prisoners; it lost on the Senate floor by an overwhelming margin (23-67). But two other proposals passed the Senate only to be deleted or weakened in conference. One would have halted all aid to Chile and the other would have required the President to report to Congress on the use of military aid by Portugal to repress independence movements in its African colonies.

Interest in the relationship between human rights and military aid increased in 1974. The Senate accepted an amendment to the foreign assistance authorization bill offered by Senator Kennedy that ended military assistance to Chile, but it rejected two proposals that would have generalized the issue of military aid and human rights. One was a second attempt by Senator Abourezk to change the nonmandatory language in Section 32 to an outright ban on military aid to governments with political prisoners, the other was an amendment by Senator Cranston to phase out military aid to military dictatorships by the end of FY1976. Both proposals were rejected by a two-to-one margin, in part because of their vague wording, but a proposal to broaden the prohibition on police training to include training in the United States was accepted without a major struggle. All this was preface, however, to the crucial human rights legislation of 1974—the addition of Section 502B to the Foreign Assistance Act of 1961. Section 502B was

[105] PL91-672, Sec. 4.

[106] On the Nixon administration's interpretation, see *Aircraft Sales in Latin America*, p. 25, *supra* n. 89. In a matter related to human rights considerations, a Vietnam-weary Congress amended the Foreign Assistance Act of 1969 (PL91-175) to limit the number of military students trained in the United States in any fiscal year to the number of foreign civilians brought to the United States as Fulbright scholars in the preceding fiscal year. In 1976, this provision was repealed.

a simple sense-of-Congress statement "that, except in extraordinary circumstances, the President shall substantially reduce or terminate security assistance to any government which engages in a consistent pattern of gross violations of internationally recognized human rights."[107] This original Section 502B was enormously significant, for it established the principle that the receipt of military aid should be linked to the recipients' human rights behavior. In addition, Section 502B provided specific examples of what was meant by a consistent pattern of gross violations of fundamental human rights: "torture or cruel, inhuman or degrading treatment or punishment; prolonged detention without charges; or other flagrant denials of the right to life, liberty, and the security of the person."[108] Although Section 502B was an addition to the Foreign Assistance Act of 1961, its definition clause was so worded as to make it applicable to FMS credits as well as grant aid.

The liberal Ninety-fourth Congress demonstrated a greater concern for the international protection of human rights than any other in United States history, and as a result 1975 and 1976 were the salad years for the human rights movement in Washington. As usual, congressional concern over this foreign policy issue focused upon the annual foreign assistance legislation. In 1975, the authorization process concentrated upon human rights in the economic aid program, and the appropriations bill contained no human rights provisions for either economic or military aid. But in 1976, Congress completed a major reevaluation of the military assistance program, building upon the work of earlier years. The human rights centerpiece of the International Security Assistance and Arms Export Control Act (PL94-329) was a completely rewritten Section 502B.

The 1976 version of Section 502B must be viewed primarily as a liberal Congress's reaction to the Ford administration's open contempt for the earlier nonmandatory section. Between 1974 and 1976, the executive branch simply ignored Congress's advice that military assistance be denied to governments engaged in gross violations of human rights. By 1976, congressional liberals were ready to act. The House battle to strengthen Section 502B was led by Representative Fraser, under whose supervision most of the section was written, and

---

[107] PL93-559, Sec. 46.

[108] The phrase "consistent pattern of gross violations of fundamental human rights" was borrowed from United Nations ECOSOC Resolution 1503, which governs the review of human rights communications by the U.N. Commission on Human Rights. See John Salzberg and Donald D. Young, "The Parliamentary Role in Implementing International Human Rights: A U.S. Example," *Texas International Law Journal* 12 (Spring-Summer 1977): 271.

by Stephen Solarz, a young liberal in his first term. They encountered no serious opposition on the House floor once a weakening amendment supported by the Democratic leadership was defeated by a close (11-11) vote during markup in the Committee on International Relations. The Senate struggle was entirely different, with spirited but unsuccessful efforts to weaken key provisions of Section 502B. The ban on aid to repressive governments emerged intact from the House-Senate conference committee—the House version was essentially identical to that of the Senate except that it did not establish a human rights office in the State Department—but in early May, the bill was vetoed by President Ford. His veto message cited five "unwise restrictions" in the bill, one of which was Section 502B.[109]

With no chance of mustering the required two-thirds majority to override the veto, the bill was returned to the two foreign affairs committees. The House then voted to retain the strong human rights provisions of the vetoed bill, particularly the provision permitting Congress to halt military aid to human rights violators with a concurrent resolution, but at the urging of Hubert Humphrey, the Senate Committee on Foreign Relations changed its provision to require a joint resolution for an aid cutoff.[110] The conference committee subsequently adopted the weaker Senate version, and the bill was signed into law on the last day of the year for which it was originally intended.[111] From 1976 to 1978, the crucial provision of Section 502B read: "It is . . . the policy of the United States that, except under circumstances specified in this section, no security assistance may be provided to any country the government of which engages in a consistent pattern of gross violations of fundamental human rights." Section 520B also required the Secretary of State to submit an annual report to Congress on the status of human rights in each country receiving military assistance, and it detailed the evidence the executive branch must consider in researching the reports.

In addition to the general human rights provisions in military assistance legislation, Congress restricted military aid to two Latin American countries prior to the beginning of the Carter administration. The Chilean government of General Pinochet was the principal focus

[109] *Weekly Compilation of Presidential Documents*, May 12, 1976, p. 829.

[110] Unlike a concurrent resolution, a joint resolution requires the signature of the President.

[111] The original authorization request was for FY1976 alone, but following the presidential veto in May the foreign affairs committees were faced with the dilemma of rewriting the FY1976 legislation and completing action on the FY1977 authorization in time to meet the May 15 deadline imposed by the new congressional budget procedures. To accomplish this, both houses combined the FY1976 and FY1977 authorization bills into a single bill, H.R. 13860 and S. 3439.

of efforts to use military aid as a tool to encourage respect for human rights. The September 1973 coup in Chile occurred as Congress was considering the foreign assistance authorization for FY1974. During floor debate on October 1, the Senate accepted Senator Kennedy's proposal to request the President to deny aid to Chile until its government ceased violating human rights. The House version of the bill had no such provision because it had been passed before the coup, but in conference House members accepted the Senate amendment after the language was softened significantly.[112]

The Foreign Assistance Act of 1974 contained a much more specific restriction on military aid to Chile for FY1975. The House version was more stringent than that passed by the Senate; it prohibited all military aid except $800,000 in IMET programs and included a ban on the issuance of commercial export licenses. The Senate prohibited all military aid including training but placed no restriction on commercial transactions. In conference, the weaker Senate version was accepted. Thus the 1974 legislation on aid to Chile made no mention of halting aid that had already been authorized but not delivered ("pipeline" aid) or of prohibiting export licenses for commercial sales.[113]

Finally, in 1976 the atrocities in Chile and the displeasure with Secretary Kissinger's failure to implement the previous year's reductions in economic aid combined to permit congressional liberals to enact new restrictions on military aid to Chile.[114] Human rights activists in both the House and Senate found no difficulty in passing an extremely strong bill prohibiting MAP, IMET, FMS credits, and the delivery of items that were already authorized by these programs. The Senate went two steps further than the House, prohibiting FMS cash sales and commercial sales of defense equipment. House-Senate conferees adopted the Senate version, but under strong pressure from House International Relations chairperson Morgan (who was himself being pressured by the Ford administration), they weakened *both* bills

[112] The Foreign Assistance Act of 1973 had an unusual legislative history. In June, the Senate attempted to force a separation of the combined authorization into its military and economic components by passing only a military aid authorization. In July when the House passed the standard combined aid authorization, the Senate had to begin work on the economic aid program. The two Senate bills were combined during the House-Senate conference.

[113] PL93-559, Sec. 25.

[114] For an atypical example of congressional ire over Kissinger's *obedezco-pero-no-cumplo* policy, see Senator Kennedy's statement in the *Congressional Record*, February 18, 1976.

by permitting the pipeline to remain open, i.e., all export licenses granted prior to June 30, 1976 were not affected by the legislation.[115]

The second pre-1977 military aid reduction occurred in 1976, when Representative Edward I. Koch mounted an unusually effective campaign to halt aid to Uruguay, using as a legislative vehicle the FY1977 foreign assistance appropriations bill. As part of its campaign against torture in Uruguay, Amnesty International asked Koch, a member of Clarence Long's key Appropriations Subcommittee on Foreign Operations, to insert into the *Congressional Record* its report on the Uruguayan government's repression of human rights. His interest piqued, Koch pursued the question of military aid to Uruguay during the hearings of his subcommittee. The State Department gave no answer to the question of why the United States should arm the government of the nation Koch called "the torture house of Latin America."[116] After considerable persuasion by Koch and a key aide, Charles Flynn, the subcommittee members voted 6 to 4 to reject the administration's $3.05 million request for military aid to Uruguay. In June, the subcommittee's position was upheld during markup by the full committee and on the House floor.

In the meantime, Senator Inouye's Appropriations Subcommittee on Foreign Operations ushered through the Senate a bill that included no reduction of the administration's request for Uruguay. Inouye argued that with so many human rights violators in the world it was useless to single out one of them for an aid reduction. Between the time that the Senate bill left Inouye's subcommittee and reached a House-Senate conference in September, however, two events occurred. First, Representative Fraser's International Relations Subcommittee on International Organizations held three hearings on human rights in Uruguay. The witnesses against aid to Uruguay were impressive, while the representatives of the Ford administration could only be labeled as pathetic.[117] Second, Koch and staffer Flynn moved vigorously to mobilize public support. Every citizen who had ever written Koch in support of his outspoken position against the war in

[115] PL94-329, Sec. 406. On the strange compromise, see the conference report, House Report 94-1272, p. 55.

[116] House Report 94-1228, p. 57. See also U.S. Congress, House, Committee on Appropriations, Subcommittee on Foreign Operations and Related Agencies, *Foreign Assistance and Related Agencies Appropriations for 1977*, 94th Cong., 2d Sess., 1976, pt. 1, pp. 806-807.

[117] Of particular value was the testimony of exiled Uruguayan parliamentarian Wilson Ferreira Aldunante, which was arranged by the Washington Office on Latin America. Ferreira also spoke with the ranking Republican on Inouye's subcommittee, Edward Brooke, and apparently convinced him that repression was so extreme in Uruguay that the Senator should drop his opposition to the aid reduction.

Vietnam received a plea to write his or her senator on behalf of the cut. Koch convinced major national organizations, including the United Auto Workers and the U.S. Catholic Conference, along with prominent individuals such as Notre Dame's President Theodore Hesberg to contact Senators Inouye and Brooke to urge that they deny the Uruguayan aid request. Faced with this type of opposition, Inouye conceded in conference, and all military aid to Uruguay was halted.[118]

As with the case of the Harkin amendment to economic aid legislation, Congress created the major piece of human rights legislation governing military aid (Section 502B) and established the principle of aid reductions for human rights violations before the inauguration of Jimmy Carter. Despite its institutional weaknesses and its subordinate role in foreign policy making, and despite the overt hostility of the Nixon-Ford administration, Congress forced the issue of human rights onto the administration's agenda with Latin America. There were glaring weaknesses in each human rights measure, but they formed a solid foundation upon which to build a human rights partnership with the Carter administration.

Congress and the Carter Administration

The inauguration of a new administration and the Ninety-fifth Congress in January 1977 promised a new era of cooperation in the drive to dissociate military assistance programs from repressive governments. This promise took concrete form on February 24, when Secretary of State Vance took advantage of his first appearance before the Senate Appropriations Subcommittee on Foreign Operations to inform Congress of the decision to reduce military aid to Argentina and Ethiopia (and economic aid to Uruguay) for their human rights violations.[119] Soon thereafter, the administration released its annual human rights reports on countries receiving military aid, and within weeks Argentina, Brazil, El Salvador, Guatemala, and Uruguay had all rejected various types of assistance on the grounds that U.S. concern over alleged human rights violations constituted unacceptable interference in the internal affairs of sovereign states. While the administration's initiatives failed to please completely many active advocates of human rights, they demonstrated a willingness to cooperate with Congress in the pursuit of what was now a mutual interest.

In Congress, the relationship between human rights and military assistance remained an issue of importance, with attention focused

[118] PL94-441, Sec. 505.
[119] U.S. Congress, Senate, Committee on Appropriations, Subcommittee on Foreign Assistance and Related Programs, *Foreign Assistance and Related Programs Appropriations, Fiscal Year 1978*, 95th Cong., 1st Sess., 1977, p. 196.

upon strengthening Section 502B and halting aid to the most egregious violators. The initial vehicle for these two interests was the FY1978 military aid authorization bill. In its 1976 form, Section 502B was a quasimandatory prohibition, a statement that the policy of the United States was to halt security assistance to gross violators of human rights. Such a policy provision is more than a statement of the sense of Congress but less than an outright prohibition. No one, however, seemed certain how much less or more. Section 502B required the executive branch to give serious consideration to the relationship between military aid and human rights but not to terminate aid to human rights violators. Seeking to create such a mandatory ban, in 1977 human rights activists on the Committee on International Relations convinced House members to amend Section 502B to prohibit military aid "for the purpose of, or which would have the effect of, aiding directly or indirectly the efforts of foreign governments to repress the legitimate rights of the population in such countries."[120] The Senate bill contained no comparable provision, and House-Senate conferees deleted the House amendment on the grounds that it was "so broad as to be impractical and impossible to implement."[121] The initial attempts by human rights activists in the Ninety-fifth Congress thereby ended in defeat.

The effort to make Section 502B mandatory was successful in the second session of the Ninety-fifth Congress. In April 1978, Representative Fraser introduced an amendment to the FY1979 security assistance authorization bill (H.R. 12514) to delete the introductory words "It is further the policy of the United States that. . . ." Fraser's initiative was strongly opposed by the chairperson of the Committee on International Relations, Clement Zablocki, who argued instead that Section 502B should be weakened to provide the administration greater flexibility and to permit arms manufacturers to contribute to an improvement in the nation's balance of payments. Fraser was also opposed by the Carter administration because, according to assistant secretary of state Douglas Bennett, a mandatory prohibition would be difficult to administer. Despite this opposition, the Fraser position prevailed in the House.

Human rights activists in the Senate were concerned with other aspects of their version of the military assistance bill, so there was no change comparable to that of the House. In the Senate-House conference, the Senate accepted the House version without serious ar-

[120] The phrase "or which would have the effect of" was added to the bill during floor debate. House Report 95-503, p. 31; *Congressional Record*, May 24, 1977, p. H4934.
[121] House Report 95-503, p. 31.

gument.[122] With final passage of the International Security Assistance Act of 1978 (PL95-384) in September, the relevant portion of Section 502B became: "Except under circumstances specified in this section, no security assistance may be provided to any country the government of which engages in a consistent pattern of gross violations of internationally recognized human rights."

The 1978 military aid authorization bill contained three other human rights provisions related to security assistance. First, the existing prohibition on police training was expanded to prohibit the export of crime control equipment to a country whose government engages in human rights violations. Second, the purpose of IMET was expanded to include education of trainees in the "basic issues involving internationally recognized human rights." The House had proposed a stronger requirement—that a course on human rights be completed by all IMET students as a prerequisite for completion of all other courses—but yielded to the Senate on this issue. Third, $300,000 in IMET funds was cut from the administration's request, with the tacit understanding that the reduction should affect Nicaragua and Paraguay. The Senate bill explicitly prohibited the use of IMET funds for training soldiers from these two nations. House-Senate conferees agreed to avoid naming countries, but their report noted that "the elimination of references to specific countries should not be interpreted as approval of the human rights practices in either Nicaragua or Paraguay."[123]

The hardest-fought human rights victory of the Ninety-fifth Congress was the 1977 reduction in military aid to Argentina. By the beginning of that year, nearly all policy makers were in agreement that the Argentine military's behavior had been uncommonly brutal following the March 1976 coup against the government of Isabel Perón. The reduction in military aid announced by the Carter administration in February encouraged Congress to seek a more stringent sanction. In the House, Representative Yatron's International Relations Subcommittee on Inter-American Affairs and the full committee rejected attempts to halt all military aid to Argentina. The committee bill did, however, reduce the administration's request by the amount proposed for FMS loan guarantees to Argentina, Brazil, El Salvador, and Guatemala "because of human rights violations . . . and because of indications by the governments of those countries that they no longer desire military assistance from the United States."[124] The issue

[122] Bruce Cameron, "The Human Rights Working Group and Human Rights Legislation," unpublished paper, 1978, p. 24.
[123] House Report 95-1546, p. 31.
[124] House Report 95-274, pp. 24-25.

of aid to Argentina then moved to the House floor, where a spirited debate and the close defeat (187-200) of an amendment by Representative Garry Studds to halt all military aid indicated that the opponents and proponents of aid to Argentina were closely matched. Opponents of the ban based their arguments upon the need to combat terrorism ("Civil wars are never polite," observed Representative Edward Derwinski). The Democratic foreign affairs leadership adopted Henry Kissinger's earlier argument that the executive branch should be provided with flexibility in dealing with issues of foreign policy.[125]

When the Senate's military aid authorization bill reached the floor of the upper chamber, it too lacked a provision banning aid to Argentina. But on the floor, Senator Kennedy introduced an extremely strong amendment that received the support of Frank Church, chairperson of the Committee on Foreign Relations. The Kennedy amendment would have halted all military aid and commercial sales to Argentina, including all aid and sales currently in the pipeline. At the request of the Carter administration, Senator Humphrey introduced a weakening substitute that would begin the ban in October 1978, would free pipeline aid, and would permit a presidential waiver.[126] Kennedy accepted the Humphrey substitute, and it passed the Senate by voice vote. In conference, the House accepted the Senate version and, with the President's signature, the Foreign Assistance Act of 1961 was formally amended to prohibit military aid to Argentina in the form of grants, credits, loan guarantees, sales, and export licenses issued after September 30, 1978.

While the foreign affairs committees worked on the FY1978 authorization for military aid, the House Appropriations Subcommittee on Foreign Operations was holding hearings on the companion appropriations bill (H.R. 7797). In 1977, the subcommittee switched its sights from Uruguay to Argentina and Nicaragua. The Carter administration had already reduced FMS credits to Argentina from $30 million to $15 million, and the Argentine government had rejected the remaining $15 million, which the 1977 authorization bill was about to prohibit for good measure. The request of the Carter administration also contained a $700,000 IMET grant for Argentina, however, and it was upon this budget item that human rights activists concentrated. Since it had already proposed its own aid reduction, the administration could not defend the IMET grant. The undersecretary

---

[125] *Congressional Record*, May 23, 1977, p. H4791.

[126] The Carter administration argued that it needed the extra year to attempt to persuade the Videla government to cease torturing its citizens.

of state for security assistance, Lucy Benson, told subcommittee chairperson Long that

> we can always not give the money even though you appropriate the moneys, and the country stays in the budget. What we would like is the opportunity, the flexibility, to be able to continue with the program if we consider it to be a good idea. We would be glad to consult with you about it before doing so.
>
> *Mr. Long.* Would you mind terribly if Congress or this committee said we would like to be the ones that decide?
>
> *Ms. Benson.* I wouldn't dream of arguing with you. [127]

Despite this weak defense by the administration, the subcommittee rejected by a vote of 8 to 5 the proposal to delete Argentina's IMET grant from the aid budget. Three liberals on the subcommittee cast the deciding votes against the amendment: Silvio Conte and Louis Stokes argued for more flexibility for the administration, while David Obey, a strong supporter of previous human rights actions, voted against reducing Argentina's aid to halt the practice of taking "a dozen different actions in a dozen different committees."[128] Despite this setback, human rights activists who had suffered the narrow 187 to 200 defeat on the issue of aid to Argentina in the authorization bill were anxious to resume their attack when the appropriations bill reached the House floor. Representatives Studds and Edward Roybal promptly offered an amendment similar to the one that had been defeated in the subcommittee, and this time the increasingly common coalition of liberal human rights activists and conservative opponents of foreign aid held together. The amendment passed by a comfortable margin of 223 to 180.

In the meantime, Senator Inouye's Appropriations Subcommittee on Foreign Operations continued its established policy of ignoring the human rights violations of recipient governments, and the administration's request passed the Senate without an attempt to match the House action against Argentina. The first House-Senate conference in September produced no compromises on a total of thirty-six differences, including the Argentine IMET reduction. In the second conference in October, the Senate yielded to the House insistence upon the cut. When the bill became law in late October, it contained the stipulation that "none of the funds appropriated . . . shall be used

---

[127] *Foreign Assistance and Related Agencies Appropriations for 1978*, pt. 1, pp. 750-751, *supra* n. 92.

[128] Obey is reported to have declared during committee markup that "the House is going bananas on this issue" of human rights. Americans for Democratic Action, *Legislative Newsletter*, July 1, 1977, p. 2.

to provide international military education and training to the Government of Argentina."[129]

During the 1977 foreign aid appropriations process, a second country, Nicaragua, was also targeted for a reduction in military aid for human rights abuses. The primary proponent of this action was Representative Koch, who a year earlier had successfully engineered the fight to end military aid to Uruguay. Working from the Ford-Kissinger budget, the Carter administration proposed $3.1 million in military aid to Nicaragua—$600,000 in IMET grants and $2.5 million in FMS credits. By a narrow 5 to 4 vote, Clarence Long's subcommittee agreed to prohibit any of this aid to Nicaragua. But, as noted earlier in the discussion of interest groups, by the time the bill reached the House floor, Somoza's supporters were more than equal to the challenge. The day after the vote to cut aid to Argentina, an amendment to restore military aid to Nicaragua easily passed by a margin of 225 to 180.[130] These two votes served as a stark indicator of the fragility of the liberal-conservative coalition that determined the fate of human rights legislation in the 1970s. Since the Senate version contained no restriction on aid to Nicaragua, the issue died at that point.

In addition to the contests over aid to Argentina and Nicaragua, the appropriations bill for FY1978 also ended MAP, IMET, and FMS aid to Ethiopia and Uruguay and terminated FMS credits for Argentina, Brazil, El Salvador, and Guatemala. Although these were House initiatives, they merely confirmed the administration's announced intentions (in the cases of Argentina and Uruguay) and the countries' own declarations (in all five cases). The Senate Appropriations Subcommittee on Foreign Operations deleted both House amendments, for chairperson Inouye remained adamantly opposed to even *pro forma* reductions. He defended this position so resolutely that the first House-Senate conference could not resolve the differences, but in the face of similar intransigence by House conferees he yielded, and in the second conference the House language was accepted.

Finally, at the initiative of the House, a provision was added to the FY1978 appropriations bill that prohibited economic as well as military aid of any type "to any country for the purpose of aiding directly the

[129] PL95-148.

[130] There was some speculation that the difference between the Nicaraguan and Argentine votes could be attributed to the anti-Semitism of Argentina's government. Of the twenty-three members of the House who identified themselves as Jewish in their congressional biographies, however, eighteen voted to halt aid to Nicaragua and nineteen voted against aid to Argentina. Only three of the twenty-three switched their votes. The influence of Jewish constituents on non-Jewish members cannot be determined.

efforts of the government of such country to repress the legitimate rights of the population."[131] As with all provisions of appropriations bills, this section applied only to expenditures during the fiscal year for which the appropriations were made.

With the exception of a repetition of this provision, the foreign aid appropriations bill for FY1979 (PL95-481) contained no mention of human rights. There were two minor controversies regarding military assistance to repressive governments. One involved a House initiative championed by Representative Leo Ryan to reduce MAP funds to the Philippines by $5 million.[132] The move was strongly opposed by Senator Inouye. House-Senate conferees compromised by deleting $2.5 million from the administration's $18.1 million request for MAP aid to the Marcos government. The second dispute was over a proposal by Senator Mark Hatfield to delete $150,000 in IMET aid to Nicaragua. Although approved by the Senate, Hatfield's initiative died without discussion in the House-Senate conference. Before the conference committee met, Representative Charles Wilson announced his intention to defeat the entire aid appropriations bill if Nicaragua were denied either economic or military aid. Unwilling to test Wilson's strength, Congress yielded to his pressure.

The Ninety-fifth Congress (1977 to 1978) did much to refine and strengthen the human rights restrictions on military assistance programs in Latin America, but it broke little new ground. Perhaps this was inevitable, for the Ninety-third and Ninety-fourth Congresses left little new ground to be broken. Nonetheless, it is notable that the only important victories for human rights activists were in strengthening Section 502B and in halting aid to Argentina. The latter effort was greatly encouraged not only by the administration's announced reduction but by the Argentine government's subsequent rejection of all FMS credits. Given these two occurrences, the fact that the prohibition on aid to Argentina was extremely difficult to achieve and that it contained a one-year delay should be interpreted as a sign of weakness in the congressional human rights forces. By the time the ban went into effect on October 1, 1978, U.S. firms had sold but not delivered to the Argentine government $3 million in ammunition, $19 million in aircraft, $3 million in communications equipment, and $7 million in ships and spare parts.[133] The pipeline was packed, and

---

[131] PL95-148, Sec. 113.

[132] Ryan's California constituents included a sizable number of Filipino immigrants. Also in his district, unfortunately, were relatives of followers of the People's Temple, who asked their congressman to investigate the sect's activities in Guyana. Ryan's murder on a remote Guyanese airfield sparked the Jonestown massacre.

[133] *Washington Post*, July 2, 1978, p. B3.

it was the decision of the Carter administration and not Congress that kept this pipeline closed in the late 1970s.

After 1976, the executive branch seized the initiative from Congress and began to determine how and where military assistance should be used to attack repressive governments in Latin America. Early analyses of the Carter administration's efforts in this area were uniformly negative. While the President was praised for his public commitment to human rights, his military aid budget was attacked by both human rights NGOs and by human rights activists in Congress. The Inter-religious Task Force on U.S. Food Policy blasted the administration's FY1978 security assistance proposals as heavily skewed toward the most repressive governments.[134] Brazil, Indonesia, the Philippines, and South Korea were all scheduled by the Carter administration to receive major assistance. After holding his criticism for nine months, the highly respected leader of the Friends' Committee on National Legislation, Edward Snyder, was quoted as saying that "with regard to giving military aid to repressive regimes, I see little difference between this administration and the Nixon-Ford approach."[135]

While this criticism was justified in the sense that military aid continued to flow to many repressive regimes, in the case of Latin America, it was first premature and then simply incorrect. It was premature because the FY1978 budget was largely the creation of the outgoing Ford administration and incorrect because, as Table 6.3 demonstrates, executive branch requests for military aid to Latin America dropped dramatically between FY1976 and FY1979. While worldwide military assistance expenditure requests remained roughly unchanged between FY1977 and FY1979, Latin America's share of the total dropped from 8.1 percent to 2.3 percent. Several factors contributed to this reduction. As mentioned several times previously, political dissent by leftist groups in several nations (Argentina, Chile, and Uruguay) had been largely exterminated by 1977, so less aid was required to contain the political groups that had been considered threats by earlier administrations. At the same time, the level of human rights violations accompanying this political repression had risen so dramatically that Congress legislated the series of reductions discussed above. By the end of 1978, the executive branch could not provide certain types of military aid to Argentina, Brazil, Chile, El Salvador, Guatemala, and Uruguay.[136] Perhaps more significantly, in

[134] *Congressional Record*, April 1, 1977, p. S5356.

[135] *Washington Post*, October 25, 1977, p. A3.

[136] By 1980, the Carter administration had executed an extraordinary policy reversal and had begun to channel large amounts of military aid to the center-right military junta in El Salvador. An excellent discussion of this reversal, which clearly reflected

TABLE 6.3
ADMINISTRATION MILITARY ASSISTANCE REQUESTS, FY1976-FY1979
(thousands of dollars)

Country	FY1976*	FY1977	FY1978	FY1979
Worldwide	$3,108,700	$2,575,500	$2,616,034	$2,398,945
Latin America	233,500	208,945	149,350	54,221
Argentina	34,920	49,300	15,700	—
Bolivia	11,920	15,105	15,500	6,777
Brazil	61,120	61,100	50,100	—
Chile	—	—	—	—
Colombia	16,750	25,700	30,000	19,450
Costa Rica	—	—	—	—
Dominican Republic	3,370	1,525	1,765	1,030
Ecuador	10,970	10,900	10,900	10,400
El Salvador	6,640	3,120	3,125	14
Guatemala	3,630	1,115	2,110	3
Haiti	200	700	700	525
Honduras	6,640	3,115	3,120	2,250
Mexico	5,100	5,200	200	200
Nicaragua	6,540	3,150	3,100	153
Panama	2,080	1,825	1,430	1,502
Paraguay	8,810	1,440	1,100	467
Peru	20,940	20,900	10,900	7,050
Uruguay	17,120	3,050	—	—
Venezuela	16,750	700	100	—
Canal Zone Schools	—	—	—	4,400

SOURCES:
U.S. Congress, Senate, Committee on Appropriations, Subcommittee on Foreign Assistance and Related Programs. *Foreign Assistance and Related Programs Appropriations Fiscal Year 1977.* 94th Cong., 2d Sess., 1976, pp. 1114, 1152-1170.
———. *Foreign Assistance and Related Programs Appropriations Fiscal Year 1978.* 95th Cong., 1st Sess., 1977, pp. 1302, 1348-1363.
U.S. Congress, Senate, Committee on Appropriations, Subcommittee on Foreign Operations. *Foreign Assistance and Related Programs Appropriations Fiscal Year 1976.* 94th Cong., 1st Sess., 1975, pp. 1448, 1481-1494.
———. *Foreign Assistance and Related Programs Appropriations Fiscal Year 1979.* 95th Cong., 2d Sess., 1978, pp. 1410, 1503-1537.
NOTE: Administration Military Assistance Requests includes Military Assistance Program, International Military Education and Training Program, Foreign Military Sales credits and guarantees, and Excess Defense Articles. Does not include the cost of MAAGs.
* Does not include the 1976 budgetary transition quarter (197T).

order to preempt action by either Congress or human rights activists within the State Department, military aid requests were reduced for

the administration's growing fear of instability in Central America, is William M. LeoGrande and Carla Anne Roberts, "Oligarchs and Officers: The Crisis in El Salvador," *Foreign Affairs* 58 (Summer, 1980): 1084-1103.

other countries with governments noted for their high levels of human rights violations. ARA decided not to request the typical $1 million to $4 million in FMS credits for Somoza's Nicaragua, for example, simply because the Bureau recognized that either HA or liberal members of Congress would put up too much of a fight.

It is difficult to determine how these variables interacted, and for that reason it is difficult to determine the extent to which the changes in Table 6.3 reflect the autonomous decisions by the Carter administration to withdraw military assistance in order to promote respect for human rights in Latin America. There were some documented cases where the administration used military assistance to Latin America for this purpose. In 1977, the United States signed an FMS agreement with Nicaragua, for example, but the State Department refused to release the funds because of the Somoza government's human rights violations. The administration delayed the actual use of the money until pressure by pro-Somoza members of Congress forced a partial release.[137] Then in late 1978, the administration placed a complete ban on military aid and export licenses for Nicaragua, making Somoza's government the third in Latin America (with those of Chile and Uruguay) to be totally cut off from U.S. military arms and services. In another case, in mid-1978 the Carter administration briefly suspended military aid to Bolivia when General Juan Pereda Asbun seized power following a disputed election.[138] Most of the repressive regimes in Latin America were pressured from time to time with delays in the approval of military aid requests, but the greatly reduced size of the military aid program decreased its utility as an instrument to attack the region's repressive governments. Once aid had been reduced, the Carter administration was forced to turn to other foreign policy tools, especially commercial arms sales, to promote its human rights policy. As for military aid, the administration could do little more than wait to see if the reductions were having their desired effect.

[137] See *Human Rights and United States Foreign Policy*, pp. 40-41, *supra* n. 62.

[138] The suspension lasted for twenty-five days. Another cutoff occurred following the García Meza coup.

· 7 ·

MULTILATERAL ECONOMIC
ASSISTANCE

IN 1970, PRESIDENT NIXON proposed to Congress "that the United States channel an increasing share of its development assistance through multilateral institutions as rapidly as practicable." An increase in multilateral aid, he continued, creates "better relations between borrowing and lending countries by reducing the political frictions that arise from reliance on bilateral contacts in the most sensitive affairs of nation-states. It will enhance the effectiveness of the world development effort by providing for a pooling of resources, knowledge, and expertise for solving development problems which no single country can muster."[1] Congress agreed to the President's proposal, and over the course of the 1970s, an increasing proportion of the total United States economic aid budget was earmarked for distribution through multilateral development banks (MDBs). As Table 7.1 indicates, on a worldwide basis about 7 percent of U.S. economic assistance was channelled through MDBs during the 1960s. Although yearly figures fluctuate widely because of the irregularity of bank replenishments and the peculiarities of the congressional authorization and appropriation procedures, during the period 1970 to 1979, the average rose to about 15 percent.[2]

Because MDBs use member contributions in part as a foundation upon which to borrow further funds in the world's private capital markets, the flow of MDB resources to Latin America that is based upon U.S. contributions is considerably in excess of this nominal percentage. In 1977, for example, the United States contributed $931 million to various MDBs; in that same year, MDB loans to Latin American governments were 3.4 times that amount, or $3,140 million. Bilateral U.S. economic aid to Latin America in FY1977 totaled

---

[1] *Public Papers of the Presidents of the United States: Richard M. Nixon, 1970* (Washington, D.C.: Government Printing Office, 1971), pp. 750-751.

[2] Averages are particularly misleading in this case, for much of the bilateral economic aid of the early and mid-1970s was in fact aid to support the war effort in Indochina. In FY1974, for example, South Vietnam and Cambodia received $930 million (or 24 percent) of the $3,906 million in total U.S. bilateral aid. It is impossible to determine how much economic aid was offered to other countries such as South Korea, the Philippines, and Thailand as payment for their support of the U.S. war effort.

$346 million. Worldwide, MDB loans amounted to $8.9 billion in FY1977; U.S. bilateral economic aid was $4.6 billion.[3] Latin America was the focus of a truly impressive growth in MDB lending during the 1970s. Table 7.2 demonstrates the extent of this growth, which appears particularly large in contrast to the declining U.S. bilateral aid program.[4]

Two MDBs provide development financing for Latin America: the World Bank Group and the Inter-American Development Bank. The World Bank Group consists of three major components: the International Bank for Reconstruction and Development (IBRD or the World Bank) provides conventional loans, the International Development Association (IDA) provides concessional loans, and the International Finance Corporation (IFC) provides support for development-oriented private investments.[5] Membership in the World Bank is conditioned upon prior membership in the International Monetary Fund (IMF), a requirement that serves to exclude countries with governments that control the convertibility of their currencies.[6] Although the three institutions have distinct functions, they are extremely closely linked at the policy and administrative level. There is a single group of governors for all three organizations (usually the finance ministers of member governments), a single group of executive directors, a common headquarters in Washington, D.C., and, in the case of the World Bank and the IDA, a common staff. The president of the World Bank is also president of both the IDA and the IFC.

Ultimate responsibility for the Bank's actions rests with the board of governors, but since the board meets only once a year, the IBRD's general operations, including its decisions on loan proposals, are han-

[3] Of the $4.6 billion in bilateral economic aid, $1.76 billion was in the form of security-supporting assistance.

[4] Brazil has been by far the largest Latin American borrower, with total loans from both banks equaling $4.67 billion during the decade 1968 to 1977. Next was Mexico ($3.41 billion) followed by Colombia ($1.82 billion) and Argentina ($1.79 billion). Together, these four countries received 23 percent of all MDB loans during the decade. Worldwide, Brazil's total was exceeded only by India's $4.73 billion; Mexico was third worldwide, Colombia sixth, and Argentina seventh. See U.S. Congress, House, Committee on Appropriations, Subcommittee on Foreign Operations and Related Agencies, *Foreign Assistance and Related Agencies Appropriations for 1979*, 95th Cong., 2d Sess., 1978, pt. 1, p. 573.

[5] Histories of the World Bank Group are plentiful. A good, concise analysis is U.S. Congress, House, Committee on Foreign Affairs, *The United States and the Multilateral Development Banks*, 93d Cong., 2d Sess., March 1974. The IBRD's annual reports are extremely useful sources of basic bank data.

[6] Yugoslavia, Romania, and the People's Republic of China are exceptions to the rule that nonmarket economies are excluded. In 1978, the World Bank had 132 member states, most of which also belonged to the IDA. There were 108 IFC members.

TABLE 7.1
COMPARISON OF U.S. BILATERAL AND MULTILATERAL ECONOMIC ASSISTANCE,
FY1962-FY1979
(millions of dollars)

Fiscal Year	Total Economic Assistance	Bilateral	Contributions to MDBs	Contributions to MDBs as a Percentage of Total
1962-1969	$33,389	$31,040	$2,349	7.0%
1970	3,676	3,196	480	13.1
1971	3,442	3,262	180	5.2
1972	3,940	3,798	142	3.6
1973	4,117	3,342	775	18.8
1974	3,906	3,092	814	20.8
1975	4,908	4,124	784	16.0
1976[a]	4,810	4,442	368	7.7
1977	5,591	4,660	931	16.7
1978	6,661	5,557	1,104	16.6
1979	6,918	5,286	1,632	23.6

SOURCE: U.S. Agency for International Development, Office of Program Information and Services, Statistics and Reports Division, *U.S. Overseas Loans and Grants and Assistance from International Organizations: Obligations and Authorizations,* July 1, 1945-September 30, 1976, p. 6; and July 1, 1945-September 30, 1979, p. 6.

[a] Includes transition quarter.

TABLE 7.2
LOANS AUTHORIZED BY IBRD, IDA, AND IDB, FY1961-FY1978

Fiscal Year[a]	IBRD[b,c] Number of Loans	IBRD[b,c] Amount (millions)	IDA[b] Number of Loans	IDA[b] Amount (millions)	IDB Number of Loans	IDB Amount (millions)
1961	27	610	2	101	73	293
1962	29	882	16	134	68	329
1963	28	449	17	260	56	258
1964	37	810	17	283	68	299
1965	38	1,023	19	309	66	373
1966	37	839	12	284	68	396
1967	46	777	17	353	60	496
1968	44	847	16	107	55	431
1969	82	1,399	29	385	67	632
1970	69	1,580	50	606	59	644
1971	78	1,921	51	584	59	652
1972	72	1,966	68	1,000	52	807
1973	73	2,051	75	1,357	57	884
1974	105	3,218	69	1,095	53	1,111
1975	122	4,320	68	1,576	70	1,375
1976	141	4,977	73	1,655	81	1,528
1977	161	5,759	67	1,308	81	1,809
1978	137	6,098	99	2,313	65	1,870

SOURCES: World Bank *Annual Reports,* 1976 and 1978; IDB *Annual Reports,* 1962-1978.

[a] FY of IBRD and IDA ends June 30; FY of IDB ends December 31.

[b] Beginning with FY1971, includes credits approved by executive directors; earlier years include only credits signed.

[c] Joint IBRD/IDA loans included only once as IBRD commitments.

dled by the twenty-one executive directors. Five of these directors represent the major contributors (France, Japan, the United Kingdom, the United States, and West Germany), while the remaining sixteen are distributed to blocs of nations. There are three directors primarily representing groups of Latin American countries. Both the governors and directors cast votes in proportion to the financial contribution of the member(s) they represent. This provides the United States with a substantial but certainly not an overwhelming influence in Bank decisions. As of 1979, the United States held 23 percent of World Bank votes, 20 percent of IDA votes, and 32 percent of IFC votes. In addition, the IBRD, IDA, and IFC staffs are dominated by U.S. citizens. Each of the six World Bank presidents has been from the United States, and U.S. citizens comprise about 27 percent of the World Bank/IDA staff. Perhaps more significant is the fact that about 40 percent of all management positions in the World Bank/IDA are filled by U.S. nationals. MDB staff members are international civil servants rather than representatives of national governments, but the presence of its citizens and the voting power of its executive director ensures that any major concern of the United States government is given serious consideration by the World Bank Group.

The Inter-American Development Bank (IDB) is the oldest of the regional development banks, established in 1959 by the United States and nineteen Latin American countries "to contribute to the acceleration of the process of economic development of the member countries."[7] Today, with forty-one members, the IDB pursues this goal by loaning its money to members through two "windows": the ordinary capital account for loans at commercial rates and the Fund for Special Operations (FSO) for loans at concessional rates.[8] The organizational structure of the IDB is not unlike that of the World Bank Group. There is a board of governors with formal authority over all IDB activities, but day-to-day decisions on loan proposals are made by the eleven executive directors. Two of these are elected by two groups of nonregional members, one is appointed by the United States, and the remaining eight are elected by eight groups of Latin American nations. Votes by both the governors and executive directors are weighted according to the size of the nation's or group of nations' contribution to the Bank. The United States holds 35 percent of the votes in the ordinary capital account and 61 percent of the votes in the FSO, making the FSO the only MDB account over which it possesses a veto. Unlike the World Bank Group, the two presidents of the IDB

[7] Articles of Agreement, Article 1, Section 1.

[8] The IDB also administers various trust funds under special agreements with individual countries. The largest of these are the $525 million U.S. Social Progress Trust Fund and the $500 million Venezuelan Trust Fund.

have been Latin Americans—Felipe Herrera of Chile (1960-1971) and Antonio Ortiz Mena of Mexico (since 1971). The executive vice president is always a United States citizen, however, and U.S. nationals comprise more than 40 percent of the Bank's professional and administrative staff.

Both the World Bank and the IDB obtain their financial resources for hard loans from borrowings on Western capital markets. Member subscriptions (both paid-in and callable capital) form the financial foundation for these borrowings. Soft-loan resources are contributed directly by member governments. As current resources are committed, the board of governors of each bank periodically votes to increase its level of activity by asking members for more money, negotiating each country's contribution at a special meeting.[9] When the necessary funds have been received—in the case of the United States, the executive branch must obtain the money from Congress—bank officials determine to whom they should be loaned. In discussing loan proposals, the banks' staffs and directors are legally bound to base their decisions upon purely economic criteria.[10] But there has never been a clear definition of these criteria; indeed, by the 1970s, it was widely acknowledged that the global distribution of resources is essentially a political consideration.[11] Nonetheless, it is significant that there exists

[9] In the course of these increases, the United States has slowly reduced its overall average proportional participation in the MDBs from a high of 41 percent to about 24 percent.

[10] The articles of agreement founding the IDB contain the following clause: "The Bank, its officers and employees shall not interfere in the political affairs of any member, nor shall they be influenced in their decisions by the political character of member or members concerned. Only economic considerations shall be relevant to their decisions, and these considerations shall be weighted impartially." Similar clauses are included in all other MDB charters: IBRD Article IV, Section 10; IFC Article III, Section 9; IDA Article V, Section 6.

[11] Before he became the Carter administration's assistant secretary of the treasury for international affairs, C. Fred Bergsten argued that politics and international economics were inseparable. See, for example, his comments in C. Fred Bergsten, *The Future of the International Economic Order: An Agenda for Research* (Lexington, Mass.: D.C. Heath, 1973), pp. 9, 30-31; and *Toward a New International Economic Order: Selected Papers of C. Fred Bergsten, 1972-1974* (Lexington, Mass.: D.C. Heath, 1975), p. 429. Once behind his desk at Treasury, however, Bergsten apparently changed his mind. See U.S. Congress, House, Committee on Appropriations, Subcommittee on Foreign Operations and Related Agencies, *Foreign Assistance and Related Agencies Appropriations for 1978*, 95th Cong., 1st Sess., 1977, pt. 1, pp. 206, 459, 513-514. For an excellent contrary opinion, see R. Peter DeWitt, Jr., *The Inter-American Development Bank and Political Influence, With Special Reference to Costa Rica* (New York: Praeger, 1977). As early as 1973, the Congressional Research Service of the Library of Congress had concluded that "it seems somewhat naive to assume that a massive switch to multilateral aid programs will 'take the politics out of foreign aid'." U.S. Congress, Senate, Committee on Foreign Relations, *Alternatives to Bilateral Economic Aid*, 93rd Cong., 1st Sess., June 18, 1973, p. 6.

a formal prohibition on the consideration of political variables in decision making, for it justifies attempts by officials of the MDBs and the United States executive branch to dissuade Congress from earmarking or restricting the use of U.S. contributions. Congress has never been convinced by this argument, for, in the perennial struggle with the executive branch over control of foreign policy, it has found that the periodic requests for new funds provide the primary opportunity to influence a broad variety of bank policies.

United States Participation

Executive Branch

Prior to a bureaucratic reorganization in 1978, the entity responsible for coordinating all forms of United States participation in the MDBs was the little-known National Advisory Council on International Monetary and Financial Policies (NAC), whose members were the Secretary of the Treasury (chairperson), the assistant to the President for economic affairs (deputy chairperson), the Secretaries of State and Commerce, the chairperson of the board of governors of the Federal Reserve System, and the president of the Export-Import Bank. The original Bretton Woods Agreements Act of 1945 (PL79-171) created the NAC's bureaucratic predecessor, which was disbanded in 1965 and then reestablished as the NAC a year later.[12] The bureaucratic victor in this death and resurrection was the Department of the Treasury, which emerged in 1966 with the power to instruct United States representatives to the MDBs, a function that had previously belonged to the entire NAC. The NAC and its successor became advisory bodies. While formal advisory decisions on MDB activities were taken in the name of NAC principals, in fact nearly all decisions were made at lower levels. Immediately below the NAC was a committee of alternates that, like the NAC, met infrequently—eight times in 1976—and then primarily to agree to major policy changes or to resolve an issue that had stymied the second support group, the NAC staff committee.

[12] Executive Order number 11269, February 14, 1966. There are a number of studies of the bureaucratic processes involved in U.S. participation in the MDBs. Of particular value are Jonathan Earl Sanford, "American Foreign Policy and the Multilateral Banks: The Actors and Issues Affecting U.S. Participation in the International Development Lending Institutions," Ph.D. dissertation, American University, 1977; U.S. Congress, Senate, Committee on Governmental Affairs, *U.S. Participation in the Multilateral Development Banks*, 96th Cong., 1st Sess., April 30, 1979; and Stephen D. Cohen, *The Making of United States International Economic Policy: Principles, Problems, and Proposals for Reform* (New York: Praeger, 1977).

The staff committee was composed of professional representatives (attorneys, economists) from each of the member agencies. It acted as the basic working unit within the NAC. The purpose of its meetings (sixty-three in FY1976) was to determine the United States position on loan proposals and other matters related to U.S. participation in the MDBs. During the two weeks prior to these meetings, each committee member circulated upcoming loan proposals within his or her own agency and attempted to resolve internal disputes. At the meeting, the strengths and weaknesses of each proposal were discussed and a decision made, usually by consensus, on how to instruct the U.S. executive director. With the exception of disputes over human rights considerations, a subject discussed below, unresolved differences of opinion were sent up to a higher level—first to the NAC alternates and then to the NAC principals. Only extremely rarely were the principals unable to reach an agreement. When they could not, the Secretary of the Treasury decided without a consensus. A dissenting principal could appeal directly to the President, but apparently this occurred infrequently. In 1978, neither Treasury nor State Department officials could recall when such an appeal had last been made. Once a consensus was reached, NAC principals gave their formal advice to the Secretary of the Treasury, who instructed the appropriate executive director. U.S. executive directors are legally bound to follow these instructions. Without instructions, they cannot vote.

During the mid-1970s, these bureaucratic procedures were modified slightly. First, Treasury revised its internal structure in recognition of the increased importance of MDB activity. The NAC was seriously reduced in power when its Multilateral Institutions Program Office (MIPO) was disbanded. MIPO had been a small Treasury-based organization charged with assessing the technical merits of loan proposals. In its place, an expanded Office of Multilateral Development Banks (OMDB) was created within the office of the assistant secretary of the treasury for international monetary affairs. Although the NAC retained the formal authority to advise the Secretary of the Treasury, OMDB obtained the crucial responsibility for coordinating the loan approval process within the executive branch. Then in 1978, the Carter administration created the Development Coordinating Committee (DCC) to oversee all economic aid programs. The DCC promptly created a Working Group on Multilateral Affairs (WGMA), chaired by the chief of OMDB. The WGMA quickly became the equivalent of an expanded NAC staff committee, with the added formal participation of AID and such executive branch departments as Agriculture and Transportation. By the early 1980s, all loan proposals were flowing from the banks' executive directors to the OMDB, which presented them to the WGMA for approval. The OMDB then notified the Secretary of the Treasury of the WGMA's position. Thus the NAC was all but eliminated from decision making on MDB loan proposals.

In a formal sense, the decision-making process on United States participation in the MDBs is truly interagency, with the Department of the Treasury acting as *primus inter pares*. In practice, however, with the important exception of human rights activities during the Carter administration, the entire procedure has been tightly controlled by the Treasury. One reason for this is Treasury's control over information. All communications from the MDBs to WGMA members flow from the various banks' staffs to the executive directors to OMDB, which is physically housed within the Treasury. Loan documents—the essential information upon which decisions are based—typically arrive at the OMDB ten to fourteen days prior to the vote by the bank executive directors. OMDB sends the material out to the various WGMA agencies so that each may formulate its independent view. As with bilateral assistance, the distribution of loan documents is done on the understanding that the responsible agency will provide all other agencies with equal access to information and equal time for its consideration.

In addition to the control of the flow of information on bank activities, Treasury also holds a special position on the WGMA by virtue of its technical expertise. While all WGMA participants generally accept—indeed, some would say they are intimidated by—the technical evaluations by MDB staffs, OMDB has the task of checking the technical and economic feasibility of each loan proposal. Since loan decisions are supposed to be made exclusively on the basis of economic criteria, this check provides Treasury with the opportunity to support or oppose a loan on the basis of arguments that it alone is in a position to verify.

Finally, Treasury dominates decision making because other agencies have decided to permit it to do so. The State Department has never acted to challenge Treasury's dominance over policy on the banks. In 1972, one official at State openly admitted that U.S. participation in the MDBs "is basically a Treasury operation."[13] This is true even when decisions are of an overtly political nature. The center of financial control over the policy of economic hostility toward Allende's Chile, for example, was the office of Treasury Secretary John Connally. Officials at the State Department's Bureau of Inter-American Affairs

[13] U.S. Congress, House, Committee on Foreign Affairs, Subcommittee on Inter-American Affairs, *Treasury Department Management of U.S. Participation in the Inter-American Development Bank*, 92d Cong., 2d Sess., September 21, 1972, p. 13.

were apparently ignorant of the entire operation.[14] During the late 1970s, the weakness of ARA in influencing bank loans to Latin American governments was particularly obvious. Lacking technical skills, ARA's personnel were no match for the highly professional team at Treasury or for the activists in State's Bureau of Human Rights and Humanitarian Affairs.

For all of these reasons, Treasury has enjoyed a dominant voice in creating and implementing United States policy toward the MDBs. In 1978, Treasury Secretary Michael Blumenthal described his primacy for the benefit of Congress: "I do not, and I would like the record to show that, exaggerate the degree of authority I have in this matter. I have complete authority . . . to direct how our executive directors vote. I can only be overruled by the President himself."[15] On issues other than human rights, during the Carter administration, there was no other governmental unit, including Congress and the White House staff, that could challenge Treasury's dominance of United States multilateral aid policy.

All this is not meant to imply that Treasury dominates other bureaus in the same way that circus lion tamers control their animals. The formal decision-making process oriented around the WGMA is supplemented by a complex network of informal, rather friendly relationships among bank officials and U.S. government agencies and among the various federal bureaucracies that participate in decision making on United States policies and procedures toward MDBs. Much of the review work on loans is conducted far in advance of the time when the banks make loan documents available for consideration by the WGMA. Participating agencies receive monthly status reports of loan proposals in preparation, with each separate loan entered on the summary from one to several years before formal approval is requested. Given this advance notice, interested agencies have the ability to influence loan proposals at an early stage of their preparation. One AID official commented to GAO researchers that so much information is presented informally that the formal approval process focuses principally on a check to see whether earlier informal comments have been taken into consideration in the final proposal, and a Federal Reserve officer remarked that the informal review is crucial because by the time a proposal reaches its final form it is too late to make

[14] U.S. Congress, Senate, Select Committee to Study Governmental Operations with Respect to Intelligence Activities, *Covert Action in Chile 1963-1973*, 94th Cong., 1st Sess., 1975, p. 35.

[15] See *Foreign Assistance and Related Agencies Appropriations for 1979*, pt. 1, p. 429, *supra* n. 4.

major changes.[16] In brief, as with bilateral aid procedures, the decision-making process on multilateral aid is wide open, with nearly every interested agency able to inject itself into the process at a variety of points. But the ability to participate should not be confused with the ability to decide, which on major issues is the near-exclusive province of the Treasury.

As the United States began to increase its relative commitment to multilateral aid, some criticism was raised over the government's decision-making processes. In a 1973 report, the General Accounting Office noted that the NAC review process lacked firm guidelines for decisions and that during the formal and informal review periods NAC agencies rarely had access to adequate information to render sound judgments on loan proposals. The GAO was particularly critical of the NAC staff committee meetings. It found that in a majority of cases questions about the wisdom of approving loans were simply left unanswered, with the NAC recommending approval on all loans. The Treasury objected so strenuously to the GAO's characterization of the NAC as a "rubber stamp" that the term was left out of the final report to Congress.[17] A 1974 study by the Congressional Research Service softened these criticisms somewhat, but it agreed with the GAO that the NAC's technical review personnel were "extremely hard pressed" and could not evaluate loan proposals thoroughly.[18]

Perhaps the single most important cause of this criticism has been the marginal adjustments of the government to the increased volume of MDB loan activity. As Table 7.2 indicates, the number of MDB loans to Latin America has grown substantially in recent years, to the point that the WGMA's workload is now quite large. In 1976, for example, its predecessor had to make 816 formal loan and policy decisions. By the late 1970s, executive directors had to vote every Tuesday and Thursday on an average of eight loan proposals. Before the U.S. representatives could cast a vote, each loan proposal had to be studied and discussed by WGMA members, so that a consensus

[16] U.S. General Accounting Office, *More Effective United States Participation Needed in World Bank and International Development Association*, Report B-161470 (Washington, D.C.: General Accounting Office, February 14, 1973), p. 25; *The United States and the Multilateral Development Banks*, p. 105, *supra* n. 5. U.S. Congress, House, Committee on Foreign Affairs, Subcommittee on Inter-American Affairs, *Foreign Policy Implications of U.S. Participation in the Inter-American Development Bank*, 91st Cong., 2d Sess., May-June 1970, p. 89.

[17] See *More Effective United States Participation Needed in World Bank and International Development Association*, pp. 29, 66-82, *supra* n. 16.

[18] See *The United States and the Multilateral Development Banks*, pp. 106-107, *supra* n. 5.

could be reached on the U.S. position.[19] Adding to this burden is the fact that loan decisions are never spaced evenly throughout the year; they tend to cluster at the end of the banks' fiscal years. In FY1973, for example, 54 percent of all World Bank and IDA loans were approved in June, and over a five-year period (1968-1972), 45 percent of all IDB loans were presented to the executive directors for approval during the final quarter.[20] Given this workload and MIPO's small staff (in 1973, it had only one full-time person assigned to evaluate the technical/economic aspects of loan proposals) the CRS was correct to suggest that automatic approval appeared inevitable. MIPO's successor, the Office of Multilateral Development Banks, is better equipped to perform its functions. In 1979, there were five professional staff members in OMDB to evaluate the technical merits of MDB loan proposals. While the strong criticism of earlier years is no longer justified, the U.S. government continues to rely heavily upon the technical evaluations of MDB economists.

The second major criticism of Treasury's decision-making process is that it lacks adequate guidelines for decisions. As late as 1972, there were simply no guidelines; the United States executive director to the World Bank noted that "we really look at each one as it comes along."[21] In response to GAO criticism, the National Advisory Council developed five criteria to appraise loan proposals:

1. priority of the project in the development process;
2. technical feasibility of the project;
3. capacity of local institutions to implement the project;
4. soundness of the project's financial plan; and
5. economic benefits of the project.[22]

Yet as the CRS subsequently discovered, officials "are selective in the

[19] It is no simple matter to study an MDB loan proposal, for each is an extremely detailed document often including a narrative description of from twenty-five to thirty pages and a variety of annexes related to such technical considerations as market demand, technical designs and specifications, revenue and cost assumptions, projected rate of return calculations, and balance of payments calculations. See *U.S. Participation in the Multilateral Development Banks*, pp. 45-46, *supra* n. 12.

[20] There were times when as many as eighty loan proposals were on a NAC agenda for a two-hour meeting. See ibid., pp. 47-48; *The United States and the Multilateral Development Banks*, pp. 106-107, *supra* n. 5; U.S. Congress, House, Committee on Banking, Finance, and Urban Affairs, Subcommittee on International Development Institutions and Finance, *International Development Institutions—1977*, 95th Cong., 1st Sess., March 1977, p. 68.

[21] *Washington Post*, December 29, 1972, p. A2.

[22] U.S. National Advisory Council on International Monetary and Financial Policies, *Annual Report 1972-73* (Washington, D.C.: Government Printing Office), pp. 57-59.

criteria they apply and emphasize on each proposal."[23] In practice, a loan is approved by the WGMA if no participating agency wishes to register an objection. If a reservation is issued, then a variety of justifications for rejection are acceptable, few of which bear any relation to the five formal criteria. These justifications are often clearly and openly political, ranging from the uncompensated expropriation of property owned by U.S.-based multinational corporations to the consistent and gross violation of human rights.

The Role of Congress

Congress's impact upon United States policy toward the MDBs has been relatively insignificant when compared to its influence over bilateral aid programs. The basic reason for this low level of influence appears to be related to the general obscurity of the banks. Until recently, MDBs were not a major component of the U.S. aid program, and Congress simply preferred to concentrate upon the more important components, especially AID. In addition to this general disinterest, which over the course of the 1970s became much less evident, congressional oversight of the MDBs has been hampered both by its procedures and by its lack of expertise. In the House, two committees share jurisdiction over MDB authorizations: the Committee on Foreign Affairs oversees foreign policy aspects of U.S. activities in the MDBs and the Committee on Banking reviews the legislation authorizing U.S. replenishments. In the Senate, the Committee on Foreign Relations exercises exclusive jurisdiction. The House and Senate Appropriations Subcommittees on Foreign Operations control the appropriations process; they include MDB funds in the annual omnibus foreign assistance appropriations bill.

These divisions of authority are common, of course, and would cause no problem were it not for the fact that appropriations for one MDB replenishment typically require several installments spaced over a number of years. For example, negotiations for the fourth replenishment for the IDA were concluded in September 1973, and Congress authorized United States participation the following July. By 1976, all nations except the United States had completed their contributions to the fourth replenishment. By 1978, a fifth replenishment had been negotiated, yet the executive branch was still trying to obtain appropriations for the fourth. Thus the administration's IDA request for FY1979 included (1) $800 million for the second installment of the fifth replenishment, (2) $375 million for the fourth installment of the fourth replenishment, and (3) $375 million for the third installment

[23] See *The United States and the Multilateral Development Banks*, p. 109, *supra* n. 5.

of the fourth replenishment. Treasury Secretary Blumenthal was therefore called to explain the entire matter to a House appropriations
subcommittee, seven of whose eleven members were not on the subcommittee in 1973 and 1974. His relative success in obtaining the
funds was due less to his pedagogic capabilities than to his announcement that if the United States did not appropriate some of its past-
due replenishments, all lending activity would cease in the IDB by
1978 and in the IDA by 1979.[24] As the Senate Foreign Relations
Committee noted a year earlier, "a negative vote in the appropriations
process would mean no U.S. commitments, no U.S. membership and
because of the large U.S. role in the organization, no IDA."[25]

Not only do most members of Congress lack a memory of previous
activities but only a very few of them possess a rudimentary knowledge
of MDB procedures and policies. Much of the responsibility for this
ignorance rests with the Treasury, which has consistently balked at
congressional requests for access to documents regarding the banks'
operations. Congress has no right to require the banks to provide
information of any type, nor can it require bank authorities to testify
at public hearings.[26] Both the GAO and the CRS have been asked
by Congress to study the MDBs, and, although the Treasury has
provided much of the requested data on the banks, it has steadfastly
refused to turn over two sets of key documents: the summaries of
meetings of the banks' executive directors and the studies by outside
consultants.[27] The essence of congressional complaints is not that this
particular information is unavailable, however, but rather that it has

[24] *Foreign Assistance and Related Agencies Appropriations for 1979*, pt. 1, pp. 418,
431, *supra* n. 4.

[25] Senate Report 95-159, p. 13.

[26] Jonathan Sanford and Margaret Goodman, "Congressional Oversight and the
Multilateral Development Banks," *International Organization* 29 (Autumn 1975): 1057-
1059. The articles of agreement founding the banks grant their officers nearly absolute
immunity from any inquiry or legal process and also protect the banks' archives and
communications "from search, requisition, confiscation, expropriation or any other
form of seizure by executive or legislative action." Articles of Agreement of the IBRD,
Article VII, Sections 4-9. In the United States, the Bretton Woods Agreements Act
(PL79-171, Sec. 11) guarantees these immunities.

[27] In June 1978, Treasury agreed to provide Congress on a continuing basis with
a variety of documents related to MDBs. U.S. Congress, House, Committee on
Appropriations, Subcommittee on Foreign Operations and Related Agencies, *Foreign
Assistance and Related Programs Appropriations for 1980*, 96th Cong., 1st Sess., 1979,
pt. 2, pp. 89-90. On the unwillingness of the executive branch to share information
from MDBs with Congress, see Sanford and Goodman, "Congressional Oversight and
the Multilateral Development Banks," pp. 1060-1061; *Foreign Policy Implications of
U.S. Participation in the Inter-American Development Bank*, p. 28, *supra* n. 16; *The
United States and the Multilateral Development Banks*, pp. vii, 6, *supra* n. 5.

no independent sources on the operations and policies of the banks. Congress must accept what the executive branch chooses to provide.

It should be noted, however, that neither Treasury's policy on particular documents nor the MDB's immunities prohibit interested members of Congress from obtaining general information on the workings of the banks. Because such information is widely distributed, at least part of the reason for Congress's ignorance may be attributed to the fact that members have not tried particularly hard to learn about the banks. For example, it was not Treasury's fault that appropriations subcommittee chairperson Clarence Long, a former professor of economics, was puzzled by the banks' need to have callable capital to serve as a financial foundation in support of borrowings on the world capital market.[28] A wealth of general information is available on the banks' operations that, as statements from hearings make obvious, most members responsible for MDB legislation have never read.

Although Congress does not participate actively in creating U.S. policy toward the MDBs, on several occasions it has added amendments to authorization and appropriation bills that restrict the freedom of action of the executive branch. Since the banks cannot accept funds that are earmarked for specific purposes or otherwise restricted in their use, Congress has instead acted to restrict the actions of the U.S. executive directors to the banks by legislating a number of very specific prohibitions on United States activity within bank councils.[29] They include directives that the United States vote against loans to countries that (1) expropriate the property of U.S. citizens or U.S.-based multinational corporations,[30] (2) fail to take adequate steps to

---

[28] See *Foreign Assistance and Related Agencies Appropriations for 1979*, pt. 1, pp. 423-424, *supra* n. 4. Nor is it easy to understand Representative Trent Lott's comment in 1979 that "it is very difficult to find out what they are doing with these funds." *Congressional Record*, September 6, 1979. The MDBs and their auditors have publicly accounted for every dollar the banks have received. The World Bank annual report in particular has come to be recognized for the extraordinary detail of reporting on its financial transactions. For further instances of this attitude among members of Congress, see also *Foreign Policy Implications of U.S. Participation in the Inter-American Development Bank*, p. 9, *supra* n. 16; *Treasury Department Management of U.S. Participation in the Inter-American Development Bank*, *supra* n. 13.

[29] During the late 1970s, earmarking—stipulating the types of projects or the specific recipients for which U.S. contributions can be used—became a major issue of congressional-executive relations regarding the MDBs. As early as 1975, IDB president Ortiz Mena refused to accept $50 million from the United States because Congress had earmarked it for distribution to cooperatives, credit unions, and savings and loan associations (PL94-11). Later in the 1970s and early 1980s, the issue centered upon prohibitions on the use of U.S. contributions to aid in the production of citrus, palm oil, and sugar, and to aid Vietnam.

[30] PL86-147, Sec. 21; PL86-565, Sec. 12.

control the production or flow of narcotic drugs through their countries to the United States,[31] (3) develop nuclear explosive devices,[32] (4) use loan proceeds to expand production of certain commodities for export,[33] or (5) violate their citizens' fundamental human rights.

HUMAN RIGHTS AND THE MDBs

Human rights activists have always argued that a borrower's disregard of its citizens' human rights is an appropriate criterion in MDB decision making. Therefore once the Harkin amendment and Section 502B had been added to legislation governing bilateral assistance, the strengthening of human rights considerations in United States policy toward the banks became a major goal of the human rights movement. The process by which this policy was created and implemented provides particularly valuable insight into the bureaucratic politics of both Congress and the Carter administration.

Human Rights Legislation

As in the case of bilateral economic and military aid, Congress was first to raise the issue of the relationship between human rights and United States policy toward the MDBs. In 1975, the Ford administration proposed to the human rights-oriented Ninety-fourth Congress a bill (H.R. 9721) to provide for increased financial contributions to the IDB and for participation in the African Development Fund. The bill emerged from its initial consideration by the House Committee on Banking in approximately the form that the administration desired, but during a brief floor debate, Representative Harkin proposed an amendment that directed the U.S. representatives to the banks to vote against any loan to any government that violates its citizens' human rights unless the loan proceeds would directly benefit needy people. This proposal came on the heels of passage earlier in the year of the original Harkin amendment to the bilateral economic assistance bill (PL94-161) and immediately after a House-Senate conference had agreed to accept a strengthening of Section 502B as part of the pending military assistance bill. No opposition to the Harkin MDB initiative appeared, and it was accepted without a roll-call vote.[34]

The bill then moved to the Senate, where the Ford administration attempted to have the Harkin amendment deleted. Assistant secretary of state William D. Rogers offered two reasons for the administration's

[31] PL86-147, Sec. 22; PL86-565, Sec. 13.

[32] PL93-373, Sec. 3.

[33] PL95-118, Sec. 901(a). See also PL95-481, Sec. 609 and *Foreign Assistance and Related Agencies Appropriations for 1979*, pt. 1, pp. 909-919, *supra* n. 4.

[34] *Congressional Record*, December 9, 1975, p. 39391.

opposition to the initiative: "In our view, the Inter-American Development Bank is not the place to deal with human rights matters [and] the introduction of a noneconomic issue into a technical and functional institution like the two regional development banks is unwise. It smacks of paternalism. . . . The great advantage of the international financial institution is its insulation from political pressures."[35] But the administration's efforts were unsuccessful, and the bill emerged from the Foreign Relations Committee with its human rights provision intact. It was subsequently accepted by the full Senate without opposition—indeed almost without mention—and was signed into law by President Ford in May 1976.[36]

It was also during 1976 that Congress began to notice that Chile had been compensated for reductions in U.S. bilateral aid with increases in multilateral development bank loans. As Table 7.3 indicates, the two MDBs increased their lending to Chile from nothing in FY1972 and FY1973 to $110.8 million in 1974. While information is unavailable on the extent to which the United States encouraged these increases, it is known that the Nixon-Ford administration opposed only one loan to Pinochet's Chile. The vote came in June 1976, one month after passage of PL94-302, on a loan that could not be interpreted as directly benefiting needy people—a $21 million industrial credit to cover the foreign exchange component of a program to expand private establishments in Chile's manufacturing sector. In this isolated case, the person responsible for directing the U.S. vote was the deputy assistant secretary of state for inter-American affairs, Joseph Grunwald, a former president of the Latin American Studies Association on leave from his position at the Brookings Institution. He simply took advantage of the unstable situation created by PL94-302. Citing the provisions of that law, Grunwald was able to overcome the strong resistance of his immediate superior, assistant secretary of state William D. Rogers, and of a number of Treasury officials. Without instructions from senior decision makers, no one at the assistant secretary level or lower wanted to be held responsible for failing to enforce the law. In addition, because there had been almost no controversy over United States policy toward the MDBs, the decision-making process was sufficiently informal that Grunwald, whose duties in ARA included all economic issues, could control the vote without attracting too much attention. But following the publicity given this vote, Secretary of State Kissinger and Treasury Secretary Simon exerted firmer control over the process, and the Ford administration

[35] U.S. Congress, Senate, Committee on Foreign Relations, Subcommittee on Foreign Assistance and Related Programs, *IDB and AFDF Authorization*, 94th Cong., 1st Sess., January 28, 1976, p. 44.
[36] PL94-302; *Congressional Record*, March 30, 1976, p. S4602.

TABLE 7.3
MDB Loan Authorizations to Chile, 1961-1979
(millions of dollars)

Year	IBRD	IDB	Total
1961	25.0	30.1	55.1
1962	0	29.5	29.5
1963	19.0	19.5	38.5
1964	0	22.7	22.7
1965	7.2	31.2	38.4
1966	60.0	45.6	105.6
1967	0	36.5	36.5
1968	11.6	11.9	23.5
1969	0	62.5	62.5
1970	19.3	3.0	22.3
1971	0	11.6	11.6
1972	0	0	0
1973	0	0	0
1974	13.5	97.3	110.8
1975	20.0	45.5	65.5
1976	33.0	25.2	58.2
1977	60.0	68.0	128.0
1978	0	54.0	54.0
1979	38.0	0	38.0

Sources: U.S. Congress, Congressional Research Service, *The Multilateral Development Banks and the Suspension of Lending to Allende's Chile*, rev. ed. (Washington, D.C.: Congressional Research Service), December 13, 1974 (reprinted in U.S. Congress, House, Committee on Foreign Affairs, Subcommittee on Inter-American Affairs, *The United States and Chile during the Allende Years*, 93d Cong., 2d Sess., 1971-1974, pp. 417-448); and U.S. National Advisory Council on International Monetary and Financial Policies, *Annual Reports*, 1971 through 1978.

never cast another negative vote or abstained for human rights reasons in any MDB.

The administration's disregard for human rights considerations in approving loans to Chile seemed particularly inappropriate to many members of Congress in light of the fact that several of America's closest allies were working to raise the issue in the banks. In February 1976, the IBRD reached its only nonunanimous decision of the year, when nine of the twenty executive directors (with 41 percent of the Bank's votes) refused to approve a $33 million credit to the Chilean copper industry. While the Scandinavian and other Western European nations (including Great Britain, France, and Germany) abstained, the United States cast its 23 percent vote in favor of the loan. Lacking legislation upon which to base their displeasure over this policy, liberal and moderate members of Congress were reduced to public statements of condemnation.

But it is notable that the February IBRD vote angered a key House liberal, Henry Reuss, the chairperson of the Banking Committee through which all MDB authorizations must pass. Reuss is reported to have commented that the loans indicated the IBRD had "succumbed to political pressure to shore up an inhuman right-wing dictatorship tottering on the edge of bankruptcy."[37] Later that year, Reuss voted against the entire foreign assistance appropriations bill, after telling his House colleagues that he no longer would support the IDB until it recognized that "the people of the United States wish to place limits on the aid they give any international organization which . . . extends financial assistance" to repressive governments.[38] There were additional voices in the congressional chorus complaining about multi-lateral loans to Chile. In late November 1976, nine members of Congress wrote Treasury Secretary Simon urging him not to support further MDB loans to Chile, and in early December, Senator Clifford Case, a widely respected liberal Republican and ranking minority member of the Senate Committee on Foreign Relations, issued a public statement favoring negative votes on two upcoming IBRD loans to Chile.[39] Simon subsequently announced that the United States would vote to approve the two loans. The turmoil over this decision was so great that the World Bank rescheduled the formal vote to permit the lame duck Ford administration to reach a compromise with its critics.[40] Apparently no compromise was possible, for on December 21 the United States voted to approve the two loans for Chile worth $60 million. The Ninety-fourth Congress had already adjourned, but several key legislators were determined not to permit another year to pass without concrete human rights provisions in legislation authorizing U.S. participation in the MDBs. Thus in 1977 a bill to replenish funds for five MDBs (H.R. 5262) became the site of the most important human rights battle of 1977.

Aware from the beginning that the bill would have to contain some human rights provision, President-elect Carter met with Representative Reuss in mid-January to discuss the issue. This meeting and subsequent ones with White House, Treasury, and State Department officials led to a very mild human rights proposal. The Carter-Reuss human rights language required that the United States, "in connection with its voice and vote" in the six MDBs to which it belonged, "shall

[37] See *International Development Institutions—1977*, p. 82, *supra* n. 20.

[38] *Congressional Record*, September 27, 1976, p. H11142.

[39] *Christian Science Monitor*, December 1, 1976, pp. 1, 42; *Miami Herald*, December 6, 1976, p. 1.

[40] The nation's prestige press was split on the issue. The *New York Times* (December 12 and 18, 1976) called for a "no" vote, while the *Washington Post* (December 19) urged that the U.S. vote "yes."

advance the cause of human rights, including by seeking to channel assistance toward countries other than those whose governments engage in a consistent pattern of gross violations of internationally recognized human rights, such as torture or cruel, inhumane or degrading treatment or punishment."[41]

When Representative Henry González's House Banking Subcommittee on International Development Institutions and Finance met in late March to begin hearings on H.R. 5262, Reuss appeared to lead the discussion on human rights. Representatives from Treasury and the State Department voiced their support for the Carter-Reuss language, while other administration officials, including the assistant secretary of state for human rights, Patricia Derian, told the subcommittee that the Harkin language passed a year earlier in PL94-302 was "clumsy" and therefore urged its repeal.[42] The next day the opposition presented its case. NGO personnel called the Carter-Reuss language "meaningless" and argued that it should be strengthened considerably.[43] Then Representative Harkin appeared as a witness and proposed a substitute human rights amendment similar to that contained in PL94-302. The question, then, was whether Congress should mandate a vote against loans to repressive governments or adopt the milder "voice and vote" language.

Chairperson Reuss led the attack on the Harkin amendment. Although his public argument against the initiative stressed his belief that the "needy people" exception was too broad a loophole, it was evident that Reuss's principal objection was to the mandatory "no" vote. In the full committee markup, the Harkin language—offered as an amendment by subcommittee member Herman Badillo—was rejected by a vote of 28 to 15, and the bill was reported to the floor with its Carter-Reuss human rights language. It never had a chance of passage, given the opposition of liberals who had been manipulated by the previous administration and had heard only the time-worn pleas for flexibility from the representatives of the Carter administration. Representative Badillo once again offered the Harkin language, and it was accepted so easily that the Speaker of the House would not permit a roll-call vote, since a recorded vote would show such an overwhelming majority that a subsequent House-Senate conference would not be able to weaken the House position.[44]

Following a lengthy discussion of human rights and multilateral assistance, the Senate Committee on Foreign Relations decided to

---

[41] See *International Development Institutions—1977*, p. 9, *supra* n. 20.

[42] Ibid., pp. 15, 64, 68, 73, 75.

[43] Ibid., pp. 80, 100.

[44] *Congressional Record*, April 6, 1977, pp. H31212-H31228.

approve the Carter-Reuss language, which in the Senate was referred to as the Humphrey-Case amendment. In its report, the committee expressed its opposition to Harkin-type language that would require "no" votes, citing as support for this position a letter President Carter had written subcommittee chairperson Humphrey: "I want to make it clear that I oppose the provision of . . . H.R. 5262, which would *require* us to vote against any loan to a country where human rights are violated. I oppose it because it will prove weak and ineffective. It would handicap our efforts to encourage human rights improvements in other countries. . . . While I appreciate and share the spirit in which this House amendment was offered, I strongly believe it represents too rigid an approach to the problem."[45] On the Senate floor, Senators Abourezk and Hatfield proposed an amendment that would delete the Humphrey-Case amendment in favor of the House-approved Harkin language. Senator Humphrey, the bill's floor manager, attacked the Abourezk-Hatfield amendment for its lack of flexibility, and the full Senate rejected it by a narrow (43-50) margin.[46] Although the Abourezk amendment was supported by liberal Senators Brooke, Church, and McGovern, the forty-three pro-Abourezk votes were contributed primarily by the Senate's most conservative members— members who hold an ideological predisposition against all forms of economic assistance. Most of the major human rights activists in the Senate, including Senators Cranston and Kennedy, voted against the Abourezk-Hatfield language. They were willing to provide the new Democratic administration with the flexibility it requested.

The House-Senate conference on H.R. 5262 was stacked against the proponents of strong human rights language. On the Senate side, supporters of the Abourezk-Hatfield amendment occupied only two of the eight conference seats, and up to that date neither of them had taken an active interest in the issue. No major proponent of human rights legislation was among the eleven House conferees; Representative Badillo was particularly conspicuous by his absence. As a result, the conference committee proceeded to eviscerate the House version of the bill. Although it retained the Harkin language, it added a prefacing phrase "where other means have proven ineffective." In addition, the President was authorized to waive the entire human rights provision if he "certifies that the cause of international human rights would be more effectively served by actions other than voting against such assistance."[47]

When the conference bill was returned to the House floor in Sep-

---

[45] Senate Report 95-159, p. 17.
[46] *Congressional Record*, June 14, 1977, pp. S9706-S9714.
[47] Senate Report 95-362, p. 5.

tember, the now-standard coalition of the most liberal human rights activists, led by Representative Harkin, and conservative anti-aid forces, led by Representative John Rousselot, an early member of the John Birch Society, were prepared to challenge its final acceptance. Representative Reuss attempted to assuage the proponents of human rights, noting that "the conferees agreed to retain every part of the House version except for the mandatory no vote." This mandatory vote, of course, was the entire issue, as both Harkin and Rousselot indicated in their prepared remarks. Other conservative speakers argued that the conference language would permit the United States to support loans to Uganda and to "Dictator Torrijos' regime in Panama," while related legislation prohibited loans to white-supremacist Rhodesia. Reuss responded by criticizing the conservatives' use of the human rights issue to undermine United States participation in the banks. He noted that conservative members had voted against the original bill when its passed the House *with* the Harkin-Badillo amendment: "Never," he complained, "have I seen the well of this House fuller of crocodile tears than it is this afternoon."

Nonetheless the coalition stayed together and the House voted 153 to 230 to reject the conference report. Among the 153 supporters of the report were Representatives Fraser, Drinan, Solarz, and Studds, all of whom were among the most active human rights proponents in the House. Voting to reject the report were virtually all House conservatives and a handful of liberals led by Representatives Harkin, Moffett, and Dellums.[48] Noting the size of the rejection vote, the Senate capitulated and accepted the original Harkin-Badillo language, and the President reluctantly signed the bill into law (PL95-118) in October 1977. It is this law that provides the foundation for all attempts by human rights activists to halt MDB loans to repressive governments.

The third piece of legislation on human rights and United States participation in international financial institutions concerned not an MDB but the International Monetary Fund (IMF), the multilateral pool of funds upon which members draw in order to pay their foreign debts when export revenues fall short of import expenses. To qualify for an IMF loan or standby agreement, a borrowing government must generally initiate a program of economic "stabilization" to alleviate the need for continued borrowing. The key components of these programs are the reduction of government expenditures and the acceptance of orthodox nonexpansionary monetary policies. At their worst, these policies lead to a period of adjustment—the "shock treatment"—

[48] *Congressional Record*, September 16, 1977, pp. H9554-H9566.

in which a nation's level of economic activity declines, unemployment rises, and social services deteriorate or disappear.[49] As in any recession in a market economy, the burden of stabilization falls most heavily upon the shoulders of citizens least able to bear it, the popular classes. In the highly mobilized nations of the Third World, these classes have displayed an increasing tendency not to endure a significant decline in their standard of living without protest. Thus at times governments overseeing IMF stabilization programs have had to overcome this reluctance through repression of dissent. It was to an examination of this relationship between the decrease in living standards accompanying IMF stabilization programs, on the one hand, and the decline in governmental respect for human rights, on the other, that Congress turned in late 1977.

The issue at hand was a proposal by the IMF to create a new supplementary financing facility (or the Witteveen facility, named after the IMF's managing director, H. Johannes Witteveen, who negotiated the facility). The purpose of this $10 billion fund was to loan money contributed to the IMF by OPEC and developed nations to Third World countries on the edge of default in debts to OPEC and developed countries. The U.S. share was slightly less than 17 percent, and the task of the Carter administration was to obtain the money from Congress. To this end, a bill (H.R. 9214) to amend the Bretton Woods Agreements Act began to wind its way through the legislative maze. Its first stop was the House Banking Subcommittee on International Trade, Investment, and Monetary Policy. There, during three days of hearings in September 1977, the subject of human rights was never raised.[50] After receiving a favorable (15-1) report, it moved on to the full committee, where Representative Perrin Mitchell offered an amendment requiring the U.S. executive director to oppose IMF transactions that would contribute to the deprivation of human rights and basic needs. Opponents of the amendment argued that such a provision would "politicize" the Fund, while Mitchell and others argued that IMF stabilization programs were not politically neutral. The committee split almost evenly on the issue, ultimately rejecting the Mitchell amendment by a narrow (17-19) margin. But in a move

[49] For an example of one such stabilization program in Argentina during 1959 to 1962, see Gary W. Wynia, *Argentina in the Postwar Era: Politics and Economic Policy Making in a Divided Society* (Albuquerque: University of New Mexico Press, 1978), pp. 99-107.

[50] U.S. Congress, House, Committee on Banking, Finance, and Urban Affairs, Subcommittee on International Trade, Investment, and Monetary Policy, *U.S. Participation in the Supplementary Financing Facility of the International Monetary Fund*, 95th Cong., 1st Sess., September 1977. Treasury Secretary Blumenthal raised the issue in response to a written question, however (see p. 59 of the report).

designed to placate the large minority, the committee agreed to place in its report a request that the administration report to Congress on the effects of IMF loan policies upon the ability of the poor in borrowing countries to obtain food, shelter, clothing, public services (health care, education, clean water), and productive employment. With that, the bill was favorably reported to the House in January 1978.[51]

Representative Harkin was waiting with a new and unusual human rights/basic needs amendment when floor debate began on the bill in late February 1978. As is common in the House, the debate took place in a nearly vacant chamber. Before Harkin could offer his amendment, Representative Mitchell, a leader of the Black Caucus, announced that he would not support any further legislation designed to promote international human rights until the Wilmington 10 were freed.[52] The ensuing debate indicated that his vote would be replaced by House conservatives who had supported earlier human rights legislation on the understanding that it would reduce the foreign assistance budget. This Harkin amendment contained three sections. The first instructed the U.S. representative to the Fund to encourage the development of stabilization programs that foster investment and employment designed to meet basic needs. The second directed the executive branch "to take all possible steps to the end that Fund transactions . . . do not contribute to the deprivation of basic human needs, nor to the violation of basic human rights . . . and to oppose all such transactions which would contribute to such deprivations or violations." The third incorporated into law the Banking Committee's earlier request for a study of the effects of Fund transactions on the standard of living of the poor.

Anticipating the Harkin proposal, the House leadership was well prepared. Prior to the debate, Speaker Tip O'Neill sent a letter to all members stating his opposition to any "politicizing" amendments. On the floor, Banking chairperson Reuss argued against its approval, using as supporting evidence a lengthy letter from Treasury Secretary Blumenthal. According to Blumenthal, IMF programs "do not deal with and cannot in any direct sense contribute to, violations of basic human rights."[53] Emphasizing the apolitical nature of the Fund, he continued:

> The IMF's Articles of Agreement require that decisions on its operations be made only on the basis of economic criteria and that it not involve itself in the political and social policies of its

[51] House Report 95-853, p. 7.
[52] *Congressional Record*, February 22, 1978, pp. H1369-H1370.
[53] Ibid., p. H1406.

members. . . . Any attempt to introduce non-economic factors into IMF decisions would, I believe, seriously undermine the effectiveness of the institution. This result would be severely damaging to U.S. economic foreign policy interests—including our human rights and human needs to objectives. Moreover, such efforts, if successful in preventing IMF financing for certain countries, could have the direct but unintended result of exacerbating the human rights and human needs situations in the individual countries concerned.[54]

Standing on the House floor, Harkin was visibly angered by Blumenthal's argument: "The State Department and the Treasury Department have opposed every single one of the human rights amendments passed by this body. . . . now . . . the Treasury Department is making the same arguments about the IMF, about the injection of politics. . . . when the IMF says that they deal only in money and not in politics, I would suggest that there is nothing in this world more political than money, how it is loaned, and under what conditions it is loaned."[55] At that point, Representative Reuss sighed and stood to announce his reluctant support for the amendment. Reuss asserted that he would have written a different amendment but that the Harkin language was acceptable in light of "the fact that we need the votes of Mr. Harkin and the doughty band of human righters who are for this amendment."[56] Harkin's proposal was accepted by voice vote, and the bill passed the House by a strong majority (267-125). The minority was dominated by the body's most conservative members.

In the Senate, the bill was referred simultaneously to both the Foreign Relations and the Banking Committees. Neither of the committee reports contained any mention of human rights.[57] On the Sen-

---

[54] Ibid.

[55] Ibid., p. H1427.

[56] Ibid.

[57] Senate Report 95-698 (Banking) and Senate Report 95-603 (Foreign Relations). The Foreign Relations report contains a highly valuable, indeed extraordinary, discussion of the concept of "conditionality," or the conditions imposed upon borrowers by the Fund. Specifically, the report discusses the manner in which IMF conditions function to protect private banks from defaults on loans to Third World governments, using the cases of Indonesia and Zaire as examples. Persons inclined to argue that the IMF employs only economic criteria in reaching policy decisions would profit from reading the report, for an ineluctable conclusion to be drawn from the experience of these two nations is that political considerations were not only a part of but were paramount in Fund decision making. See also David J. Gould, *Bureaucratic Corruption and Underdevelopment in the Third World: The Case of Zaire* (New York: Pergamon, 1980).

ate floor, Senators Abourezk and Hatfield introduced an amendment similar to the Harkin language accepted by the House. The two managers of the bill, liberal Senators Javits and Church, rose in opposition to the amendment. Both advanced the now-standard argument that the introduction of human rights language would politicize Fund activities.[58] Then, on the Harkin provision related to basic human needs, each argued—for the first time in public, I believe—that the purpose of the IMF was to force a country to initiate policies that make it increasingly difficult for citizens to meet their basic needs. "Undoubtedly . . . there would be a deprivation of basic human needs," argued Javits, for "it is inconceivable that people . . . will be able to enjoy—to obtain, as the language is—public services, including health care, education, clean water, energy resources, and transportation" after initiating an IMF stabilization program. According to Javits, the citizens of less-developed nations "should be proud of their willingness to sacrifice" their food, shelter, and health care in order that they can "put themselves in some kind of a viable economic condition."[59] Similarly, Senator Church told his colleagues in the Senate that

> if we are to amend this bill in such a way as to require the Executive Director, representing the United States at the IMF, to vote against any austerity plan, any conditionality that might adversely affect an adequate supply of food with sufficient nutritional value to avoid the debilitating effects of malnutrition, or the availability of shelter and clothing, or public services, including health care, education, clean water, energy resources, and transportation, or productive employment that provides a reasonable and adequate wage then, it seems to me, we might as well throw in the towel.[60]

The question was thus reduced to basic needs versus economic stability, and on that basis, the Senate, by a margin of 62 to 27, tabled (and thereby defeated) the Abourezk-Hatfield human rights/needs amendment.

As it had done the previous year with MDB legislation, in September 1978, the House-Senate conference removed the House human rights language from the IMF bill. They deleted entirely the second part of the Harkin amendment—the requirement that the United States oppose transactions that would contribute to the deprivation of basic needs or to the violation of human rights—and they modified the third part by deleting the list of specific subjects—food, shelter,

[58] *Congressional Record*, July 31, 1978, pp. S12097, S12145.
[59] Ibid., p. S12093.
[60] Ibid., p. S12144.

etc.—that the administration must address in its report on the impact of Fund activities upon the poor.[61] Having done this, one conferee looked at Representative Harkin, who attended the conference as an observer, and said: "I hope Mr. Harkin does not object to this language, even though we cut the heart out of it."

Harkin did object, and he attempted once again to convince the full House to reject the conference report. The House considered the report on September 28, 1978, two weeks before adjourning. Finding some crocodile tears of his own, Representative Reuss told the members that he had done the best he could in light of the Senate's opposition to the human rights/needs amendment. Given the late date, he further announced that either the conference report would be accepted or "there is not going to be any bill at all, and . . . the wretched of the world . . . are going to have the IMF window slammed down on their fingers."[62] The floor manager of the bill supplemented Reuss's remarks, noting that without the Witteveen Facility "our economic walls, along with those in other countries, would begin to crumble. . . . a negative vote by the House of Representatives today would send shock waves around the globe. . . . Let's send a strong signal to the international community and to the people of this country that we are serious about stability."[63] With that, the House accepted the conference report by a vote of 238 to 138. Among major human rights activists, only Representatives Toby Moffett and Robert Drinan joined Harkin in opposing acceptance; nearly all the rest—Fraser, Solarz, Studds—voted with the majority. The Senate accepted the conference report in fewer than five minutes, and in October H.R. 9214 became PL95-435. For the 1970s, Congress had fought its last battle over human rights and the MDBs.

Executive Branch Activity

During the period prior to 1977, there was no formal procedure used by the executive branch to incorporate human rights considerations into United States policy toward the multilateral development banks. In part this was because the appropriate officials were uninterested in efforts to promote human rights in American foreign policy, and in part it was because no bureau was responsible for making the effort to prod others into adding a human rights component to United States policy. Pre-1977 administrations simply took little interest in the subject of human rights and the MDBs. Only once prior to 1977 did the

[61] House Report 95-1613.
[62] Ibid., p. H11045.
[63] Ibid., pp. H11039, H11046.

United States oppose a loan for human rights reasons—the attempt to block an IDB loan to Chile in June 1976.

Within the Carter administration there soon developed a formal procedure for incorporating human rights considerations in policy deliberations. Beginning in April 1977, this process was controlled by the Christopher Committee, the interagency group charged with considering human rights factors in the conduct of overall foreign economic assistance policy. The WGMA (and before that the NAC) sent the committee any loan proposal to which a reviewing agency had objected for human rights reasons. At the meetings of the committee and its subordinate working group, the Bureau of Human Rights and Humanitarian Affairs generally made the first suggestion on how human rights should affect the U.S. position on a proposed loan. The Department of the Treasury, accompanied by the executive director of the bank in question, made its opinion known at an early stage of the discussion, as did the representative of the appropriate regional bureau in the State Department. Then the deputy secretary of state, Warren Christopher, decided what the United States position should be.

Since the Christopher Committee enjoyed only an advisory role, its decision could be overruled by the Treasury. But this, however, was primarily a theoretical possibility. In nearly all cases, Treasury presented its position at the committee meetings just like every other participant and then listened to the deputy secretary's decision.[64] Generally, the Carter Treasury was unwilling to quarrel needlessly with other agencies within the administration over human rights issues. Recognizing the centrality of human rights in the administration's foreign policy and deeply concerned that it not develop an "antihuman rights" label, Treasury accepted the decisions of the Christopher Committee. Only on very rare occasions was it so opposed to a decision that it requested further discussions with the deputy secretary of state.

However much the Carter Treasury may have opposed some of the more vigorous efforts of Congress and HA, it pursued the issue of human rights in bank councils with some vigor. According to Secretary Blumenthal, "at every opportunity we seek to signal the seriousness of our intentions to the other countries and to the management of the Banks. . . . Human rights objectives are being advanced by exploring with like minded countries cooperative efforts to keep off the agenda particular loans to countries which are in violation of human rights, where we feel that will send them the right kind of

[64] Cf. *Foreign Assistance and Related Agencies Appropriations for 1979*, pt. 1, pp. 428, 660, *supra* n. 4.

signal, or to discuss with those countries ways and means in which their human rights practices can be improved."[65] One Treasury official noted in 1977 that U.S. executive directors "have been raising this issue daily with their colleagues from other countries."[66] While Treasury cannot be credited with leading the executive branch's charge on behalf of human rights in MDBs, it generally supported the policy, perhaps because the Carter Treasury officials responsible for U.S. participation in the MDBs were individuals with moderately liberal credentials: the assistant secretary for international affairs, C. Fred Bergsten, the Carter administration's first chief of Treasury's OIDB, Colin Bradford, and the executive director of the IDB, Ralph Dungan.

But when human rights policy conflicted with the officials' primary role—loaning money for development purposes to Third World governments—human rights constraints were accepted rather grudgingly. The Carter administration's Treasury officials were supporters of an active human rights policy, but their primary responsibility was to help MDBs loan money. Constrained by this role, Treasury officials often reacted with guarded hostility when human rights considerations interfered with the fulfillment of their responsibility. Thus when the office personnel of the U.S. executive director of the IDB held its 1978 Thanksgiving party, a "Turkeyfest," one wall of the office was decorated with a number of paper turkeys, each inscribed with the name of an official who had offended the office during the previous year. HA's Patricia Derian and Mark Schneider were among the select group.

Exploiting President Carter's strong endorsement of human rights, the Bureau of Human Rights and Humanitarian Affairs quickly obtained considerable influence over loan proposals, especially proposals submitted by a select group of "problem" governments. HA quickly developed a reputation for extreme aggressiveness on loan proposals, prompting Representative Charles Wilson of Texas to assert that "the lunatics have taken over the asylum in the State Department and there is not much anyone can do about it."[67] While this may have been a hyperbolic evaluation of both the mental stability and political influence of HA officials, the Bureau clearly possessed a dominant role in U.S. policy making on MDB loans to the most serious human rights violators.

[65] Ibid., p. 431.

[66] U.S. Congress, House, Committee on International Relations, Subcommittee on International Organizations, *Human Rights and United States Foreign Policy: A Review of the Administration's Record*, 95th Cong., 1st Sess., October 25, 1977, p. 11.

[67] *Foreign Assistance and Related Agencies Appropriations for 1979*, pt. 1, p. 897, *supra* n. 4.

"Policy," according to State Department folklore, "is made in the cables." For MDBs and human rights in the Carter administration, policy was made in the cases before the Christopher Committee, during the case-by-case review of loans to a small number of countries. Other than the requirement that human rights be considered in policy making, there was no policy in a formal sense; rather each loan was a separate case. There were precedents, of course, but each precedent was vulnerable to challenge and modification by any decision on any subsequent case.

Table 7.4 contains a complete list of all U.S. "no" votes and abstentions for human rights reasons in the MDBs through September 1980. There was one such vote in 1976, eighteen in 1977, twenty-nine in 1978, thirty in 1979, and twenty-one in the first nine months of 1980.[68] The most striking feature of Table 7.4 is the dominant presence of Latin American nations. Of the ninety-nine votes, fifty-three were against six repressive regimes in this hemisphere—Argentina, Chile, El Salvador, Guatemala, Paraguay, and Uruguay. Argentina was the most frequent target of U.S. disapproval—fully one-fourth of all U.S. negative votes for human rights were against proposals by this single country—not only because of the nearly universal perception that the Videla government was extraordinarily repressive but also because Argentina is a relatively wealthy nation. Its loan requests therefore did not benefit needy people as frequently as those from other Latin American nations. And it should be noted that the United States did not always oppose loans to these Latin American human rights violators. In the period covered by Table 7.4, the United States opposed all six loans to Chile, twenty-three of twenty-five loans to Argentina, two of twelve loans to El Salvador, two of seven loans to Guatemala, seven of nineteen loans to Paraguay, and twelve of thirteen loans to Uruguay. The loans that were supported were for projects that directly benefited needy people.

By late 1978, efforts to protect human rights began to have the same preemptive impact of earlier United States opposition to loans to governments that had expropriated the property of U.S.-based multinational corporations. In 1977, at least half a dozen loan proposals were withdrawn from consideration after U.S. opposition became known. One of these withdrawals occurred when Treasury Secretary Blumenthal informed officials of El Salvador that he would oppose a $90 million World Bank loan for an electric power project; another involved a $14 million IDB loan for health facilities in Chile. More generally, a pattern emerged in which MDBs restricted their

[68] For comparison, in 1977, the United States voted to approve 380 loans.

TABLE 7.4

Date	Bank	Project	Amount (millions)
Afghanistan			
3/79	IDA	education	$ 20.0
4/79	ADB	cotton processing	17.9
6/79	IDA	highway	17.6
6/79	IDA	rural development	16.5
Argentina			
6/77	IBRD	industrial credit	100.0
6/77	IFC	soybean processing	9.0
10/77	IDB	gas pipeline	36.0
11/77	IDB	cellulose	54.0
12/77	IDB	petrochemicals	105.0
2/78	IBRD	grain silos	105.0
3/78	IFC	cement plant	9.0
4/78	IFC	pulp and paper plant	8.0
5/78	IBRD	agricultural credit	60.0
5/78	IFC	polyethylene plant	10.0
12/78	IDB	Yacyretá hydroelectric	210.0
3/79	IDB	science and technology	66.0
3/79	IBRD	railways	96.0
5/79	IDB	Alicura hydroelectric	155.0
5/79	IFC	Alpesca fisheries	6.0
10/79	IBRD	Yacyretá hydroelectric	210.0
11/79	IDB	gas pipeline	10.0
11/79	IDB	rural electrification	44.2
3/80	IDB	heavy equipment	55.0
5/80	IDB	roads	90.0
6/80	IBRD	oil and gas	27.0
6/80	IFC	Acindar	18.0
6/80	IDB	hydroelectricity	33.0
Benin			
5/77	IDA	roads	5.5
5/77	IDA	regional development	1.7
Central African Republic			
10/77	AfDF	education	6.3
5/79	AfDF	livestock	3.5
Chile			
6/76	IDB	industrial credit	21.0
12/77	IDB	roads	24.5
3/78	IDB	rural health	14.0
11/78	IDB	industry/tourism	17.0
11/78	IDB	agriculture credit	38.0
9/80	IBRD	agriculture credit	36.0
El Salvador			
5/78	IBRD	telecommunications	23.0
3/79	IDB	livestock	15.0

TABLE 7.4 (cont.)

Date	Bank	Project	Amount (millions)
Ethiopia			
5/77	IDA	irrigation	25.0
5/77	IDA	roads	32.0
4/78	IDA	grain storage	24.0
Guatemala			
10/79	IDB	industry/tourism	15.0
5/80	IBRD	highway maintenance	17.0
Guinea			
11/77	AfDF	hemp production	5.5
South Korea			
10/77	ADB	Asan Bay Power	1.7
12/77	ADB	mineral exploration	.2
6/80	ADB	Inchon port development	54.0
9/80	ADB	Samrangjin storage	55.0
9/80	IFC	Taihan bulk storage	9.5
Laos			
10/78	ADB	forestry	8.0
12/78	ADB	rural electric	.1
6/79	ADB	roads	.2
6/79	IDA	agriculture	10.4
10/79	ADB	agriculture	8.1
3/80	ADB	agriculture	4.5
5/80	IDA	agriculture	13.2
Paraguay			
3/78	IBRD	highways	33.0
3/78	IDB	highways	12.6
5/78	IDB	power	32.5
6/79	IBRD	highways	39.0
6/79	IFAD*	agriculture	7.5
12/79	IDB	industry/tourism	12.0
12/79	IBRD	preinvestment survey	5.0
Philippines			
11/77	ADB	hydroelectric power	29.0
12/77	ADB	Philippines Development Bank	35.0
4/78	IBRD	PISO private investment fund	15.0
5/78	IBRD	Philippines Development Bank	80.0
6/78	IFC	Cebu shipyard	2.1
10/78	ADB	mining	.1
9/79	ADB	Manila port	27.0
9/79	ADB	Manila port	.2
11/79	ADB	Mindanao power	60.7
11/79	ADB	Malangas coal	14.0
3/80	IFC	industrial gas	4.5
Uruguay			
12/77	IDB	dam	26.0
12/77	IDB	roads	3.7

TABLE 7.4 (cont.)

Date	Bank	Project	Amount (millions)
Uruguay (cont.)			
9/78	IFC	Acodike Gas	.9
4/79	IBRD	roads	26.5
5/79	IFC	Astra Fisheries	5.3
7/79	IBD	roads	35.0
12/79	IBRD	power	24.0
1/80	IBRD	Montevideo port	50.0
2/80	IDB	electricity transmission	24.0
4/80	IBRD	livestock and agriculture	24.0
6/80	IFC	Sur Investment	10.7
9/80	IDB	university education	32.5
Vietnam			
10/78	ADB	Go Cong irrigation	2.1
10/78	ADB	Binh Dinh irrigation	2.5
10/78	ADB	Tan An irrigation	7.4
11/78	ADB	water supply	4.6
Yemen P.D.R.			
2/78	IDA	irrigation	5.2
6/78	IDA	power	5.0
6/78	IDA	water supply	1.2
12/78	IDA	education	4.0
6/79	IDA	fisheries	10.0
6/80	IDA	water supply	13.2
6/80	IDA	petroleum development	9.0

SOURCE: Office of Multilateral Development Banks, Department of the Treasury.
* IFAD is the International Fund for Agricultural Development, a new MDB proposed by OPEC at the 1974 World Food Conference. It began operating in 1977, with headquarters in Rome.

processing of proposals from repressive governments to those that could be demonstrated to benefit directly the neediest citizens.

One unexpected product of these changes in United States policy toward MDB loan applications was the hostility of other MDB members, many of whom viewed the U.S. actions as intervention in the internal affairs of sovereign states. In the June 1976 vote against the IDB industrial credit to Chile, all other member governments voted for the loan, including not only Mexico, which had broken relations with Chile and had refused to attend the 1976 OAS meeting in Santiago, but also Venezuela, which at the time was developing its own reputation as a champion of human rights in Latin America. Venezuela's representative to the IDB chastised the United States for its vote, declaring that "the bank is not a forum for considering political considerations."[69] Two years later, representatives of France,

[69] *Washington Post*, July 9, 1976, p. A2.

South Korea, and Vietnam attacked U.S. officials at the Vienna meeting of the governing board of the Asian Development Bank (ADB). South Korean Finance Minster Kim Yon Hnam asserted that the Bank's purpose was economic development, and "no other considerations should be allowed to influence its operating activities."[70]

Scoldings such as these served to underscore the considerable change that occurred in United States policy toward human rights and the MDBs during the 1970s. First, Congress created a law requiring the executive branch to oppose loans to governments that violate their citizens' fundamental human rights unless the loan proceeds would directly benefit needy people. This was an unusually difficult battle for human rights activists because they were opposed not only by the Democratic congressional leadership, a common feature of all human rights battles of the 1970s, but by the human rights-oriented Carter administration as well. Nonetheless, with the help of conservative colleagues, liberal members of Congress produced a legal foundation that human rights activists inside and outside the government then proceeded to exploit. Although Congress may have been unable to add its human rights/needs amendment to legislation governing United States participation in the IMF, it raised the long-standing humanitarian concern of a relatively small number of citizens to the level of national policy debate and international diplomacy. By challenging the necessity for deprivations of basic needs that accompany IMF stabilization programs, Congress brought closer the day when the poor of the Third World will no longer be forced into even greater poverty in order to compensate for the financial mismanagement of their leaders and the detrimental impact of international market forces.

Second, the Carter administration adopted a policy of using its influence in the MDBs as an instrument to promote respect for fundamental human rights. The administration was vulnerable to criticisms that it did not use this power with sufficient vigor or consistency, that it approved many loans which violated the spirit if not the word of congressional directives, and that it was too quick to reward the marginal diminution in repression by approving a resumption of favorable votes. But there is no contesting the evidence that the Carter policy was a clear departure from that of its predecessors. The issue of human rights was raised in MDB councils, and while no loans were formally denied because of opposition from the United States, the Carter administration policy served to deter loan application by Latin America's most repressive governments. Within the U.S. government, the administration created a formal bureaucratic mechanism that

---

[70] *Washington Post*, April 26, 1978, p. A22.

served almost automatically to inject human rights considerations into any MDB loan proposal. All HA needed to do to raise a human rights issue was refuse to sign off on a loan proposal. Then the issue went to the Christopher Committee, where HA won some battles and lost others. Here the administration could be criticized for adopting a proposal-by-proposal review process, which at first simply overwhelmed officials in the newly created human rights bureau. But the administration staffed HA with aggressive personnel and provided in the Christopher Committee a forum where HA could demonstrate its vigor. Often this was not enough; sometimes it was.

· 8 ·

LINKAGES TO THE U.S.
PRIVATE SECTOR

In addition to conventional foreign policy instruments such as diplomacy and economic aid, foreign policy decision makers have at their disposal a variety of less direct tools to influence the behavior of Latin American governments. These indirect instruments are as diverse as U.S. contacts with Latin America: educational and cultural exchanges, trade, tourism, and private foreign investment. Every U.S. citizen and U.S-based corporation that affects Latin America is in theory a potential instrument of United States foreign policy. Among these instruments are four that became involved in human rights conflicts in Latin America during the 1960s and 1970s: the Export-Import Bank, the Overseas Private Investment Corporation, the Office of Munitions Control, and the American Institute for Free Labor Development. The manner in which each was used to implement United States policy toward repressive Latin American governments reveals much about the limits of humanitarian considerations in foreign policy.

The Export-Import Bank

The Export-Import Bank is the basic public sector structure used by the United States government to encourage the export of goods and services. Organized in 1934 to assist in overcoming the depression, the Eximbank is a government corporation; all of its $1 billion in capital stock is owned by the Treasury, from which it is further authorized to borrow up to $6 billion. With this financial backing, the bank borrows money from another government corporation, the Federal Financing Bank, to finance the transactions of U.S. exporters.[1]

The Eximbank employs these funds in four basic programs: direct loans, discount loans, guarantees, and insurance. Direct loans supplement private sector financing when commercial or political risks

---

[1] In the process of performing its duties, the bank regularly makes a profit. In FY1977, for example, the Eximbank supported $8.5 billion in exports while realizing a net profit of $137 million. This profit is predicated, however, upon the availability of funds at less-than-market rates from the Federal Financing Bank.

are high, when borrowers cannot meet normal commercial repayment terms, or (most frequently) when a foreign competitor for a given sale is being assisted by its export-promotion bank. In its discount loan program, the bank loans a commercial bank a sum equal to a loan by the commercial bank to finance the export of U.S. goods. The direct loan program is by far the larger of the two loan programs. In both the insurance and guarantee programs, the bank issues insurance to commercial banks and exporters that might otherwise decline to finance export sales involving unacceptable risks. An Eximbank guarantee assures a lender of repayment of principal and interest in the event a foreign borrower defaults on a loan. Armed with a bank guarantee, a foreign borrower normally finds that commercial lenders will finance transactions that prudent bankers might normally shun. Unlike a guarantee, an Eximbank insurance policy is a type of casualty insurance that protects exporters against losses resulting from defaults by foreign buyers. This insurance is issued in conjunction with the Federal Insurance Credit Association (FICA), an unincorporated cooperative composed of about fifty commercial insurance companies. Armed with a FICA policy, an exporting corporation can finance its export receivables at rates substantially lower than those available to exporters without insurance. Thus the effect of both insurance and guarantee programs is to encourage export activity by reducing the cost of credit. About $13 billion in insurance and guarantees was outstanding at the end of the 1970s.[2]

Although Eximbank is a public body with all the responsibilities for accountability that such a status requires, very little is known by the public about bank decision making. Using the exemption from the Sunshine Law (PL94-406) that permits closed meetings to protect confidential commercial or financial information, the bank's twice-

[2] U.S. Congress, House, Committee on Appropriations, Subcommittee on Foreign Operations and Related Agencies, *Foreign Assistance and Related Agencies Appropriations for 1979*, 95th Cong., 2d Sess., 1978, pt. 1, pp. 9-11; Howard S. Piquet, *The Export-Import Bank of the United States: An Analysis of Some Current Problems* (Washington, D.C.: National Planning Association, 1970), pp. 15-16. In addition to Eximbank loans, guarantees, and insurance, the U.S. government provides financial support for exporters through two other credit programs and one tax incentive program. Credit is provided through Title I of the Food for Peace program and the Commodity Credit Corporation's Short-Term Export Sales program, while tax incentives are offered through the Domestic International Sales Corporations (DISCs). For FY1977, the Congressional Budget Office estimated that the cost of these four programs (including tax revenue foregone in the case of DISCs) was $2.3 billion. U.S. Congress, Congressional Budget Office, *U.S. Government Involvement in Commercial Exports: Program Goals and Budgetary Costs* (Washington, D.C.: Government Printing Office, November 1977), p. ix.

weekly deliberations on loan proposals are strictly internal affairs. In mid-1978, Common Cause completed a year-long study of secrecy in all forty-six federal agencies that existed at the time, dubbing "The Secret Seven" those with the fewest number of meetings open to the public. The Export-Import Bank led the field: all 109 of its meetings were held in secret.[3] But while most routine decisions are made without publicity, the bank does not operate in complete solitude. One role of the National Advisory Council on International Monetary and Financial Policies is to advise the Eximbank on its lending policies. Any transaction involving Eximbank liability over $30 million is processed by the NAC in exactly the same way as the WGMA processes an MDB loan proposal. While the NAC's position is only advisory, only very rarely is its advice ignored.[4] Since 1974, the bank has also been required to inform Congress in advance of any loan or guarantee over $60 million, although Congress cannot take any action in favor of or against any transaction. The reports (ten in 1975) are simply sent to the House and Senate Banking Committees, where the staffs file them in various cabinets.

Congressional input into Eximbank activity occurs through both the authorization and appropriation processes. Authorizations, which take the form of periodic amendments to the Export-Import Bank Act of 1945 (PL79-173), are referred to the banking committees. These amendments may contain a variety of provisions, but they generally include extensions of the life of the bank and often an increase in the bank's overall lending limits. Eximbank appropriations are included, strangely, as part of the annual Foreign Assistance and Related Programs Appropriations Act. This act contains a separate title that sets the annual ceilings for the four types of bank activities and places a limit on administrative expenses. Unlike the treatment received by foreign aid agencies such as AID, the Eximbank appropriation request draws very little attention while passing through the two Appropriations Subcommittees on Foreign Operations. In 1978, for example, the House created 177 pages of hearings on the Eximbank (compared to 563 pages on the MDBs), and it did so first by padding the record and then by discussing in some detail the technical aspects of an

[3] Common Cause, "The First Year of Sunshine: Federal Agency Compliance with the Government in the Sunshine Act of 1976," mimeographed, Washington, D.C., August 1978, pp. 12-13.

[4] U.S. Congress, House, Select Committee on Foreign Aid, *Final Report on Foreign Aid*, 80th Cong., 2d Sess., 1948, p. 724; Paul Pratt, *A Handbook on Financing U.S. Exports*, 2d ed. (Washington, D.C.: Machinery and Allied Products Institute, 1976), pp. 18-19.

Eximbank-financed nuclear power plant in the Philippines. Human rights was mentioned only briefly.[5]

With little controversy surrounding its activities, with an extremely strong domestic constituency composed of agriculture, industry (particularly aircraft and heavy equipment manufacturers), commercial banks, and the National Foreign Trade Council, and with only occasional attention from Congress, the Eximbank has developed into the type of financial institution that reflects the society in which it thrives. It is business oriented—the president and the board of directors are almost always commercial bankers—reasonably efficient, and appropriately frugal. Its mission is to promote the sale of U.S. products abroad, and the bank therefore contests any attempt to restrict its lending activities. Thus the bank argues against human rights legislation not only because it would curtail financing for right-wing Latin American dictatorships but also because it could restrict trade with communist countries. Left to itself, the Eximbank would be an ardent advocate of unrestricted, government-assisted trade.

But no federal agency is left entirely to itself, and the Eximbank is regularly called upon to assist in implementing United States foreign policy.[6] While bank officials acknowledge that foreign policy considerations affect loan decisions,[7] their hermetic behavior makes it difficult to determine exactly which of these considerations impinge and how. One well-known use of Eximbank loans is as a sweetener during negotiations for military base rights. These include Portugal/Azores in 1971, Spain and Turkey in 1976, and Iceland and Panama in 1977. At times, these agreements are quite specific—an informal promise to help finance a civil air terminal in Iceland, for example—but most are general agreements to provide certain amounts of credit for a specified period. Eximbank has also responded to pressures from administration officials to halt loans. One obvious example of this type of activity during the 1970s occurred as part of the Nixon administration's hostility toward the Allende government. By mid-1971, Eximbank

[5] See *Foreign Assistance and Related Agencies Appropriations for 1979*, pt. 1, pp. 54, 125, 1130, *supra* n. 2. On the question of the relationship between Eximbank loans and foreign aid, see the opinions of two prominent human rights activists, Representatives Harkin and Badillo, in *Congressional Record*, July 27, 1978, p. H7422; and House Report 95-235, p. 22.

[6] William Charles Binning, "The Role of the Export-Import Bank in Inter-American Affairs," Ph.D. dissertation, University of Notre Dame, 1970, pp. 7-10, 287-290. In this study of bank policies between 1954 and the mid-1960s, Binning concludes that the bank "appears to have followed the basic foreign policy goals of each Administration."

[7] *Foreign Assistance and Related Agencies Appropriations for 1979*, pt. 1, pp. 60, 86, *supra* n. 2.

decision-making authority on loans to Chile had been taken over by the NAC, whose chairperson, Treasury Secretary John Connally, was assigned to coordinate the U.S. economic blockade of Chile.[8] In August, bank president Henry Kearns notified Chilean ambassador Orlando Letelier that the United States would not provide Chile with $21 million in loans and loan guarantees to finance the purchase of three Boeing jets. According to Tad Szulc, the decision to halt Eximbank credits was made by President Nixon.[9]

Until the late 1970s, the bank chose to overlook the human rights behavior of prospective borrowers. The Eximbank did not provide an inordinate proportion of its resources to repressive regimes; neither did it make any significant effort to avoid aiding governments that terrorize their citizens.[10] But Eximbank officials have always favored economically sound proposals, and they have defined the term "economically sound" from the business-oriented perspective for which they are noted: a "sound" loan is one for which there is a reasonable assurance of repayment. In the 1960s and 1970s, Latin America's more repressive regimes thereby became the region's most creditworthy borrowers. During the darkest days of their rights violations, the Argentine, Brazilian, Chilean, and Uruguayan governments paid their bills. As Eximbank president Kearns noted in 1971, "the military leadership in Brazil is as good, and in most cases better, than in other nations, despite the fact that some people think that it is a highly repressive government."[11] Kearns's opinion captures well the attitude of the bank during the Nixon-Ford administration: the violation of human rights was simply not one of the variables employed in bank decision making.

It was Congress that first raised the issue of human rights in the Eximbank. In general, Congress has adhered to an unspoken agreement that the periodic revisions of the Eximbank Act should not include country-specific amendments.[12] Over the years, however, it

---

[8] U.S. Congress, House, Committee on Foreign Affairs, Subcommittee on Inter-American Affairs, *New Directions for the 1970's—Part 2: Development Assistance Options for Latin America*, 92d Cong., 1st Sess., 1971, p. 224.

[9] *New York Times*, August 12, 1971, pp. 1, 11, and August 14, 1971, p. 3. The aircraft loans had been awaiting approval since early winter, before any major uncompensated expropriations had occurred. Chile formally defaulted on loan payments to the Eximbank on February 18, 1972.

[10] An obvious exception to this laissez-faire policy was bank activity in Chile. From an average of $1.6 million in loans during the three Allende years (FY1971-FY1973), Eximbank activity increased in FY1974 to $57.0 million.

[11] See *New Directions for the 1970's*, p. 227, *supra* n. 8.

[12] Until loans to the government of South Africa were prohibited in 1978, the Soviet Union was the only nation singled out in the act for special treatment, with Sec. 2(B)(3) requiring a report to Congress on loans over $25 million and Sec. 7(b)

has added a number of policy provisions to the bank's authorizing legislation that prohibit loans to communist countries, to countries engaged in armed conflict with the United States, to less-developed countries for the purchase of defense articles, and to any nation for the purchase of nuclear fuel reprocessing facilities. Thus when Congress decided to require that human rights considerations be included in Eximbank decision making, it was not an unprecedented intrusion of foreign policy variables in a business-oriented program.

The initial human rights provision in Eximbank legislation is a complex requirement that the bank not assist the sale of defense articles to less developed countries unless the President determines that such a sale would be in the national interest. In making this determination, the President is instructed to avoid "arming military dictators who are denying social progress to their own peoples." This weak statement was added to the Eximbank authorizing legislation in 1968.[13]

The second human rights clause had a brief but interesting history that illuminates a fundamental weakness of congressional human rights activists. In 1977, a bill (H.R. 6415) to extend the life of the Eximbank was reported out of the House Banking Subcommittee on International Trade with a clause requiring bank authorities to "take into account, in consultation with the Secretary of State, the observance of and respect for human rights in the country to receive the exports supported by a loan or financial guarantee and the effect such exports may have on human rights in such a country." Fresh from his MDB/human rights victory on the House floor a month earlier, Representative Herman Badillo criticized this provision as too weak. When H.R. 6415 was considered by the full committee, Badillo offered as a substitute a series of human rights proposals, including a Harkin-type amendment to prohibit Eximbank credits to governments engaged in gross violations of human rights unless such transactions would directly benefit needy people. Stung by his MDB defeat, Banking Committee chairperson Reuss urged acceptance of the subcommittee's weaker provision by issuing an appeal to the pocketbook.[14] After rejecting the Badillo/ Harkin amendment by a vote of 30 to 5, the committee reported the bill to the House by a vote of 38 to 1. This overwhelming approval provided Reuss with the argument he required to convince the Committee on Rules that the bill should be considered under suspension of the rules, which limits floor debate and prohibits floor amendments.

restricting loans to $300 million, none of which can be spent on any product used to produce fossil fuels.

[13] PL90-267. *Congressional Record*, February 7, 1968, p. 2433.

[14] House Report 95-235, p. 4.

On the floor, Representatives Badillo and Harkin urged defeat of the bill under suspension so that it could be amended, but it passed by a substantial (281-126) margin. In the meantime, the Senate could not break a deadlock on a number of issues concerning bank activities, including human rights and loans to South Africa, and so in August it approved a bill that simply extended the life of the bank for ninety days. Senate conferees subsequently accepted with minor refinements the House human rights language, and the House accepted the Senate's temporary extension. Senator Adlai Stevenson, the bill's floor manager, noted that the compromise was an interim measure "pending a complete review of the Bank's activities and authority."[15]

So in 1978 another Eximbank extension proposal (H.R. 12157) began to wind its way through Congress. In the House, the crucial issue was bank activity in South Africa. In committee, Representative Paul Tsongas proposed an amendment to prohibit Eximbank transactions in South Africa until significant progress had been made toward the elimination of apartheid.[16] Tsongas's initiative was amended on the floor to permit the Eximbank to continue financing exports to South African corporations that endorse the Sullivan Principles, which provide for a measure of nondiscrimination in labor practices. The complete prohibition on Eximbank lending to the South African government was retained, however, and in late July the measure finally passed the House.

While the bill was before the House, Representative Harkin offered what one member referred to as "the gentleman's annual human rights amendment."[17] The opposition argued that a human rights clause already existed in Eximbank legislation and that further restrictions would harm United States exporters rather than human rights violators. Heads nodded in agreement as Representative Hyde argued that because "this country is in a very desperate situation in terms of a trade deficit," the administration should overlook human rights considerations in making decisions on Eximbank loan applications. Banking subcommittee chairperson Neal had a similar opinion of the Harkin proposal: "This is around $1 billion in trade that this would cost us. Is that what the gentleman wants to do? Does he want to cost us that billion dollars in trade? . . . in world trade we are in a very competitive area and we have to fight for every export we get. If we are to have this very unwise language, then we would almost hobble the Bank's efforts to aid our exports. . . . It is a competitive area, and other

[15] *Congressional Record*, September 23, 1977, p. S15520.
[16] As offered to the committee by Representative Tsongas, the provision required progress toward majority rule rather than toward the end of apartheid.
[17] *Congressional Record*, July 27, 1978, p. H7422.

307

countries would certainly be happy to move in and fill the void."[18] In the most overwhelming defeat in the House of any human rights proposal during the 1970s, the Harkin amendment was rejected by a vote of 103 to 286. The House would not agree to a human rights measure that had the potential to increase the U.S. trade deficit.

In the Senate, the Eximbank review began when a bill (S. 3077) to extend the bank's life for five years and to authorize a new loan ceiling was referred to Senator Stevenson's Banking Subcommittee on International Finance. In the area of human rights, S. 3077 was indeed an innovative revision. The committee deleted entirely not only the weak human rights clause added just months earlier but also the provisions that restricted transactions with communist countries. In place of these provisions, the committee proposed that the President submit to Congress a list of countries eligible to receive bank credits. This list, which would remain effective for three years and be updated regularly, would be created after the President had considered a number of criteria, including each country's overall relationship with the United States, its creditworthiness, its policies with respect to the peaceful settlement of disputes, environmental protection, nuclear proliferation, and human rights (including specifically the right to emigrate).[19] Although Congress could not amend the list, by means of a concurrent resolution it could send it back to the President for revision. The President could remove a country from the list at any time. The purpose of this provision, which was supported primarily by Senators Stevenson and Heinz, was to provide an alternative to Congress's ad-hoc selection of the countries and issues it wished to attack and support with Eximbank financing.

The Senate could not agree on the advisability of establishing such a procedure. The Carter administration argued that publication of a list would reduce unnecessarily the flexibility of the President in foreign policy formulation and, at the same time, damage relations with a number of countries.[20] Senators Chafee, McGovern, and Thurmond then introduced a substitute to the Stevenson/Heinz listing procedure that had as its effect the elimination of all requirements that human rights be considered in Eximbank decision making. The substitute struck the Stevenson/Heinz provision, repealed the 1977 human rights legislation, and added a clause that made it difficult for the executive

---

[18] *Congressional Record*, July 27, 1978, pp. H7425-H7427.

[19] Senate Report 95-844, p. 13.

[20] Messages to this effect from deputy secretary of state Christopher and Commerce Secretary Kreps are reprinted in the *Congressional Record*, October 2, 1978, pp. H16820, H16829.

branch to restrict Eximbank financing for human rights reasons. This clause directed the administration to

> give particular emphasis to the objective of strengthening the competitive position of United States exporters and thereby of expanding total United States exports. Only in cases where the President determines that such action would be in the national interest and where such action would clearly and importantly advance United States policy in such areas as international terrorism, nuclear proliferation, environmental protection and human rights, should the Export-Import Bank deny applications for credit for nonfinancial or noncommercial considerations.

As one trade association noted in a subsequent newsletter to its members, "the enactment of this provision should result in a decrease in the use of Eximbank financing for noncommercial (i.e., 'foreign policy') considerations."[21] It is possible that Senator McGovern was unaware that he was participating in a serious weakening of human rights legislation governing the bank, for in his speech on the Senate floor, he complained only that a listing procedure would harm both U.S. exports and U.S. foreign relations. But Senator Chafee's intent was clear: he viewed his amendment as a means to reduce the President's power to deny Eximbank credits.[22] Over the opposition of most Senate liberals, the Chafee-McGovern amendment passed by a margin of 45 to 35.

Facing an extraordinarily heavy calendar and an upcoming election, in early October the Senate ceased consideration of S. 3077, and it appeared that the Ninety-sixth Congress would have to begin anew to resolve the question of human rights considerations in Eximbank lending. On October 10, the House went so far as to pass a joint resolution (H.J. Res. 157) to extend the bank's life until June 30, 1979. But then, in a move that will probably rank as one of the most successful flimflams of the Ninety-fifth Congress, leaders of the House and Senate Banking Committees decided upon a different course. They found an extremely complex bill—the Financial Institutions Regulatory and Interest Rate Control Act of 1978 (H.R. 14279)—and buried an additional title on the Eximbank in its midst. Actually, it is incorrect to say the bill was found; it was created at the very end of the Ninety-fifth Congress by combining a variety of pending bills into what is commonly known as a "Christmas tree." As one committee member told the House, "while 'sweeping up' at the House

[21] Machinery and Allied Products Institute *Bulletin* number 5789, November 2, 1978, p. 4.
[22] *Congressional Record*, October 2, 1978, pp. S16820, S16829.

Banking Committee, we found a number of bills lying around, and we present them to our colleagues today in one glorious package."[23] Deep in a discussion of the most arcane legislation imaginable (on such matters as the central liquidity facility of credit unions), this new title extended the life of the bank to 1983, increased its authorized lending limit from $25 billion to $40 billion, and added the Chafee-McGovern amendment.

H.R. 14279 was presented to and passed by the House in one day (October 11) *without* the Eximbank title. The following day, H.R. 14279 was passed by the Senate *with* many of the Eximbank provisions from S. 3077 (including the Chafee-McGovern amendment) and H.R. 12157 (but not the ban on Eximbank activity in South Africa). Then, with time too short to permit a formal House-Senate conference, H.R. 14279 was sent back to the House for approval of the Senate changes. House Banking Committee leaders added the South Africa prohibition and retained the Chafee-McGovern amendment. Finally, at 2:00 AM on October 15, the final day of the Ninety-fifth Congress, they presented H.R. 14279 to the House. The bill's floor manager informed the members that "there will not be time for more consideration, no time for more amendments to be passed between the two Houses," an evaluation seconded by a Republican leader of the Banking Committee: "All the Members can do is maybe take our word for it here tonight that we think truly it is in the best interest of the United States and our citizens and our taxpayers to support this legislation."[24] The somnolent members passed H.R. 14279 by a margin of 341 to 32. An hour later, the Senate accepted the South Africa amendment and sent the bill to the President for his signature. As PL95-630, the bill effectively ended any obligation that human rights considerations be included in Eximbank decision making.

The Carter administration never viewed trade sanctions as a primary instrument to promote human rights. In late 1978, deputy secretary of state Warren Christopher told the National Foreign Trade Convention that "restrictions on export financing should be used for foreign policy reasons only in highly exceptional circumstances." In determining these restrictions, continued Christopher, the administration operates with "a strong presumption in favor of exports." Even officials of the Bureau of Human Rights and Humanitarian Affairs agreed that restrictions on Eximbank financing should be a last resort, to be used only after diplomacy, military aid, and both bilateral and multilateral economic aid had proven unsuccessful. Thus the effect of Congress's

---

[23] *Congressional Record*, October 14, 1978, p. H13075.
[24] *Congressional Record*, October 14, 1978, pp. H13072-H13075.

1978 action was substantial in theory but, given the Carter administration's policy, minimal in practice.

It needs to be noted, however, that the Carter administration changed the Nixon-Ford policy of completely ignoring human rights considerations in bank decision making. By 1978, the Eximbank was regularly refusing to consider loan applications from Chile and Uruguay, and it had informed the governments of those countries that the refusals were based upon human rights violations. As bank president John Moore noted in 1978, "Eximbank's position has become known in the export community and as a result we receive very few applications for loans or financial guarantees in those countries."[25] Late in 1978, however, bank authorities sought permission to increase loan ceilings for both countries as a first step in reestablishing normal lending operations. Its proposal was rejected by the NAC, which, in turn, was highly influenced by State's Bureau of Human Rights and Humanitarian Affairs.

The only celebrated case of Eximbank activity on behalf of human rights involved Argentina, whose high level of human rights violations and low vulnerability to other forms of pressure made the denial of Eximbank credits a logical instrument for Carter administration human rights activists. Early in 1978, deputy secretary Christopher and bank president Moore agreed between themselves to suspend Eximbank activity in Argentina, since neither wanted to be faced with a series of case-by-case debates in the Christopher Committee. Subsequent to this decision, Argentina made an informal request for a $270 million loan to finance the purchase of hydroelectric turbines from Allis-Chalmers Corporation. The initial indication from the Carter administration was that the loan would not be approved; then Argentine President Videla met privately in Rome with Vice President Mondale when both were attending the coronation of Pope John Paul I. Negotiations were reopened, and in return for a promise by General Videla to permit the Inter-American Commission on Human Rights to conduct an in-country human rights investigation, the United States agreed to permit Eximbank financing for the Allis-Chalmers turbines. Soon thereafter, Congress passed PL95-630, forcing the administration to lift any remaining prohibition on Eximbank transactions with human rights violators.

In brief, it cannot be said that the Eximbank was used vigorously as an instrument to promote human rights during the 1970s. Overwhelming opinion in both the executive branch and Congress held

[25] *Foreign Assistance and Related Agencies Appropriations for 1979*, pt. 1, p. 1130, *supra* n. 2.

311

that the bank should be free from having to incorporate humanitarian considerations in its principal activity of facilitating United States exports. In making their case to senior policy makers, human rights activists could not compete with angry exporters and a rising red line on the nation's balance of payments graph.

Overseas Private Investment Corporation

Like the Eximbank, the Overseas Private Investment Corporation (OPIC) is a government corporation involved primarily in facilitating U.S. corporations' transactions with the Third World. Unlike the Eximbank, which finances and insures the export of goods and services, OPIC insures the overseas investments of U.S.-based multinational corporations from losses due to inconvertibility of foreign currency, to expropriation, and to damage by war, revolution, and insurrection.[26] While OPIC is not unique—Japan and more than a dozen Western European nations encourage their corporations to invest overseas by providing insurance against political risks—it is the world's largest government-sponsored political risk insurance program.[27]

Created in 1969, OPIC is only the latest in a series of government programs to insure corporate investments abroad. To encourage private sector participation in the effort to rebuild Europe, the Economic Cooperation Act of 1948 contained an insurance program that focused exclusively upon equity convertibility. In 1950, this guarantee was broadened to include loss through expropriation. Soon after, the investment insurance program became part of the State Department's International Cooperation Administration (ICA). In 1956, coverage was extended to include losses resulting from war. With Europe rebuilt, with the locus of the Cold War shifting to the Third World, with an

---

[26] OPIC has also operated a small Direct Investment Fund and is authorized by Congress to engage in several other types of activities, including investment promotion through feasibility studies and a working relationship with the International Executive Service Corps, the businessperson's Peace Corps. In 1974, Congress required OPIC to suspend most of these activities by 1980 and to concentrate upon investment insurance. PL93-390, Sec. 2(5)(A).

[27] U.S. Congress, House, Committee on International Relations, Subcommittee on International Economic Policy and Trade, *Extension and Revision of Overseas Private Investment Corporation Programs*, 95th Cong., 1st Sess., June-September 1977, p. 155; Overseas Private Investment Corporation, *Annual Report 1972* (Washington, D.C.: Overseas Private Investment Corporation, 1973), p. 11. The cross-national range is substantial. As of 1971, 3 percent of all Dutch investments in the Third World were insured, compared with 44 percent of all Japanese investments and 31 percent of all U.S. investments. More recent data are unavailable. U.S. Congress, House, Committee on Foreign Affairs, *The Overseas Private Investment Corporation: A Critical Analysis*, 93d Cong., 1st Sess., September 4, 1973, p. 3.

increasing interest in the economic development of poorer countries, and with the continuing expansion of multinational corporations, in 1959 Congress directed the ICA to focus its insurance exclusively upon investments in the Third World. This new emphasis continued throughout the 1960s, when ICA's successor, the Agency for International Development, created an aggressive Office of Private Resources that engineered a phenomenal growth in insurance coverage. During the period 1948 to 1959, the government issued $400 million in investment insurance policies; during the AID years (1961-1969), expropriation insurance alone amounted to $4.8 billion.[28]

Given this two-decade history of government support for private foreign investment alongside the clear enthusiasm of corporate officials, it is surprising that OPIC has always had to fight for its life. The original initiative to remove the insurance program from AID and place it in the hands of an independent corporation came from Senator Jacob Javits, a principal congressional champion of the multinational corporation. In 1968, a Javits-proposed amendment to the Foreign Assistance Act of 1961 requested the President to consider "the establishment of a Government corporation or a federally chartered private corporation designed to mobilize and facilitate the use of United States private capital and skills in less developed friendly countries."[29] The following year, the Nixon administration included the establishment of OPIC as part of its foreign aid authorization request. After a brief debate, the House approved by a narrow (176-163) margin legislation authorizing the creation of OPIC.[30] The Senate Committee on Foreign Relations was unreceptive to the administration's request, however. It refused to hold hearings on the subject and consequently declined to include OPIC in its version of the foreign aid authorization bill. This refusal was due not so much to hostility to the concept of OPIC as it was to the committee's concentration upon other issues, particularly the war in Vietnam, and its feeling that AID was adequately managing the investment insurance program. But Senator Javits argued that the United States should give greater prominence to the political risk insurance program by separating it from the foreign aid program. On the Senate floor, he proposed an amendment to the committee bill that was identical to the House-approved OPIC section. Despite opposition from Senators Fulbright

[28] U.S. Congress, Senate, Committee on Foreign Relations, Subcommittee on Multinational Corporations, *The Overseas Private Investment Corporation*, 93d Cong., 1st Sess., October 17, 1973, pp. 2-4.

[29] PL90-554, Sec. 502.

[30] *Congressional Record*, November 19, 1969, pp. 34904-34939, and November 20, 1969, pp. 35183-35231.

and Case, Javits' amendment was accepted by the Senate. Thus the Foreign Assistance Act of 1969 (PL91-175) authorized OPIC to assume the responsibility for insuring U.S. corporate investments in the Third World. The President formally implemented this authority in early 1971.[31]

It was not until 1973 that the Senate Foreign Relations Subcommittee on Multinational Corporations held the first Senate hearings on OPIC.[32] In the subcommittee's report, Senator Case argued that OPIC is "only a marginal contributor to the development of the poorer countries" that "tends to increase the likelihood of United States Government involvement in the internal politics of other countries in connection with the property interests of United States corporations."[33] Subsequent investigations provided additional criticisms of OPIC. One concerned the limited number of corporate beneficiaries. In 1977, the Government Accounting Office reported that "OPIC continues to provide the majority of insurance to the large 'Fortune 500' corporations. Since December, 1973, about 83 percent of OPIC's insurance coverage has gone to these firms," an observation supported by data from the Center for International policy.[34] As a result of this criticism, in 1974 and 1978 Congress attempted to increase the participation of small businesses in OPIC activity. In both years, the result defined "small business" to include some very substantial corporations. In 1978, this so angered Representative Clarence Long that he attacked the bill reported from conference as a "sham" and voted against its passage.[35]

Another criticism focused upon the type of countries in which U.S. investments were insured. The GAO found that "the success of OPIC's efforts to encourage investment in the lesser developed countries is minimal," primarily because of limited profit opportunities. In 1976, 71.5 percent of all OPIC activity involved investments in countries

[31] *Congressional Record*, December 11, 1969, pp. 38461-38474, and December 12, 1969, pp. 38684-38731. In the interim, OPIC's activities were administered by AID's Office of Private Resources. Executive Order number 11579, January 19, 1971.

[32] U.S. Congress, Senate, Committee on Foreign Relations, Subcommittee on Multinational Corporations, *Multinational Corporations and United States Foreign Policy*, 93d Cong., 1st Sess., July and August 1973, pt. 3.

[33] See *The Overseas Private Investment Corporation*, p. 33, *supra* n. 28.

[34] U.S. Congress, Senate, Committee on Foreign Relations, Subcommittee on Foreign Assistance and Related Programs, *OPIC Authorization*, 95th Cong., 1st Sess., 1977, pp. 108, 124-137. See also *Extension and Revision of Overseas Private Investment Corporation Programs*, pp. 143-159, *supra* n. 27.

[35] *Congressional Record*, April 11, 1978, pp. H2742-H2744. OPIC defends its definition in *Foreign Assistance and Related Agencies Appropriations for 1979*, 95th Cong., 2d Sess., 1978, pt. 2, pp. 1120-1121, *supra* n. 2.

with per capita annual incomes of $450 or more.[36] Additionally, several OPIC-assisted investments in very poor nations, particularly those supporting the construction of luxury resorts, aroused considerable controversy. The most notorious example was Habitation Leclerc in Haiti. Instead of going into the family cork business in France, Oliver Coquelin de Faraillon travelled to Haiti where, with $262,000 from OPIC, he developed an unusual retreat: "I wanted guests not only to feel as though they were vacationing in a Haitian Hideaway but also as though they were stepping back into another century, a lascivious and decadent past that is everyone's innermost desire to return to."[37] According to *Town and Country*, "Habitation Leclerc grew out of an illusion of his fantasy into forty-four little private bungalow suites, each with semiprivate pools scattered about the fifteen acres of lush tropical greenery. Larry Peabody filled the miniature villas with authentic antiques, and Oliver had old-print erotic drawings framed to hang in the huge bathrooms. . . . Two and a half million dollars later, Habitation Leclerc was a reality. And for those like Colie Cabot, 'it's a miracle. They've created an elegant oasis in a primitive rain forest'."[38] While OPIC officials admitted that this project was ill-advised because it contributed little to an improvement in the lives of poverty-stricken Haitians, throughout the 1970s they continued to encourage the development of luxury accommodations—ITT and TWA safari lodges in Kenya, Avis Rent-a-Car services in Malaysia and Singapore, ITT-Sheraton, Pan American-Intercontinental, and Gulf + Western hotels in Liberia, Kenya, Indonesia, the Ivory Coast, India, Brazil, Tunisia, and the Dominican Republic.[39]

Opposition to OPIC also came from organized labor, which contended that OPIC activities encouraged the export of jobs. OPIC denied that its activities resulted in lowered levels of employment in

[36] See *OPIC Authorization*, pp. 108, 110-111, *supra* n. 34. OPIC disagrees: See *Extension and Revision of Overseas Private Investment Corporation Programs*, p. 246, *supra* n. 27.

[37] *Town and Country*, January 1976, pp. 124-126.

[38] Ibid., pp. 107, 126. The ex-wife of Henry B. Cabot, Jr., and great-grandaughter of Admiral Andrew Hull Foote, Ms. Cabot notes that although "the Haitians outnumber us 100 to 1—you always feel very safe." The resort has been widely praised by that portion of the U.S. media that caters to the leisure class: "If there is a more stylish and glitteringly elegant island dining room than this small resort features, I haven't seen it yet. . . . Suspend disbelief and you'll enjoy the pretty costumes, the bright smiles and the voodoo drummer." George Lang, "Dining Out in Haiti," *Travel and Leisure*, April 1980, p. 14.

[39] Center for International Policy, "OPIC: Insuring the Status Quo," *International Policy Report* 3 (September 1977): 4. For a list of projects rejected by OPIC, see *Extension and Revision of Overseas Private Investment Corporation Programs*, pp. 123-124, *supra* n. 27.

the United States, but labor's argument attracted the support of influential congressional liberals such as Senator Frank Church, who in
1977 urged the termination of OPIC.[40] On the other hand, Senator
Hubert Humphrey sent a letter to each of his colleagues shortly before
his death, expressing concern over the AFL-CIO's opposition to OPIC:
"It is a rare occasion that I differ with my friends in the AFL-CIO,"
he wrote, but "as a friend of labor, I ask you to support the continuation
of OPIC."[41] Senator Humphrey's position was congruent with that of
the Republican Policy Committee, which endorsed OPIC in part because of its belief that, "contrary to the assertion of the AFL-CIO,"
OPIC creates rather than exports jobs.[42] Spokespersons for the Nixon,
Ford, and Carter administrations all argued that OPIC encourages a
demand for U.S. goods and services and therefore creates rather than
exports jobs. In 1977, the Carter administration quantified its argument by asserting that OPIC projects generated precisely 90,535 per-
son-years of employment in the United States during the years 1974
to 1977.[43]

The principal reason OPIC was able to withstand this substantial
opposition was not the cogency of its rebuttals or the strength of its
allies but the fact that it does not require congressional appropriations.
Since its creation, OPIC's income from insurance premiums has exceeded its costs for claims and operating expenses. In 1977, for example, its net income was $47.8 million. Thus Representative Long's
Appropriations Subcommittee on Foreign Operations conducted illuminating but unfocused hearings on OPIC in 1978, for the subcommittee has traditionally oriented its activities around the criticism and
modification of the administration's budget request. For OPIC there
is no appropriation request to criticize. Congress authorizes the existence of OPIC for a fixed number of years, however, and the periodic
reauthorization process provides the foreign affairs committees with
opportunities to evaluate OPIC activity. During the 1970s, Congress
restricted its oversight to the two occasions when OPIC required an
extension of its charter, and it was during congressional debate over

[40] The AFL-CIO position is detailed in *Extension and Revision of Overseas Private
Investment Corporation Programs*, pp. 353-359, 370-372, *supra* n. 27; *Foreign Assistance
and Related Agencies Appropriations for 1979*, pt. 2, pp. 1144-59, *supra* n. 2. Church's
mild attack is reprinted in *Congressional Record*, October 25, 1977, p. S17693.

[41] Letter dated January 9, 1978. Reprinted in *Congressional Record*, April 6, 1978,
p. S4929.

[42] *Congressional Record*, February 23, 1977, p. H1450.

[43] OPIC *Annual Report 1977*, p. 14.

the second extension in 1977 and 1978 that the issue of human rights was raised.[44]

The question of the relationship between OPIC transactions and U.S. corporate investments in countries ruled by repressive regimes would have surfaced regardless of OPIC's behavior, for the human rights implications of every foreign-assistance related program were analyzed by Congress during the middle and late 1970s. But OPIC was a special target of human rights activists, for a list of the nonsocialist Third World nations with the most repressive governments was not substantially different from a list of nations receiving disproportionate amounts of foreign capital investment and, consequently, OPIC insurance. As Table 8.1 indicates, during the three-year period 1974 to 1976 OPIC activity was concentrated in nations ruled by some of the most repressive governments on earth. No critics suggested that OPIC insurance *caused* human rights violations; rather there were charges that OPIC was assisting U.S.-based multinational corporations to take advantage of the financial benefits of repression. This point arose specifically in association with the AFL-CIO campaign against runaway plants. In a letter to their colleagues, Senators Church and Case argued that "U.S. labor is put in a competitive disadvantage by the

TABLE 8.1
OPIC Insurance by Country Receiving Investment, 1974-1976

Country	Insurance Issued	Percentage of OPIC Total
Brazil	$306,788,000	21.0
Philippines	151,378,000	10.5
South Korea	133,957,000	9.2
Indonesia	127,124,000	8.8
Taiwan	83,638,000	5.8
Dominican Republic	59,380,000	4.1
Yugoslavia	54,294,000	3.8
Total	$916,559,000	63.2

Sources: U.S. Congress, House, Committee on International Relations, Subcommittee on International Economic Policy and Trade, *Extension and Revision of Overseas Private Investment Corporation Programs*, 95th Cong., 1st Sess., June-September 1977, p. 153; Center for International Policy, "OPIC: Insuring the Status Quo," *International Policy Report* 3 (September 1977), p. 3.

[44] The original authorization was for five years. In 1974, the corporation's life was extended three more years (PL93-390), and in 1978 it was extended until 1981 (PL95-268).

repressive labor laws in force in many of the developing countries most favored by U.S. investors. All six countries which have received the most OPIC insurance since 1974 have authoritarian regimes which deny many basic trade union freedoms."[45]

Thus in 1977, when the Carter administration moved to extend OPIC's life for four years, human rights activists launched a major effort to kill OPIC or, failing that, to make the original Harkin amendment applicable to OPIC insurance activity. The issue of human rights did not arise during hearings by the House International Relations Subcommittee on International Economic Policy and Trade or the Senate Foreign Relations Subcommittee on Foreign Assistance.[46] No mention of the subject was added during the course of either committee's markup, and consequently the bills were reported to the full House and Senate without a word about human rights. In October 1977, a brief Senate debate pitted Senator Javits against Senator Church, with the argument centering upon the export of jobs.[47] Senator Church's opposition was perfunctory; after making his brief speech he left the floor, uninterested in responding to Javits' rebuttal. OPIC officials speculated that he was reluctantly fulfilling a request from the AFL-CIO. Senator Javits, conversely, was strongly committed to the continuation of OPIC because of his firm belief that multinational corporations protect free people from totalitarianism: "You have to have these enterprises to hurdle the stupidities and parochialism of the nationalities of the world or the world will go bust and become a large version of the Russian model, a dull grey prison."[48] The Senate passed its version without amendment by a 69 to 12 margin, the largest majority any OPIC legislaton had ever obtained.

The debate on the House floor was considerably more vigorous, reflecting intense anti-OPIC lobbying by human rights interest groups, particularly the Americans for Democratic Action and several church groups. After an amendment to terminate OPIC and its functions failed by a voice vote, Representative Harkin rose and apologetically ("I hope that I am not coming to the well once too often on my human rights amendment") offered an amendment to prohibit OPIC support for any project in a country with a government engaged in a consistent pattern of gross violations of internationally recognized

---

[45] Letter dated October 18, 1977. Reprinted in *Congressional Record*, October 25, 1977, p. S17693.

[46] See *Extension and Revision of Overseas Private Investment Corporation Programs*, *supra* n. 27; *OPIC Authorization*, *supra* n. 34; House Report 95-670; Senate Report 95-505.

[47] *Congressional Record*, October 25, 1977, pp. S17687-S17700.

[48] See *OPIC Authorization*, p. 70, *supra* n. 34.

human rights, unless the insured investment would directly benefit needy people. The Harkin proposal also required an annual report on the projects OPIC refused to support during the preceding year for human rights reasons and on the projects it funded despite human rights violations by employing the "needy people" clause. In the subsequent debate, the Harkin language was weakened by changing the prohibition to a directive that OPIC "take into account" the human rights violations of countries receiving OPIC-assisted investments.[49] Next it was strengthened by an amendment making the original Harkin amendment (Sec. 116) to the Foreign Assistance Act applicable to OPIC-assisted investments in cases where a foreign government is a financial participant. The twice-amended Harkin proposal then passed by a voice vote.

At that point, Carter administration officials apparently believed the bill might not pass, and they asked the House leadership to delay its consideration. For several months, officials from OPIC and the Departments of State and Treasury lobbied on behalf of the authorization. In addition, the representatives of a number of large multinational corporations invested a considerable amount of time mustering support for OPIC in the House. And one senator, Muriel Humphrey, sent a letter to each House member urging that they vote to continue OPIC. In the letter, she noted how her late husband had championed the Corporation. Four months later, the House agreed to extend the life of OPIC by a moderately comfortable margin of 191 to 165.

In conference, the Senate accepted the House human rights provision, but it insisted on a clause permitting the executive branch to ignore human rights considerations whenever OPIC insurance was determined to be in the interest of national security. Although OPIC's acting president personally assured Representative Harkin that this national security argument would never be employed in an effort to override human rights considerations, House human rights activists were apparently not convinced. When the conference report was returned to the House for approval, a handful of members made one last attempt to kill OPIC. It failed, and the conference report was accepted by a substantial (216-185) margin. Human rights activists split evenly on the final vote, with Representatives Drinan, Fraser, Solarz, and Tsongas voting approval because they did not want to place U.S.-based corporations at the comparative disadvantage of being unable to insure their investments against political risks. The

[49] As of 1978, in daily practice, OPIC officials were interpreting the phrase "take into account" as a prohibition.

Senate agreed to the conference report by a voice vote, and OPIC's life was extended until 1981.

As with most Carter administration agencies, OPIC officials made a serious effort to implement the human rights provision that Congress added to its authorizing legislation. By late 1978, OPIC had adopted the policy of not considering insurance applications for investments in several nations with governments engaged in particularly egregious human rights violations.[50] In all other proposed insurance activities, OPIC agreed to solicit the advice of the Bureau of Human Rights and Humanitarian Affairs. Whenever HA objected to a proposal on human rights grounds, OPIC prepared a formal memorandum for State's Bureau of Economic and Business Affairs (EB), setting forth the arguments why the proposal should be approved. EB then distributed the memo to all interested executive branch organizations, asking that they prepare to present their positions at a meeting of the Christopher Committee. At that meeting, the deputy secretary of state decided whether to permit the proposal to be implemented. This procedure was used rather infrequently, primarily because OPIC censored many projects in advance. In addition, because of the weak 1978 human rights clause, HA could contest vigorously only those proposals in which a repressive government had a direct financial interest. In the eight-month period from April 1978, when the OPIC human rights legislation went into effect, and November 1978, OPIC sent 106 insurance proposals to HA. Several were delayed while OPIC negotiated with HA, but only one project was finally vetoed by deputy secretary of state Christopher. This was a proposal to insure the expansion of a Phelps-Dodge facility in El Salvador. OPIC officials were of the opinion that the project would have been approved had the repressive Salvadorean government not held a 23 percent interest in the venture and had the deputy assistant secretary of state for human rights, Mark Schneider, not had a special interest in El Salvador arising out of his service in that country as a Peace Corps volunteer.

The fact that only one OPIC proposal attracted severe human rights scrutiny during a period when other government agencies were under constant pressure from human rights authorities is indicative of the weakness of the arguments advanced by OPIC's opponents. Many liberal foreign policy activists attacked OPIC because it was perceived as a symbol of government attempts to keep the Third World relatively safe for U.S.-based multinational corporations. To the extent that OPIC insured investments in nations with repressive governments,

[50] In Latin America, these included Argentina, Chile, Nicaragua, and Uruguay.

these critics took advantage of the popularity of human rights to attack their primary target, multinational investments. But they were unable to convince more than a few decision makers that OPIC played any but the most marginal role in encouraging repression. At the same time, the argument that other major Western nations supported similar insurance programs convinced many officials that OPIC was, at the very worst, a necessary evil.

COMMERCIAL ARMS SALES

Overseas commercial arms sales by U.S. corporations increased at a truly remarkable rate during the 1970s. As Table 8.2 indicates, between 1968 and 1978 the worldwide increase in U.S. commercial arms deliveries was on the order of 600 percent, an impressive growth by virtually any standard. Yet sales to Latin America did not account for much of this increase: as a proportion of total United States arms sales, sales to Latin American nations actually decreased from 5.1 percent to 2.6 percent between 1968 and 1978. Most of the nineteen

TABLE 8.2
U.S. COMMERCIAL ARMS DELIVERIES TO LATIN AMERICA, FY1968-FY1978
(thousands of dollars)

Country	1968	1969	1970	1971	1972	1973
Worldwide	$257.1	$250.8	$437.6	$480.6	$480.6	$362.1
Latin America	13.1	20.7	29.9	14.5	31.5	19.5
Argentina	3.1	5.6	7.1	1.3	13.9	11.6
Bolivia	.1	.1	.1	.4	.1	.1
Brazil	4.5	6.6	6.1	3.1	.6	.7
Chile	.4	.2	2.4	2.5	.5	.5
Colombia	1.3	2.1	7.7	2.4	.3	.6
Costa Rica	0	0	0	.1	.1	.1
Dominican Republic	0	0	0	*	*	*
Ecuador	.3	.3	1.4	.1	.1	*
El Salvador	.6	1.0	.5	.4	.1	.2
Guatemala	.4	.2	.1	.6	.5	.1
Haiti	0	0	0	.1	.1	.1
Honduras	0	*	0	*	.1	*
Mexico	.5	1.6	.8	1.1	.6	.2
Nicaragua	.2	.1	.2	.3	.2	.2
Panama	*	0	.2	.4	.3	1.7
Paraguay	0	.6	0	*	.1	.1
Peru	.7	.6	1.6	1.1	9.0	.2
Uruguay	0	.4	*	*	.1	*
Venezuela	.7	.9	1.6	.5	4.7	3.1

TABLE 8.2 (cont.)

Country	1974	1975	1976ª	1977	1978	Total
Worldwide	$502.2	$546.6	$1,407.5	$1,523.4	$1,484.9	$7,773.4
Latin America	17.6	20.7	63.7	45.7	38.7	315.6
Argentina	1.3	2.3	3.6	6.3	13.1	69.2
Bolivia	.2	.2	.2	.7	.8	3.0
Brazil	4.0	4.3	44.0	6.1	4.3	84.3
Chile	1.8	.6	1.4	1.3	0	11.6
Colombia	.8	1.0	1.2	7.1	2.4	26.9
Costa Rica	*	.1	.1	.1	.2	.8
Dominican Republic	.1	.3	*	.8	.8	2.0
Ecuador	*	1.1	2.5	.6	.9	7.3
El Salvador	.2	.2	.2	.2	.2	3.8
Guatemala	.2	.5	.3	1.0	.6	4.5
Haiti	.2	.2	.2	.5	.4	1.8
Honduras	.3	.3	.1	.1	1.1	2.0
Mexico	1.2	.8	1.0	2.4	2.1	12.3
Nicaragua	.2	.4	.8	1.6	.4	4.6
Panama	1.8	.3	.5	2.6	.9	8.7
Paraguay	.2	.2	.2	.4	.2	2.0
Peru	.4	.1	2.8	5.3	4.4	26.2
Uruguay	.2	*	.5	.4	.1	1.7
Venezuela	4.5	7.6	4.0	7.9	5.6	41.1

Sources: U.S. Department of Defense, Defense Security Assistance Agency, *Fiscal Year Series, December 1978* (Washington, D.C.: Defense Security Assistance Agency, 1978). Bound computer printout.

———. *Foreign Military Sales and Military Assistance Facts* (Washington, D.C.: Department of Defense, 1977).

ª Includes transition quarter.

* Less than $50,000.

nations listed in Table 8.2 purchased very few weapons directly from U.S. corporations; in fact, three nations (Argentina, Brazil, and Venezuela) accounted for 62 percent of the total sales of $316 million during the eleven-year span. Although large annual fluctuations make generalizations impossible, in no single year have commercial transactions equalled half the size of FMS credits from the U.S. government. Over the period 1968 to 1978, the ratio was about one dollar in government-to-government arms transfers for every seventeen cents in commercial sales.

There are three reasons why commercial arms sales to Latin America appear low. First, total military expenditures are relatively low: on the average, Latin American nations simply do not spend as much money on arms as most nations in other regions of the world. In 1976, a typical year, Latin America's share of world military expenditures was

1 percent. While the United States was spending 5.4 percent of its GNP on military goods and services, the average for Latin America was 1.8 percent. Latin America accounted for only 6 percent of world arms imports in 1976.[51]

Second, with the exception of the World War II period, Latin American nations have traditionally relied upon a variety of suppliers, particularly European nations and, increasingly, Israel. Much is often made of the fact that the U.S. share of the Latin American arms market declined from its World War II monopoly. Since the late 1960s, the United States has ranked fifth or sixth in arms shipments to the region. In general, Europe's share of sales to Latin America peaked in 1970, however, and throughout the 1970s the distribution of Latin American arms purchases was characterized by sharp annual fluctuations. In one year (1973-1974), Europe's share of the Latin American market dropped from about 70 percent to 30 percent, for example, while the U.S. share increased from less than 10 percent to over 40 percent. Most of this shift can be attributed to sales of F-5E fighter and A-37B light attack aircraft to Brazil and Chile.[52] One or two major sales of aircraft or guided missiles swing the pendulum dramatically.

Finally, United States arms sales to Latin America have not grown in proportion to the worldwide increase because the U.S. government has discouraged many of the most expensive types of commercial transfers. Beginning in 1966 and 1967, both Congress and the executive branch have acted to halt government-assisted transfers of advanced weapons. The foreign aid appropriations act for FY1968 (PL90-249) contained a formal prohibition on FMS credits to Latin American countries for the purchase of sophisticated weapons systems such as missiles and jet aircraft, a restriction added annually until 1971. In the meantime, a similar provision was added to the Foreign

[51] U.S. Arms Control and Disarmament Agency, *World Military Expenditures and Arms Transfers 1967-1976* (Washington, D.C.: Government Printing Office, July 1978), pp. 2, 9, 30, 66.

[52] U.S. National Advisory Council on International Monetary and Financial Policies, *Annual Report 1977* (Washington, D.C.: Government Printing Office, 1978), pp. 116-117; U.S. National Advisory Council on International Monetary and Financial Policies, *Annual Report 1976* (Washington, D.C.: Government Printing Office, 1977), p. 92. For an illuminating discussion of the distribution of the Latin American arms trade, see the Congressional Research Service study in U.S. Congress, House, Committee on International Relations, Subcommittee on Inter-American Affairs, *Arms Trade in the Western Hemisphere*, 95th Cong., 2d Sess., June-August 1978, pp. 227-231. For an early discussion of U.S. policy toward commercial arms trade with Latin America, see Elton Atwater, *American Regulation of Arms Exports* (Washington, D.C.: Carnegie Endowment for International Peace, 1941).

Assistance Act of 1968 (PL90-554), which remained in force until 1973. While this legislation affected only government transactions, its effect was to discourage commercial sales as well.

The policy of restraint was reversed in 1973, when President Nixon notified Congress that

> our hopes that by unilaterally restricting sales we could discourage our Latin neighbors from diverting money to military equipment and away from development needs have proven unrealistic. And the cost to us has been considerable: in friction with Latin American governments because of our paternalism, and in valuable military relationships which, in turn, provide an important channel of communication across a wide spectrum and influence our total relationship. The domestic costs are also high: in lost employment for our workers, lost profit for business, and loss of Balance of Payments advantage for our nation.[53]

Thus in June 1973, the Nixon administration announced the sale of F-5E fighters to Argentina, Brazil, Chile, Colombia, and Venezuela. Soon after, Congress responded to the President's request and repealed restrictions on *grant* military aid to Latin America. The Foreign Assistance Act of 1974 subsequently repealed the dollar *ceiling* on FMS credits to Latin America.[54] The Arms Export Control Act (PL90-629) continues to restrict FMS *credits* for the purchase of sophisticated weapons by less developed countries, however, and it also requires a halt in FMS credits to any less developed country that, in the opinion of the President, is diverting its own resources to unnecessary military expenditures.[55]

Alarmed by the growth in arms sales during the Nixon-Ford years, in May 1977 President Carter announced a new policy designed to constrain what he termed "the virtually unrestricted spread of conventional weapons." Noting that the United States at the time accounted for more than half of the $20 billion annual arms trade, the President established a set of six controls applicable to all transfers except to those countries with which the United States has major defense treaties. Of the six, only one had a significant impact upon the commercial arms trade with Latin America. The first control, a dollar ceiling on arms transfers, specifically excluded commercial sales:

[53] U.S. President (Nixon), *U.S. Foreign Policy for the 1970's: Shaping a Durable Peace; A Report to the Congress, May 3, 1973* (Washington, D.C.: Government Printing Office, 1973), p. 119.

[54] PL90-629, Sec. 33, repealed by PL93-559, Sec. 45(a). The grant-related restriction in PL87-195, Sec. 507 was repealed by PL93-189, Sec. 12(b).

[55] PL90-629, Sections 4 and 35.

"Commercial sales are already significantly restrained by existing legislation and Executive Branch policy," reported the President. Each of the next four controls (on introducing advanced weapons systems into a region, on developing advanced weapons systems solely for export, on coproduction of significant weapons, and on the retransfer of U.S. weapons to a third country) had long been a part of United States policy toward arms sales to Latin America.

The one control that affected Latin America was a prohibition on the use of embassy and military representatives abroad to promote the sale of arms. To implement this restriction, the State Department sent each embassy guidelines to be followed in contacts with commercial firms:

> Although post should treat representatives of U.S. firms selling arms with same courtesies as other U.S. businessmen and may supply basic business information and services to them (e.g., access to commercial library, names and addresses, information about local customs regulations and commercial law, etc.), mission personnel should not facilitate sale of significant combat equipment by providing such services as advice on tactics for making a sale, assistance in appointments with host government officials, or special support of any kind which might imply that USG endorses a particular sale or is likely to provide USG financing when that fact has not been established.[56]

Despite this one significant change, in general the Carter policy of restraint had a minor direct impact upon commercial sales to Latin America. It should be remembered, however, that these transfers were already quite modest.

The importance of the Carter administration's policy was not in its direct impact upon arms transfers to Latin America but in its general tone of restraint. According to the new policy, "the United States will henceforth view arms transfers as an exceptional foreign policy implement, to be used only in instances where it can be clearly demonstrated that the transfer contributes to our national security interests. We will continue to utilize arms transfers to promote our security and the security of our close friends. But, in the future, the burden

[56] U.S. Department of State, Bureau of Politico-Military Affairs, Office of Munitions Control, *Munitions Control Newsletter*, no. 61 (October 1978), p. 6. In addition, the presidential policy statement resulted in a number of changes in the International Traffic in Arms Regulations (ITAR). One such alteration (ITAR Part 123) required the approval of the Department of State before a sales proposal is made by a commercial firm to sell significant combat equipment. For a text of the Carter policy, see *Weekly Compilation of Presidential Documents* 13 (May 23, 1977), pp. 756-757.

of persuasion will be on those who favor a particular arms sale, rather than those who oppose it."[57] This shift provided the justification that the Bureau of Human Rights and Humanitarian Affairs needed to participate actively in decision making on arms export licenses to repressive Latin American governments.

Decision Making: Participants and Processes

The United States government has long been a participant in commercial arms transfers overseas through its control over export licenses. Whenever a corporation wishes to export any item on the Munitions List, it must apply to the State Department for a license.[58] Within the Department of State, the Office of Munitions Control (MC) in the Bureau of Politico-Military Affairs is responsible for processing all requests for licenses to export goods on the Munitions List. Unlike the Office of Security Assistance and Sales, its bureaucratic twin in charge of government-to-government sales, MC does not receive requests indirectly from the Department of Defense; a corporation applies directly to MC for permission to export a specific quantity of specific items to a specific nation. Once a corporation has submitted an application for an export license, MC processes it in much the same way SAS processes an FMS credit proposal. Copies of the application form are sent to any executive branch agency or bureau that has informed MC of its interest in arms export licenses. No attempt is made to exclude any participant. The reviewing organizations have twenty working days to submit a reservation, accompanied by a brief explanation of why the application should be denied or modified. If Munitions Control cannot resolve a dispute arising from a reservation, the license is delayed while the request is sent to the undersecretary of state for security assistance.[59]

When compared to its influence upon military aid policy, Congress's control of commercial arms transfers is relatively limited. In 1976,

---

[57] Weekly Compilation of Presidential Documents 13 (May 23, 1977): 756.

[58] The Munitions List is a complex document that was formally created in 1954 by the Mutual Security Act, although an equivalent list had existed since passage of the 1938 Neutrality Resolution. The list contains twenty-two categories of arms, ammunition, and implements of war, ranging from ballistic missiles and submarines to speech scramblers and dimethylaminoethoxycyanophospine, a nerve gas. The list is maintained by the Department of State with the assistance of the Department of Defense.

[59] In theory, PM cannot force the resolution of a dispute, since a reviewing organization submits its reservation at the assistant secretary or bureau level. In practice, PM attempts to negotiate a bureau-level agreement whenever possible. If this cannot be accomplished, PM writes the action memorandum to forward the issue to the undersecretary of state.

Congress sought to exert greater influence over arms sales by including in its military assistance bill a provision that all purchases of major defense articles valued over $25 million be made through government rather than commercial channels. This would have had the effect of establishing greater congressional control over large transactions, since Section 36(b) of the Arms Export Control Act permits rejection of a proposed government-to-government arms transfer by a concurrent resolution. This was one provision that President Ford cited as a cause of his veto of the first 1976 military aid authorization bill (S. 2662) on May 7, 1976: "Congress can, by duly adopted legislation, authorize and prohibit such actions as the execution of contracts or the issuance of export licenses, but Congress cannot itself participate in the Executive functions of deciding whether to enter into a lawful contract or issue a lawful license, either directly or through the disapproval procedures contemplated in this bill. . . . The President cannot . . . speak for the nation authoritatively in foreign affairs if his decisions under authority previously conferred can be reversed by a bare majority of the Congress."[60] Unable to override the President's veto, Congress ignored Ford's reservation when it rewrote the 1976 military aid authorization bill. Several key sections were modified, but the provision that large transactions—the limit was raised to $100 million in 1980—be conducted by the government was retained.[61]

In addition to this 1976 provision, the Arms Export Control Act prohibits Eximbank credits to finance military sales to any less-developed country.[62] All other congressional controls of commercial arms transfers are written in such a way that the executive branch enjoys broad discretion in determining when and under what conditions they should be applied.[63] Congress has also sought to supervise commercial arms transfers by requiring reports from the executive branch and by writing nonmandatory statements of policy. The latter are sense-of-Congress resolutions that the value of export licenses should not exceed 1976 levels and that the United States should exert its leadership "to bring about arrangements for reducing the international trade in

[60] Weekly Compilation of Presidential Documents 12 (May 7, 1976): 829.

[61] PL90-629, Sec. 38(b)(3); PL96-92, Sec. 21; PL96-533, Sec. 107(a). The requirement that sales valued at $100 million or more be made through government channels applies to "major defense articles," which are combat equipment on the Munitions List having a nonrecurring research and development cost of more than $50 million or a total production cost of more than $200 million.

[62] PL90-629, Sec. 32.

[63] An exception is Section 502B (c)(4) of the Foreign Assistance Act of 1916, under which Congress can initiate a termination of arms transfers to repressive governments. A joint resolution to this effect is subject to a presidential veto, however.

implements of war."[64] The reporting requirements are simply obligations for the executive branch to notify Congress thirty days in advance of its intention to grant an export license for any major defense equipment valued at more than $7 million or of any defense articles sold under a contract if the amount is $25 million or more.[65] Finally, Congress requires a fairly detailed quarterly listing of all export licenses for military equipment valued at $1 million or more. While all of this legislation appears to indicate considerable congressional interest in commercial arms transfers, this interest has not been translated into concrete provisions providing Congress with a major influence upon nongovernmental arms sales.

Human Rights and Commercial Arms Transfers

Given this relatively low level of congressional involvement, in the 1970s the executive branch enjoyed considerable freedom in the control of commercial arms transfers. The Nixon-Kissinger State Department used this freedom to its maximum advantage, making arms export licenses a major foreign policy instrument. Because the protection of human rights was not a central concern of that administration, however, the issue of human rights did not enter into decision making on arms transfers. In contrast, the Carter administration considered a recipient government's human rights record before authorizing export licenses. But human rights was a significant variable in only a limited number of cases. In very general terms, the value of human rights violators to U.S. national interests rather than the nature or extent of their violations determined arms sales decisions. As a result, the Carter administration maintained not one but three fairly distinct policies regarding the control of commercial arms sales to repressive regimes.

One of these was for NATO allies, Australia, Japan, and New Zealand. The human rights behavior of the governments of these countries did not enter into deliberations regarding the commercial export of defense articles. They were also exempt from many of the other restrictions placed upon arms sales. For example, sales to these allies were excluded in the calculation of the Carter administration's

[64] PL94-329, Sec. 202.

[65] PL90-629, Sec. 36(c). Congress has no power to take any action if it disapproves of the proposed commercial transaction. Because Sections 36 and 38 are extremely complex, some key members of Congress have a very vague understanding of their role in arms transfers. U.S. Congress, House, Committee on Foreign Affairs, Subcommittee on Inter-American Affairs, *Aircraft Sales in Latin America*, 91st Cong., 2d Sess., April 1970, pp. 13-21. The requirement that Congress be informed of sales over $25 million applies to "defense articles," which are defined as all articles on the Munitions List.

arms export ceiling, the key indicator of the administration's success in controlling arms transfers.[66]

A second arms export policy was for major (i.e., oil-producing) customers in the Third World and for nations such as South Korea and the Philippines that were believed to be contributing to U.S. national security. While human rights considerations entered into the decision-making process on arms exports to these nations, they were generally not of central importance. Human rights issues were given significant attention when a proposed sale was for police-type weapons, but nations in this second category could regularly buy an enormous variety of arms and still engage in the widespread violation of their citizens' rights. If a proposed sale was sufficiently large and the proposed purchaser supportive of U.S. interests in a sensitive region, almost any license request had a fairly high probability of approval.

The third commercial arms export policy was applied to small, nonstrategic customers. With the possible exception of Brazil, Mexico, and Venezuela, all Latin American nations fell into this third category. In addition to being minor purchasers, Latin American nations were believed to be the most marginal threat to national security. During the late 1970s, the governments of these countries found that their requests for export licenses were regularly denied if they were engaged in major violations of human rights.

Certainly this is not to suggest that the flow of arms was significantly restricted for any reason, including human rights. Throughout the 1970s, the overwhelming majority of license applications was approved with a minimum of delay. During FY1978, for example, only 359 applications were rejected out of a total of 23,468 formal requests.[67] While this was a significant growth (111 percent) in the rejection rate during the five years from 1973 through 1978, rejections still constituted less than 2 percent of all requests. The list of license denials is classified, but its contents during the late 1970s were fairly widely known. A few refusals were based upon the type of equipment proposed to be exported: remotely piloted vehicles, heat-seeking missiles, helicopter gunships, cluster bomb units, and some chemical weapons of war.[68] Requests to export Munitions List articles that have special

---

[66] U.S. Department of State, Bureau of Politico-Military Affairs, Office of Munitions Control, *Munitions Control Newsletter*, no. 63 (October 1978), p. 2. Congress had exempted these countries from the prohibition on exports of any major defense equipment valued at $25 million or more. PL90-629, Sec. 38(b)(3).

[67] About 1,400 of these requests were from Latin American governments.

[68] Some of these weapons are not exported because they are too dangerous—nerve gas, for example—while others, such as the hand-held, heat-seeking Redeye missile, are kept at home for fear that they could fall into the hands of terrorists.

policy implications, including silencers, incendiary munitions (napalm, white phosphorus, flame throwers), and delayed-action munitions were also generally refused.

But since exporters rarely requested permission to export items they knew to be on the disapproved list, most license denials were a reflection of the type of government making a request.[69] In the late 1970s, the Office of Munitions Control would not even accept export license requests for three Latin American nations (Argentina, Chile, and Somoza's Nicaragua) because of their human rights records. Congress forced the ban on sales to the first two countries, but the prohibition on sales to Somoza was an internal executive branch decision made in September 1978. The Bureau of Human Rights and Humanitarian Affairs provided most of the initiative to halt licenses for arms to Nicaragua, but after the late-summer eruption of violence in Nicaragua, no executive branch agency wished to be associated with a pro-Somoza position. Indeed, ARA wrote the memorandum that formally halted sales to the Somoza government. With the exception of proposed transfers to Argentina, Chile, and Nicaragua, after 1977 all other decisions on license applications were made on a case-by-case basis. Because each case was handled individually, it is difficult to generalize about policy making. When human rights considerations were involved, an objection by HA to a license for a Latin American country became a fairly accurate but far from infallible indicator that the transfer would not be made. This was particularly true of any request that involved police-type defense articles such as riot shotguns or tear gas; in these cases, the opinion of HA was tantamount to a decision by the government.[70]

Most arms transfers involve equipment such as submarine periscopes and flameproof flight suits whose utility in the support of repression is indirect, and it was over these sales to repressive governments that the major battles occurred within the Carter administration. The general position of HA was that any arms sale to an extremely repressive regime was supportive of repression; ARA and PM argued that the type of defense article should be the determining factor. This conflict arose constantly during 1977 to 1981, and it grew increasingly

[69] U.S. Congress, Senate, Committee on Appropriations, *Department of Defense Appropriations, Fiscal Year 1976*, 94th Cong., 1st Sess., April 8, 1975, pp. 174, 218, 220, 231.

[70] U.S. Congress, House, Committee on International Relations, *Foreign Assistance Legislation for Fiscal Year 1979*, 95th Cong., 2d Sess., March and April, 1978, pt. 2, p. 105. In the 1978 revision of Sec. 502B, Congress prohibited the commercial export of police equipment to countries with governments engaged in serious repression of their citizens' rights. PL95-384, Sec. 6(d)(1).

bitter as HA, with the support of deputy secretary of state Christopher, demonstrated a consistent ability to block sales to Latin America. After repeating the often-heard characterization of HA personnel as "the amateur anarchists of the building," one sales-oriented ARA official admitted that arms transfers to Latin America were now dependent on HA's approval: "Until Human Rights [HA] came along, we never had these troubles. Never have so few filled so large a space in so short a time." This view was shared by officials of the Bureau of Politico-Military Affairs, many of whom cursed with considerable vigor when an interviewer asked for a characterization of HA-PM interaction. This was perhaps an indicator of HA's success in blocking arms transfers to Latin America's repressive governments.

ARA and PM often criticized HA for its intransigence, citing two examples as evidence. One involved a request by Colt Industries to ship 5,000 sling swivels for M-16 rifles to Nicaragua. In 1976, Colt sold the Nicaraguan government 5,000 M-16s, the export license passed effortlessly through the Kissinger State Department, and the weapons were shipped to Managua. Upon their arrival, Nicaraguan officials discovered that the sling swivels—the parts by which the rifle sling is attached to the rifle barrel and stock—were rusted. They notified Colt, which offered to supply 5,000 new swivels at no cost. In the meantime, the Carter administration replaced that of Gerald Ford. In May 1977, HA refused to agree to the issuance of an export license for the replacement swivels, and its position was supported by the deputy secretary of state. In an effort to reverse the decision, ARA sent no fewer than ten memos up the State Department ladder, discussing everything from the improvement of human rights practices by the Somoza government to the damage being visited upon Colt Industries' commercial reputation. HA issued a reservation to every ARA memorandum. When the ban on arms transfers to Nicaragua went into effect in September 1978, the issue of Nicaragua's sling swivels had been sitting on the Secretary of State's desk for more than a year. In late 1978, several officials at ARA and PM were furious over HA's intransigence.

Although the second case is somewhat peculiar because of the congressional ban on arms licenses to Argentina that began on October 1, 1978, the process of decision making on license requests prior to the cutoff but after passage of the restrictive legislation is also suggestive of HA's role in decision making. During the year-long grace period, the Argentine government rushed to purchase in excess of $100 million worth of Munitions List items from U.S. manufacturers. While the export licenses for these goods were being processed, undersecretary of state David Newsom visited Argentina and in return for an agreement by General Videla to reduce repression, he agreed to arrange for approval of export licenses for several Chinook helicopters that were to be used for scientific work in Antarctica. Everyone in the State Department agreed that this carrot failed to elicit the promised behavior from the Argentine government, but it fell to HA to refuse to agree to any license requests for Argentina. Some of these refusals were outright denials, others were requests for more time to review an application. As the deadline on arms shipments approached, ARA and PM became increasingly annoyed with HA, as did the manufacturers whose sales could not be consummated. Attempts were made to obtain approval from HA on the export of certain types of noncombat items on the Munitions List, such as 37mm pilot ejection cartridges. HA refused; ARA and PM became increasingly unhappy: "Those bastards in Human Rights would rather kill an Argentine pilot than give in to us," remarked one military officer attached to PM. "What the hell kind of foreign policy is that?" Finally, deputy secretary of state Christopher accepted HA's advice to return to the stick. On the last working day of FY1978, the Argentine military attachés were called to the Pentagon and told that the State Department had denied requests for 212 licenses representing nearly $100 million worth of U.S. military equipment.

Despite these bureaucratic victories, it is important to note that HA's overall record was not particularly impressive. In general, the Bureau was ineffective in halting large sales—transfers with significant balance of payments implications—by corporations with close ties to powerful members of Congress or to the White House. HA's effectiveness was also hampered by the case approach to export license approvals. This approach, in which policy makers address each case in much the same way that an artist addresses a blank canvas, is much practiced and greatly admired in the Department of State. But as a new, relatively small bureau, HA was penalized by the case approach, for, with the exception of requests involving Argentina, Chile, and Nicaragua, in the late 1970s each license had to be handled as if it were a new issue. This process permitted sensitivity to peculiar circumstances (recent changes in the level of repression, the repressive characteristics of the item being exported, U.S. security considerations, etc.) but at the cost of efficiency and consistency. Not even a large team of artists can perform a creditable job on 23,000 canvases per year. Thus with few exceptions, in the 1970s United States policy toward commercial arms sales to Latin America consisted of general statements whose significance in decision making could not be predicted.

AMERICAN INSTITUTE FOR FREE LABOR DEVELOPMENT

Although the United States government has a long-standing interest in the development of Latin American trade unions, particularly in the training of Latin American union leaders, the American Institute for Free Labor Development (AIFLD) is a child of the Alliance for Progress. In August 1960, the AFL-CIO provided $20,000 in seed money to explore the possibility of creating an educational institution to train Latin American union leaders in various aspects of labor organizing and union operation. With the help of private foundations and corporations, the AFL-CIO inaugurated its first course in June 1961. Two months later, AIFLD was chartered as a private, nonprofit corporation. Shortly thereafter, AID created a labor advisory committee whose first official action was to recommend that the government award AIFLD $350,000 in technical service contracts—$250,000 from AID and $100,000 from the Department of Labor. AIFLD's era of dramatic growth began.

In the years since 1962, AID has provided AIFLD with nearly all of its funds, ranging from a low of about 64 percent of the total AIFLD budget in 1964 to over 90 percent, a level of AID support that has remained fairly constant since 1967. In FY1974, for example, 95 percent of AIFLD's income of $5.7 million was provided by AID grants and contracts. In FY1979, total AID funding of AIFLD reached $6.9 million, a sum representing the entire contract budget of AID's Latin America labor division. From 1962 through 1979, AID provided AIFLD with more than $80 million in technical assistance contracts and grants. By 1971, this was sufficient to rank AIFLD as the fifteenth largest recipient of AID contracts. Although more recent comparative data are not available, there is little doubt that by 1980 AIFLD ranked among the half-dozen largest AID contractors worldwide.[71] AIFLD remained a favored foreign policy instrument of the Carter administration, which in 1980 requested $8 million from Congress for AIFLD activities. According to assistant secretary of state William Bowdler, budget increases were essential because "the labor movements it

[71] Robert H. Dockery, *Survey of the Alliance for Progress: Labor Policies and Programs.* A Study Prepared at the Request of the Subcommittee on American Republics Affairs by the Staff of the Committee on Foreign Relations, United States Senate (Washington, D.C.: Government Printing Office, July 15, 1968), pp. 32-33; Hobart A. Spaulding, Jr., "U.S. and Latin American Labor: The Dynamics of Imperialist Control," in *Ideology and Social Change in Latin America,* ed. June Nash et al. (New York: Gorden and Breach, 1977), p. 67; U.S. Agency for International Development, Bureau for Population and Humanitarian Assistance, Office of Private and Voluntary Cooperation, *Voluntary Foreign Aid Programs* (Washington, D.C.: Agency for International Development, 1975), p. 12.

[AIFLD] reinforces are a key element of pluralistic democracy and an important political as well as economic force."[72]

AIFLD has two central functions. The more important of these is the training of Latin American labor leaders. In the fifteen-year period between 1962 and 1980, AIFLD trained more than 375,000 union officials from Latin America. Nearly all of this training occurred during short in-country seminars in Latin America, but more than 3,000 students have received AIFLD training in the United States. By far the most visible training program was conducted at AIFLD's Front Royal Institute in the Blue Ridge Mountains, northwest of Washington, D.C.[73] The Front Royal program was instituted in 1959 by Joseph Beirne of the Communications Workers of America. In 1966, AIFLD purchased the facility and used it until 1979 to train about 2,900 Latin American labor leaders. Because of the isolation of the Front Royal academy, AIFLD had difficulty obtaining qualified lecturers on a regular basis, and the students complained that their stay at "The Monastery" gave them little exposure to American society. Thus in 1979, Front Royal was closed and AIFLD classes moved to the George Meany Center for Labor Studies in Silver Spring, Maryland, a suburb of Washington, D.C. The Institute's classes average about forty students, with courses lasting approximately six weeks. Participants are selected by AIFLD country directors from among the outstanding graduates of in-country AIFLD programs. Courses cover the standard labor leadership subjects—union structure and finances, collective bargaining, industrial relations—plus a series of classes on comparative economic and political systems.

The second AIFLD function is to fund specific projects related to labor activity in Latin America. These include financing on a small scale a variety of social services such as union-related schools, community centers, and medical clinics. AIFLD also coordinates union-to-union assistance programs, funds the Agrarian Union Development Services to assist peasant organizing, and supports a number of cooperative housing projects for union members. None of these projects is a major developmental effort; most respond to a specific need— sewing machines for an Indian cooperative, typewriters for a union office—and are meant to be symbolic gestures of goodwill.

The executive branch controls all decision making on the size and nature of AIFLD contracts with the Agency for International Development. Specifically, the Labor Programs Division of AID's Bureau for Latin America (AID-LA) funds AIFLD. Like other private vol-

---

[72] Testimony of William G. Bowdler before the Senate Committee on Foreign Relations, April 16, 1980.

[73] About two hundred additional leaders have been trained as labor economists at AIFLD's now-defunct university programs.

untary organizations that work for AID on continuing contracts, AIFLD submits a detailed annual proposal to perform a specific set of tasks for a given sum of money. The proposal is created by AIFLD in extremely close consultation with AID's Labor Programs Division. Perhaps because the administration of AIFLD contracts is the sole activity of this division of AID-LA, the proposal typically enjoys the firm support of the bureaucracy charged with overseeing its activities. AIFLD receives its funds through a single base contract and three small grants. The contract pays for AIFLD education programs, for the maintenance of AIFLD's organization—staff salaries, office support, travel expenses—and for technical assistance to agrarian unions. The primary purpose of the grants is to disguise the source of funds that support various international trade union secretariats (ITSs). Because no ITS wishes to maintain an open link to the U.S. government, AID gives the money to AIFLD, which in turn gives the money to the U.S. unions affiliated with the various secretariats. Then each union gives the money to its ITS.

There is no congressional interest in organized labor in Latin America; therefore there is no interest in United States policy toward the subject. In addition, because AIFLD works on a contractual basis for AID, AIFLD has no corps of government employees for members of Congress to question. Should a subcommittee wish to examine AIFLD activities, it would have had to obtain its information from AIFLD president George Meany. Although Meany protested otherwise, until his death in 1980 he made it clear to Congress that he did not approve of congressional oversight of AIFLD.

The manner in which Meany obtained this freedom provides an unusually clear example of the ability of a powerful interest group to influence policy on a subject of marginal concern to members of Congress. In 1967, Senator Wayne Morse's Foreign Relations Subcommittee on American Republic Affairs launched a survey of the Alliance for Progress, the purpose of which was to determine what had gone wrong with President Kennedy's experiment in planned social change and economic development. The subcommittee hired a young Latin Americanist, Robert Dockery, to produce a study of labor policies and programs. His analysis focused upon AIFLD, touching upon a number of sensitive issues: the extent to which AIFLD was an instrument of U.S. foreign policy, the role of George Meany's virulent anticommunism in causing the rift between the United Auto Workers and the AFL-CIO, and AIFLD's ideological disputes with other trade union organizations in Latin America.[74] Infuriated by these assertions, Meany

[74] See *Survey of the Alliance for Progress: Labor Policies and Programs*, pp. 6-7, 12-13, 15-18, *supra* n. 71.

demanded that Senator Morse repudiate the study in order "to help counteract the damage resulting from the circulation of the Dockery Study on both sides of the Iron Curtain."[75] After Senator Morse's electoral defeat in 1968, the issue appeared to be closed, but then in mid-1969 the chairperson of the Senate Foreign Relations Committee, J. William Fulbright, was quoted by United Press International as suggesting that AID's support of AIFLD was "the price we paid for President George Meany's support of the U.S. Policy in Vietnam."[76] Meany then demanded and received a three and one-half hour hearing by the full Committee on Foreign Relations, at which he was the sole witness. During the hearing, Meany informed the committee's members that the AFL-CIO enjoyed an agreeable relationship with AID and the State Department, the investigation of which need not distract Congress from more pressing activities. Given the potential high costs of angering the president of the AFL-CIO, since 1969 no congressional subcommittee has had the temerity to examine the relationship between the United States government and AIFLD.[77]

The executive branch has long acknowledged its use of the private sector for foreign policy purposes, recognizing that private organizations can perform certain tasks that a government cannot.[78] AIFLD officials also admit that their organization functions in large measure as an instrument of United States policy. One of the few points in Robert Dockery's study that Meany did not contest was the assertion that "the general foreign policy objectives of the U.S. government are the same as those of AIFLD in Latin America. . . . AIFLD personnel have . . . been given de facto quasi-official status in the formulation and implementation of U.S.-Latin American labor pol-

[75] U.S. Congress, Senate, Committee on Foreign Relations, *American Institute for Free Labor Development*, 91st Cong., 1st Sess., August 1, 1969, p. 18.

[76] Ibid., p. 2.

[77] In the past, AIFLD representatives have asked to appear before congressional committees holding hearings on Latin America. See, for example, U.S. Congress, House, Committee on Foreign Affairs, Subcommittee on Inter-American Affairs, *New Directions for the 1970's: Toward a Strategy of Inter-American Development*, 91st Cong., 1st Sess., 1969, pp. 461-480. For subsequent congressional testimony by George Meany that touches upon AIFLD, see U.S. Congress, House, Committee on Foreign Affairs, Subcommittee on International Organizations and Movements, *Winning the Cold War: The U.S. Ideological Offensive*, 88th Cong., 1st Sess., April 30, 1963, pt. 2, pp. 132-158. For a laudatory appraisal of AIFLD activity, see Serafino Romualdi, *Presidents and Peons: Recollections of a Labor Ambassador in Latin America* (New York: Funk and Wagnalls, 1967); for a critical appraisal, see "Argentina: AIFLD Losing Its Grip," *NACLA's Latin America and Empire Report* 8 (November 1974): 3-23.

[78] See, for example, the report on this interaction in Bernard C. Cohen, *The Public's Impact on Foreign Policy* (Boston: Little, Brown, 1973), p. 101.

icy."[79] Nor is there is much controversy over the general aims of United States policy as they relate to AIFLD. According to AIFLD board chairperson J. Peter Grace, one of the coldest of Cold Warriors, "we need to understand that today the choice in Latin America is between democracy and communism. We must bear in mind that we cannot allow communist propaganda to divide us as between liberals and conservatives, or between business and labor, or between the American people and their government. Above all, we have to act together as Americans defending our interests abroad."[80] Earlier, Grace elaborated on AIFLD's role in achieving this goal: "Through the AIFLD business, labor and government have come together to work toward a common goal in Latin America, namely supporting the democratic form of government, the capitalistic system and general well-being of the individual."[81]

One of the most striking impressions an outsider obtains in conversations with AIFLD officials is the profound influence of the AFL-CIO's traditional anticommunism upon AIFLD policy. According to William Doherty, Jr., AIFLD's executive director, "in Latin America, the key question of our times is the future road of their revolution: Toward Communist totalitarianism or toward democracy. For the American labor movement this is one of the paramount, pivotal issues; all other questions . . . must remain secondary."[82] Although written in 1966, these words characterized the thinking of AIFLD officials throughout the 1970s. In mid-1978, George Meany spoke to AIFLD trustees on the origin and continuing purpose of the Institute. Dominating his speech was a fear of communist subversion: "We decided [in 1959] that there was a real threat to our way of life in what had happened in Cuba. . . . Because if all of South America were to go the way of Cuba, we would be pretty much isolated up here trying to preserve a decent, free way of life in the Northern Hemisphere. . . . And while we [in 1978] have come a long way, our job is not finished. Castro is very, very busy now in Africa, but that doesn't

[79] See *Survey of the Alliance for Progress: Labor Policies and Programs*, p. 16, *supra* n. 71.

[80] *American Institute for Free Labor Development: A Union to Union Program for the Americas* (Washington, D.C.: American Institute for Free Labor Development, 1980), p. 7.

[81] See *Survey of the Alliance for Progress: Labor Policies and Programs*, p. 15, *supra* n. 71. It is important to note that AIFLD is not a labor oranization but a cooperative venture between the AFL-CIO and a large number of prominent U.S.-based multinational corporations. In addition to a representative of W. R. Grace and Company, the AIFLD board contains representatives of Anaconda Copper, Gulf Oil, Johnson and Johnson, Merck, Owens-Illinois, and Pan American World Airways.

[82] Ibid., p. 13. See also *Winning the Cold War*, pp. 132-158, *supra* n. 77.

337

mean that if he is successful there he will not turn his attention again to the Western Hemisphere."[83] When and if Castro does make such a decision, AIFLD will be waiting to do battle. Latin America is the AFL-CIO's Cold War battleground, labor leaders its warriors, education its ammunition.

Underlying this policy is a belief held by AIFLD officials that a "free" trade union cannot be a "leftist" trade union and that "free trade unionism" cannot survive in a socialist state.[84] In fact, AIFLD officials reject the proposition that democratic socialism is feasible. AIFLD has therefore found itself involved, willy-nilly, in repressing the rights of union leaders whom it defines as threats to free trade unionism. Obviously, the repression of human rights is not an overt goal of AIFLD activity; rather it is more appropriate to view AIFLD's effect upon the Latin American labor movement as similar to the impact of IMET programs upon the Latin American military. AIFLD selects its students carefully, provides them with skills that are largely unavailable to other union leaders in the region, and then sends them home to defend "free trade unionism." In practice that means they are prepared to assist antileftist forces. AIFLD executive director Doherty told a radio audience in 1964 that "what happened in Brazil on April 1 did not just happen—it was planned—and planned months in advance. Many of the trade union leaders—some of whom were actually trained in our institute—were involved in the revolution, and in the overthrow of the Goulart regime."[85] No one would suggest that AIFLD made any but the most minor contribution to the Brazilian coup that led to the durable repression of Brazil's trade union movement. But AIFLD trained (and some would say indoctrinated) persons whose skills could be used to assist in the repression of Goulart's

[83] AIFLD *Report* 16 (June-July 1978): 1, 3. In 1979, as part of its ongoing campaign against what it refers to as "communism," AIFLD inaugurated a new program of activities called "Political Theories Courses" to "provide intensive and comprehensive training for trade union instructors who would become high-level educators in the complex field of ideologies as they affect trade union development." In 1979, pilot training programs were held in Colombia, Costa Rica, the Dominican Republic, and Honduras. AIFLD, *Annual Progress Report, 1962-1980: 18 years of Partnership for Progress* (Washington, D.C.: American Institute for Free Labor Development, 1980), p. 1.

[84] According to AIFLD's Doherty, "the great bulk of the 20 million organized workers in Latin America think, want, and desire almost identically with their counterpart workers in the United States. They know when industry is nationalized that collective bargaining for the most part goes out the window. They know that when the government steps in to run an industry, that the private individual, free trade unionism, and private free industry also go out the window." See *Survey of the Alliance for Progress: Labor Policies and Programs*, p. 15, *supra* n. 71.

[85] Ibid.

338

supporters in the Brazilian labor movement. One highly favorable report on AIFLD noted that in postcoup Brazil, "the new military regime promptly appointed four AIFLD graduates to clean out the Red-dominated unions and restore democratic processes."[86]

In addition to charges that AIFLD encourages repression by providing skills that are used to undermine democratic but left-leaning unions and governments, there is also the more direct allegation that AIFLD assists the Central Intelligence Agency. While other studies have made general accusations of AIFLD-CIA relations,[87] the most detailed accusations have come from Philip Agee. Agee recounts that the control of Latin American labor unions was given high priority during his CIA training. In one class, Lloyd Haskins, executive secretary of the International Federation of Petroleum and Chemical Workers and an AIFLD affiliate, lectured CIA trainees on the control of Latin American petroleum workers.[88] Once out of training, Agee apparently became quite familiar with AIFLD operations. He described AIFLD's William Doherty and AFL-CIO inter-American representative Andrew McClellan as CIA agents directed by CIA covert action staff officers and detailed the time and purpose of their visits to his post in Uruguay. One diary entry reports, for example:

> Station labour operations continue to be centered in the Uruguayan Institute of Trade Union Education, which is the Montevideo office of the AIFLD. Jack Goodwyn, Director of the Institute, is working closely with Lee Smith, the station covert-action officer, in order to develop a pool of anti-CNT labour leaders through the training programmes of the Institute. The most effective programme, of course, is the one in which trainees are paid a generous salary by the Institute for 9 months after completion of the training program, during which time they work exclusively in union organizing under Goodwyn's direction. It is this organizational work that is the real purpose of the AIFLD, so that eventually our trade union can take national leadership away from the CNT. Goodwyn's job, in addition to the training programme, is to watch carefully for prospective agents who can

---

[86] Eugene H. Methvin, "Labor's New Weapon for Democracy," *Reader's Digest*, October 1966, p. 28.

[87] Richard J. Barnet, *Roots of War* (New York: Atheneum, 1972), p. 41; Jan Knippers Black, *United States Penetration of Brazil* (Manchester, Eng.: Manchester University Press, 1977), pp. 111-124.

[88] Philip Agee, *Inside the Company: CIA Diary* (Middlesex, Eng.: Penguin Books, 1975), p. 136.

be recruited by Smith under arrangements that will protect Good-wyn.[89]

Given the very detailed nature of Agee's assertations that AIFLD and the AFL-CIO cooperate with the CIA in its covert activity in Latin America, it is notable that neither AIFLD nor the AFL-CIO offered a rebuttal. The official reply to Agee was a countercharge by Ernie Lee, the director of the AFL-CIO's international division: "We don't dignify with a response the claims of someone who is under the control of the KGB."[90] More candid respondents provided somewhat greater insight into AIFLD-CIA interaction. During the course of one interview in Washington in 1978, an AIFLD official suggested that his organization's relationship with the CIA is based upon an ad-hoc, almost accidental cooperation:

> We feel proud of the [labor organizing, cooperatives, etc.] that we're doing, so that there's so much to do in those areas that normally we don't have to run out and get ourselves into any major problems by doing what we shouldn't be doing. I'm not saying that we don't do it [collaborate with the CIA] or that we haven't done it in the past, but it's more something we do that perhaps at the time we don't realize it might be wrong. It [the action] could be construed to be correct or it could be construed to be wrong depending upon how you look at it. That situation always arises and then you have to make a value judgment, de-pending upon the perspectives and the views of the party looking at it.

Agee and others argue that the CIA's control over AIFLD activities is not nearly as capricious as this statement would suggest; rather they contend that AIFLD is the creation of the CIA, funded by AID but directed by the CIA. There is no way for an outside observer to determine which position is truthful.

This discussion of four institutionalized linkages between the United States government and its private sector was not intended to be an exhaustive analysis of the trilateral relationship between the U.S. government, its private citizens, and human rights violators in Latin America. In particular, it has not addressed the issue of the influence of corporate preferences upon foreign policy. More modest in scope, the present chapter has concentrated upon the manner in which four

[89] Ibid., p. 473. See also Black, *United States Penetration of Brazil*, pp. 119-121.
[90] Interview with Ernie Lee, Washington, D.C., May 3, 1978.

areas of public-private interaction were related to the nation's human rights policy during the 1960s and 1970s.

The overall extent of the government's exploitation of relationships betweeen its private sector and Latin America is unknown. Certain forms of cooperation are matters of public record: for example, the CIA's use of U.S.-based corporations to provide cover for its personnel and information for its analysts. It is also evident that the government on occasion asks these corporations for assistance in bringing direct pressure upon Latin American governments, as in early 1960, when Treasury Secretary Robert Anderson personally urged executives of Exxon, Shell, and Texaco not to refine Soviet crude oil in their Cuban refineries.[91] But it is not clear whether the few rather sensational public examples are typical of public-private cooperation in the pursuit of U.S. policy objectives in Latin America. Rather than dwell upon this unanswerable question, it is more illuminating to approach the issue from another perspective by looking at the potentially powerful private sector relationships that the government did *not* use during the 1970s to promote its human rights policy in Latin America.

In general, both the Nixon-Ford and Carter administrations were extremely reluctant to request private sector cooperation in efforts to pressure repressive governments to cease their human rights violations. Since the Nixon administration placed little emphasis upon the human rights component of foreign policy, its decision not to ask private corporations for assistance seems natural; but the absence of such an effort by the Carter administration was one of the most striking characteristics of its human rights policy. After 1977, the attentive public became accustomed to verbal flourishes on behalf of human rights, to cuts in economic and military aid, to pressure through MDBs, and even to an occasional halt in Eximbank or OPIC financing. In many cases, however, for every dime halted by the U.S. government, a dollar was sent to repressive governments by U.S. corporations. This vitiated the Carter human rights policy for, as even fairly friendly critics noted, "official bilateral assistance became irrelevant when billions of dollars in private resources were available for the asking."[92] Given the prominence of human rights in the administration's policy toward Latin America, it might have been expected that policy makers

[91] Philip W. Bonsal, "Cuba, Castro, and the United States," *Foreign Affairs* 45 (January 1967): 272. On the Nixon administration and Chile, see U.S. Congress, Senate, Select Committee to Study Governmental Operations with Respect to Intelligence Activities, *Covert Action in Chile 1963-1973*, 94th Cong., 1st Sess., 1975, pp. 11-13, 25.

[92] Albert Fishlow, "Flying Down to Rio: Perspectives on U.S.-Brazil Relations," *Foreign Affairs* 57 (Winter 1978-1979): 395.

would take some action when their public goals were thwarted by private actions. Yet the Carter administration did nothing.

The case of Chile attracted the most attention. In the years immediately following the 1973 coup, private investors remained wary of sending their funds to Chile. But then as Congress and, later, the Carter administration began to halt public support of the Chilean government, U.S.-based multinational corporations stepped in. Two investments in early 1978 broke the lull that had existed since the Frei administration. Exxon Corporation purchased for $107 million the state-owned La Disputada de las Condes copper complex and Goodyear Tire purchased for $34 million the state-managed CORFO-INSA tire company. Attracted by generous incentives from the Pinochet government, U.S.-based MNCs slowly began to return to Chile. By mid-1979, these investments had become so substantial that hardly anyone noticed when Anaconda Copper, now a subsidiary of Atlantic-Richfield, handed the Chilean government a check for $20 million and took control of the unexploited Pelambres copper deposit. Despite the clear U.S. government policy of halting aid to Chile, business was as usual once more.

Even more striking than corporate investments in mining and manufacturing was the support of the Pinochet government by private multinational banks. As public sources of external aid declined, private borrowings, which had been insignificant in 1974, increased to $100 million in 1975, to $520 million in 1976, to $858 million in 1977, and to an estimated $977 million in 1978.[93] Noting that these loans exceeded by far what could have been expected from official bilateral and multilateral assistance, House Banking Committee chairperson Reuss sent telegrams to six U.S. banks, suggesting that their loans "appear inconsistent" with the accepted banking policy of not interfering with U.S. foreign policy. The full explanation demanded by Reuss was never forthcoming—indeed Reuss did not pursue the matter beyond his telegram—and the United States banking community continued to finance the Pinochet government.[94]

Given the very active human rights policy of the Carter administration, it is difficult to be certain why no serious attempt was made to influence private sector transactions that supported repressive governments in Latin America. Although this foreign policy implement was used for other purposes ranging from the isolation of Cuba to the

[93] Isabel Letelier and Michael Moffitt, "Human Rights, Economic Aid, and Private Banks: The Case of Chile," mimeographed, a Report Submitted to the Subcommittee on Prevention of Discrimination and Protection of Minorities, United Nations Commission on Human Rights, April 1978, p. 14.

[94] *Washington Post*, April 13, 1978, p. A19.

promotion of majority rule in Rhodesia, apparently the costs of in-terference were too high. Facing an enormous balance of payments deficit and a highly vocal, well-connected business community, the administration was extremely reluctant to halt any potential source of foreign trade or profit. Reinforced by Congress's refusal to adopt binding human rights amendments to legislation governing public support for private transactions, the Carter administration decided that the financial and political costs outweighed the potential hu-manitarian benefits of a policy of interference.

CONCLUSION

Wʜᴇɴ Anastasio Somoza fled Nicaragua in mid-1979, he told a group of reporters awaiting his arrival in Miami that "the Nicaraguan people have not thrown me out. I was thrown out by an international conspiracy that today has a majority of communists and that today desired Nicaragua to be a communist country." At the time, most analysts disagreed with this assessment, concluding instead that the Nicaraguans were in fact responsible. Desirous of changing their government for the first time in four decades, the people of Nicaragua forced the Somoza family to take up permanent residence abroad.

While many Nicaraguans struggled for decades against the Somoza family and its National Guard, they were clearly assisted by outside forces, including the governments of Costa Rica, Cuba, Panama, Venezuela, and, in the end, the United States. No one will ever be able to determine precisely the contribution of the United States to Somoza's downfall, but there can be no doubt that the Carter administration eventually took the lead in determining the conditions under which power would be passed to the Sandinista-dominated junta. Over the course of two years, the administration very slowly, very cautiously withdrew support from the Somoza government. Then in late 1978, after it had become clear at every level of the U.S. policy-making apparatus that there would be neither peace nor stability in Nicaragua until Somoza was replaced, the administration began to work actively toward his ouster. In the end, it was U.S. ambassador Lawrence Pezzullo who informed Somoza of his options: he could continue the struggle, in which case the United States would recognize the rebel junta in a provisional capital just north of the Costa Rican border, or he could leave for Florida. If he chose to continue the fight and eventually lost, he would not be admitted to the United States.[1]

How different it seemed. With the notable exception of the Alliance

[1] It is difficult to overemphasize the fact that Ambassador Pezzullo's ultimatum came very late in the struggle. As the preceding chapters have demonstrated repeatedly, the Carter administration accepted the establishment of a Sandinista-dominated government with extreme reluctance. Only after it became evident that all other alternatives to the Somoza government had either joined the Sandinista-led coalition or demonstrated the inability to form a government, and only after the failure of an embarrassingly naive attempt to gain OAS approval of an LBJ-style inter-American peacekeeping force, only then did Carter administration officials accept the inevitable. This process of searching for an alternative to both Somoza and the Sandinistas has a number of historical precedents, including United States policy toward Cuba in late 1958.

for Progress, the Latin American policy of recent administrations had been characterized by an intervention aimed at halting social and political change, each justified by the need to counter a communist threat: Eisenhower and Guatemala, Kennedy and Cuba, Johnson and the Dominican Republic, Nixon and Chile. As the 1970s ended, few United States citizens felt any sense of pride about the behavior of their government in these interventions; many members of the attentive public were ashamed. They therefore were both pleased and surprised to note that United States policy toward Nicaragua did not appear to be a continuation of the discredited policies of the past. To many liberal citizens, the fall of the Somoza dynasty represented a major victory for progressive values in foreign policy, a symbol of the difference between the overbearing anticommunism of an earlier era and the new emphasis upon humanitarian considerations.

Like the Cuban revolution two decades earlier, the dramatic change of government in Nicaragua seemed to mark the end of yet another chapter in Latin American-United States relations and thus a convenient point at which to conclude this study of U.S. human rights policy. The downfall of Somoza may not prove to be a definitive moment in inter-American relations, but it probably will stand as the principal political event in Latin America during the human rights years. It was a logical pause that permits an assessment of United States policy toward human rights during the 1970s.

Policies are commonly judged by comparing their goals with their results. In the case of human rights, the preeminent goal of the late 1970s was to encourage a reduction in the level of gross violations of the physical integrity of the person or, failing that, to dissociate the United States from the governments responsible for the violations. An additional goal was to encourage the reconstruction or creation of liberal democratic political systems. This concluding chapter will begin by evaluating the extent to which these goals were reached by the end of the 1970s. In many Latin American countries, of course, such an evaluation is premature and should be viewed primarily as an attempt to highlight human rights practices at the beginning of the 1980s, not an attempt to balance the books on a decade of human rights activity.

The process of implementing policies often produces unexpected ancillary results that have long-term implications beyond a specific issue area. So it was that the human rights policy caused a variety of changes in foreign policy-making processes. Because each is of potential significance in determining the future of humanitarian values in United States foreign policy, it is appropriate to conclude with an analysis of the human-rights related changes that occurred in United

345

States foreign policy during the 1970s and an evaluation of their contribution to our understanding of the policy-making process.

Continuity and Change in Human Rights Practices

The Physical Integrity of the Person

In several Latin American countries, the 1970s ended with a considerable increase in the level of respect for human rights related to the physical integrity of the person—the rights to be free from torture, cruel and inhuman treatment, and prolonged detention without trial. The primary example was Brazil, where, by 1980 the use of torture by federal authorities had been reduced to extremely low levels, the physical abuse of prisoners had been curbed considerably (but still not eliminated, especially at the local level), and the widely publicized vigilantism by right-wing paramilitary groups had ceased in the area of political dissent. Extragovernmental executions of petty criminals and police abuse of groups of abandoned children remained serious problems in some urban centers. In 1978, President Ernesto Geisel annulled the arbitrary government powers granted by the series of institutional acts. His successor, João Baptista de Oliveira Figueiredo, subsequently reinstituted *habeas corpus* for political offenses. The results of these moves were sufficiently impressive to lead Amnesty International to report in late 1979 that Brazilian jails contained fewer than seventy political prisoners.[2] Soon thereafter, a Christmas amnesty granted freedom to all but about ten to twenty political prisoners who were alleged to have committed violent political crimes.

Nevertheless, some serious human rights problems continued in Brazil. While annulling the institutional acts, for example, President Geisel replaced them with safeguards (*salvaguardas*) permitting the president to initiate a state of emergency over congressional opposition. In addition, AI reported isolated but politically significant cases of torture, a number of political arrests, the harassment of returning exiles, and several ominous cases of kidnappings and disappearances of Uruguayan and Argentine exiles residing in Brazil. Nevertheless, these violations were properly viewed as exceptions to the general trend toward greater respect for the integrity of the person.

There were some significant decreases in violations of the physical integrity of the person elsewhere in Latin America, but in no case were these changes as dramatic as those that occurred in Brazil. In Cuba, President Castro announced in September 1978 that he had

[2] *Amnesty International Report 1979* (London: Amnesty International Publications, 1979), p. 51.

reached an agreement with the Cuban exile community to release all 3,000 incarcerated "counterrevolutionaries" and 600 persons imprisoned for attempting to flee the island illegally. With the release of the final 382 detainees in October 1979, there were few remaining political prisoners in Cuba.[3] Similarly, in the Dominican Republic, amnesty legislation proposed by the new government of Antonio Guzmán led to the release of about 200 political prisoners, although in late 1979 Amnesty International announced that some individuals remained in jail for political crimes. In Bolivia, the general amnesty announced by President Banzer in January 1978 apparently was implemented without exception. For a very brief period in late 1979, both the U.S. State Department and Amnesty International agreed that for the first time in living memory there were no political prisoners in Bolivian jails. In Mexico, a similar amnesty law promulgated in September 1978 led to the release of 1,589 persons in the following twelve months, but AI and a variety of Mexican human rights groups noted that only a minority of these could be classified as political prisoners and that in any event a significant number of political prisoners remained in custody. To many human rights authorities, including officials of the State Department's Bureau of Human Rights and Humanitarian Affairs, the positive human rights impact of the partial amnesty was balanced by an increase in the number of disappeared persons and the resurgence of paramilitary vigilante groups whose targets included students, labor leaders, and peasants involved in land tenure disputes, as well as individuals suspected of leftist guerrilla activity.[4]

These relatively minor changes, along with the more substantial change in Brazil and the major change in Nicaragua, were the extent of the good news regarding increased respect for the physical integrity of the person in Latin America in the late 1970s. In much of the region, the outlook for these basic human rights remained bleak, and even the few bright spots appeared only after dissenters had been eliminated or intimidated into silence, not after a decision had been reached to permit dissent. In its January 1980 *Newsletter*, Amnesty International issued a discouraging overview of human rights in 1979:

> In much of the Americas, politically motivated disappearances, extra-judicial executions and long-term detention without charge

[3] About four hundred to six hundred former public officials convicted of committing crimes during the Batista period remained in prison.

[4] U.S. Congress, House, Committee on Foreign Affairs, and Senate, Committee on Foreign Relations, *Country Reports on Human Rights Practices for 1979*, 96th Cong., 2d Sess., February 4, 1980, pp. 359-367; *Amnesty International Report 1979*, pp. 67-68.

or trial were still common, often under emergency legislation providing legal cover for repression. States of siege, special security measures or similar legislation were in force in Argentina, Brazil, Chile, Colombia, Paraguay, Uruguay, and periodically in El Salvador and Peru. Political murder and torture, sometimes by security forces or para-military death squads, were widespread.

These remarks echoed those from the International Seminar on Human Rights in Latin America, which met in Ecuador in late 1978. Seminar participants passed resolutions praising some governments but denouncing those of Argentina, Chile, Uruguay, Paraguay, Guatemala, El Salvador, and Haiti for "arbitrarily detained political prisoners, tortures, and disappeared." Each of these cases merits brief individual attention, for when combined they illustrate the extraordinary range of human rights violations in Latin America at the end of the 1970s.

Among the most serious human rights violations were those that occurred in Argentina, a primary focus of U.S. human rights policy. In late 1979, Amnesty International accused the Videla government of continuing to hold 3,000 political prisoners and of being responsible for the disappearance of 15,000 to 20,000 citizens since the 1976 coup. Assessments of the magnitude of the problem differed. The number of disappeared persons, a euphemism for political murder preceded by interrogation and torture of citizens not charged with any crime, was said by the State Department to have declined significantly in Argentina from many thousands in 1976 and 1977 to about 500 in 1978 and to 44 in 1979. But to AI, the practice remained so prominent that in 1979 its researchers could find "no significant improvement in human rights. Thousands of people are in preventive detention without charge or trial, and thousands remain unaccounted for."[5] An extremely detailed list of disappeared persons maintained by Argentina's nongovernmental Permanent Assembly for Human Rights documented 6,500 cases of disappeared persons by 1979. In the same year, a study mission of the New York City Bar Association listed the total at approximately 10,000.

Thus as the decade ended, the international outcry against abuses by the Argentine government remained extremely vocal, despite the fact that many prisoners detained under Article 23 of the Argentine constitution, which permits indefinite preventive detention "at the

[5] See *Amnesty International Report 1979*, p. 46. *Country Reports on Human Rights Practices for 1979*, p. 242, *supra* n. 4; Elena Sevilla, "Human Rights of Scientists in Argentina," paper presented at a symposium on the International Rights of Scientists, Chicago, January 23, 1980.

disposal of the executive power," were freed, tried, expelled, or permitted to exercise their constitutional "right of option" and leave the country. In August 1979, the U.S. National Academy of Sciences and the American Association for the Advancement of Science issued a joint statement condemning the human rights situation in Argentina, and throughout the year a variety of European nongovernmental human rights organizations published detailed charges of gross violations of human rights by the Videla government.[6] Perhaps the most telling commentary came in the State Department's human rights reports, which emphasized the hopeful but noted that intimidation was so strong that "an adequate defense in cases of terrorism and subversion is . . . difficult to ensure because many attorneys are reluctant to assume cases of this nature for fear of harassment and reprisals." The report continued: "There is extensive evidence . . . that torture has been routinely used by the security forces. It has been most frequent during the first days of interrogation and, according to numerous reports, has taken such forms as the use of electric shock, immersion of the head in water, mock executions, and other types of severe physical and psychological abuse. There are also credible allegations that such practices continued in 1979, with new detainees."[7] In September 1979, a six-member team from the Inter-American Commission on Human Rights conducted an on-site inspection of human rights abuses in Argentina. It confirmed the pattern of systematic repression practiced by the Argentine government.[8]

In Chile, the end of the decade saw extremely little qualitative improvement in the protection of human rights, although in quantitative terms the violations diminished considerably from the peak years of 1973 to 1977. Nonetheless, the abuses continued. In November 1979, two special rapporteurs acting for the U.N. Economic and Social Council prepared separate reports on Chile for the thirty-

[6] *Noticiero* (Madrid), no. 3 (September 1979) and no. 4 (October 1979); Human Rights Internet *Newsletter* 5 (December 1979/January 1980): 59.

[7] *Country Reports on Human Rights Practices for 1979*, p. 241, *supra* n. 4.

[8] In the mid-1970s, Argentina refused to permit the Commission to conduct an on-site investigation. Then in 1978, a bargain was struck between Vice President Walter Mondale and General Videla when both met while in Rome for the coronation of Pope John Paul I: the United States would grant export licenses for certain items on the Munitions List and reconsider Eximbank loan requests, and Argentina would permit an on-site inspection by the Inter-American Commission on Human Rights in early 1979. The Argentine government subsequently delayed the visit until September, perhaps to ensure that no report would be ready for submission to the OAS General Assembly meeting in La Paz in October. Organization of American States, Inter-American Commission on Human Rights, *Report on the Situation of Human Rights in Argentina* (Washington, D.C.: General Secretariat of the Organization of American States, 1980).

fourth session of the General Assembly. The first concluded that general human rights practices had continued to deteriorate, particularly in the abuse of power by security agencies (including electric shock torture by the National Information Center, née DINA) and the persecution of trade unionists. The second report concerned disappeared persons, focusing upon the discovery of mass graves in Lonquen, Yumbel, and Santiago's public cemetery. In December, the General Assembly accepted both reports and for the fifth time since 1973 passed a resolution expressing "its continued indignation that violations of human rights, often of a grave nature, continue to take place in Chile" and noting "its particular concern and dismay at the refusal of Chilean authorities to accept responsibility or account for the large number of persons reported to have disappeared for political reasons."

A substantial variety of human rights organizations reinforced the U.N.'s negative evaluation. Amnesty International's 1979 annual report noted that while the number of political prisoners was low as a result of earlier releases into exile, more than 1,500 persons remained missing and that throughout 1979 "serious violations of human rights continued." In addition, the OAS General Assembly adopted a resolution at its October 1979 meeting decrying "the serious limitations on the exercise of human rights" in Chile. As in the case of Argentina, the U.S. State Department was inclined to emphasize the positive aspects of Chilean human rights in its 1979 annual report, noting that confirmed disappearances had ceased, that cases of torture had declined since 1976, and that allegations of summary executions had become very rare. Nonetheless, "arbitrary detention and torture remained problems in 1979," the report continued, with about a dozen credible incidents of torture reported in 1979.[9]

In Uruguay, the violations of human rights related to the integrity of the person remained grave but certainly not as serious as they had been in 1976, when Representative Koch characterized the country as Latin America's "cesspool."[10] By 1980, there were far fewer reports of political arrests and torture, and by late 1979 a series of prisoner releases begun in 1977 had reduced the number of political prisoners to about 1,500 (State Department estimate) or 2,500 (AI). Either figure made Uruguay the nation with the highest number of political prisoners per capita in the Western Hemisphere. The State Department reported in early 1980 that torture had nearly been eliminated in Uruguay, that the level of psychological abuse during interrogation

[9] *Country Reports on Human Rights Practices for 1979*, pp. 270-277, *supra* n. 4.
[10] House Report 94-1228, p. 48.

had been reduced, and that there had been no verified instances of summary execution during 1978 or 1979. On the other hand, the report noted that *habeas corpus* remained suspended for persons arrested for subversive activities, which were extremely broadly defined to include "undermining the morale of the armed forces" or "disrespect to military authorities." The State Department reported further that the military penal code (MPC) that applied to all "crimes against the nation" regularly employed "confessional evidence frequently obtained under severe physical and psychological pressure" and that the Uruguayan bar, once among the most vigorous in Latin America, had been so intimidated that "few civilian lawyers are willing to plead cases before the military courts." The absence of civilian counsel was hardly missed, the State Department continued, since "defense counsel are limited by the system largely to sentence-bargaining and pleading for early release. There are no known cases where an accused subversive, once indicted, has been acquitted under the MPC."[11]

This official U.S. assessment of human rights in Uruguay was generally supported by other organizations. At its October 1979 meeting, the OAS General Assembly noted that human rights complaints had diminished in quantitative terms but that there were still "serious" human rights problems. Two months earlier, in August, the U.N. Human Rights Committee held its eighth session in Geneva and declared that Uruguay had violated the International Covenant on Civil and Political Rights by illegally imprisoning Luis María Bassano Ambrosini and by torturing and illegally imprisoning José Luis Massera and his family. At the Sixty-sixth Inter-Parliamentary Conference in Caracas in September 1979, representatives from seventy-eight nations received a report from the special committee on Uruguay that requested, among other things, "an end to the practice of torture and arbitrary persecution."

By the early 1980s, some progress appeared in the protection of human rights in Paraguay, although here again the level of respect for human rights had been so low that even small improvements could easily be interpreted as a significant relaxation in governmental repression. All of the organizations monitoring human rights in Paraguay noted, as AI did in 1979, that there was "a more positive balance in the field of human rights than in any year since Amnesty International began work on Paraguay in the early 1960s." The State Department agreed with this assessment: "Respect for the integrity of the individual has improved significantly over the past two years, with a few notable

[11] See *Country Reports on Human Rights Practices for 1979*, pp. 412-420, *supra* n. 4.

exceptions." It also reported that the incidence of torture had de-creased considerably toward the end of the 1970s, that although police continued to mistreat prisoners during the early stages of detention, "there have been no reports of cruel, inhuman or degrading treatment or punishment during subsequent detention in regular prison facili-ties," that almost all of the nation's six hundred political prisoners had been released—the State Department estimated there were but three in custody in late 1979—and that the incidence of confirmed disap-pearances had dropped to zero.[12]

Despite this improvement, AI also remarked that "the structure for maintaining strict control of dissent" had not been dismantled, and the State Department noted that "the human rights safeguards pro-vided for in Paraguay's Constitution have often not been honored in practice."[13] The most vigorous condemnation came from the OAS. In a highly detailed report presented to the General Assembly, the Inter-American Commission on Human Rights asserted that nearly every human right recognized in the American Declaration was vio-lated on a regular basis by the Paraguayan government of Alfredo Stroessner, including the rights to life, personal integrity, personal freedom, and a fair trial. Citing this report, the General Assembly adopted a resolution urging the government to lift the state of siege under which Paraguay has been ruled almost continuously since 1929, to establish *habeas corpus*, to release or submit to a fair trial all persons detained without charges, to end the practice of cruel and inhuman treatment of detainees, and to guarantee an independent judiciary.

Faced with the Sandinista victory in nearly Nicaragua, the Lucas government in Guatemala adopted a siege mentality that accelerated both the undeclared guerrilla warfare between left and right and the horrifyingly effective crusade by paramilitary death squads against com-mon criminals. The State Department explained the rising levels of human rights abuses by issuing a "violence as usual" commentary on Guatemalan political culture. Its 1979 annual report on human rights practices began with the assertion that "Guatemala's history has been plagued by political violence," blandly claimed that "there are no political prisoners" but neglected to explain that this was because few prisoners were taken alive, and concluded that "the overall level of both political violence and human rights violations remained lower than during the decade prior to 1976." Interspersed with these com-ments in the report were data that demonstrated exactly the opposite: "Deaths which appeared to have political overtones averaged about 20 each month," including the army chief of staff and two major

[12] Ibid., pp. 385-386.
[13] See *Amnesty International Report 1979*, p. 70; *Country Reports on Human Rights Practices for 1979*, p. 385, *supra* n. 4.

political figures, and "anti-criminal 'death squad' killings . . . averaged about forty per month." Although the May 1978 Panzos massacre, in which at least thirty-eight Indians involved in a land tenure dispute were killed by soliders, was treated in 1979 as a minor footnote, reference was made to "frequent accusations of political and personal violence" in rural areas.[14]

A number of nongovernmental human rights organizations argued that violations in Guatemala had increased alarmingly in the late 1970s. AI, for example, noted that one report had characterized 1978 as "the most violent year in the country's history." In May 1979, the Commission on Human Rights of the World Peace Council issued a condemnation of the Guatemalan government, calling on the Lucas administration "to cease repression and to dissolve the paramilitary groups." In November 1979, thirty-five representatives from eight Western European countries met in Antwerp for a Conference on Solidarity of the Human Rights Committees for Guatemala. Conference members lamented in particular that "the active leaders and members of the trade unions, student bodies, peasant organizations, religious groups and democratic parties are suffering repression, house searches, kidnappings, persecutions, death threats, torture and assassination by the army, police, and paramilitary groups maintained and led by the military dictatorship." The International Commission of Jurists asserted that "the current government has embarked on a systematic campaign to suppress dissent which has, in fact, generated a widespread climate of fear, demoralization, and the growth of clandestine opposition." Finally, in September 1979, Amnesty International launched a major campaign "aimed at ending the wave of political murder, torture, and abduction in Guatemala that has taken the lives of at least 2,000 people in the past 16 months." AI's 1979 annual report asserted that political murder and torture were widespread, death squad killings common, and dissent a form of suicide. In a December 1979 press release, AI spoke directly to the issue of the intimidation of organized labor: "To be a union leader or active member of a trade union in Guatemala today means risking one's life."[15] Universities were also targets. In late April 1980, AI's Central America Coordinating Group reported that "at least 25 professors and

[14] See *Country Reports on Human Rights Practices for 1979*, pp. 327-328, *supra* n. 4.

[15] All of these reports are summarized in *Amnesty International Report 1979*, pp. 63-66. See also Herta B. Ford, "Trade Union Repression in Guatemala," *AFL-CIO Free Trade Union News*, October 1979, p. 3; Human Rights Internet *Newsletter* 5 (December 1979/January 1980), pp. 55-56. On July 20, 1980, the Guatemalan Commission for the Defense of Human Rights dissolved itself, saying it was suicide to continue operating.

student leaders have died during March and April, 1980, [in] an apparently escalating campaign to eliminate opposition at the National University as well as at other educational institutions."

There was even less disagreement about the level of respect for the physical integrity of the person in El Salvador. Under the government of Carlos Humberto Romero, which was overthrown in October 1979, human rights violations reached totally unprecedented levels. According to the State Department, news from the countryside included "numerous reports of 'disappearances' of persons and frequent appearances of corpses, sometimes in groups and often showing signs of torture." In both rural and urban areas "a government-sponsored paramilitary organization, ORDEN, committed human rights violations, including beatings and torture, on a widespread basis." If dissenters were fortunate enough to escape summary execution by ORDEN but unfortunate enough to be apprehended by government authorities, as prisoners they were subject to "degrading treatment and punishment at stages of the judicial process from arrest to prison sentence. There were numerous accounts of persons being beaten at the time of arrest." The most notorious form of torture was burning prisoners alive. Small wonder, then, that the new government replacing that of General Romero found no political prisoners in custody.[16] Under the Romero government, dissent grew so intense that security forces resorted to mass repression. On May 8, 1979, the army opened fire on a group of demonstrators standing on the steps of the national cathedral, killing twenty-three citizens. Two weeks later, on May 22, another group of fourteen demonstrators was killed near the Venezuelan embassy. U.S. television camera crews shot extraordinary footage of the May 8 shootings, showing round after round of submachinegun fire jarring lifeless forms on the cathedral steps. These public massacres and the subsequent reappearance of a right-wing terrorist group, the White Warriors Union, marked the end of U.S. support for the Romero government.

The junta that ousted Romero in October 1979 faced the task of governing a people on the verge of civil war. At the urging of the United States, it moved to disband ORDEN and to announce an amnesty for political offenses. The State Department emphasized these conciliatory gestures in its 1979 human rights report. While it acknowledged that "there were some incidents of excessive violence by the security forces" of the new government, it asserted that there had been an overall decline in the excessive and indiscriminate use of

---

[16] See *Country Reports on Human Rights Practices for 1979*, pp. 314-316, *supra* n. 4.

force by police and military units. AI disagreed, arguing that most improvements quickly faded, especially in rural areas, where fraud, murder, and terrorism characterized Salvadorean life at the end of the 1970s. The March 1980 assassination of Archbishop Romero, an outspoken critic of right-wing terrorism, served to underscore the violent mood that characterized public life.[17]

Finally, there was Haiti, where the end of the 1970s saw no reduction in "illegal arrests, ill-treatment, and other breaches of constitutional guarantees" by the government of Jean-Claude Duvalier. "The system of authoritarian government continues," reported the State Department in early 1980, with "plausible reports of severe beatings and torture by electric shock administered to opposition political activists" and "harsh treatment by the police . . . a common substitute for legal prosecution."[18] Although political prisoners were not numerous, persons accused of political crimes were detained indefinitely without charges. The number of exiles and disappeared persons was not inconsiderable. Haiti began the 1980s as it had begun the 1970s—as the human rights basket case of the Western Hemisphere.

In summary, it cannot be said that greater respect developed for the physical integrity of the person in much of Latin America during the human rights years of the 1970s. In some countries, progress occurred in reducing the level of gross violations, while in others human rights conditions deteriorated dramatically. On balance, the gross violations of the physical integrity of the person probably declined quantitatively in the late 1970s. But this is clearly not the same as saying that there was increased respect for fundamental human rights. Violations appeared to decline when the threats to the established structure of privilege declined. Continued long enough, violations eventually became less gross because there were simply too few people left to intimidate. When the threats increased, as they did in Guatemala, El Salvador, and Colombia,[19] so too did the level of human rights vio-

---

[17] See *Amnesty International Report 1979*, pp. 61-63.

[18] See *Country Reports on Human Rights Practices for 1979*, pp. 341-342, *supra* n. 4.

[19] The human rights situation deteriorated considerably in Colombia during the late 1970s. The elected civilian government of Julio César Turbay launched a major antiterrorist campaign in 1979, primarily in response to the growing boldness of leftist guerrillas, who on January 1, 1979, stole five thousand weapons from a military arsenal. As was common throughout Latin America in the 1970s, the Colombian campaign against terrorism involved counterterrorism by the government. In late 1979, AI reported that "massive political arrests, allegations of torture, reports of extrajudicial killings, persecution of Indian peasants, and controversy generated by a new security statute were constant themes in denunciations received by Amnesty

lations. The positive correlation between increased threats and in-creased violations was perfect; there was not a single deviant case. Correlation is not causality, of course; nonetheless, it is difficult to read the preceding pages and not conclude that respect for the physical integrity of the person was (and remains) a wholly accidental bene-ficiary or casualty in the ongoing struggles of Latin American politics.

Political Liberties

In the 1970s, the protection of civil and political rights was not a central feature of United States human rights policy, but the corre-lation between increased political threats to the status quo and in-creased violations of the physical integrity of the person led many U.S. policy makers to encourage political tolerance. This may have encouraged the improvement in respect for political liberties that occurred in Latin America during the late 1970s.[20] In general, the end of the decade saw a hemispherewide trend toward increased political participation, often aptly described as decompression or *apertura*, the opening of the political process. Strict control over the pace and direction of the decompression process was the norm, but the political mood of the region at the beginning of the 1980s, while not in any sense euphoric, bore some slight resemblance to that of the twilight of the tyrants in the middle and late 1950s.

The most dramatic improvement in political liberties occurred in the Dominican Republic and Ecuador, two countries where only mod-est threats to the existing structure of privilege had arisen in the 1970s. In May 1978, the Dominican electorate ousted incumbent President Joaquín Balaguer in favor of challenger Antonio Guzmán; three months later, the Dominican Republic experienced its first peaceful change in government in recent years. In mid-1979, the Ecuadorean electorate chose Jaime Roldós to replace the military junta that had ruled the nation since the early 1970s. In neither of these cases could

---

International." While there was no evidence of disappearances or summary executions, more than a thousand persons accused of belonging to subversive organizations were detained under Article 28 of the constitution (which deals with threats to public order) and a vague Internal Security Statute promulgated by decree in September 1978. Nearly all detainees were subsequently released or tried. See *Amnesty International Report 1979*, p. 56; *Country Reports on Human Rights Practices for 1979*, p. 280, supra n. 4.

[20] The tentative wording of this sentence reflects the enormous difficulty in deter-mining the cause of such complex phenomena as political liberalization. Clearly, the role of the United States was secondary to internal political forces in each Latin American country. For a discussion of these forces in Brazil, see Peter McDonough, *Power and Ideology in Brazil* (Princeton: Princeton University Press, 1981).

the election be said to serve as a model of the democratic process. In fact, the Ecuadorean people were allowed to vote only after the most popular (and consequently most threatening) candidate, Assad Bucaram, had been removed from the ballot, and in the Dominican Republic, the electoral process was briefly interrupted by the government once it became evident that President Balaguer had been defeated. Despite these political machinations, reasonably free elections were held in two countries where reasonably free elections are traditionally rare, and in each case the electoral victor assumed power.

At the beginning of the 1980s, other Latin American nations were in the final stages of selecting new governments. The most agonizing case was that of Bolivia, which held an election in July 1978, followed by a coup (August), a countercoup (November), another election (perhaps the most democratic in Bolivian history) which produced a stalemate and an interim civilian government (July 1979), two further coups in one month (November), and then yet another interim president, who scheduled further elections in June 1980. The unusually brutal coup led by General Luis García Meza in July 1980 then aborted the entire process. Less fitful progress was occurring simultaneously in neighboring Peru, where in June 1978, citizens approved a new constitution in their first nationwide election in fifteen years. When the constitution took effect in July 1980, the Peruvian military handed power to Fernando Belaúnde Terry, the political phoenix whose Acción Popular party had scored a surprisingly large victory in the May general election.

In other Latin American countries, there was a less significant but nonetheless perceptible movement toward popular government. In Brazil, the opening initiated by President Geisel (1974-1979) accelerated under his successor. Although some critics asserted that the government's intention was to divide the opposition, most political leaders applauded the abolition of the mandatory two-party system imposed in 1965, for it encouraged a return to the coalition-oriented multiparty system that characterized Brazilian democracy prior to 1964. Further stimulation to democratic participation came in early 1979, when the government relinquished the power it appropriated in 1968 to deprive citizens of their political rights, including the rights to vote and to hold public office. Slow and uncertain was the process, but when two populist warhorses of an earlier era, Leonel Brizola and Miguel Arraes, returned from lengthy exiles in late 1979 and began to crank up what remained of their electoral machines, no one could deny that a serious opening had occurred in the political process.[21]

[21] Brizola was ex-President Goulart's brother-in-law and former governor of Rio Grande do Sul. His expropriations of an American and Foreign Power Company

Initial steps toward an eventual increase in the level of political participation occurred in other Latin American countries. In Panama, there was steady progress in the gradual return to mass electoral participation under the constitution of 1972, with the culmination scheduled for 1984 and the first presidential election by direct popular vote. In Argentina, the Videla government began what promised to be a lengthy process of transferring power to a civilian government with the announcement in December 1979 of an extremely vague political plan. Similarly, in 1979, the Uruguayan military government announced a return to constitutional rule, after the creation of a new constitution that would restrict political freedom and institutionalize a major political role for the armed forces.

In many countries, there was progress in securing political liberties other than those directly related to the conduct of liberal democratic electoral politics. Freedom of the press expanded substantially, formal prohibitions of political activity were often ignored when moderate political groups—the Christian Democrats in Chile or the United Confederation of Argentine Workers—appeared to be reconstituting their organizational structures and, at times, mildly criticizing the authorities. Freedom of movement, particularly the right to leave one's country, increased somewhat in the Southern Cone, although this freedom primarily affected only a limited number of persons with substantial financial means or a handful of prominent political figures such as ex-President Héctor Cámpora of Argentina, who in 1979 was finally granted safe-conduct out of Argentina after spending more than three years in the Mexican embassy. In general, each move toward greater freedom of expression or individual action was accompanied by severe restrictions on groups considered threatening by the existing dictatorial government. The decompression process involved a substantial measure of continued repression.

The Role of the United States

Any discussion of the role of outside forces in producing changes in human rights practices must underscore in advance the impossibility of determining causal relationships. When two phenomena occur in close temporal sequence—the ultimatum by Ambassador Pezzullo followed quickly by the departure of Somoza, for example—there is a natural tendency to attribute causality to the initial act. But we know beyond doubt that while the ambassador may have administered the *coup de grâce* to the Somoza dynasty, in no realistic sense could his

subsidiary (1959) and an ITT subsidiary (1962) formed the basis for numerous claims that Brazil was headed toward communism. Arraes was mayor of Recife and governor of Pernambuco during the Quadros-Goulart era.

action be said to have caused the Nicaraguan revolution of 1979. Exactly the same understanding should be used in evaluating all the efforts by the United States government in support of human rights during the 1970s. The United States encouraged greater respect for human rights; whether the changes in human rights behavior discussed in the preceding pages would have occurred without this encouragement cannot be determined. My view is that in many cases the changes would not have occurred, at least not as quickly as they did, but this is a view that cannot be confirmed beyond reasonable doubt. [22]

One fairly uncontroversial assertion of causality is possible, however. There is no doubt that the United States placed the issue of human rights at the center of diplomatic intercourse in the hemisphere. Because of the predominance of the United States, the agenda for inter-American relations reflects the principal concerns of the U.S. government. When in the mid-1970s these concerns focused upon human rights violations, human rights became, in the words of assistant secretary of state Viron Vaky, "a conscious factor all governments have to take into account. No longer can the factor be ignored." [23]

Once at the center of the stage, human rights considerations were assigned a concrete role in United States diplomacy. The potential for rewards was demonstrated whenever possible, as, for example, in August 1979, when both Rosalynn Carter and Secretary of State Vance attended the inauguration of Jaime Roldós in Ecuador, or a month earlier, when President Carter took the precedent-setting step of receiving President-elect Roldós in the Oval Office of the White House. Similarly, in September 1979, the President surprised many observers

[22] The Carter administration was extremely anxious to avoid strained relations by claiming to have caused improvements in human rights practices. In 1979, assistant secretary of state Vaky told Congress "there has been some progress in many areas [but] we do not take credit for that improvement; the credit belongs to the peoples and governments of Latin America and the Caribbean. But we do take satisfaction in our contribution." When pressed to detail the results of their efforts, administration spokespersons never said more than "we have made a contribution." U.S. Congress, House, Committee on Foreign Affairs, *Foreign Assistance Legislation for Fiscal Years 1980-81*, 96th Cong., 1st Sess., 1979, pt. 5, pp. 7, 175.

A *Washington Post* assessment of three and a half years of the Carter human rights policy was more willing to credit the administration: "It is remarkable how rapidly the world scene has changed since President Carter embarked on his human rights crusade. . . . Can one thank Carter for this? Not in a direct way, since cause and effect often appear so far apart. Without doubt, however, the administration's constant, if not lately so loud, articulation of the issues has given the human rights ball a mighty shove. . . . The constant refrain of human rights . . . helped provide a climate conducive to world political liberalization." *Washington Post*, August 29, 1980, p. A30.

[23] *Foreign Assistance Legislation for Fiscal Years 1980-81*, pt. 5, p. 20, *supra* n. 22.

by inviting three members of the Nicaraguan junta to meet with him at the White House, thereby publicizing his administration's acceptance of the overthrow of the Somoza government and, perhaps, identifying the United States with the progressive reforms of the new government.

The diplomatic threats were slightly more veiled than the rewards, but there is no doubt that they were communicated. The pressures were particularly strong on individual Latin American leaders opposed to improved human rights conditions, as the Somoza case demonstrates. So too does the case of El Salvador's Carlos Humberto Romero. Assistant secretary of state Vaky visited El Salvador in July 1979, specifically to urge greater liberalization in order to de-fuse civil unrest. He was followed in August by State Department trouble-shooter William Bowdler, who came close to indicating publicly that Romero stood in the way of a peaceful resolution to El Salvador's problems. In mid-October, Romero's comrades-in-arms placed him on a plane out of the country. Then, as violence increased in this unhappy land, the Carter administration repeatedly warned right-wing elements not to stage a coup against what appeared at first glance to be a centrist junta, and in early 1980 it underscored its concern by naming one of the State Department's most skillful diplomats, Robert White, as ambassador. While serving as ambassador to Paraguay, White stood out among all U.S. diplomatic personnel in Latin America for his effective work on behalf of human rights.[24]

The real test of United States intentions was not the pleading and cajoling of diplomats, however, but rather the specific actions taken when threats were ignored or, conversely, when they seemed to lead to improved human rights practices. First, the United States encouraged respect for human rights by increasing aid when significant improvements occurred. After instituting a complete halt in aid to Nicaragua during the closing months of the Somoza regime, for example, in the two and a half months between mid-July and the end of the fiscal year, economic aid to Nicaragua totaled $23,571,000 in deliveries, a relatively enormous figure. This was followed by the administration's request to Congress for a special appropriation of $75 million

[24] At the time of this writing (mid-1980), it is difficult to identify with confidence the Carter administration's policy toward El Salvador. What seems apparent is that the United States seems determined to provide the new military-dominated government with substantial amounts of military aid so that it can remain secure while instituting what the State Department refers to as "revolutionary reforms." No doubt there is some logic to this policy that escapes average mortals, but with El Salvador teetering on the edge of civil war, it would seem that a policy of providing pyromaniacs with matches so that they can fight fires reflects the design of persons who have taken leave of their reason.

to assist in Nicaraguan relief and reconstruction. The governments of Bolivia, Costa Rica, the Dominican Republic, Peru, and especially Ecuador were also rewarded. In the case of Ecuador, an aid program was initiated in FY1980 after several years of no bilateral development assistance.

The major changes in U.S. aid programs occurred when repressive governments were penalized. The governments of Argentina, Chile, Nicaragua, and Uruguay became principal targets during the late 1970s, but other Latin American governments, particularly those of El Salvador, Guatemala, and Paraguay, also learned that there were tangible costs to continued human rights violations. Nowhere were these costs more evident than in the reduction and redirection of military assistance. First, there was a substantial overall reduction in military aid to the region. The Carter administration's FY1980 military aid request was $38.7 million, the smallest amount of the decade— 30 percent less than in FY1979 and less than half the budget of FY1978, the last budget prepared by the Ford-Kissinger foreign policy team. The FY1980 budget contained no concessional MAP funds, FMS credits for only six countries (Bolivia, Colombia, the Dominican Republic, Ecuador, Panama, and Peru), and IMET grants for ten nations.[25] Second, there were country-specific restrictions. Totally excluded from military aid for human rights reasons were Argentina and Chile (by congressional action), plus Romero's El Salvador, Somoza's Nicaragua, Paraguay, and Uruguay. Haiti and Honduras were dropped from the list of FMS recipients but kept their IMET programs. The only anomaly in the FY1980 Carter budget was a proposal to provide Guatemala with $250,000 in IMET training, and Congress proceeded to delete that sum from the administration's IMET request.[26] Third, these quantitative reductions were matched by a severe control of the type of aid provided. No major weapons systems were included in U.S. military aid (although the Carter administration approved the commercial sale of at least one such system, a Vulcan-Chaparral missile system for Ecuador), and a portion of the military aid was also designed to assist civilians. For example, Bolivia's entire FMS credit in FY1979 purchased a military field hospital that also served civilians. In ad-

[25] The FY1981 budget reflected the Carter administration's increasing concern over instability in Central America and the Caribbean. The $63.6 million request reflected a large increase over FY1980.

[26] Angered over the 1977 State Department human rights report, Guatemala rejected military aid in FY1978 and FY1979 but subsequently requested that aid be resumed. *Foreign Assistance Legislation for Fiscal Years 1980-81*, pt. 8, pp. 94-99, *supra* n. 22. The administration's $6 million military aid request for El Salvador in FY1981 created fears that anomalous behavior would once more become the norm.

dition, the Carter administration turned down requests from repressive governments for a wide variety of specific armaments, particularly crowd-control equipment and antiinsurgency weapons such as rifles, rifle sights, and night vision devices. In brief, for human rights reasons, the FY1980 military aid program to Latin America bore virtually no resemblance to that of a decade earlier.

All of these changes occurred over the strenuous opposition of a few members of Congress and many administration officials. In 1979, a spokesperson for the Defense Security Assistance Agency told Congress that "our security ties with some of the most influential countries in the region have been seriously attenuated. There has been a gradual deterioration of our military relationships at a time when the region is predominantly governed by military regimes."[27] Working through Representative Yatron's Foreign Affairs Subcommittee on Inter-American Affairs, executive branch officials who identified with this position attempted to undermine the effectiveness of the human rights legislation governing military aid. In 1979, for example, assistant secretary of state Vaky asked Yatron to submit an amendment to the military aid authorization bill to permit IMET training in arms restraint and peacekeeping operations to any human rights violator and, specifically, to Argentina and Chile. The amendment was killed during markup by the full Committee on Foreign Affairs. In 1979, the subcommittee also passed another ARA-initiated amendment to the foreign assistance authorization bill, one that would have given the administration discretion to restore military aid to Chile. Although a Department of Defense spokesperson called the proposal "desirable" and applauded its approval by the subcommittee, chairperson Yatron recognized its certain defeat and withheld it during committee markup.[28]

Despite these assaults, military aid remained a major instrument of U.S. human rights policy to the end of the 1970s, simply because it appeared to be the best method of pressuring repressive governments to relent or, failing that, of placing a visible distance between the United States government and the most repressive Latin American military establishments. Thus the DSAA argument was unconvincing not because it was untrue that relations had been "attenuated," although they were probably much less seriously damaged than administration alarmists suggested, but because it was correct: the policy of the government in the late 1970s was to weaken relations with repressive governments. In this sense, the policy was effective.

[27] *Foreign Assistance Legislation for Fiscal Years 1980-81*, pt. 5, p. 29, *supra* n. 22.
[28] Ibid., pp. 39, 172-173.

To say more than that the U.S. human rights policy served to reduce relations with repressive governments is to raise once again the issue of causality. It is at least reasonable to believe that several Latin American governments became less repressive sooner than they would have had the United States not adopted a strong human rights policy. But, again, it is also reasonable to believe that the gross violations themselves responded to a dynamic—threats to the established structure of privilege—completely beyond the control of Washington. The United States government could encourage the violations, as the examples of Brazil and Chile demonstrate beyond any reasonable doubt, but once they had begun, the United States could not halt them until they had run their course. After two to three years of governmental terror, the fury of the initial repression subsided; then the United States government appeared as an effective advocate of greater respect for the physical integrity of the person and, much later and much slower, of the process of political liberalization.

This evaluation seems particularly appropriate in the cases of Argentina, Brazil, Chile, and Uruguay, but it is a less accurate description of the impact of U.S. policy in Latin American countries such as El Salvador, Guatemala, and Nicaragua, where there was a rising tide of public opposition to existing repressive regimes that *coincided* with the renewed emphasis upon human rights. This public opposition led to what appeared in mid-1980 as an authentic revolution in Nicaragua and to extraordinarily strong threats to the existing structure of privilege in El Salvador and Guatemala. I believe the human rights policy of the United States helped to create this opposition. There are no data to confirm this belief, but in the early 1980s it was widely if not universally held by foreign policy analysts. Popularity is not always the best gauge of an argument's validity, of course, but analysts who rarely found a trace of competence in U.S. foreign policy makers were caught admitting that their human rights policy had encouraged the resurgence of the opposition to repressive Latin American governments. The normally critical liberal weekly *Latin America* noted, for example, that "Carter's policy (albeit unwittingly) undermined the entire *somocista* system in Nicaragua" and that "the best the Guatemalan government can hope for is a victory at next year's US presidential polls for a Republican."[29] The United States emboldened the opposition to repression. It is here that the policy of promoting human rights promised to leave a lasting impact upon Latin America.

At the beginning of the 1980s, no one could predict with accuracy the long-term implications of encouraging opposition groups. These

[29] *Latin America Regional Report* RM 79-01, November 16, 1979, p. 5.

new threats to existing repressive governments might be crushed as they were in Uruguay, or they might emerge victorious as they did in Nicaragua. To ensure an outcome favorable to its wishes, the United States could do more—much more—just as it could have done much more in Nicaragua. The United States could have demanded that its own private sector cease financing the Somoza government, it could have launched an embargo similar to that with which it has harassed the Cuban government for two decades, it could have sent CIA assassins to Managua, it could have sent in the Marines. But in the case of Nicaragua and, the future might show, elsewhere as well, these efforts would have been superfluous. Once it had been demonstrated that the coercive power of the Somoza government would no longer be reinforced by the United States, the people of Nicaragua began to resolve their own problems of political power.

CHANGE IN FOREIGN POLICY

Why did the United States decide to cease reinforcing the Somozas, Pinochets, and Videlas of Latin America? Why in the 1970s did Congress cease writing Hickenlooper amendments to protect U.S. investors and start writing Harkin amendments to protect human rights? The answer is that there was a breakdown in the broad consensus among policy makers that core values were threatened in Latin America. In order to defend this answer, it is necessary to recapitulate the intellectual process by which it was reached.

Explaining Change: Theory

The question of why human rights became a part of United States policy toward Latin America has been addressed by focusing upon bureaucratic politics, a perspective that emphasizes the importance of bargaining among competing organizations in the determination of public policy. The bureaucratic politics perspective was chosen because it is particularly helpful in explaining how policy changes occur in response to noncrisis issues. One such issue, human rights, had been making a slow comeback in foreign policy for nearly a decade prior to the beginning of the Carter administration. New political actors oriented toward humanitarian values had appeared in Washington, primarily in Congress, and they had demanded a voice in decision making on the human rights component of foreign policy. Exactly why they appeared will be discussed in the following pages; the important point here is that these new actors obtained for themselves an expanded role in the policy-making process. As existing organizations adjusted their operating procedures to accommodate these new participants with new perspectives, the balance of decision-making power was altered substantially. Then with the inauguration of President Carter came a host of further changes in bureaucratic processes related to human rights. These adjustments—always minor, always incremental—explain much of the cumulative variation in United States policy toward human rights violations in Latin America during the 1970s.

The bureaucratic politics perspective has been criticized as superficial in the sense that it "explains" change by describing how change occurs. The perspective tends to direct the attention of researchers toward mechanistic questions related to organizational processes rather than toward the fundamental questions of *why* change occurs. But it need not be so, for behind the bureaucratic processes are real people with real values, often passionately held, eager to discuss the rationale for their behavior. For some unknown reason, however, the perspective that emphasizes the value systems of policy makers has been considered a principal intellectual rival of the bureaucratic politics model of foreign policy decision making.[30] Yet we have seen in the case of human rights that the analysis of bureaucratic victories and defeats leads almost inexorably to an examination of the core values that underlie the process of foreign policy making. This suggests that while the two approaches have different emphases, they are complementary rather than mutually exclusive.

Shared values. Studies that analyze policy-makers' value systems are likely to be refreshingly straightforward. Unlike their colleagues who support the bureaucratic politics approach, analysts adopting this perspective find it relatively easy to identify and assess United States policy toward Latin America. They recognize but refuse to concentrate upon the organizational complexity of the foreign policy-making apparatus; instead they underscore the cohesion that results from sharing a single set of core values. Rather than enumerating the bureaucratic entities involved in foreign policy decision making, these analysts refer to values that virtually every key policy maker in each organization is believed to share. This shared-value perspective leads analysts such as the Argentine sociologist Jorge Graciarena to the conclusion that

[30] Two useful essays that identify the characteristics of the bureaucratic politics perspective and compare it to other approaches to inter-American relations are Abraham F. Lowenthal, " 'Liberal,' 'Radical,' and 'Bureaucratic' Perspectives on U.S. Latin American Policy: The Alliance for Progress in Retrospect," in *Latin America and the United States: The Changing Political Realities*, ed. Julio Cotler and Richard R. Fagen (Stanford: Stanford University Press, 1974), pp. 227-233; and Jorge I. Domínguez, "Consensus and Divergence: The State of the Literature on Inter-American Relations in the 1970s," *Latin American Research Review* 13 (1978): 87-126.

"the fundamental interests of the United States as a nation and leader of the capitalist world rarely enter into the debates of the political functionaries and bureaucrats, since these interests are shared among them as a common assumption."[31] From this perspective, policy is coherent because the values that orient the thinking of policy makers are uniform throughout the policy-making apparatus.

There are only two specific core values that policy makers are said to share and that thereby provide coherence for United States policy toward Latin America: anticommunism and support for the property rights of liberal capitalism, including free trade. It cannot be denied that the United States acts with extraordinary coherence when policy makers perceive a threat from a foreign enemy in Latin America and that since World War II the enemy has been labeled communism. Nor can it be denied that during the past three decades a variety of left-leaning Latin American political movements have been attacked by the U.S. government. Anticommunism is a real and prominent value informing United States policy toward Latin America.

On the other hand, the coherence of U.S. policy on issues involving the violation of liberal property rights is less clear. As the chapter on public opinion indicates, the majority of United States citizens and their foreign policy officials favor governments that establish a minimum of restrictions on the movement and operation of private capital. Beyond that, however, the positions of the public as well as various bureaucratic actors appear to diverge. Conspicuously absent is a consensus on the concrete steps to be taken when property rights are threatened. Shared-value analysts generally fail to recognize the high level of abstraction at which this value exists and how quickly consensus breaks down in specific cases. In addition, they often seem uninterested in determining whether policy results from a dislike of communism or from the support of liberal capitalism. Instead, the separate influence of these two core values is blurred, and the impact of each on United States policy is viewed as complementary or additive.[32]

---

[31] Jorge Graciarena, "Commentary on Mitchell," in *Latin America and the United States: The Changing Political Realities*, ed. Julio Cotler and Richard R. Fagen (Stanford: Stanford University Press, 1974), p. 207.

[32] While the existence of a coherent value structure among officials who create United States policy toward Latin America is frequently advanced as an axiom, it is in reality a hypothesis that has yet to be tested with reliable data. Some data exist, but they have not been used by analysts committed to the shared-value perspective. For a sample of the available data, see Lloyd S. Etheredge, *A World of Men: The Private Sources of American Foreign Policy* (Cambridge: MIT Press, 1978); Bernard Mennis, *American Foreign Policy Officials: Who They Are and What They Believe Regarding International Politics* (Columbus: Ohio State University Press, 1971). On the

While it is difficult to dispute the existence of these shared values and probably equally difficult to contest their influence in establishing significant limits on United States policy toward Latin America, the shared-value perspective offers only a partial explanation of the policy process because it is unable to predict the content of policy whenever a threat to core values is not evident to all policy makers. What is sometimes lacking is not the near-universal dispersion of these two values among senior foreign policy makers, but rather a uniformity of perceptions that a threat to these values exists. When perceptions of a threat are fairly uniform, as in Guatemala in the early 1950s or Chile two decades later, they provide the basis for considerable policy coherence. But what about United States policy toward Batista's Cuba in 1958, toward Pinochet's Chile in 1977, and Somoza's Nicaragua in 1978, when there was little agreement among policy makers that core values were threatened? There is no doubt that many crucial issues of U.S.-Latin American relations are viewed by all policy makers as involving these two consensually held values. As the preceding chapters have suggested, in a clearly perceived crisis involving communism or, to a lesser extent, an attack upon traditional liberal property rights, the shared-value perspective is extraordinarily useful in explaining United States policy. At other times its utility is limited, and it is then that an understanding of bureaucratic politics becomes essential for clarifying the values that underlie foreign policy.

Parenthetically, the public and its foreign policy makers also hold a variety of additional but less salient values, one of which is respect for liberal human rights. Because foreign policy officials view their primary responsibilities to be furthering the nation's interests abroad and protecting national security, humanitarian values never dominate foreign policy. After Latin America has been made safe from communism and for capitalism, however, a variety of humanitarian values tends to be expressed in U.S. foreign policy. Relief for victims of natural disasters, aid for economic development, and human rights for oppressed people reflect humanitarian values whose legitimacy is unquestioned. Many ostensibly humanitarian initiatives—the Alliance for Progress, for example—clearly respond in part to perceived threats upon core values, but there also seems to be a genuine commitment by the public and their foreign policy officials to do good not because it is politically advantageous but because it is right. Public opinion and elite survey data have demonstrated repeatedly that the

general subject of values and foreign policy, see the summary analysis by Bernard C. Cohen and Scott A. Harris, "Foreign Policy," in *Handbook of Political Science*, ed. Fred I. Greenstein and Nelson W. Polsby (Reading, Mass.: Addison-Wesley, 1975), 6: 395.

relatively wealthy, secure people of the United States believe they have an obligation to help others whose lives are destroyed by an earthquake, whose children are dying from malnutrition, and whose political rights are disregarded by a government that rules through torture and intimidation. Although humanitarian values may be discarded quickly when a threat to core values is perceived, and although their relative prominence is argued continually, their right to be included among the values that inform foreign policy decision making is rarely challenged. To miss this point is to misunderstand a significant feature of United States foreign policy, especially U.S. policy toward Latin America.

Bureaucratic politics. The prominence of the bureaucratic politics perspective in the study of U.S.-Latin American relations reflects in part the undeniable fact that official involvement in Latin America is remarkably complex. Nearly every agency of the government is responsible for some aspect of United States relations with Latin America, and at least one-third of all the departments and agencies of the executive branch are deeply involved in formulating or implementing policy toward the nations of the region.[33]

After studying the activities of these organizations, a number of analysts have concluded that the policy-making process is most adequately described as decentralized, fragmented, or incoherent. In a study of U.S. economic policy toward Latin America that ranges far beyond the confines of bureaucratic politics, R. Harrison Wagner reported that "since many of those who participate in making foreign policy are more or less independent of each other and have conflicting views, it is possible that the government will undo with one hand what it is trying to do with the other, and it is likely that it will do nothing that departs from past decisions (usually compromises) until forced to do so."[34] Several major foreign policy officials have reached

[33] In the mid-1970s, no fewer than forty-five separate government entities maintained representatives in one or more U.S. embassies, outnumbering officials from the State Department (including AID) by a ratio of about five to one. U.S. Civil Service Commission, Bureau of Personnel Management and Information Systems, *Federal Civilian Workforce Statistics: Annual Report of Employment by Geographic Area* (Washington, D.C.: Government Printing Office, 1976), pp. 160-161; U.S. Civil Service Commission, Bureau of Manpower and Information Systems, *Employment by Agency and Citizenship in U.S. Territories and Foreign Countries* (Washington, D.C.: Civil Service Commission, 1976); Donald P. Warwick, *A Theory of Public Bureaucracy: Politics, Personality, and Organization in the State Department* (Cambridge: Harvard University Press, 1975), pp. 64-65; U.S. Congress, House, Committee on International Relations, Special Subcommittee on Investigations, *Congress and Foreign Policy*, 94th Cong., 2d Sess., January 2, 1977, p. 251.

[34] R. Harrison Wagner, *United States Policy toward Latin America: A Study in Domestic and International Politics* (Stanford: Stanford University Press, 1970), p. 77.

the same conclusion. In 1960, Senator Mike Mansfield blamed the regrettable state of U.S.-Latin American relations upon the foreign policy bureaucracy, "a creaky, confused and jumbled machinery."[35] A decade later, Nelson Rockefeller also faulted the bureaucracy for the incoherence that continued to characterize policy:

> With the present U.S. Government structure, Western Hemisphere policies can neither be soundly formulated nor effectively carried out. The State Department controls less than half of the decisions related to the Western Hemisphere. Responsibility for policy and operations is scattered among many departments and agencies. . . . To cope with the diffusion of authority, there has grown up a complex and cumbersome system of inter-departmental committees within which there are interminable negotiations because no one member has the authority to make a final decision. The result is that there are endless delays in decision making.[36]

Observers who note the large number of bureaucratic actors influencing foreign policy almost invariably conclude that the United States has no "policy" toward Latin America or even toward an individual nation in Latin America. Instead, the United States has a number of micropolicies. At times, these combine to form a reasonably rational whole, but often the parts are not only separate but contradictory and therefore incapable of contributing to a unified, coherent policy.[37] Consequently, the study of bureaucratic politics often becomes the analysis of how contradictory policy preferences are reconciled.

[35] "New Horizons for the Americas," *Congressional Record*, August 8, 1960, p. 15948.

[36] U.S. Congress, Senate, Committee on Foreign Relations, Subcommittee on Western Hemisphere Affairs, *Rockefeller Report on Latin America*, 91st Cong., 1st Sess., November 20, 1969, p. 5.

[37] The emphasis of the bureaucratic politics approach on fragmentation is no doubt in part a consequence of the nature of the early literature. Intellectually, the study of bureaucratic processes as a determinant of foreign policy belongs to the branch of organization theory that concentrates upon organizational decision-making processes. Much of this literature developed out of the examination of the business firm, where the core values of profit and growth are much more restricted in scope and essentially complementary rather than competitive, at least in the long term. Thus the literature on organizational decision making emphasizes how differing policy preferences are articulated and resolved in an environment of relative value homogeneity. Quite naturally, therefore, these studies tend to concentrate upon how something can be made to happen, not why it should happen. There is a general consensus on why business exists. Despite the fact that there is no similar consensus on why government exists, the emphasis upon process in organizational decision-making theory has often been translated fairly literally into the examination of public policy.

A goal of much of this volume has been to describe the reconciliation of differences on the issue of human rights during the 1970s. As with most foreign policy issues, human rights questions cut across the domain of a variety of foreign policy bureaucracies. As a consequence of shared responsibility, the nation's human rights policy came to reflect to a large extent the procedures by which conflicting organizations resolved their differences. A perspective emphasizing these negotiations therefore clarified changes in the locus of power in decision making. Looking for alternative proposals and compromises, we have used interviews, public records, and memoranda to trace the human rights policy back through the decisional process. The answer to the question of which bureaucracy prevailed (and to what extent) has told us much about the distribution of power among foreign policy organizations. This may be useful information for foreign policy practitioners who wish to make the mechanism of government responsive to senior authorities.

But most of the people who read this volume will not be foreign policy officials; they will be informed citizens interested in the foreign policy of the most powerful nation in the Western Hemisphere. For these citizens, the utility of comparing the policy preferences of bureaucratic victors and vanquished is that such a comparison reveals the dominant values of United States foreign policy. Or, stated differently, *the principal utility of the bureaucratic politics approach is that it helps to isolate and illuminate values in specific choice situations* when there is no consensus among policy makers that core values are being threatened.[38] Thus bureaucratic politics is not a theoretical perspective competitive with that which emphasizes shared values. It is a perspective that serves to determine the extent to which values are shared in any given situation and, when they are not, what the competing values are and which appear to be dominant.

Explaining Change: Practice

From the perspective of bureaucratic politics, then, what led to the breakdown in the broad consensus that core values were threatened in Latin America? The material presented in the preceding chapters indicates that there was an unusual conjunction of five events that produced the breakdown that led to the increased power of human rights in United States policy toward Latin America during the 1970s.

First there was the enormously unpopular intervention in Vietnam, which undermined citizen support for foreign policy in general. Viet-

[38] I am indebted to Harrison Wagner for indicating how the data presented in this volume tend to support this conclusion of the literature on organizational decision making.

nam labeled the United States as the primary supporter of a repressive government whose only virtue was its fanatical anticommunism. Virtually all of the human rights activists within and outside the government cut their humanitarian teeth by gnawing on the Johnson and Nixon policies toward Vietnam; indeed, the initial human rights legislation of the 1970s—on political prisoners and on military and police aid—was directed primarily at Vietnam. Having digested these victories, antiwar activists then searched for bigger bones to chew, and they found the more general issue of United States support of repressive Third World governments.

Watergate was the second event to increase the importance of human rights in the 1970s. The Nixon administration collapsed in August 1974, and the following November the people voiced their consternation by electing an overwhelmingly Democratic Congress: 291 Democrats to 144 Republicans in the House. Among the new members were Tom Harkin, Toby Moffett, Stephen Solarz, and Paul Tsongas, all of whom worked during 1975 and 1976 to add human rights amendments to legislation governing aid programs. The 1975 Harkin amendment and the strengthening of Section 502B in 1976 are Congress's principal legislative contributions to the human rights policy of the 1970s. Lacking any authority whatsoever in the area of human rights, the Ford administration was unable to defeat these congressional initiatives.

The third important event was the 1973 coup in the nation that had been the pride of Latin American democracy. On nightly television, the world was sickened by the brutality of the Pinochet government, and that alone would have turned a liberal Congress against the Nixon administration's low profile toward the junta's human rights violations. But then came the revelations concerning United States covert actions against the Allende government and its support of the junta through military aid and the Food for Peace program. Citizens who took the time to read the documents produced by congressional investigating committees were simply appalled by the behavior of their government. In my view, the Nixon-Kissinger policy toward Chile marked the darkest moment in the history of United States-Latin American relations. Although high levels of human rights violations have occurred elsewhere in the hemisphere, Chile in the 1970s provided the one case that combined the destruction of a strong democratic tradition, followed by uncommonly gross human rights violations and extensively documented U.S. complicity. As Chile became the focus of the human rights movement in the United States, it directed the attention of human rights activists to Latin America.

Fourth, by adopting human rights as the soul of his foreign policy,

President Carter legitimized a humanitarian concern in much the same way that John Kennedy had legitimized economic aid through the Alliance for Progress.[39] Like assistance to poor people, human rights had a humanitarian connotation that had been lacking for years in U.S. foreign policy. The policy braced State Department personnel who shortly before would have forfeited their careers had they voiced concern over the lack of humanitarian values in foreign policy. Numbers of latent human rights activists stepped out of the closet. In addition, the political appointees whom President Carter sent to operate the new Bureau of Human Rights and Humanitarian Affairs were people with strong, contentious dispositions. Until 1977, the few human rights personnel in the State Department were chosen for their ability to counter criticism from the public and Congress. Thereafter, they were selected because they could increase the impact of human rights in foreign policy decision making.

Briefly, the first four circumstances that influenced the success of the human rights movement in the 1970s were an extraordinarily weak administration—the only one in United States history to be driven from office by public indignation—with a Latin American policy discredited beyond redemption by the events in Chile; a liberal Congress elected to punish the Republicans for their misdeeds; and subsequently a new administration that offered a heretofore unsurpassed emphasis upon human rights in foreign policy.

The fifth unique feature was peculiar to the *late* 1970s: during the human rights years there was no credible threat to United States security in Latin America. By 1976, Latin America was dominated by repressive conservative governments. There were no Allendes or Goularts to threaten stability-oriented foreign policy officials. No government was moving to the left, no government was threatening the continued dominance of liberal capitalism. Core values were not under attack. There were only the Sandinistas in Nicaragua, with little hope in 1975 of ever overwhelming the strength of Somoza's U.S.-supplied National Guard. As the challenge to Somoza grew, so did the assertions that United States security was threatened. Apparently this argument

[39] There is no person more competent to assess this feature of U.S. foreign policy than Donald Fraser, the founder of the congressional human rights movement: "The Carter administration has built an impressive record in its efforts to introduce human rights concerns into our foreign policy," he asserted in 1979. "I do not agree with all of its decisions, and I believe it has made its share of errors. Nonetheless, compared to the past, the increased attention to human rights and the effort to shape our policies accordingly stand as a singular achievement of this administration." U.S. Congress, House, Committee on Foreign Affairs, Subcommittee on International Organizations, *Human Rights and U.S. Foreign Policy*, 96th Cong., 1st Sess., 1979, p. 298.

carried the day in Congress, for while the governments of Argentina, Brazil, Chile, El Salvador, Guatemala, and Uruguay were being sanctioned, Nicaragua remained unpunished. Although human rights forces made slow progress in the executive branch, they were forced to expend every dime of their political capital, and then it was only very late in the day that they were able to defeat in pitched battles the bureaucratic onslaughts of the Somoza lobby and its anticommunist allies in Congress. In fact, few of the human rights victories of the 1970s were won with ease.[40] Under the most positive possible circumstances, each victory was extremely difficult.

It is beyond imagination that anything resembling these five fortuitous phenomena will reoccur simultaneously during the final decades of the twentieth century. But counterbalancing the temporary nature of these five environmental factors are three structural changes in the foreign policy decision-making process that strengthen the role of humanitarian values in United States policy toward Latin America.

First, the increased influence of interest groups oriented toward humanitarian values is a reality. The monopoly once held by business groups and lobbyists for Latin American governments has been broken. As a result, United States policy can no longer be made the way it once was. The day is gone when a highly competent attorney such as Monroe Leigh can quietly slip a piece of paper into the hand of a senator and expect to see it processed without opposition into law, as he did with both Hickenlooper amendments in the 1960s. The day is gone when a Latin American dictator such as Anastasio Somoza can engage in gross violations of human rights and expect to continue to nose up to the foreign assistance trough. There may be more Hickenlooper amendments, and there undoubtedly will be times when foreign policy officials feel obliged to support a repressive dictatorship in order to protect their view of national security, but now these issues will be contested. Now there will be *institutions* employing individuals like Kay Stubbs, the young attorney affiliated with the Washington Office on Latin America, who worked for years to educate members of Congress and the State Department about the nature of the Somoza government, contesting point by point every move of the Somoza lobby and, in the end, having the satisfaction of seeing United States policy move in the direction she and the rest of the Washington

---

[40] Two exceptions to this were PL94-302, a 1976 law that added human rights considerations to U.S. participation in the Inter-American Development Bank and the African Development Fund, and PL95-88, a 1977 law that added human rights considerations to Food for Peace decision making.

human rights lobby desired.[41] Kay Stubbs returned to Nicaragua to assist in the reconstruction effort, but there remains in Washington a group of institutions, the centerpiece of which is the Washington Office on Latin America, whose recruitment functions in such a way as to be selective of dedicated, competent individuals. In the 1960s, lobbyists who championed humanitarian values in U.S. policy toward Latin America were primarily individuals—Tom Quigley, Brady Tyson, Philip Wheaton, William Wipfler—who held ties to church organizations but who acted primarily as individuals. Then these early activists were reinforced by others—Bruce Cameron, Joseph Eldridge, Jo Marie Griesgraber, and perhaps two dozen more—who represent institutionalized interest groups. The 1970s will be remembered as the decade in which forces pursuing humanitarian values in U.S. policy toward Latin America finally coalesced to form a fairly cohesive institutional structure. In the struggle for support from U.S. policy makers, the next Somoza will be faced with a serious battle. That is a major change.

A second change in the policy-making process accentuated by the human rights movement of the 1970s was the resurgence of congressional interest in humanitarian issues, which had as a natural consequence a renewed interest in selected aspects of U.S.-Latin American relations. Since about 1965, when the invasion of the Dominican Republic marked the end of a brief period of congressional concern with Latin America per se, few members of Congress have been interested in any Latin America-related issue. At the beginning of the 1980s, there is still little congressional interest in Latin America. But this condition, ostensibly lamentable, has a positive aspect. It permits aggressive, issue-oriented legislators to capture the congressional policy-making process despite their lack of strategic bureaucratic positions. Had these legislators been opposed by informed, industrious leaders of the inter-American subcommittees during the 1970s, few of the human rights proposals by Representatives Fraser, Harkin, Koch, Drinan, Solarz, and Senators Kennedy, McGovern, and Abourezk would have become law. Or, perhaps more accurately, their proposals would have been even more seriously weakened by amendments. As it was (and is), virtually any member of Congress has a reasonable chance of having his or her favorite topic become part of United States policy toward Latin America. This is a two-edged sword, or course, as human rights activists will no doubt discover. But the sword has always been there, and it has always been brandished by legislators

[41] The victory was bitter compensation for the life of her husband, Enoc Ortez Dávila, who was killed in battle by Somoza's National Guard only days before the Sandinista National Liberation Front marched into Managua.

obsessed with national security or the protection of economic interests. Only in the 1970s did persons concerned with humanitarian aspects of American foreign policy learn to wield it with proficiency.

The third change in the policy-making process was the development of a human rights bureaucracy within the executive branch. Created at congressional insistence in the years immediately prior to the Carter administration, this bureaucracy proved to be absolutely indispensable in implementing U.S. human rights policy toward Latin America during the late 1970s. Few if any of the human rights initiatives discussed in the preceding chapters would have occurred without the aggressive prodding of the Bureau of Human Rights and Humanitarian Affairs. Assisted at times by individuals occupying human rights-related positions in other parts of the foreign policy bureaucracy, during the Carter administration nothing of significance could be changed in United States policy toward repressive Latin American governments without first obtaining clearance from HA or, failing that, without successfully overcoming HA's opposition through appeals to senior foreign policy officials. But circumstances will certainly change over time, and a new administration with limited interest in the humanitarian aspects of foreign policy could quickly end the effectiveness of the human rights bureaucracy within the executive branch.

The future of human rights in United States policy toward Latin America will therefore depend upon the balance struck between the structural changes that indicate a greater political power for human rights forces—the development of interest groups, the increased congressional assertiveness in areas related to humanitarian concerns, the institutionalization of a human rights bureaucracy in the executive branch—and the ever-changing environmental factors that cannot be expected to encourage human rights initiatives to the same extent as they did in the 1970s. At the beginning of the 1980s, the great imponderable is when and under what conditions a fairly unambiguous threat to the core values of United States foreign policy makers will appear again in the Latin American environment. The course of change is difficult to predict, for there are many possible scenarios, but some repressive governments will undoubtedly be less capable than others in controlling change, and in at least one Latin American country a popular, reform-oriented movement will develop. Here, history tells us, are the makings of a threat.

Whether fighting a guerrilla war in the countryside as in Nicaragua, or elected by a slim majority as in Chile, this political movement will probably be weak in administrative skills, led by inexperienced personnel, and buffeted by a bewildering array of long-submerged political pressures. But it will nonetheless advocate reforms that threaten to

375

alter significantly the existing structure of socioeconomic privilege, not out of devotion to an abstract ideological model, but because the movement's political base is popularity among citizens who desire such a restructuring. If history repeats itself, this simple fact will be beyond the realm of comprehension by United States policy makers. Like the movements led by Allende, Arévalo-Arbenz, and Goulart, the new popular movement will advocate the nationalization of property be- cause its leaders and their followers believe that their country will be a more pleasant place in which to live if peasants do not work for landowners and if major productive enterprises are administered by the government rather than by private corporations.

No one would wish to predict the result of these attempts at reform. There could be another Cuba in 1959, another Chile in 1973, or another Nicaragua in 1979. It is impossible to know what will happen to future popular, reformist movements in Latin America.

It is far less difficult to speculate about United States policy toward these movements. Certainly the prospect of major socioeconomic re- forms will lead some part of the public and its representatives in Congress and the executive branch to perceive a threat to their core values of anticommunism and the support of private capital. These citizens will demand that their government act to neutralize the threat. The measures they suggest taking will probably differ very little from those taken during successful campaigns of the past. If the popular movement has reached power, there will be covert action using con- tacts in the military and organized labor, an unannounced economic blockade through Eximbank, OPIC, and private sector financial in- stitutions, a quiet halt in all economic aid, a boost in military assist- ance. If the popular movement has not yet reached power, there will be a frantic search for an acceptable "centrist" civilian to lead an ostensibly reformed government, a promise of economic aid to en- courage reforms, and a major military aid program.

In policy-making councils, the opposition to these hostile actions would logically consist of the same forces of the center and liberal left that championed human rights in the 1970s. Throughout the 1970s, these forces demonstrated their ability to influence United States pol- icy toward Latin America, but with the exception of Nicaragua they never faced in Latin America a circumstance in which human rights values were competing with the core values that orient U.S. foreign policy. Latin America is therefore the wrong place to assess the likely outcome of such a competition. For purposes of prediction, there are instead the cases of Iran, the Philippines, and South Korea—major defeats for human rights forces during the Carter administration. Only when communism was dead in Latin America were human rights born

376

again in U.S. policy. In Nicaragua, the single case where anticommunism was employed as a countervailing value, human rights forces were victorious not because they overcame traditional U.S. anticommunism but because they prevented Somoza from making a communist threat credible to more than a few policy makers.

This subtle distinction between outright combat and the struggle for credibility should not be missed. So long as anticommunism remains a component of national security policy, it will always defeat humanitarian values in a straightforward struggle for control of United States policy toward Latin America. Once a threat to national security is perceived, officials who perceive it must act; by definition, not to act on a national security threat is to jeopardize the nation's safety, something no administration would consider. Thus the goal of forces protecting a reform-oriented Latin American political movement from hostile acts by the United States is to break the perceptual link that permits the threat of major structural reforms in Latin America from being defined as a shift toward communism and, therefore, as a threat to the United States. The goal is influence over the perceptions of policy makers.

This is precisely the goal human rights activists reached in the case of Nicaragua. Note, however, that by late 1978 it was relatively easy for human rights forces to influence policy-makers' perceptions on Nicaragua, given the unusual barbarity of the Somoza government. With the entire Nicaraguan population in armed rebellion and with our most progressive Latin American allies—Costa Rica and Venezuela—in open support of the rebels, it was obvious that something more than a simple communist conspiracy was afoot. It will be a different matter entirely to convice senior foreign policy officials that the next popular, reform-oriented Latin American political movement is not a threat to the security of the United States.

How does a group oriented around humanitarian values wage a battle for the control of senior foreign policy-makers' perceptions? How does such a group successfully contest the assertions of rival groups, both within and outside the government, who claim to have identified a threat to the most important foreign policy value of all, national security? Here there are lessons from the human rights experience. First, they contest the issue with facts. Just as they showed policy makers and the attentive public how Anastasio Somoza maintained power through raw terror, they now demonstrate that the next progressive political movement, far from deserving hostility, merits support because it is advocating reforms designed to meet the basic needs of its citizens, reforms that we have recognized for decades as essential to long-term stability. Most foreign-policy officials know that

377

U.S. policy is to encourage stability through reform in Latin America. But they have to be reminded—individually, personally, and repeatedly, just as in the case of human rights—that what they know about social change and basic needs rather than what they have been conditioned to fear about communism should guide their actions. Certainly this argument will not convince the most enthusiastic supporters of the status quo in Latin America. Those foreign policy officials who view every Third World peasant as a potential threat to U.S. national security will always be unremitting foes of social change. Perhaps, however, the argument will serve to restrict their freedom of action.

But in no case are facts alone sufficient. Also essential is a foundation upon which to build a structure of facts. In this context, it is extremely important to note that a major source of strength of human rights activists during the 1970s was that they spoke from a position of recognized moral superiority. At a time when the moral authority of the United States government had all but disappeared, when a perverted understanding of national security had so debased the nation that few citizens were surprised when their leaders were found to be liars and criminals—shallow people who somehow came to believe that the way to protect our security was to napalm peasants, finance tiger cages, and destabilize democratic regimes—at that time, human rights forces began to talk about the felicitous consequences of a policy based upon humanitarianism. They said a people drunk with anticommunism had squandered whatever was left of their moral legacy in the mindless exercise of power. They said that a sobered people now needed to reclaim the principles they had pawned to finance their folly. They spoke with certainty of how to do some limited good in a confusing world where good is difficult to find and even harder to create. They spoke of principles all citizens understand. They spoke of human rights.

There are few principles more self-evident than that which asserts the human right to be free from torture at the hands of one's government. But there is at least one. It is that people have basic needs: to eat, to have shelter, to receive medical care, to read and write. During the twentieth century, these have become more than needs; by all but the most traditional standards, these are now human rights. And they are rights that millions of Latin Americans are systematically denied not because they are poor—Is that not the lesson of Cuba and now Nicaragua?—but because the human and financial resources of their societies are controlled by groups that are no more concerned about the moral implications of malnutrition than they are of torture. Yet, as we have seen, these are the groups that the United States has traditionally supported, not because we stand for either malnutrition or torture, but because our policy makers believe that support for the status quo in Latin America is essential to our national security. Encouraged by private interests employing the crudest form of red-baiting, the United States government traditionally pursues a policy that is patently devoid of positive long-term consequences for either the security of our nation or the well-being of the vast majority of Latin Americans.

There will be neither peace nor stability in Latin America until the basic needs of the people are met, not by another welfare program reminiscent of the Alliance for Progress, but by a fundamental restructuring of privilege, so that the right of the minority of Latin Americans to spend their vacations at Disneyworld is made subordinate to the right of peasants to eat. That is the truth with which United States policy makers must become acquainted. Until they do, human rights activists must fight a two-front war. Not only must they continue their efforts to force the United States government to cease supporting Latin American political groups that use repression to thwart change, they must fight tooth and nail against future efforts by private interests or the U.S. government to harass progressive Latin American political movements whose policies are designed to meet basic needs. This is precisely what occurred in the 1970s, and the results, while not spectacular, were nonetheless significant. The result in the case of Nicaragua and, the future might show, elsewhere as well, was that the citizens of a small nation enjoyed at least temporarily an unprecedented freedom to resolve their own problems of political power, to institute their government, as we once did, in such forms as to them seemed most likely to effect their safety and happiness.

379

BIBLIOGRAPHY

Adams, James L. *The Growing Church Lobby in Washington*. Grand Rapids, Mich.: Eerdmans, 1970.

Adler, Kenneth P., and Bobrow, Davis. "Interest and Influence in Foreign Affairs." *Public Opinion Quarterly* 20 (Spring 1956): 89-102.

Agee, Philip. *Inside the Company: CIA Diary*. Middlesex, Eng.: Penguin Books, 1975.

Allison, Graham T. "Conceptual Models and the Cuban Missile Crisis." *American Political Science Review* 63 (September 1969): 689-718.

———. *Essence of Decision*. Boston: Little, Brown, 1971.

Almond, Gabriel A. *The American People and Foreign Policy*. Rev. ed. New York: Frederick A. Praeger, 1960.

American Institute for Free Labor Development. *American Institute for Free Labor Development: A Union to Union Program for the Americas*. Washington, D.C.: American Institute for Free Labor Development, 1980.

———. *Annual Progress Report, 1962-1980: 18 Years of Partnership for Progress*. Washington, D.C.: American Institute for Free Labor Development, 1980.

Amnesty International. *Amnesty International 1961-1976: A Chronology*. London: Amnesty International, 1976.

———. *Amnesty International Report 1979*. London: Amnesty International Publications, 1979.

———. *Report of an Amnesty International Mission to Argentina, 6-15 November 1976*. London: Amnesty International, 1977.

Anderson, Charles W. *Politics and Economic Change in Latin America*. New York: Van Nostrand Reinhold, 1967.

Anderson, Jack. "Five Rose-Colored Days in Nicaragua." *Washington Post*, January 25, 1979, p. DC9.

Anton, Thomas J. "Roles and Symbols in the Determination of State Expenditures." In *Policy Analysis in Political Science*, edited by Ira Sharkansky. Chicago: Markham, 1970.

Arévalo, Juan José. *The Shark and the Sardines*. Translated by June Cobb and Dr. Raúl Osegueda. New York: Lyle Stuart, 1961.

"Argentina: AIFLD Losing Its Grip." *NACLA's Latin America and Empire Report* 8 (November 1974): 3-23.

Art, Robert J. "Bureaucratic Politics and American Foreign Policy: A Critique." *Policy Sciences* 4 (December 1973): 467-490.

———. *The TFX Decision*. Boston: Little, Brown, 1968.

———. "Why We Overspend and Underaccomplish." *Foreign Policy*, no. 6 (Spring 1972), pp. 95-114.

Atkins, G. Pope. *Latin America in the International Political System*. New York: Free Press, 1977.

381

Atwater, Elton. *American Regulation of Arms Exports*. Washington, D.C.: Carnegie Endowment for International Peace, 1941.

Baily, Samuel L. *The United States and the Development of South America, 1945-1975*. New York: New Viewpoints, 1976.

Baines, John M. "U.S. Military Assistance to Latin America: An Assessment." *Journal of Inter-American Studies and World Affairs* 14 (November 1972): 469-487.

Baldwin, David A. "Congressional Initiative in Foreign Policy." *Journal of Politics* 28 (November 1966): 754-773.

————. *Economic Development and American Foreign Policy, 1943-1962*. Chicago: University of Chicago Press, 1966.

Banfield, Edward. "Congress and the Budget: A Planner's Criticism." *American Political Science Review* 43 (December 1949): 1217-1228.

Barnet, Richard J. *Intervention and Revolution*. New York: Mentor, 1972.

————. *Roots of War*. New York: Atheneum, 1972.

Barone, Michael; Ujifusa, Grant; and Matthews, Douglas. *The Almanac of American Politics 1978*. New York: E. P. Dutton, 1977.

Bayley, David H. *Public Liberties in the New States*. Chicago: Rand-McNally, 1964.

Beals, Carelton; Oliver, Bryce; Brickell, Herschel; and Inman, Samuel Guy. *What the South Americans Think of Us*. New York: Robert M. McBride, 1945.

Bergsten, C. Fred. *The Future of the International Economic Order: An Agenda for Research*. Lexington, Mass.: D.C. Heath, 1973.

————. *Toward a New International Economic Order: Selected Papers of C. Fred Bergsten, 1972-1974*. Lexington, Mass.: D.C. Heath, 1975.

————; Horst, Thomas; and Moran, Theodore H. *American Multinationals and American Interests*. Washington, D.C.: Brookings Institution, 1978.

Bertsch, Gary K. "Monitoring the Effects of Governments on Human Dignity: Policy Evaluation in Communist Party States." *International Studies Quarterly* 20 (December 1976): 641-646.

Bilder, Richard B. "Human Rights and U.S. Foreign Policy: Short-Term Prospects." *Virginia Journal of International Law* 14 (Summer 1974): 597-609.

Binning, William Charles. "The Role of the Export-Import Bank in Inter-American Affairs." Ph.D. dissertation, University of Notre Dame, 1970.

Birns, Laurence. "Chile in *The Wall Street Journal*." *The Nation* 217 (December 3, 1973): 581-587.

————. "The Death of Chile." *New York Review of Books*, November 1, 1973, pp. 32-34.

Bishop, George F.; Oldendick, Robert W.; Tuchfarber, Alfred J.; and Bennett, Stephen E. "Pseudo-Opinions on Public Affairs." *Public Opinion Quarterly* 44 (Summer 1980): 198-209.

Black, Jan Knippers. *United States Penetration of Brazil*. Manchester, Eng.: Manchester University Press, 1977.

Black, Lloyd D. *The Strategy of Foreign Aid.* Princeton: D. Van Nostrand, 1968.

Blane, Andrew. "The Individual in the Cell: A Rebuttal to 'Politics and Amnesty International'." *Matchbox,* Winter 1979, pp. 5-6, 19-20.

Bonsal, Philip W. "Cuba, Castro, and the United States." *Foreign Affairs* 45 (January 1967): 260-276.

Brown, William A., and Opie, Redvers. *American Foreign Assistance.* Washington, D.C.: Brookings Institution, 1953.

Brzezinski, Zbigniew. "Half Past Nixon." *Foreign Policy,* no. 3 (Summer 1971), pp. 3-21.

Buergenthal, Thomas. "International Human Rights: U.S. Policy and Priorities." *Virginia Journal of International Law* 14 (Summer 1974): 611-621.

————, and Sohn, Louis B. *International Protection of Human Rights.* New York: Bobbs-Merrill, 1973.

"Building a Better Thumbscrew." *New Scientist* 59 (July 19, 1973): 139-141.

Burr, Robert N. *Our Troubled Hemisphere: Perspectives on United States-Latin American Relations.* Washington, D.C.: Brookings Institution, 1967.

Cameron, Bruce. "The Human Rights Working Group and Human Rights Legislation." Unpublished paper, 1978.

Carroll, Holbert. *The House of Representatives and Foreign Affairs.* Pittsburgh: University of Pittsburgh Press, 1966.

Center for International Policy. "OPIC: Insuring the Status Quo." *International Policy Report* 3 (September 1977).

Cheever, Daniel S., and Haviland, H. Field, Jr. *American Foreign Policy and the Separation of Powers.* Cambridge: Harvard University Press, 1952.

Chicago Council on Foreign Relations. *American Public Opinion and U.S. Foreign Policy 1975.* ICPSR Codebook 5808. Ann Arbor: Inter-University Consortium for Political and Social Research, 1977.

Clark, Paul G. *American Aid for Development.* New York: Praeger, 1972.

Claude, Richard P. "Human Rights in the Philippines and United States Responsibility." Working Paper No. HRFP-5. College Park: Center for Philosophy and Public Policy, University of Maryland, 1978.

————. "Reliable Information: The Threshold Problem for Human Rights Research." *Human Rights* 6 (Winter 1977): 169-187.

Clausen, Aage R. *How Congressmen Decide: A Policy Focus.* New York: St. Martin's Press, 1973.

Clemens, Walter C., Jr. *The Superpowers and Arms Control.* Lexington, Mass.: D.C. Heath, 1973.

Cochrane, James D. "U.S. Policy toward Recognition of Governments and Promotion of Democracy in Latin America since 1963." *Journal of Latin American Studies* 4 (November 1972): 275-291.

Cohen, Bernard C. *The Influence of Non-Governmental Groups on Foreign Policy-Making.* Boston: World Peace Foundation, 1959.

————. *The Press and Foreign Policy.* Princeton: Princeton University Press, 1963.

————. *The Public's Impact on Foreign Policy.* Boston: Little, Brown, 1973.

Cohen, Bernard C., and Harris, Scott A. "Foreign Policy." In *Handbook of Political Science*, vol. 6, edited by Fred I. Greenstein and Nelson W. Polsby. Reading, Mass: Addison-Wesley, 1975.

Cohen, Stephen D. *The Making of United States International Economic Policy: Principles, Problems, and Proposals for Reform*. New York: Praeger, 1977.

Collier, David. "Industrial Modernization and Political Change: A Latin American Perspective." *World Politics* 30 (July 1978): 593-614.

Commission on United States-Latin American Relations. *The Americas in a Changing World. A Report of the Commission on United States-Latin American Relations*. New York: Quadrangle, 1975.

Common Cause. "The First Year of Sunshine: Federal Agency Compliance with the Government in the Sunshine Act of 1976." Mimeographed. Washington, D.C.: Common Cause, August 1978.

"Congress and U.S. Foreign Policy towards Latin America." Mimeographed. Transcript of a Conference on the United States, U.S. Foreign Policy, and Latin American and Caribbean Regimes, Washington, D.C., March 31, 1978.

Congressional Quarterly. *The Washington Lobby*. 2d ed. Washington, D.C.: Congressional Quarterly, 1974.

Connell-Smith, Gordon. "The United States and the Caribbean: Colonial Patterns, Old and New." *Journal of Latin American Studies* 4 (May 1972): 113-122.

Converse, Philip E. "The Nature of Belief Systems in Mass Publics." In *Ideology and Discontent*, edited by David E. Apter. New York: Free Press, 1964.

————. "Public Opinion and Voting Behavior." In *Handbook of Political Science*, vol. 4, edited by Fred I. Greenstein and Nelson W. Polsby. Reading, Mass.: Addison-Wesley, 1975.

Cooney, John E. "Public-Relations Firms Draw Fire for Aiding Repressive Countries." *Wall Street Journal*, January 31, 1979, pp. 1, 30.

Council on Hemispheric Affairs. "For the Freedom of Thought and Person." New York: Council on Hemispheric Affairs, 1977(?).

Crecine, John P. *Government Problem Solving: A Computer Simulation of Municipal Budgeting*. Chicago: Rand-McNally. 1969.

————, and Fischer, Gregory. "On Resource Allocation Processes in the U.S. Department of Defense." Mimeographed. Ann Arbor: Institute of Public Policy Studies, University of Michigan, 1971.

Cunningham, George. *The Management of Aid Agencies*. London: Croom Helm, 1974.

Curti, Merle, and Birr, Kendall. *Prelude to Point Four: American Technical Missions Overseas, 1838-1938*. Madison: University of Wisconsin Press, 1954.

Dahl, Robert A. *Congress and Foreign Policy*. New York: Harcourt, Brace, 1950.

Davis, David Howard. *How the Bureaucracy Makes Foreign Policy: An Exchange Analysis*. Lexington, Mass: D.C. Heath, 1972.

Davis, Nathaniel. "U.S. Covert Action in Chile, 1971-1973." *Foreign Service Journal* 55 (November 1978): 10-14, 38-39; (December 1978): 11-13, 43.

Davis, Otto A.; Dempster, M.A.H.; and Wildavsky, Aaron. "A Theory of the Budgetary Process." *American Political Science Review* 60 (September 1966): 529-547.

Dawson, Raymond H. "Congressional Innovation and Intervention in Defense Policy: Legislative Authorization of Weapons Systems." *American Political Science Review* 56 (March 1962): 42-57.

de Galíndez, Jesús. "Anti-American Sentiment in Latin America." *Journal of International Affairs* 9 (1955): 24-32.

Derian, Patricia. "Foreign Policy and Human Rights." Speech to the National Foreign Policy Conference on Human Rights, Washington, D.C., February 27, 1978.

Destler, I. M. *Presidents, Bureaucrats, and Foreign Policy: The Politics of Organizational Reform.* Princeton: Princeton University Press, 1974.

Dewitt, R. Peter, Jr. *The Inter-American Development Bank and Political Influence, With Special Reference to Costa Rica.* New York: Praeger, 1977.

DeYoung, Karen, and Krause, Charles A. "Our Mixed Signals On Human Rights In Argentina." *Washington Post*, October 29, 1978, pp. C1-C2.

Dockery, Robert H. *Survey of the Alliance for Progress: Labor Policies and Programs.* A Study Prepared at the Request of the Subcommittee on American Republics Affairs by the Staff of the Committee on Foreign Relations, United States Senate, Washington, D.C.: Government Printing Office, July 15, 1968.

Domínguez, Jorge I. "Consensus and Divergence: The State of the Literature on Inter-American Relations in the 1970s." *Latin American Research Review* 13 (1978): 87-126.

————; Rodley, Nigel S.; Wood, Bryce; and Falk, Richard. *Enhancing Global Human Rights.* New York: McGraw-Hill, 1979.

Drew, Elizabeth Brenner. "Mr. Passman Meets His Match." *The Reporter* 31 (November 19, 1964): 40-43.

Einaudi, Luigi. "U.S. Relations with the Peruvian Military." In *U.S. Foreign Policy and Peru,* edited by Daniel A. Sharp. Austin: University of Texas Press, 1972.

Emerson, Rupert. "The Fate of Human Rights in the Third World." *World Politics* 27 (January 1975): 201-226.

Erickson, Robert S., and Luttbeg, Norman R. *American Public Opinion: Its Origins, Content, and Impact.* New York: Wiley, 1973.

Estep, Raymond. "United States Military Aid to Latin America." Mimeographed. Maxwell Air Force Base, Ala.: Aerospace Studies Institute, Air University, 1966.

Etheredge, Lloyd S. *A World of Men: The Private Sources of American Foreign Policy.* Cambridge: MIT Press, 1978.

Fagen, Patricia Weiss. "U.S. Foreign Policy and Human Rights: The Role of Congress." In *National Control over Foreign Policy Making,* edited by Antonio Cassese. Leyden: Sijthoff and Noordhoff, 1979.

Fagen, Richard R. "The Carter Administration and Latin America: Business as Usual?" *Foreign Affairs* 57 (Winter 1978-1979): 652-669.

———. "The United States and Chile: Roots and Branches." *Foreign Affairs* 53 (January 1975): 297-313.

Falk, Richard. *A Global Approach to National Policy.* Cambridge: Harvard University Press, 1975.

Farber, Maurice L. "Canal Issue Shows the Risks of Opinion Polling." *Los Angeles Times,* March 7, 1978, pt. 2, p. 5.

Farer, Tom J. "United States Foreign Policy and the Protection of Human Rights: Observations and Proposals." *Virginia Journal of International Law* 14 (Summer 1974): 623-646.

Farnsworth, David N. *The Senate Committee on Foreign Relations.* Urbana: University of Illinois Press, 1961.

Feinberg, Richard. "The Political Economy of the U.S. Export-Import Bank." Ph.D. dissertation, Stanford University, 1978.

Fenno, Richard F., Jr., *Congressmen in Committees.* Boston: Little, Brown, 1973.

———. "The House Appropriations Committee as a Political System: The Problem of Integration." *American Political Science Review* 56 (June 1962): 310-324.

Ferguson, Yale H., ed. *Contemporary Inter-American Relations.* Englewood Cliffs, N.J.: Prentice-Hall, 1972.

———. "The Ideological Dimension in United States Policies toward Latin America, 1945-76." In *Terms of Conflict: Ideology in Latin American Politics,* edited by Morris J. Bleachman and Ronald G. Hellman. Philadelphia: Institute for the Study of Human Issues, 1977.

———. "Reflections on the Inter-American Principle of Nonintervention: A Search for Meaning in Ambiguity." *Journal of Politics* 32 (August 1970): 628-654.

———. "Through Glasses Darkly: An Assessment of Various Theoretical Approaches to Inter-American Relations." *Journal of Inter-American Studies and World Affairs* 19 (February 1977): 3-33.

Fishlow, Albert. "Flying Down to Rio: Perspectives on U.S.-Brazil Relations." *Foreign Affairs* 57 (Winter 1978-1979): 387-405.

Ford, Herta B. "Trade Union Repression in Guatemala," *AFL-CIO Free Trade Union News,* October 1979, p. 3.

"For the Record: The Human Rights Lobby in the USA." *Latin America* 10 (October 15, 1976): 315.

Francis, Michael J. "La ayuda económica de Estados Unidos a América Latina como instrumento de control político." *Foro Internacional* 12 (April-June 1972): 433-452.

———. "Military Aid to Latin America in the U.S. Congress." *Journal of Inter-American Studies* 6 (July 1964): 389-404.

———. *Military Assistance and Influence: Some Observations.* Carlisle Barracks, Pa.: Strategic Studies Institute, U.S. Army War College, 1977.

Frankel, Charles. *High on Foggy Bottom: An Outsider's Inside View of the Government.* New York: Harper and Row, 1968.

Fraser, Donald M. "Freedom and Foreign Policy." *Foreign Policy,* no. 26 (Spring 1977), pp. 140-156.

Gallup, George H. *The Gallup Poll: Public Opinion 1935-1971.* 3 vols. New York: Random House, 1972.

————. *The Gallup Poll: Public Opinion 1972-1976.* 2 vols. Wilmington, Del.: Scholarly Resources, 1978.

Gastil, Raymond D. *Freedom in the World: Political Rights and Civil Liberties 1978.* New York: Freedom House, 1978.

George, Alexander L. "The Case for Multiple Advocacy in Making Foreign Policy." *American Political Science Review* 66 (September 1972): 751-785.

Glick, Philip M. *The Administration of Technical Assistance: Growth in the Americas.* Chicago: University of Chicago Press, 1957.

Gonzalez, Edward. "United States Policy and Policy-Making in the 200-Mile Fisheries Dispute with Ecuador and Peru." In the *Report* of the Commission on the Organization of the Government for the Conduct of Foreign Policy, vol. 3, app. I. Washington, D.C.: Government Printing Office, 1975.

Gould, David J. *Bureaucratic Corruption and Underdevelopment in the Third World: The Case of Zaire.* New York: Pergamon, 1980.

Graciarena, Jorge. "Commentary on Mitchell." In *Latin America and the United States: The Changing Political Realities,* edited by Julio Cotler and Richard R. Fagen. Stanford: Stanford University Press, 1974.

Gutteridge, William F. "The Impact of Foreign Aid upon the Political Role of the Armed Forces in Developing Countries." In *The Politics of International Organization,* edited by Robert W. Cox. New York: Praeger, 1969.

Hafer, Donald L. "Bureaucratic Politics and 'Those Frigging Missiles': JFK, Cuba and U.S. Missiles in Turkey." *Orbis* 21 (Summer 1977): 307-333.

Halperin, Morton H. *Bureaucratic Politics and Foreign Policy.* Washington, D.C.: Brookings Institution, 1974.

————. "Is the Senate's Foreign Relations Research Worthwhile?" *American Behavioral Scientist* 4 (September 1960): 21-24.

Hammond, Paul Y. "Foreign Policy Making and Administrative Politics." *World Politics* 17 (July 1965): 656-671.

The Harris Survey Yearbook of Public Opinion 1970. New York: Louis Harris and Associates, 1971.

The Harris Survey Yearbook of Public Opinion 1971. New York: Louis Harris and Associates, 1975.

The Harris Survey Yearbook of Public Opinion 1973. New York: Louis Harris and Associates, 1976.

Haviland, H. Field, Jr. "Foreign Aid and the Policy Process: 1957." *American Political Science Review* 52 (September 1958): 689-724.

Hayden, Samuel L. "Human Rights Briefing Paper." Mimeographed. Washington, D.C.: Council of the Americas, 1978.

Hayter, Teresa. *Aid as Imperialism.* Middlesex, Eng.: Penguin Books, 1971.

Hayter, Teresa. "Aid: Politics and Myths." *Latin American Review of Books* 1 (1973): 31-33.

Heilbroner, Robert L. *The Limits of American Capitalism*. New York: Harper and Row, 1965.

Held, Virginia; Morgenbesser, Sidney; and Nagle, Thomas, eds. *Philosophy, Morality and International Affairs*. New York: Oxford University Press, 1974.

Henkin, Louis. "The United States and the Crisis in Human Rights." *Virginia Journal of International Law* 14 (Summer 1974): 653-671.

Hero, Alfred O., Jr. "Foreign Aid and the American Public." *Public Policy* 14 (1965): 71-116.

Hilsman, Roger. *The Politics of Policy Making in Defense and Foreign Affairs*. New York: Harper and Row, 1971.

Hinckley, Barbara. *Stability and Change in Congress*. New York: Harper and Row, 1971.

Hirsch, Fred. *The Social Limits to Growth*. Cambridge: Harvard University Press, 1974.

Holt, Pat M. *United States Policy in Foreign Affairs*. Boston: Allyn and Bacon, 1971.

Hovey, Harold A. *United States Military Assistance: A Study of Policies and Practices*. New York: Praeger, 1965.

Hughes, Barry B. *The Domestic Context of American Foreign Policy*. San Francisco: W. H. Freeman, 1978.

Hughes, David R. "The Myth of Military Coups and Military Assistance." *Military Review* 47 (December 1967): 3-10.

Huntington, Samuel P. "Foreign Aid for What and for Whom." *Foreign Policy*, no. 1 (Winter 1970-1971), pp. 161-189.

Inter-American Development Bank. *Fifteen Years of Activities, 1964-74*. Washington, D.C.: Inter-American Development Bank, 1975.

International League for Human Rights. *Report of the Conference on Implementing a Human Rights Commitment in United States Foreign Policy*. New York: International League for Human Rights, 1977.

Jackman, M. "Education and Prejudice or Education and Response Sets?" *American Sociological Review* 38 (1973): 327-339.

Johnson, Richard A. *The Administration of United States Foreign Policy*. Austin: University of Texas Press, 1971.

Jones, Marie Thourson. "The Council of the Americas and the Formation of American Foreign Policy." In the *Report* of the Commission on the Organization of the Government for the Conduct of Foreign Policy, vol. 3, app. i. Washington, D.C.: Government Printing Office, 1975.

Joyce, James Avery. *The New Politics of Human Rights*. London: Macmillan, 1978.

Kane, William Everett. *Civil Strife in Latin America: A Legal History of U.S. Involvement*. Baltimore: The Johns Hopkins University Press, 1972.

Kegley, Charles W., Jr., and Wittkopf, Eugene R. *American Foreign Policy: Pattern and Process*. New York: St. Martin's Press, 1979.

Keohane, Robert O. "Not 'Innocents Abroad': American Multinational Corporations and the United States Government." *Comparative Politics* 8 (January 1976): 307-320.

Key, V. O., Jr. *Parties, Politics, and Pressure Groups.* 4th ed. New York: Thomas Y. Crowell, 1958.

———. *Public Opinion and American Democracy.* New York: Alfred A. Knopf, 1961.

Klare, Michael T. *Supplying Repression.* New York: The Field Foundation, 1977.

Kohen, Arnold S. "U.S. Diplomacy and Human Rights: The Cruel Case of Indonesia." *Nation* 225 (November 26, 1977): 553-557.

Kolodziej, Edward A. "Congress and Foreign Policy: The Nixon Years." *Proceedings* of the Academy of Political Science, vol. 32 (1975), pp. 167-179.

Krasner, Stephen D. "Are Bureaucracies Important? (Or Allison Wonderland)." *Foreign Policy*, no. 7 (Summer 1972), pp. 159-179.

———. "Business-Government Relations: The Case of the International Coffee Agreement." *International Organization* 27 (Autumn 1973): 495-516.

Lang, George. "Dining Out in Haiti." *Travel and Leisure*, April 1980, p. 14.

Langguth, A. J. *Hidden Terrors.* New York: Pantheon, 1978.

Larsen, Egon. *A Flame in Barbed Wire: The Story of Amnesty International.* New York: W. W. Norton, 1979.

Leacacos, John P. "Kissinger's Apparat." *Foreign Policy*, no. 5 (Winter 1971-1972), pp. 3-27.

Lefever, Ernest W. "The Military Assistance Training Program." *Annals* of the American Association of Political and Social Science, vol. 424 (March 1976), pp. 89-95.

Lehman, John. *The Executive, Congress and Foreign Policy: Studies of the Nixon Administration.* New York: Praeger, 1976.

LeoGrande, William M., and Roberts, Carla Anne. "Oligarchs and Officers: The Crisis in El Salvador." *Foreign Affairs* 58 (Summer, 1980): 1084-1103.

Lernoux, Penny. "Church Cowed by Uruguayan Military." Mimeographed. New York: The Alicia Patterson Foundation, 1975.

Letelier, Isabel, and Moffitt, Michael. "Human Rights, Economic Aid, and Private Banks: The Case of Chile." Mimeographed. A Report Submitted to the Subcommittee on Prevention of Discrimination and Protection of Minorities, United Nations Commission on Human Rigths, April 1978.

Liberation Brazil Committee. *The Brazilian Dictatorship: The Linchpin of Repression in Latin America.* London: Latin America Publications, 1977.

Linehan, Patrick E. *The Foreign Service Personnel System. An Organizational Analysis.* Boulder, Colo.: Westview Press, 1976.

Lipson, Charles H. "Corporate Preferences and Public Policies: Foreign Aid Sanctions and Investment Protection." *World Politics* 28 (April 1976): 396-421.

Lobe, Thomas. "Adventures in Social Control in the Third World." In *United States National Security Policy and Aid to the Thailand Police.* University of

Denver Graduate School of International Studies. Monograph Series in World Affairs. Vol. 14, bk. 2. Denver, 1977.

Lowenthal, Abraham F. "Foreign Aid as a Political Instrument: The Case of the Dominican Republic." *Public Policy* 14 (1965): 141-160.

————. " 'Liberal,' 'Radical,' and 'Bureaucratic' Perspectives on U.S. Latin American Policy: The Alliance for Progress in Retrospect." In *Latin America and the United States: The Changing Political Realities*, edited by Julio Cotler and Richard R. Fagen. Stanford: Stanford University Press, 1974.

————, and Treverton, Gregory F. "The Making of U.S. Policies toward Latin America." Mimeographed. Washington, D.C.: Woodrow Wilson Center of the Smithsonian Institution, 1978.

Lowi, Theodore J. "American Business, Public Policy, Case-Studies, and Political Theory." *World Politics* 16 (July 1964): 677-715.

————. "Making Democracy Safe for the World: National Politics and Foreign Policy." In *Domestic Sources of Foreign Policy*, edited by James N. Rosenau. New York: Free Press, 1967.

Luard, Evan, ed. *The International Protection of Human Rights*. London: Thames and Hudson, 1967.

McCann, Thomas P. *An American Company: The Tragedy of United Fruit*. New York: Crown, 1976.

McDonough, Peter. *Power and Ideology in Brazil*. Princeton: Princeton University Press, 1981.

Machan, Tibor R. *Human Rights and Human Liberties: A Radical Reconsideration of the American Political Tradition*. Chicago: Nelson Hall, 1975.

Maddox, James G. *Technical Assistance by Religious Agencies in Latin America*. Chicago: University of Chicago Press, 1956.

Manley, John. *The Politics of Finance*. Boston: Little, Brown, 1970.

Martin, William M., Jr. "Human Rights and Foreign Policy: The Relationship of Theory and Action." *Parameters* 8 (September 1978): 30-40.

Mason, Edward S. *Foreign Aid and Foreign Policy*. New York: Harper and Row, 1964.

Maynes, Charles William et al. *U.S. Foreign Policy: Principles for Defining the National Interest*. New York: Public Agenda Foundation, 1976.

Meek, George. "U.S. Influence in the Organization of American States." *Journal of Inter-American Studies and World Affairs* 17 (August 1975): 311-325.

Mennis, Bernard. *American Foreign Policy Officials: Who They Are and What They Believe Regarding International Politics*. Columbus: Ohio State University Press, 1971.

Methvin, Eugene H. "Labor's New Weapon for Democracy." *Reader's Digest*, October 1966, pp. 21-28.

Michaels, Albert L. "The Alliance for Progress and Chile's 'Revolution in Liberty,' 1964-1970." *Journal of Inter-American Studies and World Affairs* 18 (February 1976): 74-99.

Milbrath, Lester W. "Interest Groups and Foreign Policy." In *Domestic Sources of Foreign Policy*, edited by James N. Rosenau. New York: Free Press, 1967.

Miller, Stephen. "Politics and Amnesty International." *Commentary* 65 (March 1978): 57-60.

Miller, Warren E., and Stokes, Donald E. "Constituency Influence in Congress." *American Political Science Review* 57 (March 1963): 45-56.

Mitchell, Christopher. "Dominance and Fragmentation in U.S. Latin American Policy." In *Latin America and the United States: The Changing Political Realities*, edited by Julio Cotler and Richard R. Fagen. Stanford: Stanford University Press, 1974.

Montgomery, John D. *Foreign Aid in International Politics*. Englewood Cliffs, N.J.: Prentice-Hall, 1967.

————. *The Politics of Foreign Aid: American Experience in Southeast Asia*. New York: Praeger, 1962.

Moore, Heyward, Jr. "Congressional Committees and the Formulation of Foreign Aid Policy." Ph.D. dissertation, University of North Carolina, 1965.

Moore, Russell Martin. "Imperialism and Dependency in Latin America: A View of the New Reality of Multinational Investment." *Journal of Inter-American Studies and World Affairs* 15 (February 1973): 21-35.

Moran, Theodore H. *Multinational Corporations and the Politics of Dependence: Copper in Chile*. Princeton: Princeton University Press, 1974.

Morgenthau, Hans J. "A Political Theory of Foreign Aid," *American Political Science Review* 56 (June 1962): 301-309.

————. "To Intervene or Not to Intervene." *Foreign Affairs* 45 (April 1967): 425-436.

Morris, Roger. *Uncertain Greatness: Henry Kissinger and American Foreign Policy*. New York: Harper and Row, 1977.

Morrow, William L. "Legislative Control of Administrative Discretion: The Case of Congress and Foreign Aid." *Journal of Politics* 30 (November 1968): 985-1011.

Mosher, Arthur T. *Technical Cooperation in Latin American Agriculture*. Chicago: University of Chicago Press, 1957.

Moskowitz, Moses. *The Politics and Dynamics of Human Rights*. Dobbs Ferry, N.Y.: Oceana, 1968.

Nadel, Mark V. "The Hidden Dimension of Public Policy: Private Governments and the Policy Making Process." *Journal of Politics* 37 (February 1975): 2-34.

Nash, James A. "Church Lobbying in the Federal Government: A Comparative Study of Four Church Agencies in Washington." Ph.D. dissertation, Boston University, 1967.

Natchez, Peter B., and Bupp, Irvin C. "Policy and Priority in the Budgetary Process." *American Political Science Review* 67 (September 1973): 951-963.

Needler, Martin C. "Military Motivations in the Seizure of Power." *Latin American Research Review* 10 (Fall 1975): 63-79.

Nelson, Joan M. *Aid, Influence, and Foreign Policy*. New York: Macmillan, 1968.

Nordlinger, Eric A. *Soldiers in Politics: Military Coups and Governments*. Englewood Cliffs, N.J.: Prentice-Hall, 1977.

Novick, David. "Decision Making in the Department of Defense." *Business Horizons* 15 (December 1972): 23-33.

O'Donnell, Guillermo A. *Modernization and Bureaucratic Authoritarianism: Studies in South American Politics*. Berkeley: Institute of International Studies, University of California, 1973.

Ohlin, Goran. "Swedish Aid Performance and Development Policy." In *European Development Policies*, edited by Bruce Dinwiddy. New York: Praeger, 1973.

O'Leary, Michael Kent. *The Politics of American Foreign Aid*. New York: Atherton, 1967.

Organization of American States, Inter-American Commission on Human Rights. *Report on the Situation of Human Rights in Argentina*. Washington, D.C.: General Secretariat of the Organization of American States, 1980.

Ornstein, Norman J. "Congress and U.S. Foreign Policy toward Latin America." Mimeographed transcript of a Conference on the United States, U.S. Foreign Policy, and Latin American and Caribbean Regimes, Washington, D.C., March 31, 1978.

————, and Elder, Shirley. *Interest Groups, Lobbying and Policymaking*. Washington, D.C.: Congressional Quarterly, 1978.

Overseas Private Investment Corporation. *Annual Reports*, 1972 through 1979. Washington, D.C.: Overseas Private Investment Corporation.

Pancake, Frank R. "Military Assistance as an Element of U.S. Foreign Policy in Latin America, 1950-1968." Ph.D. dissertation, University of Virginia, 1969.

Parker, Phyllis R. *Brazil and the Quiet Intervention, 1964*. Austin: University of Texas Press, 1979.

Pastor, Robert A. "Congress' Impact on Latin America: Is There a Madness in the Method?" In the *Report* of the Commission on the Organization of the Government for the Conduct of Foreign Policy, vol. 3, app. 1. Washington, D.C.: Government Printing Office, 1975.

————. "U.S. Sugar Politics and Latin America: Asymmetries in Input and Impact." In the *Report* of the Commission on the Organization of the Government for the Conduct of Foreign Policy, vol. 3, app. 1. Washington, D.C.: Government Printing Office, 1975.

Pearson, Frederic S.; Reynolds, J. Martin; and Meyer, Keith E. "The Carter Foreign Policy and the Use of International Organization: The Limits of Policy Innovation." *World Affairs* 142 (Fall 1979): 75-98.

Perlmutter, Amos. "The Presidential Political Center and Foreign Policy: A Critique of the Revisionist and Bureaucratic-Political Orientations." *World Politics* 27 (October 1974): 87-106.

Phillips, David Atlee. *The Night Watch*. New York: Atheneum, 1977.

Pierce, Lawrence. *The Politics of Fiscal Policy Formation.* Pacific Palisades, Calif.: Goodyear, 1971.

Pike, Fredrick B. *Chile and the United States, 1880-1962.* Notre Dame: University of Notre Dame Press, 1963.

————. "Guatemala, the United States, and Communism in the Americas." *Review of Politics* 17 (1955): 232-261.

————, and Bray, Donald W. "A Vista of Catastrophe: The Future of United States-Chilean Relations." *Review of Politics* 22 (July 1960): 393-418.

Piquet, Howard S. *The Export-Import Bank of the United States: An Analysis of Some Current Problems.* Washington, D.C.: National Planning Association, 1970.

Pollis, Adamantia, and Schwab, Peter, eds. *Human Rights: Cultural and Ideological Perspectives.* New York: Praeger, 1979.

Polsby, Nelson W. *Congressional Behavior.* New York: Random House, 1971.

Powell, John Duncan. "Military Assistance and Militarism in Latin America." *Western Political Quarterly* 18 (June 1965): 382-392.

Powelson, John P. "International Lending Agencies." In *U.S. Foreign Policy and Peru,* edited by Daniel A. Sharp, Austin: University of Texas Press, 1972.

Pratt, Paul. *A Handbook on Financing U.S. Exports.* 2d ed. Washington, D.C.: Machinery and Allied Products Institute, 1976.

President's Committee to Study the United States Military Assistance Program. *Composite Report.* Washington, D.C.: Government Printing Office, August 17, 1959.

————. *Conclusions Concerning the Mutual Security Program.* Washington, D.C.: Government Printing Office, August 17, 1959.

Pressman, Jeffrey L., and Wildavsky, Aaron. *Implementation.* Berkeley: University of California Press, 1973.

Public Papers of the Presidents of the United States: Dwight D. Eisenhower, 1954. Washington, D.C.: Government Printing Office, 1960.

Public Papers of the Presidents of the United States: John F. Kennedy, 1961. Washington, D.C.: Government Printing Office, 1962.

Public Papers of the Presidents of the United States: John F. Kennedy, 1963. Washington, D.C.: Government Printing Office, 1964.

Public Papers of the Presidents of the United States: Lyndon B. Johnson, 1963-64. Washington, D.C.: Government Printing Office, 1965.

Public Papers of the Presidents of the United States: Lyndon B. Johnson, 1965. 2 vols. Washington, D.C.: Government Printing Office, 1966.

Public Papers of the Presidents of the United States: Richard M. Nixon, 1969. Washington, D.C.: Government Printing Office, 1971.

Public Papers of the Presidents of the United States: Richard M. Nixon, 1970. Washington, D.C.: Government Printing Office, 1971.

Public Papers of the Presidents of the United States: Richard M. Nixon, 1971. Washington, D.C.: Government Printing Office, 1972.

Quigley, Tom et al. *U.S. Policy on Human Rights in Latin America (Southern*

Cone): *A Congressional Conference on Capitol Hill.* New York: Fund for New Priorities in America, 1978.

Ransom, Harry Howe. *The Intelligence Establishment.* Cambridge: Harvard University Press, 1970.

Ray, Philip L., Jr., and Taylor, J. Sherrod. "The Role of Nongovernmental Organizations in Implementing Human Rights in Latin America." *Georgia Journal of International and Comparative Law,* supplement to vol. 7 (Summer 1977), pp. 477-506.

Ripley, Randall B. *Congress: Process and Policy.* New York: W. W. Norton, 1975.

Robinson, James A. *Congress and Foreign Policy-Making: A Study in Legislative Influence and Initiative.* Rev. ed. Homewood, Ill.: Dorsey, 1962.

The Rockefeller Report on the Americas. Chicago: Quadrangle Books, 1969.

Rogers, William D. *The Twilight Struggle: The Alliance for Progress and the Politics of Development in Latin America.* New York: Random House, 1967.

Romualdi, Serafino. *Presidents and Peons: Recollections of a Labor Ambassador in Latin America.* New York: Funk and Wagnalls, 1967.

Ronfeldt, David, and Sereseres, Caesar. *U.S. Arms Transfers, Diplomacy and Security in Latin America and Beyond.* Santa Monica, Calif.: RAND Corporation, 1977.

Ronning, C. Neale. "Human Rights and Humanitarian Laws in the Western Hemisphere." *Social Research* 38 (Summer 1971): 320-336.

Roper, Burns W. "The Limits of Public Support." *Annals* of the American Academy of Political and Social Science, vol. 442 (March 1979), pp. 40-45.

Rosenau, James N. "Foreign Policy as an Issue-Area." In *Domestic Sources of Foreign Policy,* edited by James N. Rosenau. New York: Free Press, 1967.

Rourke, Francis E. *Bureaucrats, Politics and Public Policy.* 2d ed. Boston: Little, Brown, 1976.

Rowe, Edward Thomas. "Aid and Coups d'Etat." *International Studies Quarterly* 18 (June 1974): 239-255.

Sack, Roger E., and Wyman, Donald L. "Latin American Diplomats and the United States Foreign Policymaking Process." In the *Report* of the Commission on the Organization of the Government for the Conduct of Foreign Policy, vol. 3, app. I. Washington, D.C.: Government Printing Office, 1975.

Salzberg, John, and Young, Donald D. "The Parliamentary Role in Implementing International Human Rights: A U.S. Example." *Texas International Law Journal* 12 (Spring-Summer 1977): 251-278.

Sanford, Jonathan Earl. "American Foreign Policy and the Multilateral Banks: The Actors and Issues Affecting U.S. Participation in the International Development Lending Institutions." Ph.D. dissertation, American University, 1977.

————, and Goodman, Margaret. "Congressional Oversight and the Multilateral Development Banks." *International Organization* 29 (Autumn 1975): 1055-1064.

Sanford, William Reynolds. "The Decision-Making Process in the Alliance for Progress." Ph.D. dissertation, University of Southern California, 1972.

Sapin, Burton M. *The Making of United States Foreign Policy.* Washington, D.C.: Brookings Institution, 1966.

Schlesinger, Arthur M., Jr. "Human Rights and the American Tradition." *Foreign Affairs* 57 (1978): 504-526.

————. *A Thousand Days: John F. Kennedy in the White House.* Boston: Houghton Mifflin, 1965.

Schoultz, Lars. "The Socioeconomic Determinants of Popular-Authoritarian Electoral Behavior: The Case of Peronism." *American Political Science Review* 71 (December 1977): 1423-1446.

Schreiber, Anna P., and Schreiber, Philippe S. E. "The Inter-American Commission on Human Rights in the Dominican Crisis." *International Organization* 22 (Spring 1968): 508-528.

Schwelb, Egon. *Human Rights and the International Community.* Chicago: Quadrangle Books, 1964.

"Senate, House Committees Differ on Foreign Affairs." *Congressional Quarterly Weekly Report* 28 (November 20, 1970): 2825-2828.

Sevilla, Elena. "Human Rights of Scientists in Argentina." Paper presented at a symposium on the International Rights of Scientists, Chicago, January 23, 1980.

Shestack, Jerome J., and Cohen, Roberta. "International Human Rights: A Role for the United States." *Virginia Journal of International Law* 14 (Summer 1974): 675-701.

Sigler, Jay Adrian. "Research Resources on Comparative Rights Policy." In *Comparative Human Rights,* edited by Richard P. Claude. Baltimore: The Johns Hopkins University Press, 1976.

Simon, Herbert A. *Administrative Behavior: A Study of Decision-Making Processes in Administrative Organization.* 2d ed. New York: Macmillan, 1957.

————. "Theories of Decision-Making in Economics and Behavioral Science." *American Economic Review* 49 (June 1959): 253-283.

Simon, Rita James. *Public Opinion in America: 1936-1970.* Chicago: Markham, 1974.

Simons, Lewis M. "U.S. to Skirt Rights Issue in Aid to Friends." *Washington Post,* September 11, 1977, p. A23.

Smith, Earl E. T. *The Fourth Floor: An Account of the Castro Communist Revolution.* New York: Random House, 1962.

Smith, James B., Jr. "Note." *Texas International Law Journal* 11 (Winter 1976): 137-146.

Smith, Joseph Burkholder. *Portrait of a Cold Warrior.* New York: G. P. Putnam's Sons, 1976.

Snyder, Richard C.; Hermann, Charles F.; and Lasswell, Harold. "A Global Monitoring System: Appraising the Effects of Government on Human Dignity." *International Studies Quarterly* 20 (June 1976): 221-260.

Somoza, Anastasio (as told to Jack Cox). *Nicaragua Betrayed.* Belmont, Mass.: Western Islands, 1981.

Spaulding, Hobart A., Jr. "U.S. and Latin American Labor: The Dynamics of Imperialist Control." In *Ideology and Social Change in Latin America*, edited by June Nash, Juan Corradi, and Hobart A. Spaulding, Jr. New York: Gordon and Breach, 1977.

Stillman, Richard J. "Woodrow Wilson and the Study of Administration: A New Look at an Old Essay." *American Political Science Review* 67 (June 1973): 582-588.

Swansbrough, Robert H. *The Embattled Colossus: Economic Nationalism and United States Investors in Latin America.* Gainesville: University of Florida Press, 1976.

Szulc, Tad. *The Illusion of Peace: Foreign Policy in the Nixon Years.* New York: Viking Press, 1978.

Tendler, Judith. *Inside Foreign Aid.* Baltimore: The Johns Hopkins University Press, 1975.

Thayer, George. *The War Business: The International Trade in Armaments.* New York: Simon and Schuster, 1969.

Theberge, James D. "A Minerals Raw Material Action Program." *Foreign Policy*, no. 17 (Winter 1974-1975), pp. 75-79.

Thorp, Willard L. *The Reality of Foreign Aid.* New York: Praeger, 1971.

Todman, Terence A. "The Carter Administration's Latin American Policy: Purposes and Prospects." Speech at the Center for Inter-American Relations, New York, February 14, 1978.

————. "Statement before the Subcommittee on Inter-American Affairs, House International Relations Committee." Mimeographed. March 1, 1978.

Treverton, Gregory F. "United States Policy-Making toward Peru: The IPC Affair." In the *Report* of the Commission on the Organization of the Government for the Conduct of Foreign Policy, vol. 3, app. i. Washington, D.C.: Government Printing Office, 1975.

Trice, Robert H. *Interest Groups and the Foreign Policy Process: U.S. Policy in the Middle East.* Sage Professional Papers in International Studies 02-047. Beverly Hills, Calif.: Sage Publications, 1976.

Truman, David B. "The Domestic Politics of Foreign Aid." *Proceedings* of the Academy of Political Science, vol. 27 (January 1962), pp. 62-72.

Tulchin, Joseph. "Inhibitions Affecting the Formulation and Execution of the Latin American Policy of the United States." *Ventures* (Fall 1967): 68-80.

Tuthill, John W. "Operation Topsy." *Foreign Policy*, no. 8 (Fall 1972), pp. 62-85.

U.S. Agency for International Development. *FY1966 Annual Report to the Congress.* Washington, D.C.: Agency for International Development, 1967.

————. *U.S. Overseas Loans and Grants and Assistance from International Organizations and Loan Authorizations, July 1, 1945-September 30, 1976.* Washington, D.C.: Agency for International Development, 1977.

————. *U.S. Overseas Loans and Grants and Assistance from International*

Organizations, July 1, 1945-September 30, 1978. Washington, D.C.: Agency for International Development, 1979.

U.S. Agency for International Development, Bureau for Population and Humanitarian Assistance, Office of Private and Voluntary Cooperation. *Voluntary Foreign Aid Programs.* Washington, D.C.: Agency for International Development, 1975.

U.S. Agency for International Development, Office of Contract Management, Support Division. *Current Technical Service Contracts as of June 30, 1974.* Washington, D.C.: Agency for International Development, 1974.

U.S. Air Force, Directorate of Military Assistance and Sales. *Information and Guidance on Military Assistance Grant Aid and Foreign Military Sales.* 12th ed. Washington, D.C.: U.S. Air Force, 1970.

U.S. Arms Control and Disarmament Agency. *World Military Expenditures and Arms Transfers 1967-1976.* Washington, D.C.: Government Printing Office, 1978.

U.S. Civil Service Commission, Bureau of Manpower and Information Systems. *Employment by Agency and Citizenship in U.S. Territories and Foreign Countries.* Washington, D.C.: Civil Service Commission, 1976.

U.S. Civil Service Commission, Bureau of Personnel Management and Information Systems. *Federal Civilian Workforce Statistics: Annual Report of Employment by Geographic Area.* Washington, D.C.: Government Printing Office, 1976.

U.S. Committee to Strengthen the Security of the Free World (Clay Committee). *The Scope and Distribution of United States Military and Economic Assistance Programs.* Washington, D.C.: Department of State, 1963.

U.S. Congress. *Country Reports on Human Rights Practices. Report Submitted to the Committee on Foreign Relations, U.S. Senate, and the Committee on International Relations, U.S. House of Representatives, by the Department of State.* 95th Cong., 2d Sess., February 3, 1978.

U.S. Congress, Congressional Budget Office. *U.S. Government Involvement in Commercial Exports: Program Goals and Budgetary Costs.* Washington, D.C.: Government Printing Office, 1977.

U.S. Congress, Congressional Research Service. *The Multilateral Development Banks and the Suspension of Lending to Allende's Chile.* Rev. ed. Washington, D.C.: Congressional Research Service, December 13, 1974.

U.S. Congress, House, Committee on Appropriations. *Mutual Security Appropriations for 1960.* 86th Cong., 1st Sess., 1959.

————. *Foreign Assistance and Related Agencies Appropriations for 1971.* 91st Cong., 2d Sess., 1970.

U.S. Congress, House, Committee on Appropriations, Subcommittee on Foreign Operations and Related Agencies. *Foreign Assistance and Related Agencies Appropriations for 1976.* 94th Cong., 1st Sess., 1975.

————. *Foreign Assistance and Related Agencies Appropriations for 1977.* 94th Cong., 2d Sess., 1976.

————. *Foreign Assistance and Related Agencies Appropriations for 1978.* 95th Cong., 1st Sess., 1977.

U.S. Congress, House, Committee on Appropriations, Subcommittee on Foreign Operations and Related Agencies. *Foreign Assistance and Related Agencies Appropriations for 1979.* 95th Cong., 2nd Sess., 1978.

———. *Foreign Assistance and Related Agencies Appropriations for 1980.* 96th Cong., 1st Sess., 1979.

U.S. Congress, House, Committee on Banking, Finance, and Urban Affairs, Subcommittee on International Development Institutions and Finance. *International Development Institutions—1977.* 95th Cong., 1st Sess., 1977.

U.S. Congress, House, Committee on Banking, Finance and Urban Affairs, Subcommittee on International Trade, Investment, and Monetary Policy. *U.S. Participation in the Supplementary Financing Facility of the International Monetary Fund.* 95th Cong., 1st Sess., 1977.

U.S. Congress, House, Committee on Foreign Affairs. *Foreign Assistance Act of 1965.* 89th Cong., 1st Sess., 1965.

———. *Foreign Assistance Act of 1967.* 90th Cong., 1st Sess., 1967.

———. *Foreign Assistance Act of 1968.* 90th Cong., 2d Sess., 1968.

———. *Foreign Assistance Legislation for Fiscal Years 1980-81,* 96th Cong., 1st Sess., 1979.

———. *Mutual Security Act of 1959.* 86th Cong., 2d Sess., 1958.

———. *The Overseas Private Investment Corporation: A Critical Analysis.* 93d Cong., 1st Sess., 1973.

———. *The United States and the Multilateral Development Banks.* 93d Cong., 2d Sess., 1974.

U.S. Congress, House, Committee on Foreign Affairs, and Senate, Committee on Foreign Relations. *Country Reports on Human Rights Practices for 1979.* 96th Cong., 2d Sess., 1980.

———. *Required Reports to Congress in the Foreign Affairs Field.* 93d Cong., 1st Sess., 1973.

U.S. Congress, House, Committee on Foreign Affairs, Subcommittee on Asian and Pacific Affairs. *Political Prisoners in South Vietnam and the Philippines.* 93d Cong., 2d Sess., 1974.

———. *The Treatment of Political Prisoners in South Vietnam by the Government of the Republic of South Vietnam.* 93d Cong., 1st Sess., 1973.

U.S. Congress, House, Committee on Foreign Affairs, Subcommittee on Inter-American Affairs. *Aircraft Sales in Latin America.* 91st Cong., 2d Sess., 1970.

———. *Assessment of Conditions in Central America,* 96th Cong., 2d Sess., 1980.

———. *Cuba and the Caribbean.* 91st Cong., 2d Sess., 1970.

———. *Foreign Policy Implications of U.S. Participation in the Inter-American Development Bank.* 91st Cong., 2d Sess., 1970.

———. *Impact of Cuban-Soviet Ties in the Western Hemisphere, Spring 1980,* 96th Cong., 2d Sess., 1980.

———. *New Directions for the 1970's: Toward a Strategy of Inter-American Development.* 91st Cong., 1st Sess., 1969.

———. *New Directions for the 1970's—Part 2: Development Assistance Options for Latin America.* 92d Cong., 1st Sess., 1971.

————. *Treasury Department Management of U.S. Participation in the Inter-American Development Bank.* 92d Cong., 2d Sess., 1972.

————. *The United States and Chile during the Allende Years.* 93d Cong., 2d Sess., 1971-1974.

U.S. Congress, House, Committee on Foreign Affairs, Subcommittee on International Organizations. *Human Rights and U.S. Foreign Policy.* 96th Cong., 1st Sess., 1979.

————. *Review of the 35th Session of the United Nations Commission on Human Rights.* 96th Cong., 1st Sess., 1979.

U.S. Congress, House, Committee on Foreign Affairs, Subcommittee on International Organizations and Movements. *International Protection of Human Rights.* 93d Cong., 1st Sess., 1973.

————. *Review of the U.N. Commission on Human Rights.* 93d Cong., 2d Sess., 1974.

————. *Winning the Cold War: The U.S. Ideological Offensive.* 88th Cong., 1st Sess., 1963.

————. *Winning the Cold War: The U.S. Ideological Offensive—U.S. Government Agencies and Programs.* 88th Cong., 2d Sess., 1964.

U.S. Congress, House, Committee on Foreign Affairs, Subcommittee on National Security Policy and Scientific Developments. *Military Assistance Training.* 91st Cong., 2d Sess., 1970.

U.S. Congress, House, Committee on Foreign Affairs, Subcommittees on Inter-American Affairs and on International Organizations and Movements. *Human Rights in Chile.* 93d Cong., 2d Sess., 1973-1974.

U.S. Congress, House, Committee on International Relations. *Foreign Assistance Legislation for Fiscal Year 1978.* 95th Cong., 1st Sess., 1977.

————. *Foreign Assistance Legislation for Fiscal Year 1979.* 95th Cong., 2d Sess., 1978.

————. *International Security Assistance and Arms Export Control Act of 1976.* 94th Cong., 2d Sess., 1976.

————. *Report of Secretary of State Kissinger on His Trip to Latin America.* 94th Cong., 2d Sess., 1976.

————. *Report of Secretary of State Kissinger on His Visits to Latin America, Western Europe, and Africa.* 94th Cong., 2d Sess., 1976.

————. *Report on Debt Relief Granted by the United States to Developing Countries.* 94th Cong., 1st Sess., 1975.

————. *Report on Developing Countries External Debt and Debt Relief Provided by the United States.* 94th Cong., 2d Sess., 1976.

————. *Survey of Activities, 94th Congress.* 94th Cong., 2d Sess., 1976.

U.S. Congress, House, Committee on International Relations, Special Subcommittee on Investigations. *Congress and Foreign Policy.* 94th Cong., 2d Sess., January 2, 1977.

————. *Human Rights and U.S. Policy: Argentina, Haiti, Indonesia, Iran, Peru, and the Philippines. Reports Submitted to the Committee on International Relations, House of Representatives, by the Department of State.* 94th Cong., 2d Sess., December 31, 1976.

U.S. Congress, House, Committee on International Relations, Subcommittee on Inter-American Affairs. *Arms Trade in the Western Hemisphere.* 95th Cong., 2d Sess., 1978.

U.S. Congress, House, Committee on International Relations, Subcommittee on International Economic Policy and Trade. *Extension and Revision of Overseas Private Investment Corporation Programs.* 95th Cong., 1st Sess., 1977.

————. *To Require Certain Actions by the Overseas Private Investment Corporation.* 94th Cong., 2d Sess., 1976.

U.S. Congress, House, Committee on International Relations, Subcommittee on International Organizations. *Chile: The Status of Human Rights and Its Relationship to U.S. Economic Assistance Programs.* 94th Cong., 2d Sess., 1976.

————. *Human Rights and United States Foreign Policy: A Review of the Administration's Record.* 95th Cong., 1st Sess., 1977.

————. *Human Rights in Indonesia: A Review of the Situation with Respect to the Long-Term Political Detainees.* 95th Cong., 1st Sess., 1977.

————. *Human Rights in Indonesia and the Philippines.* 94th Cong., 1st and 2d Sessions, 1975-1976.

————. *Human Rights in the International Community and in U.S. Foreign Policy, 1945-76.* 95th Cong., 1st Sess., 1977.

————. *Human Rights Issues at the Seventh Regular Session of the Organization of American States General Assembly.* 95th Cong., 1st Sess., 1977.

————. *Human Rights Issues at the Sixth Regular Session of the Organization of American States General Assembly.* 94th Cong., 2d Sess., 1976.

————. *Religious Persecution in El Salvador.* 95th Cong., 1st Sess., 1977.

U.S. Congress, House, Committee on International Relations, Subcommittee on International Political and Military Affairs. *U.S. Defense Contractors' Training of Foreign Military Forces.* 94th Cong., 1st Sess., 1975.

U.S. Congress, House, Committee on International Relations, Subcommittees on International Organizations and on Asian and Pacific Affairs. *Human Rights in East Timor and the Question of the Use of U.S. Equipment by the Indonesian Armed Forces.* 95th Cong., 1st Sess., 1977.

U.S. Congress, House, Select Committee on Foreign Aid. *Final Report on Foreign Aid.* 80th Cong., 2d Sess., 1948.

U.S. Congress, Joint Committee on the Library. *Annual Report of the Congressional Research Service of the Library of Congress for Fiscal Year 1975.* 94th Cong., 2d Sess., 1976.

U.S. Congress, Senate. *The Senate Committee System: First Staff Report to the Temporary Select Committee to Study the Senate Committee System.* 94th Cong., 2d Sess., 1976.

U.S. Congress, Senate, Committee on Agriculture, Nutrition, and Forestry, Subcommittee on Foreign Agricultural Policy. *Future of Food Aid.* 95th Cong., 1st Sess., 1977.

U.S. Congress, Senate, Committee on Appropriations. *Department of Defense Appropriations, Fiscal Year 1976.* 94th Cong., 1st Sess., 1975.

————. *Foreign Assistance Appropriations 1965.* 89th Cong., 2d Sess., 1964.

U.S. Congress, Senate, Committee on Appropriations, Subcommittee on Foreign Assistance and Related Programs. *Foreign Assistance and Related Programs Appropriations Fiscal Year 1977.* 94th Cong., 2d Sess., 1976.

————. *Foreign Assistance and Related Programs Appropriations Fiscal Year 1978.* 95th Cong., 1st Sess., 1977.

U.S. Congress, Senate, Committee on Appropriations, Subcommittee on Foreign Operations. *Foreign Assistance and Related Programs Appropriations Fiscal Year 1976.* 94th Cong., 1st Sess., 1975.

————. *Foreign Assistance and Related Programs Appropriations Fiscal Year 1979.* 95th Cong., 2d Sess., 1978.

U.S. Congress, Senate, Committee on Foreign Relations. *Activities of Non-diplomatic Representatives of Foreign Principals in the United States.* 88th Cong., 1st Sess., 1963.

————. *Alternatives to Bilateral Economic Aid.* 93d Cong., 1st Sess., 1973.

————. *American Institute for Free Labor Development.* 91st Cong., 1st Sess., 1969.

————. *American Republics Cooperation Act and Other Subjects.* 86th Cong., 2d Sess., 1960.

————. *CIA Foreign and Domestic Activities.* 94th Cong., 1st Sess., 1975.

————. *The Foreign Agents Registration Act: A Study Prepared by the American Law Division, Congressional Research Service, Library of Congress.* 95th Cong., 1st Sess., 1977.

————. *Foreign Aid Program: Compilation of Studies and Surveys.* 85th Cong., 1st Sess., 1957.

————. *Foreign Assistance Act of 1962.* 87th Cong., 2d Sess., 1962.

————. *Foreign Assistance Act of 1967.* 90th Cong., 1st Sess., 1967.

————. *Foreign Assistance Authorization: Arms Sales Issues.* 94th Cong., 1st Sess., 1975.

————. *International Development and Security.* 87th Cong., 2d Sess., 1961.

————. *Mutual Security Act of 1958.* 85th Cong., 2d Sess., 1958.

————. *Mutual Security Act of 1960.* 86th Cong., 2d Sess., 1960.

————. *Nomination of Lincoln Gordon to be Assistant Secretary of State for Inter-American Affairs.* 89th Cong., 2d Sess., 1966.

————. *Nondiplomatic Activities of Representatives of Foreign Governments: A Preliminary Study Prepared by the Staff.* 87th Cong., 2d Sess., 1962.

————. *Shlaudeman Nomination.* 94th Cong., 2d Sess., 1976.

U.S. Congress, Senate, Committee on Foreign Relations, Subcommittee on American Republics Affairs. *Survey of the Alliance for Progress: Labor Policies and Programs.* 90th Cong., 2d Sess., 1968.

————. *United States-Latin American Relations: Compilation of Studies.* 86th Cong., 2d Sess., 1960.

U.S. Congress, Senate, Committee on Foreign Relations, Subcommittee on Foreign Assistance and Related Programs. *Foreign Assistance Authorization.* 95th Cong., 1st Sess., 1977.

————. *IDB and AFDF Authorization.* 94th Cong., 1st Sess., 1976.

U.S. Congress, Senate, Committee on Foreign Relations, Subcommittee on Foreign Assistance and Related Programs. *International Security Assistance Programs.* 95th Cong., 1st Sess., 1978.
———. *OPIC Authorization.* 95th Cong., 1st Sess., 1977.
U.S. Congress, Senate, Committee on Foreign Relations, Subcommittee on International Operations. *Foreign Relations Authorization Act.* 95th Cong., 1st Sess., 1977.
U.S. Congress, Senate, Committee on Foreign Relations, Subcommittee on Multinational Corporations. *The International Telephone and Telegraph Company and Chile, 1970-71.* 93d Cong., 1st Sess., 1973.
———. *Multinational Corporations and United States Foreign Policy.* 93d Cong., 1st Sess., 1973.
———. *The Overseas Private Investment Corporation.* 93d Cong., 1st Sess., 1973.
U.S. Congress, Senate, Committee on Foreign Relations, Subcommittee on Western Hemisphere Affairs. *Latin America.* 95th Cong., 2d Sess., 1978.
———. *Rockefeller Report on Latin America.* 91st Cong., 1st Sess., 1969.
———. *United States Policies and Programs in Brazil.* 92d Cong., 1st Sess., 1971.
———. *U.S. Relations with Latin America.* 94th Cong., 1st Sess., 1975.
U.S. Congress, Senate, Committee on Governmental Affairs. *U.S. Participation in the Multilateral Development Banks.* 96th Cong., 1st Sess., 1979.
U.S. Congress, Senate, Committee on Government Operations, Subcommittee on Oversight Procedures. *Legislative Oversight and Program Evaluation: A Seminar Sponsored by the Congressional Research Service, Library of Congress.* 94th Cong., 2d Sess., 1976.
U.S. Congress, Senate, Committee on the Judiciary, Subcommittee to Investigate Problems Connected with Refugees and Escapees. *Refugee and Humanitarian Problems in Chile.* 93d Cong., 1st Sess., 1973.
———. *Refugee and Humanitarian Problems in Chile, Part III.* 94th Cong., 1st Sess., 1975.
U.S. Congress, Senate, Select Committee to Study Governmental Operations with Respect to Intelligence Activities. *Alleged Assassination Plots Involving Foreign Leaders: An Interim Report.* 94th Cong., 1st Sess., 1975.
———. *Covert Action in Chile 1963-1973.* 94th Cong., 1st Sess., 1975.
———. *Intelligence Activities.* Vol. 7. 94th Cong., 2d Sess., 1975.
———. *Supplementary Detailed Staff Reports on Foreign and Military Intelligence, Book IV.* 94th Cong., 2d Sess., 1976.
U.S. Department of Commerce, Office of Business Economics. *Foreign Grants and Credits by the United States Government: December 1955 Quarter.* Washington, D.C.: Department of Commerce, 1956.
U.S. Department of Defense. "Response to Senator Mike Mansfield: Information for Consideration by the Commission on the Organization of the Government for the Conduct of Foreign Policy." In the *Report* of the Commission on the Organization of the Government for the Conduct of Foreign Policy (Washington, D.C.: Government Printing Office, June 1975), vol. 5, app. N.

U.S. Department of Defense, Defense Security Assistance Agency. *Fiscal Year Series, December 1978*. Washington, D.C.: Defense Security Assistance Agency, 1978. Bound computer printout.

———. *Foreign Military Sales and Military Assistance Facts*. Washington, D.C.: Department of Defense, 1975 and 1977.

———. *Military Assistance and Sales Manual*. Publication 5105.38-M. Washington, D.C.: Department of Defense, 1978.

U.S. Department of State. *Diplomacy for the 70's: A Program of Management Reform for the Department of State*. Publication 8551. Washington, D.C.: Government Printing Office, 1970.

U.S. Department of State, Agency for International Development. *Congressional Presentation Fiscal Year 1980*. Washington, D.C.: Agency for International Development, 1979.

U.S. Department of State, Bureau of Public Affairs, Office of Media Services. *Foreign Policy and the Department of State*. Publication 8869. Washington, D.C.: Department of State, 1976.

U.S. Department of State, Bureau of Public Affairs, Office of Public Communication. *Human Rights and U.S. Foreign Policy*. Publication 8959. Washington, D.C.: Department of State, 1978.

U.S. Department of State, Office of Public Affairs. *Military Assistance to Latin America*. Washington, D.C.: Department of State, 1953.

U.S. General Accounting Office. *Assessment of Overseas Advisory Efforts of the U.S. Security Assistance Program*. Report ID-76-1. Washington, D.C.: General Accounting Office, 1973.

———. *Effectiveness of the Foreign Agents Registration Act of 1938, As Amended and Its Administration by the Department of Justice*. Report B-177551. Washington, D.C.: General Accounting Office, 1974.

———. *Impact of U.S. Development and Food Aid in Selected Developing Countries*. Report ID-76-53. Washington, D.C.: General Accounting Office, 1976.

———. *More Effective United States Participation Needed in World Bank and International Development Association*. Report B-161470. Washington, D.C.: General Accounting Office, 1973.

———. *Stopping U.S. Assistance to Foreign Police and Prisons*. Report ID-76-5. Washington, D.C.: General Accounting Office, 1976.

U.S. National Advisory Council on International Monetary and Financial Policies. *Annual Reports, 1971 through 1979*. Washington, D.C.: Government Printing Office.

U.S. President (Nixon). *U.S. Foreign Policy for the 1970's: Shaping a Durable Peace; A Report to the Congress, May 3, 1973*. Washington, D.C.: Government Printing Office, 1973.

Vance, Cyrus. "Human Rights and Foreign Policy." *Georgia Journal of International and Comparative Law*, supplement to vol. 7 (Summer 1977), pp. 223-229.

Van Dyke, Vernon. *Human Rights, the United States, and World Community*. New York: Oxford University Press, 1970.

Vogelgesang, Sandy. *American Dream: Global Nightmare. The Dilemma of U.S. Human Rights Policy.* New York: W. W. Norton, 1980.

————. "What Price Principle? U.S. Policy on Human Rights." *Foreign Affairs* 56 (July 1978): 819-841.

von Vorys, Karl. *The Political Dimensions of Foreign Aid.* Research Monograph Series no. 11. Philadelphia: Foreign Policy Research Institute, University of Pennsylvania, 1967.

Wagner, R. Harrison. "Dissolving the State: Three Recent Perspectives on International Relations." *International Organization* 28 (Summer 1974): 446-451.

————. *United States Policy toward Latin America: A Study in Domestic and International Politics.* Stanford: Stanford University Press, 1970.

Walters, Vernon A. *Silent Missions.* Garden City, N.Y.: Doubleday, 1978.

Warshawsky, Howard. "The Department of State and Human Rights Policy: A Case Study of the Human Rights Bureau." *World Affairs* 142 (Winter 1980): 188-215.

Warwick, Donald P. *A Theory of Public Bureaucracy: Politics, Personality, and Organization in the State Department.* Cambridge: Harvard University Press, 1975.

Watson, Gayle Hudgens. "Our Monster in Brazil: It All Began with Brother Sam." *Nation* 224 (January 15, 1977): 51-54.

Watts, William, and Free, Lloyd A. "Nationalism, Not Isolationism." *Foreign Policy*, no. 24 (Fall 1976), pp. 3-26.

Weiner, Harry. "Some Suggestions for Improving the Organization of the Bureau of Inter-American Affairs." In the *Report* of the Commission on the Organization of the Government for the Conduct of Foreign Policy, vol. 3, app. I. Washington, D.C.: Government Printing Office, 1975.

————. "U.S.-Brazil Relations: Non-Governmental Organizations and the Fifth Institutional Act." In the *Report* of the Commission on the Organization of the Government for the Conduct of Foreign Policy, vol. 3, app. I. Washington, D.C.: Government Printing Office, 1975.

Weiss, Peter. "Human Rights and Vital Needs." Institute for Policy Studies Issue Paper. Washington, D.C.: Institute for Policy Studies, 1977.

Weissberg, Robert. *Public Opinion and Popular Government.* Englewood Cliffs, N.J.: Prentice-Hall, 1976.

Weissbrodt, David. "Human Rights Legislation and U.S. Foreign Policy." *Georgia Journal of International and Comparative Law*, supplement to vol. 7 (Summer 1977), pp. 231-287.

Weissman, Steve. *The Trojan Horse: A Radical Look at Foreign Aid.* San Francisco: Ramparts Press, 1974.

Whitehead, Laurence. "Linowitz and the 'Low Profile' in Latin America." *Journal of Inter-American Studies and World Affairs* 17 (August 1975): 326-344.

Wilcox, Francis O. *Congress, the Executive, and Foreign Policy.* New York: Harper and Row, 1971.

Wildavsky, Aaron. *The Politics of the Budgetary Process*. 2d ed. Boston: Little, Brown, 1974.

Williams, Edward J. *The Political Themes of Inter-American Relations*. Belmont, Calif.: Duxbury, 1971.

Wilson, E. Raymond. *Uphill for Peace*. Richmond, Ind.: Friends United Press, 1975.

Wilson, Larman C. "The Principle of Non-Intervention in Recent Inter-American Relations: The Challenge of Anti-Democratic Regimes." Ph.D. dissertation, University of Maryland, 1964.

Wolf, Charles, Jr. *The Political Effects of Military Programs: Some Indications from Latin America*. Santa Monica, Calif.: RAND Corporation, 1963.

Wolpin, Miles D. *Military Aid and Counterrevolution in the Third World*. Lexington, Mass.: D.C. Heath, 1972.

―――. *Military Indoctrination and United States Imperialism.*. New York: American Institute for Marxist Studies, 1973.

Wright, James D. "Does Acquiescence Bias the 'Index of Political Efficacy'?" *Public Opinion Quarterly* 39 (Summer 1975): 219-226.

Wyman, Donald L. "Summary: U.S.-Latin American Relations and the Cases of the Countervailing Duty." In the *Report* of the Commission on the Organization of the Government for the Conduct of Foreign Policy, vol. 3, app. i. Washington, D.C.: Government Printing Office, 1975.

Wynia, Gary W. *Argentina in the Postwar Era: Politics and Economic Policy Making in a Divided Society*. Albuquerque: University of New Mexico Press, 1978.

Yankelovich, Daniel. "Farewell to 'President Knows Best'." *Foreign Affairs* 57 (1978): 670-693.

Zolberg, Aristide R. "The Military Decade in Africa." *World Politics* 25 (January 1973): 320-331.

INDEX

413

McGee, Gale, 156-157
McGovern, George, 160, 194, 197, 286, 308-310, 374
MacKenzie, Ian, 59-60
MacKenzie-McCheyne, 59-60
McNamara, Robert, 219-220, 225, 234, 237
Maddox, James G., 135n
Mahon, George, 162
Malaysia, 315
Managua, Nicaragua, 58, 62, 117, 331, 364, 374n
Mann, Thomas, 175, 187, 189-190
Mansfield, Mike, 155, 369
Mansfield amendment, 238n
Manufacturers Hanover Trust, 68
Marcos, Ferdinand, 126n, 263
Marshall Plan, 135, 141
Marstellar, Incorporated, 50-52, 54, 90
Martínez de Hoz, José, 72, 101
Marusi, Augustine R., 68
Maryknoll Fathers and Brothers, 77
Mason, Edward S., 139n
Massera, José Luis, 351
Mather, George R., 242
Matthews, Douglas, 146n
Maynes, Charles W., 25n, 116
Meany, George, 335-338
media, 20, 51-52, 55, 58
Mennis, Bernard, 366n
Mennonite Central Committee, 86, 106
Methvin, Eugene H., 339n
Mexico, 44, 118, 142, 238n, 268n, 298, 329, 347, 358
Meyer, Charles, 69, 105, 178
Meyer, Keith E., 132n
Middle East, 211, 229, 249
Miguel, Rafael, 101
Milbrath, Lester W., 48n, 104n
military aid: decision making, 221-230; historical perspective, 211-217; human rights, 247-266, 371, 376; impact assessed, 17, 29, 230-247; purpose, 217-221
Military Assistance Advisory Group (MAAG), 226, 238-247
Military Assistance Program (MAP), 213-215, 226, 228, 230, 240, 255, 262-263, 361
military base rights, 139, 304-305
Military Penal Code (Uruguay), 351
Miller, Edward G., Jr., 225
Miller, Warren E., 45-46

Miller, Stephen, 85n
Mineta, Norman, 107
Mississippi Civil Liberties Union, 126
Mitchell, John, 143
Mitchell, Perrin, 288-289
Mitrione, Dan, 180
Moffett, Toby, 287, 292, 371
Moffitt, Michael, 342n
Moffitt, Ronnie Karpen, 88
Molina, Raymond, 60, 90
Mondale, Walter, 244n, 311, 349n
Montoneros, 168
Moore, Heyward, Jr., 162n, 167
Moore, John, 311
Moran, Theodore H., 70n
Morel, Enrique, 55, 102n
Morgan, Thomas "Doc," 45, 140, 198-199, 202, 255
Morgenthau, Hans J., 140n
Morrow, William L., 162n
Morse, Wayne, 146, 156, 161n, 187, 193, 194n, 218, 251, 335-336
Mosher, Arthur T., 135n
Moynihan, Daniel, 69
Mozambique, 248
multilateral development banks (MDBs), 17, 73, 101-102, 107, 134, 141-142, 144, 149-250, 254, 255, 266, 267-300, 303, 341
multilateral diplomacy, 128-134
Multilateral Institutions Program Office (MIPO), 273, 277
multinational corporations, 48, 51, 65, 66, 72, 91, 154-157, 280, 295, 312-321, 322, 340-343
Munitions List, 326-332
Murphy, John, 58, 62, 103
Mutual Educational and Cultural Exchange (Fulbright-Hays) Act, 86
Mutual Security Act, 98, 135, 141, 213-214, 326n

narcotics control, 151, 182-183, 281
Nash, James A., 81n
National Academy of Sciences, 349
National Advisory Council on International Monetary and Financial Policies (NAC), 208n, 272-274, 276-277, 293, 303-305, 311
National Association of Manufacturers, 66n
National Chile Center, 88n

Panama Canal treaties, 38, 41, 44, 51, 70, 78, 89, 95, 117, 154-155, 157, 161, 165, 231n
Pancake, Frank R., 213n
Panzos massacre, 353
Paraguay, 15, 78, 83, 133n, 142, 195, 213, 236, 238n, 259, 295-297, 348, 351-352, 360-363
Paraguay Watch, 88n
Parker, Daniel, 192
Parker, Phyllis R., 173n
Partners of the Alliance, 138n
Passman, Otto, 138, 162-164
Pastor, Robert A., 49n, 149n, 193n
Pattison, Ned, 197n
Peabody, Larry, 315
Peabody, Rivlin, Lambert and Meyers law firm, 64-65
Peace Corps, 90, 104, 121, 126, 135n, 154, 320
Pearson, Frederic S., 132n
Pendleton, Edmund, 57
People's Republic of China, 22n, 28, 268n
People's Temple, 263n
Pepsico Corporation, 66, 101
Pereda Asbun, Juan, 266
Pérez Jiménez, Marcos, 5
Permanent Assembly for Human Rights (Argentina), 348
Perón, María Estela "Isabel" Martínez de, 259
Perón, Juan, 5, 9, 50
Peru, 169, 209, 212, 233, 249, 357, 361
Petty, John, 153
Pezzullo, Lawrence, 344, 358
Phelps-Dodge Corporation, 320
Phillippines, 87, 110-111, 118, 126n, 141, 166n, 216, 236, 263-264, 267n, 304, 329, 376
physical integrity of the person, 3n, 345, 346-356
Pinochet Ugarte, Augusto, 12, 19, 54-56, 75, 82-83, 85, 101-103, 116-117, 130, 132-134, 148n, 157, 160, 170, 171n, 177, 178n, 185-186, 189, 202, 249, 254, 343, 364, 371
Piquet, Howard S., 302n
pluralism, 8-11, 13, 88-90, 91
Point Four, 140
police in Latin America, 179-183, 236, 259

political liberties, 356-358
political purposes of foreign aid, 139-141, 232-247
Popper, David, 111
popular classes, 7-8, 10-11, 13
Popular Unity coalition (Chile), 174, 242
Porter, Charles, 250, 251n
Potomac Associates polls, 25, 38n
Powell, John Duncan, 236n
Prats, Carlos, 12
Pratt, Paul, 303n
Presidential Committee to Strengthen the Security of the Free World (Clay Committee), 140
President's Committee to Study the United States Military Assistance Program (Draper Committee), 211, 220
President's Task Force on International Development, 123
Public Opinion Studies Division, 40
public relations, 50-64
Public Studies Division, 40
Punta del Este, 176, 189

Quadros/Goulart government, 9, 168-177, 187-188, 357n-358n
Quigley, Thomas, 77, 87, 114n, 204n, 374

Ray, Philip L., Jr., 160n
Reagan, Ronald, 89
Red Scare technique, 91-92, 379
refugees, 135n, 138, 155, 186, 202
repression and economic aid, 8, 11, 13, 84, 91-92, 115-116, 168-191, 194; and military aid, 179-183, 212-213, 232-237, 247-250. See also torture
Republican National Committee, 61
Republican Policy Committee, 316
Reuss, Henry, 284-292, 306
Reuters, 51
Reynolds, J. Martin, 132n
Rhoads, Brewster, 76
Rhodesia, 343
Roberts, Carla Anne, 265n
Robinson, Kenneth, 57
Rockefeller, David, 66, 68-69
Rockefeller, Nelson, 187, 369
Rogers, William D., 68, 69, 105, 121, 161, 178n, 186, 281-282
Rogers, William P., 67

State Department (*cont.*)
Department, 221-228; and lobbyists, 51,
64, 65, 94-95; and multilateral aid, 273-
278, 284-285, 290, 293-295; power struc-
ture, 119; and public opinion, 40-43
Steptoe and Johnson law firm, 98-99
Stevenson, Adlai, 307-308
Stokes, Donald E., 45-46
Stolz, Irwin, 59
Stroessner, Alfredo, 236, 352
structure of privilege, 7, 9, 368-370, 376-
379
Stubbs, Kay, 373-374
Studds, Gerry, 151, 200, 260-261, 287, 292
sugar lobby, 49-50
Sullivan, Sarria and Associates, 59
Sullivan Principles, 307
Sunshine Law, 302-303
Swansbrough, Robert H., 70n
Sweden, 139n
Szulc, Tad, 175n, 305

Taiwan, 141
Talamante, Olga, 106
tariffs, 49, 70, 101
taxes, 9, 29-33
Taylor, J. Sherrod, 160n
television, 20, 51
terrorism, 116, 132, 220, 232
Texaco, 99, 341
Thailand, 267n
Thayer, George, 243n
Theberge, James, 104n
Thurmond, Strom, 57, 308
tiger cages, 181-182
Time, 52
Time/Yankelovich survey, 30
Todman, Terence A., 79, 117-118, 152,
203, 207, 250
Tonkin Gulf resolution, 148n
Torres, Esteban, 79
Torrijos, Omar, 287
torture, 83-84, 110-111, 130, 180-183, 236,
284, 346-356
Town and Country, 315
trade, 65, 70, 72-73, 366
Transportation, Department of, 273
Treasury, Department of, 58, 166, 224, 227,
238n, 272-280, 282-285, 293-294, 301,
319

Treaty for the Elimination of All Forms of
Racial Discrimination, 131
Treverton, Gregory, 92n, 105
Trice, Robert H., 97n
Tricontinental Conference, 193n
Trujillo, Rafael, 5, 50n, 120, 251n
Truman, David B., 32n
Tsongas, Paul, 307, 319, 371
Tunisia, 315
Tupamaros, 13, 14, 168, 180
Turbay, Julio César, 355n
Turkey, 141, 198n, 304
Tuthill, John W., 142n
Tyson, Brady, 77, 116, 374

Uganda, 118, 287
Ujifusa, Grant, 146n
United Arab Republic, 198n
United Auto Workers, 79, 257, 335
United Brands, 68
United Fruit, 98
United Kingdom, *see* Great Britain
United Methodist Church, 86
United Nations, 128-134, 144, 198
United Nations Conference on Trade and
Development (UNCTAD), 130
United Nations Commission on Human
Rights, 3, 13, 109, 116, 128, 131, 253n,
349
United Nations General Assembly, 3, 13,
114, 129n, 130, 349-350
United Presbyterian Church, 86
United Press International, 51, 59, 336
United States Catholic Conference
(USCC), 87, 257
United States Chamber of Commerce, 72
Universal Declaration of Human Rights, 3-
4, 115, 128
University of Brasilia, 180
University of Georgia, 115
Uruguay, 71n, 133n, 180, 305, 311, 320n,
329, 372; economic aid, 73, 85, 101,
114, 142, 166, 183n, 203, 257, 307; mili-
tary aid, 60, 168, 213, 238n, 255-256,
260, 262-266, 361; multilateral aid, 295-
298; political trends, 7, 13-15, 122, 358,
361-364; repression and torture, 84, 111,
195, 346, 350-351

Vaky, Viron, 359-360, 363
Valdez, Abelardo, 204-205

LIBRARY OF CONGRESS CATALOGING IN PUBLICATION DATA

Schoultz, Lars.
  Human rights and United States policy
toward Latin America.

  Bibliography: p.
  Includes index.
    1. Latin America—Relations (general) with
the United States.   2.   United States—Relations
(general) with Latin America.   3.   Civil rights—
Latin America.   4.   United States—Foreign
relations—1945-   I.   Title.
F1418.S39   327.7308   81-47154
ISBN 0-691-07630-8   AACR2
ISBN 0-691-02204-6 (pbk.)